DICE IN IRELAND REVISITED

PREJUDICE IN IRELAND

REVISITED

*Based on a National Survey of Intergroup Attitudes
in the Republic of Ireland.*

Micheál Mac Gréil

SURVEY AND RESEARCH UNIT
ST. PATRICK'S COLLEGE,
MAYNOOTH, CO. KILDARE

1996

Published in 1996 by The Survey & Research Unit,
Department of Social Studies, St. Patrick's College,
Maynooth, Co. Kildare.

Printed in Ireland by Leinster Leader Ltd., Naas, Co. Kildare.

Cover design Ms. Lesley Murray.

ISBN 0 901519 89 8

*This book is dedicated to the memory of my mother,
Mollie (Ní Chadhain) 1901-1982
whose tolerant patriotism inspired openness
and generosity towards all people.*

PREJUDICE IN IRELAND REVISITED

TABLE OF CONTENTS

Foreword

There is much speculation about "the changing face of Ireland". *Prejudice in Ireland Revisited* not only provides us with empirical data on contemporary Irish society but also, because the study replicates many aspects of Dr. Mac Gréil's previous benchmark study *Prejudice and Tolerance in Ireland* (1977), it allows us to compare Dublin of 1988-89 with Dublin of the early 1970s.[1] The use of this longitudinal design allows us to examine the extent to which Dubliners have become more or less tolerant in relation to specific issues and groups over time. Consequently, the data make an immense contribution to our knowledge of the attitudes of the people living in the Republic of Ireland.

The results presented in this work are based on interviews with a random sample of 1,005 respondents in 1988-89. The data illustrate attitudes towards a wide range of political and social issues, many of which are currently sources of debate (Northern Ireland, neutrality, disarmament, the environment, the Irish language, religion, family values etc). In addition, the research examined attitudes towards a variety of economic, ethnic, political, religious, and social groups such as alcoholics, drug addicts, gay people, the unemployed, people with AIDS, the Travellers, a range of nationalities including our fellow members of the European Union, and different races.

As well as replicating questions asked in the 1972-73 survey, the author designed three innovative new scales (the New Alienation Scale, the New Patriotic Esteem Scale and the New Feminist Scale). Further, a number of the scales and questions have been included in surveys in other countries via the International Social Survey Programme (ISSP). The author also worked with the University of Nijmegen and Professor Andrew Greeley of the University of Chicago on various aspects of the study. Consequently, scales tested and validated by others were included in the survey, including the Alienation and Anomie Scales and family and religious scales. In light of the paucity of cross-national sociological data, this aspect of the research is extremely valuable.

While many of the results are heartening, some provide cause for concern. For example, the author finds evidence of relatively high levels of both anomie (normlessness) and alienation (powerlessness). When compared with the Netherlands, anomie is higher here than in Dutch society. Dr. Mac Gréil emphasises the point that these results may help to explain the increasing suicide rate in Ireland.

The results also suggest that support for social categories requiring rehabilitation is low. In particular, attitudes towards Alcoholics, Drug Addicts and People with AIDS are relatively severe. Moreover, in some cases attitudes have hardened since the 1972-73 survey. This was true for Alcoholics, Drug Addicts and, especially, the Travellers. There are also

---

1. The previous study examines the attitudes of Dubliners only.

worrying signs of an increase in ethnocentrism and very low esteem for certain groups such as Pakistanis, Moslems, Hare Krishna, Atheists and Agnostics.

In relation to "unpopular groups", Dr. Mac Gréil discovers a "selective liberalness". That is, people who would ordinarily be considered more liberal (the young, well-educated and those with a high occupational status) were not so liberal when it came to Alcoholics, Ex-Prisoners, People with AIDS and Travellers.

Prejudice in Ireland Revisited will obviously be of interest to sociologists and other academics with an interest in prejudice and ethnic and race relations. It will also be an extremely useful text book, especially for its lucid presentation of theories of prejudice, including Mac Gréil's **momentum model of society**, and his **vacillating social situation model**. However, the book will also be of interest to policy makers, politicians and people with a general interest in Irish society or those with an interest in a specific topic or group which has been investigated here. Given its methodological rigour and the vast quantity of empirical results on Irish society, the book deserves the widest possible audience, and as Dr. Mac Gréil argues

"a prejudice exposed is a prejudice undermined."

NESSA WINSTON
Department of Social Policy and Social Work, University College Dublin.

Author's Preface and Acknowledgements

The main aim of this book is similar to that of the previous publication *Prejudice and Tolerance in Ireland* (Mac Gréil, 1977), namely, to make a positive contribution to intergroup relations in modern society in general and in Ireland in particular. This is achieved by enabling the people to get a better understanding of attitudes and opinions in relation to the various ethnic, gender, political, racial, religious and social groups and categories living in the world today. Such improvement in mutual understanding should result in more positive relations between diverse groups and should facilitate the promotion of structures and goals conducive to the co-existence within an integrated, just and pluralist society.

Like most works of its nature, *Prejudice in Ireland Revisited*, is aimed at two categories of readers, namely, the socially concerned general reader and the students of the human sciences. The latter would include students of adult and community education, anthropology, history, human geography, political science and politics, social psychology, sociology and of other related human sciences. Students in these disciplines will, hopefully, find this book to be a useful text and reference source. The comprehensive amount of data published in the different chapters should enable future researchers to replicate the survey (or part of it) and measure changes in the people's attitude syndrome. Serious academic social researchers can have access to the data file of this survey by arranging it with the author.

The broad range of general readers for whom this work is also published includes "concerned citizens", i.e., parents, community leaders, journalists, clergy, politicians, public servants, educators, those in the caring professions, leaders in industry (workers and managers), and writers and commentators on social affairs. The findings of this text should be of special interest to people involved in minority relations, in international affairs, and in tourism.

It is expected that this book will attract readership outside Ireland for two main reasons. Firstly, prejudice and tolerance are universal phenomena and few societies today are without serious challenge in the area of minority relations. Secondly, a very wide range of attitudes towards various nationalities and ethnic categories is analysed and examined in this text. Irish attitudes towards twenty-eight nationalities are measured, analysed and compared. These include the following: "Africans", "Arabs", "Belgians", "Black Americans", "British", "Canadian", "Chinese", "Danes", "Dutch", "English", "French", "Germans", "Greeks", "Indians", "Irish Speakers", "Israelis", "Italians", "Luxembourgians", "Nigerians", "Northern Irish", "Pakistani", "Poles", "Portugese", "Russians", "Scottish", "Spaniards", "Welsh" and "White Americans". The importance of measuring attitudes toward members of diverse nationalities takes on a greater urgency in a world of growing global proximity of peoples. It is of special interest

xiii

in the case of Ireland with its wide diaspora and its popularity as a holiday location.

This book addresses questions and attitudes in relation to other categories (as well as ethnic ones), i.e., religious, political and social categories and minorities. Opinions and views are also reported on and analysed concerning family relations, work, unemployment, neutrality and nuclear disarmament.

In order to facilitate a diverse readership an attempt has been made to present the findings in a readable style without oversimplifying the results. A certain amount of specific terminology or jargon could not be avoided in order to maintain the necessary degree of scientific discipline and accuracy. It is hoped that the general reader will not find this too irksome. Most key concepts have been defined and described in Chapter II.

While the book as a whole forms an integrated work, each of the major areas of research within the texts, i.e., ethnocentrism; racialism; religious attitudes and practices; attitudes towards Northern Ireland and Britain; Irish political issues and opinions; sexism and views on family life; attitudes to Travellers and other social minorities; work and social mobility; and general measures of authoritarianism, liberalness, anomie and alienation, can be treated as complete topics on their own within the text. In the belief that a good table is worth more than many pages of prose, the author has tried to satisfy the needs of those who wish to see the factual results for themselves by providing a wide assortment of tabular findings.

ACKNOWLEDGEMENTS

Prejudice in Ireland Revisited, as is the case of most major works based on primary social research, is more than the work of any one author. Rather, it is the product of the work of a wide range of contributors. These include, in the first place, *respondents* to the questionnaire-interview who gave the primary source of the data. Interviewers and their supervisors, research assistants, computer staff, typists and printers, advisors and proof-readers are also among the main collaborators in a work of this nature.

The Survey Unit of the *Economic and Social Research Institute* carried out the national survey on commission from the author. Gratitude is due to the staff of the Survey Unit and to its interviewers throughout the country for the efficient and satisfactory manner in which the data were collected and computed.

The two *Senior Research Assistants* who worked on the survey and its analysis and preparation of the findings were Dr Nessa Winston and Ms Caroline O'Kelly, M.A. Their work was first class and merits the gratitude of the author. Dr Winston also read the final draft of this book and has kindly written the Foreword.

The services of the *Computer Centre* in St Patrick's College, Maynooth, have been invaluable. The director and staff of the Centre are truly to be thanked. The patient cooperation of the author's colleagues in the

Department of Social Studies, St Patrick's College, Maynooth, has been greatly appreciated. Professor Liam Ryan and Ms Maureen Redmond (Department Secretary) merit special mention.

The main *financial support* for this work has come from private sources, i.e., the Irish Jesuit Province and Father (Professor) Andrew Greeley of Chicago, United States of America. Valuable grants were also received from "The Ireland Funds" and from the "Publications Fund" of St Patrick's College, Maynooth. As those engaged in major survey research know, it is very expensive work. The above are sincerely thanked.

The author wishes to acknowledge his indebtedness to the *writers and publishers* whose works are referred to in this book. Because of the emphasis on primary research there is limited use made here of secondary analysis, apart from the author's own 1977 publication, *Prejudice and Tolerance in Ireland.* The cooperation of the Department of Sociology of the Catholic University of Nijmegen, The Netherlands, has been a most important contribution to this research.

Finally, the author feels obliged to mention his gratitude to everyone who assisted in the preparation of the manuscript and the production of this book. The text was prepared for the printers by Ms Caroline O'Kelly and Ms Ann Gleeson. The cover was designed by Ms Lesley Murray. The manuscript was read by Mr Micheál B. Ó Cléirigh, by Reverend Frank Sammon, S.J., and by Dr Nessa Winston. The final proofs were critically examined by Mr Richard Douthwaite and Mr Eoin Garrett. Any shortcomings surviving in the text are wholly due to the author. The careful work of the staff of the Leinster Leader Limited in printing the book (despite the cumbersome nature of so many tables and complicated matrixes) is acknowledged.

In conclusion, I would like to thank my fellow Jesuits in the Sandford Lodge Community, my academic colleagues in St Patrick's College, Maynooth, and family, friends and neighbours in Loughloon (where most of the original text has been written and later amended and corrected), for their encouragement and forbearance. *Tá súil agam gur fiú an iarracht seo chun leas na ndaoine a chur chunn cinn in Éirinn agus i gcéin, le cúnamh Dé.*

Le fíor-bhuíochas,

MICHEÁL MAC GRÉIL, S.J.
Loch Chluain (Loughloon)
Cathair na Mart (Westport)
Co. Mhuigheo (Co. Mayo)

Mí na Samhna 1996

Prejudice in Ireland Revisited

CHAPTER I

Background and Previous Research

PART I: BACKGROUND

1. Biographical Background

The background to this book has been a long association by its author with the study of intergroup attitudes and prejudices. The first serious encounter with the terrible effects of social prejudice on a grand scale was an encounter with *the aftermath of racism of Nazi Germany* in the early 1960s while a student in the Jesuit scholasticate in Heverlee near Louvain in Belgium. Contact with older Jesuits who had experienced the years of the holocaust resulted in a visit to Dachau Concentration Camp in 1963 and in seeing the real evidence of the persecution of the Jews, Russians, Gypsies, Homosexuals and others, including a number of young German Jesuits who had opposed the xenophobic slaughter. Masses of people were exterminated because of anti-semitism, racism, ethnocentrism and prejudice against other minorities. The dangerous myth of the superior Aryan race had been reified into an effective policy of mass genocide. A simple question raised by a professor in a sociology class (in 1963) triggered off a pursuit for an answer. The question which the professor asked himself after witnessing (when a young teenager) a trainload of Jews (men, women and children – old and young) *en route* to a concentration camp, was: "How was it possible for a civilised society (like the Germans) to permit the practice of such blatant inhumanity towards fellow human beings?" This question has been the basic one in all the author's research into intergroup relations over the past thirty years.

The second experience was that of the *Flemish versus Walloon ethnic conflict* in Belgium and the perceptible degree of intergroup hatred and ethnic prejudice which was evident during the early 1960s in Louvain until the "taalgrens" or language boundary was agreed. While French-speaking Belgians (i.e. the Walloons) constituted the dominant group, the Flemish-speaking Belgians (i.e. the Flemish) felt they were second-class citizens. While sympathetic with the civil rights aspect of the Flemish cause (as a Flemish-speaking student in the Catholic University of Louvain) at the time, the author also sensed a very strong ethnocentrism.

The third experience or exposure to intergroup prejudice was while a post-graduate student in Kent State University (Ohio, U.S.A.) under the direction of Professor Chuck Hildebrant during 1965/66 at which time the *racial civil rights movement* was very active under the national leadership of the late Martin Luther King. The focus of an M.A. Course in Sociology was on the various aspects of ethnic, anti-Semitic and, most of all, racialist prejudice. The author's M.A. thesis was entitled "A Psycho-Socio-Cultural

Theory of Prejudice", which included a survey of prejudice among selected groups of citizens in Cleveland and Philadelphia.

The fourth and most relevant background research experience of the author was an extensive survey of *intergroup attitudes and prejudices of a random sample of Dublin urban and suburban adults* (2,017 respondents) carried out over six months in 1972-73. The findings of the Dublin survey were to become part of a Ph.D. Thesis, under the supervision of Bishop (Professor) James Kavanagh, submitted in U.C.D. in 1975. The thesis was later published under the title of *Prejudice and Tolerance in Ireland* in 1977, 1978 and 1980. The 1972-73 survey was the first major survey of a wide range of intergroup attitudes carried out on a significant population of Irish people. Its findings served as a "bench-mark" which would enable replicated research to provide a measure of intergroup attitudinal change.

2. Replication of 1972-73 Survey

The survey on which this book is based is largely a replication (of the 1972-73 survey), carried out on a random national sample of the population of the Republic of Ireland taken from the 1988 Electoral Register. The actual fieldwork took place over the period from November 1988 until April 1989. The Dublin sub-sample will provide the findings from which changes in attitudes and prejudices are calculated.

As is clear from the questionnaire (Appendix A, pp. 475 ff), the current survey contains additional questions to those used in the 1972-73 survey – partly as a result of certain omissions in the earlier data, e.g. the addition of a Srole-type Anomie Scale, an Alienation Scale, a Patriotism Scale, a new Feminist Scale, a special Anti-Traveller Scale, and more information on topics such as the family, unemployment, nuclear weapons and neutrality. Some questions were also replicated from a national attitudes survey carried out in the Netherlands by Nijmegen University. In other areas certain questions and scales from the 1972-73 survey have not been replicated due to doubts about their original validity, reliability or utility in the more recent context.

During the period since the completion of the fieldwork, a number of reports have been published in "monograph" form, i.e. covering attitudes towards the Irish Language, Education, Religious Practices and Attitudes, and Political Attitudes and Opinions. The reason for publishing these reports earlier was because of their topicality. The main contents of the above monographs dealing with attitudes are included in this book in Chapters IV, VI, VII, VIII and IX below. Attitudes to the Irish Language are part of the measures of Irish Ethnic awareness. The reason for the delay in publication of over seven years has been partially due to the length of time required for completion of data analysis and the restraints of resources and time available due to the author's heavy lecturing workload. Despite the lapse of over seven years, it is felt that the overall likelihood of substantial change in the main areas of prejudice is not very great.

As was the case in the 1972-73 Dublin survey, a number of political and religious attitudinal questions were replicated from Richard Rose's survey of Northern Irish attitudes in 1968 and published four years later in the book, *Governing without Consensus* (1972). These same questions have been replicated in the 1988-89 survey and this provides a very interesting four-way comparison, i.e. 1968 Northern Ireland, 1972-73 Dublin, 1988-89 National Sample and 1988-89 Dublin sub-sample, of the findings from Richard Rose's questions. Another interesting aspect of the Rose survey has been its timing in that its fieldwork was carried out just prior to the outbreak of hostilities in Northern Ireland in 1969.

3. The Primacy of Fieldwork

It should be stated at the beginning, that the main findings reported in this book are from the actual survey carried out in 1988-89. In other words, this book reports on primary field research and deals with very little secondary analysis. Such secondary references are chosen to compare and contrast the findings analyzed in the text.

The utility of this study is its contribution to the understanding of intergroup relations in Ireland at a very important stage in its development. It is generally believed that the study of social prejudice and the publication of the findings of objective research into it can be self-therapeutic for both research students and intelligent readers. The publication of the 1972-73 findings in *Prejudice and Tolerance in Ireland* (Mac Gréil, 1977)[1] has been quite therapeutic and resulted in a relatively large readership and numerous public and published references to the findings.

Two particular issues in Irish society at the end of the 20th Century demand the sociologist's attention, namely,

    (a)   Intergroup relations within our historical sets of groups, i.e. between Catholics, Protestants and Dissenters, on the one hand, and between Republicans, Loyalists, Socialists and Capitalists, on the other; and

    (b)   The emergence of a certain degree of heterogeneity of our modern society which includes a growing diversity of ethnic, racial and social groups, especially in the larger towns and cities.

---

1. The work was awarded the "Christopher Ewart-Biggs Memorial Prize" in 1977 for its contribution "to the promotion of peace and understanding (i) in Ireland, or (ii) between the peoples of Ireland and Great Britain, or (iii) between the partners in the European Community" (see *Deeds of the Prize*).

The opening up of Irish society to a more regular and intimate contact with various European ethnic groups has important consequences for the people's attitudes towards members of such groups – as migrant students or workers abroad or as tourists/visitors, or new residents in Ireland.

4. The Historical Dimension of Irish InterGroup Attitudes and Relations

It should be noted that the Irish have been, for over two centuries, an *emigrant people* and this affects the nature of our home social composition. Our major groups, religious and ethnic, have been historical. This is in stark contrast to those societies like Britain and the United States which have been *immigrant societies* resulting in the major minorities and groups lacking a long historical past in the host country. Commentators who criticise Ireland for being too preoccupied with history fail to grasp the predominant significance of history for intergroup understanding and relations in *emigrant societies*. At a more scientific level this characteristic is evident in the absence of the historical dimension receiving much attention in minority and intergroup sociological studies emanating from the United States and Britain. Even where the historical dimension is important, as in the case of attitudes towards the Black minority in the United States, it is largely ignored in Race Relations literature.

The Post-Reformation period of Irish history has been very much the story of inter-denominational conflict. Prior to the Reformation, the denominational dimension was not significant and groups were largely classified along ethnic, political and class (feudal) lines. The establishment of the Anglican (Protestant) Church under Henry VIII and, later, the declaration that the kingdoms of Ireland and England were to become *de jure* Protestant, while the majority of the Irish people and of their leaders remained (Roman) Catholic was ultimately to lead to a period of protracted interdenominational persecution, the remnant of which is still present in Northern Ireland. Religious-cum-political wars in Europe and political upheaval in England in the 17th Century were to add to the struggles and persecutions in Ireland. In fact, Ireland was to become the battleground for the brief war between King James II (in his struggle to retain the British crown) and King William of Orange of 1689-91. The defeat of James was to add further to the penal pursuit of Catholic clergy and religious under the reign of William and Mary and that of Queen Anne. In the mid-17th Century Irish Catholics were severely oppressed under the rule of Oliver Cromwell. Irish Catholics, although constituting the numerical majority of the population, were the "sociological minority" in Ireland until the start of the 20th Century. The folk memory of the people has retained in song and story some of the more depressing experiences especially, in the case of Irish Catholic emigrants and their descendants in Britain, in the United States, in Central Asia and elsewhere abroad in the former British Colonies. This must have a very significant unwitting bearing on popular attitudes and prejudices.

Coping with the legacy of the past is a problem not unique to Ireland. Revisionist history, which tries to play down the more painful facts in the genuine interest of creating a barrier between the past and the present for the sake of harmony, is one way of dealing with the problem. Some societies go so far as not to teach the young people the history of their people's past, e.g. the teaching of Irish history in Northern Irish public schools was very minimal until recently. At the end of the day, such avoidance of the facts of history in the "official" curricula is not the most effective way of responding. Based on the principle that "to understand is not to condone", the exposure of the population to an honest attempt at providing a true and objective account of their history with professional interpretation from recognised historians coming from different socio-politico-religious backgrounds is probably the most enlightened way to address the problem.

We are fortunate to have had serious historians and authors who have researched and published the story of Post-Reformation Ireland. Among those whose work provides a valuable contribution to understanding the development of Irish grouping would include, William P. Burke,[2] Patrick J. Corish,[3] Alan Ford,[4] R.F. Foster,[5] Thomas Hamilton,[6] William E.H. Lecky,[7] F.S.L. Lyons,[8] Anthony T.Q. Stewart,[9] John H. Whyte[10] and others. Joseph Leichty's Pamphlet, *Roots of Sectarianism in Ireland* (1993, Belfast) gives a brief overview of the chronology of socio-politico-religious events which influenced the rise of sectarianism after the Reformation in the 16th Century. The reader may disagree with the interpretation given by serious writers to the causes and effects of historical developments and facts while, at the same time, learning from the reading of their works of a variety of authors to arrive at a balanced view.

The ten authors selected above are but a representative cross-section of historians who together would give the student of Irish intergroup relations a more-or-less balanced insight into the subject. Sociologists are mainly preoccupied with an analysis of the contemporary patterns of behaviour and organisations. Their interest in history is mainly to discover the background to such patterns. When both aspects are accurately combined, it should be possible to make some predictions of social change in the years ahead. In a sense there is a built-in interdependence between sociology and history.

2. Burke, William, P., *Irish Priests in Penal Times 1660-1760*, Waterford, 1914.
3. Corish, Patrick J., *The Irish Catholic Experience, Dublin*, 1985.
4. Ford, Alan, *The Protestant Reformation in Ireland*, Frankfurt-am-Main, 1987.
5. Foster, R.F., *Modern Ireland 1600-1972*, London, 1988.
6. Hamilton, Thomas, *History of Presbyterianism in Ireland*, Belfast, 1886/1992.
7. Lecky, William E.H., *The History of England in the 18th Century*, London, 1890.
8. Lyons, F.S.L., *Ireland Since the Famine*, London, 1971.
9. Stewart, A.T.Q., *The Narrow Ground, the Roots of Conflict in Ulster*, London, 1977/1989.
10. Whyte, John H., *Church and State in Modern Ireland 1923-70*, Dublin, 1971.

5. Ireland's Social Minorities

In addition to politico-religious intergroup attitudes which occupy a central position in the minds of modern Irish commentators and community leaders, we have another area of concern, if not crisis, in relation to minority relations. The position of Irish Travellers is one case in mind which is dealt with at more length in this text. Attitudes towards the role of women and other gender problems are also explored, and are a source of much mass media and other attention in Ireland today. Other social minorities are also reported on below.

Ireland, like many Western societies, seems to be entering the "post-patriarchal" era. This has come about by a growing enlightenment within Irish society and the influence of a vocal and effective feminist missionary-like campaign being diffused into Ireland, especially from the United States and Britain. The evidence presented in this book will measure the degree of acceptance in the population of some of the sexist (pro-male) stereotypical image of women. It will be shown that there has been progress in the changing of attitudes towards gender equality in a positive sense. A special "Feminist Scale" is used for the first time. The scale was composed with the co-operation of Joy Rudd, who has carried out much research into questions relating to gender equality. The feminist movement in Ireland has won approval among a large section of the respondents. Some 64% of the National Sample agreed that "the feminist movement is very necessary in Ireland" while only 15% disagreed with the statement.

An examination of the participation of females in education has shown that 18% more females than males under 35 years of age completed second-level education while, at the same time, the profile of workers has shown a substantial shift from blue-collar to white-collar jobs. This will inevitably lead to a problem of a growing minority of the young men in heretofore semi-skilled and unskilled categories. Added to that, we see a relatively low male participation in adult education when compared with females. With the combination of low education participation rates in education among this category of new and increased "blue-collar" unemployment, the emergence of a new gender minority group, young blue-collar or working-class males, is likely to become a serious social problem.

Other social groups of categories likely to elicit a degree of prejudice are the unemployed, those with mental or physical handicap, people whose sexual orientation is homosexual or gay, alcoholics, drug addicts and people with AIDS. The attitudes of the people towards such categories greatly influences the condition and behaviour of those minorities. In the case of people suffering from physical or mental handicap a positive public attitude towards them largely determines their development and capacity to contribute their share to society.

The public attitude toward homosexuals is of special significance because of the negative manner in which members of this minority have been treated in the past. "Gay bashing" has not been an unknown phenomenon in Ireland. During the Nazi persecution of minorities in Germany in the 1930s and 1940s Gay people were imprisoned in the concentration camps of Dachau and elsewhere. The recent decriminalization of homosexual relations between consenting male adults has been a very positive move to protect such people from blackmail and from classification as criminals. The residue of "Victorian Puritanism" in Irish society will, of course, outlive the criminalization which it generated in the late 19th Century. We must also distinguish between what is seen as immoral in the eyes of some and what is defined as criminal in the name of the people. A "moral person" tends to be tolerant even of those whose behaviour he or she may disapprove of (so long as it does not intrude on the basic rights of others), while "moralistic people" tend to be authoritarian and intolerant of those with whom they disagree or of whose behaviour they disapprove. In a pluralist society it is very important to promote "morality" rather than "moralism".

The Travelling People constitute one of Ireland's most vulnerable and most discriminated against minorities. Community hostility towards this relatively weak and demographically small (around 1%) proportion of the Irish population is well chronicled in the difficulty of getting public approval of suitably located serviced halting sites. More than that, there have been a number of very nasty outbreaks of physical attack on Travellers by "local residents" in recent years which are not unlike the infamous "roughing-up attacks" on Black People in the Deep South of the United States in the pre-civil rights era. "Roughing-up" is a standard and very serious behavioural expression against minorities. It was widely practised in Germany against Jews in the 1930s and more recently against foreign migrants by the Neo-Nazi gangs. One very important response of the State to this behaviour is unambivalent instant reaction in the defence of the minority and fearless negative sanctioning of the perpetrators of the "roughing-up" attacks. "Turning the blind eye" is tantamount to approval. The Courts and the security forces have a special obligation to apply and enforce the law in defence of the minority. Otherwise, the members of the minority will feel unprotected in their own country. The State will be seen as the enemy of its own citizens! It can give a licence to those taking the law into their own hands.

PART II: OUTLINE OF TEXT

As can be seen from the Table of Contents, the following text consists mainly of the findings of primary research into intergroup attitudes and related issues in the Republic of Ireland. The layout of the work follows a certain logic, beginning with two *Introductory Chapters* dealing with the background and methodology. Chapters III to V deal with the **standard areas of social prejudice**, i.e. ethnocentrism (based on nationality and culture), racialism (based on the physical traits of the minority). Religious practice and attitudes are examined in Chapters VI and VII. Chapter VIII examines attitudes toward Northern Ireland while Chapter IX deals with other Irish political attitudes and opinions such as neutrality and disarmament. A number of new questions are examined in Chapter X, which measures sexism and the people's views on feminism and family life. Chapters XI and XII focus on *social and "class" attitudes* towards a range of stimulus categories not covered under the standard ones, i.e. Travellers, heavy drinkers, people with physical and mental handicap, the unemployed, drug addicts and others. Chapter XIII looks at measures of prejudice in general, while Chapter XIV *summarises* and *interprets* the findings.

1. Methodology and Theoretical Considerations

Chapter II deals with "Methodology and Theoretical Considerations". Because this is largely a follow-up study, it is not intended to devote as much space to theoretical considerations as was the case in *Prejudice and Tolerance in Ireland* (Mac Gréil, 1977). The points made in the 1977 text are still valid and reliable. Some additional theoretical reflections will be added in an attempt to establish more clearly the reasons for differences in prejudice scores. It will also be necessary to devote space to definitions of key concepts throughout the text and, also, to enable future researchers to replicate, compare and contrast the findings of this work with the ongoing pursuit of a greater understanding of intergroup relations and attitudes in Ireland. The benefits of such understanding for the replacement of prejudice by greater tolerance is adequate reward for all the efforts of the researcher. Without adequate understanding, remedial action to correct the social and personal injustice of prejudice and discrimination is unlikely to be successful. Political and community leaders need to be "soft-hearted and hard-headed". The methodology explains the research design and the survey techniques used for the collection and processing of the data.

2. Social Distance

Chapter III reports on the "Bogardus Social Distance Scale" results. Social distance tells of how close the sample would be willing to admit the average person of some fifty-nine stimulus categories, i.e. ethnic, political, religious, racial and social groups or categories. The levels of closeness measured go from welcoming into the family as a member to "debar or deport" from Ireland. This is the major intergroup attitudinal scale used in this survey, as it was in the 1972-73 survey. It rates very highly from the points of view of "validity" and "reliability". Coupled with this scale is a "Rationalisation Scale" devised by the author in 1965 and which gives an insight into the intergroup definition by respondents who would not welcome members of various groups or categories into the family. As anticipated, there have been a number of interesting changes in intergroup definition since 1972-73.

3. Ethnocentrism and Racialism

Chapter IV concentrates on ethnocentrism. Ethnocentrism is prejudice against a person because (s)he is perceived to belong to a particular nationality or culture. A wide range of ethnic categories is tested in the questionnaire, including the other eleven member nations of the European Union (prior to January 1995). African, American and Asian categories are also tested. With the rise of ethnocentrism in France, in Germany, in the Russian Federation and, most notably, in former Yugoslavia, a close examination of the nature and extent of Irish ethnocentrism should prove useful and interesting. Not surprisingly, it will be shown that there are signs of an overall rise in ethnocentrism in the findings, when compared with those of 1972-73. Part of the measure of Irish ethnic identity is the people's attachment to, knowledge of, and use of the Irish language. The main findings published in the monograph *State and Status of the Irish Language* (Mac Gréil, 1990) are included in Chapter IV.

Chapter V reports on the current state of racialist attitudes and prejudices, i.e. against persons perceived to have different physical attributes, e.g. colour of skin, texture of hair, shape of lips, nose and eyes, and height. One of the more positive results in this book is the significant and substantial reduction in racialist prejudice when compared with the 1972-73 findings. The defeat of apartheid in South Africa is another major piece of evidence of the decline of racialism. While the scores are significantly improved, we have still a long way to go until the race factor loses its cultural and human significance as a barrier to social intimacy. Nevertheless the findings of Chapter V are good pointers towards greater enlightenment in the Irish people.

4. Religious Attitudes

The main contents of Chapters VI and VII have already been published in monograph form, *Religious Practice and Attitudes in Ireland* (Mac Gréil, 1991), because of the need to expose some of the findings close to the time of the fieldwork. Additional pieces of information have been added to integrate religious attitudes and prejudices with the forms, i.e. ethnic, political, racial and social. Special attention is paid to the current state of anti-Semitic prejudices because of the insidious nature of this type of bias. Because the Jews have been favourite scapegoats since the growth of Christianity in Europe, they have often become the object of severe prejudice and hatred. It will be shown that Irish attitudes towards Jews have been influenced by the negative attitudes towards "Israelis" as a stimulus category.

Catholic-Protestant attitudes are measured closely and are of special significance because of the long history of sectarianism in the island of Ireland (see Leichty, 1993) and the importance of ecumenical tolerance for the just and peaceful solution of the current Northern Irish problem. The evidence will show a continued high level of mutual respect between Catholics and Protestants in Ireland. Attitudes towards Moslems and Hari Krishna followers are also measured in Chapters VI and VII, as are dispositions towards Agnostics and Atheists. In the case of these latter four categories, attitudes are quite negative. The current state of anti-Semitism is examined and analysed, as are changes since 1972-73. The attitudes towards "Israelis" are analysed for the purpose of discovering their influence on anti-semitism.

5. Political Attitudes

Many of the findings of Chapters VIII and IX have already been published in monograph form, *Irish Political Attitudes and Opinions* (Mac Gréil, 1992). Prejudices towards right-wing and left-wing ideologies in Ireland seem to be converging, i.e. it will be shown in Chapter VIII that there is very little difference between the social distance scores against Socialists and those against Capitalists. Does this mean a homogenisation of right and left-wing politics in the Republic? The standing of Communists, while still low down in the rank-order of preferences, has improved significantly since the 1972-73 survey. It is interesting to record that while the fieldwork was taking place in 1988-89, the Eastern Bloc dominated by centralist Communist regimes had not as yet collapsed, although the signs of change were present in Poland and in Russia. This fact will make this work valuable as a "bench-mark" survey in the evolution of political attitudes!

Most relevant to intergroup relations in Ireland are the findings dealing with Irish Nationalism and attitudes towards aspects of the Northern Irish problem. The special anti-British Scale reflects the people's attitudes and opinions on Anglo-Irish relations. The people were not impressed by the manner in which the British authorities dealt with the Northern Irish problem. The influence of miscarriages of justice in relation to the "Birmingham Six" and others is reflected in some of the responses.

Irish attitudes to neutrality and nuclear disarmament are very clear from the findings of Chapter IX. The people strongly favour being neutral while they are totally opposed to nuclear disarmament. All-in-all, Chapters VIII and IX give a very interesting profile of what the people wanted, and how they viewed the political scene in 1988-89. The profile of political party preferences (in Chapter IX) point to a fairly centrist range of political loyalties in Ireland, i.e., nearly all parties have a spectrum of followers from the full spread of socio-economic backgrounds.

6. Feminism and Sexism

Chapter X examines attitudes in relation to women and men and sexual orientation. Gender equality has been an issue on the Irish political agenda for many years. It has gained greater prominence since Ireland's entry into the European Union in the early 1970s. A number of questions are included in the current survey relating to feminism and the place of women in the family, in the Church, in education, in the workplace and so forth. The overall findings of Chapter X will show that the substantial majority of Irish people is positive in relation to women's rights. There may be some disagreement on a number of issues pertaining to the woman's place in the home or at work. Here opinions are more divided. Some of the findings seem to indicate changes in attitudes towards single parents. Like racialism and hostility towards those with left-wing ideologies, there is evidence of a significant *decline* in negative sexist attitudes towards women as a group. Further, their improvement in participation in education points towards a continued improvement of the status and achievement of women in Irish society. Gender as a personal variable is not as significant in determining variations in prejudice scores as it was in the 1972-73 survey. Female and male attitudes coincide in the case of many attitudes and views in the 1988-89 survey findings. Issues relating to family size, rearing of children and material standard of living are also dealt with at some length in Chapter X.

7. Travellers and Social Minorities

Chapter XI is probably the most depressing chapter in this book in that it records a growing and unacceptable level of social prejudice against Travelling People throughout the national sample. While there is an overall increase in the prejudice scores in ethnic and some religious and political categories, it is quite modest when compared with what has happened to our attitudes towards our Travelling People. In Chapter XI an attempt will be made to try to explain this deterioration. Going on the premise that the condition and status of the minority is for the most part determined by the dominant group in society (the minority's position being the response to the dominant group's posture and behaviour), there is a serious need for a major examination of Irish society's whole approach to its Travelling fellow-citizens.

The position of other social minorities, i.e. Alcoholics, Drug Addicts, Ex-Prisoners, Gay People, People with Physical or Mental Handicap, People with AIDS, and Working-Class People, is reported and analyzed in Part Two of Chapter XI. The findings are quite disappointing in the case of some of these categories, especially those perceived as deviant. The tragedy of negative public attitudes towards groups whose members *need rehabilitation and support* is a vicious circle largely because of these negative attitudes. The net result at the end of the day is likely to be a further deterioration in the condition of members of the minority. This is often referred to as the "self-fulfilling prophecy" (W.I. Thomas, 1926). The "vicious circle A-B-C-circuit" is (A) negative *attitudes*, leading to (B) negative *behaviour*, leading to (C) negative *conditions*, which in turn reinforce (A) negative attitudes and on and on it goes (Mac Gréil, 1977, p. 21).

The "vicious circle theory" can also point to the way of improving attitudes, i.e. by means of positive intervention from the State and voluntary support agencies to change the behaviour (B) and improve conditions (C), the net effect of which would be a challenging of negative attitudes (A) and their replacement by more positive ones. The extent of negativity towards particular groups and categories exposed in this book will, it is hoped, help to undermine such unreasonable and counter-productive negativity and challenge such prejudices. The author is also aware of the disappointment and possible hurt such attitudes give members of these minorities themselves. They should take courage, however, from the possibility of changing people's prejudices by means of appropriate action and reaction.

8. Underclass,[12] Unemployment and Social Mobility

Chapter XII addresses public attitudes towards unemployed people as a category and also examines a number of opinions held in relation to work and Trade Unions. The level of social mobility in the population is also measured. Comparison with the 1972-73 findings will show a growth in acceptance of the unemployed into the closer levels of social distance, which probably reflects the broader spread of joblessness in Irish society over the sixteen-year interval. Another area of substantial and significant change is the decline of manual and "blue-collar" jobs as a proportion of the occupation opportunities available. The corresponding increase in "white-collar" jobs has serious implications for the educational standards of the workforce. The relatively high proportion of young men (under 35) who do not complete second-level education (18% more than their female counterparts) raises the possibility of a lesser educated new social minority, i.e. young working-class/blue-collar males. It should also be noted that formal educational requirements for many jobs may be exaggerated and may lead to unjust discrimination against the working class.

Another problem hidden in the figures and findings of Chapter XII is the nature of Irish emigration. When the local educational participation rates are compared with the educational standards in the rural counties of certain areas of Ireland, there is clear evidence of out-migration of the talented and more highly qualified. This out-migration is also true of the whole Republic.

12. Underclass refers to categories of citizens excluded from normal participation in cultural, political and socio-economic activity due to their chronic state of relative deprivation.

In effect, we in Ireland are suffering from a "brain drain" of talented young people without a corresponding in-migration of talented people from other societies. Within Ireland there is a similar pattern of upward and outward mobility from weaker communities to the stronger ones.

9. General Measures of Prejudice and Tolerance

The findings of the national survey are completed in Chapter XIII by an examination of the general scales measuring authoritarianism (Adorno, et al, 1950), anomie (Srole, 1951), liberal/illiberal attitudes (Mac Gréil, 1977), religious fundamentalism (Rose, 1972) and other general attitudes and opinions showing high correlations with levels of social prejudice. In a number of these scales, comparisons with the 1972-73 survey show a mixed result. Certain opinions classified as liberal have become more widespread without a commensurate change in other prejudice scores. This apparent contradiction raises the question of "selective liberalness", which is not the same as overall tolerance. The totally tolerant person seems to be a member of quite a small minority. A selective liberal would, for instance, be very tolerant of some groups and very negative towards others, particularly those perceived to be conservative in outlook. In this survey an attempt is made to test respondents' degree of overall tolerance. For that reason a composite tolerance score is calculated which amalgamates all scales to discover the profile of the most tolerant and most prejudiced people. Measures of social anomie (sense of normlessness) and of alienation (a sense of powerlessness) are analysed also in Chapter XIII. Since this is the first time these aspects have been measured it is not possible to compare the findings with those of 1972-73.

10. Summary and Conclusions

Chapter XIV tries to summarise the findings and deliberations of the previous chapters and analyse and interpret the causes and implications of such information on social attitudes and prejudices in Ireland today. Part I of Chapter XIV summarises the findings under thirty-one headings.
The Thirty-one headings are as follows:
     (1) theoretical approach;
     (2) social distance and intergroup definition;
     (3) ethnocentrism;
     (4) attitudes towards the Irish language;
     (5) ethnic social distance in Ireland;
     (6) racialism;
     (7) religious background;
     (8) religiosity of the sample;
     (9) Christian Church unity;
     (10) images of God and of the world;

(11) religion in socio-political life;
(12) social distance of religious categories;
(13) anti-Semitism;
(14) attitudes towards Northern Ireland;
(15) anti-British attitudes and opinions;
(16) political party preference;
(17) socio-political categories;
(18) neutrality and nuclear disarmament;
(19) marital status and family size;
(20) feminism;
(21) family values;
(22) rearing of children;
(23) family standard of living;
(24) the Travelling People;
(25) social categories and minorities;
(26) underclass and unemployment;
(27) social mobility in Ireland;
(28) authoritarianism;
(29) Liberal-Illiberal Scale;
(30) social anomie;
(31) social alienation.

The use of regression/path-analysis is employed in Part II to establish the extent of direct causation between seven independent variables and a selection of six prejudices, i.e., ethnocentrism, racialism, anti-Semitism, sexism, anti-British and anti-Traveller prejudices. Part III of the final chapter consists of the author's concluding interpretation and commentary.

CHAPTER II

Theory and Method

As stated in the Introduction, it has not been the intention of the author to repeat here in great detail the theoretical considerations published in chapters four to seven in *Prejudice and Tolerance in Ireland* (1977). The overall relevance of such theoretical considerations are still more-or-less valid and will be referred to in the course of the chapters below where the findings are analysed and explained. That said, it is, nevertheless, necessary to give some space to a brief resume of the theoretical and conceptual frameworks applied in the explanation of the findings. It is also necessary to discuss the methodology used in the research work of this book.

PART I: CONCEPTUAL FRAMEWORK

1. CONCEPTUAL FRAMEWORK:

As in most areas of study in the human sciences there is no unanimity among authors as to the definition of key concepts used in intergroup attitudes research. For that reason, therefore, it is imperative that the key concepts and terms used in this work are defined at this stage.

The function of a precise conceptual framework is to provide the reader and the researcher with a coherent set of terms which enable the accurate diagnosis of phenomena and provide the basis for research and categories for empirical measurement. Adherence to more precise use of the concepts selected is also essential for the validity of the findings.

1.1 The Key Concepts Defined:

Prejudice is the principal concept of this study and is primarily classified as a (social) psychological topic. Few concepts have received so much attention from a wide range of social psychologists. Since prejudice is a particular type of social attitude, it is, therefore, necessary at this stage to attempt a comprehensive definition of social attitudes.

Because social attitudes have a strong social and cultural dimension it is also necessary to attempt a definition of the concepts **society** and **culture**. To complete the psycho-socio-cultural framework, it will also be necessary to define the concept **personality**. These five terms constitute the basic set of general concepts which are at the core of this study.

There are also a number of specific concepts which require some clarification for the reader at this stage. They fall into two categories, namely, types of social prejudice and intergroup postures and responses. Among the types of prejudice defined here will be the following: anti-Semitism, ethnocentrism, racialism, sexism, homophobia and xenophobia. Other forms of prejudice examined below include religious, political and social prejudices. The latter three categories do not require an elaborate definition at this stage as they are merely the application of the concept of social prejudice to religious, political and social groups.

With regard to intergroup postures and responses, students of dominant-minority relations have noted a range of postures adopted by dominant groups and responses made by minority groups. **Dominant groups** are defined as those collectivities or categories of people who exercise an excessive and disproportionate degree of power and influence over other groups living in the same society. **Minority groups** are those groups who exercise a degree of power and influence which is less than equity would require. Dominant and minority groups are not classified according to numerical strength. A numerical majority can be a sociological minority group, e.g., the Black people in South Africa prior to their liberation.

The concepts to be defined as postures and/or responses include: conflict, accommodation, avoidance, assimilation, amalgamation, discrimination, segregation, stratification and pluralism. Two other postures are also adopted from time to time in situations of intergroup conflicts, i.e., annihilation (genocide) and expulsion (transplantation). The latter, which has been redefined in the recent past as "ethnic cleansing", and has been practised over the centuries in nearly every country in the world. It was a fairly widespread phenomenon in Ireland during the 16th, 17th and 18th centuries.

The above constitute the specific concepts used in this text in relation to intergroup relations. Other more general concepts such as anomie, authoritarianism and patriotism will be defined when the subjects are discussed in Chapter XIII below.

1.2 Definition of Social Prejudice:

Ann Weber in her text *Social Psychology* defines prejudice as: "an attitude (usually negative) about people based on their membership of a particular social group" (Weber, 1992, p. 198). This very general and precise definition identifies prejudice as an attitude based on a perception of group membership. The "usually negative" in parenthesis seems to allow for positive prejudice which may refer to preferential categories of people. It is generally accepted that most intergroup prejudices are expressions of positive prejudice towards one's own group or those close to it. Weber goes on to state that prejudice "involves stereotyping, social categorisation of people, and acceptance of social norms that favour prejudice. Prejudice is acquired through learning, as part of normal socialization, and in developing social identity through group membership" (Ibid, p. 211). This adds four important points to note about the nature of social prejudice i.e.,

(a) Categorisation and stereotyping;
(b) Accepting social norms supporting prejudice;
(c) Importance of socialisation to acquire prejudice;
(d) The link between one's prejudices and one's identity.

The American social psychologist, Gordon Allport, a leading authority on social prejudice, defined it thus:

> "An avertive or hostile attitude towards a person who belongs to a group, simply because he (she) belongs to that group, and is therefore presumed to have the objectionable qualities ascribed to that group.... It is an antipathy based on a faulty and inflexible generalisation."
>
> (Allport, 1954, pp. 8, 10)

Allport's definition adds a number of further points to note in addition to Ann Weber's definition and description of prejudice, i.e.,

(a) Avertive or hostile nature of the attitude;
(b) The presumption of the group's ascribed negative qualities defining the persons prejudiced against;
(c) Faulty and inflexible generalisation.

Arnold and Caroline Rose in their book, *America Divided*, saw prejudice as being primarily a "hate attitude" (Rose and Rose 1953), while Brewton Berry in his work, *Race and Ethnic Relations*, wrote: "Antipathy would really be a more accurate term than prejudice to describe the phenomenon we are dealing with" in negative intergroup attitudes (Berry, 1965, p. 299). Most other authors dealing with social prejudice agree with the points made by Gordon Allport in his definition quoted above. Elliot Aronson, in his highly acclaimed book, *The Social Animal* (3rd edition, 1980, pp. 195 ff) emphasises the role of generalisations or stereotyping in his definition of prejudice: "We will define prejudice as a hostile and negative attitude toward a distinguishable group based on generalisations derived from faulty or incomplete information" (Aronson, 1980, p. 197).

The following operational definition draws together the notes of Allport's definition and that of a number of other authors:

> Social prejudice is a hostile (antipathetic), rigid and negative attitude towards a person, group, collectivity or category, because of the negative qualities ascribed to the group, collectivity or category based on faulty and stereotypical information and inflexible generalisations.

This summary definition is an adaptation of the one given in *Prejudice and Tolerance in Ireland* (Mac Gréil, 1977, p. 9). The points made in relation to the 1977 definition[1] are still valid although the scope is broadened

1. 1977 Summary Definition: "Social prejudice is a negative, hostile, rigid and emotional attitude towards a person simply because he/she is perceived to belong to a group and is presumed to possess the negative qualities ascribed to the group as a result of selective, obsolete and faulty evidence" (Mac Gréil, 1977, p. 9).

somewhat. Apart from juxtapositioning the adjectives "negative" and "hostile", and giving the latter priority, the main addition is that of the "group, collectivity or category" as foci of the prejudice as well as the "person". The operation of prejudice towards the "group, collectivity or category" is normally exercised in the case of social prejudice towards the individual, but there are incidents of prejudice being exercised towards the "group, collectivity or category" at one remove from a personal encounter. For example, a residential or community group's prejudice towards a group of Travellers, or towards Travellers as a collectivity or category without any contact with an individual Traveller.

The use of the phrase: "based on faulty and stereotypical information" instead of: "as a result of selective, obsolete and faulty evidence" has been seen to be a more accurate definition of the rationalisation of prejudice. The new version re-emphasises Allport's emphasis on "faulty generalisation" and points to the fact that the actual person or group who happens to be the focus of the prejudice does not come into the reckoning in the situation. The justification to self, i.e., rationalisation of the prejudice, is founded in the "faulty and stereotypical information".

Finally, the addition of "inflexible generalisations" is added from Allport's definition. It reinforces the rigidity of prejudices as social attitudes. Unlike the negative attitudes which are responsive to changes in information and wants, prejudices are frequently change-resistant and can survive in spite of having no rational basis. Prejudices become deeply rooted in the culture and in the social structure—not to mention in the interpersonal response traits.

Gordon Allport has discussed the "acting-out of prejudice" in his classic text, *The Nature of Prejudice* (1954). He sees a five-step (progressive) working out of prejudice in the behaviour of those who are prejudiced. The adaptation of Allport's extended quotation which follows traces the development from stage to stage. This five-stage development of the behavioural expression of social prejudice is relatively easy to confirm in the experience of minority groups who come under the weight of dominant group hostility. Each of the stages may be illustrated with examples in many lands and at various times. In Ireland, also, some groups have had to suffer at the hands of progressive negative behaviour. The particular importance of including Allport's "acting-out" stages here is its further illustration of the nature of social prejudice. It should be added that the below stages point to the importance of intervention at the earliest possible stage to prevent the situation deteriorating. For example, if "antilocution" is curtailed, the move towards "avoidance" will be less likely. Hence the importance of **strict control** of negative stereotyping of members of minorities in the media or on the stage. Most tolerant countries should, and sometimes do, curtail the use of negative stereotypes in the media by law.

Gordon Allport held that social prejudice was "acted out" in the following five progressively severe stages of behaviour. One stage would lead to the next if not corrected.

Stage One: "Antilocution" or Ridicule, i.e. prejudiced people tend to express their hostile feelings towards the objects of their prejudices in the company of their prejudiced friends. Such behaviour is also to be found in the ethnic jokes and other forms of ridicule. Because antilocution can lead to more severe forms of behaviour it is advisable to curb or curtail it. This includes stereotypical reporting of negative behaviour of individuals in the print and electronic media.

Stage Two: "Avoidance" or Shunning, i.e., prejudiced people at this stage will seek to avoid the company of the minority as far as possible. This can take many forms, e.g. exclusive housing and recreational activities. This leads to imposed ghettoes.

Stage Three: "Discrimination", i.e., "here the prejudiced person makes detrimental distinctions of the active sort". In time this can lead to "segregation" which is discrimination backed by law and custom.

Stage Four "Physical Attack", i.e., occasional attacks on the person or property of the minority, e.g., the "roughing up" of Travellers' camps or "gay bashing".

Stage Five: "Extermination" or Expulsion:, i.e., this is "the ultimate degree of violent expression of prejudice" according to Allport. Unfortunately, it has not been that rare a phenomenon in history.

(Allport, 1954, p. 15 f.)

1.3 Definition of Social Attitudes:

Since social prejudice is a particular type of negative attitude it shares most of the characteristics of attitudes. Few concepts in social psychology have received more attention than that of attitudes. Despite all that is written, it is not easy to decide on a clear and comprehensive definition of social attitudes.

D. W. Rajecki in his book *Attitudes* (1990) uses Allport's definition as the basic definitional source.

"Gordon W. Allport, an eminent social psychologist, provided an early and comprehensive definition of attitudes: 'An attitude is a mental and neural state of readiness, organised through experience, exerting a directive or dynamic influence upon the individual's response to all objects and situations with which it is related' ". (Allport, 1935).

(Rajecki, 1990, p. 4)

The extent to which this definition of sixty years ago is still relevant is very obvious. The tens of thousands of books and articles written on attitudes (Rajecki 1990, p. 7) in the meantime have not been able to add that much to the original Allport definition. It is clear from the above definition that an attitude is seen to be:

(a) A disposition, i.e., "a mental and neural state of readiness";
(b) The product of experience;
(c) An influence on behaviour, i.e., "exciting a directive or dynamic influence upon the individual's response to all objects and situations with which it is related".

1.3.a The Structural Approach: The approaches adopted to the definition of social attitudes in *Prejudice and Tolerance in Ireland* (Mac Gréil, 1977, pp. 11-28) were two-fold, i.e., structural and functional. The structural definition may be defined as follows:

Attitudes are positive or negative dispositions towards foci composed of evaluations, feelings and behavioural tendencies.

This proved to be a highly useful (operational) definition because of its measurable components. It was also confirmed in the findings of the 1972-73 survey that there was a strong correlation between the valency of each of the components, especially in the case of more extreme attitudes, i.e., when evaluations of the focus were "bad", feeling towards it tended towards "dislike" of the object of the attitudes and there was a behavioural tendency to "hinder" or "attack" the focus. Because of this internal consistency it was possible to assess the valency of the whole attitude from a measurement of one of its components. For instance, social distance or the closeness to which people were prepared to admit numbers of various ethnic, racial, religious, political or social groups, collectivities or categories, was seen also as a measure of the "behavioural disposition" component of the attitudes and, thereby, also a measure of the whole attitude or prejudice toward the particular focus or stimulus category.

Roger Brown's descriptive definition of the concept "attitude" was included in the 1977 publication. It too was quite comprehensive and worth repeating here:

"An attitude has always a focus; it may be a person, a group, a nation, a product, anything whatever really. When the focus is known to many as in the case of statesmen, ethnic groups, and nations, the corresponding attitude can be used for the comparative characterisation of many persons. The dimension of characterisation extends from positive (or favourable) through neutrality to negative (or unfavourable). Persons are thought of as occupying positions on this dimension corresponding to their disposition to behave favourably or unfavourably towards the focus." (Brown, R., 1965, p. 420).

(Mac Gréil, 1977, p. 11)

Figures 1A and 1B demonstrate the structural nature of attitudes and illustrate the valency of attitudes. Figure 1A highlights the valency of an

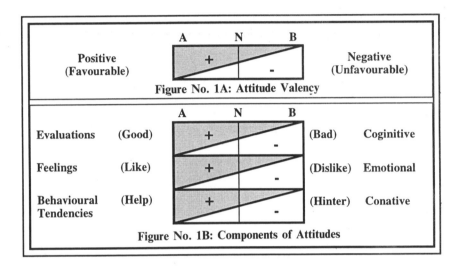

Figure No. 1A: Attitude Valency

Figure No. 1B: Components of Attitudes

attitude from positive to negative or favourable to unfavourable. The point made in Roger Brown's descriptive definition in relation to valency, i.e., ". . . from positive (favourable) through neutrality to negative (unfavourable) . . .", raises a question as to the nature of attitudinal neutrality. It is the contention of the present author that "neutrality" on the valency continuum is not a "zero point" but, rather, a situation where the positive and negative are evenly balanced.

Figure 1B shows the composite nature of attitudes in diagrammatic form. The elongated rectangle shows the continuum of valency from positive (favourable) to negative (unfavourable). Point N in the middle shows where an attitude or one of its components are equally positive and negative leading to a neutralised rather than a neutral position. This is applicable to most attitudes. Prejudice as a negative attitude tends to be different in that the positive aspect is often ignored or rationalised as an exception, with the person, group, collectivity or category being defined almost exclusively by the negative qualities ascribed to it.

Consistency between the actual location along the positive to negative continuum has proven to be greater, the closer points A or B are approached. In other words, the more positive and the more negative attitude scores within each component are the more consistent in their location on the continuum. As attitudes approach a more moderate score at point N on the continuum, the intercomponental correlation becomes less, and certain variations of location are possible (Mac Gréil, 1977, pp. 24-25).

Other characteristics of social attitudes have been discussed in *Prejudice and Tolerance in Ireland* (1977, pp. 14-23). These include the parallel structure between attitudes and culture which is defined[2] as follows:

> The interrelated set of ideas/beliefs/convictions, values, norms and symbolic meaningful systems which characterise and influence the human behaviour of a people.

The components of culture correspond to those of attitudes to the extent that the attitude syndrome of the individual or the group represents or indicates the group or individual cultural ethos or mentality. Figure 2 demonstrates the parallel structure of attitudes and culture.

When it comes to empirical measuring of attitudes there is a problem, since it is only possible to measure social behaviour. Attitudes and culture are basically non-material and are not open to direct sense perception and, thereby, to direct empirical measurement. We infer the attitudes and culture from behavioural evidence, be it in the form of expressed statements or observed interaction. The components of attitudes and culture closest to

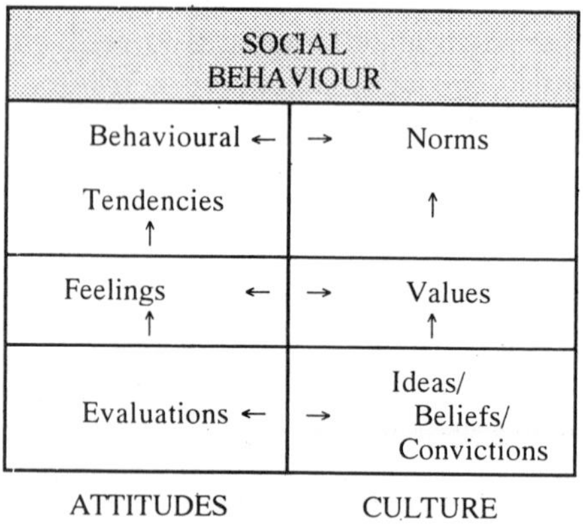

SOCIAL BEHAVIOUR	
Behavioural ← →	Norms
Tendencies ↑	↑
Feelings ← → ↑	Values ↑
Evaluations ← →	Ideas/ Beliefs/ Convictions
ATTITUDES	CULTURE

Fig No. 2: Attitude - Culture Link

2. Culture is defined on pp. 32-33 below.

behaviour are behavioural tendencies and norms. For that reason, these are the best components for measurement by inference from behaviour. It is proposed to return to the questions of "attitudes and behaviour" and "measurement of attitudes" later in this chapter.

Despite the close link between attitudes and culture, it is often possible to have a "culture-attitude lag" i.e., attitudes may change before the corresponding changes take place in the culture. For instance, attitudes toward ecumenism in Ireland had changed long before Vatican II and the World Council of Churches changed to more ecumenical values and norms. The pressure for culture-change often comes from change of attitudes among a significant group of the citizens. In like manner, changes in the culture, usually coming from outside the country, lead to changes in norms and behaviour and in turn may result in change of attitudes. For example, the impact of secular materialism on the Irish culture has led to greater commercialisation and consumerism in the people's norms. This cultural change has resulted in pressure on people's more personal and communal attitudes.

1.3.b The Functional Approach: Katz, in his article "The Functional Approach to the Study of Attitudes" (*Public Opinion Quarterly*, 24, 1960) suggested four motivational functions that were performed by attitudes:

(1) "*The adjustive function*: Essentially this function is a recognition of the fact that people strive to maximise the rewards in their external environment and to minimise the penalties . . .

(2) "*The ego-defensive function*: The mechanism by which the individual protects his ego from his own unacceptable impulses and from the knowledge of threatening forces from without and the methods by which he reduces his anxieties created by such problems, are known as mechanisms of ego-defense . . .

(3) "*The value expressive function*: The function of giving positive expression of his central values and to the type of person he conceives himself to be . . .

(4) "*The knowledge function*: Individuals not only acquire beliefs in the interests of satisfying various specific needs; they also seek knowledge to give meaning to what would otherwise be an unorganised chaotic world. . . ."

(Katz, 1960, pp. 163-204)

The four functions outlined by Katz provide a good insight into why people may hold on to certain attitudes. They also show why people may change or refuse to change their attitudes. According to Rajecki, "there is definitely a renaissance of research and writing on the functional perspective". Evidence comes from a recent volume edited by Pratkanis, Beckler and Greenwald (1989), *Attitude, Structure and Function* (Rajecki, 1990, pp. 11-12). It will be restated later that the functional aspect of social prejudice is an important theoretical consideration in explaining the existence and persistence of various degrees of negativity towards particular groups/collectivities/categories of people. Such a functional approach does not exhaust the whole gamut of theoretical explanations.

1.3.c Attitudes and Behaviour: The link between attitudes and behaviour is quite a complex issue for a number of reasons. In the first place, attitudes are both pre-reflectional and pre-behavioural. They may have a structural and functional logic but they are really a-rational. They are primarily dispositions which are positive or negative. As such, they influence behaviour in a positive or negative manner.

Since most people have a highly complex configuration of attitudes towards most major stimulus objects or categories, these attitudes have been informed by their functions and by the socio-cultural environment of the person. Not infrequently a person may possess mutually contradictory attitudes towards a focus. For example, a person with a very strong racialist prejudice against a Black person may, at the same time, have a strong Christian disposition towards all people as equal. These two mutually opposing attitudes to the Black person will, in all probability, result in a behavioural expression which will be neither strongly racialist nor strongly Christian. We have the case of Merton's "fair-weather liberal" who is not racialist but refuses to behave positively towards Black people so as not to offend wealthy White friends whom he/she sees as being financial allies. Political loyalty can also overturn or severely qualify behavioural expression of positive or negative attitudes, e.g., religious prejudice in Northern Ireland.

The link between attitudes and behaviour, is rarely, if ever, one-to-one. Neither is it non-existent. There is a higher correlation between strongly held (positive or negative) attitudes and their behavioural expression. For instance, a high level of anti-Traveller prejudice will make it unlikely that the people will permit the proper living conditions in the community (nomadic or settled) for Travellers.

The link between attitudes and behaviour is also affected by a range of other factors such as "dissonance", "self-presentation", "self-perception" and "self-justification" (see Weber, 1992, pp. 132-34). In regard to dissonance, Weber points out that

> "dissonance theory argues that mismatches among cognitive elements create dissonance, an arousing tension we are motivated to reduce. Unjustified behaviours are impossible to change once they have been enacted. Dissonant attitudes, however, are easier to alter: one need only change one's mind and the new attitude can be brought into line with the unalterable behaviour".   (Weber, 1992, p. 134)

This adoption of a new attitude to "go along with" certain behaviour patterns happens quite frequently in everyday life. The difference caused by the new attitude backing the behaviour is that it reinforces the latter continuing, as well as acting as a form of rationalisation or self-justification.

In relation to self-presentation the pressure for the "appearance" of consistency between attitudes and behaviour can be quite strong. This can often lead to a degree of hypocrisy in our lives when we are presenting ourselves "as if" we were consistent, although our attitudes may not be genuine. Politeness and raw social pressure can result in attitudinal posturing "for peace sake", "political correctness", or whatever other form of dominant pressure may prevail. People generally seek to avoid perpetual confrontation and submit to intimidation by dominant persons! This can lead to a sense of false security for the domineering person because of the "forced" attitudinal conformity of the more submissive associates.

The ongoing process of "getting to know ourselves" is greatly helped by our constant evaluation of our behaviour in relation to our "abilities, moods and attitudes".

> "Self-perception theory seems best suited to explaining newly-forming connections between attitudes and behaviour. If one's behaviour is made salient, and one's attitudes are not yet clearly formed, behaviour will shape new attitudes more than (the prevailing of) any pre-existing attitudes."
>
> (Weber, 1992, pp. 133-4)

In relation to the changing of attitudes, it should be emphasised that it is impossible to remove attitudes once they exist, that is, without removing the focus of the attitudes. All we can do is **replace** our attitudes. For example, if a person has negative attitudes towards Travelling People, it is impossible to remove such attitudes as if the Travellers no longer existed for that person. The only way to change the situation is to replace the negative attitude by a positive one or one less negative. In other words, an "attitudinal vacuum" is impossible, as long as the focus is relevant. This point will be very true for the future changing of attitudes between Unionists and Nationalists in Northern Ireland. They have no alternative but to seek what is more acceptable in each other for each side and to replace the syndrome of hate attitudes by one of positive dispositions. This is not easy because of the "rigidity" of social prejudice as an attitude.

The links between attitudes and behaviour have been highlighted over the years by many sociologists and social psychologists (W.I. Thomas, and F. Zwaniecki, 1918, Vander Zanden, 1972, Merton 1957, Weber 1992) in the context of the vicious-circle theory and the self-fulfilling prophecy theory. The latter is often referred to as the "definition of the situation" theory which states that our perception of and attitudes towards a social situation can actually lead to it changing to become as we define it.

The Vicious-Circle Theory sees a causal connection between the dominant groups' attitudes towards minorities leading to behaviour of the establishment and resulting in the conditions of living of the minority. Negative attitudes will inevitably lead to negative behaviour, which in turn results in a deterioration of the conditions of those against whom the negative

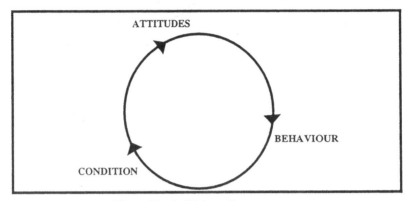

Figure No. 3: Vicious-Circle Theory

attitudes are directed. The worsening of the social and living conditions of those prejudiced against will reinforce and rationalise the negative attitudes. So, the vicious-circle theory operates and explains the deterioration of the overall position. The great thing about the vicious-circle theory is that it works in the positive direction also. For example, if attitudes toward Black people in the dominant group in Britain were to become positive, the behaviour and services would improve and the Black people would respond by improving their own education, housing, job-opportunities and general conditions. This, in turn, would challenge the racialist attitudes and further strengthen positive behaviour.

If "the vicious-circle theory" is true (and the present author finds it to be most reasonable), it stands to reason that a three-pronged approach is possible and desirable for the removal of minority inequity and discrimination. At the level of social attitudes, **community leaders**, i.e., teachers, politicians, religious leaders, and others, could address some of the more serious negative attitudes. Even academics can play an important role in exposing prejudice and thereby undermining it. For example, popular authors uch as Gordon W. Allport (1954), Gunner Mydal (1944), Robert K. Merton (1957) and others, have done much to expose the myths and fallacies of racial and other prejudiced attitudes.

Intervention at the second level of the vicious-circle refers directly to behavioural change. The role of **law** is central here. For that reason, a Minority Rights Act (regularly updated) which is fully enforced and seriously applied seems to be a *sine-qua-non* in any heterogenous society wishing long-term equity and good intergroup relations.

Finally, there is the possibility of positive intervention to improve the actual material and cultural conditions of the minority. In modern societies, **the State** is the only source of the required resources to ensure a basic minimum standard of living in line with that prevailing in society for the time being. Voluntary agencies can also contribute in this regard. Once positive interventions take place at the three points of the circle, a self-generating dynamic should amplify the pace towards equality.

The relation between "attitude" and "opinion" is that between a disposition and its expression, with the added aspects of reflection and some degree of rationalization (at least at times). Because an opinion is an oral or written expression, it is also a "behavioural phenomenon". Most attitude-measurement scales are a series of statements which express opinions or views deemed to point to certain attitudinal dispositions. Arising out of the complex relations between attitudes and behaviour it is best to seek to determine attitudes by means of multi-item scales and to arrive at a mean score for all of the items indicating a certain valency. It will be the general practice throughout this text to treat attitude-measurement differently from that of opinion-measurement. In the case of the former, the mean scale and subscale scores will be used, while when dealing with opinions, specific items and opinion-laden statements will be analysed separately.

In the case of the *Bogardus Social Distance Scale* findings, the response to each stimulus category or group will be taken as a measure of the "behavioural tendency" component of popularly-held attitudes towards the category (ethnic, political, racial, religious or social) measured. Inter-componental correlations have shown repeatedly that social-distance measures are significantly (and often substantially) correlated to scale and subscale scores in relation to members of the same category.

Finally, there are those authors who seem to disregard attitude and prejudice research (as pursued in this book) as somewhat distant. They would challenge the relevance of attitudes for behaviour and look upon them as mere conceptual constructs. Rajecki addresses this problem in Chapter Three of his book, *Attitudes* (2nd Edition 1990, pp. 77-106). The author sets the problematic thus:

> ". . . By the late 1960s evidence had accumulated that attitudes and behaviour were often inconsistent. These findings provoked something of a crisis in the field, and the status of 'attitudes' as a useful concept was called into question by some. As a reaction to these theoretical concerns of the sixties, recent work on attitude-behaviour consistency has produced what appears to be a happy ending. By now we better understand when and why attitudes and behaviour are related, or not."
>
> (Rajecki, 1990, p. 77)

The previous study, which was based on the 1972-73 survey of Greater Dublin and was published in 1977, i.e., *Prejudice and Tolerance in Ireland* (Mac Gréil), did note the reservations in relation to the complexity of "attitude-behaviour consistency" and treated the findings with great methodological care and caution. The exaggerated criticisms did not deflect attention from accurate measurement and admission of any deficiencies when they emerged. The same rigour will be observed when reporting on the data from the 1988-89 national survey on which this text is based.

1.4 Related Concepts:

To complete the conceptual framework particular to this work, it may be worth giving a brief definition and comment on a number of related concepts. Together with the two central concepts of social prejudice and social attitudes these "related concepts" go to make up the "diagnostic conceptual kit" which will enable the researcher and the reader to examine the findings and reach some conclusions at the level of explanation, i.e., through the application of theory. In addition to phenomena explained, quite a considerable range of opinions and views will be described (accurately) and discussed, and new areas of findings will be explored.

1.4.a Personality, Society and Culture: All interpersonal and intergroup interaction is dependent on and reflects the personality, the social system and the culture. The human being is psycho-socio-cultural in all aspects of social interaction.

(i) Personality: It is not easy to get agreement on the definition of personality. Walter Mischell, in his text, *Introduction to Personality* (3rd Edition, 1981), draws on the definitions of Allport (1961, p. 28), Guilford, (1959, p. 5) and McClelland (1951, p. 69) and presents the following:

> " 'Personality' usually refers to the distinctive patterns of behaviour (including thoughts and emotions) that characterise each individual's adaptations to the situations of his or her life."
>
> (Mischel, 1981, p. 2)

There were numerous theories of personality including the following:

(a) Trait Theories i.e., C. G. Jung, (1923), W. H. Sheldon (1949), H. J. Eysenck (1967);

(b) Psychodynamic Theories, i.e., S. Freud (1933), Dollard J. and N. E. Miller (1950);

(c) Social Behaviour Theories, i.e. B. F. Skinner (1953), J. B. Rotter (1966);

(d) Phenomenological Theories, K. Lewin (1936), K. Rogers (1951), G. Kelley (1955), A. Maslow (1968), G. Allport (1961).

Mischel presents and applies these theories in his text and shows the value of a more eclectic approach to the wide range of personality theories (Mischel 1981 Parts I and II, pp. 13-277).

Gordon Allport's definition of personality focused on the internal psychological systems which determine an individual's personality as:

"the dynamic organisation within the individual of those psychological systems that determine her/his characteristic, behaviour or thought."

(Allport, 1961, p. 28)

Personality is a product of socialisation and genetically inherited capacities. One's place in society and the accepted norms of the culture greatly influence the development of one's innate ability. Some psychologists, such as Sigmund Freud, place great emphasis on the inner developments of the personality while others, like George H. Mead, highlight the primary group social environment of the young person as the most important determinant of personality growth.

The different theories of personality are more complementary than contradictory in that they emphasise different features of human beings at different levels of explanation (Hayes, 1994, p. 220).

(ii) Society: Most sociologists of note have attempted to define the concept society. Talcott Parsons saw two essential requirements in a society, namely, that it be a "self-subsistent social system" and that it endure "beyond the life-span of the normal human individual" and continue in the next generation.

"A social system of this type, which meets the essential functional prerequisites of longterm persistence from within its own resources, will be called a society. It is not essential to the concept of society that it should not in any way be empirically interdependent with other societies, but it should contain all the structural and function fundamentals of an independently subsisting social system."

(Parsons, 1951, p. 19).

This definition, despite its heady jargon and tight reasoning is very comprehensive. It refers to the relatively autonomous society or, in previous terms, "sovereign state" or country. The current moves towards European integration, by weakening the autonomy of Irish society, will soon raise the question – at what point do we cease to be a "self-subsisting social system"? Once that point is reached, if it is ever reached, then we would become in Parsons' terms a territorial "community" or mere province.

The social system is operated by its members, or at least a significant proportion of them, conforming to those basic norms required for the satisfaction of society's and the members' needs. We are not free to ignore social norms necessary for the satisfaction of our collective and individual need. These norms are, in the words of sociologist, Emile Durkheim, "social facts" which he defined in his book, *The Rules of Sociological Method* (1895, translations, 1938, 1964). The following was Durkheim's own definition of "social facts".

> "A social fact is every way of acting, fixed or not, capable of exercising on the individual an external constraint; or again, every way of acting which is general throughout a given society, while at the same time existing in its own right independent of its individual manifestations."
> (Durkheim, 1964 translation, p. 13).

It should be added that there are some who would take an opposite and extreme view and say that society, as such, does not exist! This view is rejected by the present author.

(iii) Culture: Culture and society are integrally related. At its most basic level, culture is that which distinguishes human beings from all other forms of animal life, even that of the high primates. Culture is possible because of human beings' capacity "to symbol" (White 1959, pp. 6ff). It is possible to distinguish two definitions of the concept culture. One definition is what is meant when we use the concept in everyday life, while the other is what anthropologists and sociologists mean by the concept.

> "When we use the term in ordinary daily conversation, we often think of 'culture' as equivalent to the 'higher things of the mind' – art, literature, music and painting. As sociologists use it, the concept includes such activities, but also far more. Culture refers to the whole way of life of members of society. It includes how they dress, their marriage customs and family life, their patterns of work, religious ceremonies and leisure pursuits. It covers also the goods they create and which become meaningful for them – bows and arrows, ploughs, factories and machines, computers, books, dwellings."
> (Giddens, 1989, p. 30)

The content of culture is essentially non-material, although it is dependent on material media and artifacts of the vehicles of culture. The anthropologist, Mervin Harris, in his book, *Culture, People, Nature* (New York, Harper and Row, 1988) quotes (with approval) from Sir Edward Burnett Tylor's original definition of culture in his book *Primitive Culture* (London, Murray, 1871) as follows:

> "Culture taken in its wide ethnographic sense is that complex whole which includes knowledge, belief, art, morals, law, customs and any other capabilities acquired by man as a member of society. The condition of culture among the various societies of mankind, insofar as it is capable of being investigated on general principles, as a subject apt for the study of laws of human thought and action".
> (Tylor, 1871, p. 1; Harris, 1988, p. 122).

Most definitions of the concept "culture" have been influenced by Tylor's definition. Building on this definition and that of other eminent authors (Malinowski, 1930; Benedict 1935/1961; Kroeber, 1948; Kluckhohn, 1949/1971; Parsons 1954/64; Smelser, 1962) the present author, in the previous publication (1977), gave the following definition of culture.

"Culture is the interrelated set (configuration) of learned, created and borrowed beliefs, ideas, values, norms and symbolic meaningful systems, which characterise and influence the human behaviour of a people."

(Mac Gréil, 1977, p. 181).

It can be seen from this definition that culture is a composite phenomenon whose content consists of "beliefs and ideas" (i.e. cognitive component), "values" (i.e. "ethical ideals"), "norms" (i.e., "shared expectations and obligations" or the specification of values for behaviour, and "symbolic meaningful systems", (i.e., language and rituals). These components of culture are non-material. Culture defines the "ethos" of a society and the 'mentality' of its people (Benedict 1935/1961, p. 32ff.) The link between culture and social prejudice is given on pages 24-25 above.

2. TYPES OF SOCIAL PREJUDICE:

It is the basic tenet of this book that social prejudice is a universal phenomenon with manifestations in attitudes towards various groups, collectivities and categories of human beings. It has become common practice in the literature to categorise or classify types of social objects of prejudice into a number of distinct categories, namely, ethnic, political, racial, religious, sex or gender, and social. Religious prejudice is frequently subdivided into sectarianism and anti-semitism. Sex or gender prejudice is also subdivided into sexism and homophobia. Ethnic prejudice, which is normally termed ethnocentrism, is occasionally referred to as xenophobia. There has been some disagreement between authors from time to time as regards the narrow or broader meaning of some of these terms. An attempt will be made in this text to stick, as strictly as is reasonable, to the more precise meaning of each term or concept. This will be necessary to avoid ambiguity or confusion. Also, since this work is also a "follow-up" on the 1972-73 survey and report or book (Mac Gréil, 1977), it is necessary to adhere to the actual definitions and concepts used previously.

2.1 Ethnocentrism:

This concept refers to a belief or conviction that members of other nationalities or cultures are basically inferior to members of one's own nationality or culture, because of their nationality, culture or way-of-life. The definition given in *Prejudice and Tolerance in Ireland* was more specific, i.e.,

> "Ethnic prejudice consists of rigid, negative, hostile attitudes towards people who are defined as members of groups or categories that are perceived to differ from one's own group or category in matters of culture and nationality. It is basically a belief in the superiority of the members of one's own ethnic groups or categories, and a deeply held hostility towards members of these groups and categories."
>
> (Mac Gréil, 1977, p. 263).

This is quite an adequate definition. The point was also made in the 1977 text that "ethnocentrism finds expression in extreme nationalism, intolerant patriotism and exaggerated loyalty" (Ibid). It is not intended to confuse as prejudice an ordinate commitment to one's country, culture and nationality.

2.2 Political Prejudice:

This prejudice is against people defined as members of political parties, as upholders of certain political ideologies, and/or as committed to the pursuit of political goals or objectives in a manner not acceptable to the person's group. It is more than a rational objection to the party, ideology or political methodology. At the end of the day, it means that those in such parties, upholding such ideology and in favour of such methodologies are seen to be inferior to those subscribing to the acceptable parties, agreeing with the acceptable ideologies and supporting the political methodologies being accepted by, agreed to and supported by one's own political groups and categories. Political prejudice, as such, was not defined in *Prejudice and Tolerance in Ireland* (1977). In an attempt to give a definition now, the following is proposed:

> Political prejudice consists of rigid, negative, hostile attitudes towards people who are defined as members of political groups and categories that are perceived to differ from one's own political group or category in matters of party affiliation, ideological commitment and campaign methodology.

Political prejudice is not to be confused with disagreement on political issues and questions but rather a rejection of people deemed to belong to certain political groups and categories, because of their political views. Disagreement can lead to a rejection of views while prejudice leads to a rejection of people.

2.3 Racialism:

There has been some divergence of opinion on the use of this concept (see Robert Miles, *Racism after "Race Relations"*, London, Routledge, 1993). There are those who seem to use it for groups or categories with ethnic and social characteristics. The present author is not convinced of the utility of the broader use of the concept and, as in 1972-73, restricts its meaning to superficial physiognomic and genetically inherited visible body, facial features, eyes, hair, and skin traits.

The following descriptive definition from the 1977 text adequately defines the concept as used in this text:

"The use of the concept 'racial attitudes' in this study is restricted to attitudes based on response to physical characteristics, i.e., visible features, e.g., colour, size, facial features, etc. Unlike ethnic attitudes which are in response to nationality or cultural characteristics, racial attitudes are, in themselves, a-cultural. Racial prejudice then, is a negative attitude towards persons because of their membership of groups or categories perceived to differ in physical characteristics from the perceiver. It is ultimately based on the belief that certain physical characteristics, such as size, skin, colour, etc., make a person innately superior or inferior."

(Mac Gréil, 1977, p. 288).

Adopting a strictly physical (appearance) definition of racialism does not mean that all prejudice against racial groups is exclusively because of actual race. Ethnic and other associations may be involved in the mind of the perceiver. A method for determining the primary perception or definition of the category by the prejudiced respondent has been worked out via the "Rationalisation Scale" (see Chapter Three pp. 64-89 below).

2.4 Religious Prejudice:

As already noted, one religious category has been isolated in the literature as a special prejudice, i.e., "anti-Semitism" or prejudice against Jews. Anti-Semitism is one of the most studied and researched forms of social prejudice because of the genocide against Jews by the German Third Reich and its collaborators during the Second World War in Europe and because of the very long history of persecution of Jews in diaspora.

Other forms of prejudice seem to come and go, but anti-Semitism seems to continue from century to century. Jews, it could be said, are so scattered throughout the World and, at the same time, are so active, visible and weak, as well as being very successful in the areas of life they are free to pursue, that they become easy targets for scapegoating. As scapegoats they become objects of displaced aggression. The tragedy of the persecution of the Jews is that they are often attacked because they are positive, constructive and dynamic. It could also be argued that in attacking the Jews, non-Jews are attacking their perceived superior "super-ego". This is not to say that all Jews have been at all times angelic and faultless. They have the normal weaknesses and excesses of most peoples.

Religious prejudice in the broader context covers all religious affiliations and non-affiliations, as well as "agnostics" and "atheists". Religious sectarianism is a form of segregation based on perceived religious affiliation or non-affiliation. The question of prejudice against all believers becomes an issue in a world where there are explicit or implicit ideological positions adopted in professedly atheistic societies and, at the informal level, in societies where absolutist secularist policies and attitudes lead to hostile postures towards religion. Because Ireland has been to date a relatively strong religious society, i.e., a society where most people professed some form of religion and practised it regularly, most of our prejudices have been anti-religious or anti-denominational or anti-agnostic or anti-atheistic. Anti-clericalism is a fairly widespread form of religious prejudice.

With regard to a definition of religious prejudice, one could follow the example of Adorno, et al in their major work, *The Authoritarian Personality* (1950) by measuring prejudice in general and applying it to anti-Semitism or to other religions (Pennington, 1986, p. 84). At the same time, it is necessary to state what is being examined under the title religious prejudice, including anti-Semitism. The following is a tentative definition of religious prejudice.

> Religious prejudice consists of rigid, negative, hostile attitudes towards people who are seen as members of religious or religion-related groups or categories which differ from the religious or religion-related group or category of the perceiver or who are perceived not to profess belief in or be members of any religious faith or category and are, because of their membership or non-belief, deemed to be inferior to one's own group or category members.

Prejudice related to deeply held religious and ideological belief is one of the most dangerous of all prejudices and, probably, least amenable to pluralist integration. Religious prejudice is frequently used to give a so-called "spiritual" or absolutist rationalisation to other forms of prejudice.

2.5 Sexism:

Elliot Aronson in *The Social Animal* (3rd Edition, 1980) points to the facts pertaining to the constrained role of women in society and the need of society to face up to the subtle and less than subtle areas of sexist prejudice against women. As society becomes more aware "of the discrimination and stereotyping that occurs as a result of differential sex roles", . . . "sex-role stereotypes continue to crumble . . . as women widen their interests and enter new occupations the role perspectives for men are also becoming less restrictive". (Aronson, 1980, p. 205).

The recent and very welcome growth in research into sexism and social prejudice based on gender stereotypes, marks the early stages of such serious research. Sexism is deeply ingrained in the culture and in the social system. Most people, male and female, have been socialised into the accepted negative sex roles as part of their general rearing. Ann Weber in her book, *Social Psychology* (1992), gives a descriptive definition of sexism thus:

> "Sexism is discrimination based on prejudice against another gender; it typically refers to prejudice against females. Sexism is based on stereotypes that have little or no foundation in fact. Because gender roles are an important social categorisation, we seem to develop more extensive stereotypes of gender than of other group distinctions. Within a culture these stereotypes are likely to be shared and supported. Sexism and its consequences are therefore difficult but not impossible to correct."
>
> (Weber, 1992, p. 201.)

John C. Brigham, in his text *Social Psychology*, (1991) gives a very succinct definition of sexism, as follows:

> "Sexism can be defined as any attitude, action or institutional structure that subordinates a person because of his or her gender."
>
> (Brigham, 1991, p. 462).

Sexism incorporates prejudice and discrimination against males as well as against females, although, in the present time, it is widely agreed that males have had a dominant role in major positions of authority and influence in many areas of Irish society, especially in the middle and upper classes.

2.6 Homophobia:

The attitude in society towards people deemed to be homosexual (gay or lesbian) in relation to their sexual orientation must be of concern to the student of intergroup relations. In recent years in Ireland, homosexual behaviour between consenting adults over the age of seventeen years has been decriminalised after a long and arduous struggle through the Irish Court and ultimately to the European Court of Human Rights. Some psychologists see homophobia as "where a person is actively hostile to homosexuals, in a reaction formation against their own unconscious homosexual drives." (Hayes, 1994, p. 229).

Prejudice against "Gay People" has been measured in this work but it has not been possible to build an adequate theoretical or conceptual framework to find the psychological causes underpinning it. Hayes' assertion just quoted has not been tested, and the findings here are hardly adequate to explain the extent of the prejudice. It may be better to define it more generally as follows.

Homophobic prejudice consists of rigid, negative, hostile attitudes towards people who are deemed to be homosexual and possess the negatively stereotypical qualities ascribed to homosexual people.

Commenting on the nature of acting out homophobic prejudice, Ann Weber states: ". . . Anti-gay and anti-lesbian discrimination can range from subtle forms like job barriers and mandatory AIDS testing to overt violence like 'gay bashing' (unprovoked aggression against persons believed to be homosexual)".

(Weber, 1992, p. 201).

2.7 Social Prejudices:

Social prejudice is a general category covering diverse stimulus categories not covered by ethnic, political, racial, religious, sexist and homophobic prejudices. It includes a range of disadvantaged, disabled, class and socially unacceptable categories. Each category will be treated as an application of the general definition of prejudice.

The social categories which will be examined in this work will be the following:

(1) Alcoholics;   (6) People with Mental Handicap;
(2) Drug Addicts;   (7) People with Physical Handicap;
(3) Ex-prisoners;   (8) Unemployed People;
(4) Gay People;   (9) Unmarried Mothers;
(5) People with AIDS;   (10) Working Class.

Attitudes towards each of these categories will be measured in terms of social distance. Seven of the above categories were represented on the 1972-73, i.e., "Alcoholics", "Drug Addicts", "Handicapped" (not distinguishing between those with mental and those with physical handicap), "Unemployed", "Unmarried Mothers" and "Working Class".

PART II: THEORETICAL FRAMEWORK

1. MACROTHEORY:

The theoretical framework on which this research has been based has not differed greatly from that of the 1972-73 survey published in 1977 (*Prejudice and Tolerance in Ireland*), which was derived in part from a study carried out in 1966 (*A Psycho-Socio-Cultural Theory of Prejudice*) by the same author. The whole approach has been heavily influenced, at the macro level, by the structural-functional model of society and also by the theoretical reflections of the conflict structuralists.

Among the authors of the structural-functional school the following are included: Emile Durkheim (1893), Bronislaw Malinowski (1944), Alfred R. Radcliffe-Brown (1952), Talcott Parsons (1951), Leslie White (1959), Robert K. Merton (1957) and others. The main authors of the conflict school would include Karl Marx (1845/6), Georg Simmel (1908), Robert E. Park (1921), Lewis Coser (1956), Ralf Dahrendorf (1959) and others.

Sociology passed through a reaction to structural-functionalism between the late 1960s and the mid 1980s, when "microtheorising" and alternative "macrotheorising" held sway with numerous authors. By the end of the 1980s there came the "crisis of post-functionalism", which in some circles spawned a neo-functionalism revival as well as worthy critical thinking by sociologists such as Michel Foucault (1970), Jurgen Habermas (1973), Harold Garfinkel (1967), and Anthony Giddens (1973). During the 1990s we seem to have been going through a crisis in neo-Marxist structuralism after almost a decade of post-functionalism. The latter has been commented on by Jeffrey C. Alexander in his critical article "The New Theoretical Movement" in *Handbook of Sociology* edited by Neil J. Smelser (1988). The present author welcomes the return to macrotheorising at the personality-society-culture level.

2. THE MOMENTUM MODEL OF SOCIETY:

As stated above, the theoretical roots of both the 1977 work and the present study have been deeply planted in the structuralist schools. In line with the approach of 1977, neither school has been fully adopted. Instead, a new theoretical model was proposed which enabled a synthesis of both the conflict and equilibrium models.

Based on a reflection on the fundamental nature of society as the product of patterned interaction, that very interaction is seen as the very binding force of society. The nature of this interaction can be placed anywhere on the continuum from conflict to equilibrium, providing there is room for the minimum proportion of both forms of interaction. **The momentum model of society** sees society in the perpetual process of becoming or declining but never fully being. *Societas semper reformanda!*

If one assumes that society is structured, and it would be against all the evidence to deny it, it is reasonable to expect that the two major forces at work within this dynamic structure are forces leading to conformity and consent *en route* to social equilibrium and forces of dissent and non-conformity leading to social conflict. A high level of social equilibrium leads to the satisfaction of the citizens' social and personal "interests" and can lead to long periods of social stability and prosperity as long as it can maintain overall conformity. When, however, there is a significant level of social conflict there is a greater sense of "meaning" and ideas of change and vision.

The pursuit of "interests", and of "meaning" or "ideas" (in Max Weber's sense) seem to be the two primary needs of humans in society. But the real struggle is to achieve a balance of both. In the 1977 text, an attempt was made to depict in diagrammatic form the co-existence in society of "equilibrium" and "conflict" and the dynamic tension between both. Figure No. 4 demonstrates the relative position of conflict and equilibrium in a society at any particular time in history.

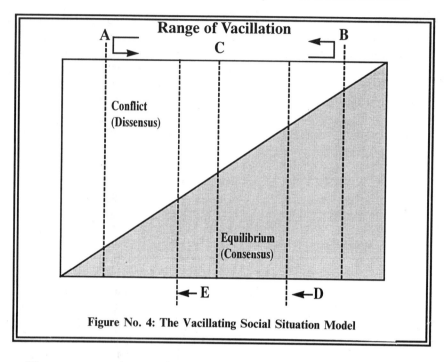

Figure No. 4: The Vacillating Social Situation Model

There are two points on the continuum beyond which the social situation cannot go. Right of point B would mean so little space for ideas or conflict that society would be totally de-radialised and under a benign or dictatorial regime where a perfectly organised bureaucratic system would only satisfy the material interests of the significant section of society. Dissent would be ruled out for all practical purposes. At such a state of imbalance between consensus and dissensus, a significant revolt is most likely with all safety-valves closed. Once the forces of conflict gather momentum, the taste of freedom (of ideas and participation) becomes socially contagious and a new situation develops and, possibly, the old order of equilibrium crushes or loses its grip, or else concedes greater dissent, e.g., collapse of East European centralist regimes.

At the other end of the spectrum or continuum, the level of dissent becomes so problematic that normal routine work is impossible. Preoccupation with ideas and revolution will not till the fields, raise the children, do the research, build the houses, provide for education, administer the welfare system, etc. If unchecked it can lead to anarchy. When point A (see Figure 4) is reached, the forces of equilibrium begin to assert themselves and a process of routinisation and ideological de-radicalisation begins to take place. The pendulum swings back with the gradual rise of bureaucrats, business people and priests replacing charismatic idealists and prophets!

Probably the healthiest position is at point C where there is a balanced tension between the prophetic and the priestly, or between the idealistic and the bureaucratic. Point D would represent a "right-of-centre" situation where there is more emphasis on "interests" than on ideas or "meaning". The left-of-centre situation at point E may be difficult to maintain, although it is a more stimulating place to live. A basic antinomy seems to exist between the pursuit of ideas/meaning and that of interests/prosperity!

The following quotation from the 1977 publication summarises the assumptions underlying the vacillating social situation model.

(1) "There are elements of conflict or dissensus present in a society at all times;

(2) "The degree of predominance of one type of element with regard to the other varies from time to time;

(3) "The rate of social change is likely to be greatest when the elements of dissensus are proportionately greater than the elements of consensus (position A) and are united in their opposition to the *status quo*.

(4) "The move towards greater consensus or equilibrium, following a major social change brought about by the elements of dissensus, is due to these elements becoming consensus-oriented, i.e., analogous to Max Weber's theory of routinization (consensus) following a charismatic-inspired (dissensus) social change. In a similar manner, the seed of dissensus springs from an over-routinized (fossilized) and meaningless consensus-dominated social system (position B), i.e., via traditionalism or bureaucratization (see *From Max Weber*, edited by H. H. Gerth and C. Wright Mills: 1948/1970, pp. 51-5, 197 ff.).

(5) "The internal *momentum* of society is largely determined by the relative position of elements of consensus and elements of dissensus, and the degree of uni-directionality between the elements of dissensus. When elements of dissensus are at cross-purposes they tend to neutralize each others' efficacy for social change.

(6) "Relative (dynamic) stability in society is only possible when the tension between dissensus and consensus is balanced and, thereby, contained (position C). The stability achieved through over-consensus (position B) is considered socially "pathological" since it contains within itself the seeds of its own destruction, i.e., it fails to provide the human need of *meaning* (just as over-dissent beyond point A on the continuum is also socially pathological)."

(Mac Gréil, 1977, pp. 153-4)

The relevance of these theoretical reflections for the study of prejudice and intergroup attitudes and opinions is obvious. Our attitudes are very functional in relation to social conformity and dissent. Prejudices are part of our attitude configuration.

3. MIDDLE-RANGE SOCIAL PSYCHOLOGICAL THEORIES:

At the middle range level of theory it will be contended that "authoritarianism" (Adorno et. al 1950) and "anomie" (Srole et. al, 1956, Merton, 1968), will be closely correlated to prejudice scores. Also, new scales purporting to measure "alienation" and "patriotism" will be explored to discover significant correlations.

3.1 Frustration-Aggression:

The social-psychological condition of "frustration" will be hypothesised again as a proximate causes of social prejudice, which is seen as a "psychological form of aggression". The frustration-aggression theory, with a strong Freudian background, has been developed by John Dollard (Dollard et. al, 1939). Insecurity, fear and anxiety (Maier 1961) are seen to be closely linked to frustration and, thereby, to social prejudice. Guilt is a psychological factor with strong links to prejudice (Allport, 1954).

3.2 Labelling and Stereotyping:

Labelling and stereotypes also play an important role in generating and reinforcing prejudice. Negative stereotypes become social stigmas against members of certain groups and categories. The authors who have contributed most to Labelling Theory include Erving Goffman (1963), Thomas Scheff (1966/1984), Edwin Lemert (1951) and others. Some of the popular negative stereotypes are tested in the chapters of this book dealing with the findings. Labelling frequently leads to the popular definition of the social minority according to perceived and ascribed negative characteristics.

3.3 Scapegoating:

The psychological functions of providing meaning, social prestige, affiliation and pathological relief add further dimensions of explanation to the variations in the scale and subscale "prejudice scores". Under the context of *meaning* prejudice can provide acceptable popular reasons for meaningless situations and causes more people to resort to *scapegoating* (Simpson C. Yinger, 1972, pp. 68 ff.). Certain minority groups are easily scapegoated and become the objects of displaced aggression, e.g., the scapegoating of Jews in times of economic and other crisis. The conditions under which scapegoating occurs have been outlined by sociologist Harry Johnson:

"(1) For some reason the true source of frustration and resentment cannot be attacked.

(2) Some other object exists that is symbolically connected with the source of frustration and is, therefore, a psychologically appropriate substitute as an object of aggression.

(3) For some reason this substitute is less well protected against attack than the true source of resentment.

It is difficult to say whether these three conditions are sufficient as well as necessary for scapegoating to occur. At any rate, the syndrome is common."

(Johnson: 1961, p. 595).

3.4 Social Prestige:

Social prestige and prejudice have a complex relation. As a "reaction formation" response to serious social and cultural deprivation, prejudice can lead people to adopt strong anti-minority dispositions, e.g. the prejudice of the Ku Klux Klan against Black People, Jews and Roman Catholics. Demagogues have exploited this tendency of the insecure disadvantaged to displace their aggression towards available scapegoats. Adolf Hitler, in his book, *Mein Kampf*, gives status to the defeated German by pointing to the superiority of the Jews:

".... For a racially pure people (the Aryans) which is conscious of its blood can never be enslaved by the Jew. In this world he will forever be master over bastards and bastards alone ...."

(Hitler, 1933/90, p. 295).

3.5 Ingroup Cohesion vs Outgroup Hostility:

Affiliation as a psychological function of prejudice is quite a serious issue. Affiliation is a dominant Western 'want' (Krech, et al 1962, p. 89-93).

"Sometimes this affiliation want becomes overpowering – the all-important want of the individual. One can almost speak of a pathological affiliation want. Schachter (1959) has pointed out that a strong affiliation want may be related to anxiety ...."

(Krech, et al, 1962, p. 91)

Graham Sumner put forward the thesis that outgroup hostility leads to ingroup cohesion (Sumner, 1906, p. 12). Robert K. Merton qualifies Sumner's thesis:

"He (Sumner) assumed, and his assumption has echoed an established truth on numerous occasions since his day, that immense loyalty to a group necessarily generates hostility to those outside the group."

(Merton, 1957, p. 398)

Some political and religious leaders, in times of crisis, may use the tactics of generating a "common enemy" to unite the people behind a cause perceived to be under threat.

Robert Merton in his Reference-Group Theory (1968, pp. 279-440) has focused on the sociological and social-psychological aspect of the relation between the member and his/her own groups and with non-membership groups. Many of the basic tenets of "Reference-Group Theory" have relevance for the understanding of social prejudice and intergroup attitudes.

3.6 The Apostate Complex:

There is one aspect of special interest, namely, the deep-seated attachments which people have had for groups which they may have left. The psychological residue of such former attachments, after membership of the group has been abandoned, may be the source of internal tension and external hostility towards the members, views and practices of the former group. Talcott Parsons seems to say that there is a *"compulsive alienation"* towards one's former group after abandoning it for a new and, maybe, opposite-oriented group (Parsons, 1951, p. 255).

If one takes the example of a devout Catholic who becomes a liberal atheist, or *vice versa*, or an active Communist who becomes an aggressive Capitalist, or *vice versa*, there is a likelihood in the case of such conversions of "over-identification" with one's new group and "compulsive alienation" towards the former group. This creates a high degree of tension because *we tend to be what we were as well as being what we are.* This is reinforced by the clash between old and new sets of friends. Also, we carry our past with us in our memories, in our interpersonal response traits, and so forth. This predicament may be called *The Apostate Complex.*

Robert K. Merton puts it very well in the context of "negative reference groups".

> "Full effective attachment to a former membership group need not, and perhaps typically does not, occur. It is then the case that former members of the group often convert it into a negative reference group towards which they are dependently hostile rather than simply indifferent. For precisely because the loss or rejection of membership does not promptly eradicate the former attachment to the group, ambivalence rather than indifference is apt to result. This gives rise to what Parsons calls 'compulsive alienation', in this, an abiding and rigid rejection of the norms of the repudiated group."
>
> (Merton, 1957, p. 295)

In the 1977 text this *dependently hostile attitude* towards one's former group was put forward as "The 'Apostate' Hypothesis". In the current text it is called the Apostate Complex, which is conducive to prejudice, not only against the abandoned group and those associated with it, but as a source of internal conflict and frustration. In a time of high ideological mobility and change of loyalties and commitment in terms of belief systems and political ideologies, this phenomenon may be more widespread than is realised. Monsignor James Horan, for instance, held the view that Irish journalists were more hostile to the Irish Catholic Church than were non-Irish non-Catholic journalists (Horan, 1992, pp. 240/2).

3.7 Fear and Anxiety:

Anxiety may be defined as a generalised state of chronic unrealistic fear. It can be caused by prolonged insecurity and a situation conducive to unresolved realistic fear due to factors outside one's control such as long-term unemployment, a breakdown in community social order, domestic disorganisation, community violence, and so forth.

Norman Maier's description of anxiety, quoted in the 1977 study (Mac Gréil, 1977, p. 94), is worth requoting here:

"In so far as the term anxiety indicates a state of generalised fear and not a reaction to some particular object in the environment, it fails to be goal-oriented and thus appears as a product of frustration. Likewise, in anxiety the object feared may give no clue as to the source of the danger."
(Maier, 1961, p. 131)

The social environment since 1972-73 has become, if anything, more conducive to anxiety in Irish society. The increase in long-term unemployment, the rise in crime, twenty years of Northern Irish 'troubles' (by 1989), AIDS, increase in the incidence of suicide, and other such developments would appear to be conducive to and indicative of greater anxiety in the population.

3.8 Personality Types:

The link between personality type and the prevalence of social prejudice has been dealt with elsewhere in this text, when analysing the authoritarian personality (see Chapter XIII).

4. SOCIAL THEORIES OF PREJUDICE AND INTERGROUP RELATIONS:

In addition to the macro and middle-range theories discussed below, i.e., structural-functionalism, conflict structuralism and the combined functional-conflict momentum model discussed below, it is possible to seek explanation for variations in prejudice scores in other more middle-range theories and theoretical models.

4.1 The Park Cycle:

A number of sociologists interested in the study of intergroup relations have adapted Park's Cycle with some success. These include, Emory Bogardus (1930, pp. 613 ff.), W. Brown (1934, pp. 34-37), Clarence E. Glick

(1955, pp. 219 ff.), Stanley Lieberson (1961, pp. 902-10), Brewton Berry (1965, pp.), Michael Banton (1967, pp. 304 ff.) and others. More recent writings on the sociology of intergroup relations have moved away from Park's four primary forms of intergroup interaction, i.e., "competition, conflict, accommodation and assimilation". The present author has found the Park approach most useful and relatively easy to apply to dominant-minority situations on the ground. As Michael Banton notes, it can be applied to all situations of intergroup interaction.

> "One virtue of this (Park's) theoretical framework is its refusal to treat race relations as different in any sociologically essential respect from relations between other sorts of groups. Park thought that patterns of race relations exemplified conflict, and to a lesser extent assimilation, but it is clear that many features could be counted as illustrations of accommodation and competition."
>
> (Banton (1967, p. 305).

Park devised the idea of a "patterned-sequence-cycle" which follows an irreversible order in minority-dominant relations, i.e.,

> *1st Stage:*   Contact;
> *2nd Stage:*   Competition between members of both groups;
> *3rd Stage:*   Accommodation;
> *4th Stage:*   Assimilation.
>
> (Park 1926, pp. 196 ff.).

This phased or staged development from the completely marginal status of the "arrived outsider" to adoption as one of the "dominant group" through assimilation was irreversible for Park. Banton quotes Park in the course of his comment on the journey into society.

> "Another seminal idea linking the study of individual behaviour to social processes was his (Park's) notion of the 'marginal man'. In describing perhaps the most general process of all, Park maintained 'the race relations cycle which takes the form to state it abstractly of contact, competition, accommodation and eventual assimilation, is apparently progressive and irreversible' (Park 1950, p. 150). Peoples may for a time live side by side, preserving their distinctive cultures, but in the long run inter-marriage will increase and the movement to assimilation will grow."
>
> (Banton 1967, p. 307).

At the time of Park's writing on the inevitable and irreversible move towards assimilation, it was generally accepted that cultural pluralism was neither possible or maybe desirable. It was the famous "melting pot" era in the United States.[3] Since the 1960s, however, the assimilationists have been challenged, and the possibility of the co-existence of diverse cultural and religious groups on a basis of equality has been deemed desirable and possible. R.A. Schermerhorn in his book, *Comparative Ethnic Relations* (1970, pp. 122-163), has coherently discussed the conditions and possibilities of fully integrated pluralism which is a rejection of assimilationism (see below page 51).

While not necessarily agreeing with the inevitable and irreversible move toward assimilation as the final stage, the Park cycle has much to offer as a model of explanation of the life-cycle of intergroup interaction. Obviously the span of time of this life-cycle can vary, for example, the slow process of integration of the groups in Ireland after almost four hundred years or sixteen generations. Are the opposing groups coming to the end of their "competition and conflict stage" in Northern Ireland and heading for a "mutual accommodation stage"? Is hostility towards Travelling People indicative of their entering into Park's "competition or conflict stage"? These are all very interesting theoretical reflections on some of Ireland's most urgent intergroup situations.

4.2 Dominant Group Postures and Minority Group Responses:

The interaction between dominant groups and the minority groups within society can be seen as a "posture-response dialectic". It should be stated very clearly that this approach only examines the actual existential situation of a dominant and a minority group co-occupying the same society at different times in the history of their interaction. This does not, of course, ignore the background to the situations examined.

Migration theory and history are essential dimensions to the explanation of the nature and state of intergroup relations. Robert Miles in his book *Racism after "Race Relations"* (1993) correctly draws attention to these dimensions. The Irish abroad have endured some of the "alienation" effects experienced by immigrants and migrants from other poorer countries around the world. As pointed out earlier in this work (see pp. 6f), Irish society today is not affected that much by major influences of migrants or immigrants. We are and have been primarily an emigrant society for over one hundred and fifty years. In addition to the emigrant character of Irish society, it is also a "post-colonial society", with a long history of the majority of being "aliens" in their own society due to religious, social and political discrimination.

Returning to the Posture-Response dialectic/paradigm, Figure 5 gives the range of options and possibilities.

In all, there are nineteen situations ranging from A, "avoiding annihilation"

---

3. Henry Pratt Fairchild in his book *Immigration* (1925) was seen by James Vander Zanden (1972, p. 25) as an effective promoter of assimilation.

Figure No. 5: Dominant Posture/Minority Response Paradigm

Dominant Postures → Minority Responses ↓	Annihilation 1.	Expulsion 2.	Segregation 3.	Stratification 4.	Assimilation 5.	Amalgamation 6.	Pluralism 7.
1. Avoidance (Withdrawn)	A	B	C	D	E	F	
2. Agression (Conflict)	G	H	I	J	K	L	
3. Accommodation (Acceptance)			M	N	O	P	
4. Assimilation (Acculturation)					Q		
5. Amalgamation (Miscegenation)						R	
6. Pluralims (Co-Existence)							S

Source: Mac Gréil, 1977, p. 142.

to S "mutual desire for pluralism". Generally speaking, in the case of A to P the initiative is in the hands of the dominant group. It is also possible to experience shift and changes in the postures of the dominant groups and in the responses of the minority groups over time. For instance, the Native American peoples (often referred to as "American Indians") have experienced all postures from genocide (annihilation) to pluralist co-existence and changes in postures, depending on the political mood of the dominant group of the day. Although separate nations in theory, they are not members of the United Nations, which might guarantee them some degree of stability in their pluralism.

An understanding of the behaviour patterns implied in the various "postures" and those predicated by the "responses" of the minorities, should make it possible to explain and, in some instances, predict, the psychological, sociological and cultural (anthropological) outcome of the intergroup interaction. Space does not permit a detailed analysis and description of the parameters of each of the nineteen situations, i.e., from A to S. In the course of the text reference can be made to the paradigm, when dealing with different groups, collectivities and categories, especially those classified as minorities.

4.3 Individual Group Postures and Responses:

4.3.a Annihilation: In the course of the history of intergroup relations this most extreme of all dominant postures has been adopted and pursued from time-to-time. The most notorious in this century has been the genocide policies of the German Third Reich against Jews and other categories including Gypsies, Homosexuals, and members of various nationalities. The inter-tribal genocide in Rwanda in the very recent past keeps the reality of such a posture before the minds of both students of intergroup relations and political and religious leaders.

4.3.b Expulsion: Expulsion has been quite a common dominant posture in the course of history. It can be due to displacement of the indigenous population to enable the plantation of favoured members of the dominant group, in other words, the occupation of captured territory. The forced migration of whole populations and the so-called "ethnic cleansing" are but examples of a dominant group policy of expulsion. Irish people have on a number of occasions been forced from their lands in the course of the 16th, 17th and 18th Centuries. Other examples of expulsion include the Moors from Spain, the Chocktaw Indians in the U.S.A., and many others. The subtle pressure to force poor people out of inner cities in response to "gentrification" programmes is also a mild form of expulsion of the weak by the strong. Denial of permanent residence and halting sites to Irish Travelling people could be classed as an indirect form of expulsion.

4.3.c Segregation: Segregation is commonly associated with formal discrimination, i.e., discrimination validated by law and custom. In other words, it is legitimised or legalised discrimination. Segregation not infrequently involves territorial or spatial apartheid. Desegregation means the removal of formal legal support for systematic discrimination, e.g., the removal of political gerrymandering in Northern Ireland.

4.3.d Stratification: Stratification has been defined by Vander Zanden as the differential ranking of people (1972, p. 221) and by Talcott Parsons as follows:

> "There is a sense in which all the elements of the relational reward system come to be integrated in terms of a ranking system in terms of esteem, just as the control of facilities is ordered in a political power system. This ranking system in terms of esteem is what we call the system of *stratification* of the society."
>
> (Parsons, 1951, p. 132).

This stratification system may be maintained by rigid income differentials, feudal systems and other forms of subordination. The most notorious form of rigid stratification is the "caste system". Informal stratification is quite widespread in most Western societies.

4.3.e Assimilation: Anthony Giddens, (1989) gives a summary definition of "assimilation" as follows:

"The acceptance of a minority group by a majority population in which the group takes over the values and norms of the dominant *culture.*"

(Giddens, 1989, p. 735)

Elsewhere in the same text Giddens, when commenting on the development of ethnic relations, notes that the process of "assimilation" of immigrants means that they "abandon their original customs and practices, moulding their behaviour to the values and norms of the majority. Generations of immigrants (to the United States) faced pressures towards being 'assimilated' in this way, and many of their children became more or less completely 'American' as a result" (Giddens, 1989, p. 271). The social policy of assimilation, which has been generally promoted by dominant groups toward "acceptable" minorities, implies "that, over time, all groups will conform to the moves, life style, and values of the dominant group" (Newman, 1973, p. 52). It is akin to "cultural absorption" of the minority by the dominant group at the expense of the former's own culture and ethnic uniqueness.

The concept of assimilation is discussed at some length in *Prejudice and Tolerance in Ireland* (1977) both as a "posture" and as a "response" (see Mac Gréil, 1977, pp. 137-9, 163-9). The summary and conclusion to the section on assimilation as a minority response is worth repeating.

"Assimilation . . . implies a voluntary move on the part of the minority group to adopt the cultural forms of the dominant group and discard its (minority) individual cultural identity. It also implies a reciprocal policy on the part of the dominant group to absorb the minority into its own culture. . . . It has been suggested that the ideologies of socialism, liberalism, and capitalism favour assimilation."

(Mac Gréil, 1977, p. 166)

4.3.f Amalgamation: While "assimilation" leads to the demise of the minority's cultural identity, "amalgamation" is seen to lead to a "hybrid" mix of the dominant and minority cultures. Since the dawn of civilisation there has been a high degree of cultural diffusion in the sense that societies have borrowed and shared cultural items and this has led to a degree of change in the respective cultures. "Amalgamation" inevitably leads to intergroup marriages or "miscegenation" between members of the groups. Amalgamation is more likely when the socio-political power of both groups is fairly balanced. In the case of imbalance of power the likelihood of assimilation of the weaker into the stronger culture is probable.

4.3.g Pluralism: The concept "pluralism" is a word used very frequently in political and sociological commentary about the ideal form of intergroup integration. Yet the evidence of its concrete realisation "on the ground" is not that impressive. It is a difficult model of integration. It is particularly relevant to the Northern Ireland situation and to other societies with diverse groups adhering to different cultural, political and religious traditions. The following definition tries to include the essential characteristics of pluralism.

Pluralism is a voluntary form of integration which guarantees equality to all and respects, protects and promotes the different cultural, political and religious traditions of the members of the groups and/or collectivities living in the same society.

As pointed out in the previous publication (Mac Gréil, 1977, pp. 134-7, 173-9), Richard A. Schermerhorn distinguished four meanings of the term "pluralism" i.e.,

(1) *"An Ideological Designation*, i.e., a desire of the minority to remain itself;

(2) *"A Political Designation*, i.e., political decisions arrived at by and implemented through diverse 'parties, lobbies or the use of media';

(3) *"A Cultural Designation*; i.e., groups distinguished by their language, religion, kinship systems, nationality etc.;

(4) *"A Structural Designation*; i.e., institutional duplication to ensure that members of different ethnic and religious groups interact mostly with their own members and preserve their group identities."

(Schermerhorn 1970, pp. 122 ff.)

The key notes in pluralism as a model of intergroup integration are the following:

(a) Group differences to be facilitated and respected;

(b) Equality of treatment for all members of different groups;

(c) Pluralist arrangement is voluntarily agreed by different groups;

(d) Duplication of facilities, i.e., language, education and religious. The preservation of distinctive group identity may require separate schools, churches, multilingual and other facilities.

Pluralism leads to a high degree of group endogamy, i.e., members of the different groups tend to marry those with similar cultural, linguistic, ethnic and religious backgrounds. This may be referred to as the principle of 'marital propinquity'.

4.3.h Avoidance/Withdrawal: This is a common minority response to dominant postures not perceived to be friendly or desirable by the members of the society. Sometimes it may be the only option open to a relatively weak minority in the face of dominant group hostility. Withdrawal from the area of danger, i.e., in the case of a threat of annihilation or forced expulsion, is unfortunately quite common, e.g. former Yugoslavia, Rwanda, and other cases of the flight of refugees. Most instances of large-scale refugee movement are examples of "minority withdrawal".

In societies where the dominant groups try to stratify and segregate minority groups, there can be a reaction of withdrawal into certain communities with little or no contact with members of the dominant groups. This can also be a reaction against forced assimilation policies, when minority groups set up their own ethnic communities, e.g. Chinatowns in U.S. cities. Some minority ghettoes may be partly due to withdrawal from the friendless social environment of the dominant group (see Mac Gréil, 1977, pp. 142 ff.)

4.3.i Aggression or Conflict: The history of intergroup relations shows that conflict is a frequent response of minority groups to the postures adopted by dominant groups at various times. The nature and intensity of the aggression or conflict is determined by the hostility of the dominant group and the approach of the minority and its relative strength. A major source of class conflict is the attempt to pursue the group's access to authority and power within the authority structure of society.

> "The authority structure of entire societies as well as particular institutional order within societies (such as industry) is, in terms of the theory here advanced, the structural determinant of class formation and class conflict."
>
> (Dahrendorf, 1959, p. 136).

The nature of minority group conflict can range from organised violent (military or paramilitary) aggression to non-violent protest. The civil rights movements around the world have engaged in conflict with dominant groups in the course of the various campaigns for ethnic, gender, political, religious, racial and/or social groups' rights. Dominant groups can also institute aggressive reaction against minority conflict. But it must be stressed that inequality and exploitation are the generic social causes of conflict in intergroup relations. Neil Smelser points to the universal inequality potential of societies.

> "One of the universal features of both relational structures and groups is that they become the basis of inequality in society. Specific kinds of institutions (religion, the military, commerce) may be regarded as especially important in the range of society's institutions, and be therefore endowed with greater resources, respect, freedom, and privilege than others."
>
> (Smelser, 1988, p. 105)

Haralambos and Holborn in their book, *Sociology: Themes and Perspectives* (3rd edition, London, 1991), summarise the Marxist approach to conflict thus:

> "Marx maintained that, with the possible exception of societies of pre-history, all historical societies contain basic contradictions which mean that they cannot survive for ever in their existing form. These contradictions involve the exploitation of one group by another: in feudal society, the lords exploit their serfs; in capitalist society, employers exploit their employees. This creates fundamental conflict of interest between social groups since one gains at the expense of another. This conflict of interest must ultimately be resolved since a social system containing contradictions cannot survive unchanged."
>
> (Haralambos & Holborn, 1991, p. 12.)

Where prejudice enters into the equation it is as a mechanism of rationalisation of inequality, as well as being a form of psychological aggression and as an irrational basis of conflict. When constructive conflict is positively directed at the source of inequality, it is likely to lead to social change which will reduce social contradictions and conflict itself.

4.3.j Accommodation or Acceptance: It is possible for minorities to accept the dominant postures of segregation, stratification, forced assimilation, and amalgamation as responses of last resort. Very weak and passive groups tend to accommodate as a mode of adaptation to a situation in which they do not see an alternative. People socialised in a deprived situation or social condition tend to become passive and suffer from "induced submissiveness" and poor social or ethnic self-esteem. At the other end of the spectrum, people socialised in privileged situations tend to possess a degree of "induced dominance". This latter quality is acquired over years of being in a position to exercise authority and of having power to influence one's own life and the lives of others.

The "accommodation and acceptance response" has met with some criticism and even derision by those who would wish for a more aggressive or conflictual response to exploitation. This has been summed up very well by Brewton Berry in his book, *Race and Ethnic Relations* (Boston, Houghton-Miffin, 1965), when he writes:

> "It is an amazing fact, but one amply attested, that some human beings have an infinite capacity to endure injustice without retaliation, and apparently without resentment against their oppressors. Instances of this phenomenon are numerous, and they come from every part of the world where one group dominates another. Militant leaders have been driven to despair by the apathy they have encountered among those they would lead to freedom; and members of dominant groups have

commented on the cheerfulness and the loyalty among those who would seem to have no reason for such sentiments."

(Berry, 1965, p. 382).

Examples of accommodation were found among the deprived Black people in the United States of America in the past. They were often referred to as "Uncle Toms", "Nannies", and "Boys". In Ireland too we had our accommodating poor peasants – both rural and urban, who "tipped the cap" to their "superiors"! The Travelling People in the past also seemed to respond to their treatment by the dominant group in a passive manner. In fact, they seemed to have been fatalistic about their relative and real deprivation. In recent years there seems to be a change of response from accommodation to conflict among some Travellers which, if it is directed in a constructive manner, could be interpreted as a positive development.

4.3.k Conclusion: The above ten postures and responses help to explain the volatility of intergroup relations, which can change in both a positive or negative manner depending on the wishes of the dominant groups and the responses of the minorities. Generally speaking, the nature of the dialectic or dialogue is mostly determined by the dominant group, which is invariably in a position to take the initiative in its own interests or apparent interests.

It is frequently said that there are "minority problems" in societies! This is a very symptomatic description of the situation. Usually intergroup relations are primarily "problems of the dominant groups". For instance, the racial problems of South Africa and of the United States were and are basically White people's problems. In Ireland the main problem of the Travelling People is a problem for the Settled People! In the case of male sexism, the primary problem is that of males as a dominant group. It is important to avoid the trap of "victimology" which seeks the explanation of social problems in the deprived and weaker sections of society rather than in the privileged and more powerful beneficiaries of the social inequality. The victimological approach keeps the spotlight away from the dominant group, which is "structurally" responsible for the deprivation of the weak, through their (the dominant group's) superfluity of power and resources.

PART III: RESEARCH DESIGN

This book reports on a national survey of Irish intergroup attitudes and prejudices carried out from November 1988 until April 1989. For the most part, this national survey has been a replication of a similar survey carried out in Greater Urban and Suburban Dublin in 1972-73. The fieldwork, i.e., the interviewing and entering of the data was carried out, on contract, by the Survey Unit of the Economic and Social Research Institute in Dublin.

1. RESEARCH APPROACH:

The research approach has been to *monitor, describe, explore* and, as far as possible, *explain* the current state of intergroup prejudice and tolerance in Ireland and the degree of attitude and prejudice changes which have taken place in the Dublin population over the sixteen years between 1972-73 and 1988-89.

In addition to intergroup attitudes and prejudices, other areas of social and personal attitudes are reported on and analysed in this work. These include authoritarianism, anomie, alienation, patriotism, attitudes towards work and unemployment, attitudes towards Irish neutrality and towards nuclear weapons, and respondents' views and opinions on issues of contemporary interest to Irish society. Certain measures of social mobility, changes in education and occupational status and the assessment of material standard of living of the people are reported on and examined in this project. Special measures of religiosity and political views and attitudes are analysed, as are attitudes and views on the Irish language. The normal demographic profile of the population (as represented by the national sample) is described and commented on in the course of this book.

2. POPULATION AND SAMPLE:

The population of the National Survey consisted of all those on the Register of Electors (over 18 years of age) in 1988 in the Republic of Ireland. A random sample of 1,347 was chosen using the ESRI "Ransam Programme". A response rate of slightly over 73% was achieved and 1,005 respondents agreed to be interviewed.

2.1 Profile of Sample:

The interviews were carried out by the E.S.R.I. field interviewers during the period of November 1988 to April 1989. The normal research procedures were followed and the fieldwork was completed to the satisfaction of the Survey Unit of the E.S.R.I. and under its supervision.

Table 1 gives the demographic profile of the sample interviewed. The below distribution of the sample, when compared with the distribution of over eighteen-year-olds in the closest census of the population (1986) by comparable variables proved to be representative (with the normal margins of error).

2.2 Commentary on Profile:

The profile of this sample of the Irish adult population (Republic of Ireland) is in itself an interesting finding. The age distribution shows a slight distortion of profile due to emigration, on the one hand, and high fertility

(in the recent past), on the other. The contrast between the demographic profile of Dublin (City and County) and that of Connaught/Ulster is disturb-
ingly great. The percentage of the adult population over fifty years of age
in Connaught/Ulster (48.6%) is nearly twice (180%) the "over fifty" adult
population of Dublin City and County (26.5%) This gives some real impres-

TABLE No. 1
PROFILE OF NATIONAL SAMPLE 1988-89

A. AGE		F. COUNTY OF RESIDENCE	
1. 18 to 35 years	392 (39.1%)	1. Dublin	277 (27.6%)
2. 36 to 50 years	271 (27.0%)	2. Rest of Leinster	255 (25.4%)
3. 51 to 65 years	194 (19.4%)	3. Munster	300 (29.9%)
4. 66 year plus	145 (14.5%)	4. Connaught/Ulster	173 (17.2%)
B. GENDER		**G. PLACE OF REARING**	
1. Females	544 (54.1%)	1. Large City (100,000 plus)	235 (23.4%)
2. Males	461 (45.9%)	2. Small City (10,000 plus)	117 (11.7%)
		3. Town (1,500 plus)	153 (15.3%)
		4. Rural (under 1,499)	498 (49.7%)
C. MARITAL STATUS		**H. POLITICAL PARTY PREFERENCE**	
1. Never Married	291 (29.0%)	1. Fianna Fail	449 (44.7%)
2. Married	624 (62.1%)	2. Fine Gael	252 (25.1%)
3. Widowed	71 (7.1%)	3. Labour	66 (6.6%)
4. Other	19 (1.9%)	4. Progressive Democrats	42 (4.2%)
		5. Workers Party	24 (2.4%)
		6. Other Party/Non-Party	35 (3.5%)
		7. Would Not Say	60 (6.0%)
		8. Would Not Vote	43 (4.3%)
		9. No Reply	34 (3.4%)
D. EDUCATION		**I. SOCIAL CLASS POSITION**	
1. Primary Only	283 (28.2%)	1. Class I ("Upper Class")	34 (3.8%)
2. Incomplete 2nd Level	348 (34.7%)	2. Class 11 ("Upper Middle Class")	105 (11.8%)
3. Complete 2nd Level	232 (23.1%)	3. Class 111 ("Middle Middle Class")	270 (30.3%)
4. Third Level	140 (14.0%)	4. Class IV ("Lower Middle Class/ Upper Lower Class")	295 (35.1%)
		5. Class V ("Lower Class")	188 (21.1%)
E. OCCUPATIONAL STATUS		**J. RELIGIOUS AFFILIATION**	
1. Semi-Unskilled Manual	156 (17.5%)	1. Roman Catholic	946 (94.2%)
2. Skilled/Routine Non-Manual	278 (31.1%)	2. Protestant*	43 (4.3%)
3. Inspectional/Supervisory	300 (33.6%)	3. Other Religion	6 (0.6%)
4. Professional/Executive	159 (17.8%)	4. No Religion	9 (0.9%)

• **Church of Ireland/Methodists/Presbyterians**

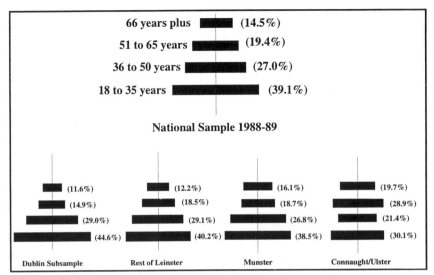

Figure No. 6: Demographic Profile of the Sample

sion of the extent of out-migration from Connaught/Ulster to Dublin, elsewhere in Ireland and abroad (see Figure No. 6). It also highlights the gross imbalance between the young workforce of Dublin and the ageing workforce in Connaught/Ulster. This age profile will influence the response of the "County of Residence" subsamples. The "Rest of Leinster" and "Munster" subsamples are relatively close to the national average.

The distribution of the "gender" variable is within the margin of error of the census over 18 year olds' distribution. Fieldwork experience has shown that females are more available and willing to be interviewed than are men. In this survey, care has been taken to ensure that all randomly chosen names, male and female, were equally pursued for interview. "Education" and "occupational status" provide an interesting distribution and show the impact of the free second-level schemes ("the O'Malley scheme") at the end of the 1960s. Comparisons with the 1972/73 survey show the very substantial increase in educational participation (see Mac Gréil, 1990).

"County of residence" shows a relatively low number of Connaught/ Ulster respondents in comparison with the other subsamples. This is due to the out-migration from this area and the older age profile of the remaining population. Without some very drastic intervention, i.e., the location of employment in the Connaught/Ulster region, the future viability of many of the smaller villages and communities will be severely challenged. The correction of the population imbalance would appear to be a major challenge for the people of Connaught/Ulster, i.e., the five counties of Connaught and the three border counties of Donegal, Cavan and Monaghan.

"Place/area of rearing" gives a most interesting result with half of the sample (49.7%) as rural reared and less than a quarter (23.4%) coming from a large city.

The "political party preferences" of the respondents are a changing phenomenon, although it appears that the proportion of respondents changing party allegiances may be lower than is sometimes stated. The late Harold Wilson, former Prime Minister of the United Kingdom, once stated that governments were changed more by selective abstention from voting than by change of allegiance. In the 1972-73 Dublin survey (Mac Gréil, 1977) the proportion of the sample who said they "voted occasionally for the party" they chose, i.e., the "floating vote", was 15%. This increased to 27% in 1988-89.

The social class position of the sample points to a predominant "middle class". The persistence of such a high proportion (21.1%) in the "lower class" category should raise questions about the selective nature of class homogenisation in Irish society. The implications of one-fifth of the sample in the poorer and more disadvantaged level of a society with greater numbers in the more privileged brackets has an obvious effect on a growing sense of "relative deprivation" (Redding, 1969, p. 5).

Religious affiliation of the sample has been very close to that of the 1981 census of the population which recorded Roman Catholics at 93.1%, protestants at 3.4%, other religions at 0.37%, no religion at 1.15% and "no information supplied" at 2.06%. The proportionate distribution of the 2.06% (not supplying information) would result in Roman Catholics at 95.1% and Protestants at 3.5% in 1981. Because of the very high level of denominational homogeneity, the "religious affiliation" is not statistically useful as an independent variable.

3. THE RESEARCH INSTRUMENT:

The research instrument is, as stated above, a questionnaire (see Appendix A) which was administered by the E.S.R.I. Survey Unit team of interviewers over a period of six months from November 1988 until April 1989. Its design followed more-or-less the same pattern as the questionnaire used in the 1972-73 questionnaire.

Questions 7 to 19, 28 and 29 were added from an international survey on religion and family. Some of the latter proved useful and relevant to the present study and are reported on below in Chapter X. Other material was not relevant, e.g., the question relating to divorce presumed that it was legally permitted in Ireland at the time, which was not the case.

3.1 Outline of Questionnaire:

The table of contents of the questionnaire given in Table 2 gives an outline of the dependent and independent variables. The dependent variables are highlighted. The international survey component are questions nos. 7 to 19, 28 and 29. The details of each question are printed in Appendix A (see pages 475ff).

TABLE No. 2
SUMMARY AND OUTLINE OF QUESTIONNAIRE (See Appendix A)

Introduction and place of residence;	Q32 FUNDAMENTALIST SCALE;
Q1 Gender of respondent;	Q33 Handing on of religion to the the children
Q2 Place of birth and rearing of self, spouse and parents and duration of present residence;	Q34 Attitudes towards religious vocations;
Q3 Primary and secondary ethnic self-identity;	Q35 ECUMENICAL UNITY;
Q4 BOGARDUS SOCIAL DISTANCE AND RATIONALISATION SCALES;	Q36 ANOMIE, ALIENATION, PATRIOTISM SCALES;
Q5 Age, marital status and family size;	Q37 Age left school;
Q6 Household census;	Q38 Type of school attended;
International Survey Component	Q39 Educational standard reached;
Q7 Family Life Scale;	Q40 ANTI-BLACK RACIALIST SCALE;
Q8 Women and work;	Q41 Community voluntary involvement;
Q9 Child-care for working mothers;	Q42 IRISH NEUTRALITY AND ANTI-NUCLEAR SCALE;
Q10 Pre-Marriage relationships;	Q43 IRISH LANGUAGE SCALE;
Q11 Marriage scale;	Q44 Use of the Irish language;
Q12 Ideal family size;	Q45 NORTHERN IRISH SCALE;
Q13 Parents and children scale;	Q46 Solutions to the Northern Irish problem;
Q14 Divorce and the law;	Q47 Assessment of Anglo-Irish agreement;
Q15 Working Mothers;	Q48 Political party preferences;
Q16 Divorce-status of respondent;	Q49 Political participation;
Q17 Divorce-status of spouse;	Q50/51 Voting patterns;
Q18 Parents (mothers) and jobs;	Q52 CONSERVATISM SCALE;
Q19 Parents income;	Q53 ANTI-BRITISH SCALE;
Q20 NEW SEXIST/FEMINIST SCALE;	Q54 ANTI-TRAVELLER SCALE;
Q21 Religious affiliation;	Q55 LIBERAL-ILLIBERAL SCALE;
Q22 Change of religious affiliation;	Q56/57 Employment and occupational status;
Q23 ANTI-SEMITIC SCALE;	Q58 ATTITUDES TO WORK, JOBS AND TRADE UNIONS;
Q24 Religion and personal development;	Q59 Satisfaction with material standards of living;
Q25 Religion and Social Advantage/Disadvantage;	Q60 Average income;
Q26 Religious worship/practice;	Q61 Ownership and type of family residence;
Q27 Participation of Roman Catholics in Mass and the Sacraments;	Q62 Inventory of Domestic Amenities;
Q28 IMAGES OF GOD;	
Q29 IMAGES OF THE WORLD	
Q30 Prayer practice;	
Q31 CLOSENESS TO GOD SCALE;	Q63 Details of the Interview process.

The reception which the interviewers received was on the whole very positive. Table 3 reports on the findings of Question 63.

TABLE No. 3
RECEPTION OF INTERVIEWERS BY RESPONDENTS

A. Where the Interview Took Place		C. Amount of Explanation Needed	
1. In the Living Room	66%	1. General Introduction	43%
2. In the Kitchen	24%	2. Gen. Intro. and Further	45%
3. In the Hallway	1%	Explanation at Beginning	12%
4. On the Doorstep	1%	3. Gen. Intro. and Further	0%
5. Other Locations	5%	Explanation throughout Interview	
NUMBER	1,005	NUMBER	1,005

B. Reception		D. Acquaintance with Survey	
1. Excellent	58%	1. Had not heard of Survey	95%
2. Very Good	25%	2. Had heard from person	3%
3. Good	10%	previously interviewed	
4. Fair (Improving Later)	3%	3. Had heard of survey from	2%
5. Fair	3%	other sources	–
6. Cool	1%		
7. Hostile	0%		
NUMBER	1,005	NUMBER	1,005

The above account of the actual reception received by the interviewers makes very satisfactory reading, and also speaks well of the approach and courtesy of the interviewers. The amount of information sought by the respondents is very reasonable in the light of the complexity and length of this "in depth" interview into some areas of personal attitudes and behaviour. With such cooperation from respondents the researcher can have much confidence. A similarly positive reaction was reported in 1972-73 in the Dublin Survey.

Considering that the fieldwork extended over a period of six months it is interesting to note that only 5% of the interviewees had any acquaintance with the survey in advance of their interview. With so few forewarned it means that the replies to questions measuring predispositions (which are both pre-reflectional and mostly implicit) were spontaneous. This adds to the quality of the replies.

Surveys of this nature, with long in-depth interviews carried out over a relatively extended period of time, have an advantage over public opinion polls, which are carried out over a relatively brief (number of days) time scale and are likely to be influenced by some transitory sensational media-exposed event or public campaign. The survey is much more likely to tap into the deeply held attitudes and opinions of the people without influence of media, sensational campaigning or the pressure of urgency. Even elections and referenda sometimes reflect the campaigns and the charismatic appeal of protagonists as much as they reflect the basic values and attitudes of the people. People can be susceptible to seductive persuasion. The surveyor, on the other hand, must interview in the "calm cool" of the respondents' home at her or his time. Ideally, a survey, properly conducted, is a consultation of the sample of people in an easy manner that gives the respondent the necessary confidence to express her or his view or opinion. For that reason the findings of Table 3 are most reassuring.

Returning to Table 2, the normal "independent variables" are included, i.e., "age", "gender", "marital status", "education", "occupational status", "social class position", "county of residence", "place of rearing" and "political party preferences" have been measured. In addition variables such as: "religious practice and beliefs", "community voluntary involvement", "political participation", "material standard of living (including income)" and "type of dwelling", have also been included.

The "dependent variables", which are those various scales and measures used to gauge prejudice and related attitudes and issues, include: ethnic self-identity, social distance and intergroup definition, sexism, anti-semitism, authoritarianism, anomie, alienation, patriotism, racialism, attitudes towards Northern Ireland, anti-British attitudes, anti-Traveller attitudes, liberalness, attitudes towards work and trade unions, and other attitudes towards religion, the Irish language and family life. These diverse prejudices and related attitudes and opinions are measured by the scales and questions highlighted in Table 2 above.

The sequence of questions is such as to enable the interviewer to bring the respondent through the series of "independent" and "dependent" variables in accordance with the guidelines of questionnaire construction and layout. Awkward and difficult questions are interspersed with non-challenging ones so as to ensure a continued flow in the interview. Sensitive questions relating to personal income and material standard of living, for instance, are held over until the end of questionnaire (Qs. 59 to 62) to prevent interruptions earlier in the interview, in the event of some respondents becoming annoyed with these questions. This is a common strategy in questionnaire construction. The most demanding (and probably the most important) question has been put early on in the interview, i.e., Question 4 seeking social distance and rationalization for fifty nine categories. This early stage for Question 4 is at a time when the interviewee is fresh.

3. CONCLUSION:

The research design of the 1988-89 survey was similar to that of the 1972-73 survey (see Mac Gréil, 1977, Chapter 3, pp. 48-78). In the above pages the research approach, population and sample, and profile of respondents were discussed. Some interesting features about the sample were noted and, as will be observed in the following chapters, these will have an influence on the levels and variations in the responses to the numerous "dependent variables".

One of the most important features of this work, as its title, *Prejudice in Ireland Revisited*, indicates, is the fact that change can be measured in the peoples' attitudes, prejudices and opinions over a period of sixteen years i.e., between 1972-73 and 1988-89. The findings of the 1988-89 survey will, in turn, become a second bench-mark for a future survey in 2004-05. In terms of ethnic and religious attitudes, it is of special value and interest that the interviews for the 1988-89 survey took place before the collapse of the Eastern Europe Communist Block and the various changes of the 1990s in Irish society, as a result of the Maastricht agreement and other developments. Because this work is seen as a benchmark, it has been deemed necessary to provide as much quantitative evidence as possible in this publication. (Hopefully, this will not be off-putting to the reader not particularly interested in such detailed reporting of findings.)

The outline of the questionnaire summarised in Table 2, and given in full detail in Appendix A, has proven to be most satisfactory in the field, as shown by the reception and performance of the respondents and interviewers. This gives the researcher greater confidence in the findings.

The times at which interviews commenced are summarised in Table 4 below. The distribution of the times of interview show an interesting pattern, and may be of use to researchers organising their fieldwork plan for future surveys. Slightly less than one-quarter of interviews took place before 1 p.m. The majority were interviewed between 1 and 7 p.m. (60.0%). The

TABLE No. 4
TIMES OF COMMENCEMENT OF INTERVIEWS

Time Commencing	Percentage	(Cumulative Percent)	Number
1. 9 a.m. to 11 a.m.	8.9%	(8.9%)	89
2. 11 a.m. to 1 p.m.	14.7%	(23.6%)	148
3. 1 p.m. to 3 p.m.	26.4%	(50.0%)	265
4. 3 p.m. to 5 p.m.	19.0%	(69.0%)	191
5. 5 p.m. to 7 p.m.	14.6%	(83.6%)	147
6. 7 p.m. to 9 p.m.	14.6%	(98.2%)	147
7. 9 p.m. to 11 p.m.	1.8%	(100.0%)	18
	Total Number of Interviews		1,005

average length of interview was slightly over one-and-a-half hours (91.7 minutes). The success of the fieldwork was due to the cooperation of respondents and the courteous skill of the team of E.S.R.I. interviewers. The researcher and the reader are indebted to both the interviewees and the interviewers who have made a work of this nature possible. The careful and professional work of the E.S.R.I. Survey Unit in the computation of the data has been most satisfactory.

CHAPTER III

Social Distance in Ireland

PART I: INTRODUCTION

"Social Distance" is one of the most reliable and valid measures of intergroup attitudes. It measures "behavioural tendency", which is an important indicator of the valency of social attitudes (Mac Gréil, 1977, pp. 11 ff.). In 1926, Emory Bogardus devised a highly valuable Social Distance Scale which has had a high level of validity and reliability as an instrument of measurement of intergroup attitudes (see Bogardus, 1947/1928[1]). In the original Bogardus Social Distance Scale, subjects were asked to indicate how close they were prepared to admit members of listed categories on a scale of seven statements, i.e.

1. *"To close kinship by marriage"*
2. *"To my club as personal chums"*
3. *"To my street as neighbours"*
4. *"To employment in my occupation"*
5. *"To citizenship in my country"*
6. *"As visitors only in my country"*
7. *"Would exclude from my country"*.

The lower the mean social distance (M.S.D.) the more preferred the category. On the basis of the mean social distance scores, Bogardus was able to give the rank ordering of preference of the ethnic and racial categories measured.

In the 1972-73 survey of intergroup attitudes in Dublin (Mac Gréil, 1977), the Bogardus Social Distance Scale was used, and proved to have high validity and reliability. The addition of a "rationalisation" question (see Question 4(b) of Questionnaire in Appendix A) was included to determine the intergroup definition by the sample of various categories. Because this was also measured in the 1972-73 survey, changes in intergroup definition over the intervening sixteen years can be analysed in the present study.

The wording of the seven Bogardus statements has been adapted to suit modern Irish society. The following are the adapted statements:

---

1. BOGARDUS, EMORY S.: "Measuring Social Distance", *Journal of Applied Sociology*, 1925, 9, pp. 299-308; *Immigration and Race Attitudes*, Boston, D. C. Heath & Co., 1928; "A Race-Relations Cycle", *American Journal of Sociology*, Vol. 35, No. 4, January 1930; "A Social Distance Scale", *Sociology and Social Research*, 1933, 17, pp. 265-71; "Changes in Racial Distances" *International Journal of Opinion and Attitude Research*, I, 1947, 1; "Stereotypes versus Sociotypes", *Sociology and Social Research*, 34, 1950.

63

1. *"Would marry or welcome as member of my family"*
2. *"Would have as close friends"*
3. *"Would have as next-door neighbours"*
4. *"Would work in the same workplace"*
5. *"Would welcome as an Irish citizen"*
6. *"Would have as visitors only to Ireland"*
7. *"Would debar or deport from Ireland"*.

In briefing the interviewers it was stressed that the respondents should understand what each level (1 to 7) meant and should be given a "prompt card" while answering. The question was to be answered briskly and respondents were asked to respond to the average person in the category rather than the best or worst person. Brisk answering would elicit dispositions, while pondering would lead to reflection. Attitudes are essentially pre-reflectional.

The change of wording in *number one* would enable people to record the desire for greatest closeness to persons who were not eligible for marriage. It also included "welcoming as members of the family" other than spouses, i.e. daughters, sons, brothers and sisters. This would be true in the case of celibates or other people for whom marriage would not be possible.

The modification of the wording in *number two* replaced "close friends" for "personal chums". The original wording was considered unsuitable for modern Ireland. Interviewers were to explain that "close friends" involved persons with whom the respondent would share confidences and discuss personal problems. In the case of *number three*, the word "street" was omitted so as to incorporate rural as well as urban neighbourhoods.

The alteration to *number four* has made the statement more inclusive and incorporates spatial as well as occupational social distance. The word "welcome" was added to the *fifth statement* to emphasise the pro-active rather than passive acceptance of a person as "citizen".

Numbers 6 and 7 are seen as negative statements by implication, i.e. would deny citizenship, and "would debar or deport". The use of the concepts "debar" and "deport" to replace the original "to exclude" was considered more explicit and covered categories within one's country and those from outside it. Because of the specifically negative nature of numbers six and seven, they will not be included in the cumulative percentages in tables giving social distance data. They will, however, be included in the calculation of the "mean social distance" score.

PART II: OVERALL SOCIAL DISTANCE:

Table 5 gives the overall distribution of answers for the fifty-nine stimulus categories tested in the 1988-89 National Survey. The categories are placed in "rank-order" of social closeness, as determined by the mean social distance score.

TABLE NO. 5
OVERALL SOCIAL DISTANCE SCORES OF TOTAL SAMPLE

STIMULUS CATEGORY	Kinship %	Friendship %	Neighbour %	Co-Worker %	Citizen %	Visitor %	Debar %	Mean Social Distance	N.
1. Roman Catholics	96.8	2.1 (98.9)	0.5 (99.4)	0.1 (99.5)	0.2 (99.7)	0.3	–	1.057	1001
2. Working Class	86.8	8.0 (94.8)	3.2 (98.0)	1.4 (99 4)	0 6 (100.0)	–	–	1. 210	1001
3. Gardaí	84.0	8.6 (92.5)	5.6 (98 1)	1.0 (99.1)	0.7 (99.8)	–	0.2	1.267	1005
4. Irish Speakers	84.4	81. (92.5)	4.1 (96.6)	1.8 (98.4)	1.4 (99.8)	0.3	–	1.287	1004
5. Unemployed	78.1	13.9 (92.0)	5.3 (97.3)	1.2 (98.5)	1.3 (99.8)	–	0.2	1.345	1001
6. English	77.9	10.6 (88.5)	5.2 (93.7)	2.5 (96.2)	1.1 (97.3)	2.1	0.7	1.475	1003
7. White Americans	78.6	8.6 (87.2)	4.6 (91.8)	2.7 (94.5)	2.1 (96.6)	3.2	0.2	1.514	1002
8. British	76.7	10.8 (87.5)	5.0 (92.5)	3.1 (95.6)	1.0 (96.6)	2.8	0.7	1.521	1004
9. People with Physical Handicaps	57.8	32.2 (90.0)	5.9 (95.9)	2.5 (98.4)	1.3 (94.7)	0.3	–	1.581	1001
10. Canadians	75.8	9.2 (85.0)	6.1 (91.1)	3.2 (94 3)	1.7 (96.0)	4.0	0.1	1.582	1003
11. Scottish	74.2	11.6 (85.8)	5.3 (91.1)	2.8 (93 9)	2.4 (96.3)	3.7	0.1	1.592	1002
12. Church of Ireland	64.5	20.3 (84.8)	9.8 (94.6)	2.3 (96.9)	1.5 (98.4)	1.4	0.2	1.609	1004
13. Northern Irish	70.9	12.8 (83.7)	7.0 (90.7)	3.2 (93.9)	3.51 (97.4)	2.2	0.4	1.637	1001
14. Welsh	72.8	10.0 (82.8)	7.8 (90.6)	3.4 (94.0)	2.2 (96.2)	3.4	0.4	1.641	999
15. Protestant	62.2	21.8 (84.0)	9.5 (93.5)	3.2 (96.7)	1.8 (98.5)	1.2	0.4	1.659	1002
16. Unmarried Mothers	61.1	21.8 (82.9)	9.7 (92.6)	3.7 (96.3)	2.7 (99.0)	0.6	0.4	1.684	1001
17. French	66.2	11.0 (77.2)	8.3 (85.5)	4.9 (90.4)	2.4 (92.8)	7.0	0.3	1.883	1004
18. Dutch	63.9	12.4 (76.3)	8.0 (84.3)	5.4 (89.7)	2.5 (92.2)	7.2	0.7	1.946	1002
19. People of Luxembourg	64.9	11.6 (76.5)	6.7 (83.2)	4.8 (88.0)	4.0 (92.0)	7.8	0.3	1.960	1002
20. Germans	62.0	13.4 (75.4)	8.3 (83.7)	5 2 (88.9)	2.5 (91.4)	8 2	0.5	1.994	1002

Prejudice in Ireland Revisited

TABLE No. 5—Continued
OVERALL SOCIAL DISTANCE SCORES OF TOTAL SAMPLE

STIMULUS CATEGORY	Kinship %	Friendship %	Neighbour %	Co-Worker %	Citizen %	Visitor %	Debar %	Mean Social Distance	N.
21. People with Mental Handicaps	34.6	43.5 (78.1)	13.2 (91.3)	4.3 (95.6)	3.5 (99.1)	0.7	0.1	2.010	999
22. Trade Unionists	63.7	8.8 (72.5)	6.3 (78.8)	10.6 (89.4)	6.4 (95.8)	2.0	2.2	2.022	994
23. Presbyterians	52.3	20.8 (73.1)	12.1 (85.2)	6.0 (91.2)	3.5 (94.7)	4.6	0.8	2.045	1004
24. Danes	61.4	11.2 (72.6)	8.3 (80.9)	5.7 (86.6)	3.9 (90.5)	9.0	0.6	2.088	1003
25. Belgians	60.2	10.7 (70.9)	9.1 (80.0)	6.3 (86.3)	4.9 (91.2)	8.0	0.8	2.122	1000
26. Methodists	49.0	22.4 (71.4)	11.9 (83.3)	6.3 (89.6)	5.3 (94.9)	4.5	0.7	2.128	1002
27. Spaniards	58.3	11.2 (69.5)	6.9 (76.4)	7.0 (83.4)	4.5 (87.9)	11.1	0.9	2.252	998
28. Polish People	54.6	13.1 (67.7)	8.3 (76.0)	7.1 (83.1)	4.7 (87.8)	11.7	0.6	2.315	1003
29. Italians	55.1	11.4 (66.5)	8.5 (75.0)	7.9 (82.9)	4.4 (87.3)	11.9	0.8	2.339	1001
30. Portuguese	51.8	14.8 (66.6)	8.4 (75.0)	7.1 (82.1)	4.6 (86.7)	12.6	0.7	2.385	994
31. Capitalists	47.8	12.0 (59.8)	10.9 (70.7)	9.2 (79.9)	6.4 (86.3)	10.2	3.4	2.587	998
32. Jews	39.5	21.9 (61.4)	11.8 (73 2)	7.9 (81.1)	6.0 (87.1)	10.9	2.1	2.599	1003
33. Greeks	44.6	15.2 (59.8)	10.4 (70.2)	9.6 (79.8)	4.4 (84.2)	14.5	1.5	2.634	1003
34. Socialists	44.9	13.2 (58.1)	11.0 (69.1)	10.4 (79.5)	7.2 (86.7)	10.3	3.1	2.650	995
35. Coloureds	34.3	24.6 (58.9)	12.5 (71.4)	9.8 (81.2)	4.0 (85.2)	12.5	2.4	2.715	1003
36. Russians	40.9	14.9 (55.8)	9.9 (65.7)	9.1 (74.8)	4.1 (78.9)	17.2	4.	2.882	1001
37. Africans	30.1	24.3 (54.4)	10.8 (65.2)	11.7 (76.9)	7.2 (84.1)	13.7	2.3	2.916	1003
38. Chinese	30.9	20.4 (51.3)	11.7 (63.0)	12.5 (75. 5)	5.8 (81.3)	16.0	2.8	3.009	1002
39. Blacks	29.7	21.3 (51.0)	12.2 (63.2)	13.4 (76.6)	5.0 (81.6)	14.5	3.9	3.019	1004
40. Agnostics	31.1	18.2 (49.3)	14.4 (63.7)	12.4 (76.1)	6.9 (83.0)	11.6	5.3	3.021	997

TABLE No. 5—Continued
OVERALL SOCIAL DISTANCE SCORES OF TOTAL SAMPLE

STIMULUS CATEGORY %	Kinship %	Friendship %	Neighbour %	Co-Worker %	Citizen %	Visitor %	Debar %	Mean Social Distance	N.
41. Unionists	33.4	16.5 (49.9)	12.2 (62.1)	10.3 (72.4)	9.1 (81 5)	11.0	7.6	3.084	1002
42. Alcoholics	13.8	30.9 (44.7)	17.8 (62.5)	17.4 (79 9)	11 7 (91 6)	5.4	3.0	3.105	1000
43. Indians (Non-Amer)	31.0	18.6 (49.6)	11.3 (60.9)	11.9 (72.8)	6.0 (75.8)	17.7	3.6	3.108	1001
44. Israelis	32.4	16.8 (49.2)	11.4 (60.6)	11.8 (72.4)	5.1 (77.5)	19.1	3.5	3.117	1001
45. Nigerians	29.1	19 6 (48.7)	12.1 (60.8)	10.9 (71.7)	7.0 (78.7)	19.2	2. 1	3.131	1000
46. Atheists	28.5	18. 9 (47.4)	14.1 (61.5)	13.1 (74.6)	5.7 (80.3)	12.4	7.4	3.152	1002
47. Black Americans/ American Negroes	26.2	19.9 (46.1)	12.9 (590)	12.9 (71.9)	7.3 (79.2)	17.0	3.7	3.212	998
48. Ex-Prisoners	23.7	15.7 (39.4)	13.6 (53.0)	20.2 (73.2)	11.4 (84.6)	9.9	5.5	3.316	1000
49. Pakistanis	24.2	18.4 (42.6)	12.1 (54.7)	12.5 (67.2)	6.7 (73.9)	22.4	3.5	3.404	998
50. Moslems	20.6	20.3 (40.9)	15.6 (56.5)	10.9 (67.4)	8.6 (76.0)	20.6	3.4	3.420	1000
51. Arabs	20.1	19.0 (39.1)	14.4 (53.5)	14.9 (68.4)	5.0 (73.4)	21.5	5.2	3.509	1001
52. Travellers	13.5	13.2 (26.7)	14.3 (41.0)	22.7 (63.7)	26.3 (90.0)	7.0	3.0	3.681	1000
53. Communists	24.4	13.4 (37.8)	11.6 (49.4)	10.6 (60.0)	5.8 (65.8)	20.2	14.1	3.769	1003
54. Gay People	12.5	22.7 (35.2)	14.0 (49.2)	15.5 (64.7)	9.4 (74.1)	10.6	15.2	3.793	999
55. Sinn Féin	17.2	8.2 (25.4)	13.3 (38.7)	12.8 (51.5)	14.9 (66.4)	10.1	23.6	4.245	995
56. Hare Krishna	12.7	12.8 (25.5)	10.0 (35.5)	13.6 (39.1)	11.4 (60.5)	22.4	17.0	4.331	997
57. People with AIDS	7.2	20.9 (21.8)	11.6 (39.7)	9.0 (48.7)	16.3 (65.0)	12.4	22.5	4.336	997
58. Drug Addicts	5.3	12.9 (18.2)	9.1 (27.3)	15.2 (42.5)	14.0 (56.5)	14.6	29.1	4.798	1003
59. Provisional I.R.A.	9.3	6.8 (16.1)	9.0 (25.1)	12.8 (37.9)	11.8 (49.7)	7.2	43.1	5.049	991

Generally speaking, the stimulus categories are ranked according to the "principle of propinquity", i.e. those closest to the respondent in terms of religion, colour, ethnic similarity, political ideology and social acceptance, scoring lowest in social distance (Mac Gréil, 1977, p. 234). Where there are exceptions to this general result, it can be assumed that there are particular factors at work which merit comment.

1. IRISH INGROUPS:

The logic of the scoring and ranking of the categories substantiates the validity and reliability of the scale. The first five and most preferred, are:

1. "Roman Catholics"	(1.057)	4. "Irish Speakers"	(1.287)
2. "Working Class"	(1.210)	5. "Unemployed"	(1.340)
3. "Gardaí"	(1.267)		

These provide a most interesting range of religious, ethnic, professional and social class categories. The very high level of acceptance of these categories puts them among the Republic's "ingroups". What this finding tells of contemporary Irish society will be discussed below.

2. BRITISH-AMERICAN CATEGORIES:

The *British-American Categories* and the "Northern Irish" are clustered together as follows in rank order of mean social distance scores:

1. "English"	(1.475)	5. "Scottish"	(1.592)
2. "White Americans"	(1.514)	6. "Northern Irish"	(1.637)
3. "British"	(1.521)	7. "Welsh"	(1.641)
4. "Canadians"	(1.582)		

Their relatively highly favoured position is both logical and interesting. The positioning of "White Americans" and "Canadians" in the overall category of "Irish and British" is probably both a historical sharing of a common colonial background, and also a result of the feedback from the experience of Irish emigrants and returned emigrants. It would not point to a perception of "White Americans" and "Canadians" as strongly multi-ethnic peoples. If the latter were the case, would it not place them in among the Western European categories? "Black Americans" were not included among the highly favoured categories!

The ranking of *"Northern Irish"* outside the Irish ingroups and in with the British-American categories is a case of deviation from the "principle of propinquity". It also reflects the dual-category perception of the Northern Irish people, i.e. Irish-British and Catholic-Protestant. While their mean social distance score is quite favourable at 1.637, with 70.9% welcoming 'Northern Irish' to kinship, it is significantly different from the status of 'Irish Speakers' at 1.287 and 84.4% welcoming to kinship.

3. EUROPEAN NATIONALITIES:

The other *Continental European Nationalities* (in rank order) are:

1. "French"	(1.883)		7. "Spaniards"	(2.252)
2. "Dutch"	(1.946)		8. "Polish People"	(2.315)
3. "People of Luxembourg"	(1.960)		9. "Italians"	(2.339)
4. "Germans"	(1.994)		10. "Portuguese"	(2.385)
5. "Danes"	(2.088)		11. "Greeks"	(2.634)
6. "Belgians"	(2.122)		12. "Russians"	(2.882)

These categories cover a wide range of scores from 1.883 to 2.882, or from 63.9% to 40.9% in welcoming to kinship. The first six categories all scored more than 60% in relation to admission to kinship. Spaniards, Poles, Italians and Portuguese were less well favoured with between 50% and 60%. The kinship scores for the Greeks (at 44.6%) and the Russians (at 40.9%) were relatively low.

4. ETHNICO-RACIAL CATEGORIES:

The *Ethnico-Racial and Racial categories* clustered together between the mean social distance scores of 2.715 and 3.404, or admission-to-kinship percentages from 34.4% to 24.2%. The ethnico-racial and racial categories include:

1. "Coloureds"	(2.715)	5. "Non-American Indians'	(3.108)
2. "Africans"	(2.916)	6. "Nigerians"	(3.131)
3. "Chinese"	(3.009)	7. "Black Americans"	(3.212)
4. "Blacks"	(3.019)	8. "Pakistanis"	(3.404)

As will be seen in Table 3 below, each of these categories has a racial rationalisation score of over 12%. The influence of the racial factor obviously contributed to their position on the Social Distance Scale and to their relatively close clustering. It is acknowledged that the concept "American Negroes" is no longer acceptable when describing "Afro-Americans". The reason it was included here was to replicate the 1972/73 Survey.

5. ARABS AND ISRAELIS:

The position of the other two ethnic categories, i.e., "Israelis" and "Arabs" provides an interesting comparison.

1. "Israelis"	(3.117)	2. "Arabs"	(3.509)

Their respective admission to kinship scores give "Israelis" 32.4% and "Arabs" 20.1% which shows a substantial difference and reflects the higher level of endogamy in relation to "Moslems".

6. SOCIAL CATEGORIES:

The range of *Diverse Social Categories* covered a wide range of mean social distance scores from 1.210 to 4.798 with admission-to-kinship scores going from 86.8% for "Working Class" to 5.3% for "Drug Addicts". Because of their diversity there is need to sub-divide the categories. The list of categories included under the general heading "social categories" includes:

1. "Working Class"	(1.210)	7. "Ex-Prisoners"	(3.316)
2. "Unemployed"	(1.345)	8. "Itinerants/Travellers"	(3.681)
3. "Physically handicapped"	(1.581)	9. "Gay People"	(3.793)
4. "Unmarried mothers'	(1.684)	10. "People with AIDS"	(4.336)
5. "Mentally handicapped"	(2.010)	11. "Drug Addicts"	(4.798)
6. "Alcoholics"	(3.105)		

7. RELIGIOUS STIMULUS CATEGORIES:

Religious Stimulus Categories are also scattered throughout the rank-order in Table 1. The principle of religious propinquity is obviously at work in the findings, i.e. the more institutional churches being preferred. Again, the range of mean social distance scores and difference in percentage welcoming to kinship are wide, from 1.057 and 96.8% respectively for "Roman Catholics" to 4.331 and 12.7% for "Hare Krishna". The list of "religious categories" includes the following:

1. "Roman Catholics"	(1.057)	6. "Jews"	(2.599)
2. "Church of Ireland"	(1.609)	7. "Agnostics"	(3.021)
3. "Protestants"	(1.659)	8. "Atheists"	(3.152)
4. "Presbyterians"	(2.045)	9. "Moslems"	(3.420)
5. "Methodists"	(2.128)	10. "Hare Krishna"	(4.331)

The relatively negative standing of "Agnostics" and "Atheists" is commented on in Chapter V below.

8. SOCIO-POLITICAL CATEGORIES:

A number of *Socio-Political Categories* are also included in the Bogardus Social Distance Scale (Table 1), i.e.

TABLE No. 6
OVERALL PERCENTAGES "WELCOMING TO KINSHIP" AND
"DENYING CITIZENSHIP"

Stimulus Category	Welcome to Kinship %	Deny Citizenship %	Mean Social Distance	Stimulus Category	Welcome to Kinship %	Deny Citizenship %	Mean Social Distance
1. Roman Catholics	96.8	0.2	1.057	31. Capitalists	47.8	13.4	2.587
2. Working Class	86.8	0.0	1.210	32. Jews	39.5	13.0	2.599
3. Gardai	84.0	0.2	1.267	33. Greeks	44.6	16.0	2.634
4. Irish Speakers	84.4	0.3	1.287	34. Socialists	44.9	13.4	2.650
5. Unemployed	78.1	0.2	1.345	35. Coloureds	34.3	14.9	2.715
6. English	77.9	2.8	1.475	36. Russians	40.9	21.2	2.882
7. White Americans	78.6	3.4	1.514	37. Africans	30.1	16.0	2.916
8. British	76.7	3.5	1.521	38. Chinese	30.9	18.8	3.009
9. People with Physical Handicap	57.8	0.3	1.581	39. Blacks	29.7	18.4	3.019
10. Canadians	75.8	4.1	1.582	40. Agnostics	31.1	16.9	3.021
11. Scottish	74.2	3.8	1.592	41. Unionists	33.4	18.6	3.084
12. Church of Ireland	64.5	1.6	1.609	42. Alcoholics	13.8	8.4	3.084
13. Northern Irish	70.9	2.6	1.637	43. Non-American Indians	31.0	21.3	3.108
14. Welsh	72.8	3.8	1.641	44. Israelis	32.4	22.6	3.117
15. Protestants	62.2	1.6	1.659	45. Nigerians	29.1	21.3	3.131
16. Unmarried Mothers	61.1	1.0	1.684	46. Atheists	28.5	19.8	3.152
17. French	66.2	7.3	1.883	47 Black Americans	26.2	20.7	3.212
18. Dutch	63.9	7.9	1.946	48 Ex-Prisoners	23.7	15.4	3.316
19. Luxembourgians	64.9	8.1	1.960	49. Pakistanis	24.2	25.9	3.404
20. Germans	62.0	8.7	1.994	50. Moslems	20.6	24.0	3.420
21. People with Mental Handicap	34.6	0.8	2.010	51. Arabs	20.1	26.7	3.509
22. Trade Unionists	63.7	4.2	2.022	52. Travellers	13.5	10.0	3.681
23. Presbyterians	52.3	5.4	2.045	53. Communists	24.4	34.3	3.769
24. Danes	61.4	9.6	2.088	54. Gay People	12.5	25.8	3.793
25. Belgians	60.2	8.8	2.122	55. Sinn Fein	17.2	33.1	4.245
26. Methodists	49.0	5.2	2.128	56. Hare Krishna	12.7	39.4	4.331
27. Spaniards	58.3	12.0	2.252	57. People with AIDS	7.2	34.9	4.336
28. Polish People	54.6	12.3	2.315	58. Drug Addicts	5.3	44.7	4.798
29. Italians	55.1	12.7	2.339	59. Provisional I.R.A.	9.3	50.3	5.049
30. Portuguese	51.8	13.3	2.385				

Note: Rank-Order correlation coefficient between M.S.D. and Kinship Score = 0.98

1. "Gardaí"	(1.267)	5. "Unionists"	(3.084)
2. "Trade Unionists"	(2.022)	6. "Communists"	(3.769)
3. "Capitalists"	(2.587)	7. "Sinn Féin"	(4.245)
4. "Socialists"	(2.650)	8. "Provisional I.R.A."	(5.049)

All of these categories scored over 16% as "political" in the rationalisation scale. Political stimulus categories tend to elicit highly polarised responses, especially in the case of unpopular groups (at the time of interview). This is clearly manifested in regard to the relatively high percentages for "denial of citizenship" in the case of a number of the less favoured of the above categories.

9. SUMMARY SOCIAL DISTANCE RATINGS:

Table 6 gives three scores in relation to each of the fifty-nine stimulus categories, i.e. percentage welcoming to kinship, percentage denying citizenship and mean social distance scores. The value of this scale is that it summarises the main findings in Table 5 and can be "read at a glance".

The very high rank-order correlation between percentages admitting to family and mean social distance ($\rho = 0.98$) scores is further evidence of the high validity of the Bogardus scale. The major exceptions to the pattern are the categories of physical and mental handicap where there is a higher level of acceptance than the percentages welcoming to kinship would indicate.

The three columns in Table 6 indicate the standing of the groups and the nature of the hostility in the sample towards certain categories. Unpopular *political* groups tend to have a more polarised response, i.e. would have a relatively high "denial of citizenship score", while unpopular social groups would have a relatively low percentage refusing citizenship despite a high mean social distance score. This diversity of pattern response is well illustrated by comparing the response of the sample to "Travellers" and to "Communists" at more or less similar mean social distance scores of 3.681 and 3.769 respectively. Such a pattern variation was also noted in the findings of the 1972-73 survey (see Mac Gréil 1977, pp. 248 and 254).

PART III: THE RATIONALISATION SCALE:

The Rationalisation Scale was first used by the present author in surveys of intergroup attitudes carried out in Philadelphia and Cleveland in the United States in 1966 (see Mac Gréil 1966, pp. 30 ff.). It was used in the 1972-73 survey and reported on in *Prejudice and Tolerance in Ireland* (Mac Gréil 1977, pp. 234-238). In both surveys it proved a most reliable instrument for measuring intergroup definition by those who did not welcome certain categories into kinship.

The procedure and the content of the rationalisation question are important. Having completed the social distance (Bogardus) scale respondents were asked the following question:

Q4(b)   *"Looking over your answers to this (Bogardus Social Distance Scale) question, there are a number of categories which you would not welcome into kinship. Which of the following would you say was your main reason for placing them at the distance indicated? (Show prompt card C and explain it).*

Reasons:

A.   Religious beliefs and/or practices;
B.   Racial – Colour of Skin, etc.;
C.   Political Views and/or Methods;
D.   Nationality and Culture (Ethnic);
E.   Economic Danger to us;
F.   Not Socially Acceptable;
G.   Way of Life;
H.   Other (Specify).

Table 7 reports the reasons given by respondents for not admitting members of the particular categories into kinship. It is suggested here that these reasons give a reflection of the popular perceptions of such categories by Irish people. These perceptions have their basis in popular stereotypes, actual or vicarious experience, or prevalent myths about the people in question. They also tell us much about the respondents themselves and their perceived reasons for rejecting members of the group into very close social distance.

It may be contested that these subjective classifications are not those of the respondents who admit members to kinship, thereby giving much credence to "negative perception". Since the main focus of this work is the explanation of intergroup *prejudice and discrimination*, the limitation of "negative perception" does not matter that much.

1. SINGLE AND MULTIPLE IDENTITIES:

The main value of this question is to establish how respondents see or define the categories. It was assumed that the *reason* given for denying closer relationship with members of a category indicates how that category is defined by the perceiver.

As can be seen from Table 8 most categories ended up with more than one definition, i.e., twenty categories had only one definition. These were "religious" and "ethnic" categories. Twenty-nine categories had dual-identity while nine had three significant identities and one category was

TABLE NO. 7
GENERAL RATIONALISATION SCALE

	Religious %	Racial %	Political %	Cultural Ethnic %	Economic %	Not Socially Acceptable %	Way of Life %	Other %	N.
	1	2	3	4	5	6	7	8	
1.Roman Catholics	63.3	0.0	13.3	3.3	0.0	0.0	16.7	3.3	30
2.Working Class	1.7	0.0	2.6	8.6	2.6	12.1	68.1	4.3	116
3.Gardaí	0.7	0.7	16.5	4.3	0.7	4.3	64.0	8.6	139
4.Irish Speakers	2.1	0.7	9.9	29.8	0.0	2.8	45.4	9.2	141
5. Unemployed	1.5	0.0	2.0	2.9	19.5	6.8	62.0	5.3	205
6.English	9.1	0.5	31.6	42.1	1.4	1.4	12.0	1.9	209
7.White Americans	1.5	1.5	5.4	63.4	2.0	0.5	24.3	1.5	202
8.British	8.99	0.9	35.6	36.0	0.9	1.3	14.2	2.2	225
9.People with Physical Handicap	0.8	0.3	0.0	2.2	3.0	18.9	56.0	18.9	366
10. Canadians	2.6	0.9	9.8	65.0	1.3	3.0	16.2	1.3	234
11. Scottish	7.0	0.4	6.1	66.4	0.4	0.8	17.6	1.2	244
12. Church of Ireland	85.0	0.3	1.5	2.9	0.0	0.9	8.5	0.9	340
13. Northern Irish	12.1	1.4	42.6	17.4	1.8	2.8	20.2	1.8	282
14. Welsh	3.9	0.0	4.3	74.1	0.8	1.2	14.1	1.6	255
15. Protestants	83.9	0.3	3.0	3.3	0.3	1.1	7.5	0.6	361
16. Unmarried Mothers	1.7	0.0	0.0	1.9	2.2	28.9	60.8	4.4	360
17. French	2.8	0.3	2.2	73.8	1.2	2.5	15.7	1.5	325
18. Dutch	4.9	0.6	3.4	72.1	1.1	1.4	14.7	1.7	348
19. People of Luxembourg	2.1	0.3	4.4	75.5	1.2	0.6	14.7	1.2	339
20. Germans	3.8	0.5	5.5	72.1	1.1	3.6	11.5	1.9	366
21. People with Mental Handicap	1.0	0.0	0.0	10	1.9	18.9	52.8	26.5	593
22. Trade Unionists	0.6	0.0	39.8	6.0	18.6	4.5	27.5	3.0	334
23. Presbyterians	84.0	0.2	2.6	2.8	0.2	1.5	8.2	0.4	463
24. Danes	3.8	1.1	3.5	68.1	1.1	3.2	18.4	0.8	370
25. Belgians	3.9	1.3	4.4	73.0	1.0	0.5	13.8	2.2	385
26. Methodists	83.9	0.4	2.6	3.4	0.4	0.8	7.2	1.2	497
27. Spaniards	1.5	3.5	2.2	76.0	1.5	1.2	13.1	0.9	404
28. Polish People	3.8	2.5	6 6	73.1	0.9	1.4	11.1	0.6	442
29. Italians	3.5	4.4	1.9	73.1	0.2	1.2	14.4	1.4	431
30. Portuguese	1.7	6.4	2.3	75.3	1.3	1.3	10.6	1.0	470
31. Capitalists	2.0	0.2	18.1	8.7	25.6	4.9	38.9	1.6	507
32. Jews	63.0	0.8	5.2	17.7	0.8	1.3	10.3	0.8	594
33. Greeks	4.8	.4.1	3.9	72.8	0.7	1.3	10.7	1.7	540
34. Socialists	4.3	0.4	39.2	8.7	14.1	5.3	26.9	1.2	531

TABLE No. 7—Continued
GENERAL RATIONALISATION SCALE

	Religious %	Racial %	Political %	Cultural Ethnic %	Economic %	Not Socially Acceptable %	Way of Life %	Other %	N.
	1	2	3	4	5	6	7	8	
35. Coloureds	2.0	49.6	1.7	35.1	0.2	2.7	8.3	0.6	641
36. Russians	7.3	1.2	20.9	52.2	4.0	2.9	10.9	0.7	579
37. Africans	7.3	3 5.5	2.9	39.7	1.2	1.7	10.9	0.8	688
38. Chinese	4.8	17.0	3.6	57.4	1.5	2.2	12.9	0.5	672
39. Agnostics	70 3	0.7	1.2	8.4	0.6	3.3	14.5	1.0	670
40. Blacks	2.9	46.2	2.0	37.5	0.3	2.7	7.5	0.8	691
41. Unionists	13.6	0.2	59.8	5.6	1.5	3.1	15.6	0.7	646
42. Alcoholics	1.0	0.1	0.0	1.4	8.1	19.4	67.4	2.6	842
43. Indians	8.3	19.3	1.8	54.4	0.4	2.7	12.6	0.3	673
44. Israelis	11.2	5.9	11.7	56.2	1.5	1.5	11.4	0.8	660
45. Nigerians	5.1	32.5	3.0	47.3	0.6	1.6	9.4	0.4	692
46. Atheists	75.5	0.7	1.0	5.0	0.1	3.6	12.5	1.5	702
47. Black Americans	3.2	39.4	2.0	38.6	0.8	4.2	11.2	0.5	715
48. Ex-Prisoners	0.0	0.0	1.6	1.1	3.1	27.3	64.3	2.5	740
49. Pakistanis	6.4	24.8	1.9	51.6	0.9	2.4	11.4	0.5	737
50. Moslems	63.3	3.3	2.6	20.3	0.4	1.8	8.0	0.2	777
51. Arabs	15.2	12.9	5.6	50.0	1.4	2.0	12.2	0.6	788
52. Itinerants/Travellers	0.6	0.0	0.0	2.3	1.8	20.3	74.2	1.0	844
53. Communists	28.2	0.8	27.4	7.1	117	5.2	18.7	0.9	737
54. Gay People	0.8	0.0	0.1	0.4	0.7	20.4	74.5	3.2	854
55. Sinn Fein	0.6	0.0	65.6	1.1	2.6	7.1	22.6	0.4	807
56. Hare Krishna	65.2	0.6	1.4	6.1	0.5	4.8	20.0	1.4	854
57 People with AIDS	0.2	0.0	0.3	0.4	3.5	25.8	51.9	17 7	894
58. Drug Addicts	0.2	0.0	0.0	0.3	6.0	20.1˙	68.4	5.0	931
59. Provisional I.R.A.	0.6	0.0	59.6	1.0	2.8	8.6	25.9	1.5	884

viewed under four identities or reasons. The categories with multiple identities fell victim to a range of prejudices. For instance the category
"Northern Irish" was refused admission to a closer relationship for political
(42.6%), ethnic/way of life (37.6%) and religious (12.1%) reasons which
points to the complexity of the attitudes of the 29% of the sample who would

TABLE No. 8
MAJOR CLASSIFICATION OF CATEGORIES

Category	Primary Classification	Second Classification	Third Classification
1. Africans	Ethnic/Way of Life (50.6%)	Racial (35.5%)	..
2. Agnostics	Religious (70.3%)	Way of Life (14.5%)	
3. Alcoholics	Way of Life (67.4%)	Socially Unacceptable (19.4%)	
4. Black Americans	Ethnic/Way of Life (49.8%)	Racial (39.4%)	
5. Atheists	Religious (75.5%)	Way of Life (12.5%)	
6. Arabs	Ethnic/Way of Life (62.2%)	Religious (15.5%)	Racial (12.9%)
7. Belgians	Ethnic/Way of Life (86.8%)		
8. Blacks	Racial (46.2%)	Ethnic/Way of Life (45.5%)	
9. British	Ethnic/Way of Life (50.2%)	Political (35.6%)	
10. Canadians	Ethnic/Way of Life (81.2%)		
11. Capatilists	Way of Life (38.9%)	Economic (25.6%)	Political (18.1%)
12. Chinese	Ethnic/Way of Life (70.3%)	Racial (17.0%)	
13. Church of Ireland	Religious (85.0%)		
14. Coloureds	Racial (49.6%)	Ethnic/Way of Life (43.4%)	
15. Communists*	Religious (28.2%)	Political (27.4%)	Way of Life (18.7%)
16. Danes	Ethnic/Way of Life (86.5%)		
17. Drug Addicts	Way of Life (68.4%)	Socially Unacceptable (20.1%)	
18. Dutch	Ethnic/Way of Life (86.8%)		
19. English	Ethnic/Way of Life (52.1%)	Political (31.6%)	
20. Ex-Prisoners	Way of Life (64.3%)	Socially Unacceptable (27.3%)	
21. French	Ethnic/Way of Life (89.5%)		
22. Gardaí	Way of Life (64.0%)	Political (16.5%)	
23. Gay People	Way of Life (74.5%)	Socially Unacceptable (20.4%)	
24. Germans	Ethnic/Way of Life (83.6%)		
25. Physically Hcp.	Way of Life (56.0%)	Socially Unacceptable (18.9%)	
26. Greeks	Ethnic/Way of Life (83.5%)		
27. Hare Krishna	Religious (65.2%)	Way of Life (20.0%)	
28. Indians	Ethnic/Way of Life (67.0%)	Racial (19.3%)	
29. Israelis	Ethnic/Way of Life (67.6%)	Political (11.7%)	Religious (11.2%)
30. Italians	Ethnic/Way of Life (85.5%)		
31. Travellers	Way of Life (7.42%)	Socially Unacceptable (20.3%)	
32. Irish Speakers	Ethnic/Way of Life (75.2%)		
33. Luxembourgians	Ethnic/Way of Life (90.2%)		
34. Jews	Religious (63.0%)	Ethnic (17.7%)	Way of Life (10.3%)
35. Methodist	Religious (83.9%)		
36. People with Ment. Hcp.	Way of Life (52.8%)	Socially Unacceptable (18.9%)	
37. Moslems	Religious (63.3%)	Ethnic (20.3%)	
38. Nigerians	Ethnic/Way of Life (56.7%)	Racial (32.5%)	
39. Northern Irish	Political (42.6%)	Ethnic/Way of Life (37.6%)	Religious (12.1%)
40. Pakistanis	Ethnic Way of Life (63.0%)	Racial (24.8%)	
41. People with AIDS	Way of Life (51.9%)	Socially Unacceptable (25.8%)	
42. Poles	Ethnic/Way of Life (85.9%)		
43. Presbyterians	Religious (83.9%)		
44. Portuguese	Ethnic/Way of Life (85.9%)		
45. Protestants	Religious (83.9%)		
46. Provisional I.R.A.	Political (59.6%)	Way of Life (25.9%)	
47. Roman Catholics	Religious (63.3%)	Way of Life (26.7%)	Political (13.3%)
48. Russians	Ethnic/Way of Life (63.1%)	Political (20.9%)	
49. Scottish	Ethnic/Way of Life (84.0%)		
50. Socialists	Political (32.9%)	Way of Life (26.9%)	Economic (14.1%)
51. Spaniards	Ethnic/Way of Life (89.1%)		
52. Sinn Féin	Political (65.6%)	Way of Life (22.6%)	
53. Trade Unionists	Political (39.8%)	Way of Life (27.5%)	Economic (18.6%)
54. Unemployed	Way of Life (62.0%)	Economic (19.5%)	
55. Unionists	Political (59.8%)	Way of Life (15.6%)	Religious (13.6%)
56. Unmarried Mothers	Way of Life (60.8%)	Socially Unacceptable (28.9%)	
57. Welsh	Ethnic/Way of Life (88.2%)		
58. Working Class	Way of Life (68.1%)	Socially Unacceptable (12.1%)	
59. White Americans	Way of Life (87.7%)		

*Fourth Category = Economic (11.7%)

Note: In the case of countries "Ethnic" and "Way of Life" are added together.

not welcome them as members of the family. A close examination of those reasons, which were given by more than 10% of respondents, is given in Table 9 which highlights the categories with multiple or singular definitions. The following summarises further the findings of Table 8.

TABLE NO. 9
STIMULUS CATEGORIES CLASSIFIED BY NUMBER OF IDENTITIES

A Single Identity	B Double Identity	C Treble Identity	D Quadruple Identity
Belgians (Eth)	Africans (Eth-Rac)	Arabs (Eth-Rel-Rac)	Communists (Rel-Pol-Wol-Ec)
Canadians (Eth)	Agnostics (Rel-Wol)	Capitalists (Wol-Ec-Pol)	
Church of Ireland (Rel)	Alcoholics (Wol-Soc)	Israelis (Eth-Pol-Rel)	
Danes (Eth)	Black Americans (Eth-Rac)	Jews (Rel-Eth-Wol)	
Dutch (Eth)	Atheists (Rel-Wol)	Nth. Irish (Pol-Eth-Rel)	
French (Eth)	Blacks (Rac-Eth)	Roman Catholic (Rel-Wol-Pol)	
Germans (Eth)	British (Eth-Pol)	Socialists (Pol-Wol-Ec)	
Greeks (Eth)	Chinese (Eth-Rac)	Trade Unionists (Pol-Wol-Ec)	
Italians (Eth)	Coloureds (Rac-Eth)	Unionists (Pol-Wol-Rel)	
Irish Speakers (Eth)	Drug Addicts (Wol-Soc)		
Luxembourgians (Eth)	English (Eth-Pol)		
Methodists (Rel)	Ex-Prisoners (Wol-Soc)		
Poles (Eth)	Gardaí (Wol-Pol)		
Presbyterians (Rel)	Gay People (Wol-Soc)		
Portuguese (Eth)	People with Phy. Hcap. (Wol-Soc)		
Protestants (Rel)	Hare Krishna (Rel-Wol)		
Scottish (Eth)	Indians (Eth-Rac)		
Spaniards (Eth)	Travellers (Wol-Soc)		
Welsh (Eth)	People with Men. Hcap. (Wol-Soc)		
White Americans (Eth)	Moslems (Rel-Eth)		
	Nigerians (Eth-Rac)		
	Pakistani (Eth-Rac)		
	People with AIDS (Wol-Soc)		
	Provisional I.R.A. (Pol-Wol)		
	Russians (Eth-Pol)		
	Sinn Fein (Pol-Wol)		
	Unemployed (Wol-Eth)		
	Unmarried Mothers (Wol-Soc)		
	Working Class (Wol-Soc)		

2. ETHNIC CATEGORIES:

A study of Tables 7 and 8 reveals much about Irish people's attitudes and perceptions of other people. Most ethnic categories have been defined as expected in ethnic, cultural and way-of-life terms, i.e.

1. "Belgians"
2. "Canadians"
3. "Danes"
4. "Dutch"
5. "French"
6. "Germans"
7. "Greeks"
8. "Irish Speakers"
9. "Italians"
10. "People of Luxembourg"
11. "Polish People"
12. "Portuguese"
13. "Scottish"
14. "Spaniards"
15. "Welsh"
16. "White Americans"

The ethnic categories which do not follow this pattern are those which are ethnico-racial or ethnico-political.

2.1. Ethnico-Racial Categories: There are clear signs of the decline in *racial* prejudice, i.e. racial in the strict sense of referring to physical appearance of colour, size, facial features and so forth. In the 1972-73 survey of ethnico-racial social distance, the *racial* rationalisation exceeded the *ethnic* one.

Tables 42 (p. 153), 92 (p. 230) and 142 (p. 328) show the extent of the change of perception of stimulus categories in the intervening fifteen years. This difference is even greater when it is considered that the findings of an urban sample is being compared with a national one. Such a change in intergroup definition will be welcomed by those working for the reduction of racialism. Giving cultural and ethnic status to a people is attributing *human characteristics* to them, while perceiving them as racial is emphasising the *physical trait*, which has been at the root of the de-humanising myth of race. It will be shown later that the standing of peoples of distinctive physical differences, i.e. so-called racial groupings, has improved significantly since 1972-73 (see Chapter IV below).

Both in terms of acceptance to closer social distance and of improvement in intergroup classification, there is convincing evidence that Irish people are becoming less racialist than previous research has shown. Why this is so is probably due to advances made by black people in Ireland and elsewhere abroad in challenging some of the negative myths and stereotypes which marred Western civilisation for over five hundred years. Of course, what is evident is not the end of racialism but the weakening of its grip and basis. Much more needs to be achieved before irrational racism is fully removed from the people's attitudes.

2.2. Ethnico-Political Categories: Ethnic categories with a strong political rationalisation include "Arabs", "British", "English", "Israelis", "Northern Irish", and "Russians". This negative political perception of the *"British"* and the *"English"* is probably as a result of Ireland's colonial past and the present "troubles" in Northern Ireland. The level of political rationalisation is substantial at 35.6% and 31.6% respectively.

The *"Israeli"* rationalisation pattern is quite complex, with 67.6% "ethnic" and "way of life", 11.7% "political", and 11.2% "religious". The latter is a reflection of the Jewish association. The 11.7% political rationalisation may be considered relatively small in the light of regular media coverage of the Middle-East conflict. When the responses to "Jews" are compared with those to "Israelis", the degree of difference is greater.

Reading this evidence, one may conclude that the Irish people see the "Jews" as less ethnic (more universal), much less political and more religious than might have been anticipated. This should be reassuring to Irish Jews, although their religious designation has changed substantially

SUB-TABLE A

	Religious	Ethnic	Political	Way-of-Life	N.
"Jews"	63.0%	17.7%	5.2%	10.3%	594
"Israelis"	11.2%	56.2%	11.7%	11.4%	660
	+51.8%	-38.5%	-6.5%	-1.1%	

when compared with the case of the Greater Dublin sample of 1972-73, when rationalisation against the Jews was 79.3% "religious" (see Mac Gréil, 1977 p. 236).

The perception of "Russians" as ethnico-political reflects the presence of the Communist association which was still largely present in 1988-89. The interviews were completed just prior to the collapse of the U.S.S.R. and the demise of the dominance of Communist ideology in Eastern Europe. In 1972-73 there was a 14.8% religious rationalisation in the Dublin survey as compared with only 7.3% in the present findings. The "ethnic/way-of-life" percentage in 1988-89 at 63.1%, is 12% greater than the corresponding score in the 1972-73 survey. This indicates a growth in the Irish people's perception of "Russians" more as an ethnic group and less as a Communist-cum-Atheistic people. It will be very interesting to compare these findings with those of the next survey planned for 2004-05, when the impact of recent and future post-Cold-War developments can be measured.

2.3. Rationalisation of "Northern Irish": The reasons given for not admitting *"Northern Irish"* to kinship provide an interesting spread, i.e. Political (42.6%), Way of Life (20.2%), Ethnic (17.4%) and Religious (12.1%). In the mind of these respondents "Northern Irish" constitute a "Politico-Ethnico-Religious" stimulus category, while "Way of Life" is a problem for some. This does not differ that much from the reasons given in the 1972-73 Greater Dublin Survey (Mac Gréil, 1977 p. 236). If this finding is representative of prejudice in the Republic against the "Northern Irish", it is clear that negative attitudes are very much more political than religious. (All this should be seen in the context of a relatively high level of acceptance, i.e. mean social distance of 1.637 in a 1 to 7 range. In the event of improvement in the "Political" and "Way of Life" aspects, the level of social distance is likely to be reduced even further.)

2.4. Rationalisation of "Arabs and Moslems": Irish attitudes towards *"Arabs"* are quite negative (mean social distance of 3.509) with only 20.1% willing to welcome them into the family through marriage. The major reasons given by the 80% who would not be willing to admit them to kinship are largely ethnic (50.0%) with "religious" (15.2%), "racial" (12.9%) and "way of life" (12.2%) accounting for most of the other 50%. There is relatively little direct contact between the majority of Irish people and their Arab fellowkind. The experience of Irish soldiers on peace-keeping duties in the Lebanon may help to provide favourable contact with Arabs and the Middle-East.

The relatively high social distance scores for "Moslems" (3.420) is practically the same as that for "Arabs". In the reasons given on the Rationalisation Scale, "religion" ranks second at 15.2%. "Ethnic" and "way of life" (62.2%), however, constitute the main defining classification by those refusing to admit "Arabs" to family through marriage.

2.5. Summary: The *single-identity* categories include ethnic and religious categories. In the ethnic categories we have Irish Speakers, Scottish and Welsh, Western European countries and the two North American countries, i.e., Canadians and White Americans. Eleven countries or nationalities failed to be identified totally by their ethnicity/way of life. Nine of these were given *double-identity*. The "British" and the "English" scored 50-30 as Ethnic-Political, which reflects the perceived involvement in the Northern Irish "troubles". "Russians" also had a double-identity, scoring 63-21 as ethnic-political. This reflects the association of "Russians" with the Communist regime of the U.S.S.R. The *six* ethnic categories where second identity was racial are discussed in detail below in Chapter V. One ethnic category, "Israelis" registered a *triple identity* scoring 68-12-11 as an ethnic-political-religious. This reflects the impact of the Middle East conflict and the close identity of "Israelis" with the Jewish religion.

3. RACIAL CATEGORIES:

The two racial-group categories, i.e., "Coloureds" and "Blacks" recorded a double identity scoring 50-43 and 46-46 as racial-ethnic respectively. This increase in the ethnic identity of these two categories is commented on in the chapter dealing with changes in racial-ethnic identity (see Chapter IV below).

4. RELIGIOUS CATEGORIES:

Four of the ten religious categories recorded a *single identity*, i.e., "Church of Ireland", "Methodists", "Presbyterians" and "Protestants". A further four, i.e., "Agnostics", "Atheists", "Hare Krishna" and "Moslems" produced a *double identity*. In the case of the first three the second identity was "way of life" with ratios between "religious" and "way of life" ranging from 65 to 20 for "Hare Krishna", to 70 to 16 for "Agnostics" and 76 to 13 for "Atheists". The significance of rejecting because of "way of life" probably reflects a disapproval of the liturgical and other life-style of the groups. The double identity for "Moslems" was 63 to 20 as "religious" - "political". This perception by 20% of "Moslems" as primarily a political category probably reflects the public reports on the Moslem states in the Middle East and in Northern Africa, especially the revolution brought about by the Ayatollah Khomeini in Iran. It is interesting to note the sensitivity of the Irish people to political activity of Moslem religious leaders.

The two remaining religious categories elicited a *triple-identity* among those denying them admission to the family. "Jews" were perceived as "religious", "ethnic" and people with a different "way of life". The ratio between the three reasons put forward for denying kinship were 63-18-10 as "religious-ethnic-way of life". The ethnic rationalisation was, obviously, associated with the Jews' identity with the State of Israel, while the "way of life" was probably reflecting the separate dietary and other perceived differences in life-style. "Roman Catholics" were also given a triple-identity of "religious", "way of life", and "political". It should be noted that the actual number of cases not admitting "Roman Catholics" to kinship was too small (at 30 cases) for further comment on distribution of "reasons".

5. POLITICAL STIMULUS CATEGORIES:

The eight political stimulus categories, i.e. "Capitalists", "Communists", "Gardaí", "Provisional I.R.A.", "Socialists", "Sinn Féin", "Trade Unionists", and "Unionists", have produced a variety of patterns of rationalisation. The inclusion of "Gardaí" and "Trade Unionists" as political is a result of the reasons offered by the respondents for not admitting them to kinship. The political role of the Trade Union movement in Ireland has been central for the past hundred years or more and the Irish Labour Party had its origins in the Trade Unions. Gardaí, like police forces in other countries, are seen as part of the executive arm of government. Because of the on-going political unrest in Ireland, the role of the Gardaí in the State's action against political violence and agitation would give them a political character.

The overall standing of the *"Gardaí"* has been exceptionally high, with 84% welcoming them to kinship. The other 16%, who would not welcome members of the "Gardaí" into their families through kinship did so mainly because of the way of life, probably the demands of their occupation and its behaviour patterns as publicly perceived. The second classification of 16.5% points to a public perception of the Gardaí as a political as well as an occupational stimulus category. The role of the Gardaí in the State's response to the paramilitary activities relating to Northern Ireland is a factor in their "political" rationalisation.

The position of "Trade Unionists" is more explicitly political in the public perception as expressed in the almost 40% choice of "political" as the primary classification. "Way of Life" (27.5%) and "economic" (18.6%) were the other two major reasons chosen. Thus, "Trade Unionists" could be aptly defined as an economic-cum-political stimulus category in Ireland.

The other six *political categories* can be sub-divided into two groups, i.e.

(1) General categories: "Capitalists", "Communists" and "Socialists"; and (2) Specific groups: "Provisional I.R.A.", "Sinn Féin" and "Unionists". The latter three are involved in the Northern Ireland situation.

5.1 Politico-Economic Categories: "Capitalists" received a relatively high mean social distance score (2.587) and would be welcomed into the family through marriage by less than half of the sample, i.e. 47.8%. This means that 52.8% would not admit "Capitalists" to kinship. Their reasons for not doing so were three-fold: "way of life" (38.9%), "economic" (25.6%) and "political" (18.1%). In a society with an espoused capitalist ideology by the majority of politicians, such a high negative attitude is surprising. The image and life-style of the "Capitalist" must not be that attractive to most people. The second and third classification would indicate a political-cum-economic image.

"Socialists", with a mean-social-distance score of 2.650, rank very close to "Capitalists" (only 0.063 higher on the continuum of 1-7 mean-social-distance scale). Some 44.9% would welcome "Socialists" into the family through kinship (2.9% less than in the case of "Capitalists"). The three main classifications of "political" (39.2%), "way of life" (26.9%) and "economic" (18.6%) are the same as "Capitalists" but in a different order. Here the political is more prominent and enjoys the primary classification.

The changes in the rationalisation of "Socialists" since 1972-73 are most interesting, i.e.

SUB-TABLE B

'SOCIALISTS'	Religious	Political	Ethnic Way-of-Life	Economic	N.
A. 1988-89 (National)	4.3%	39.2%	34.6%	14.1%	531
B. 1972-73 (Dublin)	10.2%	79.6%	2.2%	2.4%	832
A-B	-5.9%	-40.4%	+32.4%	-11.7%	

The decline in the "religious" factor and the increases in "ethnic/way of life" and "economic" shows a shift to a more secular attitude or a lessening of religious prejudice against "Socialists".

The "religious" factor is the primary classification in the case of "Communists", which is a change since 1972-73 when the "political" reason was primary.

The substantial decline in the proportion giving a "political" reason for refusing admission to kinship to "Communists" is significant and may indicate that the fear of Communism as a political threat has weakened in Irish society. The growth of the "ethnic/way of life" reason would seem to indicate an association of Communists with particular nationalities. It would appear that many still see communism as a danger to the faith. It

SUB-TABLE C

'COMMUNISTS'	Religious	Political	Ethnic Way-of-Life	Economic	N.
A. 1988-89 (National)	28.2%	27.4%	25.8%	11.7%	737
B. 1972-73 (Dublin)	33.8%	55.8%	1.6%	2.5%	1732
A-B	-5.6%	-28.4%	+24.2%	-9.2%	

should also be noted that the very high mean social distance score for "Communists" (3.769) and the small minority who would welcome them into their family through kinship (24.4%) reflect a serious level of anti-Communist bias in the population for a variety of reasons. It should be noted that the fieldwork for this survey took place just before the drastic changes in Eastern Europe.

5.2 Republican and Unionist Categories: The three specific Political Stimulus Categories were clearly classified as "political" by those who did not welcome them into their family through kinship, i.e. "Provisional I.R.A."

SUB-TABLE D

		Political %	Ethnic W.O.L. %	Religious %	N.
1. Provisional I.R.A.	A. 1988-89 (National)	59.6	26.9	N/S	884
	B. 1972-73 (Dublin)	93.3	0.9		1464
	A-B	-33.7	+26.0		
2. Sinn Féin	A. 1988-89 (National)	56.6	23.7	N/S	807
	B. 1972-73 (Dublin)	93.6	0.7		1376
	A-B	-28.0	+23.0		
3. Unionists	A. 1988-89 (National)	59.8	21.2	13.6	646
	B. 1972-73 (Dublin)	88.7	1.6	4.9	1401
	A-B	-28.9	+19.6	+8.7	

at 59.6%, "Sinn Féin" at 65.6% and "Unionists" at 59.8%. The second classification for all three was "way of life" at 25.9%, 22.6% and 15.6% respectively. some 13.6% of reasons given against admission of "Unionists" to family were "religious". (See Table 9).

The emergence of the "ethnic/way of life" reason could have two explanations. One would be a recognition of a sub-cultural or sub-ethnic difference between the respondents and the members of each of the Northern political categories measured on the Bogardus Social Distance Scale. The second reason could refer to the perceived violent and conflictual pattern of daily living for members of each of the categories in the North. In the case of Sinn Féin, which is established throughout the Republic of Ireland, it is probably associated with the paramilitary way-of-life in Northern Ireland. Both of these are hypothetical explanations and would need further analysis for verification.

The relatively low percentage of "religious" reasons in relation to "Unionists" on the rationalisation scale is yet another indicator of the weak level of sectarian anti-Protestant prejudice in the Republic and the predominance of political bias in regard to Unionists. Further analysis of these findings will be presented below in Chapter VI.

5.3 Summary: None of these eight political categories received a *single identity*. Three socio-political categories, i.e., "Gardaí", "Provisional I.R.A." and "Sinn Féin" were given a *double identity*. Gardaí were denied kinship because of their "way of life" (64%) and "political" (17%) association. It should be pointed out that the actual number denying kinship to Gardaí was only 139, representing 16% of the sample. The reasons for refusing closer social distance to "Provisional I.R.A." were 60 to 27 as "political" – "way of life". The 27% giving "way of life" probably had paramilitary behaviour in mind. The reasons for refusing closer social distance to "Sinn Féin" were weighted slightly more in favour of political, i.e., with 66 to 23 for "political" – "way of life". The very similar pattern of rationalisation for both categories reflect their strong association in the perception of the people. The high correlation between the Bogardus Social Distance scores of both categories at r = 0.73 substantiates the public perception of "Sinn Féin" and the "Provisional I.R.A." in the rationalisation Table (No. 7).

Four other socio-political categories elicited a *triple identity*. "Capitalists" were denied kinship by respondents for reasons of "way of life", "economic" and "political" on a ratio of 39-26-18 respectively. The reasons given in relation to "Socialists" were the same but in a different order i.e., "political", "way of life" and "economic" in a ratio of 39-27-14 respectively. It has been noted elsewhere that the mean social distance score of these two categories were quite close at 2.587 for "Capitalists" and 2.650 for "socialists", which is literally "too close to call" at that place on the one-to-seven continuum.

"Trade Unionists" have a pattern of rationalisation similar to that of "Socialists", i.e., "political", "way of life", and "economic" on a ratio of 40-28-19 respectively. The correlation between these two categories" social distance scores was only moderately high at r = 0.56. The final socio-political category to elicit a triple identity was "Unionists" whose pattern of rationalisation was "political", "way of life" and "religious" on a ratio of 60-16-14 respectively. This shows the predominantly political definition of "Unionists". Those who gave "way of life" as a reason were probably put off by the image of Unionists on parades or their association with hostilities in Northern Ireland. The religious identity by 14% of respondents is probably due to their religious or denominational stereotype sometimes projected by the public leadership of Unionists groups and their relations with the Orange Order.

The only category to elicit *four identities* at above the 10% level was "Communists". The four reasons receiving significant support from those who denied closer social distance to "Communists" were "religious", "political, "way of life" and "economic" at a ratio of 28-27-19-12. This means that prejudice against "Communists" in Ireland is very complex involving religious, political and socio-economically based prejudices. It is interesting to record once again that this survey was carried out just prior to the fall of the Soviet Union and the collapse of the Communist governments in the Eastern European countries.

6. DIVERSE SOCIAL CATEGORIES:

As stated above, the eleven social categories included on the Bogardus Social Distance Scale covered a very wide spectrum of social distance from "Working Class" with an M.S.D. score of 1.210 to "Drug Addicts" with a score of 4.798.

6.1 Working Class and Unemployed: All of the eleven social categories elicit a *double identity* of "way of life" and "not socially acceptable". "Way of life" does not necessarily mean deviant behaviour in every case. It can also mean different and unattractive lifestyles. "Working Class" and "Unemployed" were among the *ingroups* of Irish society. They were placed second and fifth in the rank-ordering of fifty-nine categories. The relatively small number who refused to welcome members of the "Working Class" (13%) and of the "Unemployed" (22%) into kinship gave their reasons as "way of life" and "not socially acceptable" at a ratio of 68 to 12 and 62 to 20 respectively. The relatively high status for the "Unemployed" should be welcomed as is the low proportion of those refusing closer social distance doing so for reasons of social unacceptability or snobbery. This is a big change since 1972-73, and may be due to the more widespread incidence of unemployment across the board in the Republic over the past fifteen years.

6.2 People With Handicap: "People with Physical Handicap" and those with "Mental Handicap" have been positively rated in terms of mean social distance, i.e., at 1.581 and 2.010 respectively or 9th and 21st in rank-order out of fifty-nine categories. The reasons given by those refusing closer social distance were "way of life" and "not socially acceptable" at a ratio of 56 to 19 and 53 to 19 respectively. Those with physical handicap are almost among the ingroups in popularity which must be most encouraging. Also the relatively low proportion giving "not socially acceptable" as a rationalisation among those refusing closer social distance indicates a relatively low level of social stigma in the Republic in regard to people with handicap. The correlation between the social distance scores of both categories was significant but moderate at r = 0.57.

6.3 Gay People: The response of the population to "Gay People" was very negative in terms of social distance. The mean social distance score at 3.793 and their rank-order placing at 54th out of fifty-nine categories is quite disturbing in relation to a relatively weak and vulnerable minority. The reasons given for refusing closer social distance to "Gay People" have been "way of life" and "not socially acceptable" at a ratio of 75 to 20 respectively. Perceived "way of life" or life style of Gay People is negatively perceived by the majority of the people. The social stigma against them is not as serious as a rejection of their life-style.

It will be shown below (see Chapter XI, Part II) that a plurality of the sample. (44%) were in favour of decriminalising "*homosexual behaviour between consenting adults*" with 35% against. The association of "Gay People" with AIDS is clear from the moderately high Pearson correlation (r = 0.63) between the social distance responses in relation to "Gay People" and "People with AIDS". Those supporting gay people's rights in the public media and elsewhere need to cultivate a better understanding and respect for this minority in the population and examine the approach adopted to date. The decriminalisation of this minority in recent years could, in time, get rid of the penal Victorian legacy against people perceived to be "gay".

6.4 Ex-Prisoners: It is generally accepted that public willingness to reintegrate Ex-Prisoners into society is an essential condition for the rehabilitation of Ex-Prisoners (see *MacBride Report*, 1980). Attitudes towards "Ex-Prisoners" are fairly negative in the Bogardus Social Distance Scale findings with a mean social distance of 3.316. The rationalisation of those refusing close social distance to this category were "way of life" and "not socially acceptable" with a ratio of 64 to 27 respectively. Social stigma is moderately high at 27% while the main reason is "way of life" or life style. It probably is also a rejection of perceived criminal activity.

6.5 Unmarried Mothers: The social distance scores of "Unmarried Mothers" in Irish society are low with a mean social distance of 1.659 and gaining 16th place in the rank-ordering of the fifty-nine categories. Those who refused closer social distance gave as their main reasons "way of life" and "not socially acceptable" at a ratio of 61 to 29 respectively. The moderately high social stigma of 29% is the equivalent of 10.4% of the sample viewing "Unmarried Mothers" as "not socially acceptable" which, while small in terms of the total sample, is significant. However the vast majority do not hold this view. The positive view towards "Unmarried Mothers" is held by a sample which has expressed very supportive opinions for the institutions of marriage and the family (see the findings of the "Family Values Scales" in Chapter X below). "Unmarried Mothers" have maintained their good standing since 1972-73 when they were given an ingroup status at an M.S.D. of 1.360.

6.6 "Alcoholics" and "Drug Addicts": "Alcoholics" and "Drug Addicts" as victims of compulsive behaviour, need the support of members of the community for their rehabilitation. The findings of the Bogardus Social Distance Scale in their regard is not very positive with both categories receiving a mean social distance score of over three, i.e. 3.105 for "Alcoholics" and 4.798 for "Drug Addicts". The latter is the second highest M.S.D. score in the whole scale. It is dangerously high in that it reflects quite a penal attitude that could easily spill over into hostile physical attack. The reasons given for these negative attitudes were "way of life" and "not socially acceptable" at a ratio of 67 to 19 and 68 to 20 respectively. The life-styles of both groups are rejected by over two-thirds of those not admitting them to closer social distance. In a society so tolerant of alcoholic drinking, it is surprising how negative the majority of people are to "Alcoholics". Also the very penal attitudes towards "Drug Addicts", who are often victims of the widespread use of drugs in modern urban society, is also counterproductive in terms of support for rehabilitation.

6.7 People with AIDS: Victims of AIDS are a small but growing minority in Irish society. The attitudes expressed in the Bogardus Social Distance Scale against this category are appallingly negative and totally counterproductive with regard to the humane support likely to be given to them. The two groups or categories which are moderately positively correlated to "People with AIDs" are "Drug Addicts" (r = 0.54) and "Gay People" (R = 0.63). The reasons given by respondents who refused closer social distance to "People with AIDS" were "way of life" (life style) and "not socially acceptable" at a ratio of 52 to 26 respectively. The element of social stigma is moderately substantial while life-style is the main reason for their rejection.

6.8 Itinerants/Travellers: In the course of the interview the terms "Itinerants" and "Travellers" were used because the former was the generally used concept in 1972-73. The latter is the acceptable concept today. Elsewhere in this book part of a chapter is devoted to the negative prejudice against *"Travellers"* and possible causes of this. Their rationalisation shows "way of life/life style" and "not socially acceptable" as the main reasons at a ratio of 74 to 20 respectively. This strong emphasis on "way of life" could represent a distinctive sub-culture or a rejection of a perceived "life-style". The 20% "not socially acceptable" at least shows a relatively low, if significant, percentage for "social stigma". A detailed analysis of attitudes and prejudices towards Travellers is given in Chapter XI below (see pages 323 to 341).

6.9 Summary: Rationalisation of refusal of admission or welcoming into family in the case of the eleven *social stimulus* categories has been primarily "way of life". In the case of nine of the eleven categories, the second classification has been "not socially acceptable" or, in other words, social pressure from friends, neighbours and associates. The tragic fact about the relatively deprived categories is that social support would be necessary to facilitate the improvement of their life chances. Hence the urgency to correct the status of such deprived categories. Of course, some would argue that, in the case of those deprived groups whose condition is seen to be voluntarily inflicted, the negative sanction of social unacceptability prevents greater numbers becoming so deprived. Charity would demand "love for the sinner while rejecting the sin"!

The aim of this book is not to moralise but rather to present the facts as they emerge from the findings. The level of social acceptability of five of the eleven social categories has been relatively high, i.e. they were given a low mean social distance score of 1-2 on a 1-7 scale. These are, in order of acceptability:

More Acceptable Social Categories		*Less Acceptable Social Categories*	
1. "Working Class"	(1.210)	6. "Alcoholics"	(3.105)
2. "Unemployed"	(1.345)	7. "Ex-Prisoners"	(3.316)
3. "People with Physical Handicap"	(1.581)	8. "Travellers"	(3.681)
		9. "Gay People"	(3.793)
4. "Unmarried Mothers"	(1.684)	10. "People with AIDS"	(4.336)
5. "People with Mental Handicap"	(2.010)	11. "Drug Addicts"	(4.798)

The "Less Acceptable" categories are likely to feel social ostracisation because of their high level of Social Distance. In a sense, society's attitude to these six categories constitutes very severe social bias and negative labelling.

PART IV: INTERGROUP SOCIAL DISTANCE SCORES CORRELATED

1. FACTOR ANALYSIS:

There are two standard statistical techniques for discovering how the respondents group the categories. The first of these is by means of *factor analysis* which pulls together into clusters categories receiving more or less similar reactions, at least in valency if not in intensity, although the latter can affect the factoring function, as can be seen by the large number of categories not getting the necessary variance loading (+0.5) to fall into one of the seven factors given in Table 10. A testing of the excluded categories on their own produced an interesting pattern of clustering.

Eighteen stimulus categories were clustered together in *Factor No. 1* which was made up of racial, ethnic and religious categories. It was possible to divide this factor into two sub-factors, i.e., (a) racial/ethnic and (b) religious. It was interesting to note that the three Protestant denominations were not included, i.e., "Church of Ireland", "Methodists" and "Presbyterians", which were clustered together in *Factor No. 4*. It is also interesting and it confirms the rationalisation scale that "Communists" were factored with diverse religious groups with relatively high or distant social distance scores. The fact that "socialists" did not join "Communists" in the religious cluster points to the declassifying of "socialists" as a category with religious connotations, which may have been the case in the past when the fear of socialism was identified by some/many as a threat to religion (see the biography of James Connolly).

Factor No. 2 is conceptually logical in clustering European Ethnic (i.e., from the Continent of Europe) together with "White Americans" and "Canadians". The European identity of the latter two categories probably indicates that the United States and Canada are still culturally part of Greater Europe in the minds of the Irish people. Many Irish people may feel closer to these North American categories than they do to the ethnic categories of continental Europe (as the social distance score bears out). The overall impression given by the findings would seem to indicate that Irish people do not see themselves primarily or even secondarily as European or as British (see the Ethnic self-identity scale p. 97 below) but definitely as Irish with very close attachments to "English", "Scottish", "Welsh", "White Americans" and "Canadians" and a fairly close attachment to the Western European nationalities. The cultural affiliation with the European Union is not yet very impressive in the findings. Economic and political relations do not seem to be having strong ethnic and cultural affinities. Irish people, when they look out, seem to look West as much as they look East!

Factor No. 3 draws five categories together. This combines two subgroups, i.e., "Gardaí" and "Irish Speakers" who are categories with very

TABLE No. 10
FACTOR ANALYSIS CLUSTERINGS OF STIMULUS CATEGORIES

1 Racial Ethnic Religious		2 Ethnic European		3 Irish Socio-Political		4 Religious Denomination		5 British		6 Republican		7 Handicapped	
(a) Racial Ethnic		Belgians	0.693	Gardai	0.550	Church of Ireland	0.530	British	0.798	Sinn Fein	0.834	People with Physical Handicap	0.680
Black Americans	0.758	Canadians	0.557	Irish Speakers	0.625	Methodists	0.637	English	0.741	Provisional I.R.A.	0.870		
Arabs	0.802	Danes	0.773	Trade Unionists	0.530	Presbyterians	0.658					People with Mental Handicap	0.716
Blacks	0.750	French	0.791	Unemployed	0.530								
Chinese	0.816	Germans	0.740	Working Class	0.691								
Coloureds	0.696	Italians	0.650		0.632								
Greeks	0.748	People of Luxembourg	0.785										
Indians	0.615	Polish People	0.654										
Israelis	0.764	Portuguese	0.639										
Nigerians	0.713	Scottish	0.555										
Pakistanis	0.792	Spaniards	0.702										
Russians	0.614	Welsh	0.601										
		White Americans	0.509										
(b) Religious													
Agnostics	0.622												
Atheists	0.598												
Communists	0.640												
Hare Krishna	0.593												
Jews	0.509												
Moslems	0.690												

Categories not 'factored' Alcoholics, Capitalists, Drug Addicts, Dutch, Ex-prisoners, Gay People, Travellers, Northern Irish, People with AIDS, Protestants, Roman Catholics, Socialists, Unionists, Unmarried Mothers.

low mean social distance scores (1.267 and 1.287 respectively). The remaining three provide a logical combination enjoying the common characteristic of "work", i.e. Trade Unions, Unemployed and Working Class.

Factor No. 4 consists of the three Irish Protestant Denominations who are highly to moderately highly thought of by the sample, and were given relatively low mean social distance scores, i.e., "Church of Ireland" at 1.609, "Methodists" at 2.128 and "Presbyterians" at 2.045. It is interesting to observe that the category "Protestants" was not clustered with the Protestant denominations. They are among the categories which did not get over 0.5 in any factor.

Factor No. 5 is a most significant grouping of the "British" and the "English" on their own. These two categories did not perform as did their ethnic neighbours, "Scottish" and "Welsh" who were included in categories of Factor No. 2. The Pearson correlation matrix of the fifty-nine categories, (see Appendix B below) bears out the unique response pattern of these two ethnic categories, both of them having low mean social distance scores, i.e., "English" at 1.475 and "British" at 1.521, indicating their position among Ireland's "ingroups". The Pearson correlation between both categories was very high at r = 0.80. The whole complexity of Irish intergroup relations is further analysed in Chapter VIII, below.

Factor No. 6 draws the two publicly identified Republican categories together with a very high varimax loading of 0.834 and 0.870. This bears out the high Pearson correlation between the two categories of r = 0.73. At the time of interviewing, both categories, "Sinn Féin", and "Provisional I.R.A." were extremely unpopular and publicly co-identified. The identification of "Sinn Féin" with the "Provisional IRA" (r = 0.73) is very high and probably explains the low social distance score of "Sinn Féin". It will be shown later that the sample overwhelmingly rejected the use of violence in Northern Ireland (see pp. 239ff). Hostility towards both categories was very negative with mean social distance scores of 4.245 and 5.049 for "Sinn Féin" and "Provisional I.R.A." respectively. Attitudes towards these categories would have, in all probability, improved following the ceasefire and positive peace initiatives.

Factor No. 7 brought the attitudes toward the two categories of people with handicap together. The Pearson correlation between the two categories was only moderately high at r = 0.57. Also there was a disparity between the mean social distance scores of "people with physical handicap" at 1.581 and "people with mental handicap" at 2.010.

2. PEARSON CORRELATIONS BETWEEN CATEGORIES:

The second technique by which it is possible to gauge the classification of the stimulus categories by the respondents is by means of the Pearson product-moment correlation co-efficient. Table 182 (Appendix B) is a comprehensive table giving the Pearson correlation between each stimulus category. In all there are 1,711 correlation scores on the table and it is printed in full here as a reference table. Further on in this work various groupings of categories, e.g. ethnic, racial, religious are abstracted from Table 182.

The range of correlation goes from -1.0 through 0.0 to +1.0. The degree of correlation is calculated as follows

> *rho = 0.0 to 0.2 = None or Negligent*
> *rho = 0.2 to 0.4 = Low Degree of Correlation*
> *rho = 0.4 to 0.6 = Moderate Degree of Correlation*
> *rho = 0.6 to 0.8 = Marked Degree of Correlation*
> *rho = 0.8 to 1.0 = High Degree of Correlation*
>
> (Mac Gréil, 1977, p. 283 n.)

The correlations of 0.50 and higher are printed in bold type. The very widespread level of correlation of r = 0.50 and higher shows the underpinning degree of uniformity in social prejudice. In other words, those likely to be prejudiced against religious categories are also likely to be prejudiced against ethnic, racial, social and other categories as well. If this be true, and it appears to be from an analysis of Table 182, a particular form of prejudice such as racialism is but a symptom of something deeper in the culture, in society and in the personality, which is shaped by the socio-cultural forces of rearing and living in society.

3. SUMMARY AND CONCLUSIONS:

The pattern of the findings of the social distance (Bogardus) scale was more-or-less as anticipated and repeats the findings of the 1972-73 survey. Once again, the Bogardus Scale performed very well in discerning the range of valency in the intergroup attitudes and prejudices of the national sample. Overall, there are indications of a significant growth in ethnocentrism and in certain other prejudice categories. The extent and reasons for such a change will be examined in the next chapter.

There have been a number of changes in the patterns of rationalisation over the sixteen years between 1972-73 and 1988-89. The two areas of most notable and striking change is the reduction in *"not socially acceptable"* and *"racial"* as reasons for refusing members of certain categories into 'kinship'. The shift seems to have been from "not socially acceptable" to "way of life" and from "racial" to "ethnic or nationality". The latter indicates the weakening of 'pure racialism', while the former could be attributed to a reduction of 'snobbery' or pressure to conform to neighbourhood or other prejudices.

The results of the factor analysis and Pearson Correlation matrix are also revealing and confirm previous patterns and clusterings, with notable exceptions. These results help to confirm further the validity and reliability of the Bogardus Social Distance Scale.

CHAPTER IV

Ethnocentrism in Ireland

INTRODUCTION

In this chapter it is proposed to examine in greater detail the prejudices of the Irish people towards a number of other nationalities with a view to discovering the nature of Irish ethnocentrism. Related to ethnic prejudice is the ethnic self-identity of the people and their attitudes and opinions in relation to the Irish language as Ireland's major and unique symbolic meaningful system. In addition, the findings of a special *"Irish Patriotic Esteem Scale"* will be examined.

The principal instrument used to measure Irish ethnocentrism will be the Bogardus Social Distance scale used to gauge social distance towards twenty one ethnic or nationality groups. A further six ethnic groups' social distance scores are examined in the next chapter which concentrates on racialism. The six latter groups are classified as ethnico-racial categories in the rationalisation scale. These ethnico-racial categories are: "Africans", "American Negroes/Blacks", "Chinese", "Indians", "Nigerians", and "Pakistanis".

Returning to the twenty-one ethnic nationalities for whom detailed measures of social distance are reported below it is possible to divide them into a number of ethnic groupings.

(a) *Irish and British Categories:*
   1. British*
   2. English
   3. Northern Irish
   4. Scottish
   5. Welsh

(b) *European and North American Categories:*
   1. Belgians*
   2. Canadians
   3. Danes*
   4. Dutch*
   5. French*
   6. Germans*
   7. Greeks*
   8. Italians*
   9. Luxembourgians*
   10. Poles
   11. Portuguese*
   12. Russians
   13. Spaniards*
   14. White Americans

(c) *Middle East Categories:*
   1. Arabs
   2. Israelis

* Member Country of the E.C. in 1989.

PART I: IRISH NATIONALITY AND ETHNIC IDENTITY

While it can be agreed from the history of ethnic conquest that large countries have tended to be most nationalistic, and even jingoistic, at times, and smaller countries tended to be more global and open in outlook, it is nevertheless true that small historical nations can also display great national pride and ethnocentric bias. Larger nations can neglect the outside world because of the size and strength of their own domain. An analysis of the average daily news presented in the popular print and electronic media in countries like the United States, Germany, France, Russia and China, would have proportionally very little foreign news compared with the popular media of smaller countries like Belgium, Denmark, Ireland and the Netherlands. These latter countries tend to have a higher proportion of their popular news from countries outside their own land. It could be argued that the limitation of local news in the small country forced a greater dependence on foreign news. The impact of local/provincial papers, of course, in all countries is primarily centred on the local scene.

1. NATIONALITY:

The intensity of nationalism in large countries can lead to great wars and even imperial colonisation and exploitation and the imposition of their value systems on other peoples, e.g., the "quasi-missionary" ideological zeal of the United States in Vietnam in the 1970s and a similar motivation of the U.S.S.R. in Afghanistan in the 1980s to mention but two very tragic and possibly well intentioned ethnico-political exercises. At the core of all acts of ethnic expansionism is the erroneous belief that "our way of life" is the best for the other groups even if it has to be imposed on them. This could be classified as "**offensive ethnocentrism**".

At the other end of the spectrum, there are many cases of "**defensive ethnocentrism**" which seems to emerge often in response to attempts to force assimilation on the people. A classic example of "defensive ethnocentrism" was the case of Iran where a programme of Westernisation had been imposed by a pro-Western elite. Many ordinary Moslem Persians were incensed and became understandably lured into the very violent reassertion of ethnico-religious identity under the extreme leadership of representatives of the alienated Iranians. The tragic outcome resulted in extremism and bloodshed. The rise of so-called "ethnic fundamentalism" in many countries is often a response to a sense of threat by the people to their cultural identity. The tragedy of the Balkans at present is almost a classical case of "defensive ethnocentrism". When people are secure they are not a prey to extremism. People become insecure when their identity and values seem to them to be threatened by multiple forms of "offensive ethnocentrism".

A people's nationality represents their culture with its beliefs, ideas, convictions, values, norms, and symbolic meaningful systems, which constitutes

what might be called its "ethos' (see Ruth Benedict 1932). Each culture
views the same world differently. Global bureaucracies are a force for
cultural homogenisation and usually adopt one or two macro cultures to
standardise the rest. For instance, cultural pluralists are becoming very concerned by global transmission of popular cultural ideas and the promotion
of a life style and values system which appears to be incompatible with other
cultures and traditions. This is seen as a very insidious form of "**cultural colonisation**". The attempt to impose universal rights to the transmission of
television programmes (via satellite) as part of the GATT agreement was
resisted by France because of the perceived danger to the French culture.
France was reacting in a manner which, for many, was considered
reasonable.

Ethnocentrism in Irish society has been largely a case of "defensive
ethnocentrism" and a response to a long history of colonial "offensive
ethnocentrism". The latter, for instance, almost succeeded in replacing the
native language and culture by that of the dominant group which ruled the
country from medieval times until 1921, when native administrations were
given authority on both sides of the Border. The administration in the Irish
Free State (Twenty-Six Counties) has had almost full national sovereignty,
while the administration in Northern Ireland (Six Counties State) has had
limited devolved authority from Westminster. The ethnic and cultural
residue of the colonial past left two partially distinct ethnic groups in the
island of Ireland. The Irish (Nationalist) ethnic group dominated the
Twenty-Six Counties (i.e., 90% plus of the population), while the Loyalist
ethnic group dominated the Six Counties State (i.e. 60% plus of the population).

This division of the island of Ireland led to a "double-double ethnic division" of the country. In the Twenty-Six Counties (i.e., the "Irish Free State"
and later the "Republic of Ireland") the former Loyalists must have felt a
sense of "ethnic defensiveness" while the nationalists in the Six Counties
(i.e., Northern Ireland) were also forced into an "ethnic defensive" situation. Because of the conflict in Northern Ireland, the inter-group relationship has been politicised with religious identity overtones. Because the
survey on which this book is based did not extend to Northern Ireland, the
findings analysed here only deal with the adult population living in the
Republic of Ireland in 1988-89.

2. ETHNIC SELF-IDENTITY OF IRISH PEOPLE

In research into social attitudes and opinions it is essential for the researcher to establish as far as is possible the nature of the people's self-
perception and self-identity. This is so because of the *subjective* nature of
inter-group attitudes and opinions.

Prejudice in Ireland Revisited

TABLE No. 11
ETHNIC SELF-IDENTITY

Ethnic Self-Identity	First Preference	Second Preference
1. Irish	67.5%	25.6%
2. County/City	20.6%	28.3%
3. Southern Irish	7.3%	30.1%
4. Northern Irish	0.6%	1.6%
(Irish: National/Interval)	(96.0%	(85.6%)
5. European	1.4%	9.3%
6. Other	2.6%	5.0%
Number	1,005	995

2.1 Overall Findings:

When respondents were asked the following question: *"Which of these terms, i.e., Irish, Province/County, Northern Irish, Southern Irish, Anglo-Irish, British, European, or other, best describes the way you usually think of yourself?"*, the overwhelming majority gave an Irish identification as their first preference (96%) and as their second preference (86%). Table 11 (above) gives a breakdown of the answer. This question about ethnic self-identity was originally used by Richard Rose in the survey of Northern Ireland people and published in *Governing Without Consensus: An Irish Perspective* (see Rose 1971, p. 285). The same question was replicated in the 1972-73 survey. The comparative results are reported below on Table 13 (page 99).

A follow-up question: *"Would you say you are a strong on average (first preference identification)?"* The theoretical assumption made by Rose in relation to this question was that people with secure self-identities would respond "average", while those who would protest their identity too much by answering "strong" probably had identity insecurity. The overall response to the question was as follows: "Strong" 41%; "average" 57%; "don't know" 2%. Does this indicate an element of ethnic identity insecurity in two fifths of the sample?

2.2 Ethnic Self-Identity by Personal Variables:

Table 12 gives a breakdown of Irish primary ethnic self-identity by personal variables. Neither "marital status" nor "political party preference" recorded a statistically significant variation between their subsamples in the case of the identification or its intensity. "Age" and "gender" failed to show significance in regard to identification.

2.2.a *Identification:* In the case of the personal variables showing statistically significant variation in relation to the option between a national self

Prejudice in Ireland Revisited

TABLE No. 12
PRIMARY ETHNIC SELF-IDENTITY BY PERSONAL VARIABLES

Variable	Identification		Intensity of Identiy		Number
	Irish	Internal Irish*	Strong	Average	
Total Sample	67.5%	28.5%	40.7%	57.0%	964
Age			P≤.002		
1. 35 years or less	N/S		33.3	64.0	375
2. 36 to 50 years			31.9	58.6	256
3. 51 to 65 years			51.3	41.7	187
4. 66 years plus			48.6	49.3	140
Gender			P≤.05		
	N/S				
1. Females			37.0	60.2	522
2. Males			45.1	53.3	439
County of Residence	P≤.001		P≤.005		
1. Dublin	740	22.0	42.6	54.7	265
2. Rest of Leinster	74.0	22.8	35.1	60.0	245
3. Munster	64.3	29.3	39.9	59.8	281
4. Connaught/Ulster	53.2	45.7	47.1	51.8	170
Area of Rearing	P≤.002				
			N/S		
1. Large City	69.4	24.7			221
2. Small City	67.5	25.6			109
3. Town	74.5	22.2			148
4. Rural	64.6	32.8			481
Education	P≤.001		P≤.005		
1. Primary Only	59.7	37.8	48.0	49.8	275
2. Incomplete Second	69.0	26.1	33.6	63.0	330
3. Complete Second	71.6	25.9	38.2	59.6	225
4. Third Level	72.7	20.1	48.1	51.9	129
Occupational Status	P≤.002				
			N/S		
1. Professional /Executive	73.0	19.5			147
2.Inspector/Supervisor	70.7	25.0			286
3. Skilled/Routine N-man	61.2	34.5			266
4. Semi/Unskilled	70.5	28.8			153
Social Class Position					
1. Class I	82.4	11.8			32
2. Class II	71.4	18.1			94
3. Class III	71.9	24.4			259
4. Class IV	61.4	32.2			284
5. Class V	64.4	33.5			182

* **Includes "Province/County of Rearing", "Southern Irish", "Northern Irish"**

identity, i.e., *"Irish"*, or a provincial or county self-identity some clear patterns emerge from the findings. Leinster ("Dublin" and the "Rest of Leinster") and "town-reared" respondents opt more for the national self-identity, in other words, they see themselves (74% of them) as being primarily members of Irish *society*. In contrast almost half (45.7%) of

Connaught/Ulster respondents opted for a more local *community* identity as compared to less than a quarter of Dublin and rest of Leinster people having a primary community identity. The rural-reared were also the highest (32.8%) subsample in the "place of rearing" variable to perceive themselves primarily as more provincial or county. The broader "society" primary self-identity scores are positively correlated to educational standard reached, i.e., "third-level" respondents were highest (72.7%) in opting for "Irish" as their primary ethnic self-identity while "primary only" were least (59.7%). In the case of occupational status the highest status was least regional or local in their primary identity. The lower the class-position status the higher was the proportion opting for a more local *"community"* identity.

The following table (13) shows the comparative finding of the Northern Ireland survey of 1968, the Dublin Survey of 1972-73 and the present survey at the national level and for the Dublin subsample.

TABLE No. 13
COMPARATIVE ETHNIC SELF-IDENTITY
(1968, 1972-73 and 1988-89)

SURVEY	Irish	Internal Irish	Anglo-Irish and British	Other	
1. Northern Ireland 1986*	43%	21%	35%	1%	1,291
2. Dublin 1972-73**	48%	47%	2%	3.5%	2,311
3. National Sample 1988-89	68%	29%	2%	1%	1,005
4. Dublin subsample 1988-89	74%	22%	3%	1%	265
Change (4-2)	+26%	-25%	+1%	0%	–

* Richard Rose 1971, p. 285.
** M. Mac Gréil, 1977, p. 125.

The very substantial and significant increase in the proportion of Dublin respondents seeing themselves primarily as "Irish" rather than as "Dubliners" or "Mayo people", etc., when compared with the 1972-73 is very noteworthy and marks an acute shift away from "community self-identity" to "society self-identity". This could also reflect a growth in the proportion of the population in Dublin who had become middle class.

This broader primary ethnic self-identity seems to be a trait of the middle class and suburban cultural ethos, while the "working class" and rural citizens would have a higher proportion identifying primarily with their county or city of origin, e.g., a Dublin working-class person would tend to have a stronger sense of local community than would the average suburban middle class Dubliner. If that be the case, those supporting Dublin *county* teams or *local* soccer teams would tend to get their major support from working class areas, while the *Irish* Rugby team would be more likely to attract a more middle class support from people with relatively weaker local community self-identities. Are the middle class more citizens of society while the working class are members of localised communities or counties?

The changes since 1972-73 would seem to show a decline in the proportion of those with primary local community self-identities. This indicates an increase in the trend towards the middle-class ethos, with its weakening of community identity. This could also signal a fall off in family and parish identity and a move towards a more anonymous individualism with all its virtues and miseries! In such a society hostility resulting from impassioned local loyalties may decline to be replaced by intergroup indifference and bureaucratically based contractual relations, i.e., the move from *gemeinschaft* to *gesellschaft* (see Tonnies 1955). The trend emerging in this study sees the signals of such change, i.e. from *"community"* to *"association"*.

2.2.b *The Strength of Primary Ethnic Self-Identity:* Four of the nine personal variables recorded a statistically significant variation between the scores of their subsamples. The five which reported consensus were "marital status", "area of rearing", "occupational status", "social class position" and "political party preference". Going on Richard Rose's hypothesis that those asserting that their primary ethnic self-identity as *"strong"* were "protesting too much" and manifesting a degree of insecurity in the self-identity, it could be concluded that those with the highest score for *"average"* would have the least problem about who they were. On that basis then the findings show that younger respondents are more self-secure in regard to their self-identity than are older respondents. Females are slightly (but significantly) more secure than males. Those with "incomplete second level" education are significantly more secure in their ethnic self-identity than are other educational subsamples, especially those with "third level" and "primary only". With regard to "county of residence" respondents from the "rest of Leinster" (i.e., outside Dublin) are slightly the more secure subsample.

It is interesting to compare the findings of the levels of strength in Northern Ireland (1968), Greater Dublin 1972-73, and the 1988-89 national and Dublin findings.

TABLE No. 14
COMPARATIVE STRENGTHS OF PRIMARY ETHNIC SELF-IDENTITY

SURVEY	STRONG	AVERAGE	NUMBER
1. Northern Ireland 1968*	38%	60%	1,291
2. Dublin 1972-73**	52%	47%	2,287
3. National Sample 1988-89	41%	57%	960
4. Dublin Subsample 1988-89	43%	55%	265
Change in Dublin (4-2)	-9%	+8%	

* Richard Rose 1971, p. 285.
** M. Mac Gréil, 1977, p. 125.

The changes which have taken place in Dublin between 1972-73 and 1988-89 show a modest drop in the percentage asserting a "strong" sense of identity. This would point to an improvement of their self-identity security of the Dublin sample over the intervening sixteen years (1972-73 to 1988-89).

2.2.c *Conclusion:* From the above findings on the responses to the question on perceived primary ethnic self-identity it is overwhelmingly clear that Irish people see themselves as Irish as distinct from Europeans, British or even Anglo-Irish. The majority are secure in their ethnic self-identity. The area of most change has been the 26% increase in the proportion opting for nationwide "Irish" primary ethnic self-identity. This is seen as indicating a marked increase in middle class ethos in Dublin, i.e., a shift towards *gesellschaft* and away from *gemeinschaft*.

3. NATIONAL RESPECT AND PATRIOTIC ESTEEM

The self-confidence of the Irish people as Irish is an important social-psychological measure of personal self-identity. National respect and patriotic self-esteem can constitute a doubled-edged sword. The serious absence of these qualities could indicate a degree of self-denigration, which is to be found among colonised and oppressed people and minorities. This negative condition has in the past led to "accommodation", to serious discrimination against and negative stratification of members of minorities. The much criticised "Uncle Toms", "Nannies" and "Boys" in the time of severe discrimination against Blacks in the Deep South of the United States were examples of "accommodation" to the demeaning conditions of semi-slavery. In Ireland the caricature of the "alickadoos", i.e., depicting inordinate submissiveness towards colonial dominant groups or to one's perceived "betters" exercising disproportionate power, was indicative of a lack of national pride and patriotic esteem.

The other blade of the double-edged sword is the xenophobic sense of superiority *vis-a-vis* other nationalities and cultures. This may also pass as national respect and patriotic esteem. It may become in fact a rationalisation for ethnic prejudice and can lead to ethnic persecution. The extreme example of this was the deliberate orchestration of nationalist pride and patriotic zeal of the Third Reich in Germany between 1933 and 1945. It is very important, therefore, to note and take cognizance of the positive and negative dimension of the dispositions and opinions which constitute "national respect and patriotic esteem". Table 15 is an attempt to measure national respect and patriotic esteem. This is the first time that this scale is being tested so its findings are more tentative as a result.

3.1 Overall Findings:

It is quite clear from the findings of Table 15 that the vast majority of the sample have a very positive view on Ireland. This corroborates the

TABLE No. 15
(NATIONAL RESPECT AND) PATRIOTIC ESTEEM SCALE (Cronbach Alpha = 0.53)

ITEM	Agree %	Don't Know %	Disagree %	Patriotic Score (0-200)	Number
1. Everywhere in the world Irish people are loved	46.1	17.1	36.8	109.3	1002
2. In striving for international cooperation we must take care that no typically Irish customs are lost	73.2	13.9	13.0	160.2	1003
3. (We), the Irish people, are always willing to put our shoulder to the wheel.	53.1	17.7	29.2	123.9	1000
4. Generally speaking Ireland is a better country than most other countries	63.1	15.2	21.7	141.4	1000
5. We, the Irish, have reason to be proud of our history	75.4	14.6	10.1	165.3	1003
Table Score				140.0	

extremely high percentage whose primary ethnic self-identity was Irish. Viewed in the context of the findings of the *Anomie Scale* and of the *Alienation Scale*, this relatively strong score of 140.0 or 70% on the Patriotic Scale is more than romantic, uncritical chauvinism, although an element of the latter may be hidden in these figures. Also, it should be noted that the "patriotic question" has been a very live issue in Ireland as a post-colonial society, where the country was divided on our gaining independence for twenty-six of the thirty-two counties in the early 1920s. The problem of "post-colonial attitudinal schizophrenia" has been documented elsewhere (see pp. 260ff). There may be a tendency to self-depreciation due to a long period of colonisation by a powerful nation.

3.2 Individual Items:

Before discussing the variations in the scale scores by personal variables the significance of the views expressed in each of the five items of the *Irish Patriotic Scale* will be discussed.

3.2.a *The Irish Abroad*: Ireland has been an "emigration country" for almost two hundred years. Over that time Irish people have settled abroad, especially in the English-speaking countries, e.g. England, Scotland, Wales, United States, Canada, Australia and New Zealand. For over a century there have been thousands of Irish missionaries working in Africa and Asia and, in recent times numerous Irish lay volunteers have given service in countries where there were severe deprivations. In the light of this relatively wide global presence of Irish people, it is interesting to note that respondents were divided on how we were perceived abroad. A plurality (46.1%) agreed that: "*Everywhere in the world Irish people are loved*", while a substantial minority of more than one third (36.8%) disagreed with the view expressed.

3.2.b *Preservation of the Irish Ethos*: In a time when there has been much written and said in favour of European integration and a diminution of local national sovereignty, it was instructive to measure the extent of the people's wish to preserve Irish customs and ethos. Item no. 2 set out to measure level of resistance to European cultural assimilation, which had been promoted through common institutions and attempts at common education programmes. Almost three quarters of the sample agreed with the view that: "*In striving for international cooperation we must take care that no typically Irish customs are lost*", with only 13% disagreeing with the statement. This overwhelming support for the preservation of the national ethos can only be explained by some degree of concern that the Irish way of life is in danger of being absorbed into an international super-culture. This also reflects a high esteem in the people for their uniquely Irish customs and a rejection of transnational cultural homogenisation.

The national respect expressed in the response to item no. 4 (claiming that Ireland is a better country then most others) verges on the ethnocentric. It could be interpreted as indicating a quasi-superiority complex, which may be a reaction to being so long kept under the thumb of their colonial master. It is analogous to the "black power" phase of racial liberation. Some would say that some exaggerated claims of superiority by a minority in the process of liberation is a counter reaction to previous submission to an inferior role *vis-a-vis* the dominant group (see Mac Gréil, 1977, pp. 122-3).

Almost two-thirds (63.1%) agreed with the view that: "*Generally speaking Ireland is a better country than most other countries*", while only a little over one-in-five (21.7%) disagreed with this claim to the superiority of Ireland as a country. One would have anticipated a much higher percentage in the "don't know" column in reply to such a statement!

The third item dealing with ethnic self-respect is item no. 5 which states that: "*We, the Irish people, have reason to be proud of our history*". Politicians and other public commentators frequently criticise the Irish for being too conscious of their sad history which predominantly records a struggle for independence alternated by a succession of occupations by a foreign power and plantations. It should be noted that Ireland's major minority groups are historical because of the continuous emigration out of Ireland and very little immigration into Ireland since the 17th century. It is inevitable, therefore, that history is a very important dimension to the understanding of the intergroup relations problem in this country. Intergroup relations conflict in Britain, in the United States and in societies with recent inward migration, do not have to deal with the problems associated with a long history of relations between minorities and dominant groups.

As already stated, the historical dimension is central to the intergroup question in Ireland. The reply to item no. 5 shows three quarters of the sample are proud of Ireland's history and only one tenth would disagree. This finding is important for those engaged in working out a solution which, hopefully, will be one of "integrated pluralism" and will make the basis of the next chapter in the "history of Ireland".

3.2.c *Irish Work Ethic:* Item no. 3 raises the question of the Irish people being willing to take responsibility and commit themselves to work for the country. While the majority (53.1%) agreed with the statement that: "*Irish people are always willing to put their shoulder to the wheel*", a substantial minority (29.2%) disagreed. This latter group may be pointing to an aspect of alienation or anomie which makes people reluctant to shoulder the burden of working hard for the community. This would be consistent with the desire to let others do it and with a sense of indifference. Of course, some of the negative effects of a dependency culture, due to prolonged unemployment for example, would be a degree of apathy towards work and towards responsibility for the provision of goods and services necessary for the life of the community.

3.3 "Patriotism" by Personal Variables

Table 16 gives the subsample variations within each of nine personal variables. The maximum range of "patriotic-score" is 0-200. Score ranges under 10 could be judged not significant since it represents a difference of 5% or less of the total range or 7% of the mean score. This would mean that "gender" has not varied significantly and "marital status", "place of residence" and "place of rearing" have shown significant but small score variations.

The level of "patriotic esteem" was highest among the older age category (at 25 points above the sample average). In terms of "education" there was a negative correlation between standard achieved and "patriotic score" recorded. A similarly negative correlation was recorded for "occupational status". The combination of "education" and "occupational status" in social class differences resulted in a very marked range of 44 or 24% of the mean score (140) between Class I ("Upper Class") and Class V ("Lower Class") respondents. Does this mean that those who are relatively successful acquire a greater emotional distance form the Irish ethos?

"Fianna Fáil" and "Fine Gael" supporters were above the sample average in their patriotic scores, while the Labour Party and Progressive Democrats were below the sample mean. Of the four parties Fianna Fáil supporters scored highest while Progressive Democrats scored least.

TABLE No. 16
PATRIOTIC SCALE SCORES BY PERSONAL VARIABLES (0-200)

VARIABLE	Part. Score	VARIABLE	Part. Score
A. Age		F. Education	
1. 35 years or less	132	1. Primary Only	156
2. 36 to 50 years	131*	2. Incomplete School	143
3. 51 to 65 years	150	3. Complete Second	126
4. 66 years plus	165	4. Third Level	123*
Range	34	Range	33
B. Gender		G. Occupational Status	
	N/S	1. Professional/Executive	123*
		2. Inspector/Supervisor	139
		3. Skilled/Routine Non-Man	140
		4. Semi/Unskilled	151
		Range	28
C. Martial Status		H. Social Class Position	
1. Never Married	137*	1. Class I	106*
2. Married	140	2. Class II	123
3. Widowed	154	3. Class III	138
		4. Class IV	142
		5. Class V	150
Range	17	Range	44
D. County of Residence		I. Political Party Preferences	
1. Dublin	138	1. Fianna Fáil	147
2. Rest of Leinster	132*	2. Fine Gael	141
3. Munster	147	3. Labour Party	132
4. Connaught/Ulster	142	4. Progressive Democrats	125*
Range	15	Range	22
E. Place of Rearing			
1. Large City	132*		
2. Small City	133		
3. Town	134		
4. Rural	147		
Range	15		

* Asterisk refers to the lowest per score.

As stated above this is the first time that this scale was used and further
refinement will be necessary to work out precisely what it is telling us. The

following is the *Pearson product moment correlation coefficient matrix of the five items.*

TABLE No. 17
PEARSON PRODUCT-MOMENT CORRELATION COEFFICIENT MATRIX
OF PATRIOTIC SCALE

	1	2	3	4	5
1. Irish loved everywhere	1.00	.11	.36	.15	.16
2. Preservation of Irish Customs		1.00	.22	.10	.13
3. Irish people willing to shoulder the wheel			1.00	.19	.26
4. Ireland is a better country than most				1.00	.19
5. Irish have reason to be proud of its history					1.00

Note: Significant correlations underlined

It is interesting to note that item no. 3 is the only one positively correlated to all other items. Items nos. 1 and 2 are only correlated to no. 3, while nos. 4 and 5 are correlated to each other and to no. 3. This points to the multi-dimensionality of the scale. Overall the level of correlation is not exceptionally high.

PART II: ATTITUDES TOWARDS THE RESTORATION OF THE IRISH LANGUAGE

Four measures were used to gauge the attitudes of the people toward the national language. In the first place, a special scale used in 1972-73 was repeated in the 1988-89 survey. Secondly, the respondents were asked to give their views on the potential of *"a return to the Irish language and culture as a good basis for Irish unity in the long-term."* This view was also measured in the 1972-73 Dublin survey. Thirdly, respondents were asked to indicate how their "feelings towards Irish" had changed since the time they left school. Fourthly, the levels of competence in and use of Irish were measured. Findings in relation to these four questions give a valuable indication of the present general public status of Irish in the Republic at the end of the 1980s.

1. OVERALL ATTITUDES

The respondents were asked to select one of six possible choices in regard to the future of the Irish language in the Republic. The options ranged from abandonment of Irish to it replacing English. Table 18 gives the response for three samples, i.e., the total sample of 1988-89; the Dublin sub-sample of 1988-89 and the total Dublin sample of 1972-73.

TABLE No. 18

ATTITUDES TOWARDS THE RESTORATION OF IRISH 1988/89 AND 1972/73

"With regard to the future of the Irish Language, which of the following would you like to see happen?"				
OPTIONS CHOSEN	1988/89 National Sample	1988/89 Dublin Sub-Sample	1972/73 Dublin Sample	Percentages Change
1. "The Irish language should be discarded and forgotten'	6%	4%	15%	-11%
2. "It should be preserved for its cultural value as in music and arts".	43%	52%		
3. "Spoken Irish should be preserved only in the Gaeltacht".	9%	9%	} 61% 34%	+17%
4. "Ireland should be bilingual with English as the principal language	34%	31%	33%	-2%
5. "Ireland should bilingual with Irish as the principal language".	5%	3%	10%	-7%
6. "Irish should be the principal language of use (like English is now)".	4%	3%	8%	-5%
	N=1,000	N=274	N=2,282	

Note: Deviations from total of 100% due to rounding.

The 1988-89 findings for the National sample show that 94% of the respondents are positively disposed towards Irish and wish to have it revived or preserved. Some 52% wished to see it preserved for its cultural value as in music or art or as the spoken language in the Gaeltacht. Some 43% would like to see it in daily use again – mainly as the second language of a bilingual society.

These findings point to the practically universal attachment to Irish among the population. The change in attitudes since 1972-73 shows a very significant drop (from 15% to 4%) in the percentage wishing to "discard and forget" Irish. Despite this widespread attachment to the language, there has been a lowering of idealism over the sixteen years in relation to the extent to which the people wish to restore the language to daily use. This may be due to any of a number of developments, such as the lowering of the status of Irish in the public services, the lack of Irish on more widespread media and so forth.

Only four personal variables, i.e., "education", "county of residence", "occupational status" and "political party preference" have shown significant variations in regard to respondents' choices. The higher the respondents' education and occupation, the more positive were their attitudes and expectations in relation to the Irish language. Respondents from Connaught/Ulster had the highest expectations in relation to the future of Irish, while Dublin respondents were those with the lowest expectations. In the case of "occupational status", those with higher status jobs were more favourably disposed. The improvement in the standing of Irish among the more highly statused in society indicates that Irish is becoming "fashionable".

TABLE No. 19
ATTITUDES TOWARDS THE FUTURE OF THE IRISH LANGUAGE BY
PERSONAL VARIABLES

PERSONAL VARIABLE	Irish and forgotten Value/Gaeltacht	Irish preserved for cultural language	Ireland bilingual English principal language	Irish to replace English/principal	N.
A. Education (P≤.001)					
1. Primary Only	10%	50%	30%	9%	276
2. Incomplete Second	6%	54%	31%	10%	348
3. Complete Second	3%	51%	37%	10%	230
4. Third Level	2%	51%	44%	3%	140
B. County of Residence (P≤.05)					
1. Dublin	4%	60%	31%	5%	264
2. Rest of Leinster	9%	52%	31%	8%	230
3. Munster	5%	50%	37%	9%	284
4. Connaught/Ulster	5%	42%	39%	14%	162
C. Occupational Status (≤.001)					
1. Professional/Executive	3%	49%	43%	5%	157
2. Inspector/Supervisor	4%	52%	38%	6%	299
3. Skilled/Routine Non-Manual	6%	51%	29%	13%	277
4. Unskilled/Semi-Skilled	10%	51%	31%	8%	154
D. Political Party Preference (P≤.001)					
1. Fianna Fáil	4%	52%	35%	9%	447
2. Fine Gael	9%	56%	30%	5%	250
3. Labour Party	8%	46%	35%	11%	65
4. Progressive Democrats	0%	56%	37%	7%	41
TOTAL SAMPLE	6%	52%	34%	9%	1005

Fianna Fáil supporters are not significantly different from the national average. Fine Gael and Labour supporters are significantly higher than the average in the case of those who would discard the language and Fine Gael is lower in relation to revival options. Progressive Democrat supporters had nobody wishing to discard Irish.

2. CHANGE OF ATTITUDE TO IRISH SINCE AT SCHOOL

Respondents were asked if their attitudes towards Irish had changed since they were at school. Table 20 gives a breakdown of the direction of change of feeling towards Irish for the sample. The respondents were asked: "Which of the following best describe the way you feel now?"

TABLE No. 20
"FEELINGS" TOWARDS IRISH WHEN IN SCHOOL AND NOW?

"Feeling"	When in School	Now	Percentage change since leaving school
1. Strongly in Favour	18%	19%	1%
	} 44%	} 57%	} +13%
2. Somewhat in Favour	26%	38%	+12%
3. No particular feelings	33%	29%	-4%
4. Somewhat opposed	13%	9%	-4%
	} 23%	} 15%	} -8%
5. Strongly opposed	10%	6%	-4%
	N = 973	N=973	

NOTE: Deviations from total of 100% due to rounding

It is clear from the above table that respondents' feelings towards Irish have significantly changed in the intervening years since leaving school. The percentage in favour has gone from 44% to 57%, while those opposed to Irish have dropped from 23% to 15%. This is a net change of 21% in favour of the language, i.e., the margin between those in favour and those opposed has changed from 21% "when in school" to 42% "now".

Table 21 gives the principal reasons given by those who had changed their feeling since being at school.

TABLE No. 21
REASONS FOR CHANGE IN FEELINGS TOWARDS IRISH
SINCE LEAVING SCHOOL

REASON	PERCENT	
A. Positive Changes (83%)		
1. Greater Cultural Appreciation	22%	
2. Reaching Personal Maturity	14%	
3. Removal of Compulsory Irish	12%	83%
4. Irish a National Symbol	10%	
5. Other Positive Reasons	25%	
B. Negative Changes (18%)		
1. Of Little Use/Waste of Time	11%	
2. Other Negative Reasons	7%	18%
	N=251	101%

3. IRISH AS A GOOD BASIS FOR IRISH UNITY

Respondents were asked if they agreed or disagreed with the view that: "*A return to the Irish language and culture could provide a good basis for Irish unity in the long term, even though it might provide difficulties in the short term*". This question formed part of a list of eleven questions relating to Northern Ireland. The purpose of the question was to measure the perceived importance of the language as a basis of ethnic unity or identity. The same question was included in the 1972-73 survey. Table 22 gives a breakdown of replies of the total sample and of the 1972-73 Dublin sample.

TABLE No. 22
"A RETURN TO THE IRISH LANGUAGE AND CULTURE COULD PROVIDE A GOOD BASIS FOR IRISH UNITY IN THE LONG TERM"

RESPONSE	National Sample (1988-89)	Dublin Sub-Sample (1988-89)	Dublin Sample (1972-73)	Change in Dublin Responses
1. Agree	24%	20%	18%	+2%
2. Don't Know	19%	22%	4%	+18%
3. Disagree	57%	58%	79%	-21%
	N=1,000	N=274	N=2,279	

Support for the view expressed in the statement is clearly a minority opinion. Almost one quarter of the national sample agreed that the Irish language would provide a good basis for Irish unity while more than half of the sample disagreed. The shift of opinion since 1972-73, however, has been a significant reduction of 21% in the proportion disagreeing with the view expressed in the statement. This may indicate the beginning of a growth in the perceived importance of the language as a common unifying symbol of national identity.

4.1 Self-Perceived Competence in Irish:

The findings of Table 23 indicate the level of self-perceived competence in the sample in 1988-89. If the changes in the case of the Dublin sub-sample when compared with the 1972-73 survey are a representation of the national population, the level of overall competence seems to be increasing significantly at the "middling" and "not so fluent" levels. The decline in the percentage stating they had "no Irish" or had "only a little" is also significant. The low scores in the case of "fluent" and "very fluent" probably reflect the limited opportunities for speaking the language after school. Nevertheless, some 41% of the national sample can now speak more than the "*cúpla focal*" (i.e. more than "a few words") when compared with 1972-73.

TABLE No. 23
SELF PERCEIVED COMPETENCE IN IRISH

"What would you say your competence is in the Irish Language?"					
Level of Competence	National Sample (1988-89) Sample		Dublin Sub-Sample (1988-89)	Dublin Sample (1972-73)	Change
	Actual	Cumulative			
1 Very Fluent	3%	(3%)	3% } 11% } 7%		+4%
2. Fluent	5%	(8%)	8%		
3. Middling	19%	(27%)	22% } 39% } 18%		+21%
4. Not So Fluent	14%	(41%)	16%		
5. Only a Little	40%		32%	50%	-18%
6. None	19%		20%	25%	-5%
TOTAL	N=920	N=274	N=274	N=2,282	

When levels of competence were measured by personal variables, the most significant results were found in the case of age, education and place of residence. Table 24 gives the breakdown.

TABLE No. 24
SELF-PERCEIVED COMPETENCE IN IRISH BY AGE, EDUCATION AND
PLACE OF REARING

PERSONAL VARIABLE	LEVEL OF COMPETENCE				
	Very Fluent/ Fluent 1	Middling/ Not So Fluent 2	(Cumulative) (1+2)	Only a Little 3	None 4
A. Age (P≤.001)					
1. Under 21 years	11%	45%	(56%)	34%	9%
2. 21-35 years	6%	43%	(48%	42%	10%
3. 36-50 years	11%	30%	(41%)	40%	18%
4. 50 years and older	7%	23%	(30%)	40%	30%
B. Education (P≤.001)					
1. Primary Only	4%	15%	(19%)	43%	37%
2. Incomplete Second Level	3%	28%	(31%)	52%	17%
3. Complete Second Level	9%	48%	(57%)	35%	8%
4. Third Level	26%	53%	(79%)	15%	5%
C. Place of Rearing (P≤.001)					
1. Large City	12%	39%	(51%)	31%	18%
2. Small City	5%	33%	(38%)	51%	11%
3. Town	6%	35%	(41%)	37%	22%
4. Rural	7%	29%	(36%)	45%	19%
TOTAL SAMPLE	8%	33%	(41%)	40%	18%

The negative correlation between age and competence in Irish is clear from the findings of Table 24. Only those over 50 years of age score below the national average. The positive link between education and competence is also very clearly borne out by the findings. Probably the "place of rearing" variable is the most interesting in that it would seem to indicate that the level of competence among "large city" reared is considerably higher than that among "rural" and "small city" reared. The "town" reared are in between. These findings should challenge the popular image that Irish is a rural, rustic phenomenon.

4.2 Declared Use of Irish:

Respondents were asked: "*How frequently would you say you use Irish, i.e., read, listen to or speak?*" Their replies are given in Table 25.

TABLE No. 25
DECLARED FREQUENCY OF USE OF IRISH

DECLARED FREQUENCY	TOTAL NATIONAL SAMPLE 1988-89		DUBLIN SUB-SAMPLE 1988-89		DUBLIN SURVEY 1972-73		CHANCE PERCENT
	Actual	Cum.	Actual	Cum.	Actual	Cum.	
1. Daily	7.2%	(7.2%)	4.5%	(4.5%0	7.0%	(7.0%)	–2.5%
2. Weekly	2.9%	(10.1%)	1.1%	(5.6%)	9.1%	(16.1%)	–8.0%
3. Occasionally	17.7%	(27.8%)	19.5%	(25.5%)	8.6%	(24.7%)	+10.9%
4. Rarely	22.5%		22.6%		23.4%		–0.8%
5. Never	49.7%		52.3%		52.0%		+0.3%
	N-975		N=274		N=2,282		

It is quite clear that the level of use of Irish is much lower than the level of perceived competence. With 41% able to converse in the language (at different degrees of ability) it is surprising to find the number who use Irish "weekly or more often" at 10.1% and "on occasion or more often" at 27.8%. The absence of opportunities to use Irish must result in a high proportion of people losing their ability to speak it with ease. The change in the "weekly or more frequent" use of Irish in Dublin is very significant, i.e., dropping from 16.1% to 6%. The "occasionally" percentage increased by 11% which balanced the decline at the more frequent usage. Nevertheless, the overall level of use of Irish in Dublin has decreased since 1972-73 despite the significant increase in competence.

The findings of Table 26 present the profile of the use of Irish. The pattern of use by age is not that varied and would indicate that the younger categories are not using the language proportionate to their competence. Females' use of Irish is significantly more frequent than that of males.

"County of residence" clearly shows the influence of the two Gaeltacht areas in Connaught/Ulster. In the case of this sub-sample the use of Irish is very much more frequent than it is in other territorial categories.

"Education" and "occupational status" indicate very clearly that Irish is more widely used by third level graduates and those at the top of the occupational scale. Practically half of the respondents from these two sub-samples use Irish occasionally or more often, while almost a quarter of them use it weekly or more frequently. This fact could well add to the "social status" of Irish in modern Ireland. Put another way, speaking Irish could become a sign of higher social status. Because of the close correlation between education and occupational status, the increase in participation in third level could result in the greater use of the Irish language in the future.

TABLE No. 26

DECLARED FREQUENCY OF USE OF IRISH BY PERSONAL VARIABLES

Personal Variables	DECLARED FREQUENCY OF USE					
	Weekly or Often	Occasionally		Rarely	Never	Number
		Actual	(Cum.)			
A. Age (P≤.05)						
1. 18-20 years	6%	27%	(33%)	13%	54%	54
2. 21.25 years	11%	17%	(28%)	30%	42%	329
3. 36-50 years	11%	20%	(31%)	19%	51%	266
4. 51 years plus	10%	15%	(25%)	20%	56%	326
B. Gender (P≤.01)						
1. Male	9%	14%	(23%)	23%	55%	447
2. Female	11%	21%	(32%)	23%	45%	528
C. County of Residence (P≤.05)						
1. Dublin	6%	20%	(26%)	23%	52%	266
2. Rest of Leinster	10%	16%	(26%)	21%	53%	250
3. Munster	10%	18%	(28%)	24%	49%	250
4. Connaught/Ulster	19%	18%	(37%)	22%	42%	166
D. Education (P≤.05)						
1. Primary only	9%	10%	(19%)	15%	66%	273
2. Incomplete Second Level	7%	15%	(22%)	24%	54%	238
3. Complete Second Level	9%	24%	(23%)	27%	39%	266
4. Third Level	22%	30%	(52%)	24%	24%	136
E. Occupational Status (P≤.001)						
1. Professional/Executive	23%	25%	(48%)	21%	31%	152
2. Inspector/Supervisor	9%	20%	(29%)	25%	46%	292
3. Skilled/Routine Non-Manual	7%	14%	(22%)	23%	57%	271
4. Unskilled/Semi Skilled	8%	12%	(20%	16%	64%	154
TOTAL SAMPLE	11%	17%	(28%)	22%	50%	975

Prejudice in Ireland Revisited

5. PLACE WHERE IRISH IS USED

Respondents were asked where they used the Irish language. Table 27 gives a breakdown of responses to seven pre-coded occasions. These are presented in rank-order of "yes" responses.

TABLE No. 27
WHERE OR WHEN IRISH IS USED BY RESPONDENTS
(Excluding those who never use the language)

*Where/When Irish is Used	Percent Using Irish	Where/When Irish Used.	Percent Using Irish
1. Listening to Programmes (TV/Radio)	50%	5. Reading	14%
2. At Home	45%	6. All possible occasions	13%
3. When meeting Irish-speaking friends	39%	7. Communicating with Officials	11%
4. At work	18%	8. Other	11%

Note* Respondents have answered Yes to more than one category (N-495)

The use of Irish takes place in predominantly domestic environments. The fact that 50% of respondents use their knowledge of Irish when listening or viewing radio and television underlies the media's potential in the extension of language usage. The relatively low usage at work is noteworthy. The importance of meeting other Irish speakers is confirmed by the high percentage (39%) who use Irish on such occasions and, also, indicates that a significant number of respondents have Irish-speaking friends.

6. SUMMARY AND CONCLUSIONS

The overall findings indicate a highly favourable disposition towards the language as indicated by the 94% who would wish to see it preserved or revived and by the very good standing of "Irish Speakers" as a social category. The desired future of Irish for 52% of the sample would be its preservation as part of our cultural heritage and as a spoken language in the Gaeltacht. Some 43% wished that it be revived in the daily life of the people. This is a reversal of the priorities desired by the Dublin people in a similar survey in 1972/73 when 51% opted for revival and 34% preferred preservation. The cause of this change in priority may be due to a lowering of the ideal of the revival of Irish for the whole population. Nevertheless, the present scores are quite optimistic and could well form a basis for further revival of Irish.

The significant advance in self-perceived competence in the language is noteworthy. The factors which may have contributed to this are not identified. Possibly the introduction of the oral Irish examination in the Leaving

Certificate in the early 1960s and the more positive disposition towards the language have contributed. The most discouraging result has been the apparent relatively low use of Irish in the population. The gap between competence and use is surprising. If one is to judge from the changes in the Dublin sub-sample since 1972-73, there is the anomalous situation of an increase in competence and good will, on the one hand, and a decline in the self-declared usage of the language, on the other. From the point of view of promoting the Irish language in society it seems that the greatest emphasis should be on increasing the opportunities of popular usage. With 41% of the population capable of using Irish and 28% actually using "on occasion" or more frequently, there are obvious possibilities for improvement.

As in the case of other reports on socio-cultural aspects of Irish, the findings here are both optimistic and problematic for those interested in the preservation and revival of the language. The positive change in attitudes towards Irish since leaving school provides further reason for a growing momentum in support for the language. The most serious impediment to such progress, however, is the discrepancy in frequency of use of Irish. Both the State and the voluntary Irish language movements would need to put greater effort into popular revival strategies as well as supporting minority Irish sub-populations. The central role of radio and television as occasions of use of the language is again borne out in the report. The decision by the Government to establish an all-Irish TV Channel is opportune in the light of the above. Finally, the key importance of the education'system for the transmission of the language to young people has also been confirmed.

In conclusion, therefore, the results presented here show that the country could be poised to make a significant advance in relation to the Irish language. The attitudes are positive and the level of competence is sufficient for a major move forward.

PART III: ETHNIC INTERGROUP SOCIAL DISTANCE

In parts I and II of this chapter issues pertaining to Irish nationality and ethnic self-identity have been examined and analysed. They included three main areas, i.e., ethnic self-identity, national respect and patriotic esteem, and attitudes towards the Irish language. These three areas are deemed to give the reader a more nuanced insight into important aspects of the (subjective) ethnic profile of the Irish people. Further insights will be presented when the findings of respondents' political aspirations are presented and examined in Chapters VIII and IX below (see pp. 224-290). It is also contended that Irish nationality, as in the case of most nationalities, is intrinsically related to the broader political and religious culture of the people as it evolves through the experience of history into the world of today.

TABLE No. 28

ETHNIC CATEGORIES' SOCIAL DISTANCE RESULTS

Rank Order	CATEGORY	Kinship	Friendship or Closer	Next-door Neighbour or Closer	Co-Worker or Closer	Citizen or Closer	Visitor Only	Debar or Deport	Mean Social Distance M.S.D.	Number	R/O
		1.	2.	3.	4.	5.	6.	7.	(1-7)		
1	English	77.9	88.5	93.7	96.2	97.3	2.1	0.7	1.475	1,003	1
2	White Americans	78.6	87.2	91.8	84.5	96.6	3.2	0.2	1.514	1,002	2
3	British*	76.7	87.5	92.5	95.6	96.6	2.8	0.7	1.521	1,004	3
4.	Canadians	75.8	85.0	91.1	94.3	96.0	4.0	0.1	1.582	1,003	4
5.	Scottish	74.2	85.8	91.1	93.9	96.3	3.7	0.1	1.592	1,002	5
6.	Northern Irish	70.9	83.7	90.7	93.9	97.4	2.2	0.4	1.637	1,001	6
7.	Welsh	72.8	82.8	90.6	94.0	96.2	3.4	0.4	1.641	999	7
8.	French*	66.2	77.2	85.5	90.4	91.8	7.0	0.3	1.883	1,004	8
9.	Dutch*	63.9	76.3	84.3	89.7	92.2	7.2	0.7	1.946	1,002	9
10.	Luxembourgians*	64.9	76.5	83.2	88.0	92.0	7.8	0.3	1.960	1,002	10
11.	Germans*	62.0	75.4	83.7	88.9	91.4	8.2	0.5	1.994	1,002	11
12.	Danes*	61.4	72.5	80.8	86.5	90.4	9.0	0.6	2.088	1,003	12
13.	Belgians*	60.2	70.9	80.0	86.3	91.2	8.0	0.8	2.122	1,000	13
14.	Spaniards*	58.3	69.5	76.4	83.4	87.9	11.1	0.9	2.252	998	14
15.	Poles	54.6	67.7	76.0	83.1	87.8	11.7	0.6	2.315	1,003	15
16.	Italians*	55.1	66.5	75.0	82.9	87.3	11.9	0.8	2.339	1,001	16
17.	Portugese*	51.8	66.6	75.0	82.1	86.7	12.6	0.7	2.385	994	17
18.	Greeks*	44.6	59.8	70.2	79.8	84.2	14.5	1.5	2.634	1,003	18
19.	Russians	40.9	55.8	65.7	74.8.	78.9	17.2	4.0	2.882	1,001	19
20.	Israelis	32.4	49.2	60.6	72.4	77.5	19.1	3.5	3.117	1,001	20
21.	Arabs	20.1	39.1	53.5	68.4	73.4	21.5	5.2	3.509	1,001	21

* European Community Member States at the time of the Survey.

1. OVERALL ETHNIC SOCIAL DISTANCE

In this part (Part III) the main emphasis will be more specifically centred on Irish intergroup attitudes to a selection of twenty-one ethnic and nationality categories through an analysis of social distance scores. These categories' Pearson correlations (p. 120) between their individual responses will be appraised for special significance. The analysis of social distance scores by personal variables will determine the extent to which "age", "gender", "marital status", "county of origin", "area of rearing", "education", "occupational status", "social class position" and "political party preference", affect the degree of intimacy to which members of each of the twenty-one ethnic categories are held by respondents.

As already pointed out it is possible to sub-divide the twenty-one ethnic categories into three broader nationality groupings:

(i)   Irish-British-(North) American Categories (Nos. 1 to 7);
(ii) Continental European Categories (Nos. 8 to 19); and
(iii) Middle Eastern Ethnic Categories (Nos. 20 and 21).

These twenty-one ethnic categories cover a very wide range of mean social distance (M.S.D.) scores from 1,475 to 3,509, i.e., a range of 2.025. Table 28 gives a detailed breakdown of the social distance responses to each of the twenty-one ethnic categories.

2. KINSHIP AND DENIAL-OF-CITIZENSHIP RESPONSES

While Table 28 gives the detailed responses at each of the seven levels of social closeness of the Bogardus Social Distance Scale, Table 29 abstracts three key social distance scores which highlight the responses in a summary form.

TABLE No. 29
ADMISSION-TO-KINSHIP AND DENIAL-OF-CITIZENSHIP ETHNIC SCALE

CATEGORY	Admit To Kinship %	Denial of Citizenship %	Mean Social Distance (1-7)	CATEGORY	Admit To Kinship %	Denial Of Citizenship %	Mean Social Distance (1-7)
1.English	77.9	2.8	1.475	12.Danes	61.4	9.6	2.088
2.White Americans	78.6	3.4	1.514	13.Belgians	60.2	8.8	2.122
3.British	76.7	3.5	1.521	14.Spaniards	58.3	12.0	2.252
4.Canadians	75.8	4.1	1.582	15.Poles	54.6	12.3	2.315
5.Scottish	74.2	3.8	1.592	16.Italians	55.1	12.7	2.339
6.Northern Irish	70.9	2.6	1.637	17.Portuguese	51.8	13.3	2.385
7.Welsh	72.8	3.8	1.641	18.Greeks	44.6	16.0	2.634
8.French	66.2	7.3	1.883	19.Russians	40.9	21.2	2.882
9.Dutch	63.9	7.9	1.946	20.Israelis	32.4	22.6	3.117
10. Luxembourgians	64.9	8.1	1.960	21.Arabs	20.1	26.7	3.509
11. Germans	62.0	8.7	1.994				

The advantage of the above summary table (29) is that it gives at a glance the standing of members of the various ethnic categories in the disposition of the sample.

2.1 Irish-British-North American Categories:

This kinship plus non-citizenship scale gives a very clear picture at a glance of the range of ethnic preferences and prejudices of the total sample of respondents and through them of the adult population of the Republic of Ireland in 1988-89. The first seven categories tell an interesting story. The respondents place the Northern Irish sixth in the rank-order of ethnic preferences. As pointed out a number of times, this placing of "Northern Irish" is not in accord with the "*principle of propinquity*", i.e., place in order of first preference categories closest to us in terms of space, racial appearance, religious belief, ethnic origins, and so forth. The explanation of this anomaly will be addressed below (see Chapter VIII, pp. 224ff).

The inclusion of "White Americans" and "Canadians" in with the British categories, confirms the continuity of their high place in terms of "propinquity". In other words, we see "White Americans" and "Canadians" as part of the "*White Anglo-Irish-Saxon*" ethnic neighbours.

2.2 Continental Europeans:

When we come to categories ranking 8th to 19th we are seeing respondents' range of preferences in relation to Continental European countries. The percentages "admitting to kinship" drop into the sixties for what might be classified as "*North Europeans*", i.e., "French", "Dutch", "Luxembourgians", "Germans", "Danes" and "Belgians". Apart from the Belgians and Luxembourgians, the other three nationalities (Dutch, Germans and Danes) are predominantly Protestant in tradition. The "denial of citizenship" percentages also falls within a very narrow range from 7.3% to 9.6% and fails to reach 10%. Despite the relatively low denial of citizenship proportion of these five categories, it is, nevertheless twice the figure of the first seven categories which ranged from 2.6% to 4.1%. The fact that more than one third of the total sample are not willing to welcome the Northern (Continental) European nationalities into their families through marriage does not leave much room for complacency in regard to the ethnic intergroup attitudes of Irish people towards this preferred sub-category of E.U. members!

The situation deteriorates somewhat when it comes to our dispositions towards the remaining members of the E.U. (at the time of the survey) and towards the two non-E.U. nationalities of "Poles" and "Russians". With "admission-to-kinship" proportions ranging from 58.3% (for "Spaniards") to 40.9% (for "Russians") and "denial-of-citizenship" percentages going from 21.2% (for "Russians") to 12.0% (for "Spaniards"). These findings leave much to be desired if one hopes for an open tolerant society. There are elements behind these figures which must be examined. Is it a manifestation of a degree of "defensive ethnocentrism" because of perceived threat to Irish values, symbolic systems and way of life? If the Irish abroad met with such a high percentage who were not prepared to grant them citizenship we might be very concerned. It may be argued that these restrictive attitudes toward "citizenship" for "*Southern and Eastern Europeans*" may be due to the adoption of attitudes of certain anti-migrant groups in Britain and elsewhere in Europe, i.e., the National Front and their Continental colleagues. The widespread readership of "right-wing" tabloid press and the high viewing of "right-wing" popular foreign-based television channels in Ireland could also be instrumental in propagating these closed attitudes towards foreigners outside the preferred groups. Because Ireland (Republic) is overwhelmingly Roman Catholic, one would have expected a greater openness to "Spaniards", "Poles", "Italians" and "Portuguese" on the grounds of religious propinquity alone. The negative position of attitudes towards "Greeks" and "Russians" is not easy to explain at a time of greater openness in Russia and the popularity of Greece as a holiday resort. A similar survey of social distance in other countries would probably give similar if not more negative results.

2.3 Middle Eastern Categories:

The attitudes toward "Israelis" and "Arabs" are very negative and contain a high degree of ethnic and religious intolerance. Around one quarter of the total sample would deny members of these categories Irish citizenship. Like most prejudices this is a highly irrational state of affairs and is probably reflective of a more widespread Western attitude toward Semitic peoples of both Jewish and Moslem backgrounds. One may explain low percentages admitting to family on the grounds of religious and ethnic endogamy (without justifying such endogamy) but in the case of "denial of citizenship" we are dealing with a much more nasty attitude syndrome. One cannot explain it on the grounds of violent conflict alone either, because Irish people seem to be quite open to nationalities with quite a violent reputation over the course of the past two or three generations, e.g., United States in South East Asia, Germans in two World Wars, Spanish, British, French, Italian colonial wars, etc. Ethnocentrism is often quite (unfairly) selective in designating its negative categories.

3. ETHNIC CORRELATIONS

Table 30 is probably one of the most impressive findings of the validity and reliability of the Bogardus Social Distance Scale. A perusal of this table tells the reader much about the respondents' ethnic attitudes and preferences.

Prejudice in Ireland Revisited

TABLE No. 30

PEARSON CORRELATION MATRIX OF ETHNIC SOCIAL DISTANCE SCORES

	Eng. 1.	Brit. 2.	Scot. 3.	Nth. Ir. 4.	Wel. 5.	Am. Wh. 6.	Can. 7.	Frh. 8.	Dut. 9.	Lux. 10.	Germ. 11.	Dan. 12.	Belg. 13.	Span 14.	Pol. 15.	Ital. 16.	Port. 17.	Gks. 18.	Russ. 19.	Isr. 20.	Arab. 21.	R/O
1. English	1.00	**.80**	**.55**	.47	**.50**	**.50**	**.50**	.47	.45	.45	.48	.48	.40	.45	.44	.42	.42	.39	.36	.32	.27	1
2. British		1.00	.49	**.52**	.49	.43	**.60**	.43	.44	.42	.46	.46	**.60**	.42	.42	.40	.41	.37	.35	.33	.30	2
3. Scottish			1.00	**.53**	**.74**	**.56**	**.57**	**.63**	**.61**	**.62**	**.59**	**.60**	**.54**	**.62**	**.62**	**.58**	**.57**	.49	.44	.43	.36	3
4. Northern Irish				1.00	.48	.44	.46	.45	.46	.47	.48	**.50**	.42	.47	.49	.38	**.50**	.46	.44	.38	.36	4
5. Welsh					1.00	**.63**	**.61**	**.66**	**.64**	**.67**	**.63**	**.63**	**.58**	**.62**	**.62**	**.60**	**.61**	**.52**	.46	.46	.39	5
6. American Whites						1.00	**.55**	**.57**	**.55**	**.58**	**.56**	**.57**	**.50**	**.55**	**.53**	**.50**	**.52**	.45	.41	.41	.34	6
7. Canadians							1.00	**.65**	**.61**	**.60**	**.60**	**.61**	**.60**	**.57**	**.56**	**.54**	**.57**	**.50**	.46	.44	.39	7
8. French								1.00	**.80**	**.80**	**.80**	**.77**	**.71**	**.73**	**.70**	**.70**	**.69**	**.64**	**.57**	**.57**	.47	8
9. Dutch									1.00	**.78**	**.75**	**.85**	**.74**	**.76**	**.73**	**.70**	**.71**	**.65**	**.58**	**.58**	.47	9
10. Luxembourgians										1.00	**.77**	**.80**	**.68**	**.75**	**.72**	**.73**	**.73**	**.66**	**.58**	**.59**	.47	10
11. Germans											1.00	**.75**	**.68**	**.71**	**.70**	**.67**	**.69**	**.65**	**.59**	**.54**	.48	11
12. Danes												1.00	**.74**	**.75**	**.75**	**.73**	**.73**	**.69**	**.63**	**.61**	.49	12
13. Belgians													1.00	**.67**	**.68**	**.67**	**.66**	**.67**	**.58**	**.58**	**.52**	13
14. Spaniards														1.00	**.75**	**.77**	**.78**	**.71**	**.67**	**.65**	**.51**	14
15. Poles															1.00	**.73**	**.79**	**.68**	**.70**	**.66**	**.54**	15
16. Italians																1.00	**.74**	**.71**	**.66**	**.70**	**.55**	16
17. Portuguese																	1.00	**.75**	**.71**	**.68**	**.56**	17
18. Greeks																		1.00	**.70**	**.71**	**.63**	18
19. Russians																			1.00	**.72**	**.62**	19
20. Israelis																				1.00	**.69**	20
21. Arabs																					1.00	21

NOTE: Scores over 50 in **bold type.**

3.1 Irish and British Categories:

The first five categories have been among the least correlating categories in the table. "English" and "British" had an r = 0.80 correlation between them but relatively few rho scores of over 0.5 with other categories. The "Scottish" and the "Welsh" performed more like European ethnic groups than did the "British" and "English". "Scottish" and "Welsh" had rho scores of over 0.5 with all E.U. nationalities except the "British" and the "Greeks". "Northern Irish" correlated least of all with the other ethnic categories.

Of the five "Irish and British Ethnic Categories" only the "Scottish" and the "Welsh" perform as ethnic categories in that they correlate more positively with the other European categories. The "English", "British" and "Northern Irish" seem to be influenced by uniquely non-ethnic factors which are examined elsewhere (see pp. 224ff below).

3.2 Canadian and American Categories:

It has been already pointed out that "Black Americans" were dealt with under the rubric of "Racial-Ethnic" or "Ethnic-Racial" categories (Chapter VI, pp. 143ff). "White Americans" had rho scores of over 0.50 in relation to fifteen of the twenty other ethnic categories with whom they were measured. These included all European ethnic categories except "British", "Northern Irish" and "Russians". The responses to "Canadians" also correlated with fifteen of the other twenty ethnic categories on the scale at a rho score of 0.50 or higher.

3.3 The Continental European Ethnic Categories:

The rho scores between all of the ten continental E.U. categories' responses are 0.64 or over. Five (8%) of the forty five correlations are 0.80 or over. Some 56% of them are between 0.70 and 0.79. This consistently high correlation is but another piece of evidence of the validity of the Bogardus Social Distance Scale in that it accurately grouped these categories sharing a common bond with Ireland in the European Union. Responses to the "Poles" were very similar in their correlations with E.U. member nationalities which were consistently high at 0.70 plus. Responses to "Russians" were significantly correlated (+0.50) to all continental European nationalities and to each of the two mid-Eastern ethnic categories.

3.4 The Mid-Eastern Categories:

The two Mid-Eastern categories, i.e., "Israelis" and "Arabs" share a common prejudice (in terms of social distance to the extent of r = 0.69). "Israelis" correlated impressively with all continental European nationalities and very weakly with "Irish-British-North American" categories (similar to that of the Russian responses to the same categories). The correlation between responses to "Arabs" and the last nine ethnic categories is over 0.50 and probably reflects the emergence of the stronger factor or the impact of the higher mean-social distance scores.

4. ETHNIC MEAN SOCIAL DISTANCE BY PERSONAL VARIABLES:

In most instances the trends follow the normal pattern of variation.[2] It should be noted that there is a connection between the variables that reinforce trends, e.g., older respondents did not have the same educational opportunities, are over represented in the "widowed" subsample and in the lower occupational status category, while Connaught/Ulster and people in rural areas have a higher proportion of older people due to migration trends. The direct influence of personal variables can be seen in path analysis findings in Chapter XIV (pp. 459ff below).

4.1 Gender and Marital Status (Table 31):

In the case of "Marital Status" the social distance responses failed to vary significantly between the subsamples "Never Married", "Married" and "Widowed" in any of the twenty-one ethnic categories. "Gender" differences were not significant in sixteen of the twenty-one categories. In the case of the five categories recording statistically significant variations, i.e., "Italians", "Portuguese", "Russians", "Israelis" and "Arabs", females had higher M.S.D. scores than males. In other words, females were more ethnocentric than males in these cases, for whatever reason.

4.2 Age (Table 31):

"Age" shows a statistically significant variation in the case of two-thirds of the ethnic categories. In each of the fourteen categories with significant differences between the M.S.D. scores of the different age subsamples, there

2. *Normal Trends or Patterns in Prejudice Scores or Percentages*:

Variable	High Tolerance/Low Prejudice	High Prejudice/Low Tolerance
A. Age	Young Subsample	Old Subsample
B. Gender	Mixed	Mixed
C. Marital Status	Never Married	Widowed
D. County of Residence	Dublin	Connaught/Ulster
E. Place of Rearing	Large City	Rural
F. Education	Third Level	Primary Only
G. Occupational Status	Professional/Executive	Semi/Unskilled
H. Social Class Position	Class I	Class V

is a more-or-less positive correlation between social distance and age, the senior middle aged (51 to 65 years) group was the most prejudiced against "French", "Dutch", "Spaniards", "Poles" and "Russians". The range of M.S.D. variation in the case of the "age" variables was on average much less than it was in the case of "education".

4.3 Residence and Rearing (Table 31):

The pattern of responses by "area of rearing" is uniform in all but three cases, i.e., "English", where the "town" subsample were most prejudiced; "White Americans", and "Spaniards", where "large city" respondents were least prejudiced. In twenty of the twenty-one categories (all except "English") "rural reared" respondents were significantly more ethnocentric than any other subsample. The least prejudiced subsample in nineteen of the twenty-one cases those reared in "small cities" (10,000 to 99,999 inhabitants). This is a very clear and convincing finding of the link between place of rearing and openness to people of foreign ethnic background or nationality.

Those reared in rural areas (which included towns of 1,500 or less) were unlikely to have had much contact with people from other countries. The fact that those reared in small cities were consistently more welcoming of members of other ethnic groups than were those from larger cities shows that the pattern of ethnocentrism is not negatively correlated with urbanisation (as might be expected). Does this reflect a fear of a degree of ethnic conflict in parts of Dublin or Cork, i.e., the two large cities in the Republic? It could also be related to a vicarious fear due to the racial and ethnic conflicts in cities of Great Britain and the United States. Thirdly, it might be a reaction of the "urban peasant" which is similar to that of the "rural peasant". Neither "peasant" concepts are seen to be pejorative. Rather, they refer to the community centred person whose circle of personal friendships are locally based and homogeneous.

"*County of Residence*" scores reflect the findings of "area of rearing", but more so. "Connaught/Ulster" respondents had the highest anti-ethnic scores for every category of the twenty to register a statistically significant variation. Munster respondents had the second highest scores in every case. With the exception of "Arabs", "Dublin" residents have been the most tolerant subsample in their social distance scores.

A striking feature of the residential variable has been its very wide range of variations (the highest of all the variables). The importance of the relatively high level of ethnocentrism in "Connaught/Ulster" and to a lesser extent in "Munster" needs attention because of the growing number of foreign nationals purchasing land in the North West, West and South West of Ireland. To what extent these findings are a reaction to this phenomenon is not possible to gauge.

TABLE 31
ETHNIC SOCIAL DISTANCE BY PERSONAL VARIABLES

Variable	Nth. Irish	English	British	Scottish	Welsh	White Americans	Can.	French	Dutch	Lux.	Germans	Danes	Belgians	Spaniards	Poles	Italians	Port.	Greeks	Russians	Israelis	Arabs
Total Sample	1.64	1.48	1.52	1.59	1.64	1.51	1.58	1.88	1.95	1.96	1.99	2.09	21.2	2.25	2.32	2.34	2.39	2.63	2.88	3.12	3.51
A. Age	N/S	N/S	N/S	N/S	N/S	P≤.05	N/S	P≤.001	P≤.001	P≤.001	N/S	P≤.007	P≤.008	P≤.002	P≤.007	P≤.004	P≤.001	P≤.001	P≤.001	P≤.001	P≤.001
1. 35 Years or less						1.44*		1.75*	1.76*	1.84*		1.93*	1.96*	2.03*	2.26	2.15*	2.20	2.39*	2.66*	2.79*	3.24*
2. 36 to 50 years						1.52		1.79	1.80	1.81*		1.97	1.99	2.12	2.16*	2.21	2.19*	2.44	2.67	2.92	3.32
3. 51 to 65 years						1.59		2.19	2.33	2.15		2.35	2.38	2.66	2.54	2.61	2.73	3.04	3.36	3.61	3.90
4. 66 years and over						1.61		2.03	2.23	2.32		2.40	2.47	2.56	2.49	2.72	2.82	3.14	3.27	3.70	4.13
RANGE						(0.17)		(0.57)	(0.57)	(0.15)		(0.47)	(0.51)	(0.63)	(0.38)	(0.57)	(0.62)	(0.75)	(0.70)	(0.91)	(0.89)
B. Gender	N/S	N/S	N/S	N/S	N/S	N/S	N/S	N/S	N/S	N/S	N/S	N/S	N/S	N/S	N/S	P≤.001	P≤.02	N/S	P≤.02	P≤.03	P≤.001
1. Females																2.50	2.53		3.07	3.27	3.69
2. Males																2.15*	2.21*		2.66*	2.96*	3.29*
(Range)																(0.35)	(0.32)		(0.41)	(0.31)	(.040)
D. County of Residence	P≤.02	P≤.001	P≤.006	P≤.001	P≤.001	P≤.002	P≤.001	P≤.001	P≤.001	P≤.001	P≤.001	P≤.001	P≤.001	P≤.001	P≤.001	P≤.001	P≤.001	P≤.001	P≤.001	P≤.001	P≤.001
1. Dublin	1.48*	1.50	1.44*	1.37*	1.30*	1.32*	1.35*	1.48*	1.48*	1.47*	1.56*	1.58*	1.70*	1.68*	1.76*	1.77*	1.82*	2.13*	2.21*	2.52*	3.140
2. Rest of Leinster	1.60	1.26*	1.47	1.50	1.50	1.46	1.50	1.68	1.74	1.70	1.86	1.86	1.78	1.91	2.09	2.02	2.08	2.24	2.53	2.84	3.05*
3. Munster	1.67	1.52	1.57	1.61	1.73	1.56	1.56	1.87	1.96	2.01	2.03	2.10	2.15	2.42	2.51	2.47	2.55	2.82	3.14	3.29	3.80
4. Connaught/Ulster	1.88	1.50	1.64	2.05	2.23	1.83	2.12	2.86	2.96	3.04	2.87	3.21	3.26	3.36	3.19	3.49	3.46	3.69	4.04	4.20	4.27
(Range)	(0.40)	(0.26)	(0.20)	(0.68)	(0.93)	(0.51)	(0.77)	(1.38)	(1.48)	(1.57)	(1.31)	(1.63)	(1.56)	(1.66)	(1.33)	(1.72)	(1.64)	(1.56)	(1.83)	(1.69)	(1.13)
E. Area of Rearing	P≤.03	P≤.001	P≤.008	P≤.001	P≤.001	P≤.001	P≤.001	≤.001	P≤.001	P≤.001	P≤.001	P≤.001	P≤.001	P≤.001	P≤.001	P≤.001	P≤.001	P≤.001	P≤.001	P≤.001	P≤.001
1. Large city	1.57	1.50	1.52	1.37	1.35	1.31*	1.41	1.55	1.54	1.54	1.70	1.65	1.69	1.70*	1.79	1.90	1.84	2.18	2.24	2.62*	3.25
2. Small city	1.31*	1.26*	1.29*	1.30*	1.30*	1.37	1.27*	1.44*	1.35*	1.45*	1.51*	1.59*	1.55*	1.72	1.64*	1.81*	1.77*	2.00*	2.07*	2.62*	2.97*
3. Town	1.53	1.52	1.52	1.59	1.49	1.41	1.45	1.71	1.73	1.88	1.81	1.89	1.84	2.01	2.14	2.02	2.13	2.27	2.44	2.90	3.37
4. Rural	1.75	1.50	1.58	1.77	1.91	1.68	1.78	2.20	2.35	2.31	2.31	2.48	2.56	2.72	2.78	2.77	2.87	3.11	3.16	3.54	4.38
(Range)	(0.44)	(0.26)	(0.29)	(0.47)	(0.61)	(0.37)	(0.51)	(0.76)	(1.00)	(0.86)	(0.80)	(.089)	(1.01)	(1.02)	(1.14)	(0.86)	(1.10)	(1.11)	(1.09)	(0.92)	(1.41)
F. Education	P≤.002	N/S	N/S	P≤.001	P≤.001	N/S	P≤.03	P≤.001	P≤.001	P≤.001	P≤.001	P≤.001	P≤.001	P≤.001	P≤.001	P≤.001	P≤.001	P≤.001	P≤.001	P≤.001	P≤.001
1. Primary Only	1.84			1.89	1.89		1.82	2.34	2.44	2.40	2.40	2.66	2.72	2.86	2.76	2.81	2.96	3.28	5.33	3.68	3.98
2. Incomplete Second	1.64			1.50	1.61		1.55	1.83	1.95	1.95	2.03	2.11	2.06	2.23	2.40	2.37	2.42	2.65	2.94	3.09	3.37
3. Complete Second	1.52			1.51	1.58		1.42	1.68	1.62	1.73	1.73	1.66	1.76	1.83	1.96	2.06	1.98	2.27	2.47	2.89	3.24
4. Third Level	1.40*			1.32*	1.31*		1.41*	1.43*	1.45*	1.47*	1.49*	1.56*	1.66*	1.73*	1.78*	1.76*	1.81*	1.86*	2.08*	2.42*	2.70*
(Range)	(0.44)			(0.59)	(0.58)		(0.41)	(0.91)	(0.99)	(0.93)	(0.91)	(1.10)	(1.06)	(1.13)	(0.98)	(1.05)	(1.15)	(1.42)	(1.47)	(1.26)	(1.28)

TABLE 31 (Continued)
ETHNIC SOCIAL DISTANCE BY PERSONAL VARIABLES

	Nth. Irish	English	British	Scottish	Welsh	White Americans	Can.	French	Dutch	Lux.	Germans	Danes	Belgians	Spaniards	Poles	Italians	Port.	Greeks	Russians	Israelis	Arabs
G. Occupational Status	P≤.03	N/S	N/S	N/S	P≤0.3	N/S	P≤.03	P≤.001	P≤.001	P≤.02	P≤.02	P≤.001	P≤.004	N/S	P≤.004	P≤.001	P≤.001	P≤.001	P≤.001	P≤.001	P≤.001
1. Prof/Executive	1.40*				1.33:		1.31*	1.51*	1.44*	1.51*	1.53*	1.53*	1.62*		1.72*	1.72*	1.79*	1.91*	2.04*	2.39*	2.70*
2. Insp./Super.	1.57				1.64		1.55	1.74	1.97	1.84	1.18	1.81	1.96		2.19	2.18	2.30	2.54	2.76	3.04	3.50
3. Skilled/R.N.M.	1.75				1.63		1.63	1.96	2.09	2.13	2.11	2.32	2.21		2.38	2.47	2.47	2.81	3.03	3.25	3.62
4. Semi/Unskilled	1.66				1.67		1.65	2.18	2.18	2.06	2.27	2.46	2.46		2.65	2.62	2.56	2.81	3.13	3.33	3.63
(Range)	(0.36)				(0.34)		(0.34)	(0.67)	(0.74)	(0.62)	(0.74)	(0.93)	(0.84)		(0.93)	(0.90)	(0.77)	(0.90)	(1.09)	(0.94)	(0.93)
H. Social Class Position	N/S	N/S	N/S	N/S	P≤.003	N/S	N/S	P≤.002	P≤.001	P≤.004	P≤.001	P≤.001	P≤.001	N/S	P≤.001	P≤.001	P≤.001	P≤.001	P≤.001	P≤.002	P≤.001
1. Class I					1.06*			1.12*	1.15*	1.15*	1.21*	1.12*	1.15*		1.29*	1.35*	1.21*	1.44*	1.44*	2.03*	2.26*
2. Class II					1.29			1.47	1.39	1.49	1.15	1.54	1.57		1.70	1.69	1.78	1.90	1.96	2.35	2.63
3. Class III					1.62			1.75	1.77	1.82	1.78	1.81	1.94		2.20	2.18	2.32	2.51	2.84	3.09	3.52
4. Class IV					1.62			1.89	2.02	2.06	2.04	2.20	2.18		2.33	2.38	2.38	2.73	2.90	3.10	3.58
5. Class V					1.72			2.25	2.26	2.16	2.36	2.53	2.51		2.66	2.70	2.68	2.92	3.21	3.43	3.68
(Range)					(0.68)			(1.13)	(1.11)	(1.01)	(1.15)	(1.41)	(1.36)		(1.37)	(1.35)	(1.47)	(1.48)	(1.77)	(1.40)	(1.42)
I. Political Party Preferences	N/S	N/S	N/S	N/S	P≤.003	N/S	N/S	P≤.002	P≤.001	P≤.004	P≤.001	P≤.001	P≤.001	N/S	P≤.001	P≤.001	P≤.005	P≤.004	N/S	N/S	N/S
1. Fianna Fail					1.65			1.93	2.03	1.99	2.06	2.16	2.21		2.40	2.39	2.52	2.79			
2. Fine Gael					1.97			2.07	2.07	2.15	2.09	2.31	2.34		2.69	2.59	2.62	2.80			
3. Labour Party					1.29*			1.50*	1.59	1.56	1.65	1.70	1.74		1.77*	1.71*	1.80*	1.83*			
4. Progressive Democrats					1.43			1.50*	1.43*	1.40*	1.64*	1.59*	1.45*		1.81	1.90	1.98	2.00			
(Range)					(0.36)			(0.57)	(0.64)	(0.75)	(0.45)	(0.72)	(0.89)		(0.63)	(0.88)	(0.82)	(0.97)			

* NOTE: Lowest Scores have Asterisks

4.4 Education and Ethnocentrism:

Only three categories failed to produce a statistically significant variation by educational subsamples, i.e., "English", "British" and "White Americans". All of the remaining eighteen ethnic categories recorded a very clear and totally consistent pattern of variance with a strong negative correlation between ethnocentrism and educational standard reached. The range of M.S.D. scores was very substantial (exceeding 40% of the total sample mean social distance score in most cases).

This result speaks well for the quality of Irish education (heretofore) in that it has produced a reduction in the level of ethnocentrism. The move away from liberal education in the humanities would need to be monitored in relation to its impact on the reduction of ethnic prejudice. One of the most alarming facts about human intelligence is the fact that it *is not correlated* with authoritarianism. In other words, the most intelligent person could be the least tolerant or most authoritarian in the group! In fact the people most in need of a broad liberal education in the humanities are the most intelligent, that is, if we wish to have a tolerant leadership in community and in society. Total specialisation in areas of science and technology without commensurate exposure to humanities and social criticism in the human sciences would not be in the overall interests of a tolerant and pluralist society.

The importance of education as a positive causal factor in the promotion of intergroup tolerance and the reduction of social prejudice is borne out very clearly in the performance of the "education" variable in Table 31. It is important to realise that education *per se* is not a guarantor of open tolerance. Without adequate exposure to the humanities and the critical human sciences it is conceivable that its influence could be neutral at best or negative at worst. The education curriculum is also open to the promotion of ethnocentrism, for example, imperialist propaganda to justify "offensive ethnocentrism" or the "demonisation" of the "enemies of the people". Education, which has become very much under the control of the State, can be a powerful agency for intolerance and prejudice, for example, the use of the education system to promote extremely nationalistic ideologies in the German Third Reich in the 1930s.

4.5 Occupational Status:

The social distance responses to five of the ethnic categories did not produce statistically significant variations, by "occupational status", i.e., "English", "British", "Scottish", "White American", and "Spaniards". In all other cases there was a negative correlation between "occupational status" and M.S.D. scores. The range of variations were substantial but not as wide as in the case of "Education".

Those with highest occupational status, i.e., "high professional and senior executives", were consistently the subsample with lowest M.S.D. scores across the board, while the biggest scores were recorded by "semi- and unskilled" respondents. There were two exceptions to the latter in the case of "Northern Irish" and "Luxembourgians" where the "skilled and routine non-manual" respondents scored highest.

It is a central thesis of this study that frustration and insecurity are causally linked to social prejudice which is a psychological form of aggression. Obviously, those in the lowest professions and occupations tend to be more insecure and are likely to experience more frustration. Therefore, the patterns of prejudice presented in the findings by occupational status are not surprising. A further explanation of the pattern is the fact that in this study a Pearson correlation of $r = 0.59$ was recorded between educational standard reached and occupational status.

4.6 Social Class Position:

The variations in the case of "social class position" reflect the combination of "education" and "occupational status". It is slightly more difficult to produce a statistically significant variation because of the fact of this variable having five subsamples rather than four as is the case of both "education" and "occupational status".

In all places where there is a statistically significant variation the pattern of variations is similar and consistent. The "Upper Class" (Class I) were least ethnocentric while the "Lower Class" (Class V) were most ethnocentric. The range of differences between the subsamples is very substantial (exceeding 50% of the mean social distance score of the total sample).

4.7 Ethnocentrism by Political Party Preference:

Ten of the ethnic categories, i.e., "Northern Irish", "English", "British", "Scottish", "White Americans", "Canadians", "Spaniards", "Russians", "Israelis" and "Arabs" recorded consensus across "political party preference" variables, i.e, the chi-square score was more than 0.5, which was the minimum required in this survey for establishing statistically significant variations between the subsample scores. The fact that there was consensus across political lines in so many cases is in itself a very significant.

Where political party preference did record significant variation Fine Gael supporters had highest M.S.D. scores, i.e., higher ethnic prejudice, while Labour Party and Progressive Democrats were least prejudiced. Fianna Fáil supporters were in between. The range of variations was much less than in the case of social-class-position.

5. CHANGES IN ETHNIC SOCIAL DISTANCE BETWEEN 1972-73 AND 1988-89

At the time of the 1972-73 survey Ireland was entering the European Economic Community (later designated the European Union). Therefore, the changes in the social distance scores of the Dublin sub-sample when compared with those of the 1972-73 survey (Table 32) could reflect two things, i.e., changes in overall ethnocentrism and the influence of the greater participation in the European Union on the attitudes of the people. Elsewhere below there will be evidence on certain opinions in relation to membership of the E.U. (see pp. 280ff below).

TABLE No. 32
COMPARATIVE TABLE OF ETHNIC SOCIAL DISTANCE: 1988-89* AND 1972-73

Category	Admit to Kinship %	Denial of Citizenship %	M.S.D. (1-7)	Category	Admit to Kinship %	Denial of Citizenship %	M.S.D. (1-7)
1. English				6. French**			
A. 88-89	77.9	2.8	1.475	A. 88-89	66.2	7.3	1.883
B. 72-73	87.3	2.5	1.285	B. 92-73	74.1	4.5	1.572
Difference	(-9.4)	(+0.3)	(+0.190)	Difference	(-7.9)	(+2.8)	(0.311)
2. British**				7. Germans**			
A. 88-89	76.7	3.5	1.521	A. 88-89	62.0	8.7	1.994
B. 72-73	82.4	3.2	1.413	B. 72-73	69.7	7.6	1.798
Difference	(-5.7)	(+0.3)	(+0.108)	Difference	(-7.7)	(+1 l)	(+0.196)
3. Scottish				8. Spaniards**			
A. 88-89	74.2	3.8	1.592	A. 88-89	58.3	12.0	2.252
B. 72-73	78.4	5.5	1.562	B. 72-73	66.5	8.2	1.862
Difference	(-4.2)	(-1.7)	(+0.030)	Difference	(-8.2	(+3.8)	(+0.390)
4. Northern Irish				9. Italians**			
A. 88-89	70.9	2.6	1.637	A. 88-89	55.1	12.7	2.339
B. 72-73	79.5	2.8	1.474	B. 72-73	62.2	9.0	1.973
Difference	(-8.6)	(-0.2)	(+0.163)	Difference	(-7.1)	(+3.7)	(+0.366)
5. Welsh				10. Russians			
A. 88-89	72.8	3.8	1.641	A. 88-89	40.9	21.2	2.882
B. 72-73	78.4	3.7	1.476	B. 72-73	50.8	17.2	2.509
Difference	(-5.6)	(+0.1)	(+0.165)	Difference	(-9 9)	(+4.0)	(+0.373)

* Dublin Subsample. ** E.U. Subsample

When asked if the sample agreed or disagreed with the view that: *"Ireland's position as a distinct and independent nation is threatened by our membership of the E.E.C.*", almost one third (31%) agreed, less than half disagreed (44%) and a quarter (25%) neither agreed nor disagreed. This 31%

coincides with the proportion of the population who voted against the Maastrict Treaty in the 1992 Referendum. While the plurality (44%) did not feel threatened by E.E.C. membership, the proportion that did was a very substantial minority of 31%.

In the case of each of the ten ethnic categories there has been a significant change in social distance scores over the sixteen intervening years between the two surveys. Mean social distance scores have increased while the percentages welcoming into kinship have correspondingly decreased. There is clear evidence of increased ethnocentrism between the early 1970s and the end of the 1980s. The five E.U. nationalities, i.e., the British, the French, the Germans, the Spaniards, and the Italians are not as close to the Dubliners as they were in the earlier survey. Does this mean that economic cooperation and greater international interaction does not lead to greater ethnic affinity? Does this mean that the increase in ethnocentrism is a reaction to the perceived threat to individual cultural ethos, in other words, a growing "defensive ethnocentrism"?

There has been little evidence in Ireland to date of political movements harnessing this change of attitude, as has been evidenced in France, in Germany and, to a lesser extent, in Britain. The sad case of ethnic conflict in the Balkans is a more extreme example of ethnocentrism leading to "ethnic cleansing" and "offensive" military action, as well as intensive "defensive" military reaction.

The extent of the change is difficult to classify. If one were to take as substantial a 10% decrease in the percentage willing to welcome members of the categories into the family through marriage we would have the following result:

"English"	=	a drop of 10.8% (of the 1972-73 figure);
"British"	=	a drop of 7.5%;
"Scottish"	=	a drop of 6.9%;
"Northern Irish"	=	a drop of 10.8%;
"Welsh"	=	a drop of 7.1%;
"French"	=	a drop of 10.7%;
"Germans"	=	a drop of 11.0%;
"Spaniards"	=	a drop of 12.3%;
"Italians"	=	a drop of 11.4%;
"Russians"	=	a drop of 19.5%

It is clear from the above that there has been a substantial decline in percentages "admitting to family" in the case of seven of the ethnic categories tested. The average drop for the ten categories was 10.8% of the original percentage "admitting to family" in 1972-73.

In summary, it can be said that the increase in ethnocentrism is widespread and real. It has happened at a time when there have been moves taking place to integrate the nationalities of Europe more closely, i.e, leading up to the Maastricht Treaty. This bears out the lessons of history that when attempts are made to bring different nationalities closely together under single political structures, the phenomenon of "defensive ethnocentrism" can arise. The Irish Act of Union in 1801 led to bitter ethnic prejudice against England in Ireland. The current very low level of ethnocentrism in relation to "English" and "British" may be because of the mutual independence of the Republic of Ireland and Britain? The ethnic hostilities in the former U.S.S.R. have only come to light once the centrist administration was relaxed. The challenge facing Europe in the future may well be to have inter-national cooperation that is genuinely pluralist in structure, i.e., void of "offensive ethnocentrism" at the centre and "defensive ethnocentrism" as a reaction to moves towards "Fortress Europe"!

CHAPTER V

Racialism

1. INTRODUCTION:

Racialism, which is often referred to as "Racism", is a particular type of social prejudice. It consists of a set of negative or hostile dispositions to members of a category of people seen to be different because of their physiognomic or physical appearances, i.e. colour of skin, texture of hair, shape of nose and lips, eyes, size of body. These differences are genetically inherited.

If one is truly scientific and restricts the concept "Race" to beings of more-or-less similar morphology or range of body structure capable of successful copulation and repeated reproduction, then there is only *one human race*. The misuse of the classification "Race" in popular and pre-scientific literature and myth has been part of the problem which has been very difficult to demythologise. From a purely human point of view the colour of one's skin is no more important than the size of one's boots. Yet, since the time of European expansion in the 16th Century, prejudice and discrimination based on physical differences have been a central intergroup problem.

The classification of people into so-called "Races" and their treatment on the basis of the false belief of innate superiority/inferiority have provided the rationalisation of periodic and widespread genocide, slavery, segregation, stratification and discrimination of those with "racial" differences. While there is evidence of a decline in radical racialism in many societies, there is still an extensive residue of racial prejudice and discrimination throughout the world, including Western Europe and the United States of America.

The findings analysed in this chapter show a significant decline in the level of racialism in the Republic of Ireland over the period 1972-89. The proportion of people living in the Republic who belong to the negroid or mongoloid racial groups is relatively small. This is largely due to the fact that Ireland has been mainly an "emigrant" rather than an "immigrant" society over the past three hundred years. Populations such as those living in the United States and Britain have had a different experience, with the large influx of people of African and Asian origins who were visibly different in terms of colour and physical appearance.

Because of the homogenous (in racial terms) nature of Irish society, it can be assumed that the origins of our racial prejudices are learned from Britain, the United States and elsewhere through experience abroad and through the constant inflow of biased media presentation of racialist intergroup relations abroad. Our racialism is, therefore, largely vicarious and dormant. The experience of Irish people abroad has been both negative and positive, i.e. competing with members of racial minorities, e.g. in the United States, and supporting peoples of different racial appearance, e.g. the foreign missions and overseas services. This has led to a more benevolent type of racialist prejudice (see Mac Gréil 1977, p. 347 ff).

Most of the scales used to measure racialism here were also used in the 1972-73 survey of prejudice and tolerance in Greater (urban and suburban) Dublin. This enables one to examine the degree of change which has taken place during the sixteen intervening years. The nature of changes in racialist attitudes certainly reflects greater enlightenment and a raising of the level of education in the population. The number of positive Black role-models in music, politics, religion and sport may have played a significant role in challenging the untenable racial myths of the past. Also such Irish persons as Paul McGrath (football) and Phil Lynott (music) (see Lynott and Hayden, 1995) and others must have helped to make our attitudes to Black and Coloured People more positive. The public stature of President Nelson Mandela of South Africa must also have made a positive contribution. The strong support in Ireland for the end of apartheid in South Africa over the years may also have contributed to the positive change.

It should be remembered that the reduction of racialism has taken place in a population which has recorded an increase in ethnocentrism, i.e. prejudice based on nationality, culture and way-of-life. This latter increase has been discussed in the previous chapter.

PART I: THE RACIALIST SCALE

Despite the decrease in the intensity and degree of racialism, there still remains a very significant level of prejudice based on physical appearance. Table 33 gives a breakdown of responses to the Racialist Scale. This scale is a replication of the one used in the 1972-73 survey. The changes of racialist dispositions in respect of each of the items are measured by the Prejudice Score (p-scores are given in Table 33 below).

The overall pattern of responses shows a high level of consistency when compared with the 1972-73 findings of the Dublin survey. Allowing for the fact that a national sample would be less liberal than an urban one, the reduction in the levels of racialism, when compared with the 1972-73 findings, is even more significant.

Before analysing the scale scores as measures of racial prejudice it may be useful to review briefly the performance of the individual items as separate statements of opinions held by the Irish population. All items with the exception of No. 8 record a majority in favour of Black people. In the case of No. 8 the plurality is in favour of Black people.

1. ACCOMMODATION FOR BLACK PEOPLE:

Two items relate to this question, i.e., Nos. 1 and 5. In the case of No. 1, four-out-of-five respondents stated they would *not "refuse digs (accommodation)*

TABLE No. 33
RACIALIST SCALE BY TOTAL SAMPLE (1972-3 DUBLIN SAMPLE IN BRACKETS)

STATEMENT	YES	DON'T KNOW	NO	P-Score* (0-200)	No
1. If you had a boarding house would you refuse digs (accommodation) to Black people?	<u>14.7</u> <u>(27.6)</u>	5.8 (5.7)	79.6 (66.7)	A. 35.1 B. (61.0) C. (33.7) D. -27.3	1,003 (2,281) (277)
2. Do you think that because of their basic make-up Black people could never become as good Irish people as others?	<u>16.7</u> <u>(26.5)</u>	10.0 (4.8)	73.3 (68.7)	A. 43.4 B. (58.0) C. (34.4) D. -23.6	1,000 (2,278)
3. Do you believe there should be a stricter control on Black people who enter this country than on Whites?	<u>26.8</u> <u>(39.2)</u>	8.7 (4.6)	64.5 (56.3)	A. 62.4 B. (83.0) C. (56.9) D. -26.1	999 (2,280)
4. Do you believe that the Black person is basically or inherently inferior to the White person?	<u>10.8</u> <u>(13.4)</u>	5.9 (3.8)	83.3 (82.8)	A. 27.5 B. (30.5) C. (20.3) D. -10.2	999 (2,277)
5. Would you stay in a hotel or guest house that had Black guests also?	90.9 (93 3)	2.9 (0.9)	<u>6.2</u> <u>(5.8)</u>	A. 15.3 B. (12.5) C. (10.9) D. -1.6 11	1,001 (2,276)
6. Do you believe that the Black person deserves exactly the same social privileges as the White person?	92.9 (93.5)	3.5 (2.0)	<u>3.6</u> <u>(4.5)</u>	A. 10.7 B. (11.0) C. (6.5) D. -4.5	1,001 (2,278)
7. Do you hold that by nature the Black and the White person are equal?	86.8 (88.2)	5.7 (3.2)	<u>7.5</u> <u>(8.6)</u>	A. 20.7 B. (20.5) C.(14.1) D. -6.4	1,000 (2,273)
8. Do you believe that Black people are naturally more highly sexed than White people?	<u>17.4</u> <u>(24.6)</u>	50.0 (37.5)	32.6 (37.8)	A. 84.7 B. (87.0) C (687) D.-18.3	990 (2,278)
9. Would you hold that Black people should be sent back to Africa and Asia where they belong and kept there?	<u>8.9</u> <u>(14.8)</u>	6.8 (4.4)	84.3 (80.8)	A. 24.6 B. (34.0) C. (22.1) D. -11.9	1,000 (2,278)
10. Do you agree that it is a good thing for Whites and Blacks to get married where there are no cultural or religious barriers?	52.4 (36.6)	16.2 (5.8)	<u>31.4</u> <u>(57.6)</u>	A. 79.0 B.(121.0) C. (61.2) D.-59.8	1,002 (2,276)
Scale P-Score(0-200)				A. (40.4 B 51.9) C.32.91 D.-19.0	

Note Negative percentages are underlined
*   A - P-Score of National Sample 1988-89
        B - P-Score of Dublin Sample 1972-73
        C - P-Score of Dublin Subsample 1988-98
        D - Change of P-Score C-B
Validity of Scale Crombach's Alpha = 0.79 (When item No. 8 is removed).

to Black people" if they owned a boarding house. One-in-seven said they would refuse digs. This latter percentage is a significant minority but it has almost halved in Dublin since 1972-73, dropping from 27.6% to 14.9%. This decrease is reflected in the change in the p-score (27.3). The item elicited significant variation in the case of "age", "gender", "marital status", "county of residence", and "education". The subgroups most in favour of refusing digs were older, females, widowed, Munster respondents and those with least education.

In relation to item no. 5 which asked if the respondent *"would stay in a hotel or guest house that had Black guests also?"*, the overwhelming majority (90.9%) said they would while only 6.2% said they would not stay in a mixed hotel or guest house.

If the views endorsed by these findings are reflected in behaviour, Black people should have little problem with accommodation in Ireland, unless they are unfortunate enough to meet anyone of the small minority opposed to giving digs to Black people.

2. RAW RACIALIST VIEWS

Three items measure raw racialist views, i.e. nos. 2, 4 and 7. No. 2 asks: *"Do you think that because of their basic make-up Black people could never become as good Irish people as others?"* It could be argued that this item contains an element of ethnocentrism as well as that of unadulterated racist xenophobia. There was a significant correlation (0.40) between it and item No. 9 and it did not group with the "purely racialist" items in the factor analysis. It groups under the "exclusion" factor. Still, it is conceptually very much a "racialist" item in that it refers to "their basic make-up".

Nearly three quarters (73.3%) disagreed with item no. 2 while one-in-six agreed with it. This was a marked improvement on 1972-73 when more than a quarter of Dublin respondents (26.5%) agreed with this racist view. The drop in p-score for Dublin respondents over the sixteen years between the surveys has been substantial, i.e, from 58.0 to 34.4 (23.6). This is further evidence of improved attitudes. The item had a significant variation in the personal variables of age, marital status and place of rearing and education. The normal pattern of variation between the subsamples was repeated and the range of variation in the case of "age" and "education" was very substantial.

Items nos. 4 and 7 are more unequivocally racist and had a strong anti-racist response. Five-sixths (83.3%) of the sample disagreed that *"the Black person was inherently inferior to the White person"*. Surprisingly, one-in-ten agreed with this untenable view. Since the mid-nineteenth century, reputable scientists have challenged this view and have been successful in establishing a normal distribution of qualities in various racial and other groups of human beings. Being different has sometimes being confused with being 'inferior'. The relatively recent experience of racist domination in Nazi Germany, supported by such texts as *Mein Kampf* and other pseudo-scientific pro-racist literature and propaganda has shown how dangerous any support for the views of "inherent inferiority" of a minority can be to the human rights of people. It is also a matter of concern to students of 'race relations' that there are signs of the re-emergence of neo-Nazi type groups across Europe and elsewhere abroad who would hold the view expressed in item no. 4. Fortunately, in Ireland there has been a move away from this view. The views of the Dublin respondents dropped from 13.4% in favour of the statement in 1972-73 to 8.3% in favour in 1988-89. It must be remembered that, where extremely racist views are concerned, a minority of 10% is quite substantial and needs our vigilance and attention, particularly in times of unrest or instability.

Item no. 7 addresses the question in no. 4 in a positive manner and receives overwhelming support with 86.9% in favour of the view that "*by nature the Black and the White person are equal*". The percentage who disagreed with this view was again very small at 7.5%, which would constitute some of the hard-core racialists in the sample. The Dublin respondents again recorded a drop from 8.6% in 1972-73 to 5.1% in 1988-89 against the tolerant view expressed in the statement.

Both items nos. 4 and 7 have shown a significant variation in all variables except "gender". This is a very good sign for the Black minority in that the residue of prejudice in the relatively low negative is likely to become lower in the future unless something happens to reverse the trend. The direction of subsample variations is, for the most part, as expected.

3. RACIAL EQUALITY

The item (no. 6) to get the highest positive support was the one asserting that "*the Black person deserves exactly the same social privileges as the White person*". There is not a significant difference between the 1972-73 scores and those of the 1988-89 surveys. This practically unanimous support in principle for "equality of privileges", while it may not be fully honoured in practice always, is a source of encouragement for Black people living and working in Ireland. More importantly, it should encourage political leaders **to enact equality legislation** which would guarantee in law equality of privilege for Black people.

4. SEXUAL STEREOTYPE

White racists are quite prepared to concede a degree of superiority in areas of physique and physical prowess to Black people, while denying them equality or superiority in intellectual and spiritual (i.e., the more exclusively human) traits. The racist literature of the Deep South in the United States of America in the past would highlight sexual prowess, athletic skill and natural rhythms of the "negro slaves". They even descended to discuss breeding for the production of better physical specimens, while at the same time they tried to deny Black people religious training and practice. Religion was only for "White humans". As a result of this tradition, ascribing superior physical qualities to Black people can be an inverted compliment.

Item no. 8 taps into the superior physique stereotype and examines the extent to which it lurks in the Irish culture. The response once again is quite ambivalent. While only one-in-six agreed (17.4%), half of the sample recorded a "don't know" and only one-third (32.6%) were confident enough to say no. Both the "yes" and "no" answers were lower than in the 1972-73 survey. The yes answer for Dublin respondents more than halved from 24.6% in 1972-73 to 11.6% in 1988-89. The p-score for the item dropped substantially from 87.0 to 68.7 in the intervening years. The item elicited a significant variation in each of eight variables.

5. RACIAL CLEANSING

It is topical today to discuss "ethnic cleansing" in former Yugoslavia and in Central Africa and elsewhere. In Britain in the 1960s and 1970s there was a "Back to Africa" campaign for commonwealth immigrants (after they had served their economic function). The main problem with immigrant or migrant workers is that they tend to be economically useful but socially unwelcome. Irish migrants to Britain and elsewhere have felt the impact of this status for over a century and a half. In continental Europe today we see manifestations of this, where migrant labourers were brought in to help reconstruct post-war Europe and fill the gap in the provision of workers created by war casualties and low fertility practices to do mostly menial tasks. The reaction of the dominant group to this growth of racially different minority groups has been at best ambivalent and at worst hostile. Items nos. 3 and 9 measure the respondents' views on restricting entry to Black people more than would be the case for White people and on a wish to return those here back to where they are perceived to come from originally.

The majority in the case of both items are on the side of admitting Blacks and against sending them back. In the case of item no. 3 which calls for *"stricter control on Black people who enter this country than on Whites"*, a little over a quarter (26.8%) of the sample agreed with the view while almost two-thirds (64.5%) disagreed. There was a very substantial reduction in the percentage calling for stricter immigration control on Blacks among the Dublin respondents since 1972-73, i.e., from 39.2% to 24.3% in favour of the item. The overall drop in the p-score of the item from 83.0 to 53.9 (26.1) is very substantial indeed.

The *"Back to Africa and Asia where they belong"* view got an overwhelming thumbs down from the sample. Only 8.9% agreed with it while 84.3% disagreed. The change since 1972-73 in regard to this racist view has been very substantial in the pro-Black people direction. It dropped from 14.8% to 6.5% over the sixteen years, while the item p-score went from 34.0 to 22.1, i.e, a decrease of 11.9. This must provide a good degree of reassurance to

Black people resident in Ireland and also encourage politicians to avoid discrimination in the immigration controls on Black people and protect the stability of residence and rights of those living in the Republic of Ireland.

The final item no. 10 confirms the change in attitude in the Bogardus Social Distance Scale, which is discussed below. The people are becoming more in favour of Blacks and Whites getting married *"where there are no cultural or religious barriers"*. The extent of this change since 1972-73 is phenomenal, i.e., those against went from 57.6% to 33.3% (-24.3%). The change in the p-score was also very substantial at -59.8, that is from 121.0 to 61.2.

In conclusion, therefore, the individual items of the Racialist Scale provide a good insight into a range of racist issues and views held by the people and the clear trend of a very notable decrease in the more negative aspects of these views. While the reduction of racism has to be welcomed, there is no room for complacency. We have still a good many miles to travel before we are relatively free of "man's most dangerous myth".

6. FACTOR ANALYSIS OF SCALE AND PREJUDICE SCORE (p-scores)

The item p-score is calculated by scoring two for "agreement" to negative statements or disagreement to positive ones and one for "don't know". The range of extremely negative and positive statements and those which are moderate either way results in a measure which captures a wide range of valency. A scale p-score which captures both extreme and moderate prejudice dispositions is considered to be a more discerning instrument of measurement.

TABLE No. 34
FACTOR ANALYSIS OF RACIALIST SCALE

Item Number	Varimax Loading	
	Factor 1 "Exclusion"	Factor 2 "Racialist"
1. Refuse digs to Blacks	0.55674	
2. Not as good Irish person	0.59558	
3. Stricter control of entrance	0.65195	
8. More highly sexed	0.67933	
10. Not good to marry blacks	0.65142	
4. Blacks inferior		-0.51220
(5. Refuse to stay in same hotel)		(-0.74542)
(6. Not entitled to same privileges)		(-0.79349)
8. Unequal by nature		-0.69866
9. Send back to Africa		-0.52975

In the factor-analysis of the 1972-73 data, the scale was divided into two subscales, i.e., "Hard-Core and 'Pure' Racialist Items" (Items 2, 4, 7 and 8) and "Pro-Discrimination Items" (Items 1, 3, 9 and 10). Items 5 and 6 were dropped because of the very high degree of consensus (over 90% in agreement) in the replies. This characteristic has been repeated in the 1988-89 data (Mac Gréil, 1977 pp. 349 ff.).

The factor analysis of replies of the 1988-89 survey created a different division of the scale when compared with 1972-73, with Items 1, 2, 3, 8 and 10 forming one cluster and Items 4, 5, 6, 7 and 9 grouping into a second factor.

The sub-classifications of "Exclusion" and "Racialist" are not intended to be conceptually precise. Items Nos. 5 and 6 are dropped when comparing the findings for 1988-9 with those of 1972-73.

There was a significant correlation between all the items within each of the factor groupings. In the case of "Factor 1" the range of correlation scores went from $r = 0.20$ to $r = 0.38$, while the level of correlation in "Factor 2" was higher, ranging from $r = 0.28$ to $r = 0.46$ (see Table 35).

TABLE NO. 35
CORRELATION MATRIX OF ITEMS OF RACIAL FACTORS

	Factor 1				Factor 2			
	No.1	No.2	No.3	No.10	No.8	No.4	No.7	No.9
Factor 1								
1.Refuse digs to Blacks	1.00	.38	.35	.31	.20	.28	.29	.44
2. Blacks never as good Irish		1.00	.35	.24	.22	.31	.28	.34
3. Stricter control on entrance of blacks			1.00	.38	.23	.38	.32	.40
10. Bad thing for black and white to marry				1.00	.24	.22	.22	.32
8. Blacks more highly sexed					1.00	.13	.15	.21
Factor 2								
4. Black inferior to white person						1.00	.38	.46
7. Unequal by nature							1.00	.46
9. Send back to Africa								1.00

As already stated, the real value of the factor analysis is to discover the subscales within the scale and, through an examination of the variations and extent of the p-scores for both the scale and the subscales, to gauge the personal factors which help to explain the range of attitudes.

The average p-scores of the Racialist Scale and its subscales are relatively low, i.e., Total Scale at 43.0, Exclusion Subscale at 60.7 and the Racialist Subscale at 24.0. Yet, despite these relatively low scores, the variable differences have been quite substantial and significant. This shows that there is further movement in relation to anti-Black attitudes and the direction of such movement is towards a further reduction in racialism. "Age" and "education", in particular, indicate that Irish society is continuing to become less racialist. The impact of urbanisation is also having a more

TABLE No. 36
RACIALIST SUB-SCALES BY PERSONAL VARIABLES (P-SCORES)

	Full Scale	Exclusion Subscale*	Pure Racialist Subscale**	Number
NATIONAL SAMPLE	40.4	60.7	24.0	995
A. AGE				
1. 35 years or less	26.3	39.9	15.5	386
2. 36 to 50 years	40.4	59.5	25.0	268
3. 51 to 65 years	47.2	75.6	24.9	193
4. 66 years +	69.3	100.4	44.5	143
Score Variation	43.0	60.5	29.0	
B. GENDER				
1. Female	41.9	58.4	25.5	537
2. Male	38.5	62.6	22.3	456
Score Variation	3.4	4.2	3 2	
C MARITAL STATUS				
1. Never Married	33.3	49.4	18.6	287
2. Married	40.5	62.3	23.8	618
3. Widowed	64.8	92.2	44.4	69
Score Variation	31.5	42.8	25.8	
D. COUNTY OF RESIDENCE				
1. Dublin	33.3	51.5	18.8	276
2. Rest of Leinster	36.5	55.4	25.3	250
3. Munster	42.5	64.6	22.8	298
4. Connaught/Ulster	50.6	77.6	32.7	169
Score Variation	17.3	26.5	13.9	
E. PLACE OF REARING				
1. Large City	30.9	47.8	17.2	234
2. Small City	33.8	52.9	16.5	117
3. Town	33.7	52.9	16.9	150
4. Rural	48.4	71 2	3 L4	490
Score Variation	17.5	23.4	14.9	
F. EDUCATION				
1. Primary Only	61.2	86.3	43.3	280
2. Incomplete Second	38.7	59.9	21.6	345
3. Complete Second	29.7	45.1	11.4	228
4. Rural	24.0	36.6	12.1	140
Score Variation	37.2	49.7	31.2	
G. OCCUPATIONAL STATUS				
1. Profess/Executive	30.1	44.7	18.4	158
2. Inspect/Supervisory	36.0	58.0	17.6	296
3. Skilled/Routine	40.4	60.3	25.1	276
4. Semi/Unskilled	48.2	70.0	32.3	155
Score Variation	18.1	25.3	14.7	
H. SOCIAL CLASS POSITION				
1. Class I	16.0	25.5	10.8	34
2. Class II	29.5	43.3	18.6	104
3. Class III	34.7	56.3	16.0	267
4. Class IV	40.7	61.2	24.4	292
5. Class V	49.2	7L0	33.5	187
Score Variation	33.2	45.5	22.7	

* Items 1, 2, 3, 8 and 10
** Items 4, 7 and 9
Lowest Scores are Underlined

tolerant effect. "Gender", as a variable, is not showing much variation. Female and male prejudices are converging, compared with the 1972-73 findings when women were significantly and substantially more prejudiced than men. It was suggested at the time that such differences were due to a higher level of frustration among women as a category, probably because of sexist discrimination against them in society. If that was the case then, the situation in 1988-89 indicates either lower frustration among women or higher frustration among men as a social category.

7. RACIALIST SCALE SCORES BY PERSONAL VARIABLES:

Table 36 gives a clear picture of the influence of personal variables on racialism as measured by the full scale and the two subscales. The findings speak for themselves. Only a brief commentary is necessary to explain the pattern.

7.1 Racialism by Age:

In two of the three measures, the range of variation is greater than the mean score and in the third case (the Exclusion Subscale) it equals it. Such a high level of dissent is rare. Because of the direction of the p-scores, i.e., a positive correlation with "age" in all three scales, the trend is clearly in the direction of further reduction in racialism, even allowing for the ageing process to increase prejudice to some degree. "Age" has a relatively high direct Beta score to the racialist scale, i.e., 0.26 in the regression analysis (see Figure No. 7, p. 142 below).

7.2 Racialism by Gender:

The variations by "gender" are barely significant and mixed. In the "Exclusive Subscale" males are slightly more prejudiced while women have a higher p-score for the "Racialist Subscale". The contrast between the low differences between males and female and the range of variations in the other variables is very striking. The regression path-analysis of the racialist scale by "age", "gender", "place of rearing", "education", "occupational status" and "alienation", "anomie" and "authoritarianism" does not include "gender" or "marital status" because of the "nominal" character of their subsamples (see page footnote on page 455).

7.3 Racialism by Marital Status:

"Marital status" registered a relatively large score difference. In the case of the "racialist subscale" the range of scores was higher than the mean. It is interesting to note that the scores of those "never married" and those "married" were quite small while the greatest deviation is in respect of the "widowed". The age factor as well as the frustrations, insecurity and tension of losing a partner would be the two main contributing factors affecting the high scores.

7.4 Racialism by County of Residence and Place of Rearing:

County of current residence measures the social influences of the respondents' community environment, while "place/area of rearing" captures the cultural effects of where the first sixteen years of life were spent. This latter location is classified as an urban-rural continuum. The "county of residence" is divided along traditional geographic lines. There is a very strong similarity between the p-score of both variables, despite the relatively high level of rural-urban migration, especially from the Western counties into Dublin. Connaught/Ulster has the highest scores, largely due to the age profile and the predominantly rural nature of the provinces. It is interesting to note that the degree of racialism in the small cities and the towns are not significantly different. Does this mean that small Irish cities are really large towns in ethos? Even Ireland's second largest city has many of the traits, in terms of attitudes and practices, one finds in large towns (see Religious Practice scores for Munster p. 163 below).

It is also interesting to note the Beta scores between *age* (0.19) and *place of rearing* in the path analysis figure below (p. 142). "Place of rearing" has, in turn, a Beta score of -0.14-0.17 with *education* and influence on "authoritarianism" scores is a Beta score of only 0.17. This means that the variations in Table 36 are the result of other variables like "age" and "education" which significantly influence the geographic distribution of the sample or are influenced by it.

7.5 Racialism by Education, Occupational Status and Social Class Position:

These three personal variables are very significantly related. "Social Class Position" as a five point scale is arrived at as a result of the combination of a seven-point educational scale (multiplied by four) and a seven-point occupational scale (multiplied by seven). The Beta score between "education" and "occupation" is very high at 0.57.

The nature of the variations in p-score in each of the three variables is as predicted with the lower grades in "education", in "occupational status" and in "social class" all registering the highest level of anti-racialist prejudice.

PART II: RACIAL SOCIAL DISTANCE

The original Social Distance Scale devised by Emory Bogardus (1925) was intended to measure attitudes towards ethnic and racial groups. It proved

Figure No. 7: Path/Regression-Analysis of Racialism

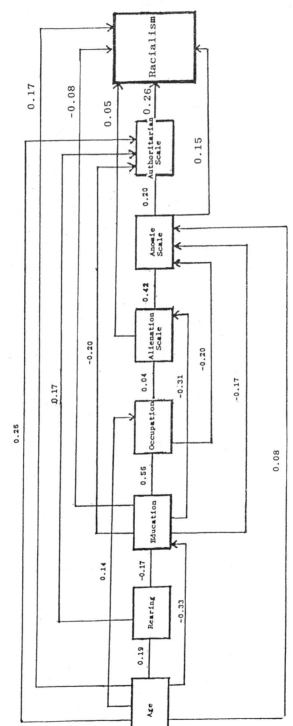

$R^2 = 0.259$ $R^2 = 0.366$ $R^2 = 0.372$ $R^2 = 0.090$ $R^2 = 0.272$ $R^2 = 0.158$ $R^2 = 0.036$

particularly suitable in relation to racial and ethnic groups in the previous Irish Survey (Mac Gréil, 1977). Social distance is a measure of behavioural tendency which is the nearest component of an attitude to behaviour.

1. OVERALL SOCIAL DISTANCE

In the course of this section the position of "Blacks" and "Coloureds" will be examined, as well as that of six ethnic-racial categories, i.e., "Africans", "Black Americans" ("American Negroes"), "Chinese", "Indians", "Nigerians" and "Pakistani". All of these categories registered a significant racial score on the rationalisation scale. With the exception of "Black Americans", the other five categories are defined primarily by their ethnic or nationality traits. This was a most significant change since 1972-73 when all of these ethnic categories were defined primarily as racial (see Mac Gréil 1977, p. 237).

Table 37 shows the results of the Bogardus Social Distance Scale for the total 1988-89 sample, for the 1972-73 Dublin sample and for the 1988-89 Dublin subsample. The change in social distance towards racial groups can be gauged by subtracting the 1972-73 score from the 1988-89.[1]

The good news of Tables 37 and 38 is the clear evidence of a significant and substantial reduction in the mean-social-distance scores for all of the eight racial and ethnic-racial categories. The one group with least movement is the "Pakistanis" who have probably been affected by their negative image in some of the English popular media, especially, the print media which have a relatively wide circulation in Ireland.

TABLE No. 37

COMPARATIVE SOCIAL DISTANCE SCORES TOWARDS RACIAL CATEGORIES
1988-89 AND 1972-73

	A	B	C	M.S.D. Variations		
	Total Sample 1988-89	Dublin Subsample 1988-89	Dublin Sample 1972-73	A - B	A - C	B - C
1. Coloureds	2.715	2.214	2.791	+0.501	-0.076	-0.577
2. Africans	2.916	2.708	2.902	+0.208	+0.014	-0.194
3. Chinese	3.009	2.527	2.891	+0.482	+0.118	-0.364
4. Blacks	3.019	2.563	2.935	+0.456	+0.084	-0.372
5. Non-American Indians	3.108	2.617	2.806	+0.491	+0.302	-0.189
6. Nigerians	3.131	2.652	2.929	+0.479	+0.202	-0.277
7. Black Americans	3.212	2.716	3.021	+0.496	+0.191	-0.305
8. Pakistanis	3.404	2.996	3.112	+0.408	+0.292	-0.116

1. Since there is a high concentration of data on this table the reader might take time to study the table which probably tells more than twenty pages of prose would.

TABLE No. 38
SOCIAL DISTANCE TOWARDS RACIAL AND ETHNIC-RACIAL CATEGORIES
1988-89

Rank Order		Kinship	Friendship or Closer	Neighbour or Closer	Co. Wkr or Closer	Citizen or Closer	Visitor Only	Db or Dp	MSD	Number
1. Coloureds	A	34.3	58.9	71.4	81.2	85.2	12.5	2.4	2.715	1003
	B	24.9	61.3	73.5	80.3	84.7	11.4	3.8	2.791	2298
	C	42.0	69.8	83.5	92.5	92.5	7.1	0.4	2,200	
Change	C-B	+17.1	+8.5	+10.0	+12.2	+7.8	-4.3	-3.4	-0.791	
2. Africans	A	30.1	54.4	65.2	76.9	84.1	13.7	2.3	2.916	1003
	B	21.5	58.4	71.1	78.5	84.1	12.0	3.8	2.902	2302
	C	36.3	58.6	69.9	81.2	86.3	13.3	0.4	2.680	
Change	C-B	+ 14.8	+0.2	- 1.2	+2.7	+2.2	+ 1.3	-3.4	-0.222	
3. Chinese	A	30.9	51.3	63.0	75.5	81.3	16.0	2.8	3.009	1002
	B	25.3	58.4	71.6	77.9	82.5	12.8	4.7	2.891	2300
	C	37.5	61.7	75.0	87.9	89.5	9.0	1.6	2.500	
Change	C-B	+ 12.2	+3.3	+3.4	+ 10.0	+7.0	-3.8	-3.1	-0.391	
4. Blacks	A	29.7	51.0	63.2	76.6	81.6	14.5	3.9	3.019	1004
	B	21.7	57.6	70.6	78.3	83.0	12.8	4.2	2.935	2297
	C	37.5	60.2	73.5	86.4	88.7	9.4	2.0	2.559	
Change	C-B	+ 15.8	+2.6	+2.9	+8.1	+5.7	-3.4	-2.2	-0.176	
5. Indians	A	31.0	49.6	60.9	72.8	78.8	17.7	3.6	3.108	1001
	B	28.5	61.4	72.7	78.3	83.5	11.6	5.0	2.806	2285
	C	39.8	60.5	73.0	84.7	87.4	9.4	3.1	2.574	
Change	C-B	+ 11.3	-0.9	+0.3	+6.4	+3.9	-2.2	- 19	-0232	
6. Nigerians	A	29.1	48.7	60.8	71.7	78.7	19.2	2.1	3.131	1000
	B	22.4	57.7	71.4	78.0	82.7	12.3	5.1	2.929	2286
	C	38.0	60.4	74.1	81.9	85.8	12.5	1.6	2.612	
Change	C-B	+15.6	+2.7	+2.7	+3.9	+3.1	+0.2	-3.5	-0.317	
7. Black Americans	A	26.2	46.1	59.0	71.9	78.2	17.0	3.7	3.212	998
	B	21.0	55.8	69.1	76.0	81.6	12.9	5.6	3.021	2298
	C	31.5	55.5	70.9	85.1	89.8	9.1	1.2	2.685	
Change	C-B	+10.5	-0.3	+1.8	+9.1	+8.2	-3.8	4.4	-0.336	
8. Pakistani	A	24.2	42.6	54.7	67.2	73.9	22.4	3.5	3.404	998
	B	23.9	53.7	65.7	73.4	79.3	13.7	7.1	3.112	2285
	C	29.5	52.7	66.5	78.7	81.1	15.0	3.9	2.953	
Change	C-B	+5.6	-1 0	+0.8	+5.3	+1.8	+1.3	-3.2	-0.159	

A = 1988-89 National Sample; B = 1972-73 Dublin Sample; C = 1988-89 Dublin Subsample.

The rank-order of the categories has broken the "principle of colour pro-pinquity", i.e., White people preferring Coloured people to Black people. For instance we prefer "Africans" and "Blacks" to "Indians". The position of "Black Americans" as second from the end is also strange and dis-appointing in that Irish people have more in common with them than with any other category on the Table. All of "Irish American" or "American Irish" are fellow citizens of "Black Americans". They are English-speaking and mostly Christian in terms of religion. "Black Americans" are positive role models in music, in comedy and in sport and athletics. The political achievements of world leaders like the late Dr. Martin Luther King inspired the Civil Rights Movement in Northern Ireland in the 1960s. Again, it is probably a vicarious bias imported from the American Irish diaspora.

The most significant change in the social distance scores has been in the increase in the percentage *admitting to family*. Refusal of admission to family was particularly true in the case of the prejudice against Black and Coloured people in the past. Racial miscegenation was severely sanctioned by all racialist regimes and dominant groups, despite the fact that there was frequent illicit sexual exploitation of Black women by White men during the slavery times in the United States and later. There was limited exploitation of Black men by White women in the Deep South of the United States and elsewhere. This opposition to interracial marriage when there are no religious or cultural differences is a very irrational form of raw racialism. Ethnic and religious endogamy is based on culture and human qualities, while racial-group endogamy is based only on physical "pure race" mythology. Giving such significance to the superficial physical aspects is sub-human and was the prime motivating ideology which sustained the attitudes and behaviour of Adolf Hitler and his "super-race" programme.

2. CORRELATIONS

TABLE No. 39
CORRELATION MATRIX OF RACIAL AND ETHNIC-RACIAL CATEGORIES

Stimulus Category	Coloureds 1	Africans 2	Chinese 3	Blacks 4	Indians 5	Nigerians 6	Black American 7	Pakistani 8
1. Coloureds	1.00	.69	.73	.81	.70	.76	.77	.67
2. Africans		1.00	.62	.72	.63	.67	.76	.62
3. Chinese			1.00	.76	.74	.72	.70	.70
4. Blacks				1.00	.74	.76	.84	.71
5. Indians					1.00	.77	.71	.77
6. Nigerians						1.00	.71	.82
7. Black Americans							1.00	69
8. Pakistanis								1.00

Note Significant Variation P≤.OOI

It is quite clear from relatively high correlation in the above matrix that the racial factor is still very much present in the social distance rating of the eight categories. The above findings also illustrate the validity and reliability of the Bogardus Social Distance scale in that the responses bring together categories with a common characteristic (having been responded to in alphabetical order). In the rank ordering of the fifty-nine stimulus categories, the racial categories were placed close together in 35th, 37th, 38th, 39th, 43rd, 45th and 49th places. The tendency in racial prejudice of "lumping all the categories together", irrespective of the vast diversity in culture, religion and nationality, is once again repeated in the 1988-89 findings, if to a lesser degree. It should be noted, however, that such "branding of all racial groups as being the same" is less severe than was the case in 1972-73 (see Mac Gréil 1977, pp. 349). This latter change is an indication of the decline of the racial factor which further substantiates the overall finding of a reduction in racial prejudice and in racial rationalisation. Nevertheless, it must be stated that, while welcoming the significant and substantial reduction in racialist prejudice, we still have a very long way to go to remove the most dangerous myth from our relationships with our fellow human beings. Race as such is not a humanly relevant factor in that there is but one human race of basically equal human beings. The highest correlation was between "Black Americans" and "Blacks" at 0.84.

3. SOCIAL DISTANCE BY PERSONAL VARIABLES:

Table 40 gives the performance of each of the subsamples within the variables recording a statistically significant variation, i.e., *chi-square* .05 or less. The percentages "admitting to kinship" and "denying citizenship" are given in the case of each category. Percentages more than 3% above the sample average are underlined. The range of difference within the variable is given to indicate the degree of diversity between the subsamples.

Because of the importance of variations within the personal variables, the amount of detail given in Table 40 is quite extensive and merits careful examination to discover the dynamic nature of racialist prejudice in Ireland and the wide range of variance in most personal variables. The general trend of such variances would indicate ongoing reduction in the extent of racialism if the current socio-cultural climate continues.

The economic and commercial illogicality of racialist prejudice has been taken on board by those with higher occupational status. If this is a reflection of what is happening in society, then industrial leaders will continue to be a major positive force against racialism. It was noteworthy that the major industrialists of South Africa exercised a leadership role in bringing about an end to apartheid, or at least forcing a move in that direction. Racialism, as with other types of intergroup prejudice and discrimination, is economically and communally highly dysfunctional because it impedes the maximum contribution of all citizens with a more-or-less similar range of talent and potential in each racial group.

Gender, Marital Status and Age: The two variables to record least variation are "gender" and "marital status". In the case of the latter, there was no significant variation in six of the stimulus categories, while the former registered no significance in the case of five categories. The meaning of such consensus between "gender" and "marital status" variables in contrast to the performance of "age", "county of residence", "place of rearing", "education", "occupational status" and "social-class-position" is very noteworthy and not that easy to explain without merely speculating.

Age as a personal variable shows a clear pattern of greater tolerance among the younger respondents and greater prejudice among the older ones. The range of difference for both "admission to kinship" and for "denial of citizenship" is both significant and substantial. This trend is a repeat of the 1972-73 findings and is a source of optimism with regard to the future continuity of the trends.

County of Residence and Place of Rearing: "County of residence" and "Place of Rearing" have recorded significant variations in all categories, as well as a very wide range of percentages. Rural-reared respondents and those living in Connaught/Ulster were markedly more reluctant to permit or welcome racial groups into close social distance. The range of scores in the case of "county of residence" is much greater than that of "place of rearing", with the most tolerant groups being "Dublin" and the "Rest of Leinster" while "Connaught/Ulster" scored negatively with between 30% and 40% consistently prepared to deny citizenship to all racial groups. On average, only 12.5% of "Connaught/Ulster" respondents would welcome racial group members into their families through marriage whereas three times that proportion (36.4%) of the respondents from "Dublin" and the "Rest of Leinster" would welcome them into kinship.

The average percentage in favour of denying citizenship to the racial groups in the case of the "Leinster" (including Dublin) respondents is three times lower than "Connaught/Ulster" at 12%. The average percentages across the eight racial-group categories admitting to kinship and denying citizenship for respondents from "Munster" was 26.9% and 21.8% respectively. Again, it is difficult to explain such a wide disparity of scoring by geographical location of residence. It is certainly not based on experience. Perhaps it is the effect of negative stereotyping coming from emigrants in Britain and the United States. Whatever the cause, it does present a challenge to teachers and community leaders in Ireland's more rural areas to undermine such a comparatively high level of racial prejudice. The path-analysis on page 142 points to the influence of other variables in the population structure of the rural-reared.

Education: The "education" variable was in line with the normal pattern or trend with one notable exception which repeated itself across the eight racial-group categories. Those with "incomplete second-level education", i.e., those with Group or Intermediate Certificate only, were more tolerant than those who had "complete second-level" i.e., those with Leaving

TABLE No. 40
SOCIAL DISTANCE TOWARDS RACIAL CATEGORIES BY PERSONAL VARIABLES

Variable	Coloureds		Africans		Chinese		Blacks		Indians		Nigerians		Black Americans		Pakistanis	
	Kinship	Deny Citizenship	Kinship	Deny Cit	Kinship	Deny Cit	Kinship	Deny Cit	Kinship	Deny Cit	Kinship	Deny Cit	Kinship	Deny Cit	Kinship	Deny Cit
National Sample	34.3	14.9	30.1	16.0	30.9	18.8	29.7	18.4	31.0	21.3	29.1	21.3	26.2	20.7	24.2	25.9
A. Age	P≤.001		P≤.001		P≤.001		P≤.001		P≤.001		P≤.001		P≤.001		P≤.001	
1. 35 years or less	42.9	8.1*	37.7	11.1*	38.6	12.9*	37.7	12.2*	38.2	15.8*	37.1	16.5*	32.7	12.7*	29.8	21.7*
2. 36 to 50 years	35.9	12.6	34.0	15.9	34.7	16.2	31.4	15.9	32.1	18.1	31.7	17.3	27.9	18.2	26.6	22.1*
3. 51 to 65	24.2*	20.6	22.7*	19.1	20.2*	25.4	21.2*	24.9	21.4*	29.7	17.3*	29.3	17.4*	28.4	15.7*	33.5
4. 66 years +	21.4*	21.4	18.8*	25.0	17.4*	30.6	15.9*	31.7	22.1*	31.0	18.1*	31.3	16.3*	37.2	16.0*	34.7
Range	21.5	13.3	18.9	13.9	21.2	17.7	21.8	19.5	16.8	15.2	19.4	14.8	16.4	24.5	14.1	13.0
B. Gender	N/S		N/S		N/S		N/S		P≤.05		P≤.05		N/S		P≤.05	
1. Male	N/S		N/S		N/S		N/S		26.8*	23.5	25.5*	24.4	N/S		20.0*	28.1
2. Female	–		–		–		–		35.9	18.7	33.3	17.6*	–		29.3	23.4
Range	–		–		–		–		9.1	4.8	7.8	6.8	–		9.3	4.7
C. Marital Status	P≤.05		N/S		N/S		N/S		N/S		N/S		P≤.05		N/S	
1. Never Married	38.5	12.4	N/S		N/S		N/S		N/S		N/S		28.7	18.3	N/S	
2. Married	32.8	14.5	–		–		–		–		–		25.0	20.0	–	
3. Widowed	26.8*	26.8	–		–		–		–		–		24.3	37.1	–	
Range	11.7	14.4	–		–		–		–		–		4.4	18.8	–	
D. County of Residence	P≤.001		P≤.001		P≤.001		P≤.001		P≤.001		P≤.001		P≤.001		P≤.001	
1. Dublin	41.7	7.6*	36.1	14.8	37.2	10.8*	37.2	11.6*	39.0	13.7*	37.7	14.9*	31.3	11.3*	29.1	20.0*
2. Rest of Leinster	42.1	8.7*	38.0	8.2*	36.2	13.8*	37.6	11.4*	37.4	14.6*	35.8	14.2*	33.6	14.6*	32.3	19.3*
3. Munster	31.3	17.7	26.0*	16.0	30.0	20.7	26.8*	19.7	28.5	22.8	26.1	24.7	24.9	23.9	21.8	28.9
4. Connaught/Ulster	16.2*	30.6	15.8*	29.2	14.6*	35.7	11.0*	37.6	12.8*	40.7	10.5*	36.3	9.2*	39.3	8.8*	40.4
Range	25.9	23.0	22.2	21.0	22.6	24.9	26.6	26.0	26.2	27.0	27.2	21.4	24.4	28.0	23.5	20.4

TABLE No. 40—Continued

SOCIAL DISTANCE TOWARDS RACIAL CATEGORIES BY PERSONAL VARIABLES

Variable	Coloureds		Africans		Chinese		Blacks		Indians		Nigerians		Black Americans		Pakistanis	
	Kinship	Deny Citizenship	Kinship	Deny Cit	Kinship	Deny Cit	Kinship	Deny Cit	Kinship	Deny Cit	Kinship	Deny Cit	Kinship	Deny Cit	Kinship	Deny
E. Place of Rearing	P≤.001		P≤.001		P≤.001		P≤.001		P≤.001		P≤.001		P≤.001		P≤.001	
1. Large City	41.3	7.3*	34.8	12.9*	35.5	9.8*	36.6	10.8*	36.2	12.5*	36.4	14.0*	30.9	9.8*	28.8	18.6*
2. Small City	42.9	9.5*	41.7	7.1*	39.3	17.9	38.1	10.7*	41.7	20.2	36.9	20.2	34.5	11.9*	33.3	26.2
3. Town	35.4	9.2*	31.5	9.2*	33.1	11.5*	31.5	10.8*	31.5	12.3*	30.0	13.1*	29.2	13.1*	26.2	16.9*
4. Rural	28.6*	25.1	25.1	20.9	26.3*	25.9	23.9*	25.1	26.0*	28.8	23.4*	27.8	21.2*	30.5	19.6*	32.5
Range	14.3	14.2	16.6	13.8	13.0	16.1	14.2	14.4	15.7	16.5	13.5	14.7	13.3	20.7	13.7	15.6
F. Education	P≤.001		P≤.001		P≤.001		P≤.001		P≤.001		P≤.001		P≤.001		P≤.001	
1. Primary Only	25.3*	24.9	22.9*	24.6	20.5	29.7	19.7	27.5	19.1	31.3	18.1	28.7	18.6	32.5	17.4	33.7
2. Incomplete Second	40.1	14.8	37.0	15.5	35.6	20.1	35.6	19.4	36.3	19.7	33.2	23.0	31.4	19.4	28.7	24.5
3. Complete Second	33.3	9.5*	28.8	10.5*	31.2	12.9	28.4	14.2	31.3	17.7	29.5	18.3	24.7	15.3	22.7	24.7
4. Third Level	46.4	5.7*	33.6	10.7*	42.1	6.4	40.7	7.1	43.6	12.1	42.1	9.3	33.6	11.4	32.4	15.8
Range	21.1	19.2	14.1	14.1	21.6	22.3	21.0	20.4	24.5	19.0	24.0	19.4	15.0	21.1	15.0	17.9
G. Occupational Status	P≤.001		P≤.05		P≤.001		P≤.05		P≤.001		P≤.001		P≤.05		P≤.001	
1. Profess/Executive	47.2	5.7*	37.7	5.7*	44.0	8.2*	42.8	7.5*	47.2	9.4	43.4	7.5	34.6	10.1	38.6	12.0
2. Inspect/Supervisory	32.6	11.7*	27.4	15.4	30.8	15.7*	28.7	17.3	27.9	16.8	28.4	19.4	25.6	18.2	21.8	22.8
3. Skilled/Routine	34.9	14.7	30.9	15.8	29.6	20.6	27.7	20.1	31.3	23.4	27.1	22.7	24.3	22.5	22.1	27.2
4. Semi/Unskilled	30.8*	20.5	30.1	23.1	26.3	23.1	26.9	20.5	26.9	26.9	24.4	28.2	22.4	23.7	21.9	35.5
Range	16.4	14.8	10.3	15.5	17.7	15.9	15.9	13.0	20.3	17.5	19.0	20.7	12.2	13.7	16.8	23.5
H. Social Class Position	P≤.001		P≤.001		P≤.001		P≤.001		P≤.001		P≤.001		P≤.001		P≤.001	
1. Class I	55.9	0.0*	35.3	2.9*	47.1	0.0*	47.1	0.0*	50.0	2.9*	50.0	0.0*	35.3	2.9*	41.2	2.9*
2. Class II	48.6	4.8*	41.9	7.6*	48.6	6.7*	45.7	6.7*	50.5	8.6*	46.7	7.6*	39.0	10.5*	41.3	12.5*
3. Class III	31.3	10.8*	25.3*	14.1	28.6	14.9	27.4	17.8	27.6*	17.2*	27.1	19.7	23.1*	17.9	20.9	23.9
4. Class IV	36.6	14.2	32.2	15.6	31.6	20.7	29.5	19.0	33.2	22.0	29.3	20.7	26.7	21.6	23.9	25.3
5. Class V	29.3*	21.3	29.8	20.2	25.5*	23.4	25.5*	21.8	23.9*	26.6	22.3*	28.7	21.3*	23.9	20.3*	34.2
Range	26.6	21.3	10.0	17.3	23.1	23.4	21.6	21.8	26.6	23.7	27.7	28.7	17.7	21.0	21.0	31.3

Notes (1) * More than 3% below the sample score;
  (2) Percentage with more than 3% above the sample average are underlined.

Certificate only. This speaks well for the graduates of our local vocational schools in that they are more tolerant in relation to racial groups. Overall, the variations by education show an optimistic trend towards a further reduction of prejudice in the future with the relatively high level of racist tolerance among *third-level graduates*, i.e., on average 39.3% would admit racial-group members to kinship and less than 10% (9.8%) would deny them citizenship.

Occupational Status: "Occupational status" has also shown, as already mentioned above, that those with the highest occupational status are relatively tolerant towards members of the eight racial and ethnic-racial groups. On average, 41.9% of higher professionals and executives would welcome a member of the eight groups into kinship, while only 8.3% would deny citizenship. The overall average for those with the lowest occupational status were 26.2% welcoming to kinship and 25.0% denying citizenship.

Social Class Position: When "education" and "occupational status" are combined into the production of the five-point *social-class-position* scale, one gets a very wide range of scores. Class I, which may be popularly called the "Upper Class", are the most tolerant subsample in all the tables with an average "admission-to-kinship" percentage as high as 45.2% and the "denial-of-citizenship" average percentage at 1.5%, which is hardly significant (statistically). The sense of personal security experienced by those at the top of the social-class-position ladder, i.e., the "Upper Class" and the "Upper Middle Class" enables them to be more tolerant and open than their less secure fellow-citizens at the bottom of the class ladder. It was found, for instance, in the United States that neighbourhood inter-racial integration was not a problem between the socio-economic equals in the wealthy class-exclusive neighbourhoods, e.g. Shaker Heights in Cleveland, Ohio, U.S.A. (see Mac Gréil 1966, p. 187 ff.).

Of course there may be another explanation for the relative tolerance of those in the top classes, namely, the pragmatic rationality of tolerance which is the only approach that makes economic and professional sense. Prejudice and the discrimination resulting from it deprive society of the talents of the various minorities, who have the ability to contribute to the cultural, economic, religious and social life of the people. This has been borne out in the United States, in South Africa, in Northern Ireland and in many other societies throughout the world. What is even more damaging to society is the very expensive negative side of deprivation in terms of costly social welfare and corrective systems resulting from deviance and even crime caused by that deprivation. In effect, potential producers are forced to become unhappy dependants consuming enormous resources and social discomfort.

Patterns and Range of Variation: The patterns of variation have been more or less the same for each of the eight categories, "Coloureds", "Africans", "Chinese", "Blacks", "Indians", "Nigerians", "Black Americans" and "Pakistanis". The relatively low position of "Black Americans" on the rank-order of the categories is a cause of concern because of the religious and ethnic propinquity of this group to the Irish

people. The following comparison (Table 41) with responses to White
Americans bears out the unpalatable influence of the racial factor.

TABLE No. 41
LEVEL OF SOCIAL DISTANCE OF BLACK AND WHITE AMERICANS

LEVEL OF SOCIAL DISTANCE	Black Americans	White Americans	Difference
1. Welcome into the family	26.2%	78.6%	-52 6%
2. Have as close friend or closer	46.1%	87.2%	-41.4%
3. Have as next-door neighbour or closer	59.0%	92.5%	-33.5%
4. Have as co-worker or closer	71.9%	95.6%	-23.7%
5. Welcome as Irish citizen, or closer	78.2%	96.6%	-18.4%
6. Welcome as visitor only	17.0%	3.2%	+14.8%
7. Would debar or deport	3.7%	0.2%	+3.5%
Mean Social Distance	3.212	1.514	+1.698

The above findings make depressing reading and highlight the level of
latent racialist prejudice in our society. They also raise serious questions
concerning the manner in which "Black Americans" are presented on the
electronic and print media, especially the foreign media disseminated in
Ireland via satellite television or imported press. These findings would also
question the other forms of racialist propaganda in relation to the "Black
Americans" originating from Irish immigrants in the United States. Whatever the source or the cause, the findings merit some study and, hopefully,
action which would lead to an improvement of image for "Black
Americans" in Ireland. The United States' Embassy in Ireland might assist
in countering the above level of prejudice against its citizens.

Another group which is out of line in relation to the severity of prejudice
against them are the "Pakistanis". When compared with the "Indians",
their neighbours in the Asian continent there is a significantly lower
preference for Pakistanis (Table 42).

TABLE No. 42
SOCIAL DISTANCE TOWARDS PAKISTANI, INDIANS AND COLOUREDS

LEVEL OF SOCIAL DISTANCE	A. Pakistani	B. Indians	C. Coloureds	A-B	A-C
1. Welcome into the family	24.2%	31.0%	34.3%	-6.8%	-10.1%
2. Have as a close friend or closer	42.6%	49.6%	58.9%	-7.0%	-16.3%
3. Have as a next-door neighbour or closer	54.7%	60.9%	71.4%	-6.2%	-16.7%
4. Have as a co-worker or closer	67.2%	72.8%	81.2%	-5.6%	-13.0%
5. Welcome as an Irish citizen or closer	73.9%	78.8%	85.2%	-4.9%	-11.3%
6. Welcome as a visitor only	22.4%	17.7%	12.5%	+4.7%	+9.9%
7. Debar or deport	3.5%	3.6%	2.4%	-0.1 %	+1.1%
Mean Social Distance	3.404	3.108	2.715	+0.296	+0.689

In the so-called racial perception, "Pakistani" would be classified as "coloured". Their presence in Ireland is relatively small in density but they are industrious and have played a positive role, mainly in Dublin society. Yet the public attitudes towards them are more negative than towards "coloureds" or towards "Indians". The relatively negative response towards Moslems (Mean Social Distance = 3.420) and the high correlation (Pearson Product-Moment Correlation) of r = 0.76 between the Pakistani and Moslem social-distance responses points to a causal link between the standing of both categories. So that each category's status can improve it will be necessary for better dialogue with and education about, Moslems and Pakistani people in Ireland. Surprisingly, in the light of the high correlation noted above between responses between "Pakistani" and "Moslems", there was a very small percentage (6.8%) giving "Religious Beliefs and Practices" as a rationalisation for refusing to welcome "Pakistani" into the family (see Table 43 below). Without Christian/Moslem ecumenical action our negative attitudes could continue, reinforced by stereotypical reports and images imported through the electronic media and cheaper foreign print. What is said here about Moslems and Pakistanis equally applies to many other categories suffering from vicariously adopted prejudices from other societies.

Before concluding the commentary on the social distance findings in relation to eight racial categories, it is well to remind the reader that the position may be negative and problematic in regard to Irish racialism but it is considerably better than it was in 1972-73. Table 38 (p. 144 above). This commentary does not exhaust the findings. The reader can examine the data and come to further interpretative conclusions. The tables are presented in as detailed a manner as is possible to facilitate further reflection on the sociological, psychological and political implications of the findings.

4. CHANGES IN INTERGROUP DEFINITION

It has been noted already above that there has been a change in the Irish people's definition of the eight racial groups since the 1972-73 survey. The nature of this change is yet further evidence of a modest but significant decline in strictly racialist attitudes. Table 43 measures the extent and direction of this change.

Intergroup definition is obtained by asking respondents for their principal reason for not admitting members of a category to closer level of social distance. This question was only asked of those not welcoming members of the category into the family through marriage or kinship. Six possible reasons were suggested, from which they would select one or name another not on the list, as their major reason for excluding members from kinship or other levels of closeness. It is held that the reason given would tell how the respondent viewed the category, i.e., its principal defining characteristic.

Table 43 gives a detailed breakdown of the reasons given for refusing a closer relationship with members of each of the racial categories by Dublin

respondents not admitting or welcoming them to kinship. The six reasons
given were:

(a) "Religious beliefs and/or practices";
(b) "Racial – colour of skin, etc.";
(c) "Political views and/or methods";
(d) "Ethnic, i.e. 'Nationality and Culture' and 'Way of Life' ";
(e) "Economic danger to us"; and
(f) "Not socially acceptable".

The percentages of the 1972-73 and the 1988-89 surveys are given so as
to measure the degree and direction of changes in intergroup perception

TABLE No. 43
COMPARISON OF RACIAL RATIONALISATIONS 1988-89 AND 1972-73

		Rel. (a)	Rac. (b)	Pol.	Ethn (c)	Econ (d)	Soc. (e)	Other (f)	N.
Coloureds	1972/73	3.3	57.2	0.7	28.6	1.8	7.7	0.7	1687
	1988/89	1.9	48.1	1.3	44.2	-	3.2	1.3	156
	Change	-1.4	-9.1	+0.6	+ 15.6	- 1.8	-4.5	+0.6	
Africans	1972/73	5.3	51.7	0.7	31.2	1.7	8.6	0.7	1783
	1988/89	6.4	36.2	2.4	52.6	1.2	0.6	0.6	171
	Change	+1.1	-15.5	+1.7	+21.4	-0.5	-8.0	-0.1	
Chinese	1972/73	4.0	46.7	2.2	37.4	1.8	6.5	1.4	1691
	1988/89	4.7	28.4	1.8	60.4	1.8	1.2	1.8	169
	Change	-0.7	-18.3	-0.4	+23.0	-	-5.3	+0.4	
Blacks	1972/73	3.8	56.5	0.7	28.3	1.7	8.3	0.8	1785
	1988/89	2.4	46.5	1.2	45.3	0.6	2.9	1.2	170
	Change	-1.4	-10.0	+0.5	+17.1	-1.1	-5.4	+0.4	
Non-American Indians	1972/73	3.6	44.7	0.8	40.2	1.4	8.4	0.9	1598
	1988/89	11.8	19.9	4.3	60.9	0.6	1.2	1.2	161
	Change	+8.2	-24.8	+3.5	+20.7	-0.8	-7.2	+0.3	
Nigerians	1972/73	4.0	52.1	0.7	32.5	1.3	8.7	0.7	1752
	1988/89	4.8	38.0	1.8	53.0	0.6	-	1.8	166
	Change	+0.8	- 14.1	+1.1	+20.5	-0.7	-8.7	+1.1	
Black Americans	1972/73	3.9	53.0	1.3	30.5	1.9	8.9	0.6	1783
	1988/89	3.3	38.7	1.1	51.9	1.1	2.8	1.1	181
	Change	-0.6	-14.3	-0.2	+21.4	-0.8	-6.1	+0.5	
Pakistanis	1972/73	3.5	46.6	2.2	35.8	2.0	9.1	0.9	1708
	1988/89	6.8	30.5	0.5	58.4	1.0	1.5	1.0	190
	Change	+3.3	-16.1	-1.7	+22.6	-1.0	-7.6	+0.1	
Average Change for Scale		+1.3	-15.3	+0.6	+20.2	-0.8	-6.6	+0.4	-

which have taken place in the intervening sixteen years. The results are very striking in a relatively short time-span. The real value of this information is that it gives an insight into how each of these categories is perceived by those prejudiced against them. With such information available, anti-racialist supporters can adopt strategies more likely to be effective in reducing further this area of irrational bias. It also reflects the manner that negative stereotyping against racial groups in the print and electronic media is aiding and reinforcing racialist prejudice in Irish society.

The major change which has taken place is the reduction of "*racial, i.e., colour of skin, etc.*" as a main reason given for not having a closer social distance and a corresponding increase in "*ethnic, i.e., nationality and culture and way of life*" as a reason. The average drop of "racial" definition for the eight categories was -15.3%, i.e., from 51.1% in 1972-73 to 35.8% in 1988-89, while the average increase in "ethnic" definition was +20.2%, i.e., from 33.1% in 1972-73 to 53.3 in 1988-89. A drop of 15.3% from 51.1% constitutes a decline of 29.5% in racial rationalisation and an increase of 20.3% from 33.1% equals a change of +61.0% in ethnic definition. This is one of the clearest indicators of a decline in racialism in Irish prejudice, which is something to be welcomed. This finding clearly reinforces and confirms the finding of the social distance scale (Table 6, p. 71 above) and of the racialist scale (Table 33, p. 133 above).

The conceptually ethnic categories, i.e., "Africans", "Chinese", "Indians", "Nigerians", "Black Americans" and "Pakistanis" are perceived to be more "ethnic" (on average) at 57.9% than the conceptual racial categories, i.e., "Coloureds" and "Blacks" (on average) at 44.8%. This was to be expected. In fact, the strong "ethnic" definitions of both "Blacks" and "Coloureds" is in line with the "Black Americans" move to redefine themselves in ethnic terms, i.e., Afro-Americans. A similar movement is also taking place in Britain. Since "ethnic" is a more human and non-biologically determined category, such moves among Black minorities being defined less as "racial" are to be welcomed, provided it does not give cultural quality to "race" itself which would be a retrograde development. This, in itself, does not remove prejudice since ethnic hatred, as we see in former Yugoslavia, can be most destructive. What is more hopeful in the case of Irish attitudes towards racial categories has been evidence of a significant and moderately substantial reduction in prejudice *as well as* a welcome shift away from the classification of people on the basis of a non-cultural characteristic such as racial features.

CHAPTER VI

Religious Practice in Ireland

INTRODUCTION

The following two chapters present and examines the findings of religious practice and attitudes among a representative national sample of the adult population of the Republic of Ireland. Some of the 1988/89 findings will be compared with those of a similar survey carried out in the Greater Dublin area during 1972/73.

The questions on religion were part of an extended interview questionnaire. A comparison between the distribution of some personal variables with those of the relevant age cohort in the Census of Population Report (1986 Census) has confirmed the representative validity of the sample interviewed.

The main aim of these chapters is to present the findings of the survey in such a way as to be of special interest to two groups: firstly, readers whose primary concerns are related to pastoral, spiritual and theological implications of religious practices and attitudes; and secondly, those who are interested in the anthropological and sociological aspects of patterned religious practices and shared religious attitudes. The areas of religious practice measured and the indicators chosen to measure attitudes are, of necessity, limited and selective. It is hoped, nevertheless, that such limitations will not distort the overall findings nor hinder valid and reliable assessment of the current situation. Most of the measures used are replicated from previous research in the field. A number of new scales are used for the first time to measure certain religious attitudes in Ireland.

Three general areas are covered in this chapter:

(a) Demographic profile of religious affiliation in Ireland;
(b) Church attendance and practice;
(c) Religion in the personal life of the people.

PART I: DEMOGRAPHIC PROFILE OF RELIGIOUS AFFILIATION

The tables in this part give a statistical profile of the sample by religious affiliation. It should be noted that the population surveyed is taken from the 1988 register of electors and covers adults over 18 years of age resident in the Republic of Ireland.

It is very clear from the above distribution that (Table 44) the population of the Republic is predominantly Roman Catholic at 94.2%, while the total proportion of the other Christian denominations is less than 5% (4.3%) of the sample. The proportion of the sample who declare "no religion" is extremely small (1.1%). Therefore, the sample is very much a religiously "professing" one. The similarity with the Census distribution (*Statistical Abstract 1988* p.50) for 1981 points to the representative quality of the sample interviewed.

TABLE No. 44
RELIGIOUS AFFILIATION OF SAMPLE

Religious Affiliation	1988/89 Total Sample	1981 ** Census of Pop.	Difference
1. Roman Catholics	94.2%	95.02%	-0.82%
2. C of I/Methodists/ Presbyterians *	4.0%	3.42%	+0.58%
3. Other Christians	0.3%	0.38%	+0.32%
4. Other Religions	0.4%		
5. No Religion	1.1%	1.17%	-0.07%
	N = 1004	N = 3,372,429 ***	

* Church of Ireland = 3.4%; Methodists/Presbyterians = 0.6%
** Source: Statistical Abstract 1988
*** A further 70,976 did not supply information on religion (see Table 45 below)

The relative stability of the proportionate distribution of the religious denominations in the Republic since the 1926 Census is given in Table 45. This table also highlights the proportionate decline in the number of Protestants in the Republic after Independence in 1921.

The most significant change in the proportionate distribution of denominations over a period of 120 years took place between 1911 and 1926. The proportionate decline in the Protestant population may have been due to a number of factors, i.e. particularly heavy Protestant casualties during World War I (1914-18), out-migration of Protestants to Northern Ireland and elsewhere, and the withdrawal of British Army garrisons in 1921.

Since 1926, the proportion of the population declaring themselves as Roman Catholic has not changed significantly. This would seem to refute the view that the Roman Catholic denomination benefited from the decline of other denominations. The very small increase in the Roman Catholic proportion and a similar decline in the Protestant percentage is within margins of error. This is also true of shifts in the other two categories. Perhaps one should not expect much variation in a society with high out-migration. If Ireland should become a society with an immigration influx of citizens, a shift in denominational spread would probably occur. As in the case of Tables 44 and 45, the relatively small percentage who declared they had "no religion" (2% or less) is indicative of the widespread importance of religion as part of the Irish person's self-identity.

TABLE No. 45
RELIGIOUS COMPOSITION OF THE REPUBLIC OF IRELAND 1861-1981 (%)

Year	Population	Roman Catholic %	Church of Ireland %	Presby- terian %	Metho- dist %	Jewish %	Other Religion %	No Religion %	No Information %
1861	4,402,111	89.4	8.5	1.5	0.4	0.008	0.22		
1871	4,053,187	89.2	8.4	1.5	0.4	0.006	0.42		
1881	3,870,020	89.5	8.2	1.5	0.5	0.001	0.32		
1891	3,468,694	89.3	8.3	1.5	0.5	0.004	0.33		
1901	3,221,823	89.3	8.2	1.5	0.6	0.09	0.36		
1911	3,139,688	89.6	7.9	1.4	0.5	0.12	0.38		
1926	2,971,992	92.6	5.5	1.1	0.4	0.12	0.33		
1936	2,968,420	93.4	4.9	0.9	0.3	0.13	0.27		
1946	2,955,107	94.3	4.2	0.8	0.3	0.13	0.27		
1961	2,818,341	94.9	3.7	0.7	0.2	0.12	0.19	0.04	0.20
1971	2,978,248	92.4	3.3	0.5	0.2	0.09	0.21	0.26	1.57
1981	3,443,405	93.1	2.8	0.4	0.2	0.06	0.31	1.15	2.06

Source: Statistical Abstract (Ireland) 1959, 1966, 1988.

TABLE No. 46
AFFILIATION DISTRIBUTION OF DUBLIN SUB-SAMPLE 1988/9 AND OF
DUBLIN SAMPLE 1972/3

Religious Affiliation	1988/9 Sub-Sample 18 yrs + A	1972/3 Sample 21 yrs + (Mac Greil) B	Change (A-B)
1. Roman Catholics	92.1%	91.0%	+1.1%
2. C of I/Methodists Presbyterians	4.7%	5.9%	-1.2%
3. Other Believers	1.2%	1.7%	-0.5%
4. No Religion	2.0%	1.4%	+0.6%
	N = 256	N = 2311	

The question of intergenerational change among members of the sample is statistically not significant and falls well within the margins of error.

TABLE No. 47
INTERGENERATIONAL CHANGE OF RELIGIOUS AFFILIATION

Religious Affiliation	Self	Father	Mother
1. Roman Catholics	94.2%	94.1%	93.9%
2. C of I/Methodists Presbyterians	4.0%	3.1%	3.7%
3. Other Believers	0.7%	0.7%	0.5%
4. No Religion	1.1%	0.1%	0.1%
	N = 1004	N = 999	N = 997

The intergenerational stability of distribution is very clear. Because of the smallness of the percentages, it would not be justified (scientifically) to give much emphasis to the one percent shift from denominations to "No Religion".

Tables nos. 44 to 47 above give a statistical profile of religious affiliation in the Republic of Ireland, and clarify how little change has taken place over the past sixty years. In the opinion of the present writer, this is indicative of two main factors, i.e. the strong place of religion in Irish self-identity, and the fact that, for the past 130 years, there has been a more-or-less continuous out-migration of population resulting in the absence of any inflow of new religious groupings. The last such inflow took place in the 17th Century. It may also be indicative of a significant degree of denominational tolerance or pluralism since the foundation of the State. Probably the higher fertility of the Roman Catholics has been neutralised by relatively higher emigration of Roman Catholic young adults over the period.

PART II: CHURCH ATTENDANCE AND LITURGICAL PRACTICE

Church membership (in the sociological sense) may be measured by the following:

(a) Participation in religious activity;
(b) Commitment to the religious beliefs and norms;
(c) Acceptance by co-believers;
(d) Formal registration of membership.

In this part it is proposed to measure (a) and (b). It is assumed that those who indicated or declared their membership of a particular denomination had undergone the formal rituals of incorporation, i.e. Baptism etc. which would satisfy criterion (d) above. The absence of evidence of "excommunication" would indicate general acceptance by co-believers of members of the various religious groups.

Part III of this chapter will attempt an assessment of the level of commitment and internalisation of beliefs and norms of the sample. In this section, participation in Church activity will focus mainly on participation in various forms of worship and sacramental life. Because of the statistical predominance of Roman Catholics, examination by subsamples (independent variables) will concern the practices of Roman Catholics only.

1. PARTICIPATION OF OVERALL SAMPLE:

The measures of participation will include formal attendance at Church Service or equivalent, Mass, Holy Communion and Confessions. Respondents were asked "How often did you attend?". They were asked to

TABLE No. 48
ATTENDANCE OF TOTAL SAMPLE AT FORMAL RELIGIOUS WORSHIP

FREQUENCY	Total Sample	Roman Catholics*
1. Daily	6.4%	6.5%
2. Several times a week	10.2% (16.6%)	8.1% (14.6%)
3. At least once a week	62.7% (79.3%)	67.0% (81.6%)
4. 1-3 times a month	5.8% (85.1%)	5.6% (87.2%)
5. Several times a year	5.9% (91-0%)	6.5% (93 7%)
6. Less frequently	5.1% (96.1%)	3.7% (97.4%)
7. Never	3.9%	2.5%
	N = 1000	N = 943

* Mass Attendance.
NOTE: Cumulative totals in brackets ( )

indicate the degree of frequency on a seven point scale from "Daily" to "Never". Table 48 gives a breakdown of the Total Sample. Reported measures of prayer are given below in Part III (see Table 64, p. 181).

TABLE NO. 49
REASONS FOR NOT ATTENDING MORE THAN "AT LEAST ONCE A WEEK"

REASON	Sub-Sample	(Percentage of Total Sample)
1. Just don't bother	62%	(10.9%)
2. Working	10%	(1.8%)
3. Complaint about Faith	7%	(1.2%)
4. Ill	6%	(1.1%)
5. Distance from place of worship	3%	(0.5%)
6. Other Reasons	12%	(2.2%)
	N= 179	(17.7%)

The findings of Tables 48 and 49 clearly show there is a relatively high level of regular participation in formal religious worship throughout the Republic of Ireland. The percentage who said they never attended formal worship (3.9% for the total sample) or do so less frequently than several times a year (5.1%) constitute only 9% of the sample.

Indifference is the biggest single reason for less frequent (less than once a week) attendance at formal worship. If one were to take those who stated they were unable to attend due to illness, to long distance from place of worship (which is particularly true of isolated rural Protestants in parts of Ireland) and to work, from those not attending more frequently, the proportion of "voluntary absentees" from weekly worship would be reduced to 14.3% of the total sample. Complaints about the Liturgy as a reason for not going frequently were given by only two respondents, i.e. 0.2% of the total sample or 1.1% of those not attending frequently. Perhaps the level of indifference may point to the failure to relate Liturgy to life and could be interpreted as an indirect critique of forms of worship.

The difference between the frequency of worship of Roman Catholics and Protestants is given in Table 50. (The numbers were too small in "other categories" for inclusion).

The frequency of participation in formal worship is significantly higher for Roman Catholics than it is for members of the Protestant Churches. This is probably explained in part by the difference in the norms prescribed by the churches in relation to participation. Roman Catholics have the obligatory sabbath norm. Should a convergence of the two norms take place, the level of expected frequency would be in Category 2, i.e. "1-3 times a month or more". Even at that level there is a significant difference between Roman Catholics and Protestants.

TABLE No. 50
ATTENDANCE AT FORMAL WORSHIP BY DENOMINATION

FREQUENCY	Total Sample	Roman Catholic	C of I/Meth/ Presbyterian	Difference
1. Weekly or more	79%	82%	55%	-27%
2. 1-3 times a month or more	85%	88%	70%	-18%
3. Several times a year or more	91%	94%	80%	-14%
4. Less often or never*	9%	6%	20%	+14%
	N = 1000	N = 944	N = 40	

*'Less often' and 'Never' had to be merged due to the small number of cases in each category.

2. ROMAN CATHOLIC PARTICIPATION

Levels of participation in Mass and in the Sacraments are generally accepted as basic measures of active Church membership. Involvement in various forms of pastoral and evangelising activity is also an important criterion. Unfortunately, it has not been possible to measure such involvement in the research on which this report is based. Measures of reported frequency of "prayer" in the normal life of the respondents will be given below as an indication of the personal (private) participation in recognised religious/spiritual activity (see Table 64). Prayer is considered to be an important manifestation of the faith and acceptance of Church/religious teaching about the "personal nature" of the Divine.

Table 51 gives the frequency of participation of the Roman Catholic sub-sample in Mass, Holy Communion and Sacramental Confession.

It is difficult for a sociologist to comment on the above findings without revealing a normative viewpoint. In the view of the present writer, Table 51 records a very positive level of liturgical and sacramental participation of the Roman Catholic adult population (as represented by the respondents). The officially sanctioned norm of participation, "as laid down" by Church Law, is weekly attendance at Mass and "worthy reception" of Holy Communion at least once annually. Roman Catholics are obliged (according to the norms of their Church) to confess their "serious sins" in Confession at least once a year. (Of course, those without serious sin are not so obliged.) These are the minimum levels of practice. The recommended levels are much higher. Monthly or more frequent reception of Holy Communion and

Sacramental Confession several times a year would be recommended in practice.

TABLE No. 51

MASS, HOLY COMMUNION AND CONFESSION PARTICIPATION BY
ROMAN CATHOLICS

FREQUENCY	Mass		Holy Communion		Sacramental Confession	
1. Daily	6.5%		5.5%		–	
2. Several times a week	8.1%	(14.6%)*	6.7%	(12.2%)	–	
3. Once a week	67.0%	**(81.6%)**	30.5%	(42.7%)	1.8%	–
4. 1-3 times a month	5.6%	(87.2%)	20.1%	**(62.8%)**	16.3	(18.1%)*
5. Several times a year	6.5%	(93.7%)	17.3%	(80.1%)	35.5%	**(53.6%)**
6. Less often	3.7%	(97.4%)	14.0%	(94 1%)	35.1%	(88.7%)
7. Never	2.5%		5.7%		11.0%	
	N = 943		N = 941		N = 941	

*Cumulative percentage in brackets, and recommended levels in bold.

The levels of "Never" or no-participation, i.e. 2.5% for Mass, 5.7% for Holy Communion and 11% for Sacramental Confessions, are relatively low but would seem to be in harmony with the distribution curve of each area of participation, namely, participation is lowest for Confessions and highest for Mass. The "Less Often" category in the case of Mass Attendance could well be persons in transition (either way) between "never" and higher participation.

Finally, before concluding from or interpreting the findings of participation as indicative of the level of Church membership, it may be necessary to discover the degree to which certain sections of the Roman Catholic population accept fully the prescribed norms of participation. This will become a more important question as the population is exposed to a diversity of worship norms, via the mass media and other contacts.

3. PARTICIPATION BY PERSONAL VARIABLES:

3.1 Mass Attendance:

The following tables examine participation in formal worship (of Roman Catholics) by "age", "gender", "marital status", "area of rearing", "place of residence", "education" and "occupation". Table 52 gives a breakdown of Mass attendance. Gender, marital status, education or occupation did not record statistically significant variations.

Age as a variable has shown a positive correlation with Mass attendance. It is, however, a J curve in that the youngest age category (18 – 20 years old) records a higher level of participation than do the 21 to 35 years old sub-sample. This pattern will repeat itself in a number of indices of participation

tion i.e. Reception of Holy Communion (Table 53) and Frequency of Sacramental Confessions (Table 54).

TABLE No. 52

MASS ATTENCDANCE (OF ROMAN CATHOLICS) BY AGE, AREA OF REARING AND COUNTY OF RESIDENCE

PERSONAL VARIABLE	Weekly or more often	1-3 times a month or more often	Several times a year or more often	Less often or never	No.
A. AGE (P≤.001)*					
1. 18 - 20 years	78%	84%	98%	2%	55
2. 21 - 35 years	71%	81%	92%	8%	320
3. 36 - 50 years	86%	90%	94%	6%	246
4. 51 yrs +	90%	92%	95%	5%	319
B. AREA OF REARING (P≤.001)+					
1. Large City (100,000+)	64%	73%	87%	13%	203
2. Small City (10,000+)	77%	87%	91%	9%	106
3. Town (1,500+)	86%	90%	94%	6%	142
4. Rural (under 1,499)	89%	92%	97%	3%	487
C. COUNTY OF RESIDENCE (P≤.001)*					
1. Dublin (Co. and City)	69%	76%	90%	10%	251
2. Rest of Leinster	78%	86%	93%	7%	238
3. Munster	90%	93%	97%	3%	286
4 Connaught/Ulster	92%	95%	96%	4%	166
TOTAL SAMPLE	82%	87%	94%	6%	941

Chi Square Scores
P≤.05 means 'probability of variation due to chance is less than one in twenty'.
P≥.001 means 'probability of variation due to chance is less than one in a thousand'.

"Area of rearing" and "county of residence" clearly indicate the negative effect of urbanisation on formal religious practice. The slightly higher percentage of weekly Mass attendance of those living in Dublin over those reared in a large city (Dublin being Ireland's major city) reflects the impact of in-migration into Dublin of those from the provinces. The 64% "weekly or more often" of those reared in a large city is the lowest percentage (18% below the national average) recorded by any subsample and probably reveals the strongest factor causing decline in Church attendance.

The implications of these findings merit further serious analysis and attention The disparity of the "large city reared" subsample is also maintained at the "1-3 times a month or more often" (14% below the national average). The weekly Mass attendance differences between Dublin (69%), the Rest of Leinster (78%) and Munster/Connaught/Ulster (91%) indicate significant geographic variations which are not wholly explained by urbanisation, apart from the Dublin factor. It should be noted that there are three strongly urbanised centres in Munster, i.e. Cork City, Limerick/Ennis/Shannon, and Waterford City. Yet, these centres do not seem to have resulted in a significant reduction in weekly Church attendances.

Figure 8: Weekly and Monthly Mass attendance by age, area of rearing and county of residence (Roman Catholics)

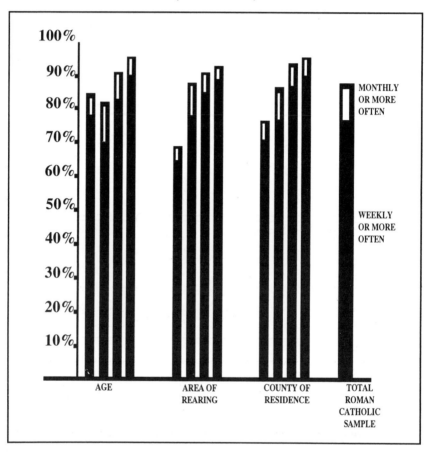

3.2 Reception of Holy Communion:

Frequent reception of Holy Communion at Mass has been promoted in the Roman Catholic Church since the time of St Pius X during the early years of this Century. Almost two-thirds (63%) of the Roman Catholics in the sample have stated that they received Holy Communion once a month. At the same time, slightly less than half (49%) of those attending Mass every Sunday do not receive Holy Communion once a week or more often.

Table 53 gives a breakdown of the frequency of reception of Holy Communion by a number of personal variables which record statistically significant variations. Figure 9 graphically illustrates the range of differences between the subsamples of each personal variable.

TABLE No. 53
RECEPTION OF HOLY COMMUNION BY PERSONAL VARIABLES

PERSONAL VARIABLE	Weekly or more often	1-3 times a month or more	Several times a year or more	Less often or never	No.
A. AGE (P≤.001)					
1. 18 - 20 years	38%	64%	78%	22%	55
2. 21 - 35 years	30%	51%	70%	30%	320
3. 36 - 50 years	44%	63%	82%	18%	246
4. 51 years +	56%	75%	90%	10%	319
B. GENDER (P≤.001)					
1. Females	55%	75%	86%	14%	518
2. Males	28%	49%	73%	27%	423
C. MARITAL STATUS (P≤.001)					
1. Never Married	38%	58%	78%	22%	271
2. Married	44%	63%	81%	19%	583
3. Widowed	65%	90%	94%	6%	68
D. AREA OF REARING (P≤.001)					
1. Large City (100,000 +)	34%	51 %	71 %	29%	203
2. Small City (10,000 +)	43%	59%	75%	25%	106
3. Town (1,500 +)	39%	64%	82%	18%	142
4. Rural (under 1,500)	48%	68%	85%	15%	487
E. PLACE OF RESIDENCE (P≤.001)					
1. Dublin (Co. and City)	40%	57%	73%	27%	251
2. Rest of Leinster	36%	60%	78%	22%	238
3. Munster	43%	64%	84%	16%	286
4. Connaught/Ulster	56%	75%	89%	11%	166
F. EDUCATION (P<.001)					
1. Primary	45%	66%	85%	15%	272
2. Incomplete Second Level	36%	57%	78%	22%	328
3. Complete Second Level	46%	67%	80%	20%	218
4. Third Level	50%	66%	77%	23%	123
G. OCCUPATION (P≤.001)					
1. Unskilled/Semi-Skilled	39%	61%	81%	19%	268
2. Skilled/Routine Non-Manual	30%	52%	75%	25%	154
3. Inspectional/Supervisory	39%	60%	78%	22%	278
4. Professional/Executive	58%	71%	84%	16%	241
TOTAL SAMPLE	43%	63%	80%	20%	941

Figure No. 9: Reception of Holy Communion by age, gender, martial status, area of rearing, place of residence, education and occupation (Roman Catholics)

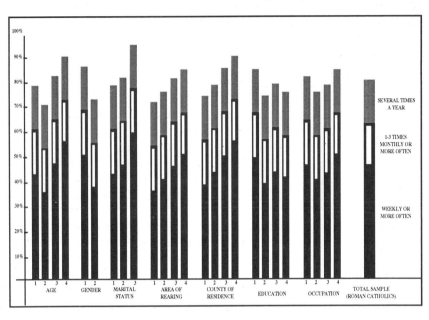

The patterns of response by "age", "area of rearing" and "county of residence" in Table 53 and in Figure 9 correspond more or less to those of Mass Attendance in Table 52 and Figure 8. The disparity between the frequencies of females and males is very substantial. The rate of weekly Communion of males is just half that of females (28% as compared with 55%). The participation rates of widowed respondents are the highest of all the subsamples. With regard to reception of Holy Communion by educational standard reached, there are a number of interesting anomalies. Some 65% of those with third level education who receive Holy Communion "several times a year or more often" (77% of the subsample) do so "once weekly or more often". In the case of respondents with only primary education, the proportion receiving Holy Communion weekly or more often is 51% of those going several times a year or more often (88% of the subsample). The comparative position of "incomplete second level" and "complete second level" is 46% and 58% respectively. In other words a higher proportion of those in the higher levels of education are more frequent receivers. This seems to indicate that those with lower education are more reluctant to receive Holy Communion every time they attend Mass than their more educated neighbours. The reasons for such reluctance have not been researched in this survey. The weakest overall performance by education is by the "incomplete second level" subsample.

The patterns of response by "occupation" mirrors that of "education" with the notable exception of the higher frequency of reception of Holy Communion by those in the top occupations than by those with higher (3rd level) education (see Figure 9). The two middle subsamples register the relatively lowest rates of reception. Again, these patterns merit pastoral analysis.

3.3 Frequency of Sacramental Confession:

Going to Sacramental Confession is part of the normal practice expected of Roman Catholics. Table 51 gives a breakdown of the Roman Catholic sample. Slightly less than one-fifth (18%) stated they went to Confession once a month or more often. Over half of the sample (54%) went "several times a year" while a further 35% stated they went less frequently. Some 11% stated they "never" went to Sacramental Confession. It is clear from this that the use of Confession as a devotional practice, i.e. monthly or more frequently, is very much a minority norm today among Roman Catholics. The "several times a year" probably means going to Confession for Christmas, Easter or on some other occasion such as "Stations" or Neighbourhood Masses, or during the "Parish Mission". Going to Confession has also become a feature of participation in pilgrimage at Knock Shrine, on Croagh Patrick, in Lough Derg and at other shrines. The "Less Often" category includes those who confess once a year.

Table 54 gives some very interesting findings in relation to variations in practice. Such differences are evident from a glance at Figure 10 which graphically illustrates the distribution by age, gender, marital status, place of residence and education.

The twenty-one to thirty-five years subsample are those with the lowest participation by *age*. Some 18% stated that they had given up going to Sacramental Confession. The reported practice of respondents over 50 years of age was very high. While 18 to 20 years old respondents' frequency patterns are low, they are not as low as the 21 to 35 years category in "monthly" practice and in relation to those still going to Confession, i.e. only 6% reported giving up the practice altogether.

The "gender" and "marital status" variables record significant variations. Males are less frequent participants than are females. The extent of the differences between the practice of females and of males, while significant, is not very substantial, unlike that of frequency of reception of Holy Communion (see Table 53, Figure 8).

The clear effect of urbanisation on the practice of Sacramental Confession is very clear in the "county of residence" variable. The percentage of those from "large cities" who no longer go to Confession is 20%, while over 10% go monthly or more often. "Town" and "rural" respondents have the highest practice while "small cities" (1,500 to 9,999) is in between these two categories and the "large city" dwellers.

TABLE No. 54
FREQUENCY OF SACRAMENTAL CONFESSION (OF ROMAN CATHOLICS) BY
PERSONAL VARIABLES

PERSONAL VARIABLE	Once a month or more often	Several times a year or more often	Less often	Never	No.
A. AGE (P≤.001)					
1. 18 - 20 years	15%	35%	60% (94%)*	6%	55
2. 21 - 35 years	8%	38%	44% (82%)	18%	321
3. 36 - 50 years	13%	50%	41% (91%)	10%	246
4. 51 years +	32%	76%	18% (94%)	6%	319
B. GENDER (P≤.00 1)					
1. Females	22%	58%	33% (91%)	9%	518
2. Males	14%	49%	38% (87%)	13%	423
C. MARITAL STATUS (P≤.001)					
1. Never Married	18%	52%	39% (90%)	10%	270
2. Married	16%	52%	36% (88%)	12%	585
3. Widowed	40%	84%	10% (94%)	6%	67
D. COUNTY OF RESIDENCE (P≤.001)					
1. Large City (100,000 +)	10%	40%	40% (80%)	20%	264
2. Small City (10,000 +)	19%	49%	38% (86%)	14%	81
3. Town (1,500 +)	26%	64%	25% (89%)	11%	122
4. Rural (under 1,500)	21%	60%	35% (95%)	6%	474
E. EDUCATION (P≤.001)					
1. Primary	27%	67%	26% (93%)	7%	272
2. Incomplete Second Level	16%	54%	35% (94%)	6%	330
3. Complete Second Level	13%	45%	44% (89%)	11%	216
4. Third Level	15%	39%	42% (81%)	19%	123
TOTAL SAMPLE (Roman Catholics)	18%	55%	35%	11%	941

*Cumulative percentages in brackets.

The differences in the "education" subsamples are significant and quite substantial. There is a clearly negative correlation between educational standard reached and reported frequency of going to Sacramental Confession.

It should be noted that the difference of frequency between Holy Communion and that of "Going to Confession" (see Table 51) is quite noteworthy. The frequency ratio at the monthly level is 62:18 or 3.4 to 1. The old practice of going to Holy Communion only after having confessed one's sins the "evening before" has been greatly modified according to the above findings.

The pastoral implications of the levels of participation appear to be serious, especially for those dealing with the urban, young, male and third level educated people.

Figure No. 10: Frequency of Sacramental Confession by age, gender, marital status, county of residence and education (Roman Catholics)

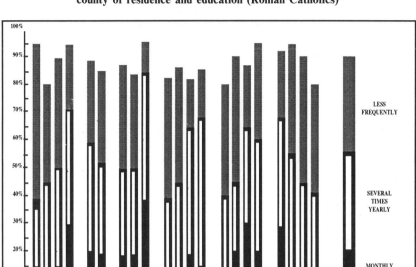

3.4 Conclusion:

The overall picture emerging from the above tables (52, 53 and 54) and figures (8, 9 and 10) shows a clear and consistent pattern among the three practices measured i.e. Mass, Holy Communion and Confession, in relation to the major personal variables. Young middle-aged (21 – 35 years old) males, never married, city reared, Dublin dwellers, skilled and routine non-manual workers and those with incomplete second level education are the subsamples recording the lowest practice frequencies in at least two of the three measures.

In the case of Sacramental Confession, those with third level education were significantly and substantially lower than respondents with lesser educational experience. This latter change of pattern raises special issues for pastoral leaders.

4. CHANGES IN LITURGICAL PRACTICE SINCE 1974:

The following Table (55) shows the trends in frequency of Mass attendance, of reception of Holy Communion and of going to Sacramental Confessions since 1974. Máire Nic Ghiolla Phádraig's findings of 1974 and Breslin and Weafer's findings of 1984 are compared with those of the current survey (1988/89).

TABLE No. 55
FREQUENCY OF SACRAMENTAL PRACTICE OF
ROMAN CATHOLICS (REPUBLIC OF IRELAND) 1974, 1984 AND 1988/9

| | 1974* | 1984** | 1988/9 | Differences | | |
	A	B	C	A-B (10 yrs)	B-C (5 yrs)	A-C (15 yrs)
1. Weekly Mass Attendance	91%	87%	82%	-4%	-5%	-9%
2a. Weekly Holy Communion	28%	38%	43%	+10%	+5%	+15%
2b. Monthly Holy Communion	66%	64%	63%	-2%	-1%	-3 %
3. Monthly Confession	47%	26%	18%	-21%	-8%	-29%
	N = 2499	N = 1006	N = 1005			

* Nic Ghiolla Phadraig, Dublin, Research and Development Unit of Irish Catholic Church.
** Breslin A. and Weafer J.A., Maynooth, Research and Development Unit of Irish Catholic Church.

The decline of 9% in (national) weekly Mass attendance over a period of fifteen years is significant but not very substantial, i.e. less than 1% per annum. It should be noted, nevertheless, that during the period 1984-1989 the rate of annual decline has reached 1% per annum, which is more than twice the annual decline of 0.4% per annum during the period 1974-84.

The frequency of monthly reception of Holy Communion has remained substantially the same over the fifteen years 1974-1989. The decline of 3% is hardly statistically significant due to the expected margins of error of each survey. The very substantial increase in the frequency of weekly reception of Holy Communion since 1974, i.e. at 1% per annum, clearly indicates a change in the level of participation of those going to Mass. The extent of the increase (15%) in weekly reception of Holy Communion is significantly higher than the decline (-9%) of weekly Mass attendance over the fifteen years 1974-1989.

There has been quite a dramatic decline in the frequency of going to Sacramental Confession at least monthly. The decline of 29% over the period represents an annual drop of almost 2% (1.9%). The figures show a slight reduction in the annual rate of decline from 2.1% per annum during the period 1974 to 1984 to 1.6% per annum during the period 1984 to 1988/9. Such a rate of decline clearly indicates a change of norm among Roman Catholics in the Republic of Ireland in relation to the practice of Sacramental Confession. The norm of monthly Confession had been reinforced by the "confraternities" and "monthly sodalities" in the parishes, which were centred around the practices of monthly Confession and monthly Holy Communion. Over the past twenty-five or thirty years most "confraternities" and "sodalities" have been discontinued. It should also be noted that the pastoral understanding of "Sacramental Confession" seems to have changed, leading to less frequent practice. The practice of Sacramental Confession has been a strong characteristic of Irish Roman Catholicism. Its decline, therefore, merits serious theological and pastoral examination and reflection.

Figure No. 11: Frequency of Sacramental Practice of Roman Catholics (Republic of Ireland) from 1974 until 1988/9

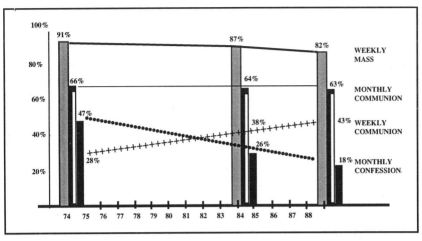

PART III: RELIGION IN THE LIFE OF THE PEOPLE

The place of religion in the "life of the people" has been measured under a number of headings:

(a) Perceived influence of religion of rearing in the respondent's growth and development and importance of handing on the faith;

(b) Perceived advantage/disadvantage of the respondent's religious affiliation in her/his "getting on" in life;

(c) Frequency of prayer and perceived closeness to God most of the time;

(d) Disposition towards vocation to the priesthood and to the sisterhood;

(e) Attitudes towards Church unity.

1. PERCEIVED INFLUENCE AND IMPORTANCE OF RELIGION IN REARING:

Table 56 gives a breakdown of respondents' replies to the following question: "Would you say that the religious beliefs in which you were brought up influenced your growth or development as a person?"

This question is a verbatim replication of a question asked originally by Professor Richard Rose in his survey of Northern Ireland in 1968 (published in Rose, *Governing Without Consensus: an Irish Perspective*, London, Faber, 1971). The same question was included by the present author in the 1972-73 survey of Greater Dublin (see in Mac Gréil, *Prejudice and Tolerance in Ireland*, 1977).

TABLE No. 56
PERCEIVED INFLUENCE OF RELIGIOUS BELIEFS IN WHICH
RESPONDENT WAS REARED (%)

Degree of Influence	Total Sample 1988/89 A	Dublin Sub-Sample 1988/89 B	Dublin Sample 1972/73 C	Difference B -C
1. An essential help to me	40.5	37.5	55.3	-17.9
2. Important but not essential	25.6 } 83.3	24.6 } 83.2	13.7 } 81.1	+10.9 } +2.1
3. Helped me somewhat	17.2	21.1	12.1	+9.0
4. Neither help nor hindrence	14.9	14.8	15.2	-0.4
5. Hindered me somewhat	1.4	0.8	2.6	-1.8
6. A serious hindrance	0.2 } 1.8	0.8 } 2.0	0.7 } 3.7	-0.1 } -1.9
7. A grave hindrance	0.2	0.4	0.4	0.0
	N = 1003	N = 256	N = 2,290	

The above results clearly indicate that "religion of rearing" is still being perceived in a very positive light by the adults of the Republic of Ireland. The consensus between the National Sample and the Dublin Subsample is very noteworthy. The perception of religion of rearing as a "hindrance" is statistically negligible. Very few respondents would seem to resent their religious formation.

The comparison between the 1988/89 subsample and the 1972/73 sample of Dublin Adults shows very little difference in overall positivity and negativity towards religious beliefs of rearing. The change of the "essential help" scores of -17.9%, while being more than balanced by the +19.9 in the other two positive categories, does, nevertheless, indicate a significant drop in the highest positive category. These findings may reflect the changes in the place of religion in the socialisation of the young over the past sixteen years in Dublin and in Ireland. The religiosity of the homes and of the schools may be modifying somewhat. Such changes would result in the decline in the "essential help" percentages. Any rise in secularism in primary socialisation will inevitably result in a reduction in the perceived importance of religion in the growth and development of the person. The evidence of the findings, however, should not be overstated in the light of the overall positive results.

A second measure, which has been tested in relation to socialisation in the faith, has been the answers to the following question: *"How important would you say it is for children to be brought up with the same religious views as their parents?"* This question had also been asked in the 1968

Northern Ireland Survey (Rose) and in the 1972-73 Greater Dublin Survey (Mac Gréil). The patterns of answering are given in Table 57.

TABLE No. 57

IMPORTANCE OF CHILDREN BEING BROUGHT UP IN THE SAME RELIGIOUS VIEWS AS THEIR PARENTS

Degree of Importance	1988-9 National Sample	1972-3 G. Dublin Sample (Mac Gréil)	1968 N. Ireland Sample (Rosé)
1. Very important	52.5% ⎫	71% ⎫	72% ⎫
2. Fairly Important	30.2% ⎭ 82.7%	12% ⎭ 83%	13% ⎭ 85%
3. Let them make up their own minds	4.4%	11 %	11 %
4. Don't know	0.5 %	1%	I %
5. Not very important	12.4%	5%	3%
	N = 1003	N = 2292	N = 1291

The findings of Table 57 are very interesting in that there is a very high positive score in favour of handing on the "religious views" of the parents to the children, i.e. plus 80%. This general positive score has been maintained in the three surveys 1968, 1972-3, 1988-9. As in the case of "perceived influence" in Table 56 above, the decrease is within the category of positive response i.e. a drop of 18.5% for "Very Important" and an increase of 18.2% in "Fairly Important". This is more clearly borne out in Table no. 58 below, where the 1988-89 Dublin Subsample is compared with the 1972-73 Greater Dublin Sample.

TABLE No. 58

CHANGE IN PERCEIVED IMPORTANCE OF CHILDREN BEING BROUGHT UP IN THE SAME RELIGIOUS VIEWS AS THEIR PARENTS IN DUBLIN BETWEEN 1972-73 AND 1988-89

Degree of Importance	1988-89 Sub-Sample	1972-73 Sample	Difference
1. Very important	45% ⎫	71% ⎫	-26% ⎫
2. Fairly important	33% ⎭ 78%	12% ⎭ 83%	+21% ⎭ -5%
3. Let them make up their own minds	7%	11%	-4%
4. Don't know	1%	1%	0%
5. Not very important	14%	5%	+9%
	N=255	N=1192	

It could be hypothesised that three things are being measured in the above tables and reflected in the internal changes. Firstly, the importance of transmitting the cultural values (which include religious views) from parents to children as an essential part of familial socialisation. Secondly, the importance of handing on the religious beliefs of parents to the young. The third aspect could be the specific obligation of bringing up the young in the denominational religious views of their family. The latter may have been affected somewhat by the advance of ecumenism. If changes are due to the decline in the perceived importance of parents handing on their religion then one might be justified in seeing them as evidence of advances in secularism. Changes due to the first hypothesis would reflect some weakening in the family as an agent of socialisation or as a change of emphasis on traditional Irish values (which included a high priority of religion). Finally, it should be noted that "same religious views" could include agnostic and atheistic views.

While Tables 57 and 58 do show a change of intensity in relation to the transmission of the family religious views to children (especially in Dublin) over the past 16 years, the overall position of handing on the faith from parents to children is still very high. This might, in part, explain the popular support in the Republic of Ireland for denominationally controlled primary education. The consistency between the findings in the Republic and those in Northern Ireland in the late 1960s and early 1970s would point to a similarity of ethos in relation to this question.

TABLE No. 59
PERCEIVED INFLUENCE OF RELIGION OF REARING IN PERSONAL
DEVELOPMENT BY AGE, GENDER AND EDUCATION

	Essential	Important but not Essential	Helped Somewhat	Total Positive
A. AGE (P≤.001)				
1. 18 - 20 yrs	31%	27%	26%	84%
2. 21 - 35 yrs	30%	29%	20%	79%
3. 36 - 50 yrs	37%	28%	17%	82%
4. 51 yrs +	55%	21%	13%	89%
B. GENDER (P≤.05)				
1. Females	44%	27%	15%	86%
2. Males	36%	24%	20%	80%
C. EDUCATION (P≤.05)				
1. Primary	47%	25%	15%	87%
2. Incomplete Second Level	37%	23%	20%	80%
3. Complete Second Level	42%	30%	14%	86%
4. Third Level	36%	27%	20%	83%
TOTAL SAMPLE	40.5%	25.6%	17.2%	83.3%

Tables 59 and 60 give a breakdown of replies by personal variables where differences have recorded an acceptable level of statistical significance (P ≤.05).

Figure No. 12: Influence of religion on rearing by age, gender and education

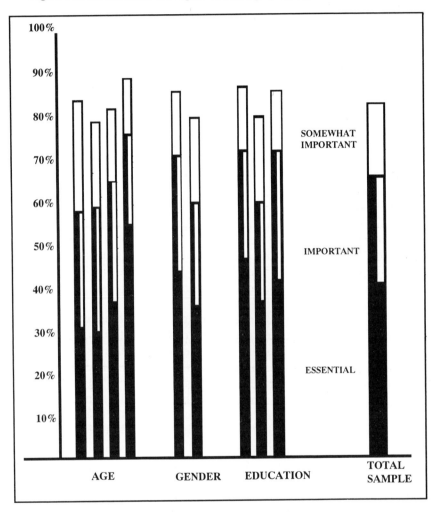

The findings of Tables 59 and 60 show that there is a positive correlation (J curve) between "age" and level of perceived influence and of perceived importance of religion. This is more manifest in the high positive scores. Females record a significantly higher degree of perceived positive influence of religion than males in their personal growth and development, while there was not any significant variation between the genders in relation to the importance of handing on religion. Dublin residents had the lowest positive scores in Table 60 while "county of residence" was not significant in the case of

TABLE No. 60

PERCEIVED IMPORTANCE OF HANDING ON OF PARENTS' RELIGIOUS VIEWS
TO THEIR CHILDREN BY PERSONAL VARIABLES

	Very Important	Fairly Important	Total Positive
A. AGE (P≤.001)			
1. 18 - 20 yrs	36%	39%	75%
2. 21-35 yrs	36%	38%	74%
3. 36 - 50 yrs	52%	32%	84%
4. 51 yrs +	73%	20%	93%
B. COUNTY OF RESIDENCE (P≤.05)			
1. Dublin	45%	33%	78%
2. Rest of Leinster	52%	29%	81%
3. Munster	61%	27 %	88%
4. Connaught/Ulster	53%	35%	88%
C. EDUCATION (P≤.001)			
1. Primary	69%	22%	91%
2. Incomplete Second Level	51%	38%	89%
3. Complete Second Level	45%	37%	82%
4. Third Level	37%	36%	73%
D. OCCUPATION (P≤.05)			
1. Unskilled/Semiskilled	59%	23%	82%
2. Skilled/Routine Non-Manual	50%	33%	83%
3. Inspectional/Supervisory	49%	37%	86%
4. Professional/Higher Executive	46%	33%	79%

Table 59. "Education" records the more significant variation in score in relation to "handing on the religious views of parents" (Table 60) with third level registering the lowest score while primary respondents were highest. The response to the question of influence (Table 59) resulted in significant variation but without a clear trend. "Occupational status" registered a slight but significant variation in Table 60, with "unskilled" respondents most likely to perceive the handing on of religious views as very important and "professional/higher executive" respondents least likely to feel that way.

The overall pattern emerging from Tables 59 and 60 shows younger, more highly educated, more prestigiously occupied, Dublin-based and male respondents slightly less positive in their responses. This would confirm a slight trend towards a more secular mentality. It must be reiterated, however, that this trend is more within the positive band and not towards a negative or hostile appraisal of religion. Nevertheless, it could indicate the beginning of a stronger secularist trend in Irish society.

2. PERCEIVED SOCIAL ADVANTAGE/DISADVANTAGE OF ONE'S RELIGION:

The question of the influence of one's religion on getting on in Irish society has been a key public issue, particularly due to allegations of

Figure No. 13: Importance of handing on parents' religious views to their children by personal variables

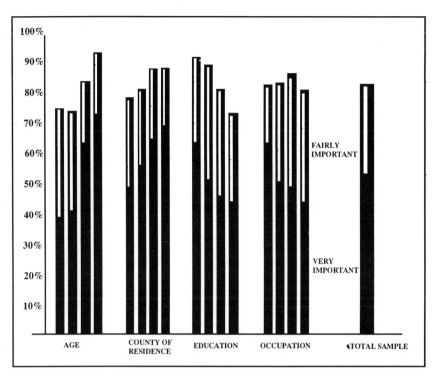

religious discrimination and sectarianism from time to time by certain political leaders and other commentators in the mass media. To examine this issue, two questions were asked of the respondents in the 1972-73 and 1988-89 surveys.

The following were the questions:

(a) *"Do you agree or disagree with the view that an applicant's religion should be considered when considering him or her for a responsible public position?"*

(b) *"Would you say that being a (respondent's religion) is an advantage or disadvantage to you in getting on?"*

The latter question had been asked by Rose in his 1968 survey of Northern Ireland. Table 61 gives a breakdown of replies to Question (a) above for the National Sample (1988/9) and shows the differences between the replies of the Dublin Subsample (1988/9) and the Greater Dublin Sample (1972/3).

TABLE No. 61

PERCEIVED IMPORTANCE OF APPLICANT'S RELIGION WITH REGARD TO A
RESPONSIBLE PUBLIC POSITION

"Do you agree or disagree with the view that an applicant's religion should be considered when considering him or her for a responsible public position?"

View	National Sample 1988-89	Dublin Sub-Sample 1988-89	Dublin Sample 1972-73	Difference
1. Applicant's Religion should be considered	16.7%	13.8%	11.6%	+2.2%
2. Don't know	5.2 %	5.9 %	0.9 %	+ 5.0 %
3. Applicant's Religion should not be considered	78.1%	80.3%	87.5%	-7.2%
	N = 1000	N = 254	N = 2281	

The evidence for 1988-9 in Table 61 reiterates the findings of the Dublin Survey of 1972-73 that the vast majority of the people **do not** favour taking an applicant's religion into consideration when he or she is considered for a responsible public position. An implication drawn from this finding would be that the vast majority (78%) would oppose religious discrimination in responsible public positions in the Republic of Ireland. The minor changes in the Dublin subsample mark a slight reduction in the anti-discrimination score, i.e. from 87.5% to 80.3% (-7.2%). This may indicate a slight reduction in the "liberal" views of the early 1970s. The variation of +2.2% in the proportion of those agreeing with the importance of an applicant's religion when applying for a job (from 11.6% to 13.8%) is at the extreme of the margin of error and cannot be given much emphasis.

The second question (b) deals with the personal experience of the respondents in relation to the role of their religious affiliation in enabling or hindering them in getting on in Ireland or in life. From the point of view of measuring experience of religious discrimination or sectarianism in its rawest sense, the negative scores, i.e. experience of "disadvantage", are the most significant.

In Table 62 the results of the two surveys in which the question was asked are given side by side. The findings are interesting in that they seem to tell us three things. In the first place, the level of perceived deprivation due to one's religion has been negligible (1.2%). In fact in the Dublin subsample, if anything, it indicates a decline (0.6%). Secondly, there has been a substantial minority (44.2%) who have seen their religion as something positive (socially). In the case of the Dublin subsample this percentage has almost doubled when compared with the 1972-73 survey, i.e. from 23.3% to 43.7%. The third point to note is the proportion who found their religion to be a neutral factor at 54.6%, while being the highest subsample, has been reduced by almost 20% since 1972-73. The similarity between the National sample and the Dublin subsample in the distribution between the variables would indicate that we may have a consensus of opinion in the findings of Table 62.

TABLE No. 62

PERCEIVED SOCIAL ADVANTAGE OF MEMBERSHIP OF A PARTICULAR RELIGION/DENOMINATION

"Would you say being a (respondent's religion) is an advantage or disadvantage to you in getting on?"

Degree of Advantage/Disadvantage	National Sample 1988- 89	Dublin Sub-Sample 1988-89	Dublin Sample 1972-73	Difference
	A	B	C	B - C
1. Great Advantage	26.6% ⎫	23.8 % ⎫	11.1% ⎫	+ 12.7% ⎫
	⎬ 44.2%	⎬ 43.7%	⎬ 23.3%	⎬ +20.4%
2. Slight Advantage	17.6% ⎭	19.9% ⎭	12.2% ⎭	+7.7% ⎭
3. Neither Adv/Disadv.	54.6%	53.5%	73.3%	-19.8%
4- Slight Disadvantage	1.0% ⎫	2.0% ⎫	2.9% ⎫	-0.9% ⎫
	⎬ 1.2%	⎬ 2.8%	⎬ 3.4%	⎬ 0.6%
5. Great Disadvantage	0.2% ⎭	0.8% ⎭	0.5% ⎭	+0.3% ⎭
	N = 1001	N = 256	N = 2280	

TABLE No. 63

PERCEIVED SOCIAL ADVANTAGE OF ONE'S RELIGION BY AGE, GENDER AND EDUCATION

Personal Variable	Great Advantage	Slight Advantage	Total Perceived Advantage
A. AGE (P≤.001)			
1. 18 - 20 yrs	27%	26%	53%
2. 21 - 35 yrs	19%	17 %	36 %
3. 36 - 50 yrs	20%	16%	36%
4. 51 yrs +	38%	17%	55%
B. GENDER (P < .05)			
1. Females	30%	16%	46%
2. Males	23%	19%	42%
C. EDUCATION (P < .05)			
1. Primary	34%	17%	51%
2. Incomplete Second Level	27%	19%	46%
3. Complete Second LeveL	120%	17%	37%
4. Third Level	22%	17%	39%
TOTAL SAMPLE	27%	18%	45%

Figure No. 14: Perceived social advantage of one's religion by age, gender and education

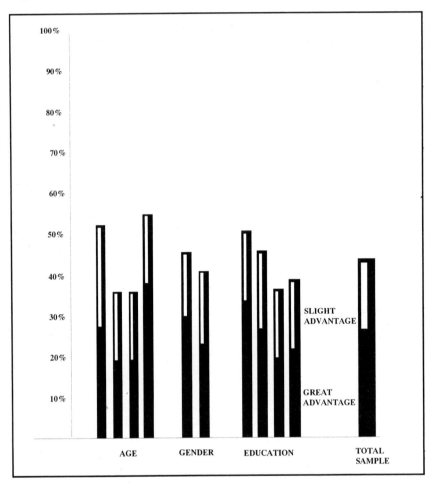

The only three personal variables to register a significant variation in perceived social advantage of membership of a particular religion (i.e. P ≤.05) were "age", "gender" and "education". Table 63 gives the breakdown of the scores of perceived social advantage by these three variables.

The scores of perceived social advantage of religion (Table 63) form a U curve in the case of age, i.e. the eldest and the youngest categories recording the highest scores. The junior and middle middle age categories are significantly lower. Does this mean that religion is becoming more relevant socially (or perceived to be such) for the younger respondents? Females have a slightly higher perception of the social advantage of religion than do men. This would be in line with the higher religiosity scores of females in general. In the case of education the lower two categories have a significantly higher score than do the higher levels.

Tables 61, 62 and 63 have given a measure of perceived social and occupational importance of religion in the Republic of Ireland in 1988-89. The overall findings of the three tables have established a non-sectarian attitude among the vast majority on the one hand, and the experience of social advantage or relevance of their religion for "getting on" in life by almost half the sample on the other. Religion is considered to be important but not hindering social advancement in the Republic.

3. PRAYER AND CLOSENESS TO GOD:

The level of perceived closeness to God is probably related to the practice of personal prayer in the life of the respondent. Table 64 gives the reported frequency of prayer. Respondents were asked "About how often do you pray?".

TABLE No. 64

FREQUENCY OF PERSONAL PRAYER OF TOTAL SAMPLE AND OF THE
ROMAN CATHOLIC SUBSAMPLE

FREQUENCY	Total Sample	Roman Catholics
1. Several Times a Day	37 %	38 %
2. Once a Day or More Often	71%	72%
3. Several Times a Week or More Often	82%	83%
4. Once a Week or More Often	90%	91%
5. Less than Once a Week	10%	9%
	N = 1001	N = 943

The findings of Table 64 are consistent with the high level of attendance at formal worship. The practice of prayer on a regular basis must indicate a strong degree of belief. The practice of prayer by Roman Catholics is not significantly different from that of the total sample. The high proportion of Roman Catholics in the sample would limit the possibility of variation but the fact that it is statistically similar would point to a universal pattern of prayer in Irish society in 1988-89.

Frequency of prayer is, on the one hand, a measure of private religious practice and, on the other, a measure of one's perceived closeness to God who is seen as personal. Table 65 and Figure No. 15 show the extent and pattern of variation between the different sub-samples of age, gender, marital status, area of rearing and education.

"Age" has shown a very significant and substantial variation between the younger and the older sub-samples. The widest range of difference is at the "several times a day" and "once a day or more often" levels of prayer frequency. The relatively low practice of prayer among the two younger sub-samples may be an issue of concern for spiritual leaders and catechists of the young today.

TABLE No. 65
FREQUENCY OF PRAYER OF ROMAN CATHOLICS BY PERSONAL VARIABLES

	Several times a day	Once a day or more often	Several times a week or more often	Once a week or more often	Less than once a week	No.
A. AGE (P≤.001)						
1. 8 - 20 yrs	19%	48%	76%	89%	11%	54
2. 21 - 35 yrs	22%	59%	74%	86%	14%	321
3. 36 - 50 yrs	33%	73%	84%	91%	9%	248
4. 51 yrs +	62%	90%	94%	97%	3%	320
B. GENDER (P≤.001)						
1. Females	44%	80%	89%	94%	6%	518
2. Males	31%	64%	76%	87%	13%	425
C. MARITAL STATUS (P≤.001)						
1. Never Married	28%	62%	79%	89%	11%	270
2. Married	38%	75%	84%	92%	8%	586
3. Widowed	79%	97%	97%	98%	2%	68
D. AREA OF REARING (P≤.001)						
1. Large C ity	31%	61%	76%	82%	18%	203
2. Small City	33%	72%	83%	90%	10%	106
3. Town	39%	71%	83%	94%	6%	143
4. Rural	42%	78%	87%	95%	5%	488
E. EDUCATION (P<.001)						
1. Primary	52%	85%	91%	96%	4%	270
2. Incomplete Second Level	31%	71%	82%	90%	10%	329
3. Complete Second Level	33%	69%	82%	90%	10%	219
4. Third Level	35%	56%	75%	86%	14%	123
TOTAL SAMPLE (Roman Catholics)	38%	73%	83%	91%	9%	943

Once again, females are substantially and significantly more frequent prayers than are males. This confirms the higher level of religiosity among female respondents. The "age" and "gender" factors contribute to the differences by "marital status". Practically all (97%) of the widowed reported praying at least "once daily". The religious practice of widowed respondents approaches that of those living a "regular life" in religious orders.

The negative impact of urbanisation on the frequency of prayer in the personal lives of respondents is borne out in the variations between the subsamples of "area of rearing". The highest frequency is given in the case of those raised in rural Ireland. This may be related to the incidence of the family rosary or regular family prayers.

Figure No. 15: Frequency of prayer by age, gender, marital status, area of rearing and education (Roman Catholic)

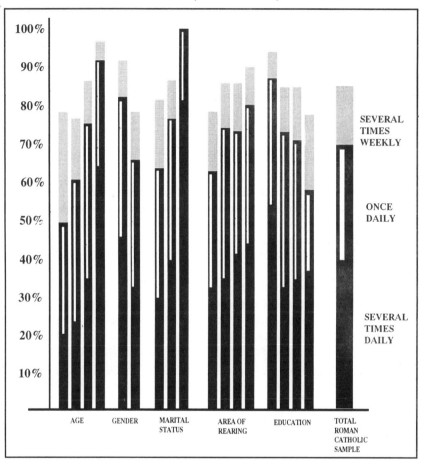

The secularising influence of third level education is evident from the findings of Table 65, where 56% of the sub-sample with "third level education" stated that they prayed "daily or more often" while 85% of those with only "primary education" did so. Does this mean that formal education is both a de-radicalising i.e. removing people from their roots, and secularising agency in Ireland?

Because of the dual importance of frequency of prayer as an indication of levels of religiosity, i.e. as a measure of both religious practice and of perceived closeness to and of God, Tables 64 and 65 and Figure 15 are very important. Table 66 measures explicit perceived closeness of God to the respondents. These findings are in response to the question: *"How close do you feel to God most of the time? Would you say extremely close, somewhat close, not very close, or not close at all?"*

TABLE No. 66
PERCEIVED DEGREE OF CLOSENESS TO GOD MOST OF THE TIME

Degree of Closeness	
1. Extremely Close	24.5 % ⎫
2. Somewhat Close	61.2% ⎬ 85.7%
3. Not Very Close	9.8 %
4. Not Close At All	2.9%
5. Non-Believer in God	1.6%

One quarter of the sample said they felt "extremely close to God" and a further 61.2% said they were "somewhat close". It could be argued that the concept "extremely close" would be perceived negatively, even by those who would see their relationship with God to be "very" close. For that reason the second degree of closeness probably signifies a higher level of closeness than the concept "somewhat close" would indicate. Over five-sixths of the sample professed a sense of closeness to God, which once again bears out the strong religious ethos of the population. Of course, it must be noted that those who did not feel close to God were not necessarily irreligious. The most heroic faith is seen by some spiritual authors as belief without a strong feeling of closeness or consolation, i.e. "the dark night of the soul".

There were a number of questions in the survey which were concerned with the perceived nature of God's relationship to people. The answers to these questions may help to give further insight into the people's existential understanding of their belief in God. Table 67 gives the responses of the sample to these questions, which have been tested in a national survey in Holland in 1985.

The findings of Table 67 clearly show that the perceptions of God's personal relations with people are significantly and very substantially more positive among the respondents of the Irish sample than they are for the Dutch sample. The level of agreement, on average, for the various statements is statistically twice as positive for the Irish.

The overall picture emerging from the findings of Table 67 point to a high degree of acceptance by the Irish respondents of a *personal God* who is perceived to be concerned about the lives of the people. At the same time, there is a significant minority who would hold that there is an autonomy of meaning in the "natural" or "secular" order.

The level of "agnosticism" or "don't knows" in relation to the particular opinions ranges from 9% to 16% for the Irish respondents, which is lower than was anticipated. The level of disbelief in God is very low as can be seen from the 6% who disagreed with item 1. As we saw in Table 66, only 1.6% stated explicitly that they did not believe in God at all.

TABLE No. 67
PERCEPTION OF GOD'S RELATIONSHIP TO PEOPLE
(OF IRISH AND DUTCH SAMPLES)

Question: *"Do you Agree or Disagree with the Following Statements?"*

Statement	Agree	Don't Know	Disagree	Mean (3- 1)	No .
1. "There is a God who wants to be our God"	83 % (48%)	11% (18 %)	6% (34%)	2.8 (2.1)	992 (2881)
	+35%	-7%	-28%	+0.7	
2. "There is a God who occupies himself with every human being personally"	78% (43%)	14% (20%)	8% (37%)	2.7 (2.0)	999 (2925)
	+35%	-6%	-29%	+0.7	
3. "God takes care that good will finally overcome evil"	73% (32%)	16% (26%)	11% (42%)	2.6 (1.9)	995 (2968)
	+41%	-10%	-29%	+0.7	
4. "Only if you believe in God, death has a meaning"	73% (34%)	9% (19%)	18% (47%)	2.6 (1.9)	999 (2832)
	+39%	-10%	-29%	+0.7	
5. "To me, life is meaningful only because God exists"	59% (21%)	11% (24%)	29% (55%)	2.3 (1.7)	996 (2900)
	+38%	-13%	-26%	+0.6	
6. "In my opinion, sorrow and suffering only have meaning if you believe in God"	48% (24%)	15% (20%)	37% (56%)	2.1 (1.6)	997 (2819)
	+24%	-5%	-19%	+0.5	

NOTE: Dutch Sample results in Brackets

4. ATTITUDES TOWARDS VOCATIONS:

It has been generally believed that *nuns* and *priests* have been held in high esteem in Ireland until quite recently. This was confirmed in the 1972-73 Greater Dublin Survey in the case of the status of priest and religious when both categories were rated within the "top ten" stimulus categories on a Bogardus Social Distance Scale of seventy categories (see Mac Gréil, 1977 pp. 230/1).

In the current (1988-89) survey, the question used to measure the standing of nuns and priests was that of finding out how welcome vocations would be in the family. A similar question was asked in the case of both nun and priest. Tables 68 and 69 give the responses to both questions.

TABLE No. 68:
PERCENTAGE OF ROMAN CATHOLICS WHO WOULD WELCOME
A NUN AND A PRIEST IN THE FAMILY

A. Question: *"Imagine you had a daughter and she came to you and said she had decided to become a nun, how do you think you would respond?"*	
Response	Percentage
1. Greatly Welcome 2. Welcome with Reservations 3. Neither Welcome nor Discourage 4. Would Discourage	} 75% 19% 6%
	N = 944

B. Question: *"Imagine you had a son and he came to you and said he had decided to become a priest, how do you think you would respond?"*	
Response	Percentage
1. Greatly Welcome 2. Welcome with Reservations 3. Neither Welcome nor Discourage 4. Would Discourage	} 79% 18% 3%
	N = 944

Almost half the Roman Catholics in the sample would "greatly welcome" a daughter or son becoming a nun or a priest while a further 28% to 30% would welcome such choices of vocation "with reservations". The percentages who would discourage such choices are very small at 6% and 3%. The variations in the percentages between nuns and priests are not very significant since they fall at the extreme of the margin of error of plus-or-minus 3%. The direction of this very slight variation shows preference to "welcoming a son becoming a priest".

These results would seem to run counter to the view that vocations have declined in the recent past due to parental discouragement. Table 69 gives a breakdown of the responses by personal variables showing significant variations in scores. In the case of "gender" there was no significant variation between the views of females and of males.

There is a significant but very slight preference for "a son becoming a priest" over "a daughter becoming a nun" in the total sample, i.e. a difference of 4% which is only 1% outside the statistical margin of error. The four personal variables of age, marital status, residence and education have recorded significant differences in scores.

Age findings form a J-curve which means that the youngest category is more positively disposed that the lower middle age category. The pattern is true in the case of "nun" and "priest". The age factor would seem to influence the score of the categories of marital status. The range of scores between the categories of "county of residence" show those living in Dublin

TABLE No. 69
REACTION OF ROMAN CATHOLICS TO VOCATION OF DAUGHTER/SON
AS A NUN OR PRIEST BY PERSONAL VARIABLES

Category 1:	"Greatly Welcome"							
Category 2:	"Welcome with Reservations"							

	Daughter to Become a Nun			Son to Become a Priest				
Personal Variable	Cat. 1	Cat.2	Total A	Cat. 1	Cat. 2	Total B	Diff. (A-B)	No.
A. AGE (P≤.001)								
1. 18 - 20 yrs	41%	29%	70%	43%	30%	73%	-3%	55
2. 21 - 35 yrs	34%	30%	64%	37%	31%	68%	4%	320
3. 36 - 50 yrs	42%	31%	73%	45%	33%	78%	-5%	246
4. 51 yrs +	61%	23%	84%	62%	24%	86%	-2%	319
B. MARITAL STATUS (P≤.05)								
1. Never Married	45%	25%	70%	47%	24%	71%	1%	270
2. Married	45%	30%	75%	47%	31%	78%	-3%	586
3. Widowed	63%	24%	87%	61%	27%	88%	1%	68
C. COUNTY OF RESIDENCE (P ≤.05)								
1. Dublin	43%	25%	68%	44%	29%	73%	-5%	252
2. Rest of Leinster	45%	27%	72%	47%	29%	76%	4%	238
3. Munster	50%	32%	82%	50%	33%	83%	-1%	287
4. Connaught/Ulster	52%	27%	79%	56%	26%	82%	-3%	167
D. EDUCATION (P≤.001)								
1. Primary	64%	21%	85%	65%	21%	86%	1%	272
2. Incomplete 2nd Level	47%	27%	74%	47%	30%	77%	-3%	330
3. Complete 2nd Level	37%	35%	72%	39%	37%	76%	4%	218
4. Third Level	28%	35%	63%	32%	33%	65%	-2%	124
TOTAL SAMPLE	47%	28%	75%	49%	30%	79%	4%	944

with the lowest scores (68% and 73%) and those living in Munster scoring highest (82% and 83%). There would seem to be a negative correlation between *educational standard* reached and positive scores of welcome. This may be due to more ambitious career expectations for daughters and sons. The higher scores of those with "Primary Level" may also reflect a category with a larger proportion of older respondents (see Mac Gréil 1990B, pp. 15ff . . . "Education by Age").

In summary, therefore it can be ascertained from the findings of Tables 68 and 69 that there is a positive disposition towards vocations to the priesthood and sisterhood in the population. The very low percentage of respondents who would discourage a son or a daughter from becoming a priest or a nun hardly substantiates the view that there is serious domestic hostility to vocations. The relatively lower support from respondents with third level education may be a significant deviation from the population norm.

Figure No. 16: Reaction to daughter/son declaring decision to become a nun/priest (A=nun, B=priest)

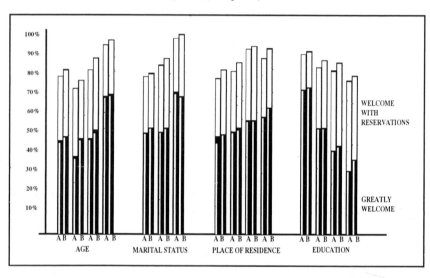

CHAPTER VII

Religious Attitudes and Perceptions

INTRODUCTION

In this chapter it is proposed to examine three further aspects of religious beliefs, attitudes and values, i.e.,

(1)   Attitudes to Christian Church Unity;
(2)   Perceptions of God;
(3)   Attitudes towards Religious Categories; and
(4)   Anti-Semitic Attitudes and Prejudices.

The significance of inter-Church attitudes in Ireland takes on a special importance in the context of Northern Ireland where political divisions have been along Christian denominational lines for over three and a half centuries. The division of Ireland into *The Irish Free State* and *Northern Ireland* in the 1920s resulted in the "Six Counties" of Northern Ireland with a dominant majority of Protestant-Unionists of 65.1% of the population as compared with the Roman Catholic-Nationalists of 33.5% while, at that time, the situation in the Twenty-six Counties of the Free State had a denominational ratio of 92.6% Roman Catholics and 7.0% who were Protestant. The following Table (70) gives a breakdown of religious denominations in Northern Ireland since 1911.

The demographic distribution of the Northern Ireland population according to religious denomination shows two features of significance, the preservation of the Catholic-Protestant ratio from 1926 until 1961 within a very narrow range and the recent increase (since 1961) of the proportionate position of Roman Catholics vis-a-vis the other major Christian denominations in the Six Counties of Northern Ireland.

The discussion on the above shift in denominational ratio in Northern Ireland in Paul Compton's article, "The Demography of Religious Affiliation", published in *Demographic Review: Northern Ireland (1995)* by the Northern Ireland Economic Council, 1995, is worth reading. The growth of "other religion" over the past three decades (see Table 70) is also a noteworthy addition to the denominational pattern. Commenting on the decline of the main Protestant denominations in Northern Ireland, Compton makes the following observation:

> ". . . (The table shows that) the main Protestant denominations, Presbyterian, Church of Ireland and Methodist, have declined more rapidly than the group as a whole, while the strength of many of those comprising the "other" category, e.g. Baptists, Church of God, has grown more significantly. . . ."

> (Compton, 1995, p. 166)

189

TABLE No. 70
POPULATION OF NORTHERN IRELAND BY RELIGIOUS AFFILIATION (1911-1991)

YEAR	Roman Catholics	Presbyterians	Church of Ireland	Methodists	Other Religions	No Religion Declared*	Number
A. Census Figures							
1911	34.4%	31.6%	26.1%	3.7%	2.6%	1.6%	1,250,531
1926	33.5%	31.3%	27.0%	3.9%	2.9%	1.4%	1,256,579
1937	33.5%	30.5%	27.0%	4.3%	3.3%	1.5%	1,279,745
1951	34.4%	29.9%	25.8%	4.9%	3.3%	1.7%	1,370,921
1961	34.9%	29.0%	24.2%	5.0%	3.3%	3.6%	1,425,042
1971	31.4%	26.7%	22.0%	4.7%	5.8%	9.4%*	1,519,640
1981	28.0%	22.9%	19.0%	4.0%	7.6%	18.5%	1,532,000
1991	38.4%	21.3%	17.7%	3.8%	7.8%	11.0%'	1,578,000
B.* Revised Distribution of "Not Stated percentage" (Paul Compton, 1995, p. 116)							
1971	36.8%	28.6%	23.5%	5.0%	5.3%	0.8%	1,519,640
1981	38.7%	26.3%	21.8%	4.6%	7.8%	0.8%	1,532,000
1991	40.6%	23.5%	19.5%	4.2%	8.4%	3.9%	1,578,000

*Revised Distribution is in accord with Paul Compton's Estimates.

YEAR	Roman Catholics	Major Protestant Denominations	Ratio
1911	34.4%	61.4%	**36:64**
1926	33.5%	62.2%	**35:65**
1937	33.5%	61.8%	**35:65**
1951	34.4%	60.6%	**36:64**
1961	34.9%	58.2%	**37:63**
1971	36.8%	57.1%	**39:61**
1981	38.7%	52.7%	**40:60**
1991	40.6%	47.2%	**46:54**

If the above changes of religious denominations were reflected in political party preferences one could say that the "balance of power" was in the hands of the "other" and "no religion" category!

PART I: ATTITUDES TO CHRISTIAN CHURCH UNITY

Ecumenism has been part of the agenda of religious debate in Ireland and elsewhere over the past thirty years. Respondents were asked two specific questions from Rose's Northern Ireland survey of 1968, i.e. *"There is a lot of talk these days about uniting the Protestant Church and the Roman Catholic Church. What do you think of this idea? (Let me make sure I have this clear)"*

(a) *Do you think that **in principle** uniting the Protestant and Catholic Church is desirable or undesirable?*

(b) *Do you think that **in practice** uniting the Churches is possible or impossible?"*

The replies in the three surveys are given in Table 71.

TABLE No. 71
ATTITUDES TOWARDS CHRISTIAN CHURCH UNITY
("IN PRINCIPLE" AND "IN PRACTICE")

Response	A 1988-89 National Sample	B 1972-73 G. Dublin Sample	C 1968 N.I. Sample	A - B	A - C
A. IN PRINCIPLE QUESTION (a)					
1. Desirable	45%	83%	45%	-38%	0%
2. Depends	27%	5%	7%	+ 22%	+ 20%
3. Don't Know	18%	4%	7%	+ 14%	+ 11%
4. Undesirable	11%	8%	42%	+ 3%	-31%
B. IN PRACTICE QUESTION (b)					
1. Possible	30%	62%	27%	-32%	+ 3%
2. Depends	27%	11%	7%	+ 16%	+ 20%
3. Don't Know	14%	5%	7%	+9%	+7%
4. Impossible	29%	22%	59%	+ 7%	-30%
	N = 1003	N = 2083	N = 1291		

The National Sample in 1988-89 is not as ecumenical as the Greater Dublin Sample was in 1972-73 according to the findings of Table 71. When the findings of the 1988-89 Dublin subsample are compared with those of the 1972-73 Greater Dublin Sample the extent of the change that has taken place is given below.

Church Unity in Principle (excluding 'Don't Knows')			
	Dublin 1988-89	Dublin 1972-73	Change
1. Desirable	63%	86%	-23%
2. Depends	23%	5%	+18%
3. Undesirable	14%	8%	+6%

The substantial change in the "desirable" percentages over the intervening sixteen years must raise questions for church and community leaders. Does it mark a certain change of ecumenical policy or a decline in the activity of the ecumenical movement in Ireland? Or is this just a reflection of a less open approach to people who may be different? The experience of more intransigent pastures of some Christian Church Groups over the 1970s and 1980s could also contribute to this change. Lack of public inter-Church solidarity on issues of "domestic" morality, i.e., indissoluble marriage and the rights of the unborn child, may have also contributed to this change? Whatever the reasons may be for the fact that almost one quarter of the Dublin subsample withdrawing their unqualified support for Christian Church Unity, it is a serious issue for the future integration of the peoples of Ireland.

TABLE No. 72
DESIRABILITY OF CHRISTIAN CHURCH UNITY IN PRINCIPLE
BY PERSONAL VARIABLES

	DESIRABLE (4)	DEPENDS (3)	UNDESIRABLE (1)	Mean Score (4-1)	No.
TOTAL SAMPLE	55%	32%	13%	3.29	827
AGE (P≤.001)					
1. 18 - 20 yrs	37%	35%	28%	2.81	43
2. 21 - 35 yrs	44%	43%	13%	3.18	270
3. 36 - 50 yrs	57%	31%	12%	3.33	225
4. 51 yrs +	66%	23%	11%	3.44	289
AREA OF REARING (P≤'.05)					
1. Large City (100,000 +)	62%	23%	15%	3.32	247
2. Small City (10,000 +)	63%	29%	8%	3.47	62
3. Town (1 ,500 +)	56%	37%	7%	3.42	110
4. Rural (under 1,500)	52%	36%	13%	3.29	408
COUNTY OF RESIDENCE (P≤.001)					
1. Dublin (Co./City)	63%	23%	14%	3.35	236
2. Rest of Leinster	63%	29%	8%	3.47	203
3. Munster	43%	45%	12%	3.19	136
4. Connaught/Ulster	52%	29%	19%	3.14	252
EDUCATION (P≤.001)					
1. Primary	63%	23%	14%	3.35	231
2. Incomplete 2nd Level	50%	36%	14%	3.22	280
3. Complete 2nd Level	46%	40%	13%	3.17	194
4. Third Level	65%	30%	5%	3.55	121
OCCUPATION (P<.001)					
1. Routine Man./Semi-Skilled	56%	27%	16%	3.21	219
2. Skilled/Non-Manual	51%	37%	13%	3.28	126
3. Inspectional/Supervisory	52%	35%	13%	3.26	262
4. Professional/High Exec.	68%	24%	8%	3.52	140

There is a positive correlation between "age" and the view that Church Unity is a something desirable. This is quite a surprising result in that many would expect older respondents to be less enthusiastic about ecumenical progress that would be the case of younger respondents.

The variations in the responses of the sub-samples classified by *area of rearing* are significant without being very substantial. The more urbanised seem to be slightly more in favour of church unity than do those raised in the smaller towns and rural areas.

Place of Residence records the highest ecumenical score for the "Rest of Leinster" and Dublin, with Munster and Connaught/Ulster less in favour.

The response by *education*, while showing a statistically significant variation between the different levels, does not, however, indicate a trend or correlation. The response is more a "U" curve with those with least and those with highest education proving more ecumenical.

The educational pattern is more or less mirrored in that of *occupational status*, the middle grades having lower "desirable" percentages than either the "routine manual/semiskilled" respondents, on the one hand or the "professional/high executive" subsample, on the other.

In summary, the evidence of Table 72, which excludes the "Don't Know" sub-sample, shows a relatively low level of opposition to Christian Church Unity i.e. those stating it would be "undesirable". Half the sample are clearly positive and one-third are positive in a qualified sense. The surprise finding of the personal variables is the finding that older subsamples were more ecumenical than were the younger ones.

**Figure No. 17: Church Unity in Principle by Personal Variables
(excluding "Don't Knows")**

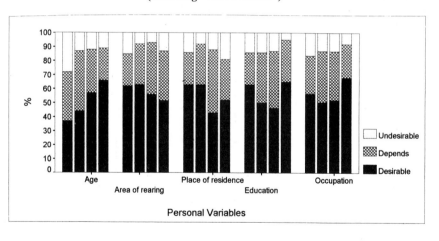

Table 73 and Figure 18 give a breakdown of the responses of three personal variables i.e. "age", "gender" and "county of rearing", in relation to the question of whether Christian Church Unity was possible in practice.

The fact that the other variables did not record significant variations would point to a moderate degree of consensus among the sample in relation to the question.

Even when one removes the "don't know" subsample, the overall positive (unqualified) optimism is slightly more than one third. This must in some way reflect the public perception of the slow or negative progress of the ecumenical movement in Ireland so far. The difference between the 55% of respondents who considered Christian Church Unity desirable (unqualified) in principle and the 35% who thought it possible (unqualified) in practice could reflect a considerable degree of "ecumenical frustration" among at least one-fifth of the Irish adult population.

TABLE No. 73
POSSIBILITY OF CHRISTIAN CHURCH UNITY IN PRACTICE BY AGE, GENDER AND AREA OF REARING (EXCLUDING "DON'T KNOWS")

	POSSIBLE	DEPENDS	IMPOSSIBLE	Mean Score	No.
	(4)	(3)	(1)	(4-1)	
TOTAL SAMPLE	35%	31%	34%	2.67	866
AGE (P<.00 1)					
1. 18 - 20 yrs	23%	25%	52%	2.19	43
2. 21 - 35 yrs	27%	34%	39%	2.49	270
3. 36 - 50 yrs	37%	26%	37%	2.63	225
4. 51 yrs +	43%	33%	24%	2.95	289
GENDER (P<.001)					
1. Females	31%	37%	33%	2.68	464
2. Males	40%	24%	36%	2.68	402
AREA OF REARING (P<.001)					
1. Large City (100,000 +)	37%	23%	40%	2.57	247
2. Small City (10,000 +)	23%	39%	38%	2.47	62
3. Town (I ,500 +)	43%	39%	18%	3.07	110
4. Rural (Under 1,500)	34%	32%	34%	2.66	408

The pattern of responses of the *age* variable again records an unexpected finding. The positive correlation between age and ecumenical optimism points to the relatively high degree of ecumenical pessimism among the younger respondents. Over 50% of the 18 to 20 year olds thought Christian Church Unity was impossible in practice.

While the mean score for males and females was the same (2.68) in the gender variable, there was more optimism at the "possible" level among males (40%) than among females (31%).

While "area of rearing" produced significant variations in the responses of the sub-samples, the pattern does not show a trend. The most ecumenically optimistic respondents were from the "town" sub-sample, while the least optimistic were those of the "small cities".

Figure No. 18: Christian Church Unity in practice by age, gender and area of rearing (excluding "Don't Knows")

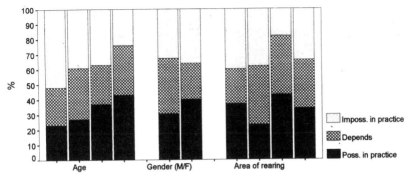

PART II: PERCEPTIONS OF GOD

1. IMAGES OF GOD

Table 74 measures the images of respondents about God. The question was taken from an international survey and the continua were devised by Professor Andrew Greeley. The following introduction and explanation was read to all respondents by the interviewers:

"There are many different ways of picturing God. We would like to know the kinds of images you are most likely to associate with God. Here is a card with sets of contrasting images. On a scale of 1 – 7 where would you place your image of God between the two contrasting images?"

TABLE No. 74
IMAGES OF GOD CONTINUA (TOTAL SAMPLE)

	1	2	3	4	5	6	7		Mean Point
1. MOTHER	2%	1%	2%	20%	10%	18%	46%	FATHER	5.7
2. SPOUSE	5%	4%	6%	19%	13%	18%	36%	MASTER	5.3
3. KING	13%	6%	3%	14%	9%	15%	40%	FRIEND	5.1
4. LOVER	17%	7%	6%	23%	11%	13%	24%	JUDGE	4.4

Figure No. 19: Images of God (Greeley Continua)

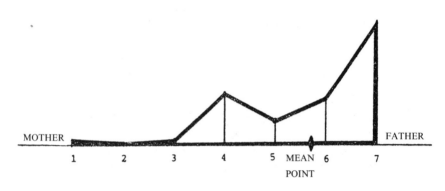

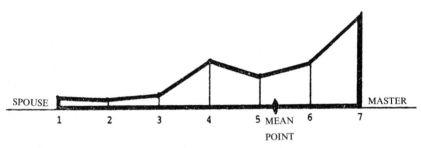

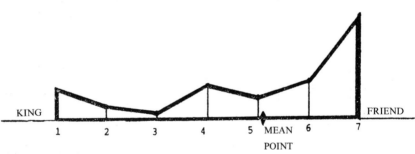

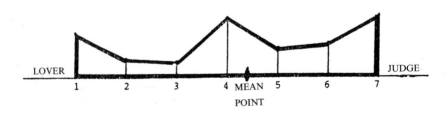

Three of the images of God which gained majority support were the biblical images of "Father", "Master" and "Judge". The biblical image of "King" lost to the image "Friend". The graphic representation in Figure No. 9 traces the relative strengths of each of the contrasted images of Mother/Father; Spouse/Master; King/Friend; Lover/Judge. The "mean point" indicated on each graph (see Figure 19) also shows the relative strength of the images. In the case of three of the pairings the mean point is between 5 and 6 on a continuum of 1 to 7, which shows a strong preference. The mean point on the fourth continuum, "Lover/Judge", is approaching the middle point of 4. This latter score and the victory of the image of "Friend" over "King" would seem to point to moderation of the strong preference for the image of "Master". The overall image of God which may be interpreted from the above would be a mixed one of respect, affection, fear and trust.

2. IMAGES OF THE WORLD AND OF HUMAN NATURE

Professor Andrew Greeley devised two further continua which were intended to measure people's image of the world and of human nature. These continua have been included in the survey examined in this book. The following question was asked of all respondents:

"People have different images of the world and human nature. We would like to know what kind of images you have. Here is a card with sets of contrasting images. On a scale of 1 to 7, where would you place your image of the world and human nature between the two contrasting images?"

TABLE No. 75
IMAGES OF THE WORLD AND OF HUMAN NATURE (TOTAL SAMPLE)

	1	2	3	4	5	6	7	
"The world is basically filled with evil and sin"	2%	5%	6%	22% Mean Point: 5.0	23%	25%	16%	"There is much goodness in the world which hints at God's goodness"

	1	2	3	4	5	6	7	
"Human nature is fundamentally perverse/corrupt"	2%	3%	4%	18% Mean Point: 5.4	17%	35%	21%	"Human nature is basically good"

The response to both issues, i.e. the perceived goodness or badness of the "world" and of "human nature" has been positive and optimistic. The sample was slightly (but significantly) more in agreement with the goodness of human nature (Mean point 5.4) than with the goodness of the world (Mean point 5.0).

Figure No. 20: Images of the World and of Human Nature (Greeley Continua)

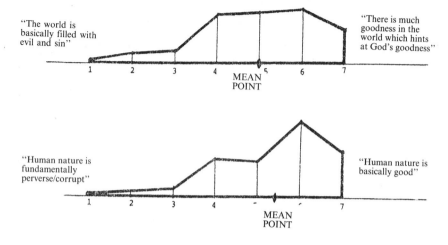

The spread of opinions, as graphically presented in Figure 20, shows how qualified the optimism of the sample is in relation to respondents' images of the world and of human nature. The relatively high percentage (one-fifth of the sample) who took a central position by opting for 4 on the continuum and the spread of the positive options, especially in the case of the image of the world, would indicate that there is a substantial lack of optimistic enthusiasm in the responses. Still, the very small number opting for the negative options, i.e. 1-3 on the continua, manifests clearly a lack of basic pessimism among the vast majority (plus-minus 90%) of the respondents. The extent to which this level of optimism is informed by faith and hope in God has not been measured explicitly in the current research. In the opinion of the author, there is a very high probability that the optimism is an expression of faith and hope coming from the people's relatively high level of religiosity (as manifest in Tables 56 to 67 above).

3. ROLE OF RELIGION IN SOCIO-POLITICAL LIFE

Questions concerning the influence of religion on the person in helping him or her to arrive at decisions or to form political ideas, have been discussed in the Irish media from time to time. Respondents were asked if they agreed or disagreed with the statements given below in Table 76. Items 1 and 2 are replicated from the Dutch Survey (Felling, Peeters, Schreuder, Eisinga and Scheepers, 1987).

TABLE NO. 76:
RELIGION AND THE SOCIO-POLITICAL LIFE OF THE PERSON
(IRISH AND DUTCH SAMPLES)*

Statement	Agree	Don't Know	Disagree	No.
1. "My (Christian) religion has a great deal of influence on my political ideas"	36% (38%)	12% (16%)	52% (46%)	1005 (1619)
2. "If I have to make an important decision, my religion would play an important role in it"	61% (50%)	12% (20%)	28% (30%)	1005 (1579)
3. "Priests, brothers and nuns should become more directly involved politically in fighting for social justice in Ireland"	49%	16%	35%	997 (1,601)

Source of Dutch Findings: Feelings, Peters, Schreuder, Eisinga and Scheepers, *Religious in Dutch Society '85*, Amsterdam, Steinmetz Archive, 1987.
* Percentages in brackets are from the findings of a Dutch national survey.

The majority (52%) of the national sample held that their (Christian) religion had not a great deal of influence on their political ideas. Still, more than one-third of the sample agreed that their religion had influenced their political views. Viewed positively the influence of religion on political ideas would be seen as interconnectedness between the clusters of cognitions within the individual, which is a sign of personal maturity. Viewed negatively, some might see such influence as intrusive leading to confessional politics.

The admission by over 60% that their religion played "an important part" when arriving at a serious (important) decision once again confirms its existential relevance in life. Less than 30% disagreed with the view expressed in Item 2 (Table 76).

The direct involvement of "priests, brothers and nuns" in political action for justice in Ireland was supported by half the sample (49%) and opposed by slightly more than one third (35%). This may challenge some of the images of Irish people as being opposed to the prophetic involvement of clergy and religious in social and political action for justice. Of course, the 35% who disagreed with this view constitute a substantial minority.

The comparison with the responses of the Dutch sample (in the case of Items no. 1 and no. 2) is indeed interesting. The differences in scores are barely significant. The Irish sample is very slightly more likely to be influenced by their religious beliefs, according to their own admission, than is the Dutch sample.

PART III: ATTITUDES TOWARDS RELIGIOUS CATEGORIES

The attitudes towards ten religious categories were measured by means of the Bogardus Social Distance Scale.

As stated earlier, this scale measures the degree of closeness to which respondents were willing to admit members of each category along a seven point continuum, i.e.

SOCIAL DISTANCE SCALE (Bogardus)						
Kinship	Friendship	Next-door Neighbour	Co-Worker	Citizen	Visitor Only	Debar/ Deport
1	2	3	4	5	6	7

A number of the religious categories measured on the Bogardus Scale in the present National survey (1988-89) were also measured in the Greater Dublin survey of 1972-73.

In Table 80 below the changes in attitudes over the intervening 16 years are calculated.

TABLE No. 77
SOCIAL DISTANCE TOWARDS RELIGIOUS CATEGORIES

Stimulus Category (in order of preference)	"Would marry or welcome as member of my family" closer"	"Would have as close friends or or closer"	"Would have as next door neighbours closer"	"Would work in the same place or closer"	"Would welcome as Irish citizen or closer"	"Would have as visitors only to Ireland"	"Would debar or deport from	Mean Social Distance (1-7)
1 Roman Catholic	97%	99%	100%	100%	100%	–	–	1.057
2 C. of I.	65%	S5%	95%	97%	99%	1%	–	1.609
3 Protestants	62%	84%	94%	97%	99%	1%	–	1.859
4 Presbyterians	52%	73%	85%	91%	94%	5%	1%	2.045
5 Methodists	49%	71%	83%	89%	94%	5%	1%	2.128
6 Jews	40%	62%	74%	82%	87%	11%	2%	2.599
6a (Israelis)	(32%)	(49%)	(60%)	(72%)	(77%)	(19%)	(4%)	(3.117)
7 Agnostics	31%	49%	63%	77%	82%	12%	7%	3.021
8 Atheists	29%	48%	62%	75%	81%	12%	7%	3.152
9 Moslems	21 %	41 %	57%	68%	76%	21 %	3%	3.420
10 Hare Krishna	13%	26%	36%	50%	61%	22%	17%	4.331

Figure No. 21: Mean social distance continuum of Responses to Religious Categories

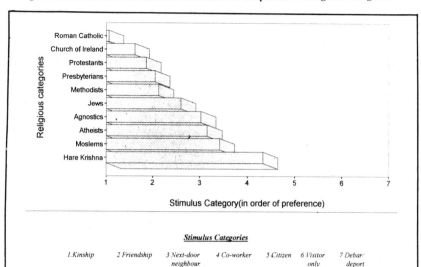

Respondents were then given a card showing the different points on the scale. The rationale for urging a brisk response was to get dispositions rather than rationalisations or reflected judgements. Attitudes are basically pre-reflectional dispositions.

The above table (77) tells a number of important things about the Irish population's attitudes to the religious categories tested. Three categories, i.e. Roman Catholics, Church of Ireland, and Protestants, have a mean social distance score under two which means closer than "friendship". Presbyterians and Methodists average very close to "friendship" also. Jews are halfway between "friendship" and "Nextdoor neighbour", while Agnostics and Atheists average close to "Nextdoor neighbour". Moslems are averaging less than halfway between "Nextdoor neighbour" and "Co-worker". The mean score for Hare Krishna is slightly further out than "Co-worker".

The rank-order of the categories, i.e. order of preference as measured by "mean social distance" scores, clearly confirms the "principle of propinquity". This "principle" states that we prefer those we perceive to be most like ourselves or nearest to our own religious self-evaluation. The percentages in the kinship column reflect the degree of "religious endogamy" in the people, namely, the preference for marriage within one's own religious group or denomination.

The responses to the stimulus categories "Jews" and "Israelis" is most interesting in that it highlights the relatively strong hostility towards "Israelis" among approximately one quarter of the sample who would deny their citizenship or debar them. Such a level of hostility is not reflected in the case of Jews. It must be assumed, however, that the rating of "Israelis" affects that of the "Jews".

TABLE No. 78
CORRELATION MATRIX OF RELIGIOUS SOCIAL DISTANCE RESPONSES

P≤.001 in all cases	Roman Catholic 1	C of I 2	Protestants 3	Presbyterians 4	Methodists 5	Jews 6	Agnostics 7	Atheists 8	Moslems 9	Hare Krishna 10
1 Roman Catholics	1.00	.21	.26	.21	.21	.18	.12	.13	.13	.09
2 Church of Ireland		1.00	.66	.59	.60	.52	.44	.44	.41	.35
3 Protestants			1.00	.71	.61	.53	.41	.45	.40	.34
4 Presbyterians				1.00	.77	.61	.49	.52	.52	.44
5 Methodists					1.00	.70	.56	.58	.59	.47
6 Jews						1.00	.57	.58	.65	.53
7 Agnostics							1.00	.80	.60	.57
8 Atheists								1.00	.60	.57
9 Moslems									1.00	.63
10 Hare Krishna										1.00

TABLE No. 79
RANK ORDER OF CORRELATION COEFFICIENTS OF RESPONSES
TOWARDS RELIGIOUS CATEGORIES

1	Agnostics with Atheists	+0.80		Church of Ireland with Jews	+0.52
2	Presbyterians with Methodists	+0.77	24 {	Presbyterians with Atheists	+0.52
3	Protestants with Presbyterians	+0.71		Presbyterians with Moslems	+0.52
4	Methodists with Jews	+0.70	26	Methodists with Agnostics	+0.49
			27	Methodists with Hare Krishna	+0.47
5	Church of Ireland with Protestants	+0.66	28	Protestants with Atheists	+0.45
6	Jews with Moslems	+0.65		Church of Ireland with Agnostics	+0.44
7	Moslems with Hare Krishna	+0.63	30 {	Church of Ireland with Atheists	+0.44
8.5 {	Protestants with Methodists	+0.61		Presbyterians with Hare Krishna	+0.44
	Presbyterians with Jews	+0.61		Church of Ireland with Moslems	+0.41
	Church of Ireland with Methodists	+0.60	32.5		
11 {	Agnostics with Muslims	+0.60		Protestants with Agnostics	+0.41
	Atheists with Muslims	+0.60	34 {	Protestants with Moslems	+0.40
13.5 {	Church of Ireland with Presbyterians	+0.59	35	Church of Ireland with Hare Krishna	+0.35
	Methodists with Moslems	+0.59	36	Protestants with Hare Krishna	+0.34
15.5	Methodists with Atheists	+0.58	37	Roman Catholics with Protestants	+0.26
	Jews with Atheists	+0.58		Roman Catholics with Ch of Ireland	+0.21
{	Jews with Agnostics	+0.57	39 {	Roman Catholics with Presbyterians	+0.21
18 {	Agnostics with Hare Krishna	+0.57		Roman Catholics with Methodists	+0.21
	Atheists with Hare Krishna	+0.57	41	Roman Catholics with Jews	+0.18
20	Methodists with Agnostics	+0.56		Roman Catholics with Atheists	+0.13
			42.5 {		
21.5 {	Jews with Hare Krishna	+0.53		Roman Catholics with Moslems	+0.13
	Protestants with Jews	+0.53	44	Roman Catholics with Agnostics	+0.12
			45	Roman Catholics with Hare Krishna	+0.09

The position of "Agnostics" and "Atheists" is quite negative in terms of social distance. More than two-thirds of the sample (69% and 71% respectively) would not welcome members of these categories into their family, i.e. "would marry or welcome as member of my family". One-fifth of the sample (19%) would deny citizenship to both categories. While these findings may reflect a religious endogamy, they also point to a serious degree of religious intolerance among a substantial minority of respondents.

Tables 78 and 79 gives the correlation coefficients between the responses to the various religious categories.

The relatively high mean social distance score in relation to Moslems (3.42) may reflect negative propaganda towards this category in British and other media. The situation in relation to the Hare Krishna (4.331) is quite negative and calls for more tolerant education in the established churches.

Figure No. 22: Response Patterns of Social Distance (Bogardus Scale 1988-89)

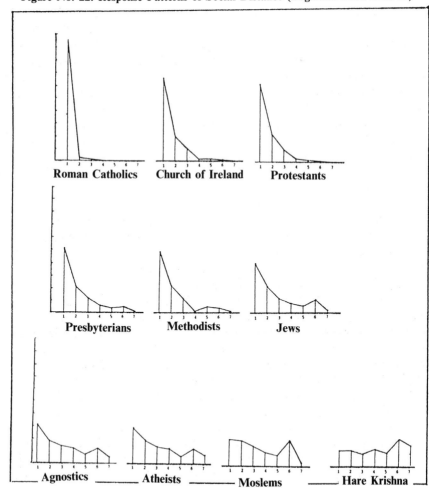

Roman Catholics   Church of Ireland   Protestants

Presbyterians   Methodists   Jews

Agnostics   Atheists   Moslems   Hare Krishna

An analysis of the above two tables points in the first instance to the internal validity of the scale in that it groups categories conceptually similar to Roman Catholics and other religious stimulus categories. This is in part explained by the practical consensus in "admission to family" (97%). The moderately high correlation (0.65) between responses towards Jews and towards Moslems is noteworthy, as is that between Moslems and Hare Krishna (0.63).

The response patterns on Figure 22 are interesting in that they show the progressive change according to the severity of the prejudice, i.e., from unimodal to bi-modal. The negative modal point is at the "visitor only" level rather than the more extreme level no. 7, namely, "debar or deport". The latter would be the modal point for "political" outgroups (see Mac Gréil, 1977, p. 248, Figure 32).

Table 80 gives a breakdown of the social distance scores of the Dublin (City and County) sub-sample (1988-89) and the scores of the Greater Dublin sample of 1972-73 in the case of eight religious categories measured in both surveys. The overall comparative figures show a small increase (+0.059) in mean social distance, which means a slightly less tolerant disposition in Dublin than was the case in 1972-73. The two categories towards which there was a decrease (a relatively small decrease) in mean social distance were Roman Catholics (−0.027) and Atheists (−0.026), i.e. the categories of both extremes of the rank order. Despite the increase in mean social distance scores for six of the eight categories, four of them recorded a small (but significant) increase in the percentage admitting into the family, i.e. Protestants (plus 6%), Church of Ireland (plus 4%), Presbyterians (plus 4%) and Agnostics (plus 3%). The percentage of Dublin respondents who would welcome Jews as members of the family was down by 4% (from 57% in 1972-73 to 53% in 1988-89).

The difference in the attitudes towards religious categories between the total sample (1988-89) and that of the Dublin sub-sample (1988-89) is quite significant and merits serious analysis. Table No. 81 points to the differences in "welcome to kinship" percentages and mean socio-distance scores of Dublin and the national sample.

It is quite clear from Table 81 that the Dublin subsample is prepared to admit all religious categories much closer than is the national sample. The degree of denominational and religious endogamy, i.e. the tendency to welcome into the family through marriage only those of one's own religion and denomination, is very high in both the National and Dublin scores. It is particularly so in relation to "Agnostics", "Atheists", "Moslems", and "Hare Krishna" categories. The position in relation to the "Jews" may be affected by the people's attitudes towards "Israelis" which are significantly and substantially less favourable (see 6a on Table 81 below).

In the above paragraphs the findings of the measures of social distance towards religious categories have been examined and analysed. The standing of the main Christian denominations has remained relatively high while

TABLE No. 80
COMPARISON OF SOCIAL DISTANCE SCORES BETWEEN DUBLIN SUBSAMPLE
1988-89 AND DUBLIN SAMPLE 1972-73 (By Stimulus Category)

	1	2	3	4	5	6	7	MS D (1-7)
1. Roman Catholics								
88/89	97%	100%	100%	100%	100%	0%	0%	1.039
72/73	96%	99%	99%	100%	100%	0%	0%	1.066
Change	+1%	+1%	+1%	–	–	–	–	-0.027
2. Protestants								
88/89	79%	90%	95%	98%	99%	1%	0%	1.395
72/73	73%	93%	98%	99%	99%	1%	0%	1.376
Change	+6%	-3%	-3%	-1%	–	–	–	+0.019
3. Church of Ireland								
88/89	77%	89%	96%	99%	99%	1%	0%	1.416
72/73	73%	93%	98%	99%	99%	1%	0%	1.397
Change	+4%	-4%	-2%	-1%	–	–	–	+0.019
4. Presbyterians								
88/89	72%	86%	91%	96%	97%	2%	1%	1.598
72/73	68%	89%	96%	98%	99%	1%	0%	1.503
Change	+4%	-3%	-5%	-2%	-2%	+1%	+1%	+0.095
5. Methodists								
88/89	67%	83%	89%	94%	97%	2%	1%	1.702
72/73	67%	88%	95%	97%	99%	1%	0%	1.552
Change	–	-5%	+4%	-3%	-2%	+1%	+1%	+0.150
6. Jews								
88/89	53%	77%	87%	93%	95%	3%	2%	1.965
72/73	57%	82%	91%	94%	97%	2%	1%	1.795
Change	4%	-5%	-4%	-1%	-2%	+1%	+1%	+0.170
7. Agnostics								
88/89	44%	63%	74%	84%	88%	9%	3%	2.488
72/73	41%	69%	81%	85%	89%	5%	6%	2.417
Change	+3%	-6%	7%	-1%	-1%	+4%	-3%	+0.071
8. Atheists								
88/89	40%	64%	74%	85%	88%	9%	3%	2.156
72/73	38%	66%	79%	83%	88%	5%	7%	2.542
Change	+2%	-2%	-5%	+2%	–	+4%	-4%	-0.026
Scale Mean								
88/89	66 1%	81.5%	88.3%	93.5%	95.4%	3.4%	1.2%	1.765
72/73	64.1%	84.9%	92.1%	94.4%	96.3%	12.0%	1.7%	1.706
Change	+2.0%	-3.4%	-3.8%	-0.9%	-0.9%	+1.4%	-0.5%	+0.059

that of "Jews" occupies a middle position (2.599). The poor standing of "Atheists" and "Agnostics" at over 3.000 and that of "Moslems" and "Hare Krishna" (at 3.420 and 4.331 respectively) is quite intolerant. The changes since 1972-73 have been fairly disappointing and reflects negatively on the degree of ecumenical progress in the intervening years. There was very little change over the sixteen years between the surveys.

TABLE No. 81
ADMISSION TO KINSHIP AND MEAN SOCIAL DISTANCE SCORES IN RELATION TO RELIGIOUS CATEGORIES OF THE TOTAL SAMPLE AND THE DUBLIN SUBSAMPLE

Stimulus Category	A National Sample 88/89		B Dublin Sub-Sample 88/89		(A - B) Difference	
	Kinship	M.S.D.	Kinship	M.S.D.	Kinship	M.S.D.
1. Roman Catholics	97%	1.057	97%	1.039	0%	+0018
2. Church of Ireland	65%	1.609	77%	1.416	-12%	+0.193
3. Protestants	62%	1.859	79%	1.395	-17%	+0.464
4. Presbyterians	52%	2.045	72%	1.598	-20%	+0.477
5. Methodists	49%	2.128	67%	1.702	-18%	+0.426
6. Jews	40%	2.599	53%	1.965	-13%	+0.634
6a. (Israelis)	(32%)	(3.117)	(45%)	(2.200)	(- 13%)	(+0.917)
7. Agnostics	31%	3.021	44%	2.488	- 13%	+0.533
8. Atheists	29%	3.152	40%	2.516	- 11%	+0.636
9. Moslems	21%	3.420	26%	2.953	-5%	+0.467
10. Hare Krishna	13%	4.331	13%	4.012	0%	+0.319
	N = 1005		N = 254			

PART IV: ANTI-SEMITISM

1. INTRODUCTION:

Anti-Semitism may be defined as prejudice against Jews and Judaism which is said to have its origin in pre-Christian times. In the ancient world the Jewish diaspora resulted in relatively small groups of Jews, who were monotheists, living among peoples who were polytheists. As minorities they were quite distinctive in faith and in practice.

The Christian era, which began from the Jewish tradition, was marked by conflict between Christianity and Jews leading to persecution. In the first wave of persecution, it was the followers of Christ who were persecuted by Jewish authorities. This was soon to be reversed, especially after the 4th Century when Christians became influential in Rome. This persecution of Jews was to continue throughout the medieval era, renaissance and "enlightenment age". The nineteenth century was also marked by continued anti-Semitism.

It was not until the reign of the Third Reich in Germany in the 1930s and 1940s that the persecution of the Jews reached its most unacceptable and horrific level with the "Holocaust". Even after the exposure of the Holocaust, anti-Semitism has not been eliminated in post-war Europe. It raises its "ugly head" in various places at different times throughout Europe, even in those parts which are seen to be "post-Christian". It seems to thrive as well in secular society as in a society in which the vast proportion of the citizens are genuine believers.

Why this pervasive form of prejudice has continued over well-nigh three thousand years without abating fully is a question which students and researchers of intergroup relations must ask. Robert S. Wistrich in his book, *Antisemitism: The Longest Hatred* (New York, Schocken Books, 1994) gives a detailed account of the history of anti-Semitism as seen from the point of view of a Jewish historian and is worth reading by all students of intergroup relations. It chronicles the various persecutions and pogroms which Jews in diaspora were forced to endure. And, yet, it does not give a totally satisfactory (sociological) explanation of this most enduring of all prejudices.

Three possible hypothetical explanations may be put forward which in some way might provide partial explanations:[2]

    (a)   The Jews as the ideal scapegoat;
    (b)   The Jews as the Ego-Ideal or Superego;
    (c)   The Jews as agents of change.

As *ideal scapegoats,* Jews in most countries have the basic characteristics of scapegoats, namely, they tend to be relatively weak (in numbers) with high visibility and can be deviously associated with areas of financial

---

2. The author acknowledges the sources of these hypothetical causes of anti-Semitism in numerous authors and from various conversations.

activity which would link them with economic failure and injustice. The classic example of this abuse of the Jews was their scapegoating by the Third Reich for the post World War I social and economic failure.

As the *ego-ideal or superego*, the Jews may appear as a challenge to others who have not achieved the same success with their own lives and talents. Because of their perpetual minority status Jews have had to be more industrious and conscientious in pursuit of education and in deferring satisfaction, while others (in the dominant group) may feel threatened and rebuked by the Jews' success. This is more than jealousy or envy. It is a constant rebuke of the non-Jews' failure. The virtuous are always perceived (at least subconsciously) by the non-virtuous as a perpetual reminder of the latter's failure. This can easily lead to an intense hatred in the form of prejudice.

The third hypothetical cause of anti-Semitism is the perception of Jews as *agents of social and cultural change*. Being a minority in diaspora, they may be perceived as being more detached from the values and norms of their society. In societies where the majority may be committed to Christian, Islamic, Communist, Hindu, and other values and norms, articulate promotion of radical change (even when many others would agree with such change) by Jews would be open to the myth that they are undermining the socio-cultural fabric. The facts of social and cultural change do not substantiate the pre-eminent role of Jews as agents of such change any more than other groups of intellectuals. Incidentally, all intellectuals are feared by many because of their promotion of change. Jews seem to be included in the paranoia towards those deemed to be agents of social change. Most repressive authoritarian regimes tend to oppress intellectuals and persecute them. Was this part of the cause of the Third Reich's inordinate hatred of the Jews?

In addition to the above three hypothetical causes of anti-Semitism, there are of course other more sociographic bases to the persecution of the Jews including many dangerous religious myths perpetuated by a literalist and fundamentalist interpretation of the Bible and the transferring of the guilt of a number of individual Jewish leaders of a particular time in relation to the persecution of Christ and his early followers to those of latter generations who are wholly innocent. Negative religious stereotypes of Jews have been transmitted to the young by Christian parents and leaders which have helped to rationalise anti-Jewish persecution.

The influence of the image of the treatment of Palestinian Moslems by the Israeli authorities has received widespread criticism in Ireland and throughout the world, especially, in relation to the plight of the refugees. This image of the persecutor rather than the persecuted is a factor likely to affect attitudes towards Jews. While there have been atrocities on both sides, the Israelis are portrayed as the dominant group and the more powerful partner in the conflict. Also, there is widespread sympathy with the dispossessed Palestinians. An effective peace process would be likely to ameliorate the Israeli image in Ireland and elsewhere. It should be noted that the 1988-89 survey preceded both this process and the Gulf War.

2. THE ANTI-SEMITIC SCALE

2.1 Overall Responses:

The following anti-semitic scale is replicated from the 1972-73 Dublin survey. Table 82 gives the responses of the total sample to this special scale.

TABLE NO. 81: ANTI-SEMITIC SCALE (1972-73 DUBLIN SCORES IN BRACKETS)

STATEMENT	Agree %	Don't Know %	Disagree %	P-Score (1-200)	Number
Question: "Now could we go on to talk about other religions. With regard to the Jews, would you agree or disagree?"					
1. That it would be good for the country to have many Jews in positions of responsibility in business.	30 (46)	35 (13)	36 (42)	106.1 (94.3)	998 (2,291)
2. That Jews are a bad influence on Christian culture and civilisation.	12 (11)	22 (6)	65 (83)	46.8 (28.0)	1,000 (2,290)
3. That Jews may have moral standards when dealing with each other, but with Christians they are ruthless and unscrupulous.	22 (22)	35 (11)	43 (67)	78.1 (55.0)	991 (2,288)
4. That it is wrong for Jews and Christians to inter-marry .	27 (28)	22 (6)	51 (66)	75.2 (61.2)	998 (2,290)
5. That golf clubs or similar organisations are justified in denying membership to a person because he/she is a Jew.	6 (5)	10 (2)	84 (93)	22.2 (12.5)	996 (2,290)
6. That the~Jjews as a people are to be blamed for the crucifixion of Christ.	20 (16)	16 (9)	64 (76)	56.0 (400)	996 (2,283)
7. That Jews do not take a proper interest in community problems and government.	16 (29)	40 (16)	44 (55)	72.4 (74.5)	994 (2,278)
8. That Jewish power and control in money matters is far out of proportion to the number of Jews.	33 (57)	43 (18)	24 (25)	109.4 (132.2)	992 (2,289)
9. That Jews are behind the money-lending rackets.	25 (49)	39 (23)	37 (28)	88.5 (121.3)	995 (2,291)
10. That we should encourage Irish Jews as much as anybody else to take up positions of importance in Irish society.	70 (85)	15 (4)	15 (11)	46.0 (26.7)	995 (2,290)
Scale P-Score	–	–	–	70.1 (64.6)	–

Cronbach's Alpha = 0.81

The percentages of the Dublin Survey (1972-73) are given in brackets for each item. With the exception of items nos. 8 and 9, i.e., the "money matters stereotype", the responses of the 1988-89 national sample were slightly more negative than those of the 1972-73 Dublin sample. A contrasting feature of the 1988-89 responses was the exceptionally high level of "Don't Knows" (averaging 28% for the scale) when compared with the replies of the 1972-73 Dublin Sample (averaging 11% for the scale). When the "Don't Knows" averages are high it may indicate a state of change in relation to the views responded to on the scale. The direction of the change cannot be asserted from the response of a sample being measured for the first time, as is the case of the 1988-89 sample. The overall level of anti-Semitism is moderately low with a scale p-score of 70.1 out of a maximum of 200!

2.2 Change in Anti-Semitism Since 1972-73:

Table 83 measures the changes in p-scores between 1972-73 and 1988-89.

TABLE NO. 83
COMPARATIVE ANTI-SEMITIC SCALE SCORES

Statement	Total Sample 1988/89 A	Dublin Sub-Sample 1988/89	Dublin Sample 1972/73 C	Differences	
				A-B	B-C
1. Responsibility in Business	106.1	84.8	94.3	+21.3	-9 5
2. Danger to Christian Culture	46.8	28.1	28.0	+18.7	+0.1
3. Ruthless with Christians	78.1	72.2	55.1	+5.9	+17.1
4. Shouldn't Inter-Marry	75.2	58.2	61.6	+17.0	-3.4
5. Deny Membership of Golf Club	22.2	11.3	12.5	+ 10.9	- 1.2
6. To Blame for the Crucifixion	56.0	39.8	40.0	+16.2	-0.2
7. Neglect Public Affairs	72.4	60.9	74.5	+11.5	-13.6
8. Excessive Control of Money	109.4	105.9	132.2	+3.5	-26.3
9. Behind Money-lending Rackets	88.5	77.6	121.3	+10.9	-43.7
10. Discourage Public Positions for Jews	46.0	25.5	26.7	+20.5	-1.2
Scale P-Score	**70.1**	**56.4**	**64.6**	**+13.7**	**-8.2**

Table 83 shows two important comparisons which are most noteworthy. The difference between the p-scores of the National Sample (A) and those of the Dublin Subsample (B) show a substantial range of variation in items nos. 1, 2, 4, 6 and 10 which indicates that respondents living outside of Dublin are significantly more anti-Semitic. The overall level of anti-Semitism in Dublin in 1988-89 is significantly lower than it was in 1972-73. Item no. 3 is the only one to show a substantial increase in the p-score. Items nos. 2, 4, 5, 6 and 10 have failed to register a significant variation. The *"money matters stereotype"* has been substantially reduced by the responses to items nos. 8 and 9.

2.3 Individual Views:

As in the case of other scales, individual items of Table 82 give an insight into particular views which are held or rejected by the public in Ireland. The combined response of the scale's items are used to measure the level of anti-Semitism or prejudice against Jews and Judaism.

2.3.a Jews in Positions of Responsibility: Three of the ten items set out to measure the views of the respondents with regard to the desirability of Jews occupying positions of responsibility in public and business life. This is a measure of trust and appreciation of Irish Jews. For purposes of measuring anti-Semitism the negative aspect of the replies are recorded.

No. 1 *Not good to have many Jews in positions of responsibility in business*	36%
No. 7 *Jews do not take proper interest in community problems and government.*	16%
No.10 *We should not encourage Irish Jews to take up positions of importance.*	15%

All three elicited a minority negative response but for No. 1 that means a plurality of the sample since only 30% rejected the negative view (see Table 82 No. 1). It is inconsistent with the responses to Nos. 7 and 10 and this is obviously due to the "money matters stereotype" which is expressed more explicitly in Nos. 8 and 9.

When measured by personal variables the pattern of replies were in line with normal patterns of responses, i.e., younger respondents, Dubliners, higher educated and those from the upper social classes were more in favour of Jews participating in positions of responsibility (see Table 84). Females had lower scores than males in the case of Nos. 1 and 7.

2.3.b Jewish-Christian Relations: The sad history of anti-Semitism records recurring incidents of Christian persecution of Jews. The rationale for such persecution has been expressed in stereotypical portraying of Jews as being responsible for the execution of Christ and of being less than ethical in the behaviour with Christians. Both groups have maintained a strong measure of religious endogamy within their respective groups.

No. 2 *Jews are a bad influence on Christian culture and civilisation.*	12%
No. 3 *Jews may have moral standards when dealing with each other, but with Christians they are ruthless and unscrupulous.*	22%
No. 4 *It is wrong for Jews and Christians to intermarry.*	27%
No. 6 *Jews as a people are to be blamed for the crucifixion of Christ.*	20%

The above responses, while very much minority positions, are nevertheless too high for an enlightened and tolerant society. The myth of deicide in item no. 6 is believed by one fifth of the sample while the response to Item no. 3 seems to indicate a certain suspicion of this minority by more than one-in-five. Table 83 records very little change in the Dublin responses to nos. 2 and 6 while the response to no. 3 increased substantially. Responses to no. 4 reflect a high level of endogamy between Christians and Jews in Ireland. This may be mutual.

In the case of personal variables the usual response patterns were recorded in regard to "age", "county of residence", "education" and "social class position".

2.3.c Money Matters Stereotype: The view that Jews are over-represented in financial dealings has a long history and has been perpetuated by Shakespeare's Shylock character. The irony of the situation has been that because of the stereotype Jews were under-represented in centres of high finance and property ownership. In the time of the Christian ban on usury, Jews were used to act as bankers and money-lenders. They could engage in that "sinful activity" to facilitate the commercial needs of "moral" Christians! In Germany during the Nazi purge of the Jews their identification with money matters was exploited by the Third Reich.

No. 8 *Jewish power and control in money matters is far out of proportion to the number of Jews.*	33%
No. 9 *Jews are behind the money-lending rackets.*	25%

It is sad to see that one third of the sample believe the statement (no. 8) about Jewish power and control in money matters and one quarter accept the "money-lending stereotype" (no. 9). Table 83 shows a very substantial reduction in both of these items between 1972-73 and 1988-89. The variations by "age", "education" and "social class position", all followed the normal patterns of p-score. The range of scores by social class position is exceptionally low. "County of residence" was mixed and males had higher scores than females.

TABLE No. 84
ANTI SEMITIC SCALE BY PERSONAL VARIABLES

Variable	Responsibility in Business 1	Danger to Christian Culture 2	Ruthless with Christians 3	Shouldn't Intermarry 4	Blame for Crucifixion 6	Neglect Public Affairs 7	Excessive Control of Money 8	Behind Money-lending Rackets 9	Discourage Public Positions 10
Total Sample	36%	12%	22%	27%	20%	16%	33%	25%	15%
A. Age	N/S	P≤.001	P≤.001	P≤.001	P≤.00i	P≤.305	P≤.001	P≤.001	N/S
1. 18 to 20 years		11	14*	18	10*	9*	23*	14*	
2. 21 to 35 years		9*	16	14*	14	12	26	14*	
3. 36 to 50 years		10	22	22	23	17	17	36	
4. 51 years plus	18	28	43	29	22	41	38		24
B. Gender	P≤.05	N/S	N/	N/S	N/S	P≤.001	P≤.001	P≤.05	N/S
1. Female	32*					14*	28*	23*	
2. Male	40					19	40	28	
C. County of Residence	P≤.001	P≤.001	P≤.001	P≤.001	P≤.001	P≤.001	P≤.001	P≤.001	P≤.001
1. Dublin	26*	6*	20*	19*	13*	12*	37	24	7*
2. Rest of Leinster	36	11	21	25	19	15	28*	23	17
3. Munster	40	14	20	26	23	20	35	22*	16
4. Connaught/Ulster	44	21	28	42	27	20	34	36	23
D. Education	P≤.001	P≤.001	P≤.001	P≤.001	P≤.001	P≤.001	P≤.001	P≤.001	P≤.001
1. Primary Only	40	18	28	43	36	24	42	43	21
2. Incomplete 2nd Level	42	16	24	28	19	17	34	24	18
3. Complete 2nd Level	29	6	16	14	12	14	26*	15	9
4. Third Level	25*	0*	16	14	12	4*	28*	8*	4*
E. Social Class Position	N/S	P≤.001	P≤.001	P≤.001	P≤.001	P≤.001	P≤.001	P≤.001	P≤.001
1. Class I		0*	15	9*	6*	0*	29*	6*	0*
2. Class II		4	14*	13	10	13	29*	17	9
3. Class III		12	21	23	19	17	33	22	15
4. Class IV		14	21	27	19	19	34	26	14
5. Class V		15	28	34	24	18	36	34	18

2.3.d Exclusion of Jews from Golf Clubs or Similar Organisations: Only 6% of the national sample would agree with denying membership of golf clubs to Jews. This percentage is so small that further statistical analysis would not be of much value.

2.4 Correlation Matrix of Scale Items:

Table 85 gives the correlation scores of each of nine items. Item no. 5 has been omitted because of its practically unanimous rejection by the sample.

TABLE No. 85
CORRELATION MATRIX OF ANTI-SEMITIC SCALE

Summary Statement		I Jews in Positions			II Jewish-Christian Relations of Responsibility				III Money-Matters	
		1	7	10	2	3	4	6	8	9
1.	Responsibility in Business	1.00	.22	.36	.38	.28	.24	.19	.19	.22
7.	Neglect public affair		1.00	.29	.37	.39	.26	.30	.31	.35
10.	Discourage public positions			1.00	.43	.34	.30	.32	.19	.32
2.	Danger to Christian Culture				1.00	.48	.36	.36	.24	.36
3.	Ruthless with Christians					1.00	.37	.31	.32	.36
4.	Shouldn't inter-marry						1.00	.32	.30	.30
6.	To blame for the crucifixion							1.00	.29	.34
8.	Excessive Control of Money								1.00	.41
9.	Behind Money-Lending Rackets									1.00

It is quite clear from the above correlation matrix that there are significant correlations (+.20) between practically all of the items and especially between those of the three subscales. This, coupled with the Cronbach Alpha score of 0.81 gives greater validity to the scale as a measure of anti-Semitic disposition.

3. SOCIAL DISTANCE TOWARDS JEWS

Reference has been made elsewhere to the social distance response to Jews in the broader context of other religious categories. In the following paragraphs it is proposed to look a little closer at the patterns of social distance against the Jews.

Table 86 compares the responses of the 1972-73 and the 1988-89 surveys. It also compares the difference between the attitudes of the national sample and that of the Dublin subsample.

TABLE No. 86
SOCIAL DISTANCE RATINGS OF JEWS IN 1972-73 AND IN 1988-89

Social Distance	National Sample 88-89 A	Dublin Subsample 1988-89 B	Dublin Sample 1972-73 C	Differences	
				A-B	B-C
1. Welcome to Kinship	40%	52%	57%	-12%	-5%
2. Welcome to Friendship or closer	61%	76%	82%	-15%	-6%
3. Welcome to Neighbourhood or Closer	73%	86%	91%	-13%	-5%
4. Welcome as Co-Worker or Closer	81%	92%	94%	-11%	-2%
5. Welcome as Citizen or Closer	87%	94%	97%	-7%	-3%
6. Welcome as Visitor Only	11%	4%	2%	+7%	+2%
7. Debar or Deport from Ireland	2%	2%	1%	.0%	+1%
Mean Social Distance	2.599	1.965	1.795	+0.634	+0.170
Number	1.003	256	2,293	–	–

There has been a substantial difference between of the responses the national sample and that of the Dublin subsample. Those living outside Dublin have a higher level of anti-Semitism found in Table 86 and this confirms the findings of Table 83 above. The change in social distance towards Jews has increased very slightly in contrast to the slight decline in the p-score of the anti-Semitic Scale in Table 83. On closer analysis the change in each of the scales is barely significant. What is disappointing is the absence of a more substantial reduction in each of scales.

The factor which probably prevented this improvement may be the negative influence of the status of "Israelis" as a category whose performance is given on Table 77 (p. 200). This is further confirmed by the high positive correlation between the social distance responses towards "Jews" and "Israelis" at r = .68.

The breakdown of social distance towards Jews by personal variables is reported on Table 87.

The combination of "education" and "age" indicate a trend towards the reduction of anti-Semitism. The most significant personal variable has been "county of residence" where the Dublin scores are very substantially different from those of Connaught/Ulster. The latter subsample responses indicate a relatively serious level of prejudice against Jews. While this may be an expression of frustration in the subsample due to numerous factors, it may also point to vicarious anti-Semitic stereotypes imported from societies outside Ireland. The proportion of Jews actually resident in Connaught/Ulster is statistically insignificant.

TABLE No. 87
SOCIAL DISTANCE TOWARDS JEWS BY PERSONAL VARIABLE

Variable	Welcome to Kinship	Deny Citizenship	M.S.D.
A. Age			
1. 18 to 35 years	43.9	10.7	2.39*
2. 36 to 50 years	42.8	10.3*	2.44
3. 51 to 65 years	32.2	18.8	2.91
4. 61 years plus	31.7*	16.6	3.06
B. County of Residence			
1. Dublin	52.5	5.1*	1.98*
2. Rest of Leinster	42.0	9.4	2.35
3. Munster	36.5	16.4	2.85
4. Connaught/Ulster	20.2*	24.9	3.51
C. Education			
1. Primary Only	29.9*	20.6	3.20
2. Incomplete 2nd Level	38.2	14.1	2.66
3. Complete 2nd Level	43.1	7.3	2.25
4. Third Level	56.4	4.3*	1.82*
D. Occupational Status			
1. Professional/Executive	54.7	6.9*	2.01*
2. Inspectional/Supervisory	38.5	9.7	2.45
3. Skilled/R. Non Manual	37.4	14.0	2.68
4. Semi/Unskilled	39.1*	19.9	3.01
E. Pol. Party Preference			
1. Fianna Fail	35.5*	14.5	2.67
2. Fine Gael	35.1*	14.3	2.80
3. Labour Party	51.5	7.6	2.12*
4. Progressive Democrats	57.1	4.8*	2.14*

Note: Highest scores are underlined, while lowest scores have asterisks (*)

SUMMARY AND CONCLUSIONS (Chapters VI and VII)

1. GENERAL REMARKS:

The profile of the sample randomly chosen reflects that of the national population which means that one religious denomination, namely Roman Catholics, constitutes over 94% of respondents interviewed. Apart from some general features, common to all denominations and religious groups, it has only been possible to examine the religious behaviour and attitudes of Roman Catholics in areas of specific liturgical practice by personal variables.

2. SUMMARY OF FINDINGS:

2.1   The demographic distribution by religious affiliation in the Republic of Ireland has been relatively stable with Roman Catholics comprising 94-95% of the population since the withdrawal of the British in 1921. Intergenerational change of religious affiliation in the sample has been statistically insignificant. This stability of denominational distribution has, in all probability, been due to two factors, i.e. firstly, the absence of significant leakage from denominations and secondly, the fact that the Republic has suffered from emigration or out-migration of its population rather than immigration over the past seventy years.

2.2   Weekly church attendance is around 80%, i.e. 79% for the total sample and 82% for Roman Catholics. This indicates a decline of 9% over fifteen years in the case of Roman Catholics, which is statistically significant if not very substantial in overall terms. Attendance once a month or more often is 85% for the total sample or 87% for Roman Catholics. Protestant church attendance is 70% monthly or more often and 55% weekly.

        Subsamples showing highest church attendance have been those over fifty years of age, those raised in rural communities, and respondents living in Munster and Connaught/Ulster. Those with lowest participation are the 21-35 year olds, respondents raised in large cities and those living in Dublin (see Table 52).

2.3   Roman Catholics' reception of Holy Communion, at 63% once a month or more frequently, has not changed significantly since 1974. While the monthly rate has remained steady, there has been a very substantial increase in frequency of weekly reception, i.e. from 28% in 1974 to 43% in 1989 (see Table 55). There is a wide variation in rate of reception by all the main personal variables. The patterns for "age", "area of rearing" and "county of residence" are more or less the same as in the case of weekly Mass attendance. Males, respondents with incomplete second level education and those with skilled and routine non-manual occupations have relatively lower participation rates.

2.4   The practice of going to Sacramental Confession by Irish Roman Catholics has suffered much over the period 1974-89, with 56% going to Confession a few times a year or more often. Some 11% of Roman Catholics stated they have given up the practice altogether. The practice of monthly Confession has gone from 47% in 1974 to 18% in 1989. Table 54 and Figure 10 give a breakdown of the categories of high and of low frequency practice. The disparities between the subsamples are very striking. Those living in Dublin, third-level respondents, and younger respondents have the lowest level of participation.

2.5 Most respondents still see religion as a largely positive influence on their lives, even though comparisons with 1972-73 data from Dublin would suggest that fewer people now see it as an essential influence (see Tables 56 and 59). A comparison between the 1988-89 and 1972/3 figures for the Dublin subsample confirm the drop in intensity while maintaining an over 80% positive response.

2.6 A similar result was recorded in response to the question on the importance of handing on parents' beliefs to children, namely a drop in intensity within the relatively high positive scores of 83% (see Tables 57 and 60). There was a significant, if not very substantial, decline in the positive scores in the case of the Dublin subsample when compared with the 1972/3 survey.

2.7 The question of perceived social advantage/disadvantage of one's religion in getting on in the Republic was measured by two questions, i.e. whether one's religion should be considered in an application for a job of public responsibility, and the respondent's own experience in relation to the matter. As in the case of the 1972-73 survey, the overwhelming majority were against considering an applicant's religion (see Table 61) and only 1% experienced their religious beliefs as a social disadvantage. At the same time, some 44% felt that their religious affiliation was a social advantage (see Tables 62 and 63).

2.8 Some 90% of the total sample stated they prayed once a week or more often, while 82% did so once a day or more often (see Tables 64 and 65). The breakdown of prayer frequency of Roman Catholics in Table 65 shows that there were significant differences between sub-samples when classified by age, gender, area of rearing, and education.

2.9 Perceived personal closeness to God is measured in Tables 66 and 67. Again the scores are very high with some 86% of the sample professing a degree of closeness and only 5% not feeling close "at all". Of the latter category, less than 2% (1.6%) said they did not believe in God. The scale reported in Table 67 compares the Irish findings with those of a similar national survey carried out in Holland in 1985. This scale shows that the Irish perceive God's personal relationship with the people very much more positively than do the Dutch.

2.10   Attitudes toward vocations to the religious and clerical life were
        measured in Tables 68 and 69. The question related to the extent to
        which Roman Catholic respondents would welcome the news that a
        daughter or son of theirs had decided to become a nun or a priest.
        Some 75% would welcome a daughter becoming a nun and 79%
        would welcome a son becoming a priest. Only 6% would discourage
        their daughter and 3% would discourage their son from pursuing
        their respective vocations. The variations by "education" have been
        the most substantial, with those reaching the higher level least
        encouraging.

2.11   Attitudes towards Christian Church Unity are reported in Tables 71,
        72 and 73. If anything, the desire for Christian Church Unity has
        lessened since 1972-73 as has optimism about its likelihood in prac-
        tice. A surprising result has been the fact that older respondents were
        more positively disposed toward ecumenical unity and more
        optimistic about it than were younger respondents (see Tables 72 and
        73).

2.12   The respondents' images of God were examined on four continua of
        Mother/Father; Spouse/Master; Friend/King; and Lover/Judge.
        Four of these images were Biblical, i.e. "Father", "Master", "King",
        and "Judge". Three of the Biblical images won majority approval
        and one, that of "King" was rejected in favour of "Friend" (see
        Table 74 and Figure 19 for the spread of responses).

2.13   The majority of the sample had a positive and optimistic vision of the
        "World" and of "Human Nature". The relative strength of this
        optimism can be gauged from Table 75 and Figure 20.

2.14   The role of religion in socio-political life was the basis of a three
        statement mini-scale tested in Table 76. While a majority of
        respondents (52%) disagree that their (Christian) religion had a great
        deal of influence on their political ideas, a substantial minority (35%)
        claimed the opposite experience. A strong majority (61%), however,
        stated that their religion "would play an important role" when mak-
        ing a political decision. A plurality (49%) favoured priests, brothers
        and nuns becoming "more directly involved politically in fighting for
        social justice in Ireland", while a substantial minority (35%) opposed
        that view.

2.15   The results of the Bogardus Social Distance Scale in relation to the
        ten Religious categories given in Table 77 are analysed in Tables 78,
        79, 80 and 81. The order of preference was predictable, namely, the
        majority denomination coming first with the established Protestant

churches next. The position of Jews is in the middle distance, while agnostics and atheists share with Moslems and Hare Krishna the bottom of the scale. The comparison of social distance scores in relation to eight of the categories points to a less liberal disposition among Dubliners in 1988-89 than was the case in 1972-73 (see Table 80). This seems to confirm the drop in ecumenist aspirations in the Christian Church Unity scale. The national sample results are compared with those of the Dublin subsample in Table 38 and show a significantly lower level of tolerance in the country as a whole than in Dublin County and City.

2.16 Attitudes towards Jews and changes in the level of anti-Semitism are examined in Part IV of this chapter (pp. 208-217). The finding of the anti-Semitic scale and measures of social distance towards Jews are presented in Tables 82-87.

3. CONCLUSIONS (CHAPTERS VI and VII):

3.1 The findings in Chapters VI and VII confirm a high degree of religious faith and practice in the Republic of Ireland. There are a number of sectors of the population which manifest weaker commitment and frequency of practice. These would include the young, middle aged, males, respondents living in Dublin, and those reared in large cities. Education is negatively related to some practices but not to others.

3.2 Perhaps urbanisation, especially in the case of Dublin, is strongly associated with a weakening of religious belief and practice, even though both belief and practice are still quite strong by international standards, even in Dublin. This is probably related to the lack of community in the capital, since religion seems to be strengthened by continuous community support.

3.3 The recent decline in vocations to the religious and clerical state *has not* so far been reflected in a corresponding decline in religious devotion and liturgical practice. In fact, the strong goodwill expressed toward vocations, especially among the so-called blue-collared and "working class" (as reflected by education), raises questions about the recruitment and training of religious and clergy and the public perception of the life of clergy and religious.

3.4 The relatively high level of prayer, reinforced by the acceptance of a very personal relationship with God, points to a higher than may be expected spirituality among the vast majority of Irish adults. There is some evidence, however, which raises questions about the practice of prayer in the homes, namely, the relatively low frequency of prayer among younger respondents.

3.5   Attitudes towards Christian Church Unity are quite positive, but less so than the present author had anticipated. This raises very serious questions for those responsible for the promotion of Church Unity. The extraordinary fact that younger respondents seem to be less ecumenical than other members of the sample points towards possible further slowing of the reunification of the whole Christian Church. This is something of special urgency to the people of Ireland in the light of the polarisation in Northern Ireland.

3.6   Religion is still very central in the personal lives of the people. They have indicated the importance of handing on the beliefs of parents to their children. Within this positive response it has been noted that its *intensity* has reduced since 1972/3. This indicates a possible reduction of the status of religion in the home or in the school. Religious belief is very much the product of *primary* socialisation. This raises questions for parents, catechists, pastors and teachers.

3.7   The response of the sample to the "Greeley Continua" in relation to the "images of God" and the optimistic/ pessimistic views of "the World" and of "Human Nature" are very interesting. God is a friendly, paternal master and judge in the view of the people, although the image of "judge" was seriously challenged by that of "lover". This benevolent image is probably related to the nature of Irish spirituality.

3.8   Intergroup (religious) attitudes reported in the Bogardus Scale show a high level of tolerance for established categories with a strong degree of religious endogamy (marrying within one's religious collectivity). The degree of exclusion from close social distance of Moslems and Hare Krishna is probably due to lack of favourable contact with these groups to date and to imported negative stereotypical thinking against them in some of the media. The position of agnostics and atheists is once again very negative and hard to explain or justify, in the light of the acceptance of faith as a *gift* from God.

3.9   It should be stated that the evidence of these chapters is, on the whole, very positive from the point of view of the state of religious beliefs and practices in Ireland (in so far as they have been reported on above). At the same time, there are sufficient indicators of drift from practice and some measures of attitudinal intolerance to caution against complacency and call for serious reappraisal of certain policies and procedures by those in pastoral and spiritual roles.

The noted drop in intensity of the importance of religion in the findings could be interpreted as an indication of future reduction in the frequency of participation in regular liturgical worship. It could be a situation of attitude-behaviour lag. At the same time the level of commitment evident in the findings of this survey is sufficient to maintain a fairly high degree of worship participation.

Because of the fact that 94% of the sample was Roman Catholic (reflecting the population distribution) it is regretted that greater detailed examination of the beliefs, practices and attitudes of those of the other Christian Churches, of other faiths and of those not professing any faith, has not been possible.

3.10   The tables and text measuring the state of anti-Semitism in Ireland try to measure this type of social prejudice and relate it to possible reasons. The main reasons given by those who would deny kinship to Jews were 63% religious and 28% ethnic/way of life. An analysis of the anti-Semitic scale shows the strength of the "money matters stereotype" had declined since 1972-73. A significant minority (20%) who still associate Jews as a people being responsible for the Crucifixion of Christ. The moderately strong ($r = 0.68$) correlation between the social distance responses to Jews and to Israelis would indicate an association between the two to the possible disadvantage of the Jews. There was an overall slight drop in p-score (1-200) of the anti Semitic Scale among Dubliners (from 64.6 to 56.4) indicates a decline in anti-Semitism in Dublin. The changes in social distance were barely significant. The most negative result has been the relatively high level of prejudice towards Jews in the more rural areas of Ireland. On balance, however, the situation overall is moderately positive with room for improvement.

CHAPTER VIII

Attitudes towards Northern Ireland and Britain

INTRODUCTION

This chapter reports on the political attitudes and opinions of a national sample of the adult population of the Republic of Ireland. Many of the questions used in the questionnaire had been part of the 1972-73 survey of the Greater Dublin adult population. The changes in attitudes during the intervening sixteen years will be noted and analysed below.

Since the end of the Irish War of Independence in 1921, the issue of the division of the island of Ireland into two separate political administrative entities, now known as the Republic of Ireland (Twenty-Six Counties) and Northern Ireland (Six Counties), has been a constant source of political irritation. The intra- and inter-community troubles of the North have occupied a central place in the attitudes and concerns of most Irish citizens. Since the outbreak of conflict in 1969, the problems have become more acute. Political and community initiatives to date have failed to provide a satisfactory solution of these problems. The impact of the strife of the twenty years 1969-1989 on the attitudes of the people of the Republic can be gauged from the findings presented in this chapter. The 1994-96 ceasefire brought a measure of improvement but has not so far resulted in a permanent solution. The ending of the IRA ceasefire early in 1996 has revived tensions again.

The attitudes and views of the people towards the Northern Ireland situation have been measured in the current research under the following headings:

(a)   Social Distance towards the Northern Irish;
(b)   Special Northern Ireland Scale;
(c)   Solutions Considered Desirable or Acceptable;
(d)   Attitudes towards the Anglo-Irish Agreement.

PART I: SOCIAL DISTANCE TOWARDS NORTHERN IRISH

Table 88 gives the social-distance responses to Irish and British categories. The placing of "Northern Irish" in fifth place in the rank-order of the mean social-distance scores of the six categories demands an explanation!

The scoring in the case of each of the six "stimulus categories" points to a relatively low level of social distance which means that each category is held in high esteem by the majority of the sample. Nevertheless, the position of "Northern Irish" raises questions. Normally, in the case of social distance scores, the principle of propinquity applies, i.e. those closest to the

TABLE No. 88
SOCIAL DISTANCE TOWARDS IRISH AND BRITISH POLITICAL ETHNIC CATEGORIES (TOTAL SAMPLE)

Stimulus Category (in order of preference)	"Would marry or welcome as member of my family" %	"Would have as close friends or closer" %	"Would have as nextdoor neighbours or closer" %	"Would work in the same place or closer" %	"Would welcome as Irish citizen or closer" %	"Would have as visitors only to Ireland" %	"Would debar or deport from Ireland" %	Mean* Social Distance
1. Irish Speakers	84.4	92.5	96.5	98.3	99.7	0.3	–	1.287
2. English	77.9	88.5	93.7	96.2	97.2	2.1	0.7	1.475
3. British	76.7	87.5	92.5	95.6	96.5	2.8	0.7	1.521
4. Scottish	74.2	85.8	91.1	93.9	96.2	3.7	0.1	1.592
5. Northern Irish	70.9	83.7	90.7	93.9	97.4	2.2	0.4	1.637
6. Welsh	72.8	82.8	90.6	94.0	96.2	3.4	0.4	1.641

*Mean Social Distance is the mean score on a scale from 1 (Kinship) to 7 (Debar or Deport).

TABLE No. 89

COMPARATIVE SOCIAL DISTANCE SCORES TOWARD NORTHERN IRISH AND RELATED CATEGORIES (1988-89 AND 1972-73)

Stimulus Category	A Total Sample 1988-9			B Dublin Sub-Sample 1988-9			Dublin Sample 1972-3			C MSD Variations		
	R/O	Kinship	MSD	R/O	Kinship	MSD	R/O	Kinship	MSD	A - B	A - C	B - C
1. English	1	77.9%	1.475	3	85.5%	1.363	1	87.3%	1.285	+0.112	+0.190	+0.078
2. British	2	76.7%	1.521	4	84.8%	1.391	2	82.4%	1.413	+0.130	+0.108	-0.022
3. Scottish	3	74.2%	1.592	2	86.3%	1.332	5	78.4%	1.562	+0.260	+0.030	-0.230
4. Northern Irish	4	70.9%	1.637	5	79.7%	1.473	3	79.5%	1.474	+0.164	+0.163	-0.001
5. Welsh	5	72.8%	1.641	1	88.2%	1.271	4	78.4%	1.476	+0.370	+0.165	-0.205

respondents in terms of ethnic, religious, and other features, should score closest on the scale. When this principle is not followed it is likely that something less favourable towards the category "out of line" is present. This can be the public image of the category as portrayed in the media or negative experience felt by the respondent in regard to it. In the case of the former, the perceived negative image some Northern Irish have of the people of the Republic could well result in counter- negativity. Whatever the explanation may be, it is clear from Table 88 that a certain degree of estrangement exists in the attitudes of the people of the Republic towards the "Northern Irish" as a stimulus category. "Irish Speakers", "English", "British" and "Scottish" ranked higher than "Northern Irish". From the point of view of inter-group relations within Ireland, this result could not be deemed very satisfactory.

A similar result was found in the 1972-73 survey of the Greater Dublin population. Table 89 gives a comparison between the findings of both surveys.

The mean social distance score of the "Northern Irish" (1.47) and the percentage welcoming to kinship (79.5%) are exactly the same for the Dublin sub-sample in 1988-89 as they were for the Dublin Sample in 1972-73. This may be viewed as disappointing when one might have expected a closer level of social distance after sixteen years.

Attitudes to the Welsh and to the Scottish have greatly improved (by 10% and 8% welcoming to kinship respectively). The rank-order of the five categories (Spearman Rank Order Correlation Coefficient r = −0.25) has changed dramatically, with the Welsh and the Scottish replacing the English and the British in the first and second positions. The deterioration of the Northern Irish from third place in 1972-73 to fifth place in 1988-89 spells the relatively negative effects of Dubliners' experience of the reported developments in Northern Ireland over the period. Such developments have resulted in distancing the Dublin people from those in Northern Ireland rather than bringing them closer.

The following Table (Table 90) gives the correlation between the social distance responses of the national sample in relation to the Irish and proximately related ethnic categories.

TABLE NO. 90
CORRELATION MATRIX BETWEEN SOCIAL DISTANCE RESPONSES

	Irish Speakers	English	British	Scottish	Northern	Welsh
1. Irish Speakers	1.00	0.34	0.30	0.38	0.40	0.41
2. English		1.00	0.78	0.51	0.45	0.50
3. British			1.00	0.45	0.39	0.47
4. Scottish				1.00	0.52	0.74
5. Northern Irish					1.00	0.48
6. Welsh						1.00

[All correlations significant at P≤.001]

TABLE No. 91
RATIONALISATION OF REFUSAL TO WELCOME AS A MEMBER OF THE FAMILY

	Religious	Racial	Political	Ethnic	Economic	Not Socially Acceptable	Other	N	Primary Classification
1. Irish Speakers	2.1	0.7	9.9	75.2	0.0	2.8	9.2	141	Ethnic
2. English	9.1	0.5	31.6	54.1	1.4	1.4	1.9	209	Ethnic/Political
3. British	8.9	0.9	35.6	50.2	0.9	1.3	2.2	225	Ethnic/Political
4. Scottish	7.0	0.4	6.1	84.0	0.4	0.8	1.2	244	Ethnic
5. NORTHERN IRISH	12.1	1.4	42.6	37.6	1.8	2.8	1.8	282	Political/Ethnic
6. Welsh	3.9	0.0	4.3	88.2	0.8	1.2	1.6	255	Ethnic

The findings of Table 90 above are more or less as predicted, i.e. a very high correlation between attitudes towards "English" and "British" (0.78) and between attitudes towards "Scottish" and "Welsh" (0.74). This indicates that the English are the predominantly British category in the perception of the respondents. The correlations between the other categories are moderately significant, with the exception of the scores between "Irish speakers" and "British" (0.30) and "Irish speakers" and "English" (0.34) which are significant but low. Respondents who would not welcome members of the six categories (in Table 88) as members of their family, were asked the following:

> "*Looking over your answers to this question, there are a number of categories which you would not welcome into kinship. Which of the following would you say was your main reason for placing them at the distance indicated?*

A. *Religious beliefs and/or practices;*	E. *Economic danger to us;*
B. *Racial – colour of skin, etc.;*	F. *Not socially acceptable;*
C. *Political views and/or methods;*	G. *Way of life;*
D. *Nationality and culture;*	H. *Other (specify)."*

The main purpose of this question was to discover which of the reasons was selected to rationalise the denial of kinship. The responses tell the researcher something about the nature of "intergroup definition".

The findings of Table 91 are most interesting in that they show the dominance of the "political" rationalisation in the case of "Northern Irish" and also in the case of "English" and "British". In the mind of the Irish refusing admission to the family, British and English are "politico-ethnic" categories, while the "Scottish" and the "Welsh" are predominantly "ethnic". One-in-eight of those who would not welcome "Northern Irish" into their family gave the reason as "religious". This 12.1% is relatively low when compared with the 42.6% who gave "political" and 37.6% with "ethnic" reasons. These figures show the weakness of religious sectarianism in Irish (Republic) attitudes towards the Northern Irish. "Irish Speakers" who were not welcomed into the family were distanced for "ethnic" reasons.

Comparisons of the rationalisation patterns between the 1988-89 study and the Greater Dublin survey of 1972-73 are given in Table 92.

The changes in the distribution of rationalisations by respondents who would not welcome members of the categories into their family highlight one very interesting factor, namely, the change in perception of the British and the English. Significantly and substantially more respondents saw these categories as "political".

Table 93 measures social distance in relation to Northern Irish by personal variables, i.e. place and county of residence, education and occupation. "Age", "gender", "marital status" and "political party preference" did not elicit statistically significant variations.

Table No. 92
COMPARISONS OF RATIONALISATIONS BETWEEN THE 1988-89 DUBLIN SUB-SAMPLE AND THE 1972-73 GREATER DUBLIN SAMPLE

		Religious %	Racial %	Political %	Ethnic %	Economic %	Not Socially Acceptable %	Other %	N
1. English	1972/3	4.0	0.4	21.2	65.3	2.2	5.8	1.0	274
	1988/9	0.0	0.0	42.5	50.0	0.0	0.0	2.5	40
	Change	-4.0	-4.0	+21.3	-15.3	-2.2	-5.8	+1.5	
2. British	1972/3	5.5	0.5	21.9	63.5	1.8	5.0	1.8	388
	1988/9	0.0	0.0	56.8	43.2	0.0	0.0	0.0	44
	Change	-5.5	-0.5	+24.9	-20.3	-1.8	-5.0	-1.8	
3. Scottish	1972/3	3.4	0.0	7.1	82.6	0.4	4.7	1.7	466
	1988/9	5.4	2.7	8.1	78.4	0.0	2.7	2.7	37
	Change	+2.0	+2.7	+1.0	-4.2	-0.4	-2.0	+1.0	
4. NORTHERN IRISH	1972/3	7.1	0.5	37.5	43.9	1.1	8.0	2.0	440
	1988/9	5.5	5.5	41.8	40.0	1.8	1.8	3.6	55
	Change	-1.6	+5.0	+4.3	-3.9	+0.7	-6.2	+1.6	
5. Welsh	1972/3	1.5	0.0	1.9	90.1	0.8	4.2	1.5	475
	1988/9	3.2	0.0	9.7	74.2	0.0	3.2	9.7	31
	Change	+1.7	0.0	+7.8	-15.8	-0.8	-1.0	+7.2	

Note: In all cases P≤.001

Those reared in "large cities" and "small cities" were more willing to welcome Northern Irish into their families than were respondents from "towns" and "rural" residents. In the case of County/Province of residence, those living in "Dublin" were most positively disposed. Education was positively correlated with percentage admitting to the family, i.e. "Third Level" respondents were 5.5% above the average while those with "Primary Only" were 6.6% below the average. Occupational status showed a mixed result, namely, those with highest and those with lowest status recording scores above the sample average. "Skilled/Routine Non-Manual" was the lowest grade scoring on admission to the family.

In summary, the main finding of the social distance scale in relation to "Northern Irish" is both positive and negative. From the *positive* point of

TABLE No. 93
SOCIAL DISTANCE TOWARDS NORTHERN IRISH BY PERSONAL VARIABLES

VARIABLE	Welcome into Family	Welcome as Friend/ Neighbour or closer	Welcome as Co-Worker/Citizen or closer	Deny Citizenship	N.
National Sample	70.9	90.7	97.4	2.6	1001
I. A. PLACE OF RESIDENCE P≤.001					
1. Large City	79.1	94.1	98.3	1.7	287
2. Small City	73.8	85.7	95.2	4.8	84
3. Town	73.1	90.8	100.0	0.0	130
4. Rural	65.2	89.6	96.6	3.4	500
B. COUNTY/PROVINCE OF RESIDENCE P≤.05					
1. Dublin	78.0	92.4	97.5	2.5	277
2. Rest of Leinster	72.5	91.7	98.0	2.0	255
3. Munster	69.1	90.6	98.3	1.7	298
4. Connaught/Ulster	60.2	86.5	94.7	5.3	171
C. EDUCATION P≤.05					
1. Primary Only	64.3	88.2	95.3	4.6	280
2. Incomplete Second Level	68.1	92.1	98.5	1.5	348
3. Complete Second Level	75.3	91.3	98.4	1.6	231
4. Third Level	76.4	92.2	97.6	2.5	141
D. OCCUPATIONAL STATUS P≤.05					
1. Unskilled/Semi-Skilled	73.5	88.3	97.3	2.6	155
2. Skilled/Routine Non-Manual	65.3	88.8	95.7	4.3	277
3. Inspectional/Supervisory	73.7	92.0	98.3	1.7	300
4. Professional/Executive	80.5	94.3	98.3	0.6	15

Note: Percentages significantly higher than the National Sample average are underlined

view, the vast majority of the national sample (70.9%) would welcome Northern Irish into the closest level of relationship, i.e. into the family, while less than 3% would deny them citizenship. In the case of those not welcoming them into the family, "religious" and "political" reasons were given by 45% of respondents. This would indicate the politico-religious identity of Northern Irish by many of those less favourably disposed to them.

"*Negatively*", as in 1972-73, respondents deviated from the "principle of propinquity" and placed Northern Irish lower down in the rank-ordering than "English", "British" and "Scottish". To correct this social distance anomaly, greater effort may be necessary for the promotion of favourable contact between people across the border. The media of mass communication could play a more positive role in the presentation of Northern Irish people to those in the Republic by strictly avoiding negative stereotyping.

PART II: SPECIAL NORTHERN IRELAND SCALE

A special Northern Ireland Scale was designed for the 1972-73 Survey of the Attitudes of Greater Dublin. This scale is not intended as a purely attitudinal scale. It measures specific *opinions* relating to the Northern problems of community and national integration.

> "The attitude scale designed especially to measure attitudes and opinions towards Northern Ireland is not strictly a prejudice scale. It would be more properly classified as an *attitude/opinion scale*. In other words, it has not been designed to elicit prejudice against any particular category with the possible exception of Item No.11 which takes "*Northerners on all sides*" as a prejudice stimulus category."
>
> [Mac Gréil 1977, p. 375]

The scale addresses a number of issues relating to Northern Ireland, i.e.

(a)   Common identity between Protestants and Catholics (Items 1, 2 and 3);
(b)   Issues relating to national unity and unity within the community (Items 4,5,6 and 7);
(c)   Role of religion, education and violence (Items 8,9 and 10);
(d)   Item 11 measures a dismissive and negative disposition.

Table 94 gives a breakdown of the responses of the total sample to each item of the scale. The eleven items divide into four sub-scales, i.e. as outlined above.

TABLE No. 94:
SPECIAL NORTHERN IRELAND SCALE (TOTAL SAMPLE)

Introduction: "Northern Ireland is a topic of interest and concern for many people. I would like to get your views on some aspects relating to the Northern problem. Would you agree or disagree with each of the following statements?"

	Agree	Don't Know	Disagree	N.
Sub Table A				
1. Catholics in Northern Ireland have more in common with Northern Protestants than they have with Catholics in the Republic.	45%	21%	34%	998
2. Northern Irish Protestants have more in common with the rest of the Irish people than they have with the British.	36%	20%	44%	997
3. Protestants in the Republic have more in common with Catholics here than they have with Protestants in Northern Ireland.	67%	16%	16%	998
Sub-Table B				
4. Northern Ireland and the Irish Republic are two separate nations.	49%	9%	42%	999
5. A return to the Irish language and culture could provide a good basis for Irish unity in the long term (even though it might present difficulties in the short term).	24%	19%	57%	1000
6. National unity is an essential condition for the just solution of the present Northern problem.	50%	25%	25%	999
7. There should be increased co-operation across the Border with the people in Northern Ireland.	90%	7%	3%	999
Sub-Table C				
8. The position and influence of the Catholic Church in the Republic is a real obstacle to Irish unity.	36%	20%	45%	997
9. Having separate Catholic and Protestant schools (Primary and Secondary Schools) has been a major cause of division in the Northern Irish community.	74%	13%	13%	1000
10. The use of violence, while regrettable, has been necessary.	16%	8%	76%	1000
Sub-Table D				
11. Northerners on all sides tend to be extreme and unreasonable.	35%	19%	46%	997

It is proposed to comment on the findings of Table 94 when examining the percentages by Sub-Scale.

2.1 Sub-Scale A: Perceived Inter-Denomination Ethnic Identity:

The findings of Items 1, 2 and 3 (Table 94) are illustrated in Figure 23 below. The perceived identity between Protestants and Catholics in the

Prejudice in Ireland Revisited

North and within the Republic is stronger than the denomination identity strengths across the Border. The ratio of common identity between *Northern Catholics* and Northern Protestants *and* that of their co-denominational members in the Republic is 45:34. In the case of the *Protestants in the Republic* and their co-citizen Catholics *and* that of their co-denominational members North of the Border, the ratio is 67:16. While the "intra-bonds" are perceived to be stronger than the "inter-bonds", it should be noted that the position in the 1972-73 Dublin sample was significantly more tilted in favour of the "intra-bonds' (see Table 95) within the Republic and Northern Ireland.

Figure No. 23: Perceived Ethnico-Religious Identity Strength in Ireland

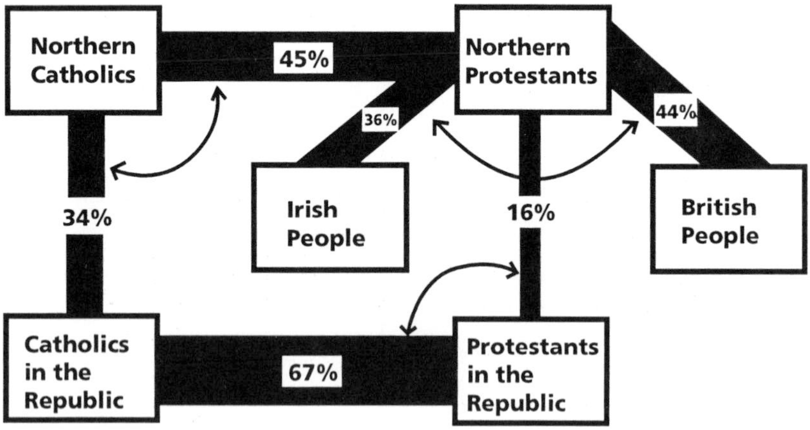

Table 95 shows the changes which have taken place in the people's perception of the "intra-" and "inter-bonds" since 1972-73. It also points out the differences between the views of the national sample and those of the Dublin sample.

It would appear that inter-denominational bondings across the Border have scored modestly higher in 1988-89 which may be indicative of a move towards greater perceived denominational solidarity throughout the whole island of Ireland.

The decline in the percentage who perceived that the Northern Protestants had more in common with the British people than they had with the Irish is also very significant and would imply a step towards their perception as having more in common with the Irish people. Respondents from Connaught/Ulster were significantly above the national average at 44% holding the view that Northern Protestants had more in common with the Irish people than with the British. "Upper Class" (56%) and "Upper Middle Class" (44%) respondents also strongly perceived Northern Protestants as

TABLE No. 95
PERCEIVED ETHNIC-DENOMINATIONAL IDENTITY 1988/89 AND 1972/73

		A Total Sample 1988/89	B Dublin Sub-Sample 1988/89	C Dublin Sample 1972/73	Diff. B/C	County of Residence (1988-89)				Social Class Position (1988-89)				
						Dublin	Rest of Leinster	Munster	Connaught/ Ulster	CII	CIII	CIIII	CIIV	CIV
1. Catholics in Northern Ireland have more in common with Northern Protestants than they have with Catholics in the Republic.	Agree:	45%	54%	59%	-5%	54%	39%	46%	29%	N/S				
	Disagree:	34%	24%	28%	-4%	24%	37%	36%	39%					
2. Northern Irish Protestants have more in common with the rest of the Irish people than they have with the British.	Agree:	36%	37%	38%	-1%	37%	25%	40%	44%	56%	44%	36%	33%	35%
	Disagree:	44%	42%	53%	-11%	42%	53%	42%	27%	24%	38%	48%	46%	37%
3. Protestants in the Republic have more in common with Catholics here than they have with Protestants in Northern Ireland.	Agree:	67%	67%	85%	-18%	67%	65%	74%	60%	79%	76%	72%	61%	62%
	Disagree:	16%	13%	8%	+5%	13%	18%	14%	21%	9%	11%	13%	19%	20%
N.		1005	277	2277	–	277	255	300	173	34	105	270	295	188

Irish. In the context of perceptions of ethnico- religious identity, it is interesting to look briefly at the respondents' own response to the question of their personal ethnic self-identity (see Table 11, p. 97 above).

2.2 Sub-Table B: Unity of Ireland:

The four statements in sub-table B of Table 94 reveal a mixed response to the ethnic unity of Ireland. Item No. 7 was practically unanimous with only 3% opposed to cross-border co-operation. The majority (50%) agreed that "National unity" was essential for a *"just solution to the present Northern problem"*. One-quarter (24%) felt that *"a return to the Irish language and culture could provide a basis for Irish unity"*. Some 57%, however, disagreed with this view. A plurality (49%) agreed that *"Northern Ireland and the Republic were two separate nations"*, with 42% disagreeing.

Table 96 shows the differences in responses between 1972-73 and 1988-89 in relation to each of the items on Sub-Table B.

TABLE No. 96
IRISH UNITY AND CROSS-BORDER CO-OPERATION (1988-89 AND 1972-73)

OPINION		A Total Sample 1988/89	B Dublin Sub-Sample 1988/89	C Dublin Sample 1972/73	Diff. B-C
1. Northern Ireland and the Irish Republic are two separate nations.	Agree:	49%	53%	43%	+10%
	Disagree:	42%	37%	55%	-18%
2. A return to the Irish language and culture could provide a good basis for Irish unity in the long term (even though it might present difficulties in the short term).	Agree:	24%	20%	18%	+2%
	Disagree:	57%	58%	80%	-22%
3. National unity is an essential condition for a just solution of the present Northern problem.	Agree:	50%	46%	58%	-12%
	Disagree:	25%	29%	36%	-7%
4. There should be increased co-operation across the Border with the people in Northern Ireland.	Agree:	90%	93%	94%	-1%
	Disagree:	3%	3%	4%	-1%
N		1004	276	2277	

As time moves on and the separation of Ireland into two administrative territories continues, it is to be expected that the perception of *"two separate nations"* would grow. This is borne out by the change in the responses of the Dublin sub-sample to item 1 above. The change in answers to the suggestion that the Irish language could provide a basis for national unity show a big decline (22%) in those disagreeing with the item, which indicates a possible growing appreciation of the significance of the Irish language and culture as a symbol of Irish ethnic unity.

The decline (12%) in the proportion of Dubliners who held that "National unity" was essential for the just solution of the present Northern problem is significant and could indicate a possible weakening of nationalist ideology in Dublin. Still, it will be shown in Table 103 (p. 246 below) that the support for a united Irish Republic as a desirable solution to the current Northern problem increased since 1972-73 in Dublin.

In relation to the desire for increased co-operation across the Border between the Republic and Northern Ireland, the extraordinarily high support has been maintained at 93%. Elsewhere in the findings some signs of estrangement from Northern Ireland are evident, but this has not led to the reduction of a desire for concrete co-operation, which must be reassuring to those who wish to see such positive inter-group behaviour. This very clear and repeated declaration of support for cross-border co-operation provides a mandate to political and other leaders for such action.

The opinions expressed in Table 97 elicited significant variations for "age", "gender", "county of residence", "education" and "political party preference". "Social class position" only elicited statistically significant variation in the case of "cross-border cooperation" with the higher classes unanimous in support of greater cooperation. Not every item was statistically significant in the case of each variable tested.

The sub-samples which were above average in agreement with the idea of *two separate nations* were females, respondents 35 to 50 years old, residents of Dublin and Munster, and supporters of the Progressive Democrats and Fine Gael. The *Irish language and culture* as a symbol of national unity was most favoured by those under 21 and over 50 years of age, residents of Connaught/Ulster, those with lower levels of education and supporters of Fianna Fáil and the Labour Party. The conviction that *National Unity was essential for the solution of the Northern problem* was held most strongly by the younger and older age groups, by Munster residents, by the two lower education sub-samples, and by Fianna Fáil supporters. There was widespread consensus in support of *increased cross-border co-operation*. In the three variables to record significant differences males, residents of Munster and Dublin, and the two highest grades of social class position were significantly above average.

2.3 Sub-Table C: Religion, Education and Violence:

The three topics raised in Sub-Table C of Table 94 have been the subject of much discussion over the past twenty-three years. What is measured is the *opinion* of respondents and not necessarily evidence of cause and effect. The plurality of respondents (45%) rejected the view that "*the position of the Catholic Church in the Republic*" was a real obstacle to Irish unity, while a minority (36%) agreed with that view. There was strong support (74%) for the opinion that "*having separate Catholic and Protestant schools is a major cause of division in the Northern Irish community*". Over three-quarters of

TABLE No. 97

IRISH UNITY AND CROSS-BORDER CO-OPERATION BY PERSONAL VARIABLES

	Northern Ireland and the Irish Republic are two separate nations. 1		A return to the Irish language and culture could provide a good basis for Irish unity in the long term (even though it might present difficulties in the short term). 2		National unity is an essential condition for a just solution of the present Northern problem. 3		There should be increased co-operation across the border with the people in Northern Ireland. 4	
	Yes	No	Yes	No	Yes	No	Yes	No
Total Sample	49%	42%	24%	57%	50%	25%	90%	3%
A. AGE								
1. Under 21	46%	43%	<u>30%</u>	46%	<u>54%</u>	25%		
2. 21 - 35	49%	39%	22%	55%	46%	27%		
3. 36 - 50	<u>55%</u>	38%	18%	<u>69%</u>	45%	<u>28%</u>	N/S	
4. 51 plus	45%	<u>48%</u>	<u>29%</u>	51%	<u>58%</u>	20%		
	{P≤.05}		{P≤.05}		{P≤.05}			
B. GENDER								
1. Female	<u>54%</u>	35%	N/S		N/S		88%	3%
2. Male	43%	<u>50%</u>					<u>94%</u>	2%
	{P≤.110}						{P≤.05}	
C. COUNTY OF RESIDENCE								
1. Dublin	<u>53%</u>	37%	20%	58%	46%	<u>29%</u>	<u>93%</u>	3%
2. Rest of Leinster	41%	<u>46%</u>	20%	<u>61%</u>	51%	20%	86%	2%
3. Munster	<u>53%</u>	41%	25%	55%	<u>57%</u>	26%	<u>93%</u>	3%
4. Connaught/Ulster	48%	<u>46%</u>	<u>35%</u>	53%	45%	25%	89%	2%
	{P≤.05}		{P≤.05}		{P≤.05}		{P≤.05}	
D. EDUCATION								
1. Primary Only					<u>56%</u>	17%	88%	3%
2. Incomplete Second Level	N/S		N/S		<u>53%</u>	23%	89%	3%
3. Complete Second Level					43%	<u>30%</u>	90%	5%
4. Third Level					45%	<u>30%</u>	<u>96%</u>	
					{P≤.05}		{P≤.05}	
E. POLITICAL PARTY PREFERENCE								
1. Fianna Fáil	46%	<u>46%</u>	<u>46%</u>	<u>28%</u>	52%	<u>55%</u>		
2. Fine Gael	<u>56%</u>	36%	37%	21%	<u>65%</u>	52%		
3. Labour Party	50%	39%	39%	<u>29%</u>	58%	39%	N/S	
4. PDs	<u>76%</u>	19%	19%	12%	<u>74%</u>	38%		
5. Workers Party	21%	<u>71%</u>	<u>71%</u>	<u>46%</u>	46%	42%		
	{P≤.001}		{P≤.05}		{P≤.05}		{P≤.05}	

Note: Percentages underlined are significantly higher than sample mean.

respondents (76%) rejected the view that "*the use of violence is regrettable but necessary*" while a minority of 16% agreed with the statement.

Table 98 compares the findings of 1988-89 with those of the 1972-73 survey of Greater Dublin.

TABLE No. 98
RELIGION, EDUCATION AND VIOLENCE IN RELATION TO
NORTHERN IRELAND (1988-89 and 1972-73)

OPINION		A National Sample 1988/89	B Dublin Sub-Sample 1988/89	C Dublin Sample 1972/73	Diff. B-C
1. The position and influence of the Catholic Church in the Republic is a real obstacle to Irish unity.	Agree:	56%	39%	41%	-2%
	Disagree:	45%	40%	53%	-13%
2. Having separate Catholic and Protestant schools (Primary and Secondary Schools) has been a major cause of division in the Northern Irish community.	Agree:	74%	73%	61%	+12%
	Disagree:	13%	15%	31%	-16%
3. The use of violence, while regrettable, has been necessary.	Agree:	16%	11%	35%	-24%
	Disagree:	76%	82%	62%	+20%

The positive position of the Catholic Church in relation to national unity has improved slightly in the opinion of the Dublin respondents. This drop of 2% in the proportion agreeing with the statement is neutralised by the decrease in the percentage disagreeing with it. The Dublin sub-sample is more critical of the role of the Catholic Church than is the national sample.

The opinions in relation to the link between separate Catholic and Protestant schools and divisions in Northern Ireland has strengthened since 1972-73, i.e. by 12%. The consequences of this view could mean a challenge to denominational *pluralism* by removing the support of structural duplication of schools. An integration of the schools, especially at the primary level, could lead to an *assimilation of denominations* or a homogenisation of beliefs, values and norms. The difference between a pluralist and an assimilationist solution is quite extensive.

Pluralism implies respect for and support of religious, political and cultural differences and a guarantee of total equality of treatment of those from diverse religious, political and cultural groups. According to Schermerborn (1970, pp. 122 ff.), pluralism may require institutional duplication such as different schools or places of worship. Assimilation implies the absorption of the religious, political and cultural traits of the minority into the overall way-of-life of the dominant group. The process by which this absorption is achieved is normally through socialisation and education. The primary and junior second-level schools play a major role in such assimilation. The future identity of any religious or cultural minority is very precarious without a pluralism of educational and religious structures. It could also be argued that subjection to common mass-media means of communication can also force assimilation of different world views into the dominant ethos of the media, which in Ireland's case is substantially foreign.

The decline of belief in *violence as a necessary, if regrettable, means of solving the Northern Irish problem* has been quite substantial over the fifteen years from 1972-73 to 1988-89, i.e. from 35% to 11% in Dublin. This may be due to one of two reasons or a combination of both. The experience of what violence had achieved had not impressed the people or their confidence in a non-violent constitutional alternative means of arriving at a solution had increased, as in the case of the Anglo-Irish Agreement.

The relatively positive response to the Anglo-Irish Agreement (see Table 105 below) could support the renewed hope in the non-violent constitutional means of solving the problem.

Attitudes towards the Provisional I.R.A. in the Republic were quite negative with a very low percentage who would welcome members into the family through kinship (9.3%) and a relatively high percentage who would deny them citizenship (50.3%). While such polarised attitudes tend to exist in relation to categories seen as politically extremist, it is nevertheless noteworthy that this rejection of the Provisional I.R.A. is not a rejection of Republicanism but rather a rejection of violent means to bring that aim about. (See Table 102 below, p. 244).

When the three items of opinion in Table 98 are tested by personal variables the findings are quite interesting (see Table 99). None of the variables recorded a statistically significant variation in the case of opinions on *separate Catholic and Protestant schools* being a major cause of division in the Northern Irish community. There seems to be widespread consensus on this issue.

The perceived position of *the Catholic Church as an obstacle to Irish Unity* elicited stronger support from males (41%), from residents of Munster (39%), and from those with third-level education (48%). This negative attitude towards the Catholic Church is substantially and significantly stronger among those in the two highest "Social Classes", i.e. "Upper Class" (59%) and "Upper Middle Class" (46%). The sample average was 36%. The Catholic Church does not seem to be the "established Church" in Ireland at present, i.e., those with high social status are more critical of it. This could encourage the Church itself to become more prophetic in relation to social issues.

The view that the *use of violence was regrettable but necessary* in relation to the solution of the Northern problem was held much more strongly by males (19%) than by females (11%), and by residents of Munster (19%) and Connaught/Ulster (23%) when compared with Dublin (11%) and the Rest of Leinster (13%). The supporters of Fianna Fáil (19%) and of the Workers Party (21%) were the parties most in agreement with the view. The sample

TABLE No. 99
RELIGION, EDUCATION AND VIOLENCE IN RELATION TO
NORTHERN IRELAND BY PERSONAL VARIABLES

	The position of influence of the Catholic Church in the Republic is a real obstacle to Irish unity.		Having separate schools has been a major cause of division.		The use of violence, while regrettable, has been necessary.	
	Agree	Disagree	Agree	Disagree	Agree	Disagree
Total Sample	36%	45%	74%	13%	16%	76%
A. GENDER						
1. Female	32%	46%	N/S		11%	81%
2. Male	41%	43%			21%	71%
	{P≤.05}				{P≤.05}	
B. MARITAL STATUS						
1. Never Married			67%	17%	N/S	
2. Married	N/S		78%	11%		
3. Widowed			70%	10%		
C. COUNTY OF RESIDENCE						
1. Dublin	39%	40%			11%	89%
2. Rest of Leinster	36%	45%	N/S		13%	76
3. Munster	35%	50%			19%	78
4. Connaught/Ulster	32%	43%			23%	65
	{P≤.05}				{P≤.001}	
E. POLITICAL PARTY PREFERENCE						
1. Fianna Fáil					19%	73%
2. Fine Gael	N/S		N/S		11%	85%
3. Labour Party					12%	73%
4. PDs					12%	83%
5. Workers Party					21%	71%
E. SOCIAL CLASS POSITION						
1. Class I	59%	32%				
2. Class 11	46%	37%				
3. Class 111	36%	47%	N/S		N/S	
4. Class IV	33%	46%				
5. Class V	31%	46%				
	{P≤.05}					

average was 16%. It should be noted that belief in the necessity of violence was very much a minority view in the case of all sub-samples.

2.4 Degree of Estrangement:

Item 11 was added to the Northern Ireland Scale in 1972-73 and again in 1988-89 to get a further indication of the degree of alienation towards the people in Northern Ireland "on all sides" of the politico-religious divide.

The discussion of the findings in relation to "social distance" (see Tables 88 to 93 above) confirmed a certain distancing of self from "Northern Irish".

Table 100 compares the findings of the two surveys, i.e. 1972-73 and 1988-89, in relation to Item 11 of Table 94.

TABLE No. 100
ATTITUDE TO NORTHERNERS ON ALL SIDES (1988-89 AND 1972-73)

STATEMENT OF OPINION		A Total Sample 1988/89	B Dublin Sub-Sample 1988/89	C Dublin Sample 1972/73	Diff (B-C)
Northerners on all sides tend to be extreme and unreasonable.	Agree: Disagree:	35% 46%	31% 50%	55% 38%	-24% +12%

While the findings of Table 100 may appear to be negative and dis-appointing to those who would aspire to a high degree of mutual respect and attractiveness between the peoples on both sides of the Border, they are, nevertheless, substantially improved when compared with the 1972-73 findings. The decline from 55% to 31% holding the view that *"Northerners on all sides tend to be extreme and unreasonable"* must indicate a change and a reduction in the sense of estrangement. If this change is also true of the views of residents of the Six Counties over the fifteen years in question towards people in the Twenty-Six Counties, then progress towards reconciliation between the Republic and Northern Ireland may well be taking place. In addition to the degree of incomprehension of the communal violence, the perceived "not an inch" mentality of certain parties to the Northern conflict is likely to cause the continuing degree of agreement with the view expressed in the statement.

A number of personal variables elicited statistically significant differences. These variations are given in Table 101. "county of residence", "political party preference" and "social class position" did not record significant variations in score, namely, there was a consensus of opinion in the case of each variable in line with the findings of the total sample. *Age* results point to the relatively low agreement with the statement among the younger respondents and the relatively high score for those over 50 years of age, i.e. three times that of those under 21 years. This relatively positive view of younger respondents may indicate a process of change in the direction of lower estrangement. *Gender* shows males with significantly higher negativity towards Northerners than that of females. The most urbanised and the least urbanised were more positive in their view than was the case of respondents resident in small cities and in towns. *Education* scores clearly show that those with high educational standards are more appreciative of Northerners than are those with lower levels. It should be noted that educational standard and age are negatively correlated which means that the age factor may also be influential in the variations between the educational sub-samples and/or *vice-versa*.

TABLE No. 101
ATTITUDE TO NORTHERNERS ON ALL SIDES BY PERSONAL VARIABLES

	Agree	Disagree	N.
Question: "Would you agree or disagree that Northerners on all sides tend to be extreme and unreasonable?"			
Total Sample	35%	46%	997
A. AGE P≤.001			
1. Under 21 years	14%	70%	56
2. 22 to 35 years	32%	46%	336
3. 36 to 50 years	35%	52%	269
4. 51 years and over	42%	38%	336
B. GENDER P≤.01			
1. Females	31%	47%	539
2. Males	40%	45%	458
C. PLACE OF RESIDENCE P≤.05			
1. Large City	31%	50%	284
2. Small City	39%	39%	84
3. Town	44%	47%	128
4. Rural	34%	45%	501
D. EDUCATION P≤.001			
1. Primary Only	41%	36%	281
2. Incomplete Second Level	45%	39%	203
3. Complete Second Level	28%	52%	310
4. Third Level	28%	58%	203

Note: Percentages significantly higer than average are underlined.

PART III: SOLUTIONS TO THE NORTHERN PROBLEM

Over the years there has been a continuous public debate on the likely solution to bring peace, justice and stability to Northern Ireland. In the 1972-73 survey of Greater Dublin, and again in the national survey of the Republic in 1988-89, respondents were asked their views on a range of seven possible solutions with the possibility of offering any other format. Table 102 gives the choices of the 1988-89 total sample.

The exclusion of "Don't Knows" assumes that those not offering an opinion for or against the "solution" in question would divide proportionately according to the distribution of choices made.

The overall findings clearly show the choice of the sample to be that of a *thirty-two county republic with one central government*. This option was considered "Desirable" by three-quarters (75%) of the respondents with "Don't Knows" excluded, and by over two-thirds (68%) with "Don't Knows" added. A further 13% and 12% respectively would consider this

TABLE No. 102
DESIRED AND ACCEPTABLE SOLUTIONS TO THE CURRENT
NORTHERN IRELAND PROBLEM ("DON'T KNOWS" EXCLUDED)

Choice of Solution	Desirable 2	Not Desirable but Acceptable 1	Total (1 + 2)	Unacceptable 0	N.	Rating Score* (1-100)
1. A thirty-two county Republic with one central government.	75%	13%	(88%)	12%	913	81.5
2. A thirty-two county Republic with provincial and central governments.	48%	30%	(78%)	22%	804	63.0
3. A Federal Republic of Northern and Southern Ireland.	42%	33%	(75%)	25%	753	58.5
4. A totally independent Northern Ireland.	22%	33%	(55%)	45%	871	38.5
5. The status quo with a devolved power-sharing Northern Administration.	19%	32%	(50%)	49%	713	35.0
6. Northern Ireland as an integral part of the United Kingdom.	10%	24%	(34%)	65%	833	22.0
7. The whole island of Ireland to be part of the United Kingdom again.	4%	3%	(7%)	93%	945	5.5

*The Rating Score is arrived at by dividing the mean score by two, i.e., 'Desirable' =2,
'Desirable but Acceptable' = 1, and 'Unacceptable' = O.

choice "Not Desirable but Acceptable", giving cumulative percentages of 88% and 80%. All the other choices are in a different "league", i.e. gaining less than 50% in the "Desirable" category (see Figure 24).

The two types of "federal" solution received substantial minority support as "Desirable" and strong cumulative majority backing as "Acceptable", i.e. 78% for a *Thirty-two County Republic with Provincial and Central Governments* and 75% accepting a *Federal Republic of Northern and Southern Ireland* ("Don't Knows" excluded). The 55% level of acceptability (22% of which is those accepting it as "Desirable") of a *Totally Independent Northern Ireland* by the sample, with "Don't Knows" excluded, is noteworthy. The opposition to options 5,6 and 7, i.e. the percentage declaring them "Unacceptable", would make them less attractive choices at present. The two "integration/reintegration" choices were decisively rejected. The response to choice No.7 practically unanimously confirms the achievement of Irish Independence for the Republic in the 1920s and totally rejects as "Unacceptable" a return of the *Whole Island of Ireland to Be Part of the United Kingdom Again*. This reconfirmation of national independence across the whole adult population may have implications for future changes in the strength of that independence.

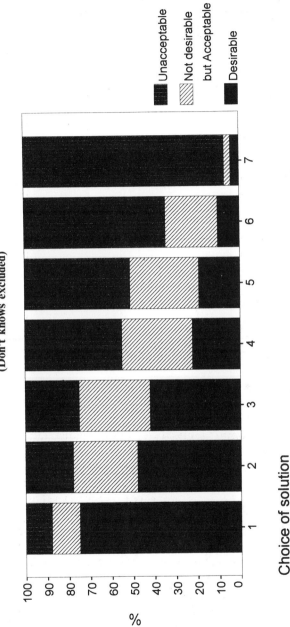

Figure 24: Responses to Listed Solutions to Northern Ireland Problem (Don't knows excluded)

Unacceptable

Not desirable but Acceptable

Desirable

Choice of solution

1: A thirty-two County Republic with one central Government
2: A thirty-two County Republic with Provincial and Central Governments
3: A Federal Republic of Northern and Southern Ireland
7: The whole Island of Ireland to be part of the United Kingdom

4: A Totally Independent Northern Ireland
5: The Status Quo with a Devolved Power-Sharing Northern Administration
6: Northern Ireland as an Integral Part of the United Kingdom

Not all of the choices in the 1972-73 Greater Dublin survey were exactly replicated for reasons of changes in the public debate and discussion of new possible solutions (see Mac Gréil, 1977, p.128). Table 103 measures the changes in opinions in Dublin over the sixteen years.

With the exception of the last option, i.e. that *the Whole Island of Ireland Return to the United Kingdom* (the pre-1922 situation), there was significant variation in each of the other five comparable options.

TABLE No. 103

COMPARISON OF RESPONSES TO NORTHERN IRELAND SOLUTIONS OF DUBLIN SUB-SAMPLE 1988-89 AND DUBLIN SAMPLE 1972-73

Choice of Solution		1 Desirable	2 Not Desirable but Acceptable	Total (1 + 2)	3 Unacceptable	N.
1. A thirty-two County Republic with one central Government.	1988-9: 1972-3:	69% 64%	15% 14%	(84%) (78%)	16% 22%	251 2259
Difference:		+5%	+1%	(+6%)	-6%	
2. A thirty-two county Republic with provincial and central governments.	1988-9: 1972-3:	49% 32%	35% 26%	(84%) (58%)	16% 42%	227 2251
Difference:		+17%	+9%	(+26%)	-26%	
3. A Federal Republic of Northern and Southern Ireland.	1988-9: 1972-3:	42% 23%	38% 31%	(80%) (54%)	20% 46%	222 2232
Difference:		+19%	+7%	(+26%)	-26%	
4. A totally independent Northern Ireland*	1988-9: 1972-3:	23% 11%	38% 16%	(61%) (27%)	39% 73%	248 2248
Difference:		+ 12%	+ 12%	(+34%)	-34%	
5. Northern Ireland as an integral part of the United Kingdom.**	1988-9: 1972-3:	10% 21%	27% 24%	(37%) (45%)	63% 55%	234 2259
Difference:		-11%	+3%	(-8%)	+8%	
6. The whole island of Ireland to be part of the United Kingdom again***	1988-9: 1972-3:	3% 5%	5% 6%	(8%) (11%)	92% 89%	262 2246
Difference:		-2%	-1%	(-3%)	+3%	

* 1972-3 wording: "Totally Independent Southern and Northern Ireland"
** 1972-3 Wording: "Northern Ireland an Integral Part of the United Kingdom with Civil Rights for All."
*** 1972-3 wording: "Whole of Ireland to Become an Integral Part of the United with regional governments in Dublin and Belfast.

3.2 Changes since 1972-73:

There was a substantial increase in support in Dublin for the federal solutions proposed in Items 2 and 3 in Table 103. The support for the non-federal republican solution (Item 1) increased also from an already high level of a positive response in 1972-73. The solution to receive the greatest proportionate increase in support, when compared with 1972-73, was the acceptance of a *"Totally Independent Northern Ireland"*. The positive support for this solution more than doubled in the intervening 15 years. *"Northern Ireland as an Integral Part of the United Kingdom"* lost support over the time between the two surveys.

3.3 Solutions by Personal Variables:

The following table (Table 104) measures the differences in responses to three options registering significant variation in more than one personal variable. "Political Party Preference" and "Social Class Position" failed to register significant variations in any of the seven options. This means that there was a consensus of views across political and social class position lines similar to the National average response. This level of consensus must add to the significance for political leaders of these findings.

In relation to the desirability of Option 1, *"a Thirty-Two County Republic with One Central Government"*, older respondents, especially those from 51 to 65 years were more in favour than were those of the two lower age-groups. The range of difference was 17.3% between the 36 to 50 years sub-sample and the 51 to 65 years one. "County of residence" was the only other personal variable to record a statistically significant difference in relation to Option 1. "Connaught/Ulster" respondents had the highest percentage for the "Desirability" of this solution (83.5%), while "Rest of Leinster" had the lowest percentage (68.9%). Both Connaught/Ulster and Munster were more "Republican" than those living in Leinster (Dublin included). This does not mean that Leinster respondents were not strongly in favour of a united Irish Republic, i.e. some 69% of Leinster respondents thought that solution to be "Desirable". It would appear from Table 104 that older people, males and those resident in Munster and in Connaught/Ulster were more "Republican" in their views and opinions.

The response to Option 4, i.e. *"a Totally Independent Northern Ireland"*, elicited statistically significant variations in the case of "age", "gender" and "county of residence". The range of variation in response to the desirability of this solution to the Northern problem went from 23.8% for those under 36 years of age to 16.7% for those between the ages of 51 and 65 years, i.e. a range of 7.1%. The percentage of females (27.8%) in favour of the desirability of a totally independent Northern Ireland was practically twice that of male respondents (13.9%). A similar level of disparity exists between the views of those resident in the "Rest of Leinster" (24%) and those in "Connaught/Ulster" (13.8%).

Prejudice in Ireland Revisited

Table No. 104
"DESIRABLE" SOLUTIONS TO THE NORTHERN IRELAND PROBLEM
BY PERSONAL VARIABLES

VARIABLE	1 Thirty-Two County Republic with One Central Government		4 Totally Independent Northern Ireland		6 Northern Ireland as an Integral Part of the United Kingdom.		N.
	Desirable	Not Acceptable	Desirable	Not Acceptable	Desirable	Not Acceptable	
National Sample	75%	12%	22%	45%	10%	66%	872
AGE	%	%	%	%	%	%	
1. Under 36 years	70.2	14.2	23.8	39.5	10.8	61.5	344
2. 36 to 50 years	69.0	149	21.4	43.2	10.4	61.0	243
3. 51 to 65 years	86.3	6.9	16.7	56.0	9.4	72.5	168
4. 66 years +	80.9	9.2	19.8	51.7	8.5	75.2	116
	P≤.001		P≤.02		P≤.01		
GENDER	N/S						
1. Females			27.8	39.1	12.4	61.1	460
2. Males			14.9	52.3	7.5	70.1	411
			P≤.001		P≤.02		
COUNTY OF RESIDENCE							
1. Dublin	69.8	15 5	22.6	39.5	9.8	62.8	248
2. Rest of Leinster	68.9	14.0	24.0	44.1	8.5	73.0	204
3. Munster	78.3	10.5	21.9	46.0	11.4	58.7	274
4. Connaught/Ulster	83.5	7.9	13.8	55.9	10.4	71.9	145
	P≤.01		P≤..05		P≤..02		
EDUCATION							
1. Primary Only					10.3	73.7	229
2. Incomplete 2nd Level	N/S		N/S		11.6	60.0	180
3. Complete 2nd Level					10.7	62.1	278
4. Third Level					7.4	62.3	184
					P≤..05		

Note: Underlined percentages are significantly above average.

Solution No.6, i.e. "*Northern Ireland as an Integral Part of the United Kingdom*", elicited significant variations in the case of the four variables on Table 104. Because of the low average numbers, the differences in the "Desirable" percentages were relatively less than those in the other two categories, i.e. "Not Desirable but Acceptable" and "Not Acceptable". From the "Not Acceptable" percentages it is clear that those in the two older age categories, males, "Connaught/Ulster" and "Rest of Leinster" residents and those with "Primary Only" education are most strongly opposed to this solution. When one combines the high "Not Acceptable" scores of all sub-samples with the low "Desirable" percentages, it is clear that this solution is overwhelmingly rejected.

In the case of Solution 2 (Table 102), i.e. "*a Thirty-Two County Republic with Provincial and Central Governments*", one variable, "county of residence" registered significant variation [P≤.008].

"A Thirty-two County Republic with Provincial and Central Governments"

		Desirable	Not Acceptable
1.	Dublin	48.9%	15.9%
2.	Rest of Leinster	*55.3%*	21.4%
3.	Munster	42.4%	*26.1%*
4.	Connaught/Ulster	42.1%	*27.7%*
	(National Sample)	(47.5%)	(22.1%)

The above variations are in marked contrast with those of the more "Republican" solution of Option 1, when examined by County of Residence on Table 104. The Connaught/Ulster respondents are less favourably disposed to the idea of Provincial Government than are the Leinster respondents (especially those in the "Rest of Leinster").

The solution calling for "the Status Quo with a Devolved Power-Sharing Northern Administration" (Solution 5 on Table 102) also elicited a significant variation in responses [P ≤.001] when measured by "County of Residence", i.e.

"The Status quo with a Devolved Power-Sharing Northern Administration"

		Desirable	Not Acceptable
1.	Dublin	16.3%	39.7%
2.	Rest of Leinster	*26.8%*	48.8%
3.	Munster	19.6%	51.5%
4.	Connaught/Ulster	13.3%	*62.9%*
	(National Sample)	(19.4%)	(49.1%)

The percentage considering this solution desirable in "Connaught/Ulster" (13.3) is half that in "Rest of Leinster". The general pattern of interprovincial variation is more-or-less similar to the other cases where "County of Residence" registered significant variation.

Conclusion: The very strong collective desire of the people for the *Thirty - two County Republic with One Central Government* is very clearly confirmed by the above findings. At the same time, there is evidence of a willingness to *accept* solutions of a "federal" nature. The preference of a *Totally Independent Northern Ireland* before the devolved Government solution may be surprising to some. Perhaps it indicates the belief in *independence* as more desirable than *dependence?* The level of consensus in relation to respondents' choices is very strong, especially consensus between supporters of different political parties and from different social-class positions.

3.4. Opinions on the Anglo-Irish Agreement:

The Anglo-Irish Agreement between the United Kingdom Government and the Government of the Republic of Ireland was signed and enacted in 1985. By the time the survey was carried out in 1988-89 it had been in operation for over three years and implemented by two Irish Governments, i.e. the Coalition Fine Gael/Labour Government under an Taoiseach, Dr Garret Fitzgerald T.D. (1982-87) and by the Fianna Fáil Government under an Taoiseach, Mr Charles Haughey, T.D. (1987-89). It was a much discussed agreement and it was to be expected that the respondents would have formed an opinion about its success or failure to date. The Unionists and the Republicans (Sinn Féin) in Northern Ireland opposed the Agreement (for different reasons).

The method used to measure respondents' appreciation of the Agreement was by means of a *continuum* It was a seven point scale, i.e. −3, −2, −1, 0, +1, +2, +3. Table 105 gives the replies of respondents.

TABLE No. 105
ASSESSMENT OF THE ANGLO-IRISH AGREEMENT (TOTAL SAMPLE)

Introduction: "How would you rate the ANGLO-IRISH AGREEMENT as providing a structure through which the Northern problem can be fairly solved? Please indicate your opinion on the following seven point scale."								
PREVENTS PROGRESS TOWARDS A SOLUTION					**PROMOTES PROGRESS TOWARDS A SOLUTION**			
		23%				52%		
Negative	9%	8%	6%	25%	19%	21%	13%	Positive
	-3	-2	-1	0	+1	+2	+3	

The overall assessment of the Agreement as reported in Table 105 and on Figure 25 indicates a positive endorsement. Over half of respondents (52%) thought it was a positive influence, while a quarter (25%) held a neutral view and slightly less than a quarter (23%) thought it to be negative. Measured on a scale of 1 to 7 the mean score in favour of the Agreement is 4.45, while the median is 5.

The next table (Table 106) gives a breakdown of the results by personal variables.

"Age" did not result in significant variations from the total sample averages. Variations between males and females, while significantly different, more-or-less balance out with *males* higher in both positive and negative replies and *females* with higher neutral replies.

"Place of rearing" findings indicate city reared were more positive in their assessment of the Anglo-Irish Agreement than were residents of small

Figure No. 25: Assessment of Anglo-Irish Agreement

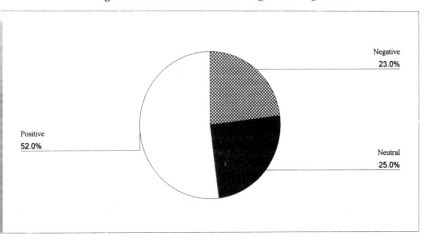

Negative
23.0%

Positive
52.0%

Neutral
25.0%

towns and rural areas. Dublin residents were ten percent more appreciative of the effects of the Agreement. Respondents living in Munster were also above average in their positive scores. Those living in Connaught/Ulster were least impressed in their assessment.

"Education" is very clearly linked to views on the Agreement. Of the sub-samples measured, "Third Level" respondents gave the third highest reply for the Agreement (72%) and the second lowest negative score (14%).

Fianna Fáil supporters' assessment of the Anglo-Irish Agreement was exactly the same of that of the national sample average. Progressive Democrats, Labour Party, Fine Gael and Workers Party supporters were all above average in favour of the Agreement. Supporters of "Other Parties" were the only sub-sample to be more Negative (49%) than Positive (29%).

"Social class position" was positively correlated with the degree of support for the Agreement and negatively correlated to the degree of conviction against the accord.

In summary, therefore, those of the Upper and Middle Class, of higher education and reared in larger urban areas were relatively more supportive of the Anglo-Irish Agreement. Political Party Preference is also a significant factor in creating variations of responses. The most significant variations in support of the Anglo-Irish Agreement were those shown in the "social-class position" variable.

3.5 Conclusions and Interpretations (in relation to Northern Ireland):

3.5a It is fairly clear from the findings of this report that the people's attitudes towards and views on *Northern Ireland* are complex and not open to simple generalisation. While there is little support for the use

TABLE NO. 106
ASSESSMENT OF ANGLO-IRISH AGREEMENT RATINGS BY
BASIC PERSONAL VARIABLES

	Promotes Progress	Neither Promotes nor prevents	Prevents Progress
	%	%	%
National Average	52	25	23
A. GENDER P≤.05			
1. Female	50	29	21
2. Male	55	20	25
B. PLACE OF REARING P≤.001			
1. Large City	61	19	21
2. Small City	57	24	19
3. Town	51	23	27
4. Rural	47	29	24
C. COUNTY OF RESIDENCE P≤.001			
1. Dublin	62	19	20
2. Rest of Leinster	46	29	25
3. Munster	56	25	19
4. Connaugh/Ulster	41	29	30
D. EDUCATION P≤.001			
1. Primary	39	31	30
2. Incomplete Second Level	51	26	23
3. Complete Second Level	60	22	18
4. Third Level	72	14	14
E. POLITICAL PARTY PREFERENCE P≤.001			
1. Fianna Fáil	52	25	23
2. Fine Gael	60	21	18
3. Labour	65	14	22
4. Progressive Democrats	74	14	12
5. Workers Party	58	21	21
6. Other Parties	29	23	49
F. SOCIAL CLASS POSITION P≤.001			
1. Class I	82	9	9
2. Class II	75	10	15
3. Class III	59	23	18
4. Class IV	45	26	28
5. Class V	38	34	28

Note: Percentages significantly above the national average are <u>underlined.</u>
* It should be noted that the Workers Party has "split" since 1989 with the establishment of the "Democratic Left" in 1992

of violence, there is overwhelming support for a Thirty-Two County Republic. Therefore, it would be against the evidence of the 1988-89 and 1972-73 surveys to conclude from a lack of support for violent methods that the "republican ideal" had weakened. The growth in support for federal solutions and for a "Totally Independent Northern Ireland" as *acceptable*, if not desirable, solution is worthy of further analysis.

3.5b As was the case in 1972-73, there is evidence of a degree of *"estrangement"* of the Northern Irish in the mind of a minority in the Republic. This is something that could be remedied by more effective favourable contact and mutual support. The Republic's media has an important role to play in this regard, as have religious and community leaders. Perhaps the bringing together of the two soccer teams into one *Island of Ireland team* would bring the grassroots on both sides of the Border together in support of one "Irish team" in international competitions and thereby provide favourable contact (as well as possibly giving us many visitors). In all major sports activities we should be one. Popular sport has an important community integration function.

3.5c The acknowledgement of a *"two nations"* situation (Northern Ireland and the Republic) could also be substantiated from evidence in the findings. This is more as a recognition of reality than as a desired socio-political solution. Catholics and Protestants were perceived to have more in common with each other within the North and within the Republic than with the co-religionists across the Border. This could be seen as a hopeful basis for Catholic-Protestant pluralist integration on each side of the Border (see Figure 23, page 234).

3.5d The negative view of separate denominational schools, although against the tenets of structural pluralism, could be interpreted more as a reaction to the painful and irrational divisions on the ground in Northern Ireland than as a desire for religious assimilation and absorption.

3.5e There is still an ambivalence toward the perceived role of the Catholic Church as an obstacle to Irish unity. For a people who are so strong in their desire for national unity and yet so strong in their religious participation and loyalty (see Chapter VI), there must be an internal tension or dilemma in relation to their nationalism and their religious allegiance. This tension was also evident in 1972-73 and has not changed very much since that time. Does it mean that despite what Unionist leaders may say, the Irish Catholics are nationalist *independently* of their perceived influence of their Church? This Irish dilemma could have positive or negative effects on the people's loyalty to the Church and on their national ideals.

PART IV: ATTITUDES AND OPINIONS RELATING TO BRITAIN

Anglo-Irish relations have dominated most of Irish history. Ireland was occupied, colonised and administered by English (and later British) authorities for seven hundred and forty-three years, i.e. from 1169 until 1922. Since 1922 the part of Ireland known as the Republic has enjoyed national autonomy while the part known as Northern Ireland has been governed from Westminster, either as a region with devolved government in Stormont or by direct rule. The latter is the current situation.

The conflict relating to British rule in Ireland has been a constant part of Anglo-Irish history, both before 1922 and since. Between 1969 and 1994 this conflict had become more militant and had adopted a para-military form. Some of the violence and conflict had "spilled over" to the Republic and England. The counter-force response of the British Government had become a source of friction and worry for the many Irish immigrants in Great Britain. A number of miscarriages of justice against Irish immigrants and visitors from Ireland had highlighted a situation likely to generate an impression among the Irish population that the Irish may not be treated fairly in Britain. This view is tested in Item 13 of Table 108 (p. 259).

SOCIAL DISTANCE SCORES OF "BRITISH" CATEGORIES

Because of the status of Britain as a former colonial power in Ireland, it is expected that the attitudes towards the British will be mixed. Such was the case in the 1972-73 survey of the attitudes of the adult population of Greater Dublin. The physical proximity of Great Britain to Ireland and the extensive and continuous contact between the peoples of Ireland and of England, Scotland and Wales should result in relatively positive attitudes and opinions by the vast majority of the Irish people, especially on issues not politically connected. This high level of positive dispositions has been already reported on in Table 88 where "English", "British", "Scottish" and "Welsh" recorded close degrees of social distance.

Table 107 gives a breakdown of this Social Distance by personal variables in relation to the British, English, Scottish and Welsh, i.e. as measured by admission to kinship and by denial of citizenship.

The changes in social distance score since 1972-73 are recorded in Table 89 (p. 226). The position of the "Scottish" and the "Welsh" improved substantially and significantly among Dublin respondents when the two surveys are compared.

The only category to elicit significant variations by *age* was the "Welsh", with the younger respondents and the senior middle-aged slightly more tolerant than the middle-aged. or the older people.

TABLE No. 107

ADMISSION TO KINSHIP AND DENIAL OF CITIZENSHIP OF BRITISH,
ENGLISH, SCOTTISH AND WELSH BY PERSONAL VARIABLES

	English		British		Scottish		Welsh*	
	Kinship	Deny Citizenship	Kinship	Deny Citizenship	Kinship	Deny Citizenship	Kinship	Deny Citizenship
National Sample	78%	3%	77%	4%	74%	4%	73%	4%
A. COUNTY OF RESIDENCE								
1. Dublin	85%	3%	83%	4%	85%	3%	87%	2%
2. Rest of Leinster	76%	2%	77%	2%	76%	2%	76%	2%
3. Munster	76%	3%	74%	5%	71%	4%	70%	4%
4. Connaught/Ulster	73%	3%	71%	3%	59%	8%	51%	9%
	{P≤.05}		{P≤.05}		{P≤.001}		{P≤.001}	
B. EDUCATION								
1. Primary Only					67%	7%	66%	6%
2. incomplete Second Level	N/S		N/S		78%	2%	76%	3%
3. Complete Second Level					74%	3%	73%	3%
4. Third Level					79%	2%	79%	3%
					{P≤.05}		{P≤.05}	
C. SOCIAL CLASS POSITION								
1. Class I			94%	0%	97%	0%	94%	0%
2. Class II			79%	4%	85%	2%	84%	0%
3. Class III	N/S		77%	3%	75%	3%	75%	3%
4. Class IV			78%	2%	74%	4%	71%	3%
5. Class V			75%	7%	71%	6%	72%	8%
			{P≤.05}		{P≤.05}		{P≤.001}	

*Social distance towards "Welsh" by age.

		Kinship	Deny Citizenship	
1.	35 years and under	75%	3%	
2.	36 to 50 years	71%	2%	
3.	51 to 65 years	74%	7%	
4.	66 years plus	70%	6%	{P≤.05}

County of residence recorded significant variations in the case of the four categories. The range of variation on admission to family through kinship was greatest in the case of "Scottish" and "Welsh". Dublin respondents were the more accepting while respondents from Connaught/Ulster were more ethnically endogamous in relation to their co-Celts, while they were much more open to "English" and "British".

Education recorded significant variations in relation to 'Scottish'' and 'Welsh'' with those with the highest standards reached being more welcoming into the family through kinship than was the case of those with least schooling.

Occupation only recorded significant differences in relation to one stimulus category, i.e., "Welsh". These variations were predictable as follows:

		Kinship	Deny Citizenship	
1.	Unskilled/Semi-skilled	73%	6%	
2.	Skilled/Routine Non-Manual	71%	4%	
3.	Inspectional/Supervisory	75%	3%	
4.	Professional/High Exec.	81%	0%	{P≤.05R

There was a 20% plus range of percentage of those welcoming "British", "Scottish" and "Welsh" into kinship between Class I and Class V of the *Social-Class Position* variable. This, again, would be predictable.

Changes in the Social Distance Scores towards "English", "British", "Scottish" and "Welsh", by Dubliners since 1972-73 have been reported already in Table 89 above, where it was noted that the relative position of "Welsh" and "Scottish" improved significantly over the intervening fifteen years. There was no significant change in the case of Social Distance Scores towards the "English" and the "British". The findings of Table 90 (p. 227) pointed to the perception of English and British by the Irish as being similar ($r = 0.78$) and likewise in the case of the "Scottish" and "Welsh" ($r = 0.74$), while the correlation between the Social Distance Scores towards the "English" *and* towards the "Scottish and "Welsh" was lower, i.e. $r = 0.51$ and 0.50 respectively. The correlation between "British" and "Scottish" and "Welsh" was $r = 0.45$ and 0.47 respectively.

The changes in the findings of the Rationalisation Scale in Table 92 (p. 230) have shown a significant increase in the *"politicisation"* of the reasons given by the minority not admitting "English" and "British" to kinship, while there was a drop in the proportion giving *ethnic or nationality* as their principal reason. The causes of these changes probably relate to the continuity of the political conflict in Northern Ireland and its spill-over in Britain since 1972-73. It is most interesting to note the great prominence of the "ethnic" nationality reasons in the case of the Celtic stimulus categories, i.e. "Scottish" and "Welsh". In the light of the current "Home Rule" and "Independence" movements in Scotland and Wales, the perceptions of both the national sample (Table 91) and the Dublin sub-sample (Table 92) in relation to the two Celtic categories are also noteworthy. (It should be cautioned, however, that these indicators come from *the relatively small percentages* not welcoming members of the categories into their family through marriage.)

CHAPTER IX

Irish Political Opinions and Issues

PART I: THE SPECIAL ANTI-BRITISH SCALE

1. OVERALL FINDINGS

In the 1972-73 survey an anti-British attitudinal scale was used to measure the evaluations, feeling and behavioural tendencies of the adults of Greater Dublin towards the British. In the analysis of these findings an apparently internal illogicality emerged from the two sub-scales, one measuring "low-esteem" of the British and the other measuring feelings of "hostility" towards them. The sub-scale scores, instead of recording a positive correlation, actually indicated a negative one. In other words, some of those who seemed most to admire or to look up to "the British" were at the same time more hostile towards them. This attitudinal inconsistency was described as an expression of "post-colonial attitudinal schizophrenia" (see Mac Gréil, 1977, pp. 374-5, 472, 524). The admiration of the former "colonial master" was in some cases also a measure of self-devaluation. In racialist and in post-racialist societies similar attitudinal contradictions have been observed, i.e. self-hatred and self-devaluation. This attitudinal incongruity might also be related to the "shoneen" mentality. An example in Ireland was the amazement felt by some members of the Ascendancy at the destructive hostility of the "formerly docile peasantry" during the Irish War of Independence. The widespread destruction of so many of the "big houses" during and after that War may have been an irrational reaction to generations of low self-esteem imposed by the system on many ordinary Irish people. It will be interesting to discover if the inter-relation between the two sub-scales has changed over the past fifteen years. One would expect it to change as Irish self-esteem grew more widespread.

It was to be expected that attitudes and opinions in the Republic towards the British would be complex. In the first place, Great Britain is geographically and ethnically (English as a common language) close to Ireland and there has been much favourable contact between the Irish and the British as a result of many Irish working in England, Scotland and Wales, and through the many people from Great Britain who visit Ireland regularly for holidays. All these factors should contribute to the "most favoured" position of the peoples of England, Scotland and Wales in the opinions and dispositions of the Irish people. The Social Distance Scales have already confirmed this high level of preference for English, British, Scottish and Welsh. On the negative side there are a number of issues which could militate against the British in the opinions and dispositions of Irish people (in the Republic), namely, the failure to solve the Northern Irish question to date and the dimension of responsibility for such failure ascribed to the British establishment. As a consequence of the military conflict resulting from the Anglo-Irish settlement of 1922 and the extension of the hostilities to Great Britain, some Irish people in Britain may fall under suspicion and sense negative discrimination. The cases of the "Guildford Four", the "Maguire Family", the "Birmingham Six", the "Winchester Three", the "U.D.R. Four" and Judith Ward, could be seen by many as manifestations of discrimination against the Irish before the British law. As already noted, Ireland for a long number of centuries suffered as a British colony to the disapproval of the majority of the Irish people.

The post-Reformation religious strife in Ireland lasted from the mid-16th Century until the mid-19th Century. Both Catholics and Presbyterians were discriminated against during the late 17th and early 18th Centuries at the hands of a pro-Anglican British Government. The Church of Ireland was disestablished in 1869 and Catholic Emancipation was not conceded until 1829 in the case of a limited franchise based on property, which meant that the property-less Catholic population were denied a vote. During the 16th, 17th and 18th Centuries there was a sequence of plantations of British people in Ireland with the consequent dispossession of native Irish, some of whom went into the poorer parts of Connaught/Ulster. The folk memory of this history is something to be reckoned with in the case of Irish attitudes towards the British, as is the folk-memory of Protestants whose ancestors were victims of sectarian violence from time to time.

The division of the island of Ireland in 1922 into the Twenty-six County Irish Free State and the Six Counties of Northern Ireland may have been aggravated further by the resulting predominance of Roman Catholics in the Twenty-six Counties and of Protestants in the Six Counties. This weakened the stimulus or challenge of arriving at a situation of integrated pluralism.

Table 108 gives the findings of the specially designed Anti-British Scale which will be analysed here both as a set of opinions and as an attitudinal scale. (The items are in the order in which they were on the questionnaire.)

Table 108 shows a wide spectrum of attitudes and opinions towards the British. Items 2, 5, 6, 9, 10 and 11 express *very positive dispositions* towards the British people, i.e. with low negative scores. On an anti-British score ranging from 0 to 200 the highest score of the six items was 43.4 for Item 10 i.e. *"I would never marry a British person"*. Incidentally, this response agrees with the Social Distance Scores in Table 88 in relation to the proportion welcoming British into the family through marriage at 77% which is only very slightly higher than the 73% disagreeing with Item 10 above.

Items on Table 108 with high (negative) anti-British scores (i.e. 100 plus) have, for the most part, political undertones. In other words, the Irish people are far from happy with the British Government or administrative establishment, particularly in its dealings with Ireland, while they seem favourably disposed to British people. The very high negative score (134.0) for Item 4, i.e. some 61% who would not prefer to *"live in Britain than any other place*

TABLE No. 108
ANTI-BRITISH SCALE BY TOTAL SAMPLE 1988-89
(AND BY THE DUBLIN SAMPLE 1972-73)

Introduction: "Now I would like to read you a number of statements about the opinions some people hold. After I read each statement could you tell me if you agree or disagree or have no opinion?"

STATEMENT	Agree %	No Opinion %	Disagree %	Anti-British Score (0-200)	N
1. If Ireland did not have its own team in the Olympic Games or international sport, I would cheer for the British.	41.8 (54 3)	10.2 (4.3)	**48.0** **(41.4)**	106.2 (87.0)	1000 (2279)
2. The British are pretty decent people.	84.7 (88.8)	10.2 (3.5)	**5.1** **(7.5)**	20.4 (19.0)	998 (2285)
3. Some British qualities are admirable, but on the whole I don't like them.	**24.1** **(22.1)**	14.4 (3 5)	61.5 (74.5)	62.7 (47.5)	999 (2286)
4. I'd rather live in Britain than any other place abroad.	27.0 (39.7)	12.0 (5 7)	61.0 (54.6)	134.0 (115.0)	1000 (2287)
5. The British are inferior in every way.	**6.1** **(5.2)**	7.4 (1 3)	86.5 (93 5)	19.6 (11.5)	998 (2284)
6. British people are slow and unimaginative.	**8.5** **(14.2)**	11.5 (5.3)	79.9 (80.5)	28.6 (33.5)	99 (2285)
7. I don't object to the British people but I don't like the British Government.	**49.4** **(36.2)**	20.6 (9 1)	30.0 (54.7)	119.4 (81.5)	996 (2285)
8. The world owes a lot to Britain.	29.1 (30.6)	19.2 (7 7)	**51.7** **(61.8)**	122.6 (131.0)	994 (2283)
9. 1 am happy to see British people get on in Ireland.	83.7 (73.9)	9.9 (5 7)	**6.3** **(20.3)**	22.6 (46.5)	995 (2283)
10. I would never marry a British person.	**15.9** **(14.5)**	11.5 (2.4)	72.5 (83.3)	43.4 (31.0)	998 (2286)
11. I would be happy if Britain were brought to its knees.	**9.2** **(17.1)**	10.6 (3.6)	80.2 (793)	29.0 (37 5)	995 (2285)
12. The British Government has been evenhanded when dealing with Northern Ireland since 1969.*	22.4	21.1	**56.5**	134.0	999
13. The British have little respect for the Irish.*	**48.1**	18.9	33.0	115.1	997
Scale P-Score (0-200)				66.0	

Note: Scores for the 1972-73 Survey of Greater Dublin Adults in brackets.
Cornback Alpha = 0.71
* These items were not included in 1972-73. Negative percentages are in **bold.**

abroad", was correlated (r = 0.30) to the view expressed in Item 1, i.e. would not cheer for the British in the event of Ireland not having a team in international sports competitions. A similar level of correlation (r = 0.28) was recorded in relation to Item 13, i.e. "*the British have little respect for the Irish*". The post-colonial residue and the "Irish bashing" in some cheaper British media as well as the much publicised miscarriages of justice in recent years (mentioned above) may have contributed to the opinions expressed in these items. The 52% who would not agree that "*the world owes a lot to Britain*", while substantially lower than the 1972-73 percentage (61.8%) for the Dublin survey, shows a lack of generosity in appreciation of Britain's positive achievements.

Only 22% agree that the "*British Government has been even-handed when dealing with Northern Ireland since 1969*" while 57% disagreed with this view. This lack of confidence of such a large proportion of the Irish population in the British Government's fair play when dealing with Northern Ireland is quite disturbing. When one bears in mind the Irish people's very positive disposition towards the British people, the negative opinion can hardly be seen as against the British people as much as against the British Government/establishment. It is therefore in the interests of positive Anglo-Irish relations in the future that British "evenhandedness" when dealing with Ireland will have to exist and be transparent to the people of Ireland.

2.1 Changes of Attitudes and Opinions between 1972-73 and 1988-89:

The replies to Items 1 to 11 show the percentages for the National Sample of 1988-89 and the Dublin sample of 1972-73, the latter scores shown in brackets. It is noteworthy that the national overall Anti-British Score for 1988-89 is 64.4 as compared with the Dublin overall score of 59.5 which reflects a slightly higher level of anti-British feeling (+4.9) in the recent national scores. The significance of the differences will be examined in the next table (Table 109) where the findings for the Dublin sub-sample (1988-89) are compared with those of 1972-73.

The results of Table 109 show a slight deterioration in attitudes towards the British in a number of items. The overall scale-score difference of +2.3 is barely significant. What is surprising about it is that it has not reduced over the fifteen years, considering the signs of more tolerant trends in the 1972-73 findings in general. One would have expected a more tolerant score because of the "liberalising" effects of greater participation in education, of joint-participation in the European Community, and of greater foreign travel.

The individual items which recorded significant degrees of change were Items 7, 4, 1, 10 and 3 (in that order). The standing of the British Government (Item 7) has dropped substantially (i.e. 35.0).

TABLE No. 109
COMPARISON OF 1988-89 AND 1972-73 RESPONSES TO THE ANTI-BRITISH SCALE

STATEMENT		Agree %	No Opinion %	Disagree %	Anti-British Score (0-200)	N
1. If Ireland did not have its own team in the Olympic Games or international sport, I would cheer for the British.	1988-89:	44.0	9.1	46.9	100.0	275
	1972-73:	53.4	4.3	41.4	87.0	2279
	Difference:	-9.4	+4.8	+5.5	+13.0	
2. The British are pretty decent people.	1988-89:	86.9	7.6	5.5	17.7	275
	1972-73:	88.8	3.5	7.5	19.0	2285
	Difference:	-1.9	+4.1	-2.0	-1.3	
3. Some British qualities are admirable, but on the whole I don't like them.	1988-89:	19.6	16.7	63.6	56.3	275
	1972-73:	22.1	3.5	74.5	47.5	2286
	Difference	-2.5	+ 13.2	- 10.9	+8.8	
4. I'd rather live in Britain than any other place abroad.	1988-89:	24.4	11.6	64.0	137.8	275
	1972-73:	39.7	5.7	54.6	115.0	2287
	Difference	-15.3	+5.9	+9.4	+22.8	
5. The British are inferior in every way.	1988-89:	5.5	6.2	88.3	17.4	274
	1972-73:	5.2	1.3	93.5	11.5	2284
	Difference	+0.3	+4.9	-5.2	+5.9	
6. British people are slow and unimaginative.	1988-89:	9.8	11.3	78.9	31.9	275
	1972-73:	14.2	5.3	80.5	33.5	2272
	Difference	-4.4	+6.0	- 1.6	- 1.6	
7. I don't object to the British people but I don't like the British Government.	1988-89:	48.0	23.3	28.7	116.5	275
	1972-73:	36.2	9.1	54.7	81.5	2285
	Difference	+11.8	+14.2	-26.0	+35.0	
8. The world owes a lot to Britain.	1988-89:	30.2	18.5	51.3	119.7	275
	1972-73:	30.6	7.7	61.8	131.0	2283
	Difference	-0.4	+10.8	-10.5	-11.3	
9. I am happy to see British people get on in Ireland.	1988-89:	85.5	8.0	6.5	22.0	275
	1972-73:	73.9	5.7	20.3	46.5	2283
	Difference:	+11.6	+2.3	-13.8	-24.5	
10. I would never marry a British person.	1988-89:	15.6	9.5	85.5	42.1	275
	1972-73:	14.5	2.4	83.3	31.0	2286
	Difference:	+1.1	+7.1	-8.4	+11.1	
11. I would be happy if Britain were brought to its knees.	1988-89:	5.8	8.7	85.5	18.1	275
	1972-73:	17.1	3.6	79.3	37.5	2285
	Difference:	-11.3	+5.1	+6.2	-19.4	
Anti-British Scale Score	1988-89:				61.8	
	1972-73:				59.5	
	Difference:				+2.3	

The Dubliners' responses to the two new items on the 1988-89 Anti-British Scale are significantly more negative than they were for the National Sample. The Dublin responses were as follows:

TABLE No. 110
DUBLIN RESPONSES TO ANTI-BRITISH SCALE NEW ITEMS (1988-89)

STATEMENT		Agree %	No Opinion %	Disagree %	Anti-British Score (0-200)	N.
1. "The British Government	Nat Sample:	22.4	21.1	**56.5**	134.0	999
has been evenhanded when	Dublin S-S:	18.2	19.6	**62.2**	142.5	275
dealing with Northern						
Ireland since 1969."	Difference:	+4.2	+1.5	-5.7	-8.5	
2."The British have little	Nat Sample:	**48.1**	18.9	33.0	115.1	997
respect for the Irish."	Dublin S-S:	**52.0**	17.1	30.9	123.3	275
	Difference:	-3.9	+ 1.8	+2.1	-8.2	

The patterns of the above responses are against the general run of score-variations between the National Sample and the Dublin Sub-Sample. In most instances the Dubliners as a category are more tolerant in their views than are those of the National Sample. The evidence of negative politicisation of Irish attitudes towards the British, already referred to above, and clearly reported in the above figures, is probably a major cause of the negative trend in some of the responses on Table 109.

2.2 Factor Analysis of Scale:

The scale, when tested, divided into three factors as given in Table 111 below. The groupings of the items are not the same in a number of items as was the case with the Greater Dublin survey in 1972-73 (see Table No.130 in Mac Gréil, 1977, p. 364).

The very high "Varimax Factor Loadings" in relation to the "Social Distance" scores (Factor 1) indicates a strong correlation between the responses which reflects the ethnic propinquity of the categories.

Factor 2 pulls together items which reflect low-esteem and envy. The factor loadings are not as high as in the case of Factor 1. Factor 3 gathers items indicating hostility and negative feelings. Factor 4 consists of two items expressing different negative attitudes.

The internal consistency/inconsistency between the various negative views expressed in the scale is best seen in the correlation matrix between the items of the scale.

The above correlations are much lower than would be expected normally from an ethnic scale. The distribution of responses between "agree' and "disagree' could have a bearing on the size of the correlations.

TABLE No. 111
FACTOR ANALYSIS OF ANTI-BRITISH SCALES

		Varimax Factor Loadings			
		Factor 1	Factor 2	Factor 3	Factor 4
1.	"English" Social Distance	-.728			
2.	"Northern Irish" Social Distance	-.744			
3.	"Scottish" Social Distance	-.900			
4.	"Welsh" Social Distance	-.855			
5.	The British are not pretty decent people (2)		.59		
6.	On the whole I don't like the British (3)		.469		
7.	The British are inferior in every way (5)		.698		
8.	The British are slow and unimaginative (6)		.673		
9.	I'm not happy if British people get on (9)		.479		
10.	I'd be happy if Britain was brought to its knees (11)		.614		
11.	I wouldn't cheer for a British team (1)			.567	
12.	I wouldn't rather live in Britain than elsewhere abroad (4)			.636	
13.	The world does not owe a lot to Britain (8)			.631	
14.	The British Government has not been evenhanded in Northern Ireland (11)			.567	
15.	I don't like the British Government (7)				.789
16.	The British have little respect for the Irish (13)				.458
	Variance	.458	3.568	1.401	1.058
	% Variance explained	14.5%	21.0%	8.2%	6.2%
	Cum % Variance explained	14.5%	35.4%	43.7%	49.9%

Note: Numbers in brackets refer to Item Number on the Anti-British Scale (see Table 108). Item 5 was not included because of distribution of responses, i.e. 6% agreeing and 87% disagreeing.

The degree and direction of inconsistency is best measured by comparing the variations in the scale and sub-scale scores by personal variables. So as to replicate the scales and sub-scales of 1972-73, only items used in both surveys are used and the 1972-73 sub-scales are tested in Table 113. The following are the adjusted sub-scales, i.e. replicating the statements tested in the 1972-73 Survey:

"Low Esteem Factor" (1972-3/1988-9)

1. "If Ireland did not have its own team in the Olympic Games or International Sports, I would cheer for the British."
2. "The British are a pretty decent people".
4. "I'd rather live in Britain than any other place abroad".
8. "The world owes a lot to Britain".
9. "I am happy to see British people get on in Ireland."

"Negative Political and Hostility Items Factor" (1972-3/1988-9)

3. "Some British qualities are admirable but on the whole I do not like them."

6. "The British are slow and unimaginative."
7. "I don't object to the British people but I don't like the British Government."
10. "I would never marry a British person."
11. "I would be happy if Britain were brought to its knees."

It should be noted that all items are scored negatively, i.e. "Agree" is scored 3 if the statement is *positive* towards the British, "disagree" is scored 1 and "no opinion" is valued 2, while in the case of a statement judged to be *negative* the values are reversed with "agree" = 3, "no opinion" = 2 and "disagree" = 1.

It is quite clear from Table 113 that the range of scale score differences for the total scales, "complete" and "adjusted", is much less than in the case of that of the two sub-scales, i.e. "low esteem" and "political/hostility". This reveals an internal neutralisation of response direction. The "political" variable is the only variable to show wide range scores for scales and sub-scales. This is largely due to the high score of "Workers Party" supporters. The range of scores in the case of the other four parties is 8.3. Also, there is very little evidence of clear patterns of anti-British scoring, even within the modest ranges of difference as is clearly borne out in Figure 26.

Figure No. 26: Anti-British Scale by Personal Variables

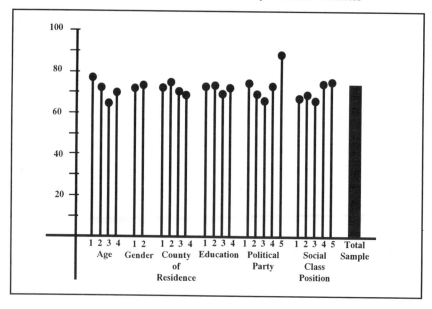

TABLE No. 112
CORRELATION MATRIX BETWEEN ITEMS OF ANTI-BRITISH SCALE

	Factor 2					Factor 3				Factor 4	
	No.2	No.3	No.6	No.9	No.11	No.1	No.4	No.8	No.12	No.7	No.13
Factor 2											
2. The British are not pretty decent people	1.00	.34	.23	.35	.30	.29	.17	.18	.10	.04	.22
3. Don't like the British on the whole		1.00	.23	.23	.31	.32	.19	.11	.08	.22	.37
6. British slow and unimaginative			1.00	.19	.26	.11	.03	-.02	-.02	.17	.22
9. Not happy to see British people get on				1.00	.22	.20	.12	.16	.08	.09	.18
11. Happy if Britain were brought to its knees					1.00	.18	.04	.12	-.05	.17	.26
Factor 3											
1. Wouldn't cheer for a British team						1.00	.30	.21	.11	17	.28
4. Would rather not live in Britain than elsewhere abroad							1.00	.22	.16	.05	.19
8. The World does not owe a lot to Britain								1.00	.17	.09	.17
12. The British Government has not been evenhanded in Northern Ireland									1.00	.10	.09
Factor 4											
7. Don't like the British Government										1.00	.23
13. The British have little respect for the Irish											1.00

The correlations between the "social distance scores", i.e. Factor 1 are given on Table 30 (p. 120). While most of the items on Table 112 above show a significant correlation (>.20), they are not very high when compared with the correlations between the social distance scores of the items of Factor 1 on Table 30.

TABLE No. 113
ANTI-BRITISH SCALE AND SUBSCALE SCORES BY PERSONAL VARIABLES

	1988-89 Complete Scale (0-200)	1988-89 Adjusted* Scale (0-200)	Low Esteem Factor (0-200)	Political/ Hostility Factor (0-200)
SOCIAL SAMPLE	73.5	68.7	81.2	56.5
A. AGE				
1. 35 years or less	78.1	73.3	93.4	53.4
2. 36 to 50 years	73.4	67.4	80.8	53.8
3. 51 years to 65 years	65.9	61.5	67.2	56.3
4. 66 years +	71.3	68.1	67.0	70.6
(Range)	(12.2)	(11.8)	(26.4)	(17.2)
B. COUNTY OF RESIDENCE				
1. Dublin	73.4	67.1	80.7	53.5
2. Rest of Leinster	77.6	72.8	85.4	60.3
3. Munster	71.9	68.1	81.4	55.4
4. Connaught/Ulster	70.5	66.1	75.4	57.8
(Range)	(7.1)	(5.7)	(10.0)	(6.8)
C. EDUCATION				
1. Primary Only	74.9	70.6	73.8	68.1
2. Incomplete Second Level	74.7	69.9	82.0	57.1
3. Complete Second Level	71.1	66.2	83.7	49.0
4. Third Level	74.3	69.0	86.5	51.4
(Range)	(3.8)	(4.4)	(12 7)	(29.9)
D. POLITICAL PARTY PREFERENCE				
1.Fianna Fáil	76.3	71.7	83.1	61.0
2.Fine Gael	71.5	65.2	69.7	46.8
3.Labour Party	68.1	60.8	68.5	53.9
4.Progressive Democrats	75.8	67.6	91.4	43.8
5.Workers Party	90.4	86.3	95.8	76.7
(Range)	(22.3)	(28.1)	(27.3)	(29.9)
E. SOCIAL CLASS POSITION				
1.Class I	69.7	61.2	84.1	38.2
2.Class 11	71.5	66.5	81.5	51.1
3.Class 111	68.1	63.0	76.5	49.5
4.Class IV	75.8	71.3	84.9	58.6
5.Class V	77.4	72.4	78.2	66.5
	(9.3)	(11.2)	(6.7)	(28.3)

* Adjusted to replicate the 1972-73 Scale. One item on the 1972-73 Scale i.e. *"British soldiers are cruel and brutal"* was dropped from the 1988-89 Scale in the course of the pilot studies of the scale. The adjusted Scale includes statements 1, 2, 3, 4, 6, 7, 8, 9, 10 and 11 of Table 22.

The 'Low Esteem' Factor consists of statements 1, 2, 4, 8 and 9 while statements 3, 6, 7, 10 and 11 make up the 'Political and Hostility Factor' (see Mac Gréil, 1977, pp. 362-75).

Footnote: The Anti-British Scale Score is arrived at by getting the 'mean of the means' of the various items and subtracting one from it and multiplying the answer by one hundred. The range of Anti-British Score is from 0 to 200. The average scale score for the National Sample at 73.5 provides the possibility of a reasonable range of responses.

Figure No. 27: Post-Colonial Attitudinal Schizophrenia Patterns by Personal Variables

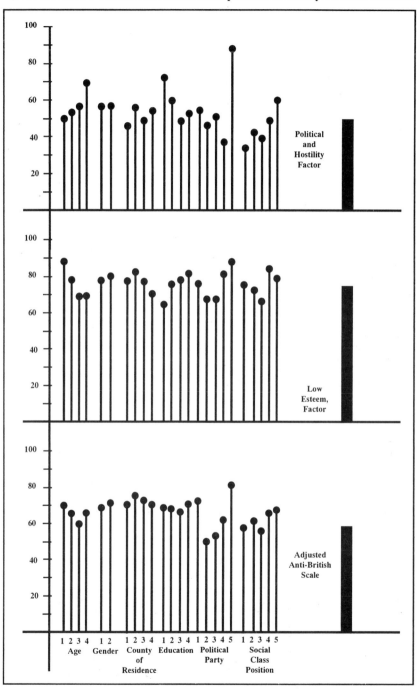

In normal circumstances one would expect two subscales measuring *negative* aspects of Irish-British attitudes to be positively correlated. Table 113 does not confirm such expectations and in the case of some ordinal variables, i.e. age, education and social class position[1] trends tend to be in the opposite direction. For instance, older respondents were more hostile but less negative in relation to esteem. More highly educated and those with higher social class position rated relatively high in "low esteem" and low in hostility compared with those in the lower educational and social class position categories. This stands out more clearly on the graphic representation of the findings on Figure 27 and confirms a degree of "post-colonial attitudinal schizophrenia".

If one examines the cross-direction of the two factor sub-scales the 1972-73 sub-sample variations are replicated.[2] The younger, more highly educated and higher socially statused respondents have lower esteem towards the British and less hospitality towards them than do those who are older, less well educated and having a lower social-class position in society. This is as one would have expected when dealing with a post-colonial situation. It may also be true of any society in the attitudes of those with less privilege towards those perceived to be enjoying the lion's share of privilege. The relatively high esteem scores are really **inverted low self-esteem perceptions**. Hence, the potential danger for society with evidently high levels of inequality. The point being made here is the potential insecurity of inequality which cannot be evaded because of its collective psychological effect on those of the "underclass".

3. CONCLUSIONS AND INTERPRETATIONS:

3.1   Attitudes towards the British are mixed. The British people are perceived as an "ingroup" while "British" and "English" when seen as political stimulus categories are viewed negatively. The so-called "shoot-to-kill" allegations in relation to incidents in Northern Ireland (i.e. the Stalker affair) and in the Gibraltar shootings, as well as the whole series of incidents of miscarriage of justice against Irish citizens and English people related to Ireland (as noted above) may have seriously undermined Irish people's confidence in British fair play. There has been a long folk tradition of distrust of British justice borne out, for example, by the treatment of those accused of the Maamtrasna Murders in 1882 (see Waldron, 1992).

There is an obvious need for the British authorities to ensure fair treatment of Irish people before the law and public redress for injustices resulting from wrongful convictions and misbehaviour by security forces. To ignore the level of resentment felt by the Irish

1. While it is accepted that educational standard is a composite component in calculating "social class position", occupational status is, nevertheless, the main component in the arrival at the different classes.

2. See Mac Gréil *op. cit.* 1977 (pp. 368-375).

population, which is implicit in the findings of Items 12 and 13 of the Anti-British Scale (Table 108, p. 259), would seriously impair proper Anglo-Irish relations. It should be noted that allegations of summary treatment of Irish offenders and alleged offenders includes people on the Loyalist and on the Republican side of the current conflict. There is a great need for much reassurance.

3.2   While the majority (52%) stated they were satisfied that the *Anglo-Irish Agreement* had been a positive development, almost the same proportion were either neutral or negative towards its contribution (see Table 105, p. 250). Probably, those with a neutral disposition were prepared to defer their judgement and give the Agreement more time to deliver results.

PART II: POLITICAL PARTY PREFERENCES 1988-89

The following table (Table 114) gives a breakdown of the party preferences of the total sample. The main difference between the findings of this survey and those of regular opinion polls is the fact that the information was collected over a relatively long period of five to six months and was part of a very extensive interview. Passing changes of opinion are thereby absorbed and neutralised. For that reason, it is not useful to compare and contrast the findings with opinion polls, apart from very general patterns. Apart from the historical value of the information contained in Tables 114 and 115, the findings also give a greater insight into the significance of political party preference as a personal variable used through this text.

TABLE No. 114
POLITICAL PARTY PREFERENCES

	Number	Percent of Total Sample	Excluding Undecided Respondents
1. Fianna Fáil	449	45%	52%
2. Fine Gael	252	25%	29%
3. Labour Party	66	7%	8%
4. Progressive Democrats	42	4%	5%
5. Workers Party	24	2%	3%
6. Other/Non-Party	35	4%	4%
7. Would/Could Not Say	60	6%	–
8. Would not Vote	43	4%	–
9. No Reply	34	3%	–
TOTAL	1005	100%	101%

At the time of interview, 87% of the sample expressed a voting preference. The distribution of their preferences for the political parties who were represented in the last Dáil was as given in Table 114. The 4% who indicated preference for "Other/ Non-Party" are presented collectively because of the small numbers involved (35 respondents). It is worth noting that less than half of those not giving a preference said they were undecided or refused to give a preference.

TABLE No. 115
POLITICAL PARTY PREFERENCE BY PERSONAL VARIABLES

	Fianna Fáil	Fine Gael	Labour Party	Progressive Democrats*	Workers' Party*	Other/Non Party*	N.
Total Sample	52%	29%	8%	5%	3%	4%	868
A. GENDER P≤.05							
1. Female	52%	31%	8%	6%	1%	2%	454
2. Male	51%	27%	7%	4%	4%	6%	414
B. PLACE OF REARING P≤.001							
1. Large City	43%	28%	10%	7%	5%	7%	176
2. Small City	44%	24%	13%	10%	4%	5%	100
3. Town	55%	28%	11%	2%	0%	5%	131
4. Rural	56%	31%	5%	4%	2%	3%	458
C. EDUCATION P≤.05							
1. Primary Only	57%	26%	6%	2%	4%	4%	250
2. Incomplete Second Level	53%	27%	9%	5%	2%	4%	297
3. Complete Second Level	48%	35%	5%	7%	2%	4%	195
4. Third Level	44%	29%	11%	7%	4%	5%	126
D. OCCUPATIONAL STATUS P≤.02							
1. Unskilled/Semi-skilled	56%	22%	11%	3%	3%	5%	284
2. Skilled Manual	56%	22%	8%	6%	5%	4%	143
3. Intermediate Non-Manual	48%	37%	6%	5%	2%	3%	209
4. Professional/Managerial	45%	34%	6%	7%	3%	6%	257

* Because of the relatively small number of respondents in these categories, the reader is advised to be cautious in concluding too much from the sub-sample distributions.

The difference between *male and female* voting intentions is significant, but not very great. Females are proportionately higher for Fine Gael and for the Progressive Democrats, while males are proportionately higher for the Workers' Party and for "Other/Non-Party". Fianna Fáil proportions are practically the same for males and females.

Place of rearing was the variable to show the greatest variation (statistically) in party preferences. Fianna Fáil supporters are proportionately more represented in categories of "Town" and "Rural" and under-represented among the "Large City" and "Small City" categories. Fine Gael's supporters are slightly over- represented among those reared in

"Small Cities". Labour Party support is largely urban-reared, as is that of the Progressive Democrats and the Workers' Party. It should be noted that some of those who were reared in "rural" or "town" areas are now resident in cities and large towns.

Fianna Fáil support among respondents with "primary only" or "incomplete second" *levels of education* is higher than the sample average, while it is below average in the "complete second" and "third level" sub-samples. Fine Gael's strongest representation is in the "Third Level" category. Labour Party supporters are also more strongly represented in the "third level". Variations in the case of the Progressive Democrats tend to be in favour of the two higher level groupings. The Workers' Party has greater representation at both the lower and at the higher levels. Because of the small but significant variations, a note of caution must be made.

Voting preferences by occupational categories also resulted in a significant variation. Fianna Fáil has above average support in the "blue collar" categories, while Fine Gael has stronger than average support in the "white collar" categories. Labour also has above average support in the "blue collar categories". The Progressive Democrats' strongest category is "professional/managerial". "Skilled manual" is the category most disposed to the Workers' Party.

PART III: ATTITUDES TO SOCIO-POLITICAL CATEGORIES

1. SOCIAL DISTANCE SCORES

As noted in chapter three (pp. 70/1 above), there were a number of socio-political categories in the list of stimulus categories towards which social distance was measured in the 1988-89 National Survey. These included "Gardaí", "Trade Unionists", "Capitalists", "Socialists" and "Communists". The responses towards political categories on the Bogardus Social Distance Scale tend to be more "polarised", especially in the case of categories with a substantial level of negativity towards their perceived views or actions.

Table 116 shows a very wide range of preferences towards the various political categories measured. The **Gardaí** are very highly thought of and could be classified as an "ingroup" in the Republic. It would be difficult to find a police force in any other country with such high national standing. This is all the more significant because of the fact that police in Ireland were perceived by many as agents of a "foreign" Government, "Great Britain", until less than seventy years before the survey was carried out in 1988-89. The Gardaí are unarmed and relate closely to the people in many parts of the Republic. This contributes to their relatively very high standing. It would be expected from these findings that public confidence in and co-operation with the Gardaí should present little problem. The residue of public hostility towards the police in the Republic coming from pre-independence

TABLE No. 116
SOCIAL DISTANCE TOWARDS SOCIO-POLITICAL CATEGORIES

SOCIAL DISTANCE	Gardaí	Trade Unionists	Capitalists	Socialists	Communists
1. "Would marry or welcome as member of my family"	84.0	63.7	47.8	44.9	24 4
2. "Would have as close friends" (or closer)	92.6	72.5	59.8	58.1	37.8
3. "Would have as nextdoor neighbour" (or closer)	98.2	78.8	70.7	69.1	49.4
4. "Would work in the same workplace" (or closer)	99.2	89.4	79.9	79.5	60.0
5. "Would welcome as an Irish citizen" (or closer)	99.8	95.8	86.4	86.6	65.7
6. "Would have as a visitor only to Ireland"	0.0	2.0	10.2	10.3	20.2
7. "Would debar or deport from Ireland"	0.2	2.2	3.4	3.1	14.1
Mean Social Distance	1.267	2.022	2.517	2.650	3.764
Number	1005	994	998	995	1003

days would seem to be very little. The relatively low (serious) crime rate[3] in the Republic may be in part thanks to the public respect for our unarmed Gardaí. This is not to ignore the problems of urban crime in Ireland today. Since the time of this survey there would appear to have been an increase in organised crime, especially, drug-related violent crime.

Trade Unionists, while just outside the "ingroup" category, score quite positively when compared with categories below them. The fact that 36% would not welcome a "Trade Unionist" as a member of the family, in a country where there is a very high union participation rate, raises questions with regard to a residual prejudice against organised labour among a minority of the people in the Republic. The 74% who would welcome them into the family puts them in a relatively favoured position.

Capitalists fare significantly worse than "Trade Unionists", with over fifty percent (52%) not welcoming them into the family through marriage. This negative image of "Capitalists" must raise serious questions for the status of the dominant ideology prevalent among Ireland's economic elite and throughout the Western "developed" world. Some 13.4% would deny citizenship to "Capitalists" as compared with only 4.2% in the case of Trade Unionists. Do these findings mean a distaste for the "capitalist ideology" among half of the population?

3. The homicide rate in the Republic (population 3.537 million) for the years 1986 to 1990 was as follows: 1986 14 murders; 1987 29 murders; 1988 20 murders; 1989 17 murders; 1990 17 murders. Source: *Garda Commissioner's Report*.

The next category in rank order of preference is **Socialists** with very little difference of percentages between them and "Capitalists". Practically the same proportion (13.4%) would deny them citizenship. The percentage not welcoming "Socialists" to kinship is 55%, just 3% higher than the figure for "Capitalists". These figures would seem to reflect the moderate alienation of over half the sample from both the right and left wings of the socio-economic political spectrum. Of course, it could also be stated that there is a balance of public status for those seen to be on the left and on the right. Political scientists and economic theorists might investigate the significance of these findings for the success and/or failure in the eyes of the people of current economic policies.

The attitudes of the Irish population to **Communists** were significantly more negative than in the case of "Capitalists" or "Socialists". Approximately one-quarter of the sample (24.4%) would welcome "Communists" into their family through marriage, while a third (34.3%) would deny them citizenship. This stimulus category ("Communists") is a complex one, as is shown in the rationalisation figures given in Table 117 with religious (28.2%), political (27.4%), way of life/culture (25.8%) and economic (11.7%) reasons given to rationalise people's refusal to welcome them into a kinship relationship. The presence of the "religious" reason probably reflects the people's refusal (71%) to admit people perceived to be atheistic (see Mac Gréil 1991 pp 57-63).

In the case of all five stimulus categories in Table 117 a significant proportion gave a "political" rationalisation. "Trade Unionists" and "Socialists" had the highest political profile. Economic reasons were significant in the case of each category 1 to 5 with "Capitalists" scoring highest (25.6%). "Ethnic/cultural/way-of-life" was the highest reason in the case of "Gardaí" and "Capitalists". In all cases, "way of life" was given as the biggest component of the composite set of reasons for refusing to welcome into the family. As already noted above, "Communists" elicited a relatively strong proportion giving religion as their main reason for not admitting members into the family. It is interesting to note the relatively small percentage who gave "not socially acceptable" as their reason in all cases.

The findings of Table 117 give an insight into the intergroup perceptions of those in the sample refusing categories to "kinship" which, in turn, is a valuable measure of *intergroup definition*. For example, should the religious and political scare in relation to "Communists" dissipate, their social distance rating would most likely improve.

Polarised scores and patterned replies are to be expected in the case of political categories about whom there are strong views in the community. It would, however, appear that the Irish sample has viewed only one of the five categories in a polarised manner, namely "Communists". The high scoring of 6 and 7, i.e. the denial of citizenship categories in the case of "Communists" shows that this category still elicits strong negative responses (see Figure 28).

TABLE No. 117
RATIONALISATIONS OF SOCIO-POLITICAL CATEGORIES

	Religious	Racial	Political	Ethnic Cultural	Economic	Not Socially	Other	N
1. Gardaí	0.7	0.7	16.5	68.3	0.7	4.3	8.6	139
2. Trade Unionists	0.6	0.0	38.9	33.5	18.6	4.5	3.0	334
3. Capitalists	2.0	0.2	18.1	47.6	25.6	4.9	1.6	507
4. Socialists	4.3	0.4	39.2	35.6	14.1	5.3	1.2	531
5. Communists	28.2	0.8	27.4	25.8	11.7	5.2	0.9	737

Note: Percentages over 8% are Underlined

TABLE No. 118
SOCIAL DISTANCE TOWARDS SOCIO-POLITICAL CATEGORIES
BY PERSONAL VARIABLES

	Trade Unionists %		Capitalists %		Socialists %		Communists %	
	Kinship	Deny Citizenship	Kinship	Deny Citizenship	Kinship	Deny Citizenship	Kinship	Deny Citizenship
National Sample	63.7	4.2	47.8	13.6	44.5	13.3	24.4	34.3
A. AGE								
1. Under 36	N/S		N/S		47.6	12.5	30.4	27.8
2. 36 - 50					46.1	8.9	28.0	29.2
3. 51 - 65					42.9	18.3	14.9	43.8
4. 66 +					38.0	17.6	14.0	49.0
(Range of Difference)					(9.6)	(9.4)	(16.4)	(21.2)
					{P≤.5}		{P≤.001}	
B. GENDER								
1. Female	N/S		42.8	15.6	41.2	16.5	21.0	37.6
2. Male			53.7	11.4	49.3	9.6	28.4	30.4
(Range of Difference)			(10.5)	(4.2)	(8.1)	(6.9)	(7.4)	(7.2)
			{P≤.005}		{P≤.00f}		{P≤.01}	
C. COUNTY OF RESIDENCE								
1. Dublin	71.2	2.2	60.6	9.7	54.0	6.5	35.0	23.8
2. Rest of Leinster	70.1	4.0	51.2	17.5	51.6	15.5	32.2	31.4
3. Munster	58.7	5.7	43.3	10.3	41.6	13.1	15.4	41.8
4. Connaught/Ulster	50.9	5.3	29.6	20.1	26.0	21.9	11.6	42.8
(Range of Difference)	(20.3)	(3.5)	(31.0)	(10.4)	(28.0)	(15.4)	(23.4)	(19.0)
	{P≤.001}		{P≤.001}		{P≤.001}		{P≤.001}	
D. PARTY POLITICAL PREFERENCE								
1. Fianna Fáil	61.9	4.7	N/S		45.9	14.0	21.7	35.9
2. Fine Gael	58.5	5.6			36.5	17.3	19.8	38.9
3. Labour Party	80.3	3.0			66.7	4.5	42.4	19.7
4. Progressive Democrats	64.3	2.4			42.9	7.1	28.6	28.6
(Range of Difference)	(18.4)	(3.2)			(30.2)	(10.2)	(22.6)	(19.2)
	{P≤.05}				{P≤.001}		{P≤.001}	
E. SOCIAL CLASS POSITION								
1. Class I	N/S		79.4	2.3	79.4	2.9	41.2	8.8
2. Class II			62.9	11.4	57.1	7.6	41.0	22.9
3. Class III			46.8	9.3	44.8	10.8	23.0	31.5
4. Class IV			45.7	14.7	43.9	12.1	24.4	34.9
5. Class V			43.0	19.4	40.1	18.7	18.7	4L7
(Range of Difference)			(36.4)	(17.1)	(34.3)	(15.8)	(22.5)	(32.9)
			{P≤.001}		{P≤.001}		{P≤.001}	

Figure No. 28: Social Distance Patterns towards Socio-Political Categories

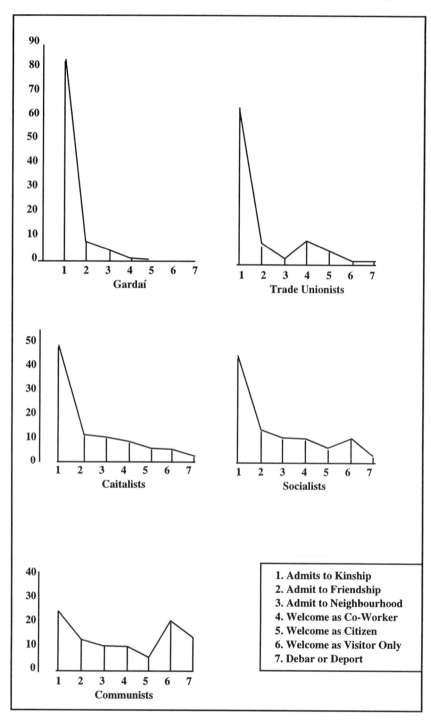

There was general consensus in relation to the social distance responses towards "Gardaí". In the case of the other four socio-political categories, the breakdown of responses by personal variables is given in Table 118 (above).

"County of residence" and "political party preference" registered significant variations in social distance towards "**Trade Unionists**". In the case of "county of residence", Dublin and the Rest of Leinster were most positive while Connaught/Ulster was least so. The supporters of the Workers' Party were most favourably disposed while Fine Gael were least.

"Gender", "county of residence" and "social class position" registered significant variations in the social distance scores towards "**Capitalists**". Those most in favour of "Capitalists" were Class I and II of "social class position", Dubliners and males, while those least favourably disposed were respondents from Class V, from Connaught/Ulster and females. The biggest range of scores between subsamples were in "Social Class Position" and "county of residence".

Socialists elicited significant variations in all five personal variables on Table 118. The range of percentage variation in admission to kinship went from 39.3% in the case of social class position to 8% in the case of gender. The subsamples most in favour of "Socialists" were Class I (Upper Class), Workers' Party supporters, residents of Dublin, males and those under 36 years of age. Those most negatively disposed to "Socialists" were Class V, supporters of Fine Gael, females and older respondents.

The pattern of responses to "**Communists**" were similar to those of "Socialists". All variables had significant differences. It is very interesting, if not ironic, to note a higher level of welcome for "Socialists" and "Communists" among those more privileged (Classes I and II) than among the lower classes (IV and V) and those with least education, while the policies of both categories are understood to work for the more deprived. This confirms the view that insecurity (of lower classes) rather than ideological incompatability is the strongest determinant of prejudice.

Table 119 measures the changes in social distance scores between the 1972-73 survey and that of 1988-89. "Capitalists" were not included as a stimulus category in the 1972-73 survey.

Social distance scores towards "Gardaí" did not change significantly in Dublin over the sixteen years interval between 1972-73 and 1988-89. There was a slight disimprovement in the standing of "Trade Unionists" and "Socialists". The standing of "Communists" in Dublin improved substantially and significantly since 1972-73.

2 CONCLUSIONS AND INTERPRETATIONS

2.1   Attitudes towards the "Gardaí" show a high level of respect in the population. This indicates good relations between the Gardaí and the various communities (urban and rural) in the Republic since the foundation of the State. Our sad history of political unrest relating to Northern Ireland has not undermined public confidence in our police force.

TABLE No. 119
DIFFERENCES IN SOCIAL DISTANCE TOWARDS SOCIO-POLITICAL
CATEGORIES IN DUBLIN BETWEEN 1972-73 AND 1988-89

Socio-Political Stimulus Category		Would marry or welcome as member 1. %	Would have as close friend or closer 2. %	Would have as nextdoor neighbours or closer 3. %	Would work in same place or closer 4. %	Would welcome as Irish citizen or closer 5. %	Would have as visitors only to Ireland 6. %	Would debar or deport from Ireland 7. %	Mean Social Distance (1-7)	N
1. Gardaí	1988/9	84.1	93.8	98.5	98.5	99.6	0.0	0.4	1.270	277
	1972/3	85.5	93.6	97.5	98.1	99.5	0.2	0.3	1.260	2299
	Difference	-1.4	+0.2	+1.0	+0.4	+0.1	-0.2	+0.1	+0.010	
2. Trade Unionists	1988/9	71.2	78.9	86.6	94.3	97.9	0.4	1.8	1.735	274
	1972/3	78.2	87.6	91.8	95.8	98.1	0.8	1.1	1.503	2288
	Difference	-7.0	-8.7	-5.2	-1.5	-0.2	-0.4	+0.7	+0.232	
3. Socialists	1988/9	54.0	68.5	80.1	89.2	93.5	5.1	1.4	2.161	276
	1972/3	62.3	75.0	82.1	86.4	90.4	4.9	4.7	2.085	2269
	Difference	-8.3	-6.5	-2.0	+0.8	+3.1	+0.2	-3.3	+0.076	
4. Communists	1988/9	35.0	49.1	61.7	72.9	76.1	12.3	11.6	3.168	227
	1972/3	22.9	41.3	52.8	57.5	64.0	8.8	27.2	3.885	2287
	Difference	+12.1	+7.8	+8.9	+15.4	+12.1	+3.5	-15.6	-0.717	

2.2 The public standing of "Capitalists", "Socialists", and "Communists" is interesting from a number of points of view. The people are almost equally attached to the so-called "right" and "left". It could be interpreted as a perfect example of a more balanced centralist position, especially in the light of the wide spectrum of supporters from all "class" positions shown in the political party profiles given in Table 118. The relatively low scores for "Capitalists" in a society often promoted and portrayed in official public relations campaigns as a predominantly "liberal capitalist society" must raise questions about the representativeness of the elite expressing this view. The counter position expressed in the support for "Socialists" probably has its roots in the traditions of Michael Davitt (Land Movement), of James Connolly and James Larkin (Labour Movement) and the strong social justice ethos of Christian Churches and other concerned groups. This is yet another manifestation of the complexity of the ethos of modern Ireland. It is also noteworthy that the standing of "Communists" improved in Ireland at the very time Communist governments were being undermined in Eastern Europe.

PART IV: ATTITUDES AND OPINIONS TOWARDS NEUTRALITY AND DISARMAMENT

The questions relating to National neutrality and opposition to nuclear weapons have been topical in Ireland for many years. The State's neutral stance during the 1939-45 War and its subsequent refusal to join NATO are concrete manifestations of Irish neutrality. The issue of our position had been discussed in the media, especially in relation to the process of European integration *via* the European Community. In this section of the report the opinions of the people are presented in relation to questions concerned with neutrality, nuclear disarmament and the effects of the EEC on Irish independence.

1. NEUTRALITY AND INDEPENDENCE SCALE

Table 120 gives the overall response of the sample to neutrality and national independence, as well as measuring the support for and appreciation of our Defence Forces' active involvement in the peace-keeping work of the United Nations.

The overwhelming support (84%) for, and the very small opposition (6%) to, Irish neutrality in wars between other countries reinforces Ireland's abstention from military alliances since our independence. This opinion (item no.3) meets with consensus in all *age* groups, *education* categories, and by supporters of various *political parties*. The endorsement of the Defence Forces' involvement in U.N. peace-keeping gets similar consensus, as in the case of neutrality. The high level of support for a more active independent foreign policy gets consensus when measured by age, education and party political preference.

The combined impact of the findings of items nos. 1, 2 and 3, points to the active nature of Irish neutrality as expected by the vast majority of the people. The Government should take courage from the reply to item no. 2 in its pursuance of an independent foreign policy.

TABLE NO. 120
OVERALL RESPONSE TO IRELAND'S NEUTRALITY AND INDEPENDENCE

Attitude/Opinion	Agree	Neither Agree nor Disagree	Disagree	Number (N)
1. "The Irish Defence Forces should continue their peacekeeping work with the United Nations".	87%	8%	5%	1,001
2. "Irish Governments should be more actively pursuing an independent foreign policy".	60%	28%	11%	1.000
3. "Ireland should continue to maintain its neutral stance in wars between other countries".	84%	10%	6%	1,003
4. "Ireland's position as a distinct and independent nation is threatened by our membership of the EEC.*".	31%	25%	44%	999

*More recently referred to as the E.U.

The responses to the item dealing with the *"perceived threat of the E.E.C. to Irish independence and distinctiveness"* are quite varied. A plurality (44%) does not perceive the E.E.C. as a threat, while significant percentages (31% and 25%) either agree or are not sure. This item has elicited a significant variation when measured by "age", "gender", "education", "political preference", "occupation" and "place of residence". Table 121 gives a breakdown of responses to item no. 4 of Table 120 by these variables.

This table shows that the widest range of opinions on the perceived threat of EEC membership to Ireland's independence is in the case of *Occupational Status* and *Education* where there is a negative correlation in each case. Dublin residents are significantly less likely to perceive a threat from membership than those from the other parts of Ireland. The above findings may also be indicative of the degree of positivity or negativity towards the European Community in the population. If that be so, the Irish people are significantly divided in their attitudes.

CONCLUSION AND INTERPRETATION:

In the light of current developments in relation to the implications of accelerated moves towards greater integration within the European Union

TABLE No. 121
MEMBERSHIP OF THE EEC AND NATIONAL INDEPENDENCE
BY PERSONAL VARIABLES

Statement: "Ireland's position as a distinct and independent nation is threatened by our membership of the EEC"

Personal Variable	Agree	Neither Agree nor Disagree	Disagree	(N)
Total Sample	31%	25%	44%	999
A. AGE [P≤.01]				
1. Under 36 years	29%	23%	48%	77
2. 36 to 50 years	31%	26%	43%	315
3. 51 - 65 years	30%	17%	53%	269
4. 66 years +	32%	29%	39%	337
B. GENDER [P≤.001]				
1. Female	31%	30%	39%	541
2. Male	31%	18%	51%*	457
C. COUNTY OF RESIDENCE [P≤.001]				
1. Dublin	30%	19%	52%	275
2. Rest of Leinster	32%	32%	36%	253
3. Munster	36%	18%	47%	299
4. Connaught/Ulster	23%	35%	42%	171
D. EDUCATION [P≤.001]				
1. Primary Only	36%	35%	30%	279
2. Incomplete Second Level	33%	23%	44%	347
3. Complete Second Level	27%	22%	50%	232
4. Third Level	22%	11%	66%	140
E. POLITICAL PARTY PREFERENCE [P≤.001]				
1. Fianna Fáil	30%	25%	45%	448
2. Fine Gael	27%	22%	52%	251
3. Labour Party	46%	17%	38%	66
4. Progressive Democrats	24%	10%	67%	42
F. OCCUPATIONAL STATUS [P≤.001]				
1. High Professional/Managerial	16%	14%	70%	96
2. Low Professional/Managerial	31%	14%	55%	161
3. Intermediate Non-Manual	35%	22%	43%	209
4. Skilled Manual	33%	23%	44%	143
5. Semi-skilled Manual	32%	35%	32%	161
6. Unskilled Manual	34%	36%	31% .	121

Underlined figures indicate majority against the view expressed.

the findings on *"Irish Neutrality and Independence"* reveal a very strong attachment to both ideals and a desire for a more active independent neutral stance by our Government on international affairs. If this is what the people really desire, then any serious diminution of either aim must be because of other incentives such as socio-economic gain or a feeling that the preservation of these ideals as something desirable is no longer possible. The consequences of such a situation could be serious in the future, should the new EEC arrangements not work out to the people's expectations and satisfaction. At the time of the survey (1988/89) the plurality (44%) of respondents did not perceive the EEC as a *"threat to Irish independence and distinctiveness"*, although 31% did see it as a threat.

2. ATTITUDES TOWARDS NUCLEAR DISARMAMENT

2.1 Overall Findings:

In Table 122 the findings of the overall sample are given in relation to five items which measure the people's views on nuclear weapons, their perceived effectiveness as protectors of peace or as threats to it, and how nuclear (weapons) free Ireland should be.

TABLE No. 122
OVERALL RESPONSE TO NUCLEAR WEAPONS AND WAR (TOTAL SAMPLE)

Attitude/Opinion	Agree	Neither Agree nor Disagree	Disagree	Number (N)
1. "The presence of nuclear weapons is more a threat to peace in Europe than its guarantee".	79%	12%	9%	1,000
2. "Ships and planes carrying nuclear weapons should be banned from visiting or passing close to Ireland".	86%	8%	6%	1,003
3. "Nuclear weapons are necessary for our protection".	15%	13%	71%	998
4. "A nuclear war is likely in my lifetime".	27%	27%	46%	999
5. "Ireland should never allow nuclear weapons on its soil".	83%	9%	7%	1,003

Items nos. 2 and 5 unequivocally establish the overwhelming support in the population for a total ban on the presence of nuclear weapons on Irish soil or on planes and ships passing over or near this country. Only seven and six percent respectively would dissent from the view that would prohibit nuclear weapons in Ireland. Apart from occupational status, where a comparatively higher proportion (17%) of "higher professional and managerial" respondents would disagree, and the case of gender (where only 3% of females disagreed with banning nuclear weapons as compared with 10% for males), there has been general consensus across the board.

The people's lack of confidence in nuclear weapons as a means of protection and prevention of war is again clearly borne out in items nos. 1 and 3, where the vast majority see such weapons as more a threat to peace in Europe and disagree with their necessity for our protection. Again there is a high degree of overall consensus on both these items when measured by education, political preference and occupational status. Female respondents are significantly less confident in the protective value of nuclear weapons than are males.

Item no. 4, i.e. "*A nuclear war is likely in my lifetime*", has produced a most divided result. The fact that some 54% of the sample either agreed with or were not sure about this view could indicate a basis for a sense of anxiety or insecurity in the population. Hence, the relevance of, and need for, world nuclear disarmament. There was consensus for this view in the case of education, political preference, place of residence and occupational status. There was significant variation in the case of age and gender. Young and middle-aged people were more convinced that a nuclear war would happen in their lifetime than were those over 51 years old. In the case of gender, some 51% of males did not see nuclear war happening in their lifetime as compared with 42% of females who held that view.

2.2 Consensus in Opposition to Nuclear Weapons:

The finding of Table 123 reports an extraordinary degree of consensus across the different personal variables in relation to a relatively high level of public opposition to Irish involvement with nuclear weapons and to the capacity of nuclear arsenals to promote world or European peace. Even where there is a statistically significant degree of dissent, the range of such variation is relatively small, e.g., in the case of item no. 2 which responds to the statement: "*Ships and planes carrying nuclear weapons should be banned from Ireland*".

These findings would create problems for the State in the event of Ireland becoming involved in military alliances with nuclear powers in Europe. It would be highly unlikely that the people of Ireland would favour Irish Defence Forces being part of a pan-European security force with a nuclear weapons dimension. When the findings of this scale are added to the response in Table 120 to the statement: "*Ireland should continue to maintain its neutral stance in wars between other countries*", i.e., 84% agreeing and 6% disagreeing, it is very clear that the Irish people are pro-neutrality and anti-nuclear.

It should be noted that the collapse of the "Eastern Bloc" in 1989 and subsequent years may have lowered the anxiety with regard to "*a nuclear war in my (respondent's) lifetime*" (item no. 4). The resumption of nuclear tests by France in 1995 and the intimation by President Chirac that it would be in the interests of the defence of Europe that French nuclear weapons were up-to-date, may revive our personal anxiety in relation to nuclear war while the UN assembly ban on nuclear testing (September 1996) may counter this anxiety!

Prejudice in Ireland Revisited

TABLE No. 123
IRISH OPINIONS ON NUCLEAR WEAPONS BY PERSONAL VARIABLES
(percentages agreeing)

PERSONAL VARIABLES	1 Nuclear weapons, presence is a threat to peace in Europe.	2 Ships and planes carrying nuclear weapons should be banned from Ireland.	3 Nuclear weapons are not necessary for our protection.	4 A nuclear war is likely in my lifetime	5 Ireland should never allow nuclear weapons on its soil.
Total Sample	79%	86%	71%	27%	83%
A. AGE 1. 35 years or less 2. 36 to 50 years 3. 51 to 65 years 4. 66 years plus (Range)	N/S	N/S	P≤.05 76.9% 72.3% 67.0% 63.2%* (13.7%)	P≤.001 31.6% 30.9% 20.2% 16.7%* (14.9%)	N/S
B. GENDER 1. Female 2. Male (Range)	P≤.001 82.1 % 75.8%* (6.3%)	P≤.001 89.2% 82.5%* (6.7%)	P≤.05 72.8% 70.2%* (2.6%)	P≤.001 26.8% 27.4%* (0.6%)	N/S
C. MARITAL STATUS 1. Not Married 2. Married 3. Widowed (Range)	N/S	P≤.05 81.4%* 87.1 % 95.8% (14.4%)	N/S	P≤.05 26.7% 28.3% 14.3%* (14.0%)	N/S
D.COUNTY OF RESIDENCE 1. Dublin 2. Rest of Leinster 3. Munster 4. Connaught/Ulster (Range)	P<.001 82.6% 66.5%* 86.3% 79.9% (19.8%)	P<.001 85.1% 76.8%* 91.3% 92.4% (15.6%)	P<.001 80.3% 59.1%* 74.3% 71.3% (21.2%)	N/S	P<.001 85.5% 74.4%* 87.7% 86.0% (13.3%)
E. EDUCATION 1. Primary Only 2. Incomplete Second Level 3. Complete Second Level 4. Third Level (Range)	N/S	P≤.05 89.0% 87.4% 83.6% 81.3%* (7.7%)	N/S	N/S	N/S
F. OCCUPATION 1. Professional/Executive 2. Inspector/Supervisor 3. Skilled/Routine Non-Manual 4. Semi/Unskilled (Range)	N/S	P≤.001 79.1%* 88.3% 84.9% 87.2% (8.1%)	N/S	N/S	N/S
G. POLITICAL PARTY PREFERENCE 1. Fianna Fáil 2. Fine Gael 3. Labour Party 4. Progressive Democrats (Range)	P≤.05 N/S	86.6% 87.6% 87.9% 83.3%* (4.6%)	N/S	N/S	N/S

* Lowest percentage in each category; highest percentage is underlined.

2.3 Conclusion and Interpretation:

The degree of *opposition to nuclear armament* in the population is exceptionally high and overwhelming. Any formal association of Ireland in military alliances with nuclear arsenals would not only be contrary to the clear popular desire for military neutrality (84% *for* and 5% *against*), but also against the strong statement of nuclear pacificism which would even ban ships and planes carrying nuclear weapons from visiting Ireland (86%) and also ban nuclear weapons ever on Irish soil (83%). These results must place very heavy responsibility on a "representative" Irish Government to *represent* the will of its people. The findings should also encourage our representative government to take independent positions on matters of international importance. Pragmatic arrangements which would compromise Ireland's "nuclear pacifism" would also have negative consequences in the future.

PART V: SUMMARY OF FINDINGS OF CHAPTERS VIII AND IX

1. NORTHERN IRELAND

1.1 The findings of the 1988-89 survey, when compared with those of the 1972-73 survey, show *an overall level of pattern consistency* in the people's political attitudes as measured by the various scales. The complexity of these attitudes and opinions has also been confirmed in the findings.

1.2 The *"Northern Irish"*, while esteemed highly by the national sample, have not been as favoured as the "English", "British" and "Scottish" on the Bogardus Social Distance Scale. This anomaly indicates negative elements in the popular perception of "Northern Irish" by a minority of people in the Republic.

1.3 The general pattern of perception of *common identity* between Catholics and Protestants vis-a-vis their fellow-citizens, within Northern Ireland and within the Republic of Ireland, has been quite similar to what it was in the 1972-73 survey. There was a slight strengthening in cross-border religious identity. There was also an increase in the percentage who would see Northern Protestants having more in common with the Irish than with the British, while the majority would still see them as British.

1.4 The *primary ethnic self-identity* of the people of the Republic is 96% Irish (with 29% opting for a local county or city identity). Only 1.4% saw themselves primarily as "European". The "social class" position factor was a significant determinant of the primacy of local rather than national ethnic self-identity, i.e. lower grades identified themselves more with their local county or city, while the upper class grades saw themselves more as "Irish".

1.5   While half the sample saw *"national unity"* as an essential condition for the just solution of the Northern problem (with 25% disagreeing), 49% agreed that *"Northern Ireland and the Republic are two separate nations"* (with 42% disagreeing). Nine of every ten supported *"increased co-operation across the border"* (with 3% disagreeing). A return to the Irish language as a basis for Irish unity was supported by 24% (with 57% disagreeing).

1.6   Some 16% agreed that *"the use of violence,* while regrettable, is necessary", with 76% disagreeing. In the case of the Dublin subsample, there was a very substantial drop in the proportion agreeing with this view since 1972-73, when 35% agreed as compared to 11% in 1988-89. Attitudes towards the Provisional IRA were very negative, with 9% welcoming them into kinship and 50.3% who would deny them citizenship.

1.7   Almost three-quarters (74%) of the sample thought that *"having separate Catholic and Protestant schools (primary and secondary schools) has been a major cause of division in the Northern Irish community"* (with 13% disagreeing), while the view that *"the position and influence of the Catholic Church in the Republic is a real obstacle to Irish unity"* was rejected by 45% to 36%.

1.8   The opinions of the national sample in relation to the "desirable" *political solution of the Northern problem* clearly favoured a "thirty-two county republic with one central government". Seventy-five percent saw it as "desirable', while a further 13% held that it was "acceptable but not desirable', which means that it was accepted by 88% of the sample. No other solution elicited 50% or more as "desirable', although the two federal options were acceptable to a majority, i.e. provincial federation accepted by 78% and a North-South federation acceptable to 75%. A "totally independent Northern Ireland" was considered acceptable to 55% and the "status quo with devolved power-sharing" would be accepted by 50%. The first four solutions recorded an increase in support, when compared with the findings of 1972-73.

1.9   Opinions on the *Anglo-Irish Agreement* (enacted in 1985) were interesting. The majority (52%) supported the view that it "promoted progress towards a solution", while 23% thought that it "prevented progress towards a solution". A quarter (25%) of the sample held a neutral position in regard to the Agreement. On a continuum of 1 to 7 in favour of the Agreement, the mean score for the sample was 4.45 with the median at 5. Those most in favour of the Anglo-Irish Agreement were those with higher levels of education and with higher social class status. Urban respondents were more appreciative of the Agreement than were the rural and "provincial" subsamples.

2. ATTITUDES AND OPINIONS TOWARDS BRITAIN AND THE BRITISH

2.1   Attitudes towards *the British categories*, i.e. "English", "British", "Scottish" and "Welsh", were on the whole quite positive. Over 70% of the sample would welcome members of each category into their families through kinship, i.e. "English" 78%; "British" 77%, "Scottish" 74%; and "Welsh" 73%. The proportion of the national sample who would deny citizenship to members of these categories was as low as 3-4%.

Respondents from Dublin were most in favour, while those from Connaught/Ulster were least favourably disposed. Social class position also registered significant differences, with those with lower class status being least favourably disposed. The standing of "Scottish" and "Welsh" among Dublin respondents improved significantly since 1972-73.

2.2   The special Anti-British Scale produced very interesting results. When compared with the findings of the 1972-73 survey, the 1988-89 findings for the Dublin sub sample show increased negativity in the attitudes towards the British in areas with political or behaviourial-tendency connotations.

2.3   The opinion that the **British Government** had been *"evenhanded when dealing with Northern Ireland since 1969"* was rejected by 56.5% (with 22.4% agreeing), while almost half of the sample (48.1%) agreed with the opinion that *"the British have little respect for the Irish"* (with 33% disagreeing). The scores for the Dublin sub-sample were even more negative in relation to both these items. Opinions expressed in the case of these items indicate a high level of negative perception of British-Irish political relations at the time of the survey.

2.4   There was *relatively little variation* between the levels of Anti-British scale scores when examined by personal variables. A similar result was found in 1972-73. The repeated anomalous result was, once again, due to the counter-balance between "low esteem" and "political hostility" sub-scales. This negative correlation between two negative sub-scales has been named the "post-colonial attitudinal schizophrenia pattern".

3. SOCIO-POLITICAL ATTITUDES AND OPINIONS·

3.1   Popular support for the *political parties* was as follows: Fianna Fáil 52%; Fine Gael 29%; Labour Party 8%; Progressive Democrats 5%; Workers Party 3%; Others and Non-Party 5%. (Those not decided on voting at the time of interview were excluded from the above distribution). The demographic profile of each party's popular support highlights the social (class) status differences between the parties. The majority of Fianna Fáil and of Labour Party supporters are "blue-collar" or "working-class", while both Fine Gael and the Progressive Democrats seem to appeal more to "white-collar" and "middle or upper class" voters.

3.2   Attitudes towards the *"Gardaí"* were again very positive, with 84% welcoming members of the force into their families through kinship. The "Garda" have maintained this "in group" status in Irish society since 1972-73.

3.3   Attitudes towards *"Trade Unionists"* were only moderately positive, with 63.7% welcoming members into the family through kinship. Their standing in Dublin, although higher than in the national sample, has suffered a slight disimprovement since the 1972-73 survey.

3.4   The three socio-political categories, *"Capitalists"*, *"Socialists"* and *"Communists"* were also tested for social distance on the Bogardus Scale. There was very little difference between the social standing of "Capitalists", with 47.8% welcoming them to kinship, and "Socialists" who would be welcomed into the family by 44.9%. "Communists" were much lower at 24.4% welcoming to kinship. When the 1972-73 findings for Dublin were compared with those of 1988-89, the "Socialists" had declined slightly from 62.3% to 54.0% for kinship. "Communists", however, improved their standing by over 50%, with an increase in the proportion welcoming them into their families through kinship rising from 22.9% in 1972-73 to 35% in 1988-89.

4. NEUTRALITY AND NUCLEAR DISARMAMENT

4.1   Attitudes towards *Irish neutrality and independence* are given in Table 123 where the peace-keeping role of the Defence Forces is overwhelmingly endorsed (87% for and 5% against). The majority (60%) favoured a more active "independent foreign policy" for the Irish Government (with 11% against). Some 84% believed that *"Ireland should continue to maintain its neutral stance in wars between other countries"* (with 6% against). There was mixed opinion in relation to Ireland's membership of the EEC threatening our "position as a distinct and independent nation", 31% agreeing that it was a threat and 44% disagreeing with this view.

4.2 The people's views on the *nuclear disarmament question* were given in Table 123. The overwhelming majority was against nuclear weapons. The view that nuclear weapons were "more a threat to peace than its guarantee" was endorsed by 79% (and opposed by 9%). Eighty-three percent held the view that "Ireland should never allow nuclear weapons on its soil" (7% in favour), while 86% held that "ships and planes carrying nuclear weapons should be banned from visiting or passing close to Ireland".

5. GENERAL CONCLUSION AND INTERPRETATIONS

Finally, when all the findings are put together, it is very difficult to reduce the views and opinions of the Irish people into simple general categories. Irish political attitudes and opinions are quite complex. On certain issues one finds very strong consensus, while on other questions there is a degree of ambivalence and, at times, even contradiction. The findings of Chapters VIII and IX would seem to indicate that the political views of the people (both rural and urban) are far more sophisticated and nuanced than some commentators would have us believe.

The findings discussed above raise as many questions as they answer. Nevertheless, it is hoped that some modest contribution has been made here to the reader's understanding of the views and expectations of the Irish people. Such a contribution will, it is hoped, make it more reasonable to change what is obviously impeding the creation of a peaceful and just Irish society, based on *integrated pluralism*. The balance of the findings are, in the opinion of the author, more positive than negative. National and community leaders, who act in the name of the people, can learn much from and be guided by the people's opinions gathered together here. A national survey is, among other things, a consultation of the adult members of the population.

CHAPTER X

Sexism, Feminism and Family Life

INTRODUCTION

One of the fastest growing areas in sociology and in the other human sciences over the past twenty years has been the subject of sexism and its counter-movement "feminism". It has become a topic of serious study for students of intergroup attitudes and behaviour. Unlike other stimulus categories, women permeate all age groups, ethnic and racial groupings, social classes, political and religious affiliations and other categories such as education and occupation. Because of the varying degrees of action and reaction surrounding issues relating to gender equality, it is very important to research and present the factual results in an objective and non-polemical manner, as is the main objective of this chapter.

The special "New Feminist Scale" has been devised specially for the 1988-89 survey. The author wishes to acknowledge the contribution of Ms. Joy Rudd in the construction of this chapter.

The "Family Life Scales" were included as part of a broader international survey of family attitudes and have some bearing on attitudes to women in the Republic of Ireland. While they do not measure sexism in the same way that the "Feminist Scale" purports to do, the opinions expressed in the four scales are a useful measure of family values and the perceived (desired) role of women within the family in the Republic of Ireland. It is clear from the findings that there is a relatively high esteem for the parenting role of women without underrating their right to careers in gainful employment. The findings of the family scales will be presented more as opinions expressing family values than as statements implying prejudice against women.

PART I: MARITAL STATUS AND FAMILY SIZE

Before proceeding with an examination of the Feminist and Family Scales there are a number of facts pertaining to the profile of the sample which reflect the current state of Irish society (at the end of the 1980s).

1. MARITAL STATUS AND FAMILY SIZE

As can be seen from the following table, the proportions in the marital status sub-samples are more-or-less in line with the distribution in the Census reports. It is worth noting the relatively low proportion who said they were separated or divorced. The proportion of "widowed" is slightly under-represented, probably due to the unavailability of the very old for interview.

TABLE No. 124
MARITAL STATUS OF SAMPLE

Status	National Sample 1988/89	Dublin Subsample 1988/89
1. Never Married	29%	31%
2. Married	62%	61%
3. Divorced/Separated	2%	3%
4. Widowed	7%	5%
No.	1,005	277

TABLE No. 125
SIZE OF FAMILY

Number of Children	Present Family of Respondents * with Children	Family where youngest child is 6 or over **	Family of Origin of Sample ***	Inter-generational Change
1	13.2%	4.8%	3.5%	+1.3%
2	22.2%	19.7%	6.0%	+13.7%
3	21.6%	21.3%	10.9%	+10.4%
4	18.1%	21.6%	16.4%	+5.2%
5	7.8%	9.1%	14.9%	-5.8%
6	7.2%	9.6%	13.6%	-4.0%
7	4.4%	6.7%	10.7%	-4.0%
8	2.9%	3.8%	7.0%	-3.2%
9+	2.6%	3.3%	16.9%	-13.6%
No.	653	417	961	

*Mean Family Size of Present Families with Children: 3.58;

**Mean Family Size of Present Families with Children with the youngest child 6 years or over: 4.11

*** Mean Family Size of Family of Origin of Sample: 5.80

When comparing the above figures, it should be noted that many current families may not yet be complete at the time of interviewing. If one were to assume that families whose youngest child is six years or older have completed child-bearing, the mean size for such families would be 4.11, which marks a significant incremental drop in average family size of 1.69. While this is very substantial, it still leaves the Irish average family size much

Prejudice in Ireland Revisited

TABLE No. 126
IDEAL SIZE OF FAMILY BY PERSONAL VARIABLE

VARIABLE	NUMBER OF CHILDREN					Desired Mean Family Size	Number
	Two %	Three %	Four %	Five %	Six + %		
TOTAL SAMPLE	20.1	29.6	37.6	6.5	6.1	3.51	962
A. Age: P≤001							
1. 35 years and less	20.6	37.0	34.4	5.3	2.6	3.34*	378
2. 36 to 50 years	26.1	30.7	32.6	5.4	5.4	3.70	261
3. 51 to 65 years	15.9	20.9	45.1	6.6	11.5	3.88	182
4. 66 years plus	13.0	18.8	47.1	11.6	9.4	3.95	138
B. Gender: P≤.004							
1. Female	19.7	25.4	42.6	5.9	6.5	3.61	524
2. Male	20.5	34.7	31.7	7.3	5.7	3.48*	438
C. Marital Status: P≤.02							
1. Never Married	15.0	34.6	36.8	8.2	5.4	3.60	280
2. Married	22.4	28.6	36.8	5.9	6.4	3.53*	595
3. Widowed	20.3	14.5	49.3	7.2	8.7	3.78	69
D. County of Residence: P≤.001							
1. Dublin	21.4	35.7	34.2	6.4	2.3	3.40*	266
2. Rest of Leinster	24.4	30.0	34.0	6.4	5.2	3.46	250
3. Munster	18.7	28.2	37.7	7.4	8.1	3.67	284
4. Connaught/Ulster	13.6	21.6	48.8	5.6	10.5	3.88	162
E. Education: P≤.001							
1. Primary Only	17.5	22.2	41.5	7.3	11.6	3.87	275
2. Incomplete Second	23.4	27.9	37.5	6.6	4.5	3.45	333
3. Complete Second	17.8	35.6	36.9	5.3	4.4	3.48	225
4. Third Level	20.3	39.8	31.3	7.0	1.6	3.32*	128
F. Occupation: P≤.03							
1. Professional/Executive	15.2	37.2	37.2	7.6	2.8	3.32*	145
2. Inspector/Supervisor	21.1	34.6	31.1	8.7	4.5	3.26	289
3. Skilled/Routine N-Man	22.6	28.1	38.9	5.2	5.2	3.48	270
4. Semi/Unskilled	22.1	21.5	41.6	6.0	8.7	3.66	149
G. Social Class Position: P≤.02							
1. Class I	13.8	37.9	37.9	10.3	0.0	3.44	29
2. Class 11	19.8	41.7	32.3	4.2	2.1	3.30*	96
3. Class 111	17.8	34.0	33.6	10.4	4.2	3.53	259
4. Class IV	22.6	28.9	38.3	4.5	5.6	3.37	287
5. Class V	23.8	22.1	39.2	6.6	8.3	3.62	181

No respondent suggested one child as an ideal number.
*Lowest mean family size; Highest mean family size is underlined.

higher than that in other Western countries. The demographic significance of such a drop in fertility, coupled with constant emigration, is obvious. Of course, increase in life-expectancy counters some of the effects of lower fertility and emigration. Table 125 is worth careful analysis to discover where the greatest changes are taking place. The proportion of families with only *two* children has trebled, while those with only *three* have doubled. The really big decline is in the proportion of families with six or more children, which shows an inter-generational drop of 24.8%, i.e. from 48.2% to 23.4%

2. IDEAL FAMILY SIZE

When asked what respondents considered to be the ideal family size, the answer was 3.51 which was 0.6 lower than the current 4.11 average for complete families or almost equal to the average size of all families with children. The figure of the ideal number of children, seen to be 3.51, would indicate a reluctance in the population to reduce family size to that of around 2.00 which is prevalent in most Western populations. The very drastic decline in birth-rate in the Republic of Ireland since the 1970s and early 1980s (from 73,000 to < 50,000) is not only due to the desired birth-rate but also to socio-economic factors such as emigration, both parents with jobs, unemployment and increase in the age of marriage because of career demands. A positive change in the distribution of income and increase in job-opportunities could, and probably would, result in an increase in births in Ireland. In any event, the relatively high figure of respondents' "ideal number of children" is indicative of a pro-children outlook in the population.

The trend of the inter-subsample variations is negatively correlated with liberal attitude scores or positives correlated with p-score variations. In other words, the "more liberal" respondents desired smaller families. The range of variation between the subsamples in relation to the "desired mean family size" is over 0.5 in the case of "age" (0.61) and "education" (0.55) which points towards a further downward trend in the years ahead unless there is a change of view in relation to desirable family size. It is interesting to observe that, in socio-economic terms those best placed to support a family, i.e., Class I & II (Upper and Upper-Middle Classes), the senior professionals and respondents with third-level education, were the subsamples (within their variables) with lowest "ideal family size", while at the other end of the spectra one found the highest "desired mean family size". In other words, the less well-off respondents were more pro-children than those with high education and more prestigious occupations. This negative correlation between social mobility and family size could have far-reaching consequences for the future of Irish society.

PART II: THE NEW FEMINIST SCALE

Table 127 below gives the responses of the whole sample to the twelve items on the New Feminist Scale. Percentages underlined are deemed to

TABLE No. 127
THE NEW FEMINIST SCALE

Statement	Agree %	Don't Know %	Disagree %	Mean p-score (1-200)	N.
1. A woman's proper place is in the home.	40.5	13.6	46.0	94.5	1003
2. It is bad that there are so few women in Government in this country	75.4	12.5	12.1	36.7	992
3. Generally speaking, women think less clearly than men.	12.0	6.3	81.7	30.3	990
4. Women work better than men in the caring professions.	70.5	11.3	18.2	47.7	996
5. People should be employed and promoted strictly on the basis of ability, regardless of sex or gender.	96.3	2.7	1.0	4.7	996
6. The feminist movement is very necessary in Ireland.	64.1	21.2	14.6	50.5	998
7. Some equality in marriage is a good thing but by and large the husband ought to have the main say in family matters.	29.6	9.6	60.8	68.9	1002
8. Education and vocational training are less important for girls than boys.	9.9	3.7	86.4	23.6	997
9. A woman should be as free as a man to propose marriage.	76.3	10.1	13.6	37.3	1000
10. Husbands and wives should have equal say in how to spend family money, irrespective of who earns it.	96.3	1.7	2.0	5 7	1003
11. Women should be allowed to become priests in the R.C. Church.	34.0	14.6	51.4	117.4	1002
12. The emigration of young women is less serious for the country than that of young men.	14.4	9.4	76.3	38.1	1003
Scale p-score				46.3	

Percentages underlined are seen to be indicative of intolerance or prejudice.
Cronbach Alpha = 0.56

signify an intolerant attitude towards women. It should be pointed out that the level of intensity of the anti-feminist attitude expressed by the different items varies enormously as is indicated by the actual responses.

1. INDIVIDUAL ITEMS OF OPINION:

In scales measuring prejudice and attitudes towards women, the value of individual items is very limited. The most reliable indicators of anti-feminist attitudes are the scale and sub-scale scores which are calculated from the cumulative response scores. An examination of the performance of individual items has value as a measure of current opinion on particular issues.

1.1 Consensus Items: Two items, i.e. numbers 5 and 10, were practically unanimous and got a statistically insignificant negative or anti-sexist response. For that reason they will be removed from the scale when measuring variable differences. Nevertheless, they are important responses to show that in the view of a national representative sample of adults in the Republic of Ireland sex or gender is totally irrelevant in relation to (a) unemployment and promotion at work and (b) husbands and wives having equal say in *"how to spend family money, irrespective of who earns it"*. Whether or not these attitudes are borne out in actual practice would demand a very extensive survey. It is possible that there can be an attitude-behaviour lag in times of social change. Such a lag, however, is likely to diminish over time due to pressure from the public attitudes.

1.2 Caring Professions: Some disagreement with the scoring of item no. 4 *"Women work better than men in the caring professions"* is anticipated from those who are opposed to the identification of women with the caring professions, i.e. nursing, social and community work, teaching, etc., as anti-feminist. People holding such an opinion might score agreement with item no. 4 as negative. The opposite argument could be stated, namely, that it is complimentary to women to hold the view that their capacity for caring is greater than that of men. The item does not imply that they are less competent in other professions. The tendency to down-grade parenting and the caring professions is more an economic-production-market based view and could well have serious sexist overtones. For that reason it was thought more appropriate to underline the negative score of 18.2% as indicative of being, on balance, anti-feminist. This item failed to group with others in the factor-analysis of the scale.

1.3 Woman's Place in the Home: Another item which is likely to cause controversy is the scoring of item 1, *"A woman's proper place is in the home"*. The scoring of a positive response to this statement as indicative of an anti-women attitude may be seen as denigrating the domestic role of women in charge of the home. There are many who genuinely see full-time home duties as superior to careers outside the home. This is not a question of prejudice or sexism but an area of value-judgement. There is, however, a view that *exclusive restriction* of women to the purely domestic role is an anti-women attitude and behaviour and an implicit denial of the woman's right to gainful employment outside the home. The inclusion of the adjective "**proper**" in the item indicated an element of exclusiveness and, thereby, make it more negative than positive. The relatively balanced scoring of 40.5% *for* and 46.0% *against* could indicate an element of ambivalence in the respondents. Nevertheless, the factor analysis of the items bore out the decision to underline the positive score as negative.

1.4 Women in Government: There is very strong support for the view that *"It is bad that there are so few women in Government in this country"*. Three-quarters of respondents held the view while only one-eighth of them disagreed. This level of dissatisfaction should in time have an effect. In recent years there have been two women in a Cabinet of fifteen ministers. Currently there are four women among the eighteen junior ministers. Since ministers are appointed from the Members of the Dáil and Seanad, it will be necessary to increase female presence in the two Houses of Parliament as a first step in responding to the public unease expressed in item no. 2. Most candidates for Parliament have to be sanctioned by the various political parties in order to contest elections. Therefore, it is up to the political parties to present more women for the electorate to choose from in General Elections. It should be noted that shortly after this survey, in 1990 a woman, Mrs. Mary Robinson, was elected President of Ireland, which would bear out the sentiment expressed in the above item.

1.5 Rejection of Negative Stereotype: The stereotypical image that *"generally speaking, women think less clearly than men"* has been overwhelmingly rejected by the respondents. This is a raw sexist view and may well have its origin in denial to women in the past of access to serious study in philosophy, theology, humanities and the sciences. The stereotype was a rationalisation of educational discrimination. This is not to say that men were denied access to a range of skills and subjects at the expense of other areas of human socialisation. The view expressed in item no. 3 is happily very much a minority view in Ireland today.

1.6 The Feminist Movement: Public attitudes in Ireland towards the Feminist Movement are very positive. Almost two-thirds of the sample (64.1%) thought that *"the Feminist Movement is very necessary in Ireland"*, while only one-seventh disagreed with that view. This opinion implies that there was need for the emancipation of women in certain areas. Looking at the differences in relation to this item (6) by personal variables, age and gender show the widest range of scores. The 51-65 year-olds were most in agreement, while the women respondents outscored the men by 70.8% to 56.1%, i.e. a difference of 14.6%. It is interesting to note that education did not record a statistically significant level of variation.

1.7 Equality in Marriage: The response to the view that *"Some equality in marriage is a good thing but by and large the husband ought to have the main say in family matters"* was rejected by three out of five respondents. The almost 30% who supported that view was higher than one would have expected from the responses to other items. It marks a significant minority supporting a strongly patriarchal view. Significant variation was recorded in all variables except marital status.

1.8 Support for Women's Education and Training: The vast majority (86.4%) of respondents rejected the view that *"education and training are less important for girls than for boys"*. In practice in Ireland today, there has been a rapid increase in the proportion of women participating in higher education. In the recently published *Report of the Steering Committee on the Future Development of Higher Education* (Dublin, H.E.A., 1995) there is the following information on changes in participation in higher education in the Republic of Ireland since 1965/66 by sector and gender.

TABLE No. 128
FULL-TIME THIRD LEVEL STUDENT NUMBERS BY SECTOR AND BY GENDER
FOR YEARS 1965/66, 1980/81 AND 1993/94

	1965/66			1980/81			1993/94		
	M. %	F. %	Total No.	M. %	F. %	Total N.	M. %	F. %	Total No.
1. Universities *	71.8	28.2	16,007	56.7	43.3	26,104	47.4	52.6	52,300
2. RTCs/DIT **	75.4	24.6	1,007	66.8	33.2	10,910	57.4	42.6	34,673
3. Colleges of Educ.***	39.3	60.7	1,679	16.4	83.6	3,164	51.1	48.9	1,220
TOTAL	69.1	30.9	18,693	56.3	43.7	40,178	51.4	48.6	88,193

* Includes National College of Art & Design and Royal College of Surgeons in Ireland;
**RTCs refers to Regional Technical Colleges; DIT refers to the Dublin Institute of Technology
***Includes other Colleges aided through the Higher Education Authority.
SOURCE: H.E.A., 1995 Table 1, Appendix

The changes in the proportion of women participating in higher education in Ireland have been very substantial and indicate a trend towards superiority for women in the very near future. The change from 28.2% in the universities in 1965/66 to 52.6% in 1993/4 radically alters the position of women. In the more technological areas of higher education there has also been an increase from 24.6% in 1965/66 to 42.6% in 1993/4, which counters some of the anti-technological bias in female education. Of course, it can still be argued that within these colleges men and women may opt for different courses. This is often as much a matter of choice as it is a matter of deterministic bias. The changes in the colleges of education from a predominantly female population, i.e. 60.7% in 1965/66 and 83.6% in 1980/81 to a more balanced distribution in 1993/94, i.e. males 51.4% and females 48.6% may help to correct the gender imbalance in the Irish teaching profession at the primary level.

All in all, it can be said that the view expressed in item no. 8 supporting equality of participation in education and training is well on the way to being achieved and even surpassed in the case of women. If present trends continue, it is envisaged that certain categories of men will become educationally deprived when compared with their female contemporaries. Another area of female superiority in participation is that of voluntary adult education where one gets in the region of 80% female participation. (See MacGréil, 1990.) This may be somewhat balanced by greater male participation in certain areas of FÁS-sponsored training courses which attract a majority of male participation. One of the most significant developments in Irish Adult Education in recent years has been at the local community level where women's groups have taken the initiative in organising "grass-roots" community education, where women are trained in the skills of community and personal development. The low participation of men from more deprived backgrounds in adult education is a matter of serious concern at present.

1.9 Proposal of Marriage: Traditionally in Ireland, as in many other societies, the decline of arranged marriages has led to a system of voluntary partner selection. It was generally felt that the man proposed marriage and the woman was free to accept or refuse the offer. With the advance of equality, it was expected that the initiative should be shared and either intended partner could feel free to propose marriage. Item no. 9, "*A woman should be as free as a man to propose marriage*", was included to see how far this equality of nuptial initiative had advanced in Ireland. The answer is very clear. Over three-quarters (76.3%) answered Yes, while slightly more than one-in-eight (13.6%) said no. The interesting thing about this response was that men were more in favour of equality (86.7%) than were women respondents (67.5%).

1.10 Women's Ordination to the Priesthood: The question of the eligibility of women for ordination to the priesthood in the Roman Catholic Church has become a widely discussed issue in the print and electronic media in recent years, probably more intensively since the time of the Survey in 1988-89. Item no. 11 measures the views of the people on the issue. Some 34%, slightly over one-third of all respondents, agreed that "*Women should be allowed to become priests in the Roman Catholic Church*", while 51.4% disagreed. Among Roman Catholics, 31% were in favour. If the "don't knows" were excluded, 39.8% would be in favour of women's ordiantion and 60.2% would be opposed to it.

In the 1972/73 survey of Dublin attitudes, 26.7% of respondents would have agreed. The response of the Dublin subsample in the 1988/89 survey shows 41.9% in favour of women's ordination which is a very substantial increase (15.2%) over the intervening sixteen years. The trend in the population in favour of women's ordination is very much in the "favourable" direction.

1.11 Women and Emigration: The relative value to the community and the country of women and men is tested in item no. 12 where respondents were asked whether they agreed or disagreed with the view that *"The emigration of young women is less serious for the country than that of young men"*. Over three-quarters (76.3%) of the sample disagreed and only one-in-seven (14.4%) agreed. This is consistent with the generally pro-female views expressed in many of the other items.

2. ITEMS OF NEW FEMINIST SCALE BY PERSONAL VARIABLES:

In examining the various items by personal variables it is important to note that each statement is seen as an expression of an opinion rather than an accurate measure of prejudice. The latter is measured by means of scale and sub-scale scores which are analysed below. Items 5 and 10 are dropped because of the statistically high level of consensus in the answers.

Table 129 gives the distribution of responses.

When items are treated individually below it is as expressed opinions that each item is examined, as was the case in the previous paragraph.

2.1 Women at Home: This statement (item no. 1) elicited a statistically significant variation, i.e. $p \leq .05$, in each of the six personal variables. The range of difference was greatest in the case of "age" and "education". The normal prejudice-score trends happened in each variable except in the case of gender where there were fewer women (36.3%) agreeing that the *"woman's place is in the home"* than was the case for men.

2.2 Women in Government: Because of the low percentage (12.1%) who disagreed with item no. 2, it was not surprising that there was so much consensus in relation to the response to the statement that it was *"bad there are so few women in Government in this country"*. Half of the variables recorded no significant variation, i.e. "age", "marital status" and "education". The range of difference in the four remaining variables is not that great, except in the case of "gender" where 16% of males did not regret that there were not more women in Government, while only half that proportion (8%) of females held a similar view. The responses of the Dublin sub-sample and of those with highest occupational status or members of social class position I

TABLE No. 129

FEMINIST SCALE BY PERSONAL VARIABLES (Negative Percentages)**

VARIABLE	Women at Home No. 1	Women in Government No. 2	Women's Unclear Thinking No. 3	Caring Profession No. 4	Feminist Movement No. 6	Husband's Role No. 7	Education for Women No. 8	Women Proposing Marriage No. 9	Ordination of Women No. 11	Emigration of Women No. 12
NATIONAL SAMPLE	40.5	12.1	12.0	70.4	14.6	29.6	9.9	13.6	51.4	14.4
A. AGE										
1. 35 years or less	20.6*	N/S	10.0	61.2*	14.6	19.6*	7.9*	7.4*	37.8*	11.7*
2. 36 to 50 years	36.3		9.4*	69.8	19.3	23.0	7.8	13.4	55.7	11.9
3. 51 to 65 years	58.2		16.4	79.4	9.3*	41.2	11.9	17.6	65.5	16.5
4. 66 years or more	78.6		16.8	85.2	13.3	53.8	16.8	25.5	64.1	23.4
	P≤.001		P≤.05	P≤.001	P≤.001	P≤.001	P≤.05	P≤.001	P≤.001	P≤.05
B. GENDER										
1. Female	36.3*	8.4*	10.0*	67.2*	12.2*	26.0*	6.5*	20.7	N/S	11.6*
2. Male	45.4	16.4	14.4	74.4	17.5	34.0	14.0	5.2*		17.6
	P≤.05	P≤.001	P≤.001	P≤.05	P≤.001	P≤.001	P≤.001	P≤.001		P≤.05
C. MARITAL STATUS										
1. Never Married	36.6*	N/S	N/S	N/S	N/S	N/S	N/S	8.3*	51.2	N/S
2. Married	40.0							13.8	50.6*	
3. Widowed	63.4							31.4	62.0	
	P≤.001							P≤.001	P≥.05	
D. COUNTY OF RESIDENCE										
1. Dublin	30.1*	12.8	7.4*	N/S	17.8	19.9*	9.5*	10.5*	41.2*	10.9*
2. Rest of Leinster	37.6	12.3	10.3		9.0	25.9	7.5	10.8	49.2	12.9
3. Munster	44.3	12.4	16.4		19.7	34.7	12.5	15.7	53.9	19.7
4. Connaught/Ulster	54.7	10.1*	14.3		8.9*	42.1	9.9	16.2	66.9	12.8
	P≤.001	P≤.05	P≤.001		P≤.001	P≤.001	P≤.001	P≤.001	P≤.001	P≤.001

FEMINIST SCALE BY PERSONAL VARIABLES (Negative Percentages)**

VARIABLE	Women at Home No.1	Women in Government No.2	Women's Unclear Thinking No.3	Caring Profession No.4	Feminist Movement No.6	Husband's Role No.7	Education for Women No.8	Women Proposing Marriage No.9	Ordination of Women No.11	Emigration of Women No.12
E. PLACE OF REARING										
1. Large City	29.4		12.7			17.8*			40.0*	10.5
2. Small City	27.4*	N/S	10.8*	N/S	N/S	23.8	N/S	N/S	48.7	9.5*
3. Town	36.2		11.5			33.8			50.0	15.4
4. Rural	50.1		12.1			36.3			57.7	17.1
	P<.001		P≤.05			P<.001			P<.001	P<.05
F. EDUCATION										
1. Primary Only	69.4		18.5	81.1		49.3	16.6	17.3	67.1	22.6
2. Incomplete Second	38.4	N/S	11.7	72.2	N/S	26.5	11.3	16.3	48.4	16.7
3. Complete Second	25.0		6.5*	64.1		21.6	5.1	10.2	47.3	7.8
4. Third Level	18.7*		11.1	59.0*		12.9*	3.6*	7.9*	34.3*	2.9*
	P≤.001		P≤.001	P≤.001		P≤.001	P≤.001	P≤.05	P≤.001	P≤.001
G. OCCUPATIONAL STATUS										
1. Profession/Executive	27.7*	13.9		61.8*		18.4*	5.7*		37.7*	7.0*
2. Inspector/Supervisor	34.7	10.1*	N/S	65.8	N/S	24.4	8.8	N/S	48.5	11.7
3. Skilled/R. N-M	40.1	13.5		71.7		29.6	9.8		53.4	16.5
4. Semi/Unskilled	53.2	11.1		79.4		42.9	17.3		58.3	26.9
	P<.001	P≤.05		P≤.03		P≤.001	P≤.003		P≤.02	P≤.001
H. SOCIAL CLASS POSITION										
1. Class I	23.5	26.5		64.7*		14.7*	5.9		29.4*	2.9*
2. Class II	21.9*	9.6		58.3		18.7	5.8*		39.0	5.8
3. Class III	32.3	8.2*	N/S	64.8	N/S	21.9	6.7	N/S	44.8	9.6
4. Class IV	41.0	13.7		71.9		30.3	11.2		55.4	16.6
5. Class V	54.3	13.0		79.0		42.6	15.5		57.8	27.1
	P≤.001	P≤.003		P≤.004		P≤.001	P≤.005		P≤.003	P≤.001

* Lowest Percentage. Highest Percentages underlined.

** Percentages are the negative responses, i.e., where statements are pro-feminist the "disagreements" percentages are recorded or *vice versa*.

are out of pattern and are the least concerned subsample. What is this saying about power complacency?

2.3 Women as Unclear Thinkers: Again, a relatively small percentage of the sample agreed with the negative stereotype that *"women think less clearly than men"*. The variations for "age", "gender" and "county of residence" are more-or-less predictable. "Place of residence" and "education" were slightly different from the norm i.e. a bigger proportion of third-level respondents (11.1%) subscribed to the stereotype than did those with complete second-level education. The range of variation in the case of "place of rearing" was too low for comment

2.4 Women in the Caring Professions: Despite the high percentage (70.4%) agreeing with the view that *"women work better in the caring professions"*, there was consensus in the case of "marital status", "county of residence" and "place of rearing". The pattern of answering in the case of the variables recording significant variation indicates that the view expressed is negative and "gender-typing". Yet because such a high percentage agreed with the view and it failed to cluster with other items in the "factor analysis" (see Table 130), it must be concluded that its negative connotations are not seen by most who agreed with it. For many it was seen as a compliment to women and not gender-typing, that is, according to the contextual performance of item no. 4.

2.5 The Feminist Movement: One in seven (14.6%) did not agree that *"the Feminist Movement is necessary"*. There was general consensus on this view in five of the eight variables. The patterns in "age" and in "county of residence" were out of form. Connaught/Ulster respondents were the most appreciative of the Feminist Movement while the Munster subsample was the least convinced of its necessity.

2.6 Husband Having Main Say in Family Matters: Because the sample is more divided on this view, there is more room for greater variance. Only "marital status" returned a "no-significance" (N/S) on the chi-square score. The patterns of variation on the other seven personal variables are true to the prejudice-score pattern with the exception of women being less in favour of the view than were men. The range of variation between the age and education sub-samples has been very substantial, i.e. in "age" between 53.8% and 19.6% (34.2%) and in "education" between 49.3% and 12.9% (36.4%) for or against the husband's *"main say in family matters"*. Whenever there is such a strong coincidence of "age" and "education" performance there is a clear indication of substantial opinion change, which in this case is away from patriarchal authority and power.

2.7 Education and Training for Boys and Girls: The percentage in favour of item no. 8 is barely 10%. Surprisingly, it registered statistically significant variation in six of the eight variables. "Marital status" and "place of rearing" recorded no significant variation. The patterns of variation between all the sub-samples of the other (six) variables are in line with expected trends except in the case of gender where females were less than half the score of males.

2.8 Women's Right to Propose Marriage: This view contravenes the traditional folkway which gave the man the informal right to propose marriage to the woman. Only one-in-seven of the sample would oppose the giving of this right equally to both parties. In the five variables with significant variation, "age", "gender", "marital status", "county of residence" and "education", the normal patterns were repeated. It was most interesting to discover the wide disparity between females and males, with females (20.7%) being four times as opposed to this assertion of egalitarianism as were the males (5.2%). Is this the one case in the ten items of Tables 128/9 where men were more "feminist" than women?

2.9 Ordination of Women: The statement in favour of the ordination of women as priests in the Roman Catholic Church was opposed by 51.4% of the sample with 34% in favour of it. The only variable to register no significant variation was "gender" which suggests that men and women hold the same view on the question. The variation patterns between the subsamples within each variable are strictly along the anticipated prejudice-score trends. Once again, the signs of further change in the direction of opinions favouring ordination are clearly indicated in the range of percentages for "age" and "education", i.e. 37.8% to 64.1% (−26.3%) for "age" and 34.3% to 67.1% (−25.8%) for education.

2.10 Emigration of Women: The value of people to Irish society can be measured by the people's regret or sense of loss on their emigration from Ireland. One-in-seven (14.4%) of the sample agreed with the anti-feminist view that *"the emigration of young women is less serious for the country than that of young men"*, while three-quarters (76.4%) disagree with the view expressed. All variables except "marital status" recorded statistically significant variations between the subsamples. All variations were in line with normal p-score trends. The range of variation between subsamples was especially wide in the cases of "education", "occupation" and, consequently, "social class position".

This concludes the examination of individual items of the New Feminist Scale as expressions of negative scores for each item by personal variables. As stated above, the measure of anti-feminist attitudes or prejudices is analysed from the scale and sub-scale scores. The latter are decided from the factor analysis of scale scores.

3. FEMINIST SCALE AND SUB-SCALE SCORES:

Nine of the twelve items on the New Feminist Scale have pulled together into three factors which are conceptually named:

(a)   Fundamental Sexism;
(b)   Domestic/Religious Attitudes;
(c)   Political Attitudes.

In Factor 1, four items, i.e. 3, 7, 8 and 12, are drawn together. Factor 2 has three items, i.e. 1, 9 and 11, while Factor 3 has but two items, i.e. 2 and 6. Table 130 gives the varimax loading of the various items.

TABLE No. 130
FACTOR ANALYSIS OF THE NEW FEMINIST SCALE

ITEMS	Varimax Loading		
	Factor I Fundamental Sexism	**Factor 2** Domestic/ Religious	**Factor 3** Political
Women think less clearly than men (3)	.60365		
Husband should have the main say (7)	.56637		
Education less important for girls (8)	.68663		
Emigration of women less serious (12)	70726		
A woman's proper place is at home (1)		.58115	
Women free to propose marriage (9)		.66680	
Women allowed to become priests (11)		.71101	
Few women in Government bad thing (2)			.73747
Feminist movement very necessary (6)			.73868

The two consensus items, nos. 5 and 10, have been omitted. The item (No. 4) referring to women being better than men in caring professions has not grouped with any other item, thereby explaining the ambivalence referred to above. The varimax loadings are all over 0.5 and the alignments of items are conceptually reasonable. The correlation matrix (Table 131) more or less confirms the factors. With the exception of the correlation between items nos. 1 and 9, all items within the factors scored significant correlations of $r = 0.2$ or over. There were a number of significant correlations between items of different factors.

Having established the sub-scales by means of factor analysis and inter-item correlation, the next task is to discover how the respondents differed in their view by personal variables. Eight such variables were used, i.e. "age",

TABLE No. 131
CORRELATION MATRIX BETWEEN ITEMS OF FEMINIST SCALE

	Factor 1				Factor 2			Factor 3	
	No.3	No.7	No.8	No.12	No.1	No.9	No.11	No.2	No.6
Factor I - Fundamental Sexism									
3. Women think less clearly	1.00	.24	.29	.27	.20	.02	.08	.30	.12
7. Husband should have main say		1.00	.25	.24	.40	.08	.20	.09	.01
8. Education less important for girls			1.00	.35	.19	.33	.08	.10	.04
12. Emigration of women less serious				1.00	.24	.44	.07	.09	-.04
Factor 2 - Domestic/Religious									
1. A woman's place is in the home					1.00	.16	.27	.15	.29
9. A woman should be free to propose marriage						1.00	.25	.05	.04
11. Women should be allowed to become priests							1.00	.15	.10
Factor 3 - Political									
2. So few women in Government is a bad thing								1.00	.29
6. The Feminist Movement is very necessary									1.00

"gender", "marital status", "county of residence", "place of rearing", "education", "occupation" and "social class position". The measure used to test variations between subsamples is the scale and subscale scores. These scores are the mean scores of all the items in the scales or subscales calculated on a range of 0-200. The higher the score, the more negative or prejudiced the response. (See Table 132).

Since it would have been too complicated to calculate scale and sub-scale statistical significance, it was decided to select a minimum level of significance required to be a score variation within each variable of at least ten. Variables registering less than ten are deemed "not significant" (N/S)

The patterns of score variations are for the most part in line with most prejudice scales reported in this book. There are, however, three notable exceptions. *Firstly,* men are more negative than women, despite their lower prejudice scores in other areas. This could be seen as the "principle of pro-pinquity" working, i.e. one opting in favour of one's own gender in the case of women's responses. It should be noted that the score variations are relatively low in all scales and sub-scales except in the case of the political sub-scale. *Secondly,* education scores are out of line with the "third level"

TABLE No. 132
THE NEW FEMINIST SCALE AND SUB-SCALE BY PERSONAL VARIABLES
(with score variations of 10 plus)

	Scale P-Score (1-200)	Fundamental Sexism	Domestic/ Religious	Political	N.
National sample	46.3	40.2	83.1	43.6	1003
A. AGE					
1. 35 years or less	37.6*	30.9*	57.4*	41.2*	394
2. 36 to 50 years	43.9	32.4	80.8	47.3	270
3. 51 to 65 years	52.6	50.7	106.2	35.1	194
4. 66 years +	65.9	66.3	126.2	54.7	145
Score Variation	28.3	35.4	68.8	19.6	
B. GENDER					
1. Female	40.9*	33.2*	75.9*	33.3*	543
2. Male	52.1	48.5	89.4	55.8	460
Score Variation	11.2	15.3	13.5	22.5	
C. MARITAL STATUS					
1. Never Married	45.8		76.7*		289
2. Married	45.6*	N/S	81.9	N/S	623
3. Widowed	56.9		119.1		71
Score Variation	11.3		42.2		
D. COUNTY OF RESIDENCE					
1. Dublin	39.5 *	30.2*	68.1*		276
2. Rest of Leinster	48.9	39.1	92.7	NIS	255
3. Munster	48.2	45.4	84.2		299
4. Connaught/Ulster	52.1	49.0	99.7		171
Score Variation	12.6	18.8	31.6		
E. PLACE OF REARING					
1. Large City	40.0*	27.3*	67.4*		286
2. Small City	43.3	35.4	73.0	N/S	84
3. Town	46.0	44.5	80.8		130
4. Rural	51.4	47.3	94.2		503
Score Variation	11.4	20.0	26.8		
F. EDUCATION					
1. Primary Only	61.2	63.3	113.7	48.5	283
2. Incomplete Second Level	49.8	42.3	93.8	45.3	281
3. Complete Second Level	38.0	28.0	67.0	37.9*	296
4. Third Level	32.9*	19.2*	53.5*	42.9	139
Score Variation	28.3	44.1	60.2	10.6	
G. OCCUPATION					
1. Professional/Executive	37.9*	27.6*	61.6*		158
2. Inspectional/Supervisory	41.8	32.5	75.4		300
3. Skilled/Routine	47.4	43.3	83.3	N/S	277
4. Semi/Unskilled	55.5	59.0	98.6		156
Score Variation	17.6	17.6	31.4	37.0	
H. CLASS					
1. Class I	36.8*	27.8*	54.9*	53.7	34
2. Class 11	35.7	24.2	56.8	42.0	104
3. Class 111	39.1	28.0	71.6	40.0*	270
4. Class IV	48.1	44.2	84.7	46.4	294
5. Class V	55.5	58.3	99.3	43.0	188
Score Variation	19.8	34.1	44.4	13.7	

Note: Highest p-scores are underlined; Lowest scores have an asterisk*

respondents having a more negative score in relation to the political sub-scale than the "complete second level" respondents. *Finally*, this latter anomaly is reinforced by the "social class position" response which shows the highest socio-economic class most negative of all the classes towards women having greater political power. At the same time, it must be noted that these variations are within an overall low intolerance score of 43.6 out of 200 on average in the case of the political subscale.

The range of score variation is highest for the personal variables of "age" and "education". "Age" is the highest (68.8) in the case of the "domestic/religious subscale" while "education's" range in the case of the "fundamental sexism subscale" is greatest at 44.1 (which is even greater than the overall average subscale score of 40.2). It is also interesting to repeat that the range in the case of the "political subscale" is greatest in the case of the "gender" variable at 22.5.

The trend of scores in relation to **sexism** is optimistic with the clear indica-tions in the "education" and "age" variables. The younger and more highly educated are more tolerant and, if this position is maintained as the sub-samples graduate, then the relatively low scores would be likely to improve further as time passes. That is, of course, unless there is a reversal of attitudes or a slowing-down of tolerance as has happened in the case of attitudes towards ecumenism and ethnic prejudices reported elsewhere in this text (see Tables 72 and 73 above). Reaction to political action by feminist groups can also become a factor affecting public attitudes.

In summary, it can be stated from the findings of the **New Feminist Scale** that the level of sexism in the adult population is relatively low, although still real. Since this is the first time that this scale has been used, it is not possible to compare its findings with those of previous studies. The findings also show that there is support for the work of the Women's Movement in Ireland to date and an awareness of its importance. There is a high level of consensus in relation to a number of central issues and the extent of "raw" sexism is quite small in people's attitudes. The issues relating to the domestic role of women is not eliciting the same level of consensus as is the case with other issues. Society must address the structural issues in relation to the best way of integrating the domestic and career needs of both men and women and their family dependants, in order to achieve a just balance. The next sec-tion deals with public attitudes towards the whole question of family, mar-riage and the rearing of children.

PART III: FAMILY VALUES

In this section it is intended to report on the findings of four special "Family Life Scales" which were included in the 1988-89 National Survey as part of a nine-nation survey of family values.

1. WORKING MOTHERS

The first scale (Table 133) deals with the issue of "working mothers", i.e., mothers having gainful employment outside the home. The findings show consistent support for the domestic role of mothers, i.e. items nos. 2, 3, 4, 5 and 6. Even item no. 7 shows a substantial minority (41.3%) agreeing with the view: "*A husband's job is to earn money; a wife's job is to look after the home and the family*" (a plurality of 45.5% disagreed with the view expressed). This support for the mother's role in the home is also accompanied by very strong support for the "working mother". It is a clear case of accepting the right of mothers to work outside the home and the personal benefits gained by such activity while, at the same time, establishing a degree of priority for the domestic role and its importance for the children, especially those of a young age. To accommodate this dilemma presents problems for employers of working mothers in ensuring that flexibility of normal working hours are geared to facilitating the domestic needs of the employees.

The differences between the views of female and male respondents show a relatively modest variation in most items. The trend of the variation is that of female support for working mothers being greater than male support. The item to elicit the biggest variation was item no. 10 which asserts enjoyment in having a job "*even if I didn't need the money*". Women were not as enthusiastic as the total sample and even less so when compared to men. The "work ethic" is significantly stronger among men. The majority/plurality position in favour or against the items was not altered although the strength or weakness varied.

Family Life Scale II (Table 134) examines in greater detail the views of respondents in relation to the domestic situations conducive to mothers working outside the home. The findings are consistent with those of Family Life Scale I.

The question asked in relation to this scale was: "*Do you think that women should work outside the home full-time, part-time or not at all under these circumstances?*" The pro-work scores are arrived at by assigning "full-time work" three points, "part-time work" two points, "can't choose" one point, and "stay at home" zero points. This gives an interesting order of pro-work, i.e., in rank order of pro-work scores:

1.	After marriage before children	259
2.	After children leave school	224
3.	After youngest child at school	167
4.	When children under school age	99

The majority favouring work for mothers preferred part-time work while the children were at home or at school. Again, this finding has implications

TABLE No. 133
FAMILY LIFE SCALE I (Working Mothers)

STATEMENT		Agree %	Don't Know %	Disagree %	N.
1. A working mother can establish just as warm and secure a relationship with her children as a mother who does not work		54%	7.9	38.0	1,004
	M: F:	N/S	N/S	N/S	
2. A pre-school child is likely to suffer if his or her mother works.		51.4	9.6	39.1	1,004
	M: F:	58.3 45.6	9.6 9.6	32.3 44.9	[P≤.001]
3. All in all, family life suffers when the woman has a full-time job.		52.8	10.3	37.0	1,004
	M: F:	N/S	N/S	N/S	
4. A woman and her family will all be happier if she goes out to work.		21.3	29.1	49.5	1,003
	M: F:	N/S	N/S	N/S	
5. A job is alright, but what most women really want is a home and children.		56.0	14.1	30.0	1,001
	M: F:	60.6 52.0	15.0 13.3	24.4 34.7	[P≤.002]
6. Being a housewife is just as fulfilling as working for pay.		63.8	15.2	21.0	1,001
	M: F:	63.2 64.4	19.4 11.6	17.4 24.0	[P≤.001]
7. Having a job is the best way for a woman to be an independent person.		57.7	13.2	29.2	1,001
	M: F:	N/S	N/S	N/S	
8. Both the husband and the wife should contribute to the household income.		64.1	15.3	20.3	1,000
	M: F:	N/S	N/S	N/S	
9. A husband's job is to earn money; a wife's job is to look after the home and family.		41.3	13.3	45.5	1,003
	M: F:	46.3 37.0	13.7 12.9	40.0 50.1	[P≤.005]
10. I would enjoy having a job even if I didn't need the money.		71.2	7.0	21.8	995
	M: F:	82.0 62.1	5.8 8.1	12.2 29.8	[P≤.001]

TABLE No. 134

FAMILY LIFE SCALE II (When Mothers Should Work Outside the Home)

Circumstances		Work Full-time %	Work Part-time %	Can't Choose %	Stay at Home %	Mean Pro-Work Score (0-300)	N.
1. After marrying and before there are children.		74.3	16.9	2.6	6.2	259	1003
	M:	71.7	17.2	4.3	6.7	254	
	F:	76.4	16.8	1.1	5.7	264	P<.02
2. When there is a child under school age.		8.9	33.4	5.1	52.6	99	1002
	M:						
	F:	N/S	N/S	N/S	N/S	–	–
3. After the youngest child starts school.		21.3	49.5	3.9	25.4	167	1001
	M:	18.3	44.0	6.3	31.4	149	
	F:	23.8	54.1	1.8	20.3	181	P<.001
4. After the children leave home.		63.3	24.1	5.7	6.9	244	999
	M:	56.6	25.3	9.8	8.3	230	
	F:	68.9	23.1	2.2	5.7	235	P<.001

Note: Majority score Underlined

for those individual and institutional employers open to the employment of "working mothers" to provide a wide range of part-time work. Trade unions, employers and the state have a responsibility in responding to this opinion of the people. In the case of items nos. 1 and 4, the percentage stating that mothers should stay at home is so small that it is hardly significant. Of course, it would not be accurate to interpret these results as "obligatory". They are rather seen as the respondent's indication of "approval" in the event of married women opting to work "full-time" or "part-time" or "stay at home". Females were significantly more in favour of mothers working in the case of items nos. 1, 3 and 4. The widest range of difference was in the case of no. 3. It should be noted that the above responses might change if there were more flexible work-times and better equipped workplaces for mothers with young children

2. THE INSTITUTION OF MARRIAGE

The institution of marriage has, in recent times, been the subject of public discussion and the growth of births outside marriage would indicate that its function as the exclusive incorporating ritual for family is being challenged by a minority of people. Although the percentage of people whose marriages are being formally separated is relatively small in Ireland, the overall trend seems to be on the increase. The opinions measured in Family Values Scale

TABLE No. 135
FAMILY LIFE SCALE III (Marriage)

STATEMENT		Agree %	Don't Know %	Disagree %	Total N.
1. Married people are generally happier than unmarried people.		45.6	25.1	29.2	1,004
	M:	51.3	24.8	23.9	
	F:	40.8	25.6	33.6	P≤.001
2. Personal freedom is more important than the companionship of marriage.		15.7	17.8	66.6	1,003
	M:				
	F:	N/S	N/S	N/S	
3. The main advantage of marriage is that it gives financial security.		22.3	11.6	66.2	1,002
	M:	23.1	14.8	62.0	
	F:	21.5	8.8	69.7	P≤.006
4. The main purpose of marriage these days is to have children.		30.9	9.3	58.8	1,000
	M:				
	F:	N/S	N/S	N/S	
5. It is better to have a bad marriage than no marriage at all.		5.0	2.5	92.5	1,003
	M:				
	F:	N/S	N/S	N/S	
6. People who want children ought to get married.		82.8	4.7	12.4	998
	M:				
	F:	N/S	N/S	N/S	
7. A single mother can bring up her child as well as a married couple.		42.3	10.4	47.3	1,002
	M:				
	F:	N/S	N/S	N/S	
8. A single father can bring up his child as well as a married couple.		25.9	10.3	63.9	1,001
	M:				
	F:	N/S	N/S	N/S	
9. Couples don't take marriage seriously enough when divorce is easily available.		68.8	7.8	23.5	1,002
	M:				
	F:	N/S	N/S	N/S	
10. Homosexual couples should have the right to marry one another.		24.9	19.3	55.9	1,001
	M:				
	F:	N/S	N/S	N/S	

III indicate the degree of support for marriage, particularly in relation to children. The overall message emerging from the findings of this table is one of extensive support for marriage and the family in the population. An examination of each item should give a good insight into different aspects of marriage and the family. Because of the insignificantly low percentage (5%) agreeing with item no. 5 (*it is better to have a bad marriage than no marriage at all*), it is unnecessary to deliberate on the statement further, apart from acknowledging the almost total disagreement with it.

2.1 Happiness and Marriage: Item no. 1 (Table 135) compares the perceived level of happiness between "married" and "unmarried" by asking the question whether respondents thought that *"married people are generally happier than unmarried people"*. A plurality agreed that they were happier (45.6%), while a substantial minority disagreed (29.2%). It is interesting to note that female respondents were less optimistic than were their male counterparts. When the female response was tested by marital status, there was a very wide variation.

"Married people are generally happier than unmarried people"

FEMALE SUBSAMPLE	Agree	Don't Know	Disagree	
	%	%	%	N.
1. Never Married	20.7	23.7	55.6	135
2. Married	44.7	26.7	28.5	333
3. Widowed	65.6	25.0	9.4	64
(Variation)	(44.9)	(3 .0)	(46.2)	P≤.001

One rarely finds such a range of variation as the above findings of women by marital status. The position of the married females is very close to the national average. Women who had "never married" were most pessimistic as a category while the "widowed" were most positive.

2.2 Personal Freedom vs Companionship: The findings in relation to item no. 2 indicate a strong vote in favour of "companionship" in marriage. The scores of female respondents are not significantly different from those of males. When one looks at females by marital status there is a stronger score in favour of "personal freedom" by the "never married" subsample.

All subsamples of females opted for "companionship" with those who had the experience of marriage being more strongly in favour of it as opposed to personal freedom, i.e., in favour of "companionship".

2.3 The Advantage of Financial Security in Marriage: The response to item no. 3 clearly rejected financial security as the main advantage of marriage.

"Personal freedom is more important than the companionship of marriage"

FEMALE SUBSAMPLE	Agree	Don't Know	Disagree	
	%	%	%	N.
1. Never Married	23.0	23.0	54.1	135
2. Married	12.3	15.7	72.0	332
3. Widowed	12.5	14.1	73.4	61
(Variation)	(10.7)	(8.9)	(19.3)	P≤.005

The responses of women were more strongly opposed to the view expressed by the item than were those of the men in the sample. When the female responses are measured by marital status, the "widowed" were most in favour of marriage for financial support.

"The main advantage of marriage is that it gives financial security"

FEMALE SUBSAMPLE	Agree	Don't Know	Disagree	
	%	%	%	N.
1. Never Married	16.3	7.4	76 3	135
2. Married	21.0	8.7	70.3	333
3. Widowed	34.4	12.5	53.1	64
(Variation)	(18.1)	(5.1)	(23.2)	P≤.05

The variations between "Never Married" and "Married" are not very great. The low scoring in favour of "financial security" by women respondents tells much about modern attitudes towards marriage and probably reflects the growing number of women in gainful employment in Ireland today.

2.4 Children and Marriage: Items nos. 4 and 6 address this question. The majority of the sample have disagreed with the view (item no. 4) that: *"The main purpose of marriage these days is to have children"*. Again the views of female respondents are not significantly different from those of males (see Table 135). The widowed female respondents are much more in favour of the primacy of children as the purpose of marriage.

"The main purpose of marriage these days is to have children"

FEMALE SUBSAMPLE	Agree %	Don't Know %	Disagree %	N
1. Never Married	23.3	6.0	70.7	133
2. Married	28.9	8.1	66.3	332
3. Widowed	48.4	14.1	37.5	64
(Variation)	(18.1)	(5.1)	(23.2)	P≤.05

In the light of the overwhelming support (82.8%) for item no. 6 which clearly states that *"people who want children ought to get married"*, the findings of item no. 4 do not mean that children are not important for marriage, but rather that they are not the *"main* purpose" of it. The "never married" (female) category of respondents are the most opposed to the view expressed in the item. A plurality of "Widows" hold that children are the main purpose of marriage. Because of the way the statement is written, including "these days", responses may be a commentary on what is happening as much as an expression of attitude.

Returning to the views expressed in item no. 6, there is consensus between the genders on the desirability of the people who want children getting married. Female respondents expressed strong support for this view in all categories of "marital status".

"People who want children ought to get married"

FEMALE SUBSAMPLE	Agree %	Don't Know %	Disagree %	N
1. Never Married	74.6	5.2	20.1	134
2. Married	83.0	4.2	12.7	330
3. Widowed	90.6	6.3	3.1	64
(Variation)	(16.0)	(2.1)	(17.1)	P≤..02

This is a very strong vote in favour of marriage as an environment for raising children. Respondents know their mind, as is evidenced by the very low percentages in the "Don't Know" column. The child-rearing function of the family with married parents is greatly supported in the response to the above item.

2.5 Single Parents: Items nos. 7 and 8 refer to the capability of single parents to bring up children when compared with married couples doing so. There is substantially more confidence in the ability of the "single mother" to bring up her child than in the "single father" to bring up his child. In the case of both items there is little or no significant difference between the views of men and women on the views expressed. A plurality disagreed with the view that a single mother could rear her child as well as a married couple (47.3% against and 42.3% for) while a majority 63.9% did not have confidence in the single father.

There was *no* significant variation among female respondents in relation to item no. 7 when tested by marital status. In the case of Item 8 there was a statistically significant variation in the responses:

"A single father can bring up his child as well as a married couple"

FEMALE SUBSAMPLE	Agree	Don't Know	Disagree	
	%	%	%	N
1. Never Married	31.6	14.3	54.1	133
2. Married	25.6	9.3	65.1	332
3. Widowed	15.6	7.8	76.6	64
(Variation)	(16.0)	(6.5)	(22.5)	P≤.04

While a higher percentage of those who "never married" agreed with the statement the majority of that category disagreed. The view of the "married" females are again in between those of the "widowed" who have very little confidence in the ability of the "single father", and the "never married".

2.6 Easily Available Divorce:[3] With regard to respondents' views in relation to item no. 9, it must be stated that at the time of this survey, divorce was banned in the Irish Constitution. Only 1% of the sample stated they were divorced. A similar percentage stated their partner had been divorced. The opinion expressed in item no. 9 is highly critical of divorce being easily available. There was no significant difference between the responses of males and females in relation to the topic. There was also a consensus among female respondents when tested by marital status in relation to the view that *"couples don't take marriage seriously enough when divorce is easily available"* (68.8% agreeing and 23.5% disagreeing). It is interesting to compare these findings with the results of the 1995 referendum on divorce in the Republic of Ireland when 50.3% voted for and 49.7% voted against.

3. Other questions on divorce from the international questions were not fully meaningful in that they assumed the existence of the availability of legal divorce in Ireland which was not the case at the time in 1988-89.

2.7 Right of Homosexual Couples to Marry: The right to marry for homosexual couples has been an issue of public controversy in the United States and in other countries where the *Family Values Scales* were tested. The issue has not been one of major concern in Ireland to date, although during the 1980s the legal ban on homosexual behaviour between consenting adult males was successfully challenged in the European Court. Through the media most respondents would have become aware of the issue of the "right to marry" of homosexual couples. The right is rejected in the findings by 55.9% against the 24.9% for. Women were not significantly different from men in their responses. There was also a consensus among female respondents when measured by marital status in relation to the rejection of the view that "homosexual couples should have the right to marry one another".

It should be noted that when the sample were asked in relation to the criminalisation of homosexual behaviour a plurality of 44% agreed to the view that: *"Homosexual behaviour between consenting adults should not be a crime"* as opposed to the 35% who thought it should be criminalised. While this latter view may be seen as positive, it is still very disappointing that the latent hostility towards "gay people" is so strongly expressed in the social distance scores of this category elsewhere in this text (see Table 149 below). Such hate attitudes towards a relatively vulnerable minority merits serious concern among fair-minded people. The recent history of Europe provides some very disturbing evidence of "gay-bashing" and even the murder and mutilation of persons seen to be homosexual, especially male homosexuals. The evidence of the 1988-89 survey is mixed.

PART IV: REARING OF CHILDREN

The previous three "Family Life Scales" dealt with the two central questions of "Working Mothers" and "the Institution of Marriage". This fourth scale has as its focus the views of respondents towards the "Rearing of Children" and their relative importance as an integral part of the family. It is very clear from the findings of Table 136 that the Irish adult population places great value on children for their own sake. These findings at the same time show that "people who have never had children" (Item no. 6) can also have worthwhile lives.

1. VALUE OF CHILDREN

Four of the six items (nos. 1, 2, 3 and 5) elicited practically total consensus in the positive direction. Only 3.5% agreed with the view that: *"children are more trouble than they were worth"*. This is an eloquent expression of a love of children irrespective of their difficulty in rearing. Less than 3% disagreed

TABLE No. 136
FAMILY LIFE SCALE IV (Rearing of Children)

STATEMENT/ITEM	Agree %	Don't Know %	Disagree %	Total N %
1. Children are more trouble than they are worth.	3.5	4.9	91.6	1,004
2. Watching children grow up is life's greatest joy.	87.1	8.5	2.8	1,003
3. Having children interferes too much with the freedom of parents.	7.8	8.7	83.6	1,004
4. A marriage without children is not fully complete.	48.2	17.6	34.3	1,005
5. It is better not to have children because they are such a heavy financial burden.	2.7	4.0	93.3	1,002
6. People who have never had children lead empty lives.	29.4	16.2	54.4	1,004

with the opinion that: "*watching children grow up is life's greatest joy*". This gives an insight into the people's priority of child-rearing as a meaningful and fulfilling experience. There was very little agreement (7.8%) with the statement that: "*having children interferes too much with the freedom of the parents*". This confirms the response to item no. 1 and reinforces the high value we place on children in Ireland.

The response to item no. 5 shows a disposition in the population rejecting the view that children are too heavy a financial burden. Only 2.7% agreed with the view that: "*It is better not to have children because they were such a heavy financial burden*". The combination of these four findings portrays the Irish people as being very positively disposed towards children. If this were fully translated into supportive behaviours and structures, there would be very little child-neglect and much less child-abuse. Unfortunately, the lack of adequate support for the poorer families and children of deprived homes in the cities and elsewhere again points to an attitude-behaviour lag. Nevertheless, the pressure of such positive pro-children attitudes and values must make it more possible for national and community leaders to institute programmes and provide domestic-oriented services which help parents in the rearing of their children.

2. CHILDLESSNESS

One possible effect of a society which values children to the extent measured in items nos. 1, 2, 3 and 5, would be the negative perception of childlessness. The two items, nos. 4 and 6, try to gauge the views of the adult population of the Republic of Ireland in relation to a marriage without children and to adults who never had children. Item no. 4 deals with the former and shows a plurality (48.2%) agreeing with the statement while a substantial minority (34.2%) did not agree, women disagreeing slightly more than men. Item no. 4 was the only item to register a statistically significant variation by gender, with 38% of female respondents as compared with 30% of males disagreeing with the statement. When the responses of females were measured by marital status it was found that never married females were significantly and substantially more opposed to the statement.

Item No. 4: "Marriage without children is not fully complete"

Female Respondents	Agree	Don't Know	Disagree	Number
1. Never Married	37.0%	14.8%	48.1%	135
2. Married	47.1%	17.4%	35.4%	333
3. Widowed	51.6%	20.3%	28.1%	64
(Variations)	(14.6%)	(5.5%)	(20.0%)	P≤.05

Apart from the contrasting views of the "never married" and the "widowed", there is an exceptionally high percentage of "don't knows", which would indicate a degree of ambiguity among a substantial minority of respondents.

The final item of Scale IV, i.e., item no. 6, has a more substantial rejection at 54.4% with less than 30% agreeing with the view. Again there is a significant proportion of respondents answering "don't know" which indicates some ambiguity. Marital status has been very significant as a variable among female respondents.

Item No. 6: "People who have never had children lead empty lives"

Female Respondents	Agree	Don't Know	Disagree	Number
1. Never Married	13.3%	13.3%	73.3%	135
2. Married	31.8%	14.1%	54.1%	333
3. Widowed	45.3%	20.3%	34.4%	64
(Variations)	(32.0%)	(7%)	(38.9%)	P≤.001

The range of variations show how divided the opinion of the three marital subsamples are. This support for childless people is to be seen in the context of the extraordinarily positive support for children within families.

PART V: FAMILY STANDARD OF LIVING INDICATORS

It may be useful at this stage to give the reader a description of the material standard of living of the respondents. This is done in relation to three indicators, i.e.,

(a) Average Household Income;
(b) Type and Ownership of Residence;
(c) Inventory of Domestic Appliances/Amenities;

The above indicators will be measured by age, gender, marital status, area of residence and social class position.

1. HOUSEHOLD INCOME

Table 137 gives the distribution of Household income (at 1988-89 values) for the sample.

There is a very wide range of household income. One third of the sample had a household income of less than £116 per week or £27.5 per person after tax. Allowing for an inflation of 17.8% between 1989 and 1995, this average weekly salary would be worth less than £135.5 weekly or £32.4 per person per week. That works out at less than £5 a day per person. The top 20% have over £10 per person per day after tax. The findings of this table show how far Ireland is from a situation of equality in income distribution. The average income of the top category is more than five times that of those at the bottom.

The above figures of income distribution concern what is referred to as **"market income"**. The material standard of living must also take "non-cash" income such as health, education, travel, telephones, and services provided from the State funds into account. Callan and Nolan (1992) comment on the impact of the latter on income equality in Ireland:

"Final income is once again more equally distributed than market income, the differences being concentrated in the larger share of the lowest quintile and the smaller share of the top quintile"

(Callan and Nolan, 1992, p. 196)

This having been acknowledged, however, does not justify the maldistribution on Table 137 above. The bottom 21% had a weekly average household income (after tax) of £76 in 1988-89 values or £96 in 1995 values. By any criteria, this must be below the poverty line.

Table No. 137

PROFILE OF HOUSEHOLD WEEKLY INCOME (AFTER TAX)

AVERAGE WEEKLY/INCOME (Post Tax)	Number of Persons in Household Mean Size of Household = 3.86 (Median = 3.2)										Total No. of Households	Mean Size of Household	Weekly Income Per Member	Weekly Income Per Person at 1995 values*
	1	2	3	4	5	6	7	8	9	10				
1. Under £38	9	1	–	–	–	–	–	–	–	–	10(1.3%)	1.50	£25.3	£29.8
2. £39-57	26	8	1	1	–	2	–	–	–	–	38(6.0%)	1.60	£30.0	£35.4
3. £58-75	15	13	8	3	2	2	–	–	–	–	45(11.7%)	2.51	£26.5	£31.2
4. £76-96	9	23	14	17	9	4	–	–	–	2*	78(21.5%)	3.31	£26.0	£30.6
5. £97-115	2	32	10	8	22	8	7	2	–	–	91(32.9%)	3.86	£27.5	£32.4
6. £116-134	4	11	13	12	13	6	1	4	1	1	66(41.2%)	4.15	£30.1	£35.5
7. £135-153	9	10	23	14	16	7	5	3	–	1	88(52.3%)	3.94	£36.5	£43.0
8. £154-173	3	6	12	10	9	8	3	1	1	2	55(59.2%)	4.47	£36.6	£43.1
9. £174-192	3	13	15	21	7	11	2	1	2	1	76(68.7%)	4.09	£44.7	£52.7
10. £193-230	–	16	9	22	11	15	3	1	3	–	80(78.8%)	4.35	£45.2	£53.2
11. £231-287	3	9	13	8	11	3	7	2	–	–	56(85.8%)	4.11	£63.0	£74.2
12. £288-383	–	11	7	15	17	4	3	2	2	–	161(93.5%)	4.38	£76.6	£90.2
13. £384-479	–	3	2	11	5	2	1	1	–	2	27(96.9%)	4.67	£92.4	£108.8
14. £480-575	–	1	2	4	5	1	1	–	–	–	14(98.6%)	4.43	£119.1	£140.3
15. £576-671	–	–	–	1	1	1	–	–	–	1	4(99.1%)	6.75	£92.4	£108.8
16. £672 plus	–	1	1	–	2	1	1	1	–	–	7(100.0%)	5.14	£130.7 plus	£154.0
	83	157	130	147	130	76	36	18	11	8	796	3.86	£44.1	£51.9

*The cumulative inflation consumer price index from February 1989 to February 1995 was 17.8

2. TYPE AND OWNERSHIP OF RESIDENCE

Ireland is one of the countries with the highest home-ownership in Europe. This is borne out by Table 138 which distributes the sample by ownership of place of accommodation.

TABLE No. 138
OWNERSHIP OF ACCOMMODATION OF SAMPLE

STATUS	PERCENTAGE	
1. Owner Occupied (fully paid for)	50.6%	
2. Being bought out (by mortgage)	29.0%	} 85.7%
3. Being bought out (by L.A. Tenant Purchase Scheme)	6.1%	
4. Local Authority Rented.	8.7%	
5. Privately Rented Accommodation.	4.4%	} 13.1%
6. Other.	1.2%	1.2%
Number	992	

With 85.7% of the sample living in accommodation that is owned by the family, the Republic of Ireland is predominantly a home-owning society. Almost 30% of the sample are in houses still paying mortgages while a further 6.1% are in the process of buying out their Local Authority house under the "Tenants' Purchase Scheme". The proportion of people renting accommodation is relatively small at 13.1% (a third of whom are in privately rented accommodation).

The distribution of the sample by type of accommodation (Table 139) also presents an interesting profile of households.

The very high percentage (96.9%) of the national sample who live in houses must also be fairly unique. In some Western societies quite a proportion of the population live in flats. It is also interesting to note that the numbers living in "semi detached" and in "terraced houses" were the same which would seem to indicate a high proportion of urban residents lived in suburbia.

TABLE No. 139
TYPE OF ACCOMMODATION OF SAMPLE

ACCOMMODATION	PERCENTAGE	
1. Detached House	54.0%	
2. Semi-Detached House	21.9%	} 96.9%
3. Terraced House	21.0%	
4. Flats	1.9%*	
5. Caravans	0.5%	} 3.1%
6. Other	0.7%	

*Some 0.2% were "high rise flats".

3. DOMESTIC APPLIANCES/AMENITIES:

One way of assessing a person's material standard of living is to discover the extent to which certain domestic appliances and amenities are available in the home. The following table (140) gives the proportion of houses or homes with the following domestic amenities.

TABLE No. 140
DOMESTIC AMENITIES AVAILABLE IN THE HOMES OF RESPONDENTS (1988-89)

AMENITY/FACILITY	PERCENTAGE
1. Indoor Flush Toilet	95.4%
2. Bath or Shower	93.9%
3. Colour T.V.	87.7%
4. Washing Machine	83.7%
5. Telephone	62.4%
6. Central Heating	61.6%
7. Spin Dryer	37.6%
8. Hi-Fi Radio/Recorder	36.9%
9. Video Recorder/Player	32.9%
10. Microwave Oven	15.1%

Items nos. 1 and 2 *Toilet* and *Bath or Shower* have become standard household facilities. The *Colour T.V.* and the *Washing Machine* are now in the homes of six out of every seven Irish citizens according to the findings. *Domestic Telephones* and *Central Heating* were reported to have been in just over 60% of the homes. Less than half of the homes with washing machines reported having a *Spin Dryer*. A little more than one third of the sample had *Hi-Fi Radio/Recorders* and *Video Recorder/Players*. Less than one in six said they had *Microwave Ovens*.

It is difficult to comment on the findings of Table 140 beyond pointing out the distribution of amenities. Once most people have access to a useful domestic amenity, as is the case for the first six of the above facilities, then the absence of such facilities leads to a sense of "relative deprivation". Not to have a *domestic telephone* or a *central heating system* is becoming a real deprivation. In modern Ireland, a telephone and central heating are no longer seen as luxuries, they have become part of the basic standard of living *for all*, as well as being a reality for the majority. This would be much more so in the case of *colour T.V.* and *washing machines*. This rejects the elitist view that only those who can afford such amenities are entitled to them, which denies equality of access to the basic standard of living. The greater the majority with the amenity, the greater the sense of relative deprivation of the minority denied such amenity. The fact that only 60.2% had domestic telephones in 1988-89 was surprising. The aim of universal domestic telephonisation was still far from the stage of achievement in a modern Western "developed" society!

CHAPTER XI

Travellers and Other Social Categories

PART I: THE TRAVELLING PEOPLE – IRELAND'S APARTHEID

The Travelling People constitute a relatively small but ubiquitous minority of nomadic or quasi-nomadic people in Ireland. In all, they make up around one per cent of the national population of the 3,878 families (1994), 46% are in houses, 25% are in "halting sites" and 28% are on the roadside (see Fogarty, 1996, pp. 6ff.).

The history of the Irish Travelling People is poorly documented. What is generally accepted is the fact that they are of Irish ethnic origin whose cultural traits had much in common with that of dispossessed peasants. Because of the various plantations and forced evictions from the land by the landlords, some people were obliged to take to the roads during the seventeenth, eighteenth and early nineteenth centuries. Following the Great Famine of the late 1840s there were further movements of people from their homes, some of whom are believed to have taken up a nomadic lifestyle. Joining this group of nomads were a number of travelling tradespeople and horse dealers. Very few of those on the roadside were of Romany background or of what is called the "Gypsies". The very recently arrived "New Age Travellers" are so recent as not to have integrated into the Irish Travelling People.

1. CULTURAL DIFFERENCES

There are a number of very clear differences in the way of life of the members of the Irish Travelling Community and that of the Settled Community. Their adherence to what Tonnies called *"gemeinschaft"* model of community distinguishes them from many of the settled community who are living a *"geselleschaft"* model (Tonnies, 1955). The latter is more conducive to contemporary urban, middle-class, nuclear-family based individualism. 'Gemeinschaft' is more conducive to community, working-class and extended-family based collectivism. Resulting from this socio-cultural difference there are a number of inevitable misunderstandings and difficulties in the relationship between the Settled People and the Travelling Community. This is particularly so in the larger urban areas.

The accepted norms of modern Irish society appear to be less domestic or community-oriented than they were. They tend to be dominated by middle-class and more individualist norms suitable for competitive living in a free market capitalist "Western World". Despite the rhetoric of liberalism, there is little evidence of tolerance towards minorities whose lifestyle is basically collectivist and domestic and community-oriented. Private property is an important symbol of value in our society and manifests the strength of our individualism.

In the author's experience of the Irish Travelling People,[1] private personal property was not of major significance and did not have the same significance as it had among the Irish Settled Community. Unless more attention is paid to matters of cultural difference between the Travelling People and their Settled neighbours, it is difficult to see a satisfactory *pluralist integration* of this important native minority into Irish society.

2. OFFICIAL POLICY TOWARDS TRAVELLERS

The official national policy towards Irish Travelling People has been one of "resettlement" with a strong emphasis on assimilation, i.e. that the Travellers cease to live their nomadic and extended-family lifestyles, and become absorbed into modern Irish sedentary life. This has succeeded in a number of cases and some Travellers have voluntarily accepted the dominant group's posture of assimilation in their regard. After a number of generations, the offspring of the Settled Travellers may "pass as" Settled People and may even become hostile to those of their own people who refuse to assimilate. Assimilation, of course, is the opposite to pluralism as a mode of integration. The latter respects, preserves and promotes the cultural differences between the Travellers and the Settled Community without distinction in access to cultural, economic and social amenities.

There seems to have been a growing awareness of their pluralist rights among many of the Travelling Community over the past decade. This has enhanced the self-esteem of many Travellers but it has met with little progress in Settled Society so far. It may be too early to expect results from the Travellers' demand for a pluralist solution. The evidence in the tables below does not show sufficient respect for the Travelling People and for their way of life to assume a voluntary dominant pluralist posture towards them.

3. CHALLENGES OF INTEGRATED PLURALISM

For pluralist integration to succeed, a number of conditions have to be put in place, i.e.

(1) Pluralist policy adopted by the State;
(2) Equality of treatment of Travellers in all aspects of their personal, social, cultural and economic affairs;
(3) Institutional duplication to facilitate the different way of life and transmission of the culture of the group;
(4) Full participation in the structures of Irish society which have a bearing on the life of the people.

The adoption of a **pluralist policy** by the State will necessitate a statutory commitment to the right of Travelling People to full integration into Irish

1. The author spent two months on the roadside with the Travelling People in 1968-69 and shared their life style.

society without sacrificing their own cultural way of life, i.e. nomadic or mobile residence, facilities for the education of young Travellers in the culture of their group and enabling Travellers to take up gainful employment appropriate to a nomadic lifestyle. If, for instance, the halting sites for Travellers were of sufficiently high standard, they might be shared with holiday makers touring Ireland with caravans. It would provide members of the Settled Community with an opportunity to get to know and respect the Travellers' way of life. Travellers would avail of caravan sites as halting sites in the off-tourist seasons. Travellers could be given work on the public caravan sites and trained in serving the nomadic residential needs of travelling tourists. There are many other areas of work which could be encouraged among the Travellers, e.g. metal crafts, street stalls for popular domestic goods, minor tarmacadam work, collection of scrap metal, and others.

The second condition of **equality of treatment** is obvious and is enshrined in *Bunreacht na hÉireann* and in other proclamations and international declarations. The protection of the civil and human rights of members of minority groups needs to be enacted in law and enforced with great diligence and vigilance. It is generally accepted that the obligation for the maintenance of equality of treatment is that of those with the political power to ensure it. *Public declarations of equal rights are as valuable as they are enforced!* Universal equality of welfare rights will inevitably result in some curtailment of the consumer choice of the privileged (Karl Mannheim, 1939). In the case of Irish Travellers' rights to serviced halts, the local residents are at times very vocal in denying permission to have such halts built in their area, often because of the perceived resultant curtailment or threat to the settled people's "consumer choices"!

The third condition of pluralism is **structural duplication** which means that a number of services may need to be duplicated to facilitate the preservation of cultural differences. Most important of these would be the education services. Ideally, each cultural minority should have its own school system as is the case of denominational schools and of Irish language schools, where the culture of the group is handed on to the young by teachers of the same background. This may be difficult in the beginning. If Travellers are exposed to educational material from the dominant culture only, it could well "deradicalise" the young, i.e. remove them from their cultural roots. A common educational system, especially at the primary level, provides very strong pressure for assimilation and cultural absorption into the settled community. This would do violence to the cultural heritage of the group. This is true of other groups in Ireland, i.e. religious groups and Irish language groups.

The fourth condition for pluralist integration relates to the **sharing in the decision-making process** in society. Pluralist integration implies equality. In all matters which affect their welfare, members of the minority are entitled to proportionate participation in the various levels of political and administrative power. Equally, Travellers are entitled to access on the basis of equality to public services, i.e. housing, transport, medical, educational, religious, recreational, legal, economic and commercial. This is not the case in Irish society where Travellers are often denied access to jobs, to education, even to public houses and many other such services.

While the most desirable solution of any genuine cultural minority living in a society with a large dominant group is that of "**integrated pluralism**", such a solution may be little more than an aspiration, unless both the dominant group and the minority pursue it. The evidence of the 1972-73 survey of the adult population of Greater Dublin pointed to a situation more akin to *lower caste* in regard to the position of Travellers in the attitudes of respondents. There was little evidence at the time of strong protest from the Travellers themselves against their "lower caste status", despite their vicarious representation by various support groups among the Settled Members of society. This seems to have changed and there is a growing awareness among Travellers themselves of their rights.

4. LOWER CASTE STATUS

An analysis of the 1988-89 responses will focus on the changes in attitude among the members of the dominant group towards the Travelling People, especially in relation to the shift towards pluralist integration from a "caste position". The characteristics of **a caste** include:

  (i) While social classes may exist within a caste there is no mobility out of the caste;

 (ii) One is born into one's caste and has to remain in it irrespective of individual merit;

(iii) There is a more-or-less strict adherence to caste endogamy, i.e. one does not marry outside one's caste;

 (iv) A relatively strong norm of apartheid is maintained within society in relation to the members of the caste, especially in the case of housing and residence;

  (v) There may also be a stratification or delineation of the place of members of the caste in the workforce;

 (vi) Consequent on the need for the maintenance of separation and apartheid, access to education and other systems may be restricted, e.g. denial of access to "public houses" and places of entertainment where close personal contact may take place;

(vii) A caste can be located at any point on society's social stratification ladder.

It will be interesting to apply the above criteria to the place of Travelling People in Irish Society. It is the view of the present author that Irish Travellers are still seen and treated as a "**lower caste**" in society and there is an urgent need to change the caste status to one of equality but difference, i.e. *integrated pluralism*. The pluralist solution would be less rigid towards the admission of some inter-marriage with members of the Settled Community who would wish to adopt the cultural lifestyle and values of Travellers. Likewise, there would be some movement from the Travelling Community into the Settled People and vice-versa. A parallel example of pluralist integration would be the Irish Language minority who adopt Irish as their ordinary and principal language.

PART II: CURRENT ATTITUDES TOWARDS TRAVELLERS

Table 141 gives the social distance scores of the 1988-89 National Sample, of the 1988-89 Dublin sub-sample and the 1972-73 Dublin sample. From the findings of Table 141 it is possible to gauge the closeness of the dispositions of settled people towards Travellers and the changes in that closeness since 1972-73.

TABLE No. 141
SOCIAL DISTANCE TOWARDS TRAVELLERS IN 1988-89 AND IN 1972-73

	Family	Friendship or Closer	Neighbour or Closer	Co-Worker or Closer	Citizen or Closer	Visitor Only	Debar\ Deport		
	1	2	3	4	5	6	7	M.S.D.	N
A. National Sample	13.5	26.7	41.0	63.7	90.0	7.0	3.0	3.681	1,000
B. Dubin Sample 1972-73	29.0	51.1	64.3	75.5	93.4	2.8	3.8	2.904	2,302
C. Dublin Subsample 1988-89	16.4	29.2	42.3	70.8	90.5	5.1	4.4	3.551	274
Change (C-B)	-12.6	-21.9	-22.0	-4.7	-2.9	+2.3	+0.6	+0.647	

The findings of Table 141 are surprisingly negative and show a substantial deterioration in the Dublin sample since 1972-73. It is difficult to comprehend that our attitudes towards our fellow-Irish citizens could be so negative. It is a classic case of severe anti-minority prejudice. Our national and community leaders, as well as our mass media of communication, have serious questions to answer. Something is radically wrong with the Government's policy and its implementation. A new Commission of Enquiry into the Treatment of Travellers is urgently needed with extensive terms of reference and Traveller participation. Only one in seven of *the national sample* would welcome a Traveller into the family through marriage, while 59% (three out of five) would not welcome Travellers as next-door neighbours. One in ten would deny citizenship to Irish Travellers. Travellers could hardly rank as "neighbours" among the majority of the Irish people as represented in these figures.

The changes in prejudice against Travellers in Dublin over the 16 years between the surveys are substantially negative. There is a massive deterioration in the percentage welcoming Travellers into kinship (from 29% in 1972-73 to 16.4% in 1988-89) and a drop of one third in the proportion welcoming them as next-door neighbours or closer. The substantial increase in Mean Social Distance Score of 0.647 is hardly credible. By moving over the M.S.D. of 3.5, Travellers have entered the "outgroup" category. This leaves many questions to be answered by Dublin Corporation and County Council. While there is some evidence of a slight growth in overall intolerance between the two surveys in the overall, as shown in other chapters of this book, it is not anywhere near the proportions shown in the above Table. The figures speak for themselves.

While it is not the primary duty of the sociologist to make normative criticism, it is nevertheless his/her duty to point out a serious deterioration in the position of a relatively weak minority in a society growing in wealth and power. Should this rate of deterioration continue over the next sixteen years, the Travellers could end up not as a "lower caste" but as an "outcast" minority.

It is still not too late to act at a number of levels. A logical prerequisite to change is to face up to the current reality. Something very negative has happened to Irish attitudes towards its major minority since 1972-73 which is not in line with the public image of a more tolerant society as often stated by some commentators. The overall evidence of this survey shows how selective our tolerance can be.

1. INTERGROUP DEFINITION OF TRAVELLING PEOPLE:

Table 142 gives the findings of the rationalisation scale in relation to the National Sample (1988-89).

TABLE No. 142
RATIONALISATION OF REFUSAL TO WELCOME A TRAVELLER AS A MEMBER OF THE FAMILY

	Religious	Racial	Political	Ethnic/ Way of Life	Economic	Not Socially Acceptable	Other	N.
A. National Sample 1988-98	0.6%	0.0%	0.0%	76.5%	1.8%	20.3%	1.0%	844
B. Dublin Sample 1972-73	0.3%	0.2%	0.1%	32.4%	3.4%	62.1%	1.6%	1,592
C. Dublin Subsample 1988-89	0.2%	0.0%	0.0%	74.4%	1.5%	22.9%	1.0%	223
Change (C-B)	-0.1%	-0.2%	-0.1%	+42.0%	-0.9%	-39.2%	-0.6%	

"Way of life" is the dominant reason for three-quarters of those not welcoming Travellers into the family (77%), while a fifth of the respondents gave "not socially acceptable" as their main reason. The perceived "way of life" of Travelling people may be negative for two reasons, i.e. they are different in values, outlook and structures, or they display an unacceptable "**poverty culture**". The latter is largely due to the refusal of society to treat Travellers equally. The Travellers' authentic cultural qualities may be difficult to perceive, so long as they are forced to live in the poverty trap. Incidentally, no respondent saw the Travellers as "racially" different and less than 2% saw them as an economic threat.

There has been a very interesting change in the pattern of rationalisation since the 1972-73 survey. There has been a shift in perception from being "not socially acceptable" to "way of life" in the case of Dublin respondents. This change in perception is noteworthy. The Travellers are now more socially unacceptable. Probably their demands for accommodation and their demands for greater access to the social facilities such as education, leisure, work and other social benefits may be eliciting a more focused response on behalf of the Settled Community which this sample represents. The patent neglect of Travellers' rights and the disruption of their former stratified integration in Irish society may also be responsible for some anti-social behaviour by some Travellers. This in turn becomes an element in the vicious circle and may lead to a further deterioration in the prejudices against Travellers.

The rank-ordering of Travellers at 52nd of the 59 categories on the Bogardus Social Distance Scale at a mean social distance score of 3.681 (in the "outgroup category" of 3.500+) gives the extent of intergroup hatred and hostility in the population (see Table 5, pp. 66f.). At such a level one can expect periodic outbreaks of emotionally inflamed physical attack by groups of Settled People[2] and also explain the failure of those responsible for the protection of people's rights from taking courageous action to protect Travellers. The desperately deprived conditions under which some Traveller families are forced to live, due to the lack of welcome towards them in Irish communities is, at the end of the day, the primary responsibility of the Settled Community and its political, statutory and voluntary leadership. This is what one would expect with regard to the treatment of a relatively weak, easily identifiable minority group.

Some 10% of respondents would go so far as denying Irish Travellers citizenship. Unlike the Black People in South Africa, who were the numerical majority and, thereby, strong in a professed ethos of majority democracy, Irish Travellers are a minuscule numerical minority. The history of the liberation of the deprived has shown that it is much more serious for a minority to suffer from the tyranny of a numerically majority dominant group than it is to be under the tyranny of a numerically minority dominant group. The position of Irish Travellers is in some way akin to the position of Catholic Nationalists in Northern Ireland prior to the Civil Rights Movement in the late 1960s i.e., where the dominant group was also numerically so and could call on the legitimation of their "majority democracy" position.

2. Such outbreaks of physical attack and abuse are examples of stage four in Allport's stages of acting-out social prejudice (see page 21).

The dominant group can use the argument of majority rule but true democracy, however, is not majority rule but, rather, social consensus which insists that all groups get their rights on the basis of equality. The lack of articulate and effective support from elected public representatives in Ireland for the rights of Travelling people reflects the tyranny of the majority opinion in this regard, which the findings of this survey clearly show.

Again, the level of consensus has been exceptionally high in that "gender", "marital status", "place of rearing" and "occupational status" failed to produce statistically significant differences between the subsamples. In the case of the variables which did record significant variations, the clearest pattern was for age (see Table 144, Section II below). Connaught/Ulster was clearly the most negative subsample while respondents from "Leinster" (excluding Dublin) were the most favourably disposed towards Travellers. "Education" and "social class position" subsample patterns were mixed. One would have expected a more clearly defined pattern by education and class!

2. THE TRAVELLERS SCALE:[3]

The following seven-item scale has been adapted from a previoius scale. The responses to it have been most discerning, resulting in a mean score of 266.5 out of a maximum of 500 which is the equivalent of 53.5%. This enables the maximum degree of variation in the different personal variables. (See Tables 143 and 144).

As is the case with other scales, the scale and sub-scale scores are the most reliable measures of social prejudice as they are arrived at by getting the cumulative scores of a number of responses to items or statements. The examination of individual items gives insight into the range of opinions or views held on specific issues. The changes in responses between 1977 and 1988-89 are not that significant in most cases. Item no. 6 was the one with greatest diffference. The items are classified into two categories, i.e., those indicating "personal factors" and those referring to "social status" (see Tables 145 and 146).

2.1 Individual Items:

2.1.a *Personal Respect*: Item no. 1 shows that the overwhelming majority (86.8%) expressed respect for the Traveller as a person. The degree of agreement, i.e. "strong", "moderate" or "slight" divides the positive response with one-quarter giving the minimum agreement. Only 13.2% said that they would not respect the Traveller. This minority attitude to a group of human beings is pathetic and definitely not Christian.

This item elicited significant variations by "gender", "county of residence", "place of rearing", "occupation" and "social class position". Women,

---

3. This scale has been adapted from the original scale of E. E. Davis, et al., 1984, which was tested on a National Sample survey of over 2,000 respondents in 1977.

TABLE No. 143
TRAVELLERS SCALE (1977 Survey Findings* in brackets)

	AGREEMENT			DISAGREEMENT					
	Strong	Mod	Slight	Slight	Mod	Strong		p-score	
	6 %	5 %	4 %	3 %	2 %	1 %	Mean	(1-500)	N.
1. Would respect this person	22.6 (21.2)	39.4 (29.3)	24.8 (26.7)	5.3 (9.1)	5.7 (6.3)	2.2 (6.8)	4.612	138.8	997
	86.8 (77.2)			13.2 (22.2)					
2. Would be reluctant to buy a house next door to this person	32.1 (35 4)	26.4 (17 8)	16.1 (16 9)	8.1 (10 6)	9.3 (8 8)	8.0 (9 9)	4.397	339.7	994
	74.6 (70.1)			25.4 (29.3)					
3. Would be hesitant to seek out this person's company	23.4 (34.3)	31.5 (20.6)	21.5 (21.6)	8.0 (10.4)	9.0 6.2)	6.5 (6.2)	4.328	332.8	998
	76.4 (76.5)			23.5 (22.8)					
4. Would be willing to employ this person	10.4 (11.9)	25.5 (17.3)	21.0 (25.6)	12.1 (15.0)	17.3 (11.4)	13.7 (18.0)	3.584	241.6	992
	56.9 (54.8)			43.1 (44.4)					
5. Would exclude this person from my close set of friends	17.0 (28.0)	27.5 (17.4)	18.4 (22.1)	12.9 (14.8)	15.8 (8.3)	8.3 (8.5)	3.922	292.2	992
	62.9 (67.5)			37.0 (31.6)					
6. Would consider this person competent to serve on a jury	11.9 (7.5)	21.1 (9.4)	18.7 (14.5)	13.9 (16.5)	19.1 (15.0)	15.2 (36.1)	3.471	252.9	984
	51.7 (31.4)			48.2 (67.6)					
7. Would avoid this person in social situations	13.5 (25.1)	24.1 (18.3)	18.3 (21.9)	14.5 (16.2)	18.6 (9.2)	11.1 (8.6)	3.662	266.2	995
	55.9 (65.3)			44.2 (34.0)					
Scale p-score								266.5	

* Davis, E. E., Grube, J. W. and Morgan, M., *Attitudes towards Poverty and Related Social Issues in Ireland,* Dublin, ESRI (No. 117), 1984, p.185.
Cronbach's alpha = 0.80
Note: Negative or prejudiced percentages are in bold figures

Munster people, rural-reared, semi-skilled or unskilled and the lower class expressed most respect for a Traveller. This is out of line with the pattern of "liberal" attitudes. Also the fact that "education" and "age" did not record variations of significance reflects a degree of non-liberalness.

TABLE No. 144
TRAVELLERS SCALES BY PERSONAL VARIABLES (% in agreement)
SECTION I: TRAVELLERS SCALE

	Respect	Reluctant to buy house next door	Hesitant to seek out company	Willing to employ	Exclude from close set of friends	Consider competent to serve on a jury	Avoid in social situations	
	1.	2.	3.	4.	5.	6.	7.	N.
National Sample	86.8	74.6	76.4	56.9	62.9	51.7	55.9	970
A. AGE								
1. 35 years or less				62.6	55.8	61.5		382
2. 36 to 50 years				57.2	65.8	49.6		263
3. 51 to 65 years	N/S	N/S	N/S	52.4	66.5	44.1	N/S	187
4. 66 years +				46.5	72.7	39.0		138
				P≤.05	P≤.001	P≤.001		
B. GENDER								
I. Female	89.1					54.7		527
2. Male	84.0	N/S	N/S	N/S	N/S	48.2	N/S	443
	P≤.05					P≤.05		
C. MARITAL STATUS								
1. Never Married			71.4			57.2	49.8	278
2. Married	N/S	N/S	77.8	N/S	N/S	50.6	57.9	609
3. Widowed			87.0			41.8	62.9	66
			P≤.05			P≤.05	P≤.05	
D. COUNTY OF RESIDENCE								
1. Dublin	81.4	80.7		59.6	56.8	57.8	52.7	267
2. Rest of Leinster	88.2	70.7		56.6	70.0	50.8	52.4	246
3. Munster	90.2	71.3	N/S	60.7	57.6	56.6	54.1	291
4. Connaught/Ulster	87.2	78.3		46.2	72.2	34.9	69.2	166
	P≤.05	P≤.05		P≤.05	P≤.001	P≤.001	P≤.05	
E. PLACE OF REARING								
1. Large City	80.3					58.4	53.0	276
2. Small City	85.4					57.8	57.1	80
3. Town	91.5	N/S	N/S	N/S	N/S	54.8	45.3	123
4. Rural	89.4					46.2	60.0	491
	P≤.05					P≤.05	P≤.05	
F. EDUCATION								
1. Primary Only	48.0			48.01		42.6		273
2. Incomplete Second	58.2			58.2		51.3		273
3. Complete Second	N/S	N/S	N/S	57.8	N/S	54.1	N/S	289
4. Third Level				69.8		65.9		135
						P≤.001		
G. OCCUPATIONAL STATUS								
1. Profess/Executive	80.5							295
2. Inspect/Supervisory	86.3							293
3. Skilled/Routine	87.7	N/S	N/S	N/S	N/S	N/S	N/S	261
4. Semi/Unskilled	91.7							152
	P≤.05							
H. SOCIAL CLASS POSITION								
1. Class I	88.2	72.7	67.6			67.6		33
2. Class 11	78.1	81.9	79.0			58.1		105
3. Class 111	85.1	77.8	79.6	N/S	N/S	57.1	N/S	264
4. Class IV	88.1	72.8	76.5			43.4		277
5. Class V	91.0	67.6	67.6			51.1		184
	P≤.05	P≤.05	P≤.05			P≤.05		

Percentages other than national sample underlined

TABLE No. 144—Continued
SECTION II: SOCIAL DISTANCE TOWARDS TRAVELLERS BY
PERSONAL VARIABLES

Variable	Admit to Family %	Deny Citizenship %	M.S.D.	Variable	Admit to Family %	Deny Citizenship %	M.S.D.
National Sample	13.5	10	3.681	National Sample	13.5	10	3.681
A. AGE				C. EDUCATION			
1. 35 years or less	<u>17.6</u>	7.7*	3.409	1. Primary Only	9.6*	<u>12.1</u>	3.922
2. 36 to 50 years	13.0	9.3	3.736	2. Inc. Second	<u>17.7</u>	10.7	3.568
3. 51 to 65 years	9.9	12.5	3.912	3. Complete Second	9.9	9.1	3.685
4. 66 years plus	8.3*	<u>14.5</u>	4.028	4. Third Level	17.3	5.8*	3.453
B COUNTY OF RESIDENCE				D. SOCIAL CLASS POSITION			
1. Dublin	16.4	9.5	3.551	1. Class I	<u>17.6</u>	2.9*	3.294
2. Rest of Leinster	<u>18.1</u>	7.9*	3.386	2. Class 11	17.3	9.6	3.606
3. Munster	11.4	9.0	3.786	3. Class 111	8.9*	8.9	3.719
4. Connaught/Ulster	5.8*	<u>15.6</u>	4.139	4. Class IV	17.5	10.3	3.572
				5. Class V	14.4	<u>13.3</u>	3.739

*Lowest percentage; Highest percentage is underlined.

2.1.b Living Next-Door to Travellers: Three-quarters of the sample said they *"would be reluctant to buy a house next-door to a Traveller"*. This view reinforces the social distance, where 59% said they would not "welcome Travellers as next-door neighbours". This finding highlights the opposition in Irish society to the provision of serviced halting sites or housing the Traveller families which lies at the root of the prevention of members of the minority from improving their social and personal condition.

When tested by personal variables, only *two* of the eight variables on Table 144 showed significant variation, i.e. "county of residence" and "social class position". Those least opposed to Travellers were people living in the "Rest of Leinster", i.e. outside County Dublin, and those of the lowest social class position. The overall level of consensus is quite discouraging for those who would hope that younger and more educated people would be more tolerant as is the case of other categories of prejudice! Our liberalness seems to be very selective.

2.1.c Shunning the Company of Travellers: In Allport's progressive sequence of the effects of prejudice, avoidance or shunning the company of members of the minority was the second in a five-point continuum of negativity (see p. 21 above). In relation to this continuum, Allport points out that if the popular media are allowed to publish *negative information* against a minority group, it will inevitably lead to *avoidance and shunning* of the members of the minority which, in turn, facilitates and even rationalises *discrimination* against the group.

Items nos. 3 and 7 measure the disposition in the population towards avoiding and shunning the company of Travellers as human persons. Again the findings are predominantly negative. Over three-quarters of the sample *"would be hesitant to seek out"* the company of Travellers, while 55.9% *"would avoid a Traveller in social situations"*. These attitudes manifest a disposition towards Travellers almost as an "untouchable caste" in Irish society. As one who lived a short time with the Travellers, the present author would say that those who shun the company of members of this minority are depriving themselves of rich cultural and personal experiences.

Only two personal variables registered significant variation in relation to item nos. 3, i.e. "marital status" and "social class position". The sub-variables most "reluctant to seek out the company" of Travellers were "widowed" and the middle middle class, i.e. Class III. In the case of item no. 7, ("avoid a Traveller in a social situation") three of the eight variables recorded significant variations, i.e. "marital status", "county of residence" and "place of rearing". Those most eager to avoid Travellers in social situations were widowed, residents of Connaught/Ulster and rural-reared respondents. Again the level of consensus by age and education is very worrying because of the lack of evidence of any movement towards an improvement in the position. One would begin to question the degree of socialisation in tolerance to Travellers in the families, churches and schools.

Item no. 5 is also indicative of avoidance and shunning but has the added dimension of group membership. The consequences of the opinion expressed in this statement would be to discourage well-disposed members of the Settled Community from developing close friendship with Travelling People. The response, at 62.9%, agreeing with the view that they *"would exclude Travellers from my close set of friends"* is relatively severe. This bears out the psychological function of prejudice in relation to group membership (see Mac Gréil, 1977 p. 104-6). Group pressure is strong.

At least this item elicited a significant variation by age with the younger categories slightly more tolerant. The only other variable to register significant differences was county of residence with Dublin respondents the most tolerant and Connaught/Ulster members most in favour of the item. Again the variation was only slight between the sub groups and education had consensus across the standards reached.

2.1.d Willingness to Employ Travellers: The response to item no. 4 is a source of some optimism in that a clear majority (56.9%) of respondents indicated a willingness to employ a Traveller. Three variables recorded a significant variation in relation to this item, i.e. age, county of residence and education. Young people, residents of Munster and those with third-level education were most willing to employ a Traveller, while older respondents, residents of Connaught/Ulster and those with primary education only were least willing to employ them.

If these findings were translated into behaviour, leading to an improvement in job-opportunities for Travellers, the net effect on public attitudes would be very significant. Positive behaviour such as increased job-opportunities would lead to a marked improvement in the living conditions and a reduction in the extent of the "culture of poverty" of Travellers. In turn, the improved condition would challenge the negative attitudes and make Travellers more acceptable.

2.1.e Competence of Travellers to Serve on a Jury: The sample is divided in its response to the statement "*Would consider a Traveller competent to serve on a jury*". With 51.7% in favour and 48.2% against, the margin of error of ±3% would make the answer almost too close to call. Still, the positive side is 3.5% greater than the negative. This, again, is the source of some optimism and should give Travellers a modicum of satisfaction.

Interestingly, unlike the other items, this one elicited significant variations in seven of the eight personal variables, i.e. "age", "gender", "marital status", "county of residence", "place of rearing", "education" and "social class position". The patterns of variation were standard in most cases. Younger respondents, females, never married, Dublin residents, city-reared, third-level educated and those in the Upper Class (Class I) were most in favour of Travellers being competent to serve on a jury. Occupation was the only variable not recording significant variation between the different levels of occupational status.

2.1.f Final Comment: This concludes the examination of the seven items of the *Traveller Scale*. The overall result is quite negative save the good results in Items 1, 4 and 6. It is not a pleasant task for a sociologist to unveil unpleasant findings but, based on the principle that "a prejudice exposed in a prejudice undermined", the above pages will, it is hoped, help to undermine the above unfair and irrational anti-Traveller views and attitudes found at present within the Irish Settled Community.

2.2 Factor Analysis of Traveller Scale:

A factor analysis of the Traveller Scale resulted in all items grouping into two factors which could be designated a four-item "social" factor consisting of items nos. 1, 4, 6 and 7 and a three-item "personal" factor composed of items nos. 2, 3 and 5. Table 145 gives the "varimax loading" for each factor (0.5 being the minimum loading for grouping).

Table 146 gives the correlation matrix of the seven items. There is a significant correlation between all the items with the factors.

2.3 Scale and Sub-Scale Scores by Personal Variables (Table 147):

The p-score (prejudice score) for the scale was 266.5 on a 1 to 500 range, which is very close to half the range and, as stated above, therefore open

TABLE No. 145
FACTOR ANALYSIS OF THE TRAVELLERS SCALE

	Varimax Loading	
	Factor 1 Social	Factor 2 Personal
Would respect this person (1)	.68311	
Would be willing to employ this person (4)	.79541	
Would consider competent to serve on a jury (6)	.77201	
Would avoid this person in social situations (7)	.61374	
Would be reluctant to buy a house next door (2)		.86871
Would be hesitant to seek out their company (3)		.85707
Would exclude from close set of friends (5)		.57027

TABLE No. 146
CORRELATION MATRIX BETWEEN ITEMS OF TRAVELLERS SCALE

Factor 1	Factor 1				Factor 2		
	1.	4.	6.	7.	2.	3.	5.
1. Would respect this person	1.00	.44	.34	.35	.19	.24	.30
4. Would be willing to employ		1.00	.53	.43	.23	.30	.41
6. Would consider competent to serve on a jury			1.00	-.41	.18	.25	.36
7. Would avoid this person in social situations				1.00	.31	.42	.60
Factor 2							
2. Would be reluctant to buy a house next door					1.00	.62	.39
3. Would be hesitant to seek out their company						1.00	.45
5. Would exclude from close set of friends.							1.00

to the widest variation. The p-score for the "social sub-scale" is lower at 225.1, while the personal sub-scale p-score is higher at 321.7. In other words, the total sample was not as prejudiced to the same extent when allowing "social" roles and status to Travellers, e.g. worker or member of a jury, as when Travellers would enter their own "personal" lives as friend, companion or next-door neighbour. This fear or rejection of Travellers entering our personal lives must be in part built on negative stereotypes and uninformed mythology in regard to this group of ordinary but different Irish people whose only major distinction has been that of being forced (by the Settled Community) to live on the margins of Irish society. It also points to the absence of real and normal interpersonal contact between Travelling People and members of the Settled Community.

Strategies and policies adopted by those who have been engaged in trying to help Travelling People have failed in the basic task of establishing favourable contact between Travelling and Settled People on a personal level. It would appear from the p-score of the "personal subscale" that this is an area requiring serious attention, that is, if the prejudices are to be replaced by more positive attitudes. Table 147 gives a breakdown of scale and sub-scale p-scores by personal variables. If one were to take 10% of the p-score as a minimum significant variation for each variable, it is clear that there is a very low range of difference for most variables. This point has already been noted when looking at the differences in relation to individual items. In other words, there is a relatively high level of consensus in the people's anti-Traveller prejudices.

2.3.a Consensus Variables: Gender and Occupational Status: The personal variables showing least variation are "gender" and "occupational status". The convergence of male and female prejudice scores is much greater than was anticipated. "Occupational status" also fails to reach the 10% variation minimum in relation to the whole scale score or the subscale p-scores. "Education" and "age" are normally the most discerning of variables in detecting change of attitudes. In the case of the Travellers Scale and sub-scales they are relatively low, especially in the case of the "personal sub-scale".

2.3.b Age: With regard to the pattern of variable variations, an examination of the underlined scores gives a predictable result. In the case of *age* the highest p-scores are in the oldest category of 66 years and over, with the lowest in the youngest category of 35 years or less. The *marital status* differences with "widowed" highest and "never married" lowest are probably influenced by the age factor.

2.3.c County of Residence and Place of Rearing: *County of residence* was the variable to elicit the greatest variation in the three p-scores. Connaught/Ulster respondents consistently scored highest of the four categories. Munster was the lowest for the full scale scores. Munster and "Rest of Leinster" scores had equally low scores in the case of the "social" sub-scale. Dublin and Munster scores were almost equally lowest in the case of the "personal" p-score. Only one p-score (social sub-scale) showed significant variation in the *place of rearing* variable. Rural respondents were highest while town respondents were least prejudiced on the social sub-scale.

TABLE No. 147
TRAVELLER SCALES BY PERSONAL VARIABLES (P-Scores)

	Scale	Social Subscale	Personal Subscale	N.
National Sample	266.5	225.1	321.7	970
A. AGE				
1. 35 years or less	247.5	206.0	301.8	382
2. 36 to 50 years	272.5	225.3	336.7	263
3. 51 to 65 years	277.6	240.3	325.7	187
4. 66 years +	292.7	256.7	342.3	138
(Score Variation)	(45.2)*	(50.7)*	(40.5)*	
B. MARITAL STATUS				
1. Never Married	251.1	211.4	304.3	278
2. Married	272.0	229.6	328.4	609
3. Widowed	283.3	244.7	334.3	66
(Score Variation)	(32.2)*	(33.3)*	(30.0)*	
C. COUNTY OF RESIDENCE				
1. Dublin	255.3	218.0	304.4	267
2. Rest of Leinster	266.2	214.9	334.1	246
3. Munster	253.5	214.3	306.7	291
4. Connaught/Ulster	307.7	269.5	357.3	166
(Score Variation)	(54.2)*	(55.2)*	(52.9)*	
D. PLACE OF REARING				
1. Large City		221.4		276
2. Small City	N/S	210.0	N/S	80
3. Town		206.2		123
4. Rural		234.3		491
(Score Variation)		(31.1)*		
E. EDUCATION				
1. Primary Only	282.6	251.7		273
2. Incomplete Second	257.9	217.5	N/S	273
3. Compete Second	267.1	222.3		289
4. Third Level	250.1	192.8		135
(Score Variation)	(32.5)*	(58.9)*		
F. SOCIAL CLASS POSITION				
1. Class I	225.9	180.9	302.0	33
2. Class 11	261.9	212.4	327.9	105
3. Class III	272.8	223.9	337.4	264
4. Class IV	268.3	233.8	315.9	277
5. Class V	257.5	223.9	301.8	184
(Score Variation)	(46.9)*	(52.9)*	(35.6)*	

*Above the minimum 10% of p-score variation. Note: The highest p-score in each variable is underlined.

2.3.d Education: The full scale and the Social Sub-scale registered significant variations (plus 10% of mean p-score) in the case of *education*. In both instances there was a negative correlation between educational standard reached and prejudice scores, with "primary only" highest and "third level" lowest. There was no significant variation in the case of the Personal Sub-scale. This consensus across educational lines in the most severe area of anti-Traveller prejudice again questions the quality of education as an agent of tolerance towards Ireland's major minority group (in terms of social prejudice). The public attitudes towards Travellers raise serious questions for educators and media controllers as well as for parents, religious leaders and other community and political leaders. Since prejudice is something we learn, the sources of rearing, teaching and general opinion formation must be questioned when negative responses such as those in this chapter are discovered in a representative sample of the adult population.

2.3.e Occupational Status: Occupational status was another variable to show high consensus. This is also against the norm because those in more secure social positions, and thereby deemed to enjoy greater self-actualization, would be in a better psychological position to be tolerant than would their fellow-citizens at the bottom of the occupational scale who seem to suffer more frustration and insecurity. In most other scales there is a negative correlation between prejudice scores and occupational status.

2.3.f Social Class Position: Social class position (which is calculated on the criteria of educational standard and occupational status) did record a significant score variation in all three areas. The "middle middle-class" (i.e. Class III) seemed to be the most prejudiced in the case of the full scale and the Personal Sub-scale.

The "lower middle-class/upper lower-class" (i.e. Class IV) have the highest p-score for the Social Sub-scale. It is not unexpected to find a relatively low, if significant, variation because of the direct influence of educational standard reached and occupational status.

2.3.g Final Comment: As a final comment on the analysis of the prejudice scores above, there are two findings worthy of emphasis. *Firstly*, there is a relatively severe measure of social prejudice against Travellers in Ireland today, which is untenable in terms of satisfactory inter group relations. *Secondly*, there is relatively little variation within the personal variables which points to a level of consensus which, if not disturbed, is likely to remain for a long time. This relatively high degree of consensus questions the universality of the tolerance of "liberal" respondents.

2.4 Travellers' Own Way of Life:

The "pluralist integration" of Travellers into Irish society has begun to replace the arguments in favour of their "assimilation" into Irish social and cultural life. The assimilationist point of view insists that through education, housing and participation in the workforce, the Irish Travelling People would take on the norms and values of the Settled Community and end up as an integral part of that society. This would obviously imply their ceasing to be nomadic and over a few generations their becoming absorbed through inter-marriage and socialisation into the culture and structures of Irish (Settled) society. Many, if not most, who promote this long-term policy do not accept that Travellers have a distinctive culture or way of life other than "the culture of poverty", which is worth preserving.

Over the past decade or more a pluralist policy has emerged, coming mainly from people working with Travellers' education and development and from articulate members of the Irish Travelling Community. These people argue that Travellers have a distinctive group culture which is not to be confused with the "culture of poverty". With regard to the latter, the advocates of integrated pluralism also wish to see an end to the "culture of poverty" in a society which has become relatively affluent.

The cultural uniqueness of the Irish Travelling people is a topic of a book in itself and some valuable work has already been written about it. Among the cultural traits which are becoming relatively unique to Irish Travellers is *their nomadic lifestyle, their strong extended-family structure, their traditional trades and crafts, their folk memory, their songs and music, and other symbolic systems of meaning and communication.* The extent to which they also share some of the cultural traits of Romany Gypsies would be the result of contact made in Great Britain.

The very strong oral tradition is a most valuable linguistic asset which should be recorded before it is interfered with by the advance in literacy and familiarity with the written word. The exclusively aural and oral nature of their language and communication is something worth retaining on record. The ballads and songs of non-literate people are especially interesting, and probably more true to the original use of language than we find in literate societies. Literate people lack the same flexibility in their use of language and are constrained by rigidly imposed syntax and vocabulary (see Sapir, *Culture, Language and Personality*, University of California Press, 1958).

One item in the survey was included to discover how tolerant respondents would be to Travellers living their unique way of life. The overwhelming majority agreed with the Travellers' right to be different (Table 148).

This response is so strongly endorsed that it is not very useful to carry out a more detailed examination by variables. You may ask how meaningful this expression of tolerance of Travellers' right to "*live their own way of life decently*" is in the light of earlier rejection of that way of life. It does seem to be somewhat contradictory or maybe "politically correct". At the very minimum, it is evidence of a latent or dormant disposition in the population towards pluralism. Those promoting pluralism could begin from that and reassure the people that such a development would be to everybody's advantage.

TABLE NO. 148
TRAVELLERS' RIGHT TO OWN WAY OF LIFE

Question: Would you agree or disagree with the following statement:
"Itinerants/Travellers should be facilitated to live their own way of life decently?"

	National Sample 1988/89	Dublin Sub Sample 1988/89	Dublin Sample 1972/73	Change
1. Agree	93.0%	90.9%	87.5%	+3.4%
2. Don't Know	5.1%	8.0%	2.0%	+6.0%
3. Disagree	1.9%	1.1%	10.5%	-9.4%
No.	998	277	2,280	
P-score (1-200)	8.9	10.2	23.0	-12.8%

CONCLUSION

The picture emerging from the above examination of the Irish people's prejudices against the Travellers is one of **caste-like apartheid**. There may be some evidence of tolerance in "Social Sub-scale" results which would indicate a disposition of letting Travellers enjoy rights – so long as they do not come too close to the Settled People in a personal capacity. Marriage, friendship and even nextdoor neighbourhood is ruled out by the majority.

The high degree of consensus in the personal variables is indicative of a more static or permanent negative disposition towards Travellers. The scores of the scales and Sub-scales were conducive to maximum variation. This points to the selective nature of liberalness which, strictly speaking, is contradictory because of the expectation of the universality of liberal attitudes. This selectivity will be reconfirmed in further evidence presented in this chapter.

The evidence of growing hostility towards Travelling People may be indicative of their moving into the second stage of the **"Park Cycle"**, i.e., in conflict with the dominant group for rights of housing, jobs, education, cultural amenities, etc. (See Parke 1926, pp. 126 ff.). If that be the case and the conflict can be made constructive and non-violent, we may be witnessing a move towards some degree of equitable accommodation on the part of the dominant group and concessions being made to the Travellers as an integral, but different, section of Irish society.

PART III: OTHER SOCIAL CATEGORIES

Under this broad classification there are ten diverse social categories against whom intergroup attitudes and prejudices have been measured by the Bogardus Social Distance Scale. They include the following (in alphabetical order):

1. Alcoholics;	6. People with Mental Handicap;
2. Drug Addicts;	7. People with Physical Handicap;
3. Ex-Prisoners;	8. Unemployed;
4. Gay People;	9. Unmarried Mothers;
5. People with AIDS;	10. Working Class.

It is possible to sub-classify six of the above into three pairs of categories, i.e.,

(a)	*Compulsive Behaviour:*	Alcoholics and Drug Addicts;
(b)	*People with Handicap:*	Mental and Physical;
(c)	*Work Related:*	Unemployed and Working Class.

The remaining four, i.e., "ex-prisoners", "gay people", "people with AIDS" and "Unmarried Mothers" are unique categories in their own right.

1. SOCIAL DISTANCE OF SOCIAL CATEGORIES:

Table 149 gives the social distance responses to each of the ten categories in rank-order of mean social distance scores.

With regard to the first five categories on Table 149 ("Working Class", "Unemployed", "People with Physical Handicap", "Unmarried Mothers" and "People with Mental Handicap") there is a fairly positive attitude towards them, i.e., an M.S.D. score of 2.000 or less. Categories nos. 1 and 2 would classify as "in groups" in Irish society because of their MSD of less than 1.500. Categories nos. 3 and 4 are on the margin of in-group status.

The public attitudes to "alcoholics", while fairly negative, are problematic because of the reluctance of many (63.3%) to have a more intimate relationship, i.e., at the "kinship" or "friendship" levels. Rehabilitation of people with compulsive behaviour problems requires good personal and community support. Such attitudes could result in causing those with alcoholic tendencies to indulge even further in their compulsive behaviour.

The position of "Ex-Prisoners" and "Gay People" is almost that of outgroups whose M.S.D. is normally 3.500 plus. The negative severity of the attitudes is best manifested by the percentages denying citizenship to each category, i.e., 15.4% to "Ex-Prisoners" and 25.8% to "Gay People".

The final two categories are in a most precarious position because of the enormous hostility of the dispositions towards them. Some 34.9% would deny citizenship to "People with AIDS" while 43.7% would do so to "Drug Addicts". When one considers that many in each of these categories may be victims of circumstances and all of them in need of extensive social support, the appalling severity of such public attitudes becomes more apparent.

It has already been noted (see pp. 85f.) that the reasons for negative attitudes put forward by respondents were primarily "way of life" and secondarily "not socially acceptable". The "way of life" in most cases refers

TABLE No. 149
SOCIAL DISTANCE OF SOCIAL CATEGORIES

Rank Order	CATEGORY	Kinship 1 %	Friendship or Closer 2 %	Neighbour or Closer 3 %	Co-Worker or Closer 4 %	Citizen or Closer 5 %	Visitor Only 6 %	Debar or Deport 7 %	M.S.D. (1-7)	N
1.	Working Class	86.8	94.8	98.0	99.4	100	0.0	0.0	1.210	1,001
2.	Unemployed	78.1	92.0	97.3	98.5	99.8	0.0	0.2	1.345	1,001
3.	People Phy. Handicap	57.8	90.0	95.9	98.4	99.7	0.3	0.0	1.581	1,001
4	Unmarried Mothers	61.1	82.9	92.6	96.3	99.0	0.6	0.4	1.684	1,001
5	People with Men. Handicap	34.6	78.1	91.3	95.6	99.1	0.7	0.1	2.010	999
6.	Alcoholics	13.8	44.7	62.5	79.9	91.6	5.4	3.0	3.105	1,000
7.	Ex-Prisoners	23.7	39.4	53.0	73.2	84.6	9.9	5.5	3.316	1,000
8.	Gay People	12.5	35.2	49.2	64.7	74.1	10.6	15.2	3.793	999
9.	People with AIDS	17.2	28.1	39.7	48.7	65.0	12.4	22.5	4.336	997
10.	Drug Addicts	5.3	18.2	27.3	42.5	56.5	14.6	29.1	4.798	1,003

to a socially unacceptable "lifestyle". The obvious area for social rehabilitation must therefore be in changes in lifestyle.

2. CHANGES IN SOCIAL DISTANCE SCORES SINCE 1972-73:

Six of the ten categories were included in the 1972-73 survey, i.e., "alcoholics", "Drug Addicts", "People with Handicap", "Unemployed", "Unmarried Mothers" and "Working Class". The following table (150) measures the changes in social distance between 1972-73 and 1988-89 in relation to each of six categories. The major changes in rationalisation are also included in Table 150.

With the notable exception of "Working Class" and "Unemployed", whose status has relatively improved, the other eight social categories have disimproved over the sixteen years between 1972-73 and 1988-89. The rise in popularity of the "Working Class" is at a time when there has been a serious decline in the proportion of skilled, semi-skilled and unskilled manual jobs in the Irish economy with the resulting unemployment, a drop in the percentages in the "**Working Class**" (see Table 156, p. 370). It could be explained by a sense of class solidarity or a "romantic attachment" to the diminishing proletariat. The extent of the decline of the "Working Class" jobs in Dublin as percentage of occupations has been as follows:

OCCUPATIONS	Dublin Sample 1972-73	Dublin Subsample 1988-89	Change
1. Skilled Manual/Routine Non-Manual	36.6%	27.9%	-8.7%
2. Semi/Skilled/Unskilled Manual	23.3%	13.4%	-9.9%
Total Working Class Jobs	59.9%	41.3%	-18.6%

Measured in terms of social class position, the decline in the Working/Lower Class categories of the Dublin subsample has been even more striking, i.e., Class IV declined from 45.8% in 1972-73 to 27.5% in 1988-89 which equals -18.3%. The lowest class on the Social Class Position scale, Class V dropped by only 3.7%, i.e., from 21.1% in 1972-73 to 17.4% in 1988-89. Could the great attachment to the "Working Class" mean a certain disillusionment with the lifestyle of the ever-expanding "Middle Class" and a degree of nostalgic longing for the more *gemeinschaftlich* way of life of the "Working Class"?

The rise in respect for the "**Unemployed**" may be due to the opposite reason for the similar trend in relation to the "Working Class", namely, this is a category of growth in the population over the period from 1972-73 to 1988-89. Between 1972 and 1989 the rate of unemployment (percentage of workforce on the "Live Register") had risen from 6.2% in 1972 to 18.2% in

TABLE No. 150

CHANGES IN SOCIAL CATEGORIES' SOCIAL DISTANCE BETWEEN 1972-73 AND 1988-89. (DUBLIN RESPONDENTS)

	Kinship 1.	Friendship or Closer 2.	Neighbour or Closer 3.	Co-Worker or Closer 4.	Citizen or Closer 5.	Visitor Only 6.	Debar or Deport 7.	Mean Social Distance (1-7)	RATIONALISATION			Number not admitting to Kinship
									Way of Life (Lifestyle)	Not Socially Acceptable	Economic	
	%	%	%	%	%	%	%		%	%	%	
1. Working Class												
1972-73	89.8	96.2	98.8	99.7	100	—	—	1.155	24.4	65.9	1.5	205
1988-89	92.8	97.1	98.9	99.6	100	—	—	1.116	63.2	10.5	10.5	19
(Change)	(+3.0)	(+0.9)	(+0.1)	(-0.1)	—	—	—	(-0.039)	(+38.8)	(-55.4)	(+9 0)	
2. Unemployed												
1972-73	68.8	87.7	94.7	96.6	99.1	0.3	0.6	1.536	7.7	37.7	52.3	679
1988-89	86.3	95.7	97.5	98.6	100	—	—	1.220	55.6	2.8	30.6	36
(Change)	(+7.5)	(+8.0)	(+2.8)	(+2.0)	(+0.9)	(-0.3)	(-0.6)	(-0.316)	(+47.9)	(-34.9)	(-21.7)	
3. Handicapped												
1972-73	77.1	95.4	98.8	99.5	99.8	0.2	—	1.294	41.2	36.5	9.8	468
*1988-89	65.6	91.7	95.3	99.3	99.6	0.4	—	1.486	43.5	22.8	3.3	92
(Change)	(-11.5)	(-3.7)	(-3.5)	(-0.2)	(-0.2)	(+0.2)	—	(+0.192)	(+2.3)	(-13.7)	(-6.5)	
4. Unmarried Mothers												
1972-73	79.0	91.4	97.0	98.0	99.2	0.2	0.6	1.360	8.0	76.2	2.5	436
1988-89	70.4	88.4	92.1	98.9	100	—	—	1.502	64.2	16.0	7.4	81
(Change)	(-8.6)	(-3.0)	(-4.9)	(+0.9)	(+0.8)	(-0.2)	(-0.6)	(+0.142)	(+56.2)	(-66.2)	(+4.9)	
5. Alcoholics												
1972-73	21.7	57.3	73.3	81.7	91.6	2.6	5.8	2.801	21.6	59.3	14.6	1,753
1988-89	14.5	48.0	63.6	83.3	92.0	5.5	2.5	3.011	71.7	21.0	1.3	233
(Change)	(-7.2)	(-9.3)	(-9.7)	(+1.6)	(+0.4)	(+2.9)	(-3.3)	(+0.210)	(+50.1)	(-48.3)	(-12.3)	
6. Drug Addicts												
1972-73	20.4	48.3	60.2	67.5	76.4	3.3	20.3	3.475	19.6	65.3	7.2	1,773
1988-89	5.1	20.4	30.5	50.9	65.5	12.7	21.8	4.495	64.2	20.8	1.2	259
(Change)	(-15.3)	(-27.9)	(-29.7)	(-16.6)	(-10.9)	(+9.4)	(+1.5)	(+1.020)	(+44.5)	(-44.5)	(-6.0)	

* People with Physical Handicap.

1985 to 16.5% in 1989. Despite better employment chances for the better educated, etc., there was a marked increase in white-collar unemployment. It had probably reached a stage where most families in Ireland had been affected directly by the new situation of "structural unemployment" across the board. Similar conditions were beginning to happen across the European Union.

The changes recorded in the rationalisation scale for both categories have marked a collapse of "not socially acceptable" as a reason. In other words, there is evidence here of the decline of social stigma attached to "Unemployed People". Also the "economic" reason has declined. This is positive news for Irish society in that the "Unemployed" will be able to feel more acceptable in society. It might also point to the public acceptance of a reasonable "minimum incomes system" for all citizens.

The position of social distance scores towards "**People who are Handicapped**" has disimproved slightly, while still remaining within the "ingroup" category of 1.500 or less. This is wholly due to the reluctance of an extra eleven percent to admit members of this category into their families. Of all categories people with handicap need the support of the domestic environment. The drop in "not socially acceptable" as a reason for refusing to welcome people who are handicapped in to the family must be a positive indication of the reduction of the public stigma against them.

The standing of "**Unmarried Mothers**" remained very high with an M.S.D. on the margin of "ingroup status" at 1.502. The drop of 8.6% of those who would welcome "Unmarried Mothers" into their families, is in line with the overall increase in prejudice as expressed by social distance scores. The big change of note in the findings of Table 7, (p. 74) has been the very substantial switch of 60% away from "not socially acceptable" (76.4% in 1972-73 in Dublin) to "way of life" or "lifestyle" as the main rationalisation. The lifestyle rather than the person has been the reason put forward.

The social distance scores for "**Alcoholics**" have deteriorated slightly, but in line with general prejudice trends. Again, it is at the kinship/family level that disimprovement took place, i.e., a drop of 7.2%. This drop has been more than compensated in the middle stages, i.e., at "co-worker" level. The drop in social stigma of 48.3% is also positive. Almost three-quarters of those who would not welcome "Alcoholics" into their family through kinship would do so for "lifestyle reasons". The overall standing of "Alcoholics" is not conducive to their rehabilitation and a greater understanding of the compulsive nature of their condition is required. An improvement of their social distance is therapeutically desirable. It is ironic that in a society like Ireland where alcoholic drink is strongly promoted and apparently very acceptable, the very negative attitudes towards "Alcoholics" prevails. This shows the cruel irony of the permissive attitudes toward alcohol advertising in a society intolerant of Alcoholics!

The position of "**Drug Addicts**" in Dublin society has deteriorated very substantially during the period from 1972-73 to 1988-89. The consequences of this very negative attitude in relation to the rehabilitation of so many people – mostly young adults and many teenagers, in such a hostile environment are very serious. Some 34.5% of respondents would deny citizenship to "Drug Addicts"! This is the situation in a city like Dublin which prides itself in great tolerance in other areas. Again, it is "lifestyle" which seems to be the main rationalisation for the very penal attitudes revealed in these figures. It must be stated that drug addiction is possible for most people exposed to drug-taking. Very often, potential addicts are introduced to drugs in glamorous situations such as commercialised entertainment functions deemed to be popular and stimulating. The "pop-culture" to which young people are being exposed has become largely a commercialised form of charged entertainment outside the control or influence of parents, teachers or community leaders.

In the light of adult society's responsibility for the protection of the young people from exposure to early introduction to addictive and illicit drugs, the above attitudes towards victims of drug addiction may be an exercise in scapegoating and the shirking of blame by the permissive adult society. Such attitudes toward "Drug Addicts" are very likely to lead to further and more devastating addiction. In other words, the drugs problem is not primarily the problem of the young addict. It is mainly the problem of adult society!

3. SOCIAL DISTANCE BY PERSONAL VARIABLES

One of the most surprising and, some might say, disappointing aspects about the findings of Table 151 is the **very high level of consensus** between the responses of the subsamples of the variables: "age", "gender", "marital status", "education", "occupational status", "social class position" and "political party preferences". Apart from the attitudes towards "Gay People", "People with AIDS", and "Drug Addicts", the above personal variables registered "no statistical significance" in relation to the social categories. "County of residence" and "area of rearing" were the exceptions in that they elicited significant variations for most social categories.

3.1 Working Class: Only one personal variable recorded significant variations in relation to "Working Class". This is not unusual for a category with such a low social distance score of 1.210 with 86.8% admitting to kinship.

The one variable in question is *"county of residence"*. The range of difference at 0.15 was relatively low. "Rest of Leinster" respondents were least welcoming while "Dublin" respondents were practically unanimously in favour of the "Working Class". "Munster" and "Connaught/Ulster" scores were in between.

3.2 Unemployed: Three personal variables recorded statistically significant variations in relation to the "Unemployed", i.e., "gender", "county of residence" and "place of rearing". Consensus prevailed in all the other variables.

TABLE No. 151

SOCIAL CATEGORIES' SOCIAL DISTANCE BY PERSONAL VARIABLES (MEAN SOCIAL DISTANCE SCORES)

VARIABLE	Working Class	Un-employed	Physically Hdcp.	Unmarried Mothers	Mentally Hdcp.	Alcoholics	Ex-Prisoners	Gay People	People with AIDS	Drug Addicts
Total Sample	1.210	1.345	1.581	1.684	2.010	3.105	3.316	3.793	4.336	4.798
A. AGE	N/S	N/S	N/S	N/S	N/S	N/S	N/S	P≤.001	P≤.001	P≤.001
1. 35 years or less								3.37*	3.83*	4.44*
2. 36 to 50 years								3.52	4.23	4.69
3. 51 to 65 years								4.49	4.88	5.24
4. 66 years plus								5.55	5.19	5.38
(Range)								(2.18)	(1.36)	(0.94)
B. GENDER	N/S	P≤.03	N/S	N/S	N/S	N/S	P≤.01	P≤.05	P≤.04	N/S
1. Female		1.38					3.47	3.63*	4.02*	
2. Male		1.30*					3.14*	3.98	5.04	
(Range)		(0.08)					(0.33)	(0.35)	(1.02)	
C. COUNTY OF RESIDENCE	P≤.02	P≤.001	P≤.001	P≤.001	P≤.008	N/S	P≤.001	P≤.001	P≤.001	P≤.02
1. Dublin	1.12*	1.22*	1.49*	1.50*	1.95		2.88*	3.13*	3.83*	4.49*
2. Rest of Leinster	1.27	1.32	1.51	1.66	1.90*		2.90	3.67	4.09	4.86
3. Munster	1.23	1.44	1.66	1.79	2.05		3.64	3.96	4.55	4.82
4. Connaught/Ulster	1.23	1.42	1.72	1.83	2.20		4.06	4.76	5.15	5.14
(Range)	(0.15)	(0.22)	(0.23)	(0.33)	(0.30)		(1.18)	(1.63)	(1.32)	(0.65)
D. PLACE OF REARING	N/S	P≤.001	P≤.001	P≤.001	N/S	P≤.001	P≤.001	P≤.001	P≤.001	P≤.001
1. Large City		1.26	1.48	1.51		3.02	2.81	3.22	3.71*	4.47
2. Small City		1.21*	1.41*	1.31*		2.55*	2.79*	2.97*	3.79	4.24*
3. Town		1.31	1.52	1.54		3.05	3.20	3.37	3.95	4.51
4. Rural		1.43	1.69	1.90		3.29	3.70	4.38	4.88	5.17
(Range)		(0.22)	(0.28)	(0.59)		(0.74)	(0.91)	(1.41)	(1.17)	(0.93)

Table No. 151—Continued

SOCIAL CATEGORIES' SOCIAL DISTANCE BY PERSONAL VARIABLES (MEAN SOCIAL DISTANCE SCORES)

VARIABLE	Working Class	Un-employed	Physically Hdcp.	Unmarried Mothers	Mentally Hdcp.	Alcoholics	Ex-Prisoners	Gay People	People with AIDS	Drug Addicts
E. EDUCATION	N/S	N/S	N/S	P≤.03	N/S	N/S	N/S	P≤.001	P≤.001	P≤.001
1. Primary Only				1.90				4.56	5.05	5.30
2. Incomplete Second				1.71				3.84	4.43	4.82
3. Complete Second				1.55				3.27	3.78	4.53
4. Third Level				1.40*				3.02*	3.62*	4.19*
(Range)				(0.50)				(1.54)	(1.43)	(0.93)
F. OCCUPATIONAL STATUS	N/S	N/S	N/S	N/S	N/S	N/S	P≤.04	P≤.001	P≤.001	P≤.02
1. Prof/Executive							2.96*	3.30*	3.76*	4.42*
2. Insp/Super							3.26	3.57	4.09	4.69
3. Skilled R. Non-Man							3.25	3.97	4.44	4.91
4. Semi/Unskilled							3.61	4.10	4.97	5.17
(Range)							(0.65)	(0.80)	(1.21)	(0.75)
G. SOCIAL CLASS POSITION	N/S	N/S	N/S	N/S	N/S	N/S	N/S	P≤.001	P≤.001	P≤.001
1. Class I								2.44*	2.79*	3.55*
2. Class 11								3.25	3.83	4.40
3. Class 111								3.52	4.01	4.79
4. Class IV								3.97	4.49	4.79
5. Class V								4.18	4.91	5.25
(Range)								(1.74)	(2.12)	(1.70)
H. POLITICAL PARTY PREFERENCE	N/S	N/S	N/S	N/S	N/S	N/S	N/S	P≤.007	P≤.007	P≤.001
1. Fianna Fáil								3.95	4.44	4.78
2. Fine Gael								4.08	4.55	5.04
3. Labour Party								3.18	3.77*	4.18*
4. PDs								2.93*	3.81	4.55
(Range)								(1.15)	(0.78)	(0.86)

Note: Highest scores ares are underlined. Lowest scores have asterisks (*).

The "gender" variable shows females were slightly more prejudiced against "Unemployed" than males. The range of difference was as low as 0.08. In the case of "county of residence", "Munster" residents were the most negative subsample while Dubliners were most in favour. "Rural-reared" respondents scored highest in "place of rearing" while those from "small cities" were best disposed to the "unemployed". The range of difference was again relatively small at 0.22.

3.3 People with Physical and Mental Handicap: "People with Physical Handicap" registered significant differences between the scores of sub-samples only in the case of "county of residence" and "place of rearing". The other handicap category, "People with Mental Handicap", attracted consensus in all variables except "county of residence". One would have expected variations in the case of "age" and "education" going on the assumption that young and highly educated would have been more tolerant and open to members of these categories. This again points to the selective nature of liberalness.

"Connaught/Ulster" respondents were the most negative subsample under "county of residence" in the case of both categories. Dublin respondents thought most positively of those with physical handicap while the "Rest of Leinster" were best disposed to the other category. The range of difference was moderate at 0.23 and 0.30. As already stated, attitudes towards people with handicaps are generally very favourable. This may be due in part to the fact that they constitute a social minority which cross class boundaries.

3.4 Unmarried Mothers: This is another category which received favourable scores on the social distance scale. It had consensus in six of the nine personal variables, i.e., "age", "gender", "marital status", "occupational status" and "political party preference". In the three variables which produced statistically significant variations a moderate range of difference was recorded.

"County of residence" subsamples were according to the normal pattern of prejudice scores with "Connaught/Ulster" scoring highest and "Dublin" having the least prejudice against "unmarried mothers". "Rural-reared" respondents were also the most prejudiced while those from "small cities" were those with the lowest scores among the "place of rearing" subsamples. The range of variation here was moderately high at 0.59. The patterns of social distance in the "education" variable follow the normal p-score pattern and the range of difference again was moderately high at 0.50 (i.e., half a stage on the seven point social distance scale).

3.5 Alcoholics: The performance of this category by the nine personal variables has been extraordinary in that, despite its relatively high mean social distance score of 3.105, it failed to elicit significant variation in seven out of the eight personal variables. This means that the attitude expressed here is a consensus attitude and unlikely to change unless the people reflect more openly on the problem of compulsive alcohol consumption. It will be very disappointing to those hoping for a more positive attitude towards alcoholics as victims of compulsive behaviour and addiction. Negative attitudes lead to negative behaviour which in turn results in the deterioration and isolation of the "Alcoholic" and, possibly forcing him or her on to a "skid row" type existence. Ireland's "drink culture" seems problematic!

"Place of rearing" did elicit a moderately high range of difference between the scores of the subsamples, i.e., 0.74 or three-quarters of a social distance stage. "Rural reared" were the most negative subsample while "small city" respondents were the least so disposed.

3.6 Ex-Prisoners: The very negative attitudes towards "Ex-Prisoners" again failed to attract significant variations in social distance scores from the variables of "age" and "education", where one would have expected greater understanding and tolerance from younger and more educated people. This means that liberalness is selective towards "Ex-Prisoners". If this be so, it is hardly open and tolerant liberalness.

One of the necessary conditions of the successful reintegration of "Ex-Prisoners" into society is the positive support of the public. Included in such support are open and tolerant attitudes. Recidivism, i.e., return of ex-prisoners to prison, in Ireland is around 58% at the present time and unlikely to reduce significantly without post-prison care and support for "Ex-Prisoners" to enable them reintegrate into their own communities. While prejudice at the level indicated by the above findings exists in Irish society, it is difficult to reverse the negative labelling of the "Ex-Prisoner". While labelling does not cause deviance, it does, nevertheless, reinforce a career of deviance or crime.

The variable "gender" produced a significant variation with females more negative than males. The range of variation was moderate at 0.33 i.e., one-third of a social distance stage. The range of variation by "county of residence" was very substantial at 1.18. The pattern of prejudice or negativity is similar to that of the other categories, that is, lowest scores came from respondents from the Rest of Leinster and the highest scores given by Connaught/Ulster respondents.

"Place of rearing" also produced a high range of variation of 0.91 which is almost one social distance stage. "Rural" respondents were most prejudiced while "small city" scores were most tolerant. "Occupational status" had a moderately high range of variation at 0.65 or two-thirds of a social distance stage. The pattern of prejudice was negatively correlated with the occupational status of respondents.

"Education", "social class position" and "political party reference" had consensus of prejudice against ex-prisoners. This reinforces the stable nature of attitudes towards this category and the selectivity of so-called liberal attitudes.

3.7 Gay People: As already stated, the level of homophobia indicated in the above findings is quite alarming, taken at the face value of the mean social distance of the national sample at 3.793, i.e., in the category of "outgroups" (over 3.500). That being said, there are strong variations in eight of the nine variables. The pattern of variations between subsamples shows some signs of growing tolerance in the population which, if they continue, means that the level of prejudice against "Gay People" should reduce over time.

The "age" variable elicited a score variation of over two stages on the social distance continuum (i.e., 2.18). There was a clearly negative correlation between age and severity of the social distance score. Males were more negative towards "Gay People" than were females. "Gender" produced a moderate range of variation of 0.35 or one-third of a social distance stage. "Marital status" is the only personal variable not to record a statistically significant variation.

"County of Residence" and "place of rearing" score very high ranges of variation of 1.63 and 1.41 respectively. Standard or normal patterns of prejudice against social categories were repeated for both variables. This rural-urban divide is very clearly marked in most of the social category scores, especially in the case of "Gay People" which must present serious problems for men perceived to be gay in rural communities.

"Education", "occupational status" and "social class position" produce a model set of response patterns, strictly along the normal prejudice trend. Higher education, high occupational status and "upper class" respondents all show significantly more tolerance towards "Gay People" than do those at the other end of the variable scales. The ranges of variation for the three variables were also quite substantial at 1.54 ("education"), 0.80 ("occupational status") and 1.74 ("social class position").

The "political party preferences" produced a very interesting mix of prejudices. Fine Gael supporters were most negative while the Progressive Democrat supporters were most tolerant towards "Gay People". The range of difference was high at 1.15. In all, the evidence of these findings heralds quite a dynamic state of the attitudes towards "Gay People". The most tolerant subsample being the Social Class I at 2.44 on the social distance scale (of 1 to 7), while the most intolerant score was the 5.55 of the over 66 years age group.

3.8 People with AIDS: The position of "People with AIDS" is very unsatisfactory in the attitudes of the Irish people. It is difficult to comprehend how a people with a reputation for hospitality like the Irish could express so hostile an attitude towards people who are weak, vulnerable and desperately in need of support. It is probably a mixture of fear, blame and anger towards people who have become the victims of a fatal illness which is communicable through sexual intercourse, blood transfusion and unsterilised hypodermic needles. In the public mind it is probably associated with promiscuity and drug injection. It is a relatively new disease and this causes the problem of "fear of the unknown".

The presentation of these findings of attitudes of the people towards "People with AIDS", "Gay People" and "Drug Addicts" creates a real problem for the present author in relation to the likely effects of publishing such findings on the welfare of the members of the categories in question. *The belief of the author is that the best way to undermine such destructive prejudices is to expose them.* This is done in the hope of challenging the untenable and irrational dispositions that good people can have towards minorities who need their respect and support. Having confronted these prejudices people would be more likely to modify them!

There is a degree of hope in the findings of Table 151 in relation to the category under review. The attitudes are dynamic and, hopefully, in the process of changing towards greater tolerance. "Education" (1.43), "age" (1.36), "occupational status" (1.21) and "social class position" (2.12) are key variables with very high ranges of difference between their subsamples and showing a pattern of variation in each case likely to result in greater tolerance in the future.

"Gender" responded to "People with AIDS" by registering a significant variation of over one stage (1.02). Males were substantially less tolerant than females toward people with AIDS. Incidentally, this was the only social category to elicit a statistically significant variation by "marital status". "Political party preferences" had a significant range of 0.78. Fine Gael scored highest while supporters of the Labour Party scored least.

"County of residence" and "place of rearing" repeated the pattern of the previous social categories with the exception of Dublin respondents scoring the lowest hostility in the "county of residence" variable subsamples. The ranges of difference at 1.32 and 1.17 were both high.

3.9 Drug Addicts: The attitudes towards "Drug Addicts" are so negative overall that they go beyond the level of outgroup. Considering that 43.7% of respondents would deny them citizenship means they are being pushed out of society. Many people want nothing to do with them. Of course this is disastrous for the "Drug Addicts" themselves and is also likely to exasperate the drugs problem. As already stated, drug addicts need support and tolerance not intensive hatred. As in the case of the two previous categories, there has been a fairly wide degree of score variation in the case of seven of the nine personal variables. "Gender" and "marital status" have shown consensus and failed to record statistically significant variations.

"Age", "education", "occupational status", and "social class position" had high ranges of score differences and recorded trends along the normal patterns. This, again, is a source of hope for a less severe level of prejudice against "drug addicts" in the future.

"County of residence" and "place of rearing" repeated the pattern of responses to "Gay People" but with lower ranges of difference at 0.65 and

0.93 respectively. "Political party preferences" had a moderately high range of difference of 0.86 or six-sevenths of a social distance stage. Fine Gael scored most negative while the Labour Party supporters were most tolerant towards "Drug Addicts".

3.10 Conclusion: The social distance measures against the social categories tells much about the level of tolerance in Irish society and the need for some self-examination. The absence of dissent in relation to the "People with Mental and People with Physical Handicap" and to "Unmarried Mothers" may be in part due to the fact that their standing in Irish society is relatively high. Nevertheless, one would have expected greater tolerance from young, educated and economically secure respondents (Class I and II) than from those older respondents, those with less education and those at the bottom of the socio-economic ladder.

Consensus in relation to "Alcoholics" and "Ex-Prisoners" is very difficult to understand because of the relatively high Mean Social Distance scores of each. It certainly raises again questions about the possibility of "selective liberalness". Such negative consensus against two social categories in desperate need of positive social support for their rehabilitation must be very disappointing. One could go further to suggest that the pervasive nature of these intolerant attitudes may well be a causal factor in the categories' problems. This could well be a classic case of the negative operation of the *vicious cicle* and "self-fulfilling prophecy" theories (see pages 28ff. above). It could well lead to a process of reinforcing members of the categories such as "Alcoholics" and pressurising "Ex-Prisoners" into a career in crime. This can happen through the process of labelling and "self-fulfilling prophecy"!

CHAPTER XII

Underclass, Unemployment and Social Mobility

PART I: THE SOCIO-ECONOMIC CONTEXT

The problem of unemployment has become a major challenge facing free-market capitalist Western societies. Ireland is not very different from other Western industrial societies. At the time of the previous study, unemployment in the Dublin area was as low as 3% of the workforce. Table 152 gives the changes in inflation and unemployment over the period. In fact, at that time, Irish employers were recruiting among Irish migrant workers in Manchester and elsewhere in Britain.

The general air of optimism and progress was to be shortlived. By the mid 1970s unemployment figures began to rise and out-migration of many of the Irish workforce returned in the late 1970s and during the 1980s. People were led to believe that the adjustments in world oil prices in 1974, and again in 1979, played a significant role in the crisis in job and economic development. High annual inflation and a significant growth in Ireland's national debt further aggravated the employment scene.

TABLE No. 152
INFLATION AND UNEMPLOYMENT TRENDS IN THE REPUBLIC OF IRELAND
1972-1989

YEAR	INFLATION RATE	UNEMPLOYMENT RATE	YEAR	INFLATION RATE	UNEMPLOYMENT RATE
1972	8.6%	6.2%	1981	20.4%	9.9%
1973	11.4%	5.7%*	1982	17.1%	11.4%
1974	17.0%	5.4%	1983	9.2%	15.3%
1975	21.0%	7.3%	1984	7.6%	16.8%
1976	18.0%	9.0%	1985	4.7%	18.2%
1977	13.6%	8.8%	1986	4.0%	18.2%
1978	7.6%	8.1%	1987	2.6%	17.6%
1979	13.2%	7.1%	1988	2.5%	17.0%
1980	18.2%	7.3%	1989	3.9%	16.5%

Sources: Leddin and Walsh 1992, p. 20;
I.P.A. Yearbook and Diary 1992, p. 104.
* Unemployment rates in Dublin were lower than the national average.

By the second half of the 1980s things began to stabilise and inflation gradually decreased with the re-emergence of continuous growth in national production. There is a significant negative rank-order correlation between inflation rates and unemployment rates over the eighteen years 1972-89, i.e., *Rho* = −0.61. There was also a significant shift in the nature of unemployment, i.e., a decline in blue-collar work and a marked increase in the services. The spread of micro-electronics and automation, as well as a move towards the replacement of native industries by new multinational projects, and a series of mergers and rationalisations of major employers such as the Irish Sugar Company, and others have been factors which militated against high employment. Quite a number of well-established companies were closed down, e.g., Irish Shipping, Ford's factory in Cork, and others. The impact of all these changes resulted in serious disruption in the occupational careers of many Irish workers and a steady increase in the numbers failing to get work. By the time of the current survey (1988-89) the numbers out of work (on the live register) was approaching 300,000, or 17% of the workforce. All this had happened despite strong economic indicators such as **inflation, interest rates, gross national production** and **credit balance of payments**. The correlation between positive economic indicators and job-creation ceased to be convincing. Some would even go so far as to say that one of the functions of high unemployment was its impact on keeping down inflation and the cost of employment. A former British Chancellor of the Exchequer publicly admitted as much in the House of Commons in the recent past!

The welcome increase in the number of women back into the labour force was not met with a proportionate increase in the job-market. What should have been an occasion of greater economic activity became a function of greater unemployment. Many young women entered the workforce to join with the young men on the dole queue! Part of the reaction to the scarcity of jobs was a new emphasis on education and training as a route to scarce employment. There was an explosion in the proportion of the age cohort waiting on at school and college (see Table 128). The competition for jobs increased and kept apace of the increased education and training of youth. This process has continued during the 1990s. The current rate of unemployment in the Republic of Ireland is only slightly lower than in 1989.

PART II: WORK, UNEMPLOYMENT AND POVERTY

Ireland has been a member of the European Union since 1973. The E.U. became part of the solution as well as being a source of the problem through its creation of the open labour and goods market. In the context of this growing crisis in jobs with the resultant effects on family and personal incomes (see Table 137, p. 320 above), the following scale was composed and used to elicit the views and opinions of a representative sample of the people of the Republic of Ireland. Table 153 below give the sample's response to a series of different opinion statements.

This table is not presented as a prejudice scale in the strict sense. Because of the diversity of topics, it is used as a set of items/statements which measure public opinions on a number of issues seen to be related to the current challenge of unequal distribution of incomes (see Table 137 above) and the respondents' perception of respective roles of the State, the Trade Unions, the Private Sector and the poor themselves. (The selection of ten items from a broader range of sixteen in the questionnaire was influenced by repetition and unrelated issues).

TABLE No. 153
WORK, UNEMPLOYMENT AND POVERTY SCALE

Statement/Item	Agree %	Don't Know %	Disagree %	N.
1. There are plenty of jobs in this country for those who are prepared to work.	37.5	8.9	53.6	998
2. It would be better for the country if the State owned and controlled more businesses and companies.	29.3	17.5	53.2	999
3. The poor person is generally responsible for his/her state of poverty	11.8	11.0	77.3	994
4. Trade Unions have too much power in this country	43.0	20.5	36.5	997
5. The private sector of Irish industry has failed to deliver jobs	63.5	19.5	17.1	996
6. Management is more to blame than workers for high unemployment	52.7	24.8	22.4	994
7. The Government should see to it that differences between higher and lower incomes are greatly reduced	83.2	7.9	8.8	997
8. Only the tough and the resolute get on in this country	56.1	16.7	27.2	998
9. Trade Unions should advise their members on how they should vote in General Elections in the light of workers' interests	24.1	10.4	65.5	997
10. Trade Unions are essential for the protection of workers' welfare and rights.	77.1	13.6	9.3	998

2.1 The Earned Reputation Theory:

In societies which are dominated by free-market, private-property and open-competition ideologies, there are many who hold the view that people deserve what they get and what they lose. In other words, those who fail to make it really do not try and must take responsibility for their poor state. This view often underpins and "justifies" inequalities in income distribution, in education and in unequal access to social and cultural services. A corollary of the justification of the poor being responsible for their poverty is the belief in the entitlement of the wealthy and those with privileges to their relative advantage. This view can be summed up in the *"Earned Reputation Theory"*.

Items nos. 1, 3, 7 and 8 measure elements of this view. The belief or myth of there being plenty of jobs available if people were prepared to work is often proffered as an explanation of unemployment. "They just don't want to work" is the most common expression of this view. How true is the content of this view? The 1972-73 survey proved, in the opinion of the present author, that when jobs were available people were only too anxious to work. At that time unemployment was between two and three percent of the workforce in Dublin, which may be the maximum level of the so-called unemployables – many of whom became unemployable through the influence

TABLE No. 154
WORK, UNEMPLOYMENT AND POVERTY BY PERSONAL VARIABLES

VARIABLE	1. Plenty of Jobs %	2. More State-owned companies %	3. The poor responsible for their poverty %	4. Trade Unions have too much power in Ireland. %	5. Private sector failed %	6. Management is more to blame for unemployment %	7. The government should see to it that differences between higher and lower incomes are greatly reduced %	8. Only the tough and resolute get on in this country. %	9. Trade Unions should give political advice to members %	10. Trade Unions essential for workers' rights %
TOTAL SAMPLE	37.5	29.3	11.8	43.0	63.5	52.7	83.2	56.1	24.1	77.1
A. Age	N/S	$P \leq .05$	N/S	$P \leq .001$	N/S	$P \leq .05$	N/S	$P \leq .05$	N/S	$P \leq .05$
1. 35 years or less		30.3		37.8*		50.0		50.4*		75.3
2. 36 to 50 years		24.4*		38.7		48.9*		57.8		79.7
3. 51 to 65 years		31.3		51.8		63.2		62.0		81.8*
4. 66 years plus		31.3		53.1		53.8		60.4		70.1*
B. Gender	$P \leq .05$ N/S		N/S	$P \leq .05$	$P \leq .001$	N/S	$P \leq .001$	N/S	$P \leq .05$	$P \leq .05$
1. Females		34.1		40.7*	65.6		84.3		24.4	76.4*
2. Males		23.7*		45.8	61.0*		82.0		23.7*	77.9
C. Marital Status	N/S	N/S	N/S	N/S	N/S	$P \leq .05$	N/S	N/S	N/S	$P \leq .05$
1. Never Married						49.1*				72.8
2. Married						55.3				80.1
3. Widowed						43.5				71.4*

TABLE No. 154—Continued

WORK, UNEMPLOYMENT AND POVERTY BY PERSONAL VARIABLES

	1	2	3	4	5	6	7	8	9	10
D. County Of Residence *(sig.)*	N/S	P≤.05	N/S	P≤.05	N/S	P≤.001	N/S	P≤.05	N/S	N/S
1. Dublin		25.5*		39.9		45.1*		61.5		
2. Rest of Leinster		28.2		33.3*		48.4		55.3		
3. Munster		29.6		37.5		59.3		49.2*		
4. Connaught/Ulster		36.6		48.5		60.0		60.8		
E. Education *(sig.)*	P≤.05	P≤.001	P≤.001	P≤.05	P≤.001	P≤.001	P≤.001	P≤.001	P≤.05	N/S
1. Primary Only	39.1	42.5	17.4	48.9	72.0	65.3	89.3	67.5	25.4	
2. Incomp. Second	39.9	33.3	12.4	44.0	66.0	58.6	84.5	57.8	24.4	
3. Comp. Second	36.2	16.8	7.4	37.1	56.7	42.0	83.5	44.6*	19.5*	
4. Third Level	30.2*	13.7*	6.5*	38.8*	51.1*	30.4*	67.4*	48.2*	28.1	
F. Occupational *(sig.)*	N/S	P≤.001	N/S	P≤.05	P≤.001	P≤.001	P≤.001	N/S	P≤.05	N/S
1. Professional/Executive		11.3*		44.7	53.5*	38.4*	71.7*		23.9	
2. Inspector/Supervisor		22.3		47.0	61.7	49.3	83.6		19.4*	
3. Skilled/Routine N-Man		31.3		39.4	67.0	58.1	87.4		23.1	
4. Semi/Unskilled		49.4		37.8*	69.9	62.8	88.5		26.9	
G. Social Class Position *(sig.)*	P≤.05	P≤.001	N/S	N/S	P≤.001	P≤.001	P≤.001	P≤.05	P≤.001	N/S
1. Class I	23.5*	2.9*			47.1*	23.5*	58.8*	44.1*	20.6	
2. Class II	39.0	13.3			53.3	38.4	72.1	47.6	29.5	
3. Class III	39.3	17.8			59.3	45.4	81.8	54.6	18.6*	
4. Class IV	40.1	31.5			66.9	60.7	88.8	58.3	21.7	
5. Class V	33.5	48.9			71.8	62.6	88.3	63.8	26.7	
H. Political Party Preference *(sig.)*	P≤.05	P≤.05	N/S	P≤.05	N/S	P≤.05	P≤.05	N/S	N/S	N/S
1. Fianna Fáil	42.0	34.1		43.4		56.5	87.3			
2. Fine Gael	37.8	25.5		50.2		52.6	80.0			
3. Labour Party	21.2*	31.8		30.3*		54.5	92.4			
4. Progressive Democrats	29.2	11.9*		52.4		33.3*	76.2*			

Note: Highest percentages are underlined while lowest scores have asterisks (*).

of long periods of joblessness even, at times, crossing generations. Also, we have the evidence of people being offered work at subsistence incomes and at unsociable hours. The willingness to work is there when the work is available and the pay and conditions are reasonable. Work for many is their best form of adult self-expression and self-fulfilment, not to speak of its role in enabling people to contribute to the general well being of society.

2.1.a Unemployment is voluntary? In response to the statement: "*There are plenty of jobs in this country for those who are prepared to work*", the majority (53.6%) disagreed, while a very substantial minority (37.5%) agreed. This is quite a disturbing proportion who believed that unemployment was voluntary, which is one implication of this finding. One very negative latent effect of this view is its capacity to weaken the collective effort to work for an improvement in the problem of work creation and work distribution. The latter could be brought about by statutory curtailment of double-jobbing, excessive overtime and the promotion of more job-sharing. Such statutory control would appear to be *imperative* in the current situation in many countries today.

There is some degree of consensus in relation to the view expressed. Table 154 shows no statistically significant variation for "age", "gender", "marital status", "county of residence" and "occupational status". The range of inter-subsample variation in favour of the view for "education" was relatively low. The absence of dissent and the relatively low range of variation in the "education" variable are indicators of less than liberal or tolerant attitude towards unemployment.

The pattern of differences between the "social class positions" was not regular, while the differences between the views of followers of Fianna Fáil and Fine Gael, on the one hand, and those of the Labour Party and Progressive Democrats, on the other hand, were substantial, with Labour Party supporters least likely to agree with unemployment being voluntary at 21%.

2.1.b The poor are responsible for their poverty? Item no. 3 is the second item which measures the degree to which the "earned reputation theory" applies to the sample's perception of the poor being the cause of their condition. Slightly less than one-in-eight (11.8%) agreed with the extreme view that: "*The poor person is responsible for his/her state of poverty*", while over three-quarters (77.3%) disagreed with it. The overwhelming rejection of this extreme expression of the "earned reputation theory" is encouraging for those who would like to see more active support of a more radical approach, i.e., the location and removal of the causes which are outside the victims in the inequitable distribution of wealth, jobs and facilities and the removal of such causes.

Only one personal variable recorded a statistically significant variation between subsamples on this item, namely, "education" where, ironically, the lower educated were more in favour of the statement at 17.4%, while those at the top of the education scale were least in favour at 6.5%. The consensus across the board in the case of all the other personal variables is in itself most noteworthy. This shows a degree of self-depreciation among one sixth of the poorly educated.

2.1.c State intervention for more income-equality? The next item (no. 7) which relates to the "earned reputation theory of poverty", is in line with item no. 3 just discussed above, i.e.,: *"The Government should see to it that differences between higher and lower incomes are greatly reduced"*. The overwhelming support for this view, i.e., 83.2% in agreement and only 8.8% disagreeing, confirms the view of item No. 3 in that it sees it to be necessary and effective for the State to intervene to correct the imbalance in income distribution in Ireland. This could be evidence in favour of a minimum income for the poor and some curtailment of maximum income levels among the wealthy.

There was considerable variation in five of the eight personal variables reported on Table 154. Females were slightly more in favour and less opposed to State intervention than were males. The range of variation in support for State intervention by "education" and by "social class position" exceeded 20%, i.e., in "education" 89.3% of those with primary only were in favour, as compared with 67.4% of those with Third Level (a difference of 21.9%) and in "social class position" 88.3% of the lower class were in favour while only 58.8% of the upper class would agree with State intervention (a difference of 29.5%). In the case of "occupational status" there was a difference of 16.8% between the support of those at the bottom of the scale and those at the top. In other words, those with greatest needs wanted intervention most, while those with greatest power and security favoured it least. The view of the supporters of the political parties show Labour Party and Fianna Fáil more in support than those who backed Fine Gael and the Progressive Democrats. It must be noted, however, that the vast majority of supporters of all political parties supported the need of Government intervention to redress the imbalance between "higher and lower incomes". Could the government not respond to this opinion in the population by the introduction of a more progressive tax system geared towards greater redistribution of wealth in Irish society?

2.1.d The self-made man/woman psychology: The fourth item to measure the "earned reputation theory" is support for perceived macho-individualism. The response elicited from the statement of item no. 8, i.e., *"Only the tough and the resolute get on in this country"*. Over half of the sample (56.1%) agreed with the view expressed, while 27.2% disagreed. This could be interpreted to mean a perceived lack of social solidarity in the case of "getting on" in Irish society. The response here is not necessarily in agreement with the macho-individualist sentiment, it is rather a collective comment by a representative sample of the adult population on the current state of affairs. It seems that the "psychology of the self-made man and woman" is thriving in Ireland. This is an implicit tenet of capitalist free-market ideology in line with the "Protestant Ethic" motivation of Max Weber. Item no. 3 on Table 177 (pp. 417ff below) further confirms the belief in self-reliance.

The performance of this item (no. 8) by personal variables is most interesting, having resulted in a statistically significant variation in half of the variables, i.e., "age", "county of residence", "education", and "social class position". There was consensus in the case of "gender", "marital status", "occupational status" and "political party preference". The range of difference was greatest in the case of "social class position" with lower class respondents at 63.8% and upper class at 44.1% (a variation of 19.7%) and of "Education" with those with "primary only" at 67.5% and "third level" with 48.3% (a variation of 19.3%). Three-fifths of older respondents perceived it was only "the tough and the resolute" who got on while two-fifths of younger respondents thought so. Dublin and Connaught/Ulster were the residential subsamples most in agreement with item no. 8 while Munster respondents were least in favour. In general, therefore, it is confirmed in each of the four variables registering significant variations that the more deprived subsamples tend to be more in agreement with the opinion expressed in the statement. It is further evidence of a relatively high level of *anomie* in the sample (see Chapter XIII, part III, below). The overall response to this item of opinion would seem to indicate the perception of a relatively high level of individualism in Irish society today!

2.2 State Ownership and Private Enterprise:

In a mixed economy like the Irish one, the question of the State vs Private Ownership of the means of production and the State as employer are being constantly reviewed and discussed. In the present context, questions are raised as to the relative significance of the State and Private Industry as job-providers. The proportion of those gainfully employed by the State in public service and in the semi-State industries in 1988 was in the region of 45% of those at work. This left 55% engaged in jobs provided by the "private sector".

Items nos. 2 and 5 address the question of the respective roles of the public and the private sectors in relation to the economy, job-creation and preservation. These are very general expressions of opinions and do not in any way suggest a definitive measure of public opinion. They are selective and very general.

2.2.a More State Ownership and Control of Industry? Item no. 2 addressed this question and elicited a most interesting response. It should be noted that this question was asked in a time when the opposite was happening in Britain with the massive privatisation of industry and utilities and the question of moves in a similar direction were being forced on to the agenda in Ireland.

The view that: "*It would be better for the country if the State owned and controlled more businesses and companies*" was rejected by slightly over half of the sample (53.2%) and accepted by three-in-ten (29.3%). Seven of the eight personal variables (Table 154) recorded statistically significant differences between the responses of the subsamples. The poorer or weaker subsamples, i.e., those in lower social class positions (Class V) than respondents from the upper and middle classes, expressed more confidence in State ownership and control.

The "age" variable was out of line with normal trends in that the most opposed subsample was the "lower middle-aged" sub-category (35 to 50 years old), while there was no significant differences between the pro-State support of the other three subsamples, i.e., the younger, senior middle-aged and older subsamples. Does this mean that 35 to 50 years are the strongest entrepreneurial years? Females were significantly more in favour of State ownership and control than were males. In regard to "county of residence", Connaught/Ulster were most in favour of the State while "Dubliners" were least so inclined. Does this reflect the farmers' underdeveloped state of economic development when contrasted with the industrial and business expansion of the Dublin area?

The largest ranges of differences were recorded in the case of "education" (28.8%), "occupational status" (38.1%), "social class position" (46.0%) and "political party preference" (22.2%). These ranges of difference in two cases exceed the mean sample percentage for the State intervention of 29.3%. Almost half of respondents in the "semi/unskilled occupation" (49.4%) and of the "lower social class position" (48.9%) were in favour of more State control and ownership of businesses. In contrast to the support of the socio-economically weak for State intervention, those in the strongest position were practically unanimously against such a position, i.e., only 2.9% of the Upper Class and 11.3% of the higher professionals and senior executives ("Upper Middle Class") favoured greater State ownership and control. This shows that there is an ideological as well as an income divergence between the rich and the poor. Also, this opinion attracted a relatively high "don't know" percentage (17.5%). "Education's" subsample differences went along similar lines, i.e., those most deprived educationally were most in favour (42.5%) of State intervention while those with Third Level education were least in favour (13.7%).

The views of the supporters of the political parties were also very interesting with Fianna Fáil supporters highest (34.1%) and Labour second (31.8%). Progressive Democrats were the least supportive at less than one-in-eight (11.9%). What this says about the ideologies of party supporters is noteworthy!

2.2.b Failure of Private Sector to Deliver Jobs? Dependence on the Private Sector (as opposed to the Public Sector, i.e., the State) to preserve and create jobs for the workforce has been a central plank of the economic policies and strategies of Western (capitalist) economies. In the so-called Eastern economies, dependence for job-creation was on the public sector. In generalised terms, while the Western economies failed to produce sufficient jobs for all of the workforce, they appear to have produced greater wealth for the majority of their people. While the Eastern economies may have failed to produce great wealth for the majority of their people, they appear to have delivered on-going full employment for their workforce. The public perception in the West seems to have valued wealth for the majority over jobs for all! In the previous paragraph it was seen that the majority (who represent mostly those who benefitted economically from the system of private capitalism) opposed the increase of the State's role in the ownership and control of industry and commercial business. Item no. 5, which is discussed here tests the public perception of the Private Sector to deliver on the so-called "jobs front".

When the sample was asked their opinion on the statement, "*The Private Sector of Irish Industry has failed to deliver jobs*", almost two-thirds (63.5%) thought it had failed, while one-in-six (17.1%) disagreed with the view expressed. A further 19.5% could not make up their minds. When this result is put together with the previous one, where greater State involvement is rejected by the majority, it is interesting to ask the question of where do the people see the delivery of jobs coming from at present or in the future? Both sources are deemed either ideologically unacceptable or pragmatically incapable of creating jobs for the workforce. Could this be the basis of the jobs dilemma facing Western "advanced" economies?

"Age", "marital status", "county of residence" and "political party preference", as personal variables failed to elicit statistically significant variations between their subsamples in relation to item no. 5. In other words, there was consensus within these variables.

The range of variation differed in the case of the subsamples recording statistically significant variations. Females were slightly more pessimistic about the private sector's delivery of jobs than were males. The range of variation by "education" was very substantial, with 72% of those with primary only agreeing with the view expressed in item no. 5 while those with third-level were 21% less at 51% agreeing. The position for "occupational status" was a gap of over 16%, i.e., 69.9% of those who were semi- or unskilled workers agreeing that the private sector had failed to deliver jobs, while 53.5% of the higher professionals and executives so agreed. The range of difference for "social class position" was even greater at 24.7% with those at the bottom of the scale overwhelmingly in agreement (71.8%) with the view expressed in contrast with the "upper class", with less than half the sample (47.7%) in agreement with the view expressed.

2.3 The Role of Trade Unions and Management:

At the time of this survey, Trade Unions and Employers/Managers constituted, with the Farmers, the three *social partners* of the Government in relation to the development and maintenance of the Irish economy insofar as it applied to industrial activity, social services, and general guidelines to wages and income taxation. In previous paragraphs questions relating to the State and the Private Sector in the context of job-creation were measured. In this paragraph, the opinion of the respondents are examined in relation to their perception of Trade Unions and of Management.

2.3.a Importance and Role of the Trade Unions: Items nos. 4, 9 and 10 address the standing and role of Trade Unions. Beginning with the latter item (no. 10), respondents were asked if they agreed or disagreed with the view that: *"Trade Unions are essential for the protection of workers' welfare and rights"*. The response of the whole sample to this opinion was overwhelmingly in favour (77.1%) and less than one-in-ten were against (9.3%). The very high appreciation of Trade Unions reflects the relatively high proportion of the workforce who are unionised, i.e., 55% in 1995. This confirms the relatively high ranking of "Trade Unionists" on the Bogardus Social Distance Scale with a mean social distance score of 2.002 on a 1 to 7 scale. Nine-in-every-ten (89.3%) would welcome Trade Unionists as Co-Workers or closer, while almost two-thirds of respondents (63.7%) would welcome Trade Unionists as members of their families.

Such positive appreciation of the role of Trade Unions in Ireland does not necessarily reflect the public perception of their role in society, as will be seen below when examining the response to item no. 4. Returning to no. 10, only three personal variables recorded significant variation, i.e., "age", "gender", and "marital status" while the other five variables, i.e., "county of residence", "education", "occupational status", "social class position" and "political party preference" all recorded consensus between the subsamples. With regard to "age", the senior middle-aged (51 to 65 years) were most appreciative of the positive role of Trade Unions at 81.8% while the older age group (66 and older) were least appreciative at 70.1%. Males were slightly more favourably disposed to Trade Unions than were females. Married respondents were significantly more appreciative of the role of Trade Unions than were either those "Never Married" or "Widowed".

Item no. 4 is critical of the perceived excessive power of Trade Unions. A plurality of the sample (43.0%) agreed that *"Trade Unions have too much power in this country"*, while over one-third of the sample (36.5%) disagreed with the view expressed here. One-fifth of the respondents neither agreed nor disagreed with the statement. This idea of excessive Trade Union power was very prevalent in the conservative British media and also referred to occasionally in the Irish print and electronic media, especially in times of protracted industrial strikes and subsequent factory closures, where organised workers were blamed or scapegoated for the collapse of the businesses. Only two personal variables registered consensus or no significant variation in relation to item no. 4, i.e., "marital status" and "social class position".

Older respondents were more critical of Trade Union power than were younger ones and females were less critical than males. Connaught/Ulster respondents were the residential subsample with the highest level of agreement (48.5%) and those living in "the rest of Leinster" were least in agreement (33.3%). There was a counter trend between "education" and "occupation" i.e., a *negative correlation* between the level of education and the degree of criticism, while in occupational status there was a *positive correlation* between the status of the occupation and the level of agreement with the statement assigning excessive powers to the Trade Unions. In other words, the occupationally strong were most critical of Trade Union power while those at the bottom of the occupational ladder were more appreciative of such power. The negative correlation in the case of levels of education probably reflects the growing strength of Trade Union membership among the more highly educated workers in the services.

The responses of the political subsamples were interesting. Progressive Democrats and Fine Gael supporters were most critical of Trade Union power scoring 52.4% and 50.2% respectively in agreement with item no. 4. The Labour Party were the least critical (30.3% in agreement) while Fianna Fáil supporters scored the sample average at 43.4%.

The third item (no. 9) dealt with the role of Trade Unions in relation to their advising members how to vote at General Elections. The sample strongly rejected the view that: "*Trade Unions should advise their members on how they should vote in General Elections in the light of workers' interests*". Two-thirds of respondents (65.5%) disagreed with this view while one-quarter (24.1%) agreed. The political affiliation of some of the major Irish Trade Unions with the Labour Party and the qualification "in the light of workers' interests" notwithstanding, the heavy rejection of this item is a significant expression in favour of Trade Union detachment from national party political contests and elections.

The performance of the personal variables shows consensus, i.e., the absence of statistically significant variation, in the case of four variables, namely, "age", "marital status", "county of residence" and "political party preferences". Cross-party consensus was quite unexpected. The variations in the case of "gender" were more in the disagreement and "don't know" percentages than in those of agreement. The "education" subsample with most support for political intervention during General Elections was the third level subsample while those with complete second level were least supportive. In "occupational status" subsamples, semi-/unskilled were most supportive while the inspector/supervisor subsample agreed least with the view. The "social class position" variations showed Class II ("Upper Middle Class") as those most agreeing with item no. 9 with Class III (Middle Middle Class") least in agreement. The results reflect, among other things, the multi-party affiliations of unionised workers in Ireland. This must raise questions for Trade Union leaderships when they make public suggestions with regard to voting in General Elections and Referenda!

2.3.b Management Versus Workers and Unemployment: At various times workers are blamed for high unemployment, either due to work practices or wage demands not conducive to competitiveness. At other times management are blamed for the loss of jobs due to lack of planning or failure to adapt structures and business practices to current requirements. Item no. 6 provokes the respondent to agree or disagree with the view that: *"Management is more to blame than workers for high unemployment"*. The majority of the sample (52.7%) agree with this opinion while less than one-quarter (22.4%) disagree. The exceptionally high level of "Don't Knows", i.e., one-quarter of the sample (24.8%), points to the ambiguity and possible ambivalence in the minds of many in relation to which party to blame most. Nevertheless, it indicates that the public perception of management in relation to unemployment needs much improvement! Just as item no. 4 expressed unease with Trade Unions, item no. 6 does likewise for management. The extent to which there is an element of scapegoating in both cases is not established.

There was a very dynamic response to this item in all personal variables except "gender" where chi-square was greater than .05 and, thereby not statistically significant. Variations by "age" did not follow the normal chronological pattern. A similar result was recorded in relation to "marital status" where married respondents were most critical of management while the widowed were least critical. The inter-subsample variation by "county of residence" found Dubliners least critical (45.1% in agreement) and "Connaught/Ulster" respondents most critical (60.0% agreeing).

The pattern for the "education" variable in relation to the blaming of management more than the workers for unemployment, showed those with least education were most (65.3%) in agreement. In the case of "age" the youngest subsample were least (30.4%) critical of management. The volatility of the opinions is to be found in the high variety in a number of personal variables including, especially, "education" and "age".

The variations for "occupational status" and "social class position" were predictable in that those with managerial roles or aspirations were less inclined to blame management for unemployment more than they would blame workers. The range of difference between the semi/unskilled at 62.8% and the high professionals and executives at 38.4% was 24.4% while the difference between Class V ("Lower Class") at 62.6% and Class I ("Upper Class") at 23.5% was as high as 39.1%.

The responses of the "political party preferences" show Fianna Fáil (56.5%), Labour Party (54.5%) and Fine Gael (52.6%) all relatively in agreement, while the Progressive Democrats were much more on the side of management at 33.3%.

The public perception of management as contributing more to unemployment than the workers may be due in part to the restructuring of jobs via modernisation, rationalisation and a greater degree of automation, on the one hand, or to a perception of poor management failing to maintain production and jobs. That management is not being viewed positively in promoting and preserving jobs merits further research and analysis. It clearly undermines a concept of co-operative worker-management relations.

2.3.c Conclusion: The roles of Trade Unions and Management, as perceived by the sample, are mixed. On the one hand, Trade Unions are seen as a necessary guarantor of worker's welfare and rights. On the other, they are seen to have too much power and should not advise workers on their political choices in General Elections. Management are seen to be more to blame for unemployment than are workers by a majority.

PART III: SOCIAL MOBILITY IN IRELAND

1. SOCIAL CLASS POSITION SCALE

Social Class Position is calculated on the basis of educational standard reached and occupational status according to the Hollingshead criteria which was used to stratify the Dublin Sample of the 1972-73 survey. Education was classified into seven categories and multiplied by a factor of four. Similarly, occupational status was divided into seven ordinal categories and multiplied by a factor of seven. The whole sample fell in the forty nine cells on figure no. 28 below.

Figure 29: Social Class Position Matrix (Hollingshead)

EDUCATION ⟶ OCCUPATION ↓	1 Post-Grad. (4)	2 Grad. (8)	3 Incomplete U/Grad. (12)	4 Complete Second (16)	5 Incomplete Second (20)	6 Complete Primary (24)	7 Incomplete Primary (28)
1. High Professional etc. (7)	I II	I 15	II 19	II 23	II 27	II 31	III 35
2. Executive, etc. (14)	II 18	II 22	II 26	II 30	III 34	III 38	III 42
3. High Inspect. etc. (21)	II 25	II 29	III 33	III 37	III 41	III 45	IV 49
4. Supervisory, etc. (28)	III 32	III 36	III 40	III 44	IV 48	IV 52	IV 56
5. Skilled-Manual Routine Non-Manual (35)	III 39	III 43	III 47	IV 51	IV 55	IV 59	IV 63
6. Semi-skilled Manual (42)	III 46	IV 50	IV 54	IV 58	IV 62	V 66	V 70
7. Unskilled Manual (49)	IV 53	IV 57	IV 61	V 65	V 69	V 73	V 77

Figure No. 28: Social Class Position Matrix (Hollingshead)

The scores in each of the cells indicate the sum of the weighted *scores of education* and *occupational status*. Hollingshead argued that in modern society, which had moved from an ascribed social status to an achieved social status, (Hollingshead, 1949; Hollingshead and Redlick, 1958) social class was best measured by a cumulative education and occupational status.

Hollingshead divided the cumulative scores of the forty nine combinations into five classes.

Class	Points Range	Popular Designations
Class I	11 - 17 points	"Upper Class"
Class II	18 - 31 points	"Upper Middle Class"
Class III	32 - 47 points	"Middle-Middle Class"
Class IV	48 - 63 points	"Working Class"*
Class V	64 - 77 points	"Lower Class"

*"Working Class" = "Lower Middle/Upper Lower Class"

2. SOCIAL CLASS DISTRIBUTION OF SAMPLE

Using the Hollingshead criteria Table 155 gives the "Class' distribution of the Total Sample (1988-89), the Dublin subsample (1988-89) and the Dublin Sample (1972-73).

TABLE No. 155
SOCIAL CLASS POSITION DISTRIBUTION 1988-89 AND 1972-73

Social Class Position	Total Sample 1988-89	Dublin Subsample 1988-89	Dublin Sample 1972-73	Change %
1. Class I ("Upper Class")	3.8%	6.9%	3.1%	+3.8%
Class 11. ("Upper Middle Class")	11.8%	15.0%	11.0%	+4.00%
3. Class 111 ("Middle-Middle Class")	30.2%	33.2%	19.1%	+14.1%
4. Class IV ("Working Class")*	33.0%	27.5%	45.8%	-18.3%
5. Class V ("Lower Class")	21.2%	17.4%	21.1%	-3.7%
Number	893	247	2.264	–
Mean Social Class Position	3.560	3.335	3.711	-0.376

*"Working Class"= "Lower Middle/Upper Middle Class"

There has been a substantial upward mobility in the Dublin adult population since 1972-73. The main move has been from the "Working Class" ("Lower Middle and Upper Lower Class") (Class IV) to the "Middle Middle Class". The "Lower Class" (Class V) dropped a relatively small percentage, i.e., down 3.7% since 1972-73. Figure No. 30 highlights the process of class homogenisation at work as predicted in the 1977 publication (see Mac Gréil, 1977, pp. 192-206). The mean social class position has improved by more than one third of a stage or class. This is quite significant.

Figure No. 30: Social Class Position of Dublin Adults in 1972-73 and 1988-89

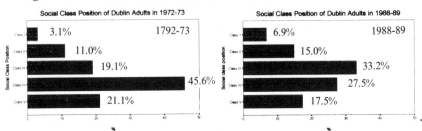

The decline of the "Working Class" i.e., Class IV and V, in Dublin between 1972-73 and 1988-89 is due to two main developments. Firstly there has been a very substantial and significant drop in the proportion of the workforce in "blue-collar" and manual work. The following distribution of the Dublin Sample 1972-73 and the Dublin subsample in 1988-89 shows decline in skilled and routine non-manual work as a proportion.

TABLE No. 156
DECLINE OF "WORKING-CLASS JOBS"

Occupational Grade	Dublin Sample 1972-73	Dublin Subsample 1988-89	Change
1. High Professional/Executive	16.8%	21.0%	+4.2%
2. Inspectional/Supervisory	23.3%	37.8%	+I 5 .5%
3. Skilled/Routine Non-Manual	36.6%	27.9%	-8.7%
4. Semi/Unskilled Manual	23.3%	13.4%	-9.9%
Number	2,270	262	

When this change in the nature of the jobs in the workforce is added to the very substantial increase in the standard of education of the young adults today compared with those of the early 1970s we can detect a double force at work in Dublin society (as in most Western societies) towards upward social mobility and the class *homogenisation* predicted by John Goldthorpe in 1967 (pp. 648-51). The traditional "class" structure of a *pyramid* with more than half of the population in the lower class position is changing to a *diamond-shaped* structure with the vast majority in the middle class category. What is likely to dampen upward mobility is a counter move through unemployment and brain drain in the rest of Ireland, especially in the West and North-West.

Figure No. 31: Social Class Position of Total Sample (1988-89)

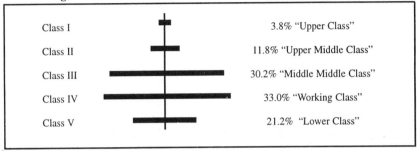

Class I	3.8% "Upper Class"
Class II	11.8% "Upper Middle Class"
Class III	30.2% "Middle Middle Class"
Class IV	33.0% "Working Class"
Class V	21.2% "Lower Class"

As was the case of the Dublin Sample in 1972-73, the 1988-89 National Sample, it could be argued, represents a transitional phase en route to the projected diamond structure. The Dublin subsample is a little further along the way toward a massive middle class. There is one anomaly emerging to challenge the homogenisation theory or thesis, namely, the failure of the "Lower Class" (Class V) to decline (−3.7%) in proportion to the very substantial increase in the "Middle Middle Class", i.e., +14.1%, in the Dublin changes over a period of sixteen years between 1972-73 and 1988-89 (see Table 155). Also the "Upper Class" proportion of the Dublin subsample more than doubled, i.e., from 3.1% in 1972-73 to 6.9% in 1988-89.

If one takes Class IV and V to more-or-less represent the "Blue Collar and Working Class"[1] then just slightly more than half the national sample (54.2%) may be categorised as "Working Class", while only 44.5% of the Dublin subsample is now so classified. The latter shows a very substantial drop since 1972-73 of 22.4%, i.e., 66.9% in 1972-73 to 44.5% in 1988-89. This in effect means a drop of one-third in the "Working Class" proportion of the adult population of Dublin City and County over a period of merely sixteen years. The "embourgeoisement" of the Dublin population is happening at a relatively accelerated pace. This has implications for many aspects of Dublin society, including political, educational, occupational, familial, economic, recreational, health care and religious areas of life. A major change in class structure affects every significant domain of life, particularly the family, where intergenerational change becomes a source of social dissonance (see, Brody, *Iniskillane* 1974).

The most dysfunctional aspect of the changes in the "*social class position*" structure is the fact that around one-fifth are still in a "lower class" status. In a previous chapter dealing with "Feminism, Sexism and Family Life" (pp. 319 f.) the household incomes (post-tax) of the sample are given. They

---

1. This included "Routine Non-Manual Workers" as well as "Manual Workers".

range from under £29.80 to £154.00 plus per person per week (at 1995 prices). It is interesting to note that the bottom 21.5% had an average post-tax weekly income of £30.60 per person per week. This indicates a comparatively low and barely subsistence income for a fifth of the population. If one takes a proportion of the population with lower status (21.2%) and with subsistence income (21.5%) as major poverty indicators, it is fair to state the Irish poverty line is slightly higher than 20% or one-fifth which involves over 700,000 of the national population.

Respondents were asked how they would place themselves on the social class ladder. It is interesting to note that they exaggerated their ratings in both directions. Fewer saw themselves as "Upper" or "Upper Middle Class" at the top of the ladder or as "Lower Class" at the bottom.

TABLE No. 157
SELF-RATED SOCIAL CLASS POSITION OF TOTAL SAMPLE

Question: "How would you rate yourself on the following Social Class Scale?"

Social Class Scale	Self-Rated	Calculated from Education and Occupation	Difference
Class I "Upper Class"	0.7%	3.8%	-3.1%
Class II "Upper Middle Class"	3.9%	11.8%	-7.9%
Class III "Middle Class"	49.5%	30.3%	+19.2%
Class IV "Working Class"	42.1%	33.1%	+9.0%
Class V "Lower Class"	3.8%	21.1%	-17.3%
Mean	3.442	3.56	+0.12

Table 157 shows the difference between the distribution of the sample by their own perceived class status and the actual distribution according to the Hollingshead criteria of "*occupational status*" and "*education*". The most striking difference between the two distributions is the underrating at the top and at the bottom of the scale. The mean rating difference is slightly higher up the scale at 3.44 for the subjective self-rating than the case of the objective rating distribution at 3.56. One interpretation from Table 157 is the aspirational popularity of "Middle Class" and "Working Class". In the Bogardus Social Distance Scale (see page 65 above) the "Working Class" was rated the second most popular category (next to "Roman Catholics") out of fifty nine categories, with 86.8% welcoming working class people into their families through marriage. It was the only category on the Bogardus scale with nobody "denying citizenship" to its members. In other words, Working Class status is very highly respected in Ireland.

If one were to combine Class IV and V (45.9%) to constitute the "Working Class" then the proportion perceiving themselves as "working class" is 8.5% lower than the percentage (54.4%) so classified by the Hollingshead scale (Table 155).

Figure 32: Self-Related Social Class Position

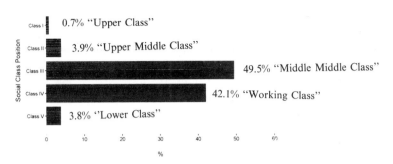

3. SOCIAL CLASS MOBILITY

While it is possible to detect some indication of social class mobility from the upward trend in occupational and education status from an analysis of the changes in the Dublin Social Class structure between 1972-73 and 1988-89, it is not in itself an adequate measure of social class mobility in the population. The method used to calculate social class mobility is the difference experienced between the generations in relation to social class positions. The criteria used here are the occupational and educational status of the respondent and that of his or her father. The very high proportion of mothers whose occupation was household duties has not made it possible to use their occupational status as a point of reference. Perhaps, in the future it will be imperative to calculate the occupational status of both parents.

3.1 Occupational Status:

The following Table 158 gives the distribution of occupational status of respondents, their parents and spouses. In the case of mothers and wives, the occupations before or after marriage were asked for. Respondents recorded occupations for only 56.5% of their mothers either before or after marriage. In the case of spouses there is a higher proportion of wives with occupations (before or after marriage) than was the case of the mothers, i.e., over 80%. This reflects the intergenerational changes in extra-domestic occupations of women.

While the above figure of intergenerational occupational status change shows a substantial gender disparity in both generations there has been a drop of 0.127 in the disparity status score, i.e., from 0.927 for parents to 0.800 for spouses. Respondents' mothers and fathers were on average significantly more different in relation to occupational status than was the case between wives and husbands among respondents themselves. The gender disparity within the total sample takes into account those who "never married" and are also likely to be younger than the married and widowed respondents (whose spouses occupation are examined above).

TABLE No. 158
OCCUPATIONAL STATUS OF RESPONDENTS, THEIR PARENT AND THEIR SPOUSES

Occupational Status	Self	Fathers A	Mothers B	Difference (A-B)	Husbands C	Wives D	Difference (C-D)
1. Unskilled, etc.	17.5%	18.7%	36.9%	- 18.2%	12.2%	23.5%	- 11.3%
2. Semiskilled, etc.	13.3%	6.4%	22.3%	-15.9%	9.1%	26.1%	-17.0%
3. Skilled/Routine Non- Manual	17.8%	28.6%	11.0%	+17.6%	31.2%	11.8%	+19.4%
4. Supervisory, etc.	10.8%	14.1%	6.6%	+7.5%	11.4%	11.4%	0.0%
5. Inspectional, etc.	22.8%	15.5%	14.7%	+0.8%	14.7%	20.2%	-5.5%
6. Executive, etc.	9.7%	8.4%	6.2%	+2.2%	9.9%	5.1%	+4.8%
7. High Professional, etc.	8.1%	8.4%	2.3%	+6.1%	11.2%	1.8%	+9.4%
N.	893	938	564	–	394	272	–
Scale Status Score (1-7)	3.696	3.604	2.677	+0.927	3.809	3.009	0.800

TABLE No. 159
OCCUPATIONAL STATUS BY GENDER

Occupational Status	Self	Males A	Females B	Difference (A-B)
1. Unskilled, etc.	17.5%	12.7%	22.1%	–9.4%
2. Semiskilled, etc.	13.3%	8.8%	17.7%	–8.9%
3. Skilled/Routine Non-Manual etc.	17.8%	26.8%	9.1%	+17.7%
4. Supervisory, etc.	10.8%	10.0%	11.5%	–1.5%
5. Inspectional, etc.	22.8%	18.6%	27.0%	–8.4%
6. Executive, etc.	9.7%	10.7%	8.8%	+1.9%
7. High Professional, etc.	8.1%	12.5%	3.8%	+8.7%
N.	893	441	452	
Scale Status Score (1-7)	**3.696**	**3.948**	**3.451**	+0.497

It is very interesting to note that the occupational status score variation between males and females in the sample (Table 159) is slightly more than half (53.7%) of what it was between respondents' fathers and mothers. This, at least, is evidence of progress, although the disparity is still quite substantial at 0.497 or half a class stage. Females are over-represented in subsamples nos. 1, 2, 4 and 5. Males outnumber females in subsamples nos. 3, 6 and 7. The difference in subsamples nos. 4 and 6 are barely significant. Females are very much under-represented in the "higher professional" and in the "skilled manual/routine non-manual" categories and over-represented in the "unskilled", "semi-skilled" and "inspectional" categories.

3.2 Educational Mobility:

Since "education" and "occupational status" are the two basic criteria used in this study to measure one's position on the Hollingshead Scale (see Figure no. 29, p. 368), it is necessary, at this stage, to present the findings in relation to the educational standard and mobility of the sample.[2]

3.2.a Age Left School: The first indicator used in the survey to measure the educational standards of the people was "age-left-school", i.e., the age when they ended their formal education. Table 160 gives a breakdown of "age-left-school" of the total sample together with corresponding proportions from the 1986 census of population of people over 15 years of age.

TABLE No. 160
AGE LEFT SCHOOL (1988-89 NATIONAL SAMPLE AND
1986 CENSUS OF POPULATION)

AGE LEFT SCHOOL	National Sample (1988-89)	National Census (1986)
Under 15 years	28%	29%
15 years	11%	13%
16 years	16%	18%
17 years	20%	13%
18 years	15%	15%
19 years	2%	3%
20 years	2%	2%
21 years plus	5%	7%
Number	N = 986	N = 2,160,596
Estimated Mean Age	X= 16.23 years	X= 16.52 years

The National Census distribution and that of the National Sample are within the statistical margin of error of each other. They both show that the average age-left-school for the adult Irish population (Republic of Ireland) is around sixteen and a half years of age. Table 161 gives a breakdown of the changes in age-left-school of the Dublin adults since the 1972-73 survey.

TABLE No. 161
CHANGES IN AGE-LEFT-SCHOOL IN DUBLIN BETWEEN 1972/7 AND 1988/89

AGE LEFT SCHOOL	Dublin Sub-Sample 1988/9	Dublin Sample 1972/3	Percentage Difference
1. Under 15 years	24.4%	40.4%	-16.0%
2. 15 years of age	7.4%	12.2%	-4.8%
3. 16 years of age	17.7%	14.4%	+3 3%
4. 17 years of age	21.0%	11.1%	+9 9%
5. 18 years of age	18.5%	11.9%	+6.6%
6. 19 years and older	11.0%	10.0%	+1.0%
Number	N = 277	N = 2,271	

2. A full report on *Educational Participation in Ireland* (based on the findings of the late 1988-89 survey) was published by The Survey and Research Unit, Department of Social Studies, St. Patrick's College, Maynooth, in February, 1990.

The changes in "age-left-school" in Dublin between 1972-3 and 1988-9 are significant. The drop in the proportion of the population who left at the younger ages and the increases in the numbers who went on to 17 and 18 years are evidence of increased participation. The increase in the post-19 years category may be less than expected. The relatively small increase in the latter category could also reflect the *"brain drain"* from the Republic of those receiving post-graduate education.

3.2.b Standard Reached: The second and most meaningful criterion by which participation has been measured was highest standard reached. Seven levels were indicated on an ordinal scale, i.e.,

Educational Participation Ordinal Scale:

1. *Incomplete Primary/National;*
2. *Complete Primary/National;*
3. *Incomplete Second Level (includes Group and Intermediate Certificates);*
4. *Complete Second Level;*
5. *Incomplete Undergraduate Third Level;*
6. *Complete Undergraduate Third Level;*
7. *Post-Graduate Level.*

This ordinal scale of standards was used in both the 1988/9 and the 1972/3 surveys. This scale is not a record of certificates or degrees. Because of the high correlation between "age-left-school" and "educational standard reached" (r = 0.75), the latter is taken as a sufficient and, probably, more meaningful indicator of educational participation. It will, therefore, be used throughout this report as the main measure. Table 162 gives the overall standard of education of the total sample.

The mean standard reached (3.302) by the sample was in the category of "Incomplete Second Level", i.e., slightly higher than Intermediate or Group Certificate Level. This would confirm the findings in Table No. 160, which stated that the estimated mean "age-left-school" was over 16 years. One adult in seven had participated in third-level education, while slightly less than two in five completed second level or went higher. These figures, it should be noted, do not include those who may have emigrated after participating in third-level studies or after completing second level education, i.e., *"brain drain"*.

3.2.c Change in Educational Participation: The measure of change in educational participation since the introduction of "free education" under the late Minister for Education, Mr. Donagh O'Malley, T.D., may be gauged when the Dublin subsample (21 years plus) is compared with the Dublin sample

(21 years plus) measured in 1972-73. None of the respondents in the latter sample were eligible to benefit from the "O'Malley scheme". Table 163 gives the details of the 1988-9 subsample and of the 1972-73 sample.

TABLE NO. 162
OVERALL STANDARD OF EDUCATION

Standard Reached	Percent		Cumulative Scores "More Than"	"Less Than"
1. Incomplete Primary	4.5%	} 28.0%	100.0%	4.5%
2. Complete Primary	23.5%		95.5%	28.0%
3. Incomplete Second Level		34.8%	72.0%	62.8%
4. Complete Second Level		23.1%	37.2%	85.9%
5. Incomplete U/Grad	4.5%		14.1%	90.4%
6. Complete U/Grad	7.8%	} 14.1%	9.6%	98.2%
7. Graduate	1.8%		18%	100.0%
Number	N= 1,000		—	—

TABLE NO. 163
STANDARDS OF EDUCATION OF DUBLIN ADULTS: 1988-89 AND 1972-73

Standard Reached	Dublin Sub-Sample 1988-9 (over 21 years)		Dublin Sample 1972-3		Percent Difference	
1. Incomplete Primary	5.1%	} 21.6%	4.8%	} 50.7%	+0.3%	} -29.1%
2. Complete Primary	16.5%		45.9%		-29.4%	
3. Incomplete Second Level	31.0%		24.7%		+6.3%	
4. Complete Second Level	29.4%		17.5%		+ 11.9%	
5. Incomplete U/Graduate	5.1%		1.5%		+3.6%	
6. Complete U/Graduate	9.4%	} 18.0%	3.6%	} 7.2%	+5.8%	} +10.8%
7. Postgraduate	3.5%		2.1%		+1.4%	
(Mean Ed. Score)*	(3.551)		(2.845)		(+0.706)	
Number	N = 256		N = 2,280			

*Score range is 1-7.

The findings in Table 163 point to a substantial improvement in the standard of participation at the second and third levels in the sixteen intervening years between 1972-3 and 1988-9. This would indicate that the greater access policy introduced in the late 1960s seems to have borne fruit. Most noteworthy may be the change in third level from 7.2% in 1972-3 to 18.0% in 1988-9, a factor of 2.5 or an increase of 150%, in the case of the proportion of the Dublin adult population with third level experience. As was the case in 1972-3, a significant proportion of the more highly educated now resident in Dublin are migrants from the other counties of the Republic. The evidence of the Clancy Report should bear out this migration of educated adults into Dublin, i.e., the discrepancy between young age cohort participation in third-level education in the rest of the country, on the one hand, and the levels of education in the resident adult population in these parts (see Clancy 1982).

3.2.d Changes in Dublin Subsample: Table 164 measures the intergenerational educational mobility of the Dublin subsample (21 years and over) in 1988/9 and that of the Dublin sample of 1972/3 to discover what change had taken place. An increase in the range of difference could be anticipated.

TABLE No. 164
INTERGENERATIONAL EDUCATIONAL MOBILITY IN DUBLIN IN 1988/89 AND IN 1972/73

Standard Reached	Respondents		Change (Fathers)		Change (Mothers)	
A. 1972-3 Dublin Sample						
1. Complete Primary	50.7%		-28.4%		-28.8%	
2. Incomplete Second Level	24.7%		+16.8%		+16.9%	
3. Complete Second Level	17.5%	} 24.7%	+7.6%	} +11.7%	+5.8%	} +11 9%
4. Third Level	7.2%		+4.1%		+6.1%	
Number	N = 2280		N = 2077	N = 2089		
B. 1988-9 Dublin Sample						
1. Complete Primary	21.6%		-41.9%		-39.1%	
2. Incomplete Second Level	31.0%		+17.9%		+11.2%	
3. Complete Second Level	29.3%	} 47.3%	+15.0%	} +24.0%	+15.3%	} +27 9%
4. Third Level	18.0%		+9.0%		+12.6%	
Number	N = 255		N = 244		N = 242	

| C. Mean Education Scores (1-4) | | | | | Variations From Parents | |
	Respondent		Fathers	Mothers	Fathers	Mothers
1. 1988/9 National Sample	2.33		1.38	1.38	+0.95	+0.95
2. 1988/9 Dublin Sub-Sample	2.44		1.68	1.64	+0.76	+0.80
3. 1972/3 Dublin Sample	1.81		1.37	1.35	+0.44	+0.46

Allowing for the very general categories and the arbitrariness of the scoring, the findings of Table 164 indicate that the intergenerational gap has widened substantially since 1972/73. The extent of the intergenerational gap in the National Sample is the equivalent of almost one level of education, i.e., 0.95 on the 4 point ordinal scale. It is interesting to note that the parents of those resident in Dublin (1988/9) reached a substantially higher level average than that of the National Sample or that of the 1972/3 Dublin sample. This would also have been true had Dublin residents' parents' standards of 1972/3 been compared with those of the whole country at the time. The parents of the National Sample in 1988/9 have more or less the same scores as had the parents of the 1972/3 sample. Half of the parents of Dublin respondents in 1972/3 were reared outside Dublin. A similar pattern has emerged in the case of the high proportion of the parents of Dublin respondents having been reared outside Dublin. It should be noted that half of the Dublin sample (1972-73) were reared outside Dublin and one-third of the respondents were themselves reared in the provinces.

3.2.e Intergenerational Gap by Gender: The following table examines the differences in the standard of education between female respondents and their mothers, and between male respondents and their fathers.

TABLE NO. 165
STANDARD OF EDUCATION OF RESPONDENTS AND THEIR PARENTS
BY GENDER

STANDARD REACHED	MALE RESPONDENTS			FEMALE RESPONDENTS		
	Self	Father	Change*	Self	Mother	Change*
1. Primary Only	31.1%	77.8%	-46.7%	25.6%	70.3%	-44.7%
2. Incomplete Second Level	35.9%	9.1%	+26.8%	33.8%	15.2%	+18.6%
3. Complete Second Level	16.2%	7.7%	+8.5%	29.0%	10.4%	+18.6%
4. Third Level	16.8%	5.4%	+11.4%	11.6%	4.0%	+7.6%
Educational Mean	(2.18)	(1.40)	(+0.78)	(2.27)	(1.50)	(+0.77)
Number	N = 457	N = 428		N = 544	N = 519	

*Change in overall distribution of subsamples.

The mean educational scores have gone up by the same amount in the case of males and of females. The intergenerational gap between male respondents and their fathers has been significantly greater at the "incomplete second level" and at the "third level" than it was for females and their mothers. Female respondents, however, made considerably more advance at the "complete second level" than did male respondents.

TABLE No. 166

VERTICAL INTERGENERATIONAL SOCIAL MOBILITY BY GENDER AND COUNTY OF RESIDENCE

	Total Downward	Downward Mobility Classes*			No Mobility Retain Fathers** Position	Upward Mobility Classes*				Upward	Total Movement	Net N
	%	-3 %	-2 %	-1 %	%	+1 %	+2 %	+3 %	+4 %	%	%	
TOTAL SAMPLE	23.2	0.5%	3.6	19.1	39.5	26.0	8.8	2.1	0.4	37.3	+14.1%	797
A. Gender												
1. Females	27.8	0.7	5.9	21.3	33.3	28.6	9.8	0.5	0.0	38.9	+11.1	409
2. Males	18.3	0.3	1.3	16.8	46.1	23.2	7.7	3.9	0.8	35.6	+17.3	388
B. County of Residence												
1. Dublin	22.8	0.8	3.0	18.1	37.6	24.9	11.4	3.4	0.0	39.6	+16.8	237
2. Rest of Leinster	20.6	0.5	2.0	18.1	42.7	27.1	6.5	2.0	1.0	36.7	+16.1	199
3. Munster	22.9	0.0	4.8	18.2	39.0	26.0	10.4	1.3	0.4	38.1	+15.2	231
4. Connaught/Ulster	28.5	0.8	3.8	23.8	39.2	26.2	4.6	1.5	0.0	32.3	+3.8	130

* Classes refer to the Hollingsheed Five Class Scale (see Page ???)

** The Father's Social Class Position was used as a reference point for measuring the intergenerational change because of the very low proportion of mothers who remained in the workforce after marriage.

3.3 Social Class Mobility:

In the case of *social class mobility* the impact of education is added to that of occupational status to determine the level of movement between the generations. The above Table 166 measures the vertical mobility experienced by the sample. The measure of mobility experienced by the Dublin Sample in 1972-73 is added for purposes of comparison.

TABLE No. 167
COMPARATIVE VERTICAL MOBILITY 1972-73 AND 1988-89

INTERGENERATIONAL MOBILITY	1988-89 National Sample	Dublin Samples		Change
		1972-73	1988-89	
1. Upward Mobility	37%	33%	40%	+7%
2. Retained Father's Position	40%	49%	38%	-11%
3. Downward Mobility	23%	18%	23%	+5%
Net Mobility	Upward 14%	Upward 15%	Upward 17%	——

The findings of Table 166 reflect most of all the advances in education over the past thirty years and the proportionate decline in manual ("blue collar") occupations. This is seen clearly in the change in the Dublin sub-sample (Table 167) where there was an increase in the proportion experiencing upward mobility from 33% in 1972-73 to 40% in 1988-89. The drop of 11% in the proportion retaining their father's status was very substantial. These changes were somewhat neutralised by the increase of 5% (from 18% to 23%) who recorded downward mobility. Overall the net upward improvement was only 1% higher than it was in 1972-73.

When one examines the finding of Table 166 by "**county of residence**" the level of social mobility in Dublin is much greater than that in Connaught/Ulster. The net increase in Dublin is almost four-and-a-half times as great as it was in Connaught/Ulster, i.e., 16.8% as compared with 3.8%. Vertical mobility rates (net upward move) in Munster and the rest of Leinster work out very close to the Dublin score. The percentage retaining the father's class was highest in the case of "rest of Leinster". This once again points to the substantial extent of *brain drain* from Connaught/Ulster because the educated are leaving the area.

The net upward vertical class mobility for "males" was significantly higher for males than for females. The pattern of movement both ways for males and females was very noteworthy and different. Males have a very high percentage maintaining the father's social class (46.1%), contrasted with 33.3% for females. The proportions experiencing upward and downward mobility were much greater among females than among males. Females were the subsample with the lowest proportion retaining the previous generation's status, i.e., 33.3%. Such a low percentage retaining parents social class position is a relatively new phenomen in social mobility research.

While the advance in educational participation has been a major contributor to vertical upward social mobility, the "white-collarisation" of work resulting from the growth of service jobs, as manifested in Table 156 ("*The Decline of 'Working-Class' Jobs*") on page 370 above, is another factor affecting social class vertical mobility. The biggest area of expansion is in the "Inspectional" and "Supervisory" grades. This marks a relatively new phenomenon in social class mobility, i.e., the crossing of the Blue-White collar line. In the 1972-73 evidence most mobility was up-and-down within each of the broad categories of "middle class" and "working class". In the 1988-89 evidence there is a significant exodus from the "working class" into the "middle class". Whether this is just part of the process of *class homogenisation* or a temporary adjustment because of the process of "white-collarisation", it may be too soon to say.

All these factors could well lead to a new post-industrial social class position classification. The addition of a third criterion, i.e., "**area and length of residence**" within or close to the city has already been added to education and occupational status as determinants of one's social class position. This criterion is fraught with difficulties and students of social stratification, including Hollingshead, have tried to address it. Most large cities have their clearly delineated segregated housing along social class position lines. The urban, suburban and exurban "ghettoes of the rich and powerful" are well known to real estate agencies and housing developers. Another criterion of one's social class position is "**one's recreational life-style**", including everything from health food to family size to media tastes to philanthropic altruism, etc. (see Johnson, H., 1961, pp. 474-5). In this research, it has not been possible to measure these further criteria.

While the above findings (Tables 166 and 167) show a relatively high degree of upward, static and downward social mobility, it should be noted that it contains a pointer to a very extensive source of frustration as well as satisfaction. Most of those who experienced downward or static mobility would normally have expected moves in the opposite direction. This includes the majority (at least 70%) of the sixty-two percent who did not achieve upward social mobility (Mac Gréil 1977, pp. 200 ff.). This seems to be the inevitable consequence of any *laissez-faire* social-class-position mobility system that seems to operate in Ireland and in most open free-market capitalist societies. This is an enormous built-in source of frustration-instigated aggression emanating from the social structure. The capacity of Irish society at present is to satisfy less than forty percent of its people's upward mobility aspirations! There is no such thing as universal upward mobility. "Open" is not infrequently confused with "universal". The dream of a "classless" society is very far removed from Ireland at the end of the twentieth century according to the above findings as it ever has been in the past!

4. SOCIAL CLASS POSITION BY PERSONAL VARIABLES

Apart from the problems of social class mobility, it is very useful to look at the variations in social class position by personal variables (excluding education and occupational status which are components of the five-class scale). *Occupational status* is not to be identified with *employment status*.

4.1 Social Class By Age:

It is quite clear from the findings of Table 168 that older respondents are of lower social class position than are younger members. This is due in large measure to educational opportunities. The older subsample is substantially under-represented in Class II ("Upper Middle Class") and over-represented in Class V ("Lower Class"). This might well have social and psychological consequences for the older citizens of Irish society. In terms of range of difference between the subsamples, the most substantial variation is between those under fifty years of age and those over it. The differences of mean class scores between subsamples one and two and between three and four are relatively speaking insignificant.

4.2 Gender:

Females are, on average, rated lower in the social class position scale than are males. Unlike "age", the gender variation is due rather to "occupational status" than to "education". The pattern of gender variation is very revealing. Females are substantially under-represented in Class I ("Upper Class") and in Class IV ("Working Class") while they are significantly over-represented in Class III ("Middle Class") and in Class V ("Lower Class"). In the case of Class II ("Upper Middle Class") there is only a 1.4% difference between the genders.

4.3 Marital Status:

The "marital status" variations reflect a combination of the "age" and "gender" variables. Married respondents scored very close to the national (total sample) average. The relatively high class position of the "never married" is probably due to their proportionately high participation in fulltime careers as well as their (average) higher level of education. This, of course, is countered by those in the pre-career stage (including students). The "widowed" represented those with lowest social class position and were substantially under-represented in Class I, Class II and Class IV. They were very substantially over-represented in Class V ("Lower Class").

TABLE NO. 168
SOCIAL CLASS POSITION BY PERSONAL VARIABLES

Personal Variables	Social Class Position					Mean
	I %	II %	III %	IV %	V %	Score
TOTAL SAMPLE	3.8	11.8	30.2	33.0	21.2	3.560
A. AGE P≤.001						
1. 35 years or less	3.4	11.7	33.0	37.5	14.3	3.476
2. 36 to 50 years	4.0	18.2	26.9	30 4	20 6	3.455
3. 51 to 65 years	4.1	5.2	32.0	29 7	29 1	3 744
4. 66 years or older	3.5	7.8	27.0	30.4	31.3	3.783
(Range)						(0.307)
B. GENDER P≤.001						
1. Female	1.5	11.1	34.7	26.1	26.5	3.650
2. Male	6.1	12.5	25.7	40.2	15.5	3.464
(Range)						(0.186)
C. MARITAL STATUS P≤.01						
1. Never Married	5.2	12.7	29.9	36.7	15.5	3.446
2. Married	3.5	12. 1	30.2	31.9	22.4	3.575
3. Widowed	2.2	2.2	37.0	19.6	39.1	3 913
(Range)						(0.467)
D. COUNTY OF RESIDENCE P≤ .01						
1. Dublin	6.9	14.1	33.2	28.6	17.2	3.351
2. Rest of Leinster	3.1	10.6	29.2	34.5	22.6	3.628
3. Munster	2.6	12.5	32.5	33.2	19.2	3.540
4. Connaught/Ulster	1.4	7 9	22 3	38.8	29.5	3.871
(Range)						(0.520)
E. PLACE OF REARING P≤.01						
1. Large City	5.0	13.2	30.1	35.2	16.4	3.448
2. Small City	4 8	21 0	20.0	35 2	19 0	3.429
3. Town	2.9	15.8	36.0	28.8	16 5	3.403
4. Rural	3.3	7.5	30.9	33.0	25.3	3.696
(Range)						(0.267)
F. POL. PARTY PREFERENCE P≤.05						
1. Fianna Fáil	4.3	8.9	28.2	35.4	23.2	3.641
2. Fine Gael	4.1	14.9	36.9	28.8	15.3	3.365
3. Labour Party	5.0	10.0	20.0	36.7	28.3	3.733
4. Progressive Democrats		21.1	31.6	36.8	10.5	3.368
(Range)						(0.365)

4.4 County of Residence:

This was the variable to record the highest range of variation in class mean score, i.e., 0.520 which means more than half a class stage. Dublin is very clearly the most privileged subsample while Connaught/Ulster is the most deprived. The range of imbalance in the case of Class I is a factor of five against Connaught/Ulster. In Class II it is a factor of two against the North West. There is a corresponding over-representation of Connaught/Ulster in Class V. "Rest of Leinster" and "Munster" are very close to the national average. If these figures are representative of the overall socio-economic position of the Irish population, then it is possible to see Ireland developing at three levels geographically, i.e., Dublin as the over-privileged location, Rest of Leinster and Munster with a moderate development profile and Connaught/Ulster as under-privileged. This finding seriously questions the equity of the decision of the Irish Government to have all of Ireland classified as one region in the case for development assistance under the Structural and Cohesion Funds from the European Union. Some might see the current gross class imbalance as due in part to the preferential application of resources to the benefit of the stronger regions of Ireland. All indicators in these findings would seem to indicate a further deterioration of the regional imbalance within the Republic of Ireland! These findings clearly point to substantial social-class-position inequality in the Republic of Ireland along regional and provincial lines. This result seems to be a far remove from the ideals of equality initially aspired for an independent Ireland during the early years of the 20th Century!

4.5 Place of Rearing:

What is most notable about the difference between "place of rearing" and "county of residence" is the range of variation of the former which is just half that of the latter. Those from "town" backgrounds were those with highest status. Respondents reared in "large cities" had a lower social status than those living in Dublin, while respondents reared in rural backgrounds had a higher social class position than those living in Connaught/Ulster. All this is an indication of internal *brain drain* to the cities and/or away from the rural areas.

4.6 Political Party Preference:

The supporters of the Progressive Democrats and Fine Gael have the highest (mean) social class position while Labour Party supporters have the lowest mean score. Followers of Fianna Fáil are much closer to Labour Party followers in terms of social class position than they are to either Fine Gael or Progressive Democrat followers. In terms of "middle" and "working" class support, the distribution by party goes as follows:

POLITICAL PARTY	Upper and Middle Class (Classes I, II and III)	Working Class (Classes IV and V)
1. Fianna Fáil	41.4%	58.6%
2. Fine Gael	55.9%	44.1%
3. Labour Party	35.0%	65.0%
4. Progressive Democrats	52.7%	47.3%
(National Sample)	(45.8%)	(54.2%)

4.7 Conclusion:

The above examination of social class position by personal variables is a necessary insight into the profile of Irish society as it is evolving and has developed since independence in the 1920s. The structural division along stratified socio-economic lines is leading to quite serious regional and other divisions. It seems (as noted in 4.4 above), that the Republic of Ireland has not so far achieved the ideal of equality espoused in *Forógra 1916 (The 1916 Declaration of Independence)* which vowed to treat all citizens equally! Membership of the E.U. has not corrected the imbalance so far.

5. SATISFACTION WITH MATERIAL STANDARD OF LIVING

It is generally accepted that people tend to exaggerate their declared satisfaction with their current standard of living. The sample were asked: "*How about your material standard of living? Would you say that your (family's) income at present is very satisfactory, fairly satisfactory, not very satisfactory, poor or very poor?*" The following table (169a) gives the responses of the sample to the question.

TABLE No. 169a
SATISFACTION LEVEL OF MATERIAL STANDARD OF LIVING

Level of Satisfaction	Percentages	
1. Very Poor	2%	
2. Poor	5%	} 27%
3. Not Very Satisfactory	20%	
4. Fairly Satisfactory	62%	} 73%
5. Very Satisfactory	11%	
Number	1,001	

The above findings show a relatively satisfied national sample, despite the fact that more than half of the respondents had a weekly take-home income of less than 36.50 in 1988-89 values, or 43.00 at 1995 values. This would seem to confirm the view of respondents' tendency to exaggerate their declared satisfaction with their standard of living. A possible reason for this is the reluctance of people to admit failure as would be implied by declaring dissatisfaction.

The following question is likely to elicit a more realistic response, since it is seen to move by commentary on sources outside the self, i.e., the poor performance of the state or the economic systems. Table 169b gives a breakdown of the responses to this question: *"With regard to the years ahead, do you expect the standard of living of the average person in this country to improve or disimprove over the next five years"?*

TABLE No. 169b
EXPECTED CHANGE IN STANDARD OF LIVING OVER FUTURE FIVE YEARS

Level of Improvement Expected	Percentage		Anomie (1-200)	Alienation (1-200)
1. Disimprove Greatly	2.9%	} 21%	126.1	131.0
2. Disimprove Somewhat	18.1%		125.8	122.4
3. Neither Improve nor Disimprove	19.6%		104.2	112.4
4. Improve Somewhat	53.2%	} 59.5%	95.7*	109.0*
5. Improve Greatly	6.3%		96.8	113.6
Number	1,002		Range = 30.4	Range = 22.0

Note: Highest scores are underlined and lowest scores have asterisks (*).

The above finding reports that the level of relative optimism in the National Sample is around 60% (59.5%) while pessimism is at a little more than one-fifth (21%). A further fifth see no change in their standard of living.

When this variable is correlated with "Anomie" and "Alienation" (as measured by the scales on pages 416 and 418 below) it is clear that optimism in regard to improvements of standard of living is negatively correlated with both scale scores. This is as hypothesised because of the strong element of pessimism and despondency in both "anomie" and "alienation". When the findings of Table 169b were correlated with social class position, the result was surprising in that it failed to elicit a statistically significant variation.

CHAPTER XIII

General Measures of Prejudice and Tolerance

INTRODUCTION

In the course of this chapter the general level of tolerance in the population is measured and variations in such tolerance are examined and, as far as the data work, explained. The main scales used are the following:

    (a)   The New Authoritarian Scale;
    (b)   The Liberal-Illiberal Scale; and
    (c)   The Social Anomie and Alienation Scales.

The first two scales are replicated from the 1972-73 survey and the range of difference between the Dublin subsample (1988-89) and the 1972-73 sample will indicate certain changes in prejudice and tolerance over the intervening sixteen years. The trends in the 1972-73 findings pointed towards an increase in tolerance and in "liberalness". It has been anticipated that there would be such an increase in tolerance and "liberalness". The Social Anomie Scale, i.e., measuring normlessness, and the Alienation Scale, i.e., measuring powerlessness, were only included in the 1988-89 survey and were omitted from the 1972-73 questionnaire.

1. THE NEW AUTHORITARIAN SCALE

1.1 Overall Findings

This scale was first used in the 1972-73 survey and was based on an adaptation of the more elaborate scales devised by Adorno *et al* (1950). As an indication of prejudice, it was very impressive in the previous study (see Mac Gréil 1977, pp.503 ff.). The four subscales within the New Authoritarian Scale represent four related aspects of authoritarianism, namely, "*Religious Fundamentalism*", "*Pro-Establishment Conservatism*", "*Fascist-type Submission and Aggression*", and "*Moralism and other Issues*". As in all scales measuring social attitudes, the cumulation scale and subscale p-scores are seen as the real indicators of authoritarianism. Individual item responses are useful indicators of *views* held in the population in relation to particular issues of contemporary relevance.

Table 170 gives responses from both the 1988-89 and the 1972-73 surveys and records the changes which have taken place over the period between the surveys. The scale and sub-scale variations have been significant, but not very substantial. In the total scale, the p-score dropped by only 11.6 points from 102.6 in 1972-73. Still, it means that the overall level of authoritarianism in the Dublin subsample is roughly 11% less than it was in 1972-73, that is, when measured by the "**New Authoritarian Scale**".

The subscale variations are also interesting, i.e.

(a)	Religious Fundamentalism	−4.9 or − 4.5% of 1972-73 scores.
(b)	Pro-Establishment Conservatism	−26.0 or −21.3% of 1972-73 scores.
(c)	Fascist-Type Submission	−12.9 or −19.4% of 1972-73 scores.
(d)	Moralistic etc.	−14.9 or −14.1% of 1972-73 scores.

The subscales with the greatest level of change has been the "*Pro-Establishment*" and the "*Fascist-type*" subscales with drops of approximately 20% of the scores recorded in 1972-73. In other words, Dublin residents are substantially less conservative and less fascist in their attitudes than they were sixteen years earlier. Of course the drop in "Pro-Establishment" could mean a higher degree of disillusion with political and other national and local leaders. It could also mean a growing political cynicism. The changes in "*Religious Fundamentalism*" (overall) are not that significant at -4.5% while "*Moralism*" has experienced a fairly substantial reduction at -14.1% over the sixteen years. There is no evidence in these findings of a rise of the so-called religious rightist attitudes. If anything, there has been a reduction in that area. It must be remembered that these findings refer to the Dublin subsample which are the appropriate scores for comparison with the 1972-73 findings.

1.2 Individual Items:

Before analysing the influence of personal variables on the scale and subscale p-scores, it is proposed to look at the response to each of the individual items as **statements of opinion** held in the population. Table 171 gives a breakdown of the responses to each item by the personal variables of "age", "gender", "marital status", "county of residence", "place of rearing", "education", "occupational status", "social class position", and "political party preference".

1.2.a Fatalism: Item no. 1 measures fatalism which expresses the view that: "*Everything that happens must be accepted as the Will of God*". More than half of the sample (52.6%) agreed with this view, while more than one-third (35.1%) disagreed. Responses by variables (except gender) showed significance in the case of "age", "marital status", "county of residence", "place of rearing", "education", "occupation", "social class position " and "political party preference". Respondents who were older, widowed, from Connaught/Ulster, rural-reared, lowly educated, with lowest skills, lower class and support Fianna Fáil, were most in agreement. As in the case of every item on the scale, the proportion who "don't know" is

TABLE No. 170
NEW A-SCALE
(A=1988-89 Total Sample; B=1972-73 Dublin Sample; C=1988-89 Dublin Subsample)

		Agree %	Don't Know %	Disagree %	A-Scale (1-200)	N
A. Religious Fundamentalism and Dogmatism						
1. Everything that happens must be accepted as the Will of God.	A	52.6	12.3	35.1	117.5	1003
	B	58.8	1.6	39.7	119.0	2289
	C	39.1	13.0	47.8	93.3	276
Variance (C-B)	D	-19.7	+11.4	+8.1	-25.7	
2. The miracles in the Bible happened just as they are described there.	A	60.0	21.2	18.7	141.3	1003
	B	57.1	9.3	33.7	123.5	2289
	C	47.5	22.1	30.4	118.4	276
Variance (C-B)	D	-9.6	+12.8	-3.3	-5.1	
3. Men whose doctrines are false should not be allowed to preach in this country.	A	48.2	17.9	33.9	114.3	997
	B	43.8	4.9	51.3	92.5	289
	C	41.7	18.1	40.2	101.6	276
Variance (C-B)	D	-2.1	+13.2		+9.1	
4. A thing is either right or wrong and none of this ambiguous woolly thinking.	A	51.9	16.9	31.3	120.6	996
	B	48.4	2.2	49.4	99.0	277
	C	38.8	21.6	39.6	101.2	276
Variance (C-B)	D	-9.6	+19.4	-9.8	+2.2	
Fundamentalist Subscale Score B	A	–	–	–	123.4	–
	B	–	–	–	108.5	–
	C	–	–	–	103.6	–
Variance (C-B)	D	–	–	–	-4.9	–
B. Pro-Establishment Disposition and Conservatism						
5. Our system of government is good because it is traditional.	A	43.9	17.8	38.3	105.6	1005
	B	44.0	4.8	51.2	93.0	2277
	C	42.5	14.2	43.3	102.0	275
Variance (C-B)	D	-I 5	+9.4	-7.9	+9.0	
6. It keeps things peaceful here.	A	67.5	12.5	20.0	147.6	998
	B	78.3	2.5	19.2	159.0	2278
	C	61.5	13.8	24.7	138.6	275
Variance (C-B)	D	-16.8	+11.3	+5.5	-20.4	
7. Its goals are usually good ones.	A	56.2	17.7	26.1	130.0	999
	B	71.3	4.1	24.6	147.0	2278
	C	55.3	17.5	27.3	129.5	275
Variance (C-B)	D	-16.0	+14.4	+2.7	-17.5	
8. It is in the hands of people who are good leaders.	A	44.0	18.4	37.6	106.4	998
	B	57.5	7.6	35.0	122.5	2277
	C	36.7	21.1	42.2	96.5	275
Variance (C-B)	D	-20.8	+13.5	+7.2	-26.0	
Pro-Establishment Score	A	–	–	–	122.4	
	B	–	–	–	130.5	
	C	–	–	–	116.7	
Variance (C-B)	D	–	–	–	-13.8	

Tᴀʙʟᴇ Nᴏ. 170—Continued

C. Fascist-type Submission and Aggression.						
9. There should be a very strict control of RTE.	A	40.0	17.9	42.1	97.9	998
	B	28.8	3.5	67.7	61.5	2282
	C	38.2	17.1	44.7	95.7	275
Variance (C-B)	D	+9.4	+13.6	-23.0	+34.2	
10. Gardaí should be armed always.	A	29.6	12.5	57.9	71.7	1000
	B	31.9	1.0	66.2	66.0	2279
	C	24.4	9.5	66.2	55.1	275
Variance (C-B)	D	-7.5	+8.5	0.0	-10.9	
11. Punks and Skinheads should be locked up.	A	13.3	9.4	77.2	36.1	997
	B	39.2	6.6	54.2	85.0	2276
	C	7.7	9.1	83.2	24.9	274
Variance (C-B)	D	-31.5	+2.5	+29.0	-60.1	
12. Student protest should be outlawed.	A	21.1	15.3	63.6	57.5	992
	B	25.2	3.3	71.4	54.0	2276
	C	11.7	14.7	73.6	38.5	273
Variance (C-B)	D	-13.5	+11.4	+2.2	-15.5	
Fascist Subscale Score	A	–	–	–	65.8	
	B	–	–	–	66.5	
	C	–	–	–	53.6	
Variance (C-B)	D	–	–	–	12.9	
D. Miscellaneous Authoritarian (Moralistic).						
13. Communism should be outlawed in Ireland.	A	52.5	15.0	32.5	120.0	1000
	B	53.6	4.4	42.0	111.5	2280
	C	41.8	13.8	44 4	100.4	273
Variance (C-B)	D	-11.8	+9.4	+2.4	-11.1	
14. The more active you are in politics, the harder it is to be a good Christian.	A	31.2	18.4	50.4	80.9	999
	B	45.2	10.8	44.0	101.0	2288
	C	25.0	19.9	55.1	71.4	275
Variance (C-B)	D	-20.0	+9.1	+ 11.1	-29.6	
15. Homosexual behaviour between consenting adults should be a crime.	A	35.1	20.9	43.9	91.2	999
	B	39.9	14.9	45.2	94.5	2277
	C	28.0	15.3	56.7	70.1	
Variance (C-B)	D	-11.9	+0.4	+11.5	-24.4	
16. Prostitution should be a prosecutable crime.	A	63.9	14.7	21.5	142.4	996
	B	51.7	10.2	38.1	113.5	2271
	C	53.5	14.5	32.0	118.9	274 1
Variance (C-B)	D	+1.8	+4.3	-5.9	+5.4	
Moralistic Subscale Score	A	–	–	–	108.6	
	B	–	–	–	105.0	
	C	–	–	–	90.2	
Variance (C-B)	D	–	–	–	-14.8	
TOTAL A-SCALE	A	–	–	–	105.1	
	B	–	–	–	102.6	
	C	–	–	–	91.0	
Variance (C-B)	D	–	–	–	-11.6	

Cronbach Alpha = 0.78

much higher than it was in the 1972-73 survey. There was a significant and substantial reduction in support of the "fatalist" view in the 1988-89 survey of Dublin when compared with the 1972-73 findings.

1.2.b Literalism: Item no. 2 measures agreement with the literal acceptance of the Bible, i.e., *"The miracles in the Bible happened just as they are described there"*. Three-fifths agreed while approximately one-fifth (21.2%) "didn't know" and a further fifth (18.6%) disagreed. All variables registered significant variation. The trend by variable mirrored that of "fatalism" (Item no. 1). Women were more in agreement with the "literalist" view than were men. The variation between the scores of 1972-73 and of 1988-89 were barely significant due to the high proportion of "Don't Know" replies.

1.2.c Intolerance of False Doctrines: There was a plurality of the sample in agreement with the opinion that *"Men whose doctrines are false should not be allowed to preach in this country"*, i.e. 48.2% in favour and 33.9% against. When one takes the disagreement percentage into account, the intolerance of false doctrines has increased since 1972-73. The response disagreeing decreased by 11.3% in the case of the Dublin sample. All variables except "gender" recorded significant variations. Trends in the subsample differences for prohibition of preachers of false doctrines followed the normal prejudice pattern in the case of age, marital status, education, occupation and class. Fianna Fáil and Fine Gael supporters showed the top score with the majority of 53% and 52% in favour of the view while P.D. supporters were least censorious. "County of residence" and "place of rearing" recorded town-reared and those outside Leinster most in favour of banning preachers of false doctrine. There was no significant variation between the views of males and females. There was a slight increase in intolerance of false doctrines since 1972-73.

1.2.d Black and White Thinking: One of the characteristics of authoritarianism is intolerance of cognitive ambiguity (Krech *et al* p. 46). Item no. 4 measures such intolerance in the state and: *"A thing is either right or wrong and none of this ambiguous woolly thinking"*. Slightly more than half of the sample (51.9%) agreed with this view, while a little less than one-third (31.3%) disagreed with it. There was a very big increase in the proportion of Dubliners (a factor of ten) who gave "don't know" as their reply, i.e., from 2.2% in 1972-73 to 21.6% in 1988-89. Apart from gender, all the other personal variables recorded significant variations between their sub-samples along the "normal prejudice trends". In the case of political party supporters the patterns are similar to those in the case of "false doctrines". The increase of 2.2 in the item score is not statistically significant but the fact that a significant decrease was not recorded is not an optimistic indicator to those looking for greater tolerance of cognitive ambiguity, which is a precondition of pluralist coexistence of groups with diverse outlooks with regard to what is right and what is wrong.

1.2.e Traditional Quality of Government: The next four items on the scale measure the level of "pro-establishment conservatism", which according to Adorno *et al* correlated with authoritarian traits. The statements used here are replicated from the 1968 survey of Northern Ireland attitudes (Rose, 1972, p. 493) and from the 1972-73 survey of Greater Dublin (Mac Gréil 1977). As was the case in the 1972-73 survey, this factor is the weakest indicator of overall authoritarianism. It is necessary to distinguish between "tolerant" patriotism and authoritarianism.

The support for the view that *"our system of Government is good because it is traditional"* of 43.9% was a plurality of the sample with 38.3% against the view. All personal variables recorded statistical significance between their subsamples. The trends are in line with most score differences. Fianna Fáil supporters are substantially more supportive (58% in favour) of the traditional system of government than is the case for supporters of all the other parties. This may be partially explained by the fact that Fianna Fáil was in government at the time. Changes since 1972-73 show a rise in support for the view or, more accurately, a decline in the percentage disagreeing with the view.

1.2.f Protector of peace in Ireland: Slightly more than two-thirds of the sample agree that the Irish system of government *"keeps things peaceful here"* while one-fifth disagree. This is a significant vote of confidence in the system operating under the Irish Constitution (*Bunreacht na hÉireann*) and could spell trouble for those wishing to change our system of government. At the same time, there has been a significant drop of support in the Dublin respondents of 16.8% for the view and a small percentage increase (5.7%) in those not agreeing with the view expressed in item no. 6. All variables had significant variation. Older, male, widowed, rural, lower educated and those with occupations with lowest status, were most in agreement. Fianna Fáil supporters and those at the bottom and at the top of the social class position scale were most in support of the peaceful role of the government system. The latter consensus between Class I and Class V is a unique finding.

1.2.g Government's Good Goals: Item no. 7 asked respondents if they agreed that the government's *"Goals were usually good ones"*. Over half of the sample (56.2%) agreed while a little more than a quarter of respondents (26.1%) disagreed. While this level of agreement shows a substantial drop (–16%) since 1972-73, it is, nevertheless, still a majority in support of our government's goals. The decline in support could show a growing sense of alienation among a significant proportion of the population. The "age" variable shows younger subsamples less in favour of the government's goals than were the older respondents. "Education", "occupational status" and "social class position" did not record any significant variation. Fianna Fáil respondents were most in favour of the government's goals (70%) which may again be due to the fact of that party being in Government at the time.

TABLE No. 171

RESPONSES TO THE NEW AUTHORITARIAN SCALE BY PERSONAL VARIABLES (% IN AGREEMENT)

	Fundamentalism				Pro-Establishment				Fascist-Type				Moralistic-Type			
	1	2	3	4	5	6	7	8	9	10	11	12	13	14	15	16
Total Sample	53	60	48	52	44	68	56	44	40	30	13	21	52	31	35	63
A. AGE	P≤.001	P≤.001	P≤.001	P≤.001	P≤.001	P≤.001	P≤.001	P≤.001	P≤.001	P≤.05	P≤.001	P≤.001	P≤.001	P≤.001	P≤.001	P≤.001
1. 35 years or less	41*	51*	38*	42*	35*	53*	48*	35*	28*	31	5*	13*	41*	22*	24*	60
2. 36 to 50 years	45	57	44	46	40	68	57	39	37	23*	9	16	47	33	32	56*
3. 51 to 65 years	67	70	58	63	50	86	61	55	51	30	17	28	66	44	46	71
4. 66 years +	79	77	70	75	69	83	69	63	62	38	38	43	76	36	58	81
B. GENDER	N/S	P≤.05	N/S	N/S	P≤.05	P≤.001	P≤.05	N/S	P≤.001	P≤.05	N/S	P≤.05	P≤.001	P≤.001	N/S	P≤.05
1. Female		64			43	64*	55*		42	33		22	56	26*		66
2. Male		55*			36*	72	58		37*	26*		19*	48*	37		62*
C. MARITAL STATUS	P≤.001	P≤.05	P≤.05	P≤.001	P≤.05	P≤.05	N/S	N/S	P≤.001	N/S	N/S	P≤.05	P≤.001	P≤.001	P≤.05	N/S
1. Never Married	49*	53*	42*	45*	39*	62*			30*			18*	44*	26*	31*	
2. Married	52	62	50	54	45	70			44			22	54	33	35	
3. Widowed	80	75	61	67	60	74			49			29	71	41	49	
D. COUNTY OF RESIDENCE	P≤.001	P≤.001	P≤.001	P≤.001	P≤.05	P≤.04	P≤.05	P≤.001	P≤.05	P≤.001	P≤.05	P≤.001	P≤.001	P≤.05	P≤.001	P≤.001
1. Dublin	39*	48*	42*	39*	43	62*	55	37*	38*	24*	8*	12*	42*	25*	28*	54*
2. Rest of Leinster	50	62	48	50	42*	66	51*	45	42	27	13	26	53	28	38	64
3. Munster	60	66	53	58	43	70	57	42	41	33	16	26	56	37	36	69
4. Connaught/Ulster	65	66	51	65	51	77	64	58	65	37	19	21	62	35	42	72
E. PLACE OF RESIDENCE	P≤.001	P≤.001	P≤.001	P≤.001	P≤.05	P≤.05	P≤.05	P≤.001	N/S	P≤.05	P≤.001	P≤.001	P≤.001	N/S	P≤.001	P≤.001
1. Large City	40*	47*	39*	39*	42*	60*	54	35		24	8	13	42		26*	55
2. Small City	49	60	41	36	31	61*	42*	33*		23*	7*	12*	31*		26*	51*
3. Town	55	66	57	55	45	72	62	43		28	8	19	56		31	65
4. Rural	60	66	53	61	47	72	58	51		34	19	28	61		43	71

TABLE No. 171—Continued

RESPONSES TO THE NEW AUTHORITARIAN SCALE BY PERSONAL VARIABLES (% IN AGREEMENT)

	Fundamentalism				Pro-Establishment				Fascist-Type					Moralistic-Type		
	1	2	3	4	5	6	7	8	9	10	11	12	13	14	15	16
Total Sample	53	60	48	52	44	68	56	44	40	30	13	21	52	31	35	63
F. EDUCATION	P≤.001	P≤.001	P≤.001	P≤.001	P≤.001	P≤.001	N/S	P≤.001	P≤.001	P≤.001	P≤.001	P≤.001	P≤.001	P≤.001	P≤.001	P≤.001
1. Primary Only	73	77	69	68	59	84		58	52	38	27	35	75	40	50	75
2. Incomplete Second	55	64	49	57	45	67		44	41	33	11	24	54	31	35	65
3. Complete Second	38	50	38	41	35	52*		34	28*	25	6	10	42	24*	26	61
4. Third Level	29*	33*	23*	27*	25*	61		33*	33	13*	5*	4*	20*	28	22*	45*
G. OCCUPATIONAL STATUS	P≤.001	P≤.001	P≤.001	P≤.001	P≤.001	P≤.05	N/S	N/S	P≤.001	P≤.001	P≤.001	P≤.001	P≤.001	P≤.05	P≤.05	P≤.05
1. Profess/Exec	40*	47*	34*	40*	33*	65			34*	15*	6*	6*	31*	29*	31	59
2. Inspec/Superv.	47	54	43	46	42	62*			36	26	11	20	50	31	29*	56*
3. Skilled/Routine	50	62	52	54	44	68			44	30	14	23	55	35	35	65
4. Semi/Unskilled	72	74	61	66	57	75			47	42	22	29	67	31	41	72
H. SOCIAL CLASS POSITION	P≤.001	P≤.001	P≤.001	P≤.001	P≤.001	P≤.05	N/S	N/S	P≤.001	P≤.001	P≤.001	P≤.001	P≤.001	P≤.05	P≤.001	P≤.05
1. Class I	29*	30*	18*	15*	29*	74			38	9*	0*	0*	15*	15*	27*	44*
2. Class II	35	41	32	37	29*	56*			29*	16	6	6	31	33	27*	56
3. Class III	46	56	40	47	40	60			35	25	9	17	46	28	29	58
4. Class IV	53	63	51	54	46	68			44	30	15	24	56	36	34	66
5. Class V	69	73	65	65	56	77			47	39	23	29	69	34	45	71
I. POLITICAL PARTY PREFERENCE	P≤.001	P≤.001	P≤.001	P≤.001	P≤.001	P≤.001	P≤.001	P≤.001	P≤.001	N/S	N/S	N/S	P≤.001	N/S	P≤.05	P≤.05
1. Fianna Fáil	60	66	53	56	58	79	70	68	48				55		35	68
2. Fine Gael	53	61	52	56	41	68	54	30	36				60		39	67
3. Labour Party	39	50	39	35	27*	64	48	24	35				39		41	53
4. PDs	26*	33*	22*	21*	31*	60	41	12	21*				26*		14*	52*
5. Workers Party	46	50	42	46	25	58	33*	8*								

Note: Highest scores are underlined; Lowest scores have asterisks (*).

1.2.h Dependence on Leaders: Belief in the strong leader has often been interpreted as a trait of the authoritarian personality and a surrender of shared power among the people and their communities. At the same time, it could be agreed that a positive response to item no. 8, i.e., "*It (the government) is in the hands of people who are good leaders*", is an appraisal of the qualities of the leaders of today. The plurality (44%) of the total sample agreed with the statement with 37.6% against the view. The position of the Dublin sample (1988-89) reversed the national response with a plurality against. There was a very substantial drop in support for "good leaders" since 1972-3, i.e., −21%. Four of the nine variables ("gender", "marital status", "occupational status" and "social class position") did not have statistically significant variations. The variations were along normal patterns.

1.2.i Censorship: The sample was split almost evenly on the view that "*there should be a very strict control of R.T.É*", i.e., 40.0% in agreement and 42.1% disagreeing. When compared with the findings of the 1972-73, the Dublin subsample was more in favour of "very strict control" of the national radio and television service. This increase in the pro-censorship view may reflect a growing sense of distrust of R.T.É. All personal variables except "place of rearing" recorded a statistically significant variation. The normal pattern of variation between subsamples occurred in the case of "age", "marital status", "county of residence" and "occupational status". Females were more in favour of censorship than were males. Other variables were irregular in their differences.

1.2.j Arming the Gardaí: Item no. 10 addresses a question which, at times, has been controversial in the Irish media. The rejection of support for the view that "*Gardaí (Police) should be armed always*" was impressive with a two-to-one vote against it, i.e. 29.6% for and 57.9% against. The context of the time of the survey was one of paramilitary violence in Northern Ireland and a growth in armed robberies in the State.

The Republic of Ireland's police (the Gardaí) have been unarmed since the foundation of the State. The success of the unarmed police policy is manifest in the relatively low rate of homicide in Ireland and the rarity of Garda being murdered in the exercise of their duty – some thirty Gardaí have been killed since the foundation of the State. All this should be evaluated in the context of the presence of paramilitary activity in the country at various periods during that time.

It could be argued that violence committed by the criminal is much less serious than a corresponding level of violence on behalf of the upholder of law and order. The criminal's violence is already negatively viewed or sanctioned because of its association with criminal behaviour. When the agents of the State are seen to resort to violence and carry lethal weapons in the course of their normal duties they implicitly make such behaviour and demeanour more socially acceptable. The very opposite is likely to be the effect on the public of an unarmed police and, it could be argued, that Ireland's relatively low homicide rate and very low police mortality rate bear out both the effective and pedagogical influence of non-armed police. This argument can be extended to the case of capital punishment and excessively penal prison sentencing and prison regimes.

The variations were statistically significant for all variables except "marital status" and "political party preference" of respondents. The normal variation patterns were recorded in the case of "age", "county of residence", "place of rearing", "education", "occupational status" and" social class position". The range of difference in the case of education was very substantial, and this was again reflected in the case of social class position. There was substantially less support for arming the Garda in 1988-89 in Dublin than was the case in 1972-73.

1.2.k The Locking up of Punks and Skinheads: Item no. 11 shows a drastic drop in hostility towards those perceived as "skinheads" or "punks". Because of the fact that fads and fashions change and yesterday's "way out" radically appearing group can become fashionable over time, it is not given the same significance as other views on this scale. It has been included for purposes of scale replication. This is not to deny that this category is not still viewed as an outgroup by some people. The addition of "punk" to the item, i.e. "*Punks and Skinheads should be locked up*", was an attempt to add a contemporary category perceived to be viewed negatively in the population. "Punks" would be the successors to the "skinheads" of the 1970s as representing those whose demeanour would arouse a hostile reaction in the late 1980s. The retention of "skinheads" was done for the purpose of replication.

Three of the nine personal variables failed to record statistically significant variations in relation to item no. 11, i.e., gender, marital status, and political party preference. All the variables with significant variations between the scores of their subsamples were in line with the normal trends. The overall result of opinions on this topic has been a relatively low level of support across the board for the "locking up" of punks or skinheads. The trend is also positive.

1.2.l Outlawing of Student Protest: Intolerance of public protest which is seen to challenge the established order is taken to be an indicator of intolerance of change or of any threat to change. Item no. 12 which measures opinions on student protest is therefore of interest. In the past, categories most associated with protest have been peasants, poor people and organised general workers. Over the years since the 1960s, students have on occasion protested in solidarity with those (at home and abroad) perceived to be deprived, or against State behaviour deemed to be seriously unacceptable. The growing phenomenon of mass third-level education in Ireland

and elsewhere in the Western world must inevitably increase the political muscle of this group of potential protestors likely to protest or revolt. The issues taken up by student groups have included human rights, anti-racialisim, anti-war and nuclear disarmament. They have become a force to be reckoned with, especially, where third-level students are allowed to develop a critical awareness of society. In the opinion of the present author recent changes in further and higher education tend to suppress somewhat the freedom to develop critical social and political awareness in the interest of a more competitive, pragmatic and examination-centred regime.

The proportion of the age cohort in full-time third-level education (entry rates) in 1994-95 was 41.9%. This ratio is expected to rise to 53% by 2010. This will mean that third-level students will represent the majority of the age cohort. The growing number of mature students entering the third-level programme will make it the natural norm to graduate from a university or college.

The growing tolerance of student protest since 1972-73 has been significant, i.e., the percentage agreeing that *"student protest should be outlawed"* has dropped from 25.2% to 11.7% in the Dublin sample while the proportion disagreeing with the statement shifted slightly from 71.4% to 73.6%. All variables except political party preference recorded significant variations and followed normal patterns, except in the case of "county of residence", where the highest intolerance was in Munster and the Rest of Leinster. Females were slightly more in favour of outlawing student protest than were their male counterparts.

1.2.m Outlawing of Communism: Item no. 13 was classified in the 1972-73 findings in the miscellaneous authoritarian factor with moralistic overtones. Over half of the 1988-89 national sample (52.6%) agreed with the view that *"Communism should be outlawed in Ireland"* while one third (32.5%) disagreed. This reflected a high degree of intolerance against Communism in the population and was probably the fruit of a combination of economic, political and religious propaganda arising from the Cold War and a fear of socialist change in Western capitalist society. It is necessary to recall that the survey of 1988-89 was completed just before the collapse of the Communist regimes of Eastern Europe. The change in the views of the Dublin sample since 1972-73 has been significant, with a plurality now against outlawing Communism i.e., 44.4% against and 41.8% for, in contrast to the majority in favour of outlawing in 1972-73, i.e., 52.6% for and 42.0% against. This shows a substantial reduction in intolerance of Communism in Ireland by 1988-89. It would be interesting to measure this view in the post-1989 era. The growth of tolerance would probably have continued and the trend accelerated somewhat.

All variables recorded significant variations for item no. 13 and the variations adhered to the normal patterns. Females were more anti-Communist than males and Fine Gael supporters were the political subsample most in favour of outlawing Communism. The patterns for "age" and "education" showed a very wide range of difference and indicate a trend towards greater tolerance of Communist ideology.

1.2.n Compatibility of Politics and Christianity: The popular association of corruption and ambivalence of political involvement is becoming less acceptable in Ireland, according to the responses to item no. 14. The majority of the sample (50.4%) disagreed with the view that: "*The more active you are in politics, the harder it is to be a good Christian*", while 31.2% agreed. The change in the opinions of the Dublin sample have been very substantial and significant, i.e., from a plurality in agreement in 1972-73 (45.2% for and 44.0% against) to a majority disagreeing in 1988-89 (55.1% against and 25% for). This level of change should encourage people to embrace politics in a more active manner and also reflects a positive view of the work of Irish politicians.

"Place of rearing" and "political party preference" were the only two variables not to elicit a statistical variation in relation to item no. 14. "Education" and "marital status" were the only variables to follow the normal pattern of variation between the subsamples. In "age" the senior middle-aged (57-65 years) were the most negative. Males thought less of politics than did females, while Munster residents had the highest level of agreement with the statement among the "county of residence" subsamples. The skilled and routine non-manual occupational status scored highest in the "occupational status" variable and this was reflected in the "social class position" scores also.

The response of the population (sample) to this item has positive implications for both politics and for Christian belief and practice. This is expressed elsewhere in the text (see Chapter VI, pp. 198ff.). Traditionally, Roman Catholics were seen to be "other-worldly" oriented (Max Weber's "other-worldly asceticism") and not that concerned about the affairs of this world. The Decree of the "*Church in the Modern World*" of Vatican II (see Vatican II 1965) has a more positive view of the world endorsing Christian involvement and the participation of Christians in political actions, e.g. "liberation theology", civil and social rights of workers, of farmers, of the unemployed, and others. In other words, the majority of the sample see Christianity as a religion capable of full engagement in political activity by believers in the pursuit of the common good. Elsewhere in the survey, 50% of the sample agreed with the view that: "*Priests, brothers and nuns should become more directly involved politically in fighting for social justice in Ireland*", while 35% disagreed.

1.2.o Decriminalisation of Homosexuality: A plurality of the sample disagreed with the view that: "*Homosexual behaviour between consenting adults should be a crime*", i.e., 43.9% against and 35.1% for. This result is very close to the responses of the Dublin sample in 1972-73, i.e., 45.2% *vs* 39.9%. Prior to the 1988-89 survey, the European Court of Human Rights ruled against the criminalisation of this behaviour in the Republic of Ireland as outlawed in the Victorian criminal legislation of the second half of the 19th century (which was in force at the time of the survey). Homosexual behaviour between consenting adults (over 17 years) has been legalised in the Republic in the early 1990s.

When the findings of the Dublin subsample are compared with those of the 1972-73 Dublin sample a very substantial and significant change of view has taken place. The proportion in favour of criminalisation has dropped from 39.9% to 28.0%, while the percentage against it has risen from 45.2% to 56.7%. While this will be seen as a big advance in tolerance, nevertheless, the minority in favour of criminalisation is, nationwide, over one-third (35.1%) and in Dublin over one-quarter (28.0%). Because of the history of cruelty and discrimination against homosexuals, who are a very vulnerable minority, open to scapegoating and maltreatment, the positive trends in the above figures do not provide a basis for complacency in the defence of the homosexual or "gay" minority. The position of "gay people" on the Bogardus Social Distance Scale has been very negative (see p. 352), probably due in part to their public association as a category more susceptible to contracting AIDS.

All variables except "gender" elicited significant variations between the scores of the subsamples. The patterns or trends in relation to item no. 15 are normal. The Labour Party supporters are the political subsample most in favour (41%) of criminalisation, with Fine Gael supporters only 2% behind them at 39%. Fianna Fáil are third with the sample average of 35% and Progressive Democrat supporters were least in favour at 14%.

1.2.p Criminalisation of Prostitution: Almost two-thirds of the sample (63.9%) agreed with the view that: *"Prostitution should be a prosecutable crime"*, while only a little more than one fifth (21.5%) disagreed with this penal statement. Item no. 16 is rare in the sense that the percentage in favour of criminalisation of prostitution marginally increased (with the 3% margin of error) when the 1988-89 Dublin subsample is compared with the 1972-73 sample. This hardening of attitudes towards prostitutes has happened at a time when the attitudes have become more permissive toward premarital sex (see Table 173, pp. 406f. below). Also there has been an increase in the availability of pornographic literature, films and video – mostly so-called "soft-porn". One would have expected a corresponding decrease in the proportion in favour of the continuation of the criminalisation of prostitution. Decriminalisation could enable the State to register those engaged in this behaviour, protect them from exploitation by violent individuals, and monitor their health and condition in relation to sexually transmittable diseases. Some interpret the criminalisation of prostitution as discrimination against women, mainly from a poorer background. It is quite an illiberal view, i.e., that two-thirds of the sample favour criminalisation of prostitution. Decriminalisation is not the same as moral approval. It would lead to the protection and control of prostitution.

This item (no. 16) elicited a statistically significant variation in the case of all variables except "marital status". The patterns of variation were along normal lines. Females were slightly more in favour of criminalisation than were their male counterparts. Fianna Fáil and Fine Gael supporters shared the most penal view at 68% and 67% (respectively) in favour of criminalisation of prostitution. Of the thirty-two subsamples showing significant variation *only two* were below 50% in their pro-criminalisation response, i.e., "third level education" and "Class I" ("Upper Class") subsamples. This widespread support for criminalisation of prostitution is difficult to understand, unless it expresses some hidden psychological insecurity in relation to the control of sexual behaviour between adults, at a time when other forms of sexual permissiveness and promiscuity seem to be tolerated and subliminally promoted in the popular media and elsewhere.

1.3 Authoritarian Scores Analysed:

The examination of the responses to the individual items of the **New Authoritarian Scale** was seen as an exercise in reporting and commenting on *opinions* or *views* expressed in relation to contemporary issues. In this section it is proposed to analyse the *attitudes* deemed to measure authoritarianism through the findings in relation to the cumulative scale and subscale scores. Table 172, which measures the scale and subscale p-scores of the 1988-89 national sample, the 1972-73 Dublin sample and the 1988-89 subsample also records the changes which have taken place in authoritarian measures during the period 1972-73 to 1988-89. It also gives the scale and subscale scores (1988-89) by personal variables.

Taking a variation of 5% of the mean scale and subscales scores as the minimum required for significant variations between subsamples, it can be seen from the above findings that, once again, gender has been singularly the variable with the least range of variation. This *gender* consensus contrasts with the finding of the 1972-73 survey, where females were significantly higher than males in all columns (see Mac Gréil 1977, p. 427). There has been a significant and substantial range of scores in the "age" variable similar to that of 1972-73 (*ibid*). The pattern of the variation is constant and consistent in relation to scale and subscale scores. It clearly shows that there is a positive correlation between age and authoritarianism (as measured by this scale).

The pattern in "marital status" is consistent across the board with the widowed highest and those who never married lowest. The influence of the age factor is obviously present as well as pressures due to the frustration of being widowed.

"County of residence" and "place of rearing" record a consistency in the subsample variations of both variables. Those reared in rural communities have highest authoritarian scores while those reared in large cities have lowest scores. In other words, there seems to be a negative correlation

AUTHORITARIAN SCALES AND SUBSCALES BY PERSONAL VARIABLES

	Personal Variable	Scale Score	Religious Fundamentalism	Pro-Establishment Conservatism	Fascist Authoritarian	Moralism and Miscellaneous
	1. Total Sample 88/89	105.1	123.4	122.4	65.8	108.6
	2. Dublin Sample 72/73	102.6	108.5	130.5	66.5	105.0
	3. Dublin Subsample 88/89	91.0	103.6	116.7	53.6	90.2
	Variation (3-2)	-11.6	-4.9	-13.8	-12.9	-14.8
A.	Age:					
	1.35 years or less	89.6*	106.7*	106.2*	51.5*	93.7*
	2. 36 to 50 years	96.6	113.6	117.7	55.2	97.2
	3. 51 to 65 years	121.0	142.5	136.0	78.2	128.4
	4. 66 years plus	142.6	163.2	156.6	107.4	142.3
	Range of Variation	53.0	56.5	50.4	55.9	48.6
B.	Gender:					
	1. Females	N/S	N/S	N/S	70.3	N/S
	2. Males				60.6*	
	Range of Variation				9.7	
C.	Marital Status:					
	1. Never Married	97.2*	113.6*	116.4*	58.9*	100.0*
	2. Married	106.3	125.4	123.6	66.8	108.6
	3. Widowed	132.3	158.0	145.7	89.0	138.0
	Range of Variation	35.1	44.4	29.3	301	38.0
D.	County of Residence:					
	1. Dublin	90.4*	102.1*	114.6*	53.8*	89.9*
	2. Rest of Leinster	108.8	125.9	122.7	69.9	112.4
	3. Munster	107.5	131.8	119.3	68.3	112.6
	4. Connaugh/Ulster	120.0	140.4	139.8	75.0	124.9
	Range of Variation	29.6	38.3	25.2	21.2	35.0
E.	Place of Rearing:					
	1. Large City	88 5*	97.4*	106.4*	53 3	95.6
	2. Small City	90.4	107.5	109.7	55.0	90.4*
	3. Town	98.7	119.5	117.2	53.1*	104.8
	4. Rural	118.5	140.9	134.4	78.5	119.7
	Range of Variation	30 0	43.5			
F.	Education:					
	1. Primary Only	132.9	157.6	145.7	92.1	136.9
	2. Incomplete Second	107.1	129.9	121.2	66.9	109.6
	3. Complete Second	89.0	103.8	107.3	50.3	94.9
	4. Third Level	72.2*	74.1*	103.8*	36.6*	70.8*
	Range of Variation	60.7	83.5	41.9	55.5	66.1
G.	Occupational Status:					
	1. Professionai/Executive	85.9*	97.0*	113.4*	42.7*	87 9*
	2. Inspector/Supervisor	97.9	114.1	116.8	59.5	99.9
	3. Skilled/Routine N-M	107.3	127.3	121.5	67.8	113.3
	4. Semi/Unskilled	124.9	152.6	135.8	86 8	125.2
	Range of Variation	39.0	55.6	22.4	44.1	37.3

TABLE No. 172—Continued
AUTHORITARIAN SCALES AND SUBSCALES BY PERSONAL VARIABLES

	Personal Variable	Scale Score	Religious Fundamentalism	Pro-Establishment Conservatism	Fascist Authoritarian	Moralism and Miscellaneous
H.	Social Class Position					
	1. Class I	70.3*	64.4*	124.3	30.2*	60.3*
	2. Class 11	81.3	90.2	103.3*	40.6	87.7
	3. Class 111	95.8	113.8	114.0	57.3	97.0
	4. Class IV	107.5	127.7	122.4	68.0	113.3
	5. Class V	125.3	151.9	137.7	85.2	117.6
	Range of Variation	55	87.5	34.4	55.0	57.3
I.	Political Party Preference-					
	1. Fianna Fáil	117.1	132.8	150.5	72.0	112.8
	2. Fine Gael	104.0	126.4	112.1	65.2	113.0
	3. Labour Party	90.0	99.6	95.0	59.9	97.7
	4. P.Ds	70.3*	71.3*	84.5*	48.8*	75.0*
	Range of Variation	46.8	61.5	66.0	23.2	38.0

between urbanisation and authoritarianism as regards environment of rearing. A similar trend is possibly at work in the case of "county of residence" where Connaught/Ulster respondents are the subsample with the highest a-scores (authoritarian scores) across the board. Dublin respondents have the lowest a-scores. The range of variations is relatively lower in the case of both variables when compared with age and education. On average it is only half of the range for education.

"Education" is the personal variable to exercise most influence on authoritarianism. This is consistent with the findings in relation to ethnocentrism, racism and other forms of prejudice. Once again, it shows the impact of Irish education on the reduction of intolerance and authoritarianism over a long period. This confirms the findings of the 1972-73 survey (see Mac Gréil, p. 427). The negative correlation between education and authoritarianism is so striking that it merits serious reflection on the vulnerability of many of those with less education to more fundamentalist and simplistic views. It also points to the liberalising effects of the Irish education system in which respondents participated. Of course, there were disappointing exceptions to this positive effect of education in relation to attitudes toward a number of social categories (see previous chapter). This positive aspect of Irish education heretofore should be appreciated by those wishing to change its ethos and curriculum. It should be remembered that there is no proven correlation between human intelligence and intolerance. Socialistion and education seem to be the determining factors of authoritarianism and intolerance, as well as structures and ideologies which benefit from closed-mindedness.

"Occupational status", while negatively correlated with the a-scores patterns, has not as substantive a range of subsample variations as in the case of education. "Social class position", which is established according to a combination of education and occupation, shows a clear negative correlation between it and authoritarianism (as measured here). The range of scores would indicate a certain counter action between the two variables, in that the range of variation is actually less than that of education in all cases except the "Religious Fundamentalism" subscale.

The "political party preferences" patterns of a-score variations are interesting in that the "Progressive Democrat" supporters have the lowest a-scores across the board. This also reflects the educational profile of this subsample (with 55% of its supporters with complete second level or higher as compared with 37% of the total sample in that educational bracket). "Fianna Fáil" registers the highest a-scores in all scales except in the case of "Moralistic/Miscellaneous Authoritarian" subscale where Fine Gael supporters take the lead. It is interesting to note an exceptionally high range of variation of a-scores for the "Pro-Establishment Conservative" subscale when compared with the figures for the other personal variables. The contrast between Fianna Fáil supporters and those of the other parties may reflect the fact that Fianna Fáil was in Government at the time of the survey, whereas the other parties were in opposition.

PART II: THE LIBERAL-ILLIBERAL SCALE

2.1 Overall Scale:

This is a scale of sixteen items which was used in the 1972-73 survey to measure the extent of illiberalness in the Dublin sample at that time. The scale was replicated in the 1988-89 survey. By means of factor analysis, most of the items were incorporated with other scales, e.g. the "New Authoritarian Scale"and others. It is, therefore, proposed to concentrate on the scale's cumulative performance as measured by mean p-score (0-200) and analyse the trend and extent of variations between the subsamples of each personal variable. It is also proposed to examine the changes which may have taken place among Dubliners since the 1972-73 survey.

Table 173 shows the performance of the sixteen items in the national sample 1988-89, the Dublin sample 1972-73, and the Dublin subsample of 1988-89. This enables us to measure the change in p-score among Dubliners over the intervening sixteen years from 1972-73 to 1988-89. The scale score shows a drop of 12.5 in illiberalness, i.e. an increase in liberal attitudes. The items to experience most change include a massive increase (+34.7) for very strict control of RTÉ. As already discussed in the Authoritarian Scale, then there was a decline in support for locking up punks and skinheads (-60.1) and a reduction of 52.1 in favour of the view that *"pre-marital sex is always wrong"*.

The difference between the responses of the Dublin subsample in relation to pre-marital sex and the views of those from outside of Dublin is almost a factor of two, i.e. 66.9 in Dublin and 111.1 outside Dublin.[1] Two other issues experiencing substantial decline were opposition to Catholic priests being free to marry and to the criminalisation of homosexual behaviour between consenting adults. The relatively substantial reduction in the anti-dole score may reflect the expansion of unemployment since 1972-73. Opposition to women getting equal pay for equal work has been practically wiped out.

Eight of the sixteen items on the *Liberal-Illiberal Scale* have been incorporated into the *New Authoritarian Scale* as a result of factor analysis i.e., items nos. 1, 2, 5, 7, 10, 11, 15 and 16.

The comparison of scores between the responses of the Dublin Subsample (1988-89) and the Dublin Sample (1972-73) shows a drop in the level of illiberalness (as measured by the scale) of 12.5 or 17.3% of the 1988-89 mean scale score. It is difficult to assess the significance of such a change – apart from stating that the trend revealed in 1972-73 has continued, probably at a lower intensity than was expected at that time. The performance of individual items has been very uneven.

When the 1972-73 findings were published in 1977, some critics challenged the author with regard to his labelling of certain items or opinions as "liberal" or "illiberal", especially items which were contrary to religious orthodoxy. Apart from the fact that non-conformity to standing and widely held opinions correlates with a more "liberal" point of view, and is, therefore, useful as a measure of liberal-illiberalness, agreement or disagreement by large numbers of people is not interpreted to mean that the statement measured is right or wrong. The popular is not necessarily the true or the false in matters of religious or political points of view.

2.2 Individual Points of View:

Two items received practically unanimous support from the respondents and are, therefore, not examined by personal variables. The potential for variation in each case is minimal.

"Women should get equal pay for equal work" gets unanimous agreement, i.e., 97.4% agreeing and 0.6% disagreeing. It would be interesting to have tested how prepared the population was to put this statement of justice into effect. Ninety-three percent agreed that: *"Itinerants/Travellers should be facilitated to live their own way of life decently"*, while less than 2% disagreed with the opinion expressed. Considering the weight of other negative information given in Chapter VII above, this extremely positive response towards Travellers may sound a bit hollow. The refusal by residents to

1. This difference in relation to the acceptance of pre-marital sex by Dublin respondents and by those from the rest of Ireland in some way reflects the territorial variations of the support for amending the Irish Constitution (November 1995) to permit Divorce.

TABLE No. 173
THE MODIFIED LIBERAL-ILLIBERAL SCALE

	Statement	Total Sample 1988-89 (A) Scale Scores (0-200)	Dublin Sample 1972-73 (B) Scale Scores (0-200)	Dublin Subsample 1988-89 (C) Scale Scores (0-200)	Variation in Dublin Score (C-B)	Percentages (Total Sample)			Total Sample Number
						Agree %	Don't Know %	Disagree %	
1.	There should be a very strict control of R.T.E	97.9	61.0	95.7	+34.7	40	17.9	42.1	998
2.	Communism should be outlawed in Ireland.	120.0	111.5	100.4	-11.1	52.5	15.0	32.5	1,000
3.	An applicant's religion should be considered when considering him/her for a responsible public position.	38.6	24.0	33.5	+9.5	16.7	5.2	78.1	1,000
4.	Catholic priests should be free to marry.	85.8	98.0	70.5	-27.5	50.7	12.9	36.4	999
5.	Homosexual behaviour between consenting adults should not be a crime.	91.2	94.5	70.1	-24.0	43.9	20.9	35.1	999
6.	Obedience to the directives of the clergy should be the hallmark of the true Catholic.	105.5	95.5	96.1	+0.6	44.1	17.2	38.6	999
7.	Gardaí should be armed always.	71.7	66.0	55.1	-10.9	29.6	12.5	59.7	1,000
8.	Itinerants/ Travellers should be facilitated to live their own way of life decently.	8.9	23.0	10.7	-12.3	93.0	5.1	1.9	999
9.	The Dole should be abolished.	43.1	49.0	31.1	-17.9	16.4	10.3	73.3	1,000
10.	Punks and skinheads should be locked up.	36.1	85.0	24.9	-60.1	13.3	9.4	77.2	997

TABLE No. 173—Continued
THE MODIFIED LIBERAL-ILLIBERAL SCALE

		A	B	C	C-B	%	%	%	N
11.	A thing is either right or wrong and none of this ambiguous woolly thinking.	20.6	99.0	101.2	+2.2	51.9	16.9	31.3	997
12.	Women should get equal pay for equal work.	3.2	22.1	1.2	-21.3	97.4	2.0	0.6	998
13.	The unmarried mother is more to blame than the unmarried father	32.3	24.0	25.2	+1.2	11.2	9.8	79.0	998
14.	Pre-marital sex is always wrong.	100.1	119.0	66.9	-52.1	43.7	12.6	43.6	997
15.	Prostitution should remain a prosecutable crime.	142.4	113.5	118.9	+5.4	63.9	14.7	21.5	996
16.	Student protests should be outlawed.	57.5	54.0	38.5	-15.5	22.1	15.3	63.6	992
	Scale Scores	87.8	71.2	58.7	-12.5				

Travellers' requests to get sites and accommodation highlights the gap between the view expressed above and behaviour! Nevertheless, both women and Travellers can take some satisfaction from the extremely high support for their rights expressed in these two items. It is something that these groups could build on in their endeavours to elicit more supportive behaviour in the community for these minorities.

2.3 Individual Items by Personal Variables:

Eight items (nos. 1, 2, 5, 7, 10, 11, 15 and 16) included in the New Authoritarian Scale have already been examined in paragraph 1.2 above, and items nos. 8 and 12 have not been tested by personal variables because of the consensus in favour of the views they express. The remaining six items (nos. 3, 4, 6, 9, 13 and 14) are examined below (Table 174) as opinions or views held in the Irish population on topical issues.

2.3.a One's Religion and Job Application: This has been a very controversial issue in Ireland in the past, because of allegations of discrimination against particular religious denominations or groups. The inclusion of item no. 3 in the 1972-73 survey and again in 1988-89 was for the purpose of measuring the degree to which one's religion determined one's employability. It should

be stated that religiosity could be genuinely taken as one of many positive per
sonality traits without any element of sectarianism, i.e., in the sense that i
might be seen to point to a deeper sense of spiritual values and responsibility

Elsewhere in the survey, respondents were asked if they would say thei
religious affiliation was an advantage or a disadvantage to them "in gettinj
on". Only *one percent* said it was a disadvantage which is the measure o
sensed discrimination on account of one's religious affiliation. The majorit
(55%) felt religion was neither an advantage nor a disadvantage, while 44%
thought religion was a great (27%) or slight (18%) advantage. The respons
to item no. 3 of Table 174 does not contradict the positive perception o
religion while rejecting a sectarian view.

The overwhelming majority (78%) of the sample disagreed that "*an applicant's religion should be considered when considering her/him for a responsibl
position*". Only one-in-six agreed with the view expressed. The latter figure
marks a slight increase in the 1972-73 Dublin survey agreement percentage
of 11.7%.

"Gender" and "county of residence" failed to register a statistically
significant variation, while all other personal variables did. The pattern of
responses were consistent with the moral liberal patterns in the case of
"education", "occupational status" and "social class position". "Age"
responses found those of 36 to 50 years least in favour and the "66 years
plus" subsample with greatest support for the view. Rural-reared
respondents were strongest supporters of item no. 3 while "small city"
people were least in favour of considering a person's religion when applying
for a responsible public position. Fianna Fáil and Fine Gael (in that order)
were above the mean percentage while the Labour Party and Progressive
Democrat supporter shared the lowest score.

2.3.b Catholic Priests' Freedom to Marry: The overall majority (52.5%) were
in favour of the view that "*Catholic Priests should be free to marry*". One-
third (32.5%) were in favour of the retention of obligatory celibacy. The
percentage in the case of the 1988-89 Dublin subsample was 59.3%, which
was 12.6% up on the 1972-73 percentage of 46.7%. This increase was significant and substantial.

All variables except "gender" recorded significant variations. Supporters
of the Labour Party and those with third-level education were the subsamples most in favour at 65.2% and 64.0% respectively. "Age" was the
variable with the widest range of variation i.e., 58.9% of the younger subsample agreeing to priests marrying while only 28.5% of the older subsample
would agree making a range of 30.4% (or 60% of the mean score for the total
sample). Married respondents were the most in favour in the "marital
status" variable. "Education" recorded a range of 27% between those with
primary only and those with third-level education. The combination of age
and education would lead to the prediction of a fairly strong trend in favour
of permitting priests to marry in the future in Irish society. The other

TABLE No. 174

LIBERAL-ILLIBERAL ITEMS BY PERSONAL VARIABLES (Percent Agreeing)

VARIABLE	Applicants' Religion should be considered etc. No. 3	Catholic priests should be free to marry No. 4	Obedience to the direction of the clergy should be the hallmark of the true Catholic No. 6	The Dole should be abolished No. 9	The unmarried mother is more to blame than the unmarried father No. 13	Pre-marital sex is always wrong No. 14	N.
Total Sample	16.7	50.7	44.1	16.4	11.2	43.7	999
A. Age	P≤.002	P≤.001	P≤.001	P≤.001	P≤.001	P≤.001	
1. 35 years or less	15.2	58.9	30.3*	12.3*	5.7*	19.5*	392
2. 36 to 50 years	12.2*	53.0	36.3	15.5	10.4	38.9	271
3. 51 to 65 years	19.2	44.8	60.6	24.4	14.1	67.5	194
4. 66 years plus	26.4	28.5*	73.6	18.8	22.9	85.4	145
B. Gender			P≤.05				
1. Female	N/S	N/S	44.6	N/S	N/S	N/S	544
2. Male			43.6*				459
C. Marital Status	P≤.05	P≤.05	P≤.01			P≤.001	
1. Never Married	17.0	48.6	38.5*			32.8*	291
2. Married	15.6*	53.5	45.0	N/S	N/S	45.4	624
3. Widowed	30.0	34.3*	64.3			75.7	71
D. County of Residence		P≤.001	P≤.01	P≤.001	P≤.001	P≤.001	
1. Dublin		59.3	36.7*	10.5*	8.7*	26.9*	277
2. Rest of Leinster	N/S	51.0	42.5	12.9	11.4	38.6	255
3. Munster		51.0	49.3	19.1	10.4	53.0	300
4. Connaught/Ulster		35.7*	49.4	26.2	16.3	62.2	173
E. Place of Rearing	P≤.002	P≤.001	P≤.001	P≤.05	P≤.001	P≤.001	
1. Large City	14.6	58.4	31.8	13.3	8.6	25.4*	235
2. Small City	7.7*	53.8	30.8*	14.5	8.5*	26.7	117
3. Town	13.2	52.0	34.9	10.5*	9.9	41.4	153
4. Rural	21.0	46.1*	56.0	20.2	13.5	57.0	498
F. Education	P≤.001	P≤.001	P≤.001		P≤.001	P≤.001	
1. Primary Only	26.3	37.0*	69.8		18.2	67.0	283
2. Incomplete Second	16.4	52.2	42.7	N/S	10.9	41.7	348
3. Complete Second	9.5*	56.9	30.2		6.0*	28.9	232
4. Third Level	10.1	64.0	19.4*		6.5	26.8*	140
G. Occupation	P≤.05	P≤.001	P≤.01		P≤.01		
1. Professional/Executive	10.7*	57.2	32.9*		8.2*		159
2. Inspector/Supervisor	14.0	57.7	37.3	N/S	8.0*	N/S	300
3. Skilled/R. Non Manual	18.7	50.0	45.7		10.1		278
4. Semi-Unskilled	19.2	46.5*	60.3		16.7		156
H. Social Class Position	P≤.05	P≤.05	P≤.001		P≤.05	P≤.02	
1. Class I	5.9*	58.8	20.6*		2.9*	29.4*	34
2. Class II	10.5	62.9	27.6		9.6	33.7	105
3. Class III	13.0	57.0	35.3	N/S	8.9	40.7	270
4. Class IV	18.6	50.8	46.1		9.8	41.5	295
5. Class V	19.7	45.5*	62.2		16.0	50.0	188
I. Political Party Preference	P≤.05	P≤.01				P≤.001	
1. Fianna Fáil	20.0	44.2*	N/S	N/S	N/S	49.0	449
2. Fine Gael	17.1	54.8				50.2	252
3. Labour Party	9.1*	65.2				29.2	66
4. Progressive Democrats	9.5	61.9				21.4*	42

variables were as predicted in accordance with the liberal pattern in other items and other scales. Fianna Fáil supporters were least in favour of priests marrying (44.2%) while those supporting the Labour Party were most in favour (65.2%).

2.3.c Docility to the Directives of the clergy: A plurality of respondents (44.1%) agreed with the view that "*Obedience to the directives of the clergy should be the hallmark of the true Catholic*" as compared with 38.6% who disagreed. There was a drop of 8% between the 1972-73 support of the Dublin sample and the 1988-89 national sample. The Catholic Church's demands on obedience has been qualified somewhat by the assertion of freedom of conscience in the Vatican II decrees. Nevertheless, those "in the seat of Moses" still attract a strong loyalty among many Irish respondents.

"Age", "education" and "social class position" produced the widest ranges of variation between their subsamples. The other variables performed along the patterns of "liberal" trends. Such trends are not in favour of the magisterial role of the clergy in the life of the Church and would seem to prefer a more participative approach to religion.

2.3.d Abolition of the Dole: Only one-in-six (16.4%) agreed with the opinion that: "*The dole should be abolished*", while almost three quarters (73.5%) disagreed with it. In 1972-73 there was similar opposition to this rather extreme statement, but the percentage for it was 6.4% higher at 22.8%.

There was a very high level of consensus in relation to this view. Only three of the nine personal variables recorded a statistically significant variation, i.e., "age", "county of residence" and "place of rearing". The senior middle-aged (51 to 65 years) were the most penal in outlook while the younger subsample (18 to 35 years) were least in favour of abolishing the dole. Connaught/Ulster respondents were most in favour of abolition while Dublin were least so inclined. This is a poor reflection on the concrete situation in that the proportion of the workforce drawing the dole was higher in Connaught/Ulster than in Dublin in 1988-89. The "rural-reared" were highest and "town-reared" lowest in their support for the abolition of dole.

Overall unemployed people should take satisfaction for the very strong and widespread support for those on the dole throughout the country. Those who seek its abolition fail to understand the need for income support for those out of work. The exceptionally high status of the "unemployed" in the social distance scale (see p. 65) confirms the positive attitude towards the dole or income support.

2.3.e Blaming the Unmarried Mother: The overwhelming majority (79%) of the national sample rejected the negative opinion that "*The unmarried mother is more to blame than the unmarried father*", while only one-in-nine (11.4%) agreed with this very intolerant view. This is a repetition of the 1972-73 performance for the Dublin subsample (see Table 173 above).

Three personal variables did not record statistically significant variations between their subsamples, i.e., "gender", "marital status" and "political party preference". In the case of the six personal variables recording significant variations, the patterns of responses were consistent with the normal pattern of prejudice responses. The range of difference in the case of "age", "social class position", and "education" was greater than the sample average percentages, i.e., 17.4%, 13.1% and 11.7% respectively. This is indicative of a strong trend to reduce further the level of support for this penal view towards women in the years following the survey. This evidence of positive opinion-change is to be welcomed.

2.3.f Pre-Marital Sex Wrong? The sample was equally divided (43.7% for and 43.6% against) in relation to the view that *"pre-marital sex is always wrong"*. This finding is open to a wide range of interpretations. Some twenty-five years after the sexual revolution, some might find it strange that half the sample expressing a pro or contra opinion would still support this ethical stand.

Two personal variables did not record statistically significant variations between their subsamples, i.e., "gender" and "occupation". The range of variation in the case of "age" has been extraordinarily high at 65.9%, which is 150% of the national sample mean of 43.7%. Only one-in-five of those under 35 years of age (19.5%) agreed with the statement, while 85.4% of those over 65 years agreed *"that pre-marital sex was always wrong"*. There was a very substantial difference of opinion between the senior (51 to 65 years) and junior (36 to 50 years) middle-aged categories. Such intergenerational divergence of opinion must be extremely rare. Does it mean that the young people are out of touch with the values of the elderly people in matters pertaining to sexual behaviour? The new norms are certainly not coming from traditional Irish society. They are the product of cultural diffusion.

This finding raises serious question for Christian Churches who counsel the unethical nature of pre-marital sex. Such teaching seems to have fallen on deaf ears among the young. The arrival of the lethal and sexually transmitted disease or condition of AIDS does not seem to have made that much impact in the area of positive attitude towards pre-marital sexual continence. Of course, disagreement with this item does not mean that young people would themselves engage in pre-marital sex!

The variations in the other six variables have been consistent with the normal patterns. In the case of "political party preferences", the supporters of "Fine Gael" were most in favour of the view expressed while "Progressive Democrat" supporters were least in agreement. There was a drastic drop in support of the view in the case of the Dublin subsample at 26.9% for when compared with the 57.6% in favour in 1972-73. The Dublin support for the opinion expressed in item no. 14, at 26.9%, contrasts with the attitudes of those resident outside Dublin, where 49.2% agree that "pre-marital sex is always wrong". The implication of the very substantial increase in pre-marital sexual permissiveness over the sixteen intervening years may also have implications for marriage and the family in Ireland in the future.

2.4 Illiberalism by Personal Variables:

Going on the basis of a minimum significant range of variation equalling 5% or less of the mean scale score, i.e. 5% of 72.1 = 3.6, all nine personal variables registered a significant variation. **Gender** has the lowest range of variation at 6.3 (or 8.7% of the sample mean score). Females were slightly more illiberal than males according to these findings.

Age and **education** were the two variables recording the widest range of variations, 50.4 and 54.1 respectively (or 70% and 75% of the scale mean score). The strong positive correlation between age and illiberalness, and an equally strong negative correlation between education and illiberalness, would combine to indicate a very strong move away from the illiberal attitudes.

The age and gender factors combined to give the variations in the **marital status** variable, as well as the frustrating effects of the relative deprivations of old age and loss of partner.

County of residence and **area of rearing** reproduced the normal patterns of variation with the more "rural" and "Connaught/Ulster" respondents registering the highest illiberal scale scores. "Large city" and "small city" reared subsamples had virtually the same score each. It is interesting to observe that the range of variation in both of these variables is about half that of "education" and "age". This goes to re-emphasise the central significance of these two latter variables on the level of illiberal attitudes.

The performance of the **occupational status** variable was consistent with the normal patterns in other scales measuring prejudice and related issues. Those in the more secure positions were less illiberal than those with occupations at the bottom of the occupational status scale. Despite the strong correlation between "education" and "occupational status" i.e. r = 0.59, the range of variance of the latter is only 58% of that of the former variable.

The pattern and range of variance by **social class position** reflects the combined influence of education and occupation. The range of variance is very substantial with Class I (the "Upper Class") scoring the least illiberal scores of all the subsamples in the table. These findings substantiate the view widely held in society that **liberalness** is mostly a middle and upper class attitude, not shared by the working and lower classes. The score of the "Lower Class" (Class V) is more than twice that of the "Upper Class" (Class I) in the above table.

Political Party Preferences as a variable elicited a significant variation of scores, with Fianna Fáil supporters highest and Progressive Democrats lowest. Fine Gael scores were only 3.7 points lower than Fianna Fáil, while Labour Party respondents occupy a central position very close to Class III ("Middle Middle Class") on the Social Class Position scale.

TABLE No. 175

PERSON CORRELATIONS BETWEEN ITEMS OF THE LIBERAL/ILLIBERAL SCALE

Item No. and Summary	1	2	3	4	5	6	7	8	9	10	11	12	13	14	15	16
1. Strict control of R T E.	1.00	.31	.16	.22	.25	.35	.13	N.S	.08	.19	.18	.09	.13	.30	.21	.27
2. Outlaw Communism		1.00	.23	.25	.28	.40	.24	N.S	.11	.29	.32	.06	.18	.35	.32	.30
3. Consider religion of applicants.			1.00	.16	.10	.27	.17	N.S	.07	.24	.09	N.S	.18	.17	.15	.23
4. Catholic priests should be free to marry.				1.00	.30	.30	N S	N.S	N S	.16	.16	.10	.16	.32	.22	.19
5. Homosexual behaviour should not be a crime.					1.00	.28	.14	N.S	.10	.27	.24	.12	.16	.38	.28	.25
6. Obedience to clergy is hallmark of true Catholic.						1.00	.21	N.S	.07	.23	.29	.10	.20	.40	.30	.32
7. Gardaí should be armed.							1.00	N.S	.12	.21	.18	N.S	15	.11	.19	.24
8. Itinerants facilitated to live their own.								1.00	N.S	N S	N.S	.13	.11	N.S	N.S	N.S
9. Dole should be abolished.									1.00	.14	.13	N.S	.11	.15	.08	.11
10. Punks/Skinheads should be locked up.										1.00	.19	N.S	.29	.29	.19	.38
11. A thing is either right or wrong.											1.00	N.S	.16	.33	.24	.24
12. Women should get equal pay.												1.00	.10	N.S	N.S	.09
13. Unmarried mother more to blame than unmarried father.													1.00	.24	09	.26
14. Pre-marital sex wrong.														1.00	.38	.32
15. Prostitution a crime.															1.00	.24
16. Outlaw student protest.																1.00

TABLE No. 176
ILLIBERALNESS BY PERSONAL VARIABLES (Sample Mean P-Score=72.1)

	Variable Scale	P-score (0-200)		Variable Scale	P-Score (0-200)
A.	Age:		**F.**	Education:	
1.	35 years or less	57.6*	1.	Primary Only	97.4
2.	36 to 50 years	63.1	2.	Incomplete Second	72.5
3.	52 to 65 years	87.3	3.	Complete Second	58.6
4.	66 years plus	108.0	4.	Third Level	43.3*
Range		50.4	Range		54.1
B.	Gender:		**G.**	Occupational Status:	
1.	Females	75.0	1.	Professional/Executive	55.6*
2.	Males	68.7*	2.	Inspector/Supervisor	65.0
			3.	Skilled/Routine Non-Man	74.3
			4.	Semi/Unskilled	87.2
Range		6.3	Range		31.6
C.	Marital Status:		**H.**	Social Class Position:	
1.	Never Married	66.6*	1.	Class I	37.5*
2.	Married	72.3	2.	Class II	52.7
3.	Widowed	96.3	3.	Class II	63.9
			4.	Class IV	74.3
			5.	Class V	86.6
	Range	29.7	Range		49.1
D.	County of Residence:		**I.**	Political Party Preference:	
1.	Dublin	58.2*	1.	Fianna Fáil	78.1
2.	Rest of Leinster	73.0	2.	Fine Gael	74.4
3.	Munster	76.3	3.	Labour Party	60.5
4.	Connaught/Ulster	86.0	4.	P.Ds	47.6*
	Range	27.8	Range		30.5
E.	Place of Rearing:				
1.	Large City	58.0*			
2.	Small City	58.4			
3.	Town	64.4			
4.	Rural	84.5			
	Range	26.5			

Lowest scores have asterisks; Highest scores are underlined.

PART III: SOCIAL ANOMIE AND ALIENATION SCALES

One of the most serious omissions in the 1972-73 survey of prejudice was the absence of a scale capable of measuring **anomie**. In co-operation with Ruben Konig, of the Social Research Department, the Catholic University of Nijmegen, a special scale was composed to measure social anomie in the sample. This scale is based on the original anomie scale developed by Srole. Anomie is a concept devised by Emile Durkheim to describe the sense of normlessness in the population following a breakdown of social stability and an accepted moral order. Srole and R.K. Merton have both developed this concept. The latter used it to explain social deviance resulting from a situation where the socially accepted norms and means are seen to be inadequate for the successful pursuit of the generally accepted cultural goals (Merton 1968). Some of the symptoms of anomie are pessimism, mistrust, anxiety and a general lack of confidence in self or friends or in the social order. It can lead to a sense of frustration, despondency, mild paranoia and even suicide. Durkheim classified one type of suicide as "anomie suicide".

3.1 The Anomie Scale

The following seven item scale (Table 177) was included in the questionnaire from the Nijmegen questionnaire. Because of its high level of validity and reliability it will be used as the "official" measure of anomie in this book. In addition to this special scale, a broader scale of alienation-related views and opinions will also be examined here to supplement the Anomie Scale. The reason for the broader scale is to delve further into the attitude syndrome of the people with a view to a better understanding of the current state of Irish culture as reflected in our attitude syndrome.

While the mean p-score of the scale is 103.8, or 51.9% of the maximum which is ideal for variance potential, it, nevertheless, indicates a relatively high level of anomie in the population. This, in turn, could point to a certain breakdown in the moral order of Irish society. People may, as a result, be left somewhat rudderless and less secure than would be desirable. These findings, provide a cause for concern. The people's cultural stability may have been undermined by a long period of social and cultural change and demoralisation (in the literal sense). Further research into this area would be required, before determining the causes and the cure for such widespread anomie in Irish society. "*Aggiornamento*" has its human costs? Anomie is positively correlated with various forms of social prejudice. An increase in the incidence of suicide, for instance, would be an indicator of rising anomie in society (see Durkheim, 1897). Recent trends in reported suicide would seem to confirm an underlying problem in Irish culture today. It would be worthwhile to retest the Durkheimian hypothesis in this context.

TABLE No. 177
THE ANOMIE SCALE*

	ITEM	Agree	Don't Know	Disagree	P-Score (0-200)
1.	These days a person doesn't really know whom he/she can count on.	<u>54.2%</u> (29.1)	10.7% (27.9)	35.1% (43.1)	119.1 (86.1)
2.	Everything changes so quickly that I often have trouble deciding what are the right rules to follow.	<u>52.8%</u>	13.4%	33.8%	119.0
3.	People were better off in the old days when everyone knew how he/she was expected to act.	<u>41.8%</u>	13.0%	45.3%	96.6
4.	There is little use in writing to public officials for anything.	<u>55.3%</u> (22.4)	15.2% (26.0)	29.5% (50.6)	125.8 (71.7)
5.	The lot of the average person is getting worse not better in Ireland today.	<u>56.9%</u> (39.9)	14.5% (28.8)	28.6% (31.3)	128.3 (108.6)
6.	It's hardly fair to bring children into the world with the way things look for the future.	<u>20.2%</u> (9.0)	11.1% (21.4)	68.7% (69.6)	51.5 (39.4)
7.	You sometimes can't help wondering whether any effort is worthwhile.	<u>37.2%</u>	12.7%	50.1%	87.1%
	Scale P-Score				103.8

Cronbach's alpha = 0.71
Notes: Responses indicating anomie are underlined. Dutch Survey figures in brackets.

3.2 Individual Items:

3.2.a Public Distrust: Most social philosophers would hold that public trust is an essential element of social security and a sense of confidence. Its absence tends to create a sense of chronic fear or anxiety which leads to anomie. Social norms are dependent on the expectation of others responding in a normative manner.

The response to item no. 1, "*These days a person doesn't really know whom he/she can count on*", received majority support (54.2%) with a little over one-third of the sample disagreeing. This reply reveals a low level of social and personal trust which could depict a lack of community support. It could also indicate the impact of living in a highly competitive social environment which one might expect in a society imbued with the competitive free market ethos. Widespread competition is dissociative.

The response to item no. 4 extends this lack of confidence to public officials when 55.3% agree that: "*There is little use in writing to public officials for anything*", with 29.5% disagreeing. This reply raises serious questions concerning the people's expectations from the elaborate public service, which must surprise those in charge of these services.

It is consistent with the answers to items nos. 1 and 4 that over one-third of the sample (37.2%) agree with the very despondent statement: *"You sometimes can't help wondering whether any effort is worthwhile"*. Just half (50.1%) of the sample disagreed with item no. 7. Those in public leadership roles must take these findings seriously and find ways of reassuring the people who seem to feel fairly isolated in Irish society today.

3.2.b Normlessness and Pessimism: While many commentators seem to herald current social changes as leading to a brighter and better future, the opinions of the majority of the national sample do not see the changes in a very positive light. It would appear that there is a serious "culture-lag" in changing Irish society from the responses to items nos. 2, 3, 5 and 6. Durkheim, who originated the concept of "anomie", detected a similar sense of **normlessness** and pessimism in late 19th Century Europe.

The response to the view that: *"Everything changes so quickly that I often have trouble in deciding what are the right rules to follow"* was quite anomic. Over half of the sample (52.8%) agreed while one-third (33.8%) disagreed. One of the possible causes for this degree of normlessness may be the gradual undermining or growing withdrawal of commitment to the moral norms of religion and the failure of the secular alternative to fill the ethical vacuum. Respondents were divided on whether *"people were better off in the old days when everybody knew how he/she was expected to act"*. A plurality (45.3%) disagreed, while 41.8% agreed with item no. 3. It is quite clear from these findings that the level of social mobility and improvements in standards of living of many that these benefits have not impressed a large proportion of the sample. Many would seem to say "they got more out of less" in the past!

Item no. 5 focuses on the future, and again records a two-to-one pessimistic answer. In response to the opinion that: *"The lot of the average person is getting worse not better in Ireland today"*, 56.9% agreed and 28.6% disagreed. This refers to more than their own expectations of improvements in the standard of living, where 59.2% anticipated improvement "over the next five years" (see Table 170, Chapter XII, page 387). In other words, "the lot of the average person" is perceived to get worse, despite anticipated improvement in standard of living! The ingredient is the lack of cultural consolidation in the area of such things as trust and norms for social living!

The most severe test of pessimism is made in item no. 6 where respondents were asked to agree or disagree with the view that: *"It's hardly fair to bring children into the world with the way things look for the future"*. Over two thirds (68.7%) of the sample disagreed with this extremely pessimistic view while one-in-five (20.2%) agreed with it. This latter percentage, while a minority, is still relatively high in the light of the severity of the pessimism expressed in the view.

As in the case of item no. 5, the Dutch National Survey figures have shown a substantially lower level of anomie in their responses to items nos. 1, 4, 5 and 6, than was the case in the Republic of Ireland.

3.3 The Alienation Scale:

The following scale has been devised to capture further nuances relating to anomie and alienation in the population. It is seen as supplementary to the Anomie Scale. In all there are thirteen items in this scale. *Alienation*, as measured here, is defined as **a sense of powerlessness** which, when coupled with *anomie*, leaves the individual in a depressed and hopeless situation. Thankfully, one rarely finds people or groups who are totally alienated and anomic. What is found in research is rather the degree of alienation and of anomie.

TABLE No. 178
THE NEW ALIENATION SCALE

ITEM	Agree %	Don't Know %	Disagree %	P-Score (0-200)
1. With everything so uncertain these days it seems as though anything could happen.	81.8	8.5	9.8	172.0
2. Most people can still be depended on to come through in a pinch.	81.0	9.1	10.0	29.0
3. If you try hard enough you can usually get what you want.	72.8	11.8	15.5	42.7
4. Most people don't care what happens to the next fellow.	33.2	13.5	53.3	79.9
5. Parents are not strict enough with their children in Ireland today	62.3	17.0	20.6	141.7
6. Nowadays, more and more people are prying into matters that should remain personal and private.	69.5 (46.9)	13.0 (25.3)	17.6 (27.8)	151.9 (119.1)
7. What this country needs most are a few courageous fearless, devoted leaders in whom the people can put their faith.	82.3	9.0	8.8	173.5
Scale P-Score				112.9

Cronback Alpha = 0.36
Notes: Answers underlined refer to indicators of alienation.
Dutch Survey Scores in Brackets.

Since this is an experimental scale (Table 178) which captures a relatively wide range of responses, a note of caution must be sounded when making conclusions. At the same time, the individual items and the scale itself expose a certain degree of alienation, or a sense of powerlessness, in the sample. The Cronbach Alpha is low but significant at 0.36.

This is hardly surprising when one considers the state of Ireland and that of the world in 1989 with the threat of nuclear proliferation, the cold war still unresolved, the desperate plight of the exploited and neglected developing world, the growing worries about the environment and the continuing intransigence of those involved in the Northern Ireland "Troubles". We may add to that the inability of Irish society to provide gainful employment for a substantial proportion of its labour force i.e., 15% to 17% at the time, despite some improvement in the economic indicators. The resulting brain-drain through emigration was (and still is) leaving large sections of Irish society facing de-population. When one adds to this the rise of the problems of neglected areas of our cities, i.e., drugs, crime, and domestic stress. The heady days of the 1960s and 1970s with its sexual revolution and the "hybrazil" of the EEC being reached, were to be shattered by the continuity of high unemployment, the Northern "Troubles",the rise in promiscuity and drugs related problems such as AIDS, homelessness and other failures. In such an environment one expects to find relatively high *anomie* and *alienation* in the population.

While the above litany of potential causes of alienation may appear very stark on their own, there were some positive developments which are also reflected in the above responses. These included increased participation in education, improvements in social welfare and assistance, moves towards the ending of the Cold War (without awareness of some of the negative consequences which have followed it, e.g. the former Yugoslavia debacle), some initiatives towards a resolution of the Northern Ireland problem, a marked improvement in the standard of living of the majority of the people and a growing awareness of the futility of nuclear proliferation. The rise of consumerism and individualism, while contributing to the material standard of living of many people may have had a negative effect on the sense of community and neighbourhood support. Table 178, then, should be interpreted as a reflection on the socio-cultural environment of the people towards the end of the 20th Century (i.e., in 1988-89).

3.3.a Uncertainty and Insecurity: Two of the strongest characteristics of a sense of alienation are feelings of uncertainty and of insecurity. Should the latter persist, it can lead to *anxiety* which is best defined as a state of chronic unrealistic fear. The two items which measure these feelings are nos. 1 and 6. The overwhelming majority of respondents (81.8%) agree with the view that: *"With everything so uncertain these days it seems as though anything could happen"*. Only one-in-ten (9.8%) disagreed with this statement. Such a degree of uncertainty means that the people felt that it was well nigh impossible to predict or control future developments, i.e., indicating a sense of powerlessness.

This insecurity was indicated in item no. 6 in reaction to perceived surveillance of the ordinary people's lives. More than two-thirds of the sample (69.5%) agreed to the view that, *"Nowadays, more and more people are prying into matters that should remain personal and private"*, while one-in-six disagreed with it. Such a level of perceived intrusion by means of electronic and other surveillance by the State, by the media, and by other powerful bureaucracies could easily lead to a degree of paranoia. This clearly indicates the need for some legislative protection of the privacy of the individual. The psychological health of the people would demand it. It is interesting to note that the Dutch national sample were much less convinced that their lives were being pried into by "big brother" or "big sister".

3.3.b Self-Reliance: Item no. 3 seems to put great faith in the ability of the individual "to make it" through self-effort. The success of Irish emigrants abroad and that of new Irish entrepreneurs after the War of Independence, has placed a high premium on the "mentality of the self-made man/woman" (see Table 154 above and commentary on item no. 8, pp. 361ff). This is an inevitable reaction in a society lacking commercial support, equality and solidarity. "It is everyone for her/himself and God for us all", to quote the proverb. It is also a by-product of the American "street corner to the White House" mentality. Despite its obvious heroic and positive dimension, it is also a reflection on the lack of universal communal co-operation and solidarity. It does, however, support the competitive individualism of capitalist ideology.

Almost three-quarters of the sample (72.8%) agreed that, *"If you try hard enough you can usually get what you want"*, while slightly less than one-sixth (15.5%) disagreed with the view expressed. This is a vote of confidence in the ability of the individual to succeed, which reflects a central value of United States' culture (see R.K. Merton, 1968, pp. 220ff). If that belief exists, why does it not manifest itself in local community revival and socio-economic progress? Is it that people do not feel they have the power or the possibility to engage in their community and county development?

3.3.c Mutual Support: One of the key supports in life is the security of mutual support, not only in times of need but also in daily life. Items nos. 2 and 4 address the extent of mutual support available. In the case of item No. 2 four-fifths (81.0%) agreed with the view that: *"Most people can still be depended on to come through in a pinch"*, while only 10% disagreed. This overwhelming belief in solidarity in crisis seems to co-exist with a sense of isolation in ordinary times. It reflects well on society that such confidence in crisis exists. But it is not sufficient to reassure many of the people, however. Nevertheless, it is a piece of evidence which modifies the level and intensity of alienation in Irish society.

The opinion expressed in item No. 4 probes the level of perceived concern for others in the population. When asked if they agreed or disagreed with the view that: *"Most people don't care what happens to the next fellow"*, the response was mixed. Over half of the sample (53.3%) disagreed with the statement, while exactly one-third (33.2%) agreed with it. The remaining 13.5% neither agreed nor disagreed. For a third of the sample to define most people as uncaring is substantial, and a serious reflection on the experience of such a large section of society. It probably measures the growing individualism and a sense of isolation felt by many. It is a good indirect measure of alienation.

3.3.d Discipline and Leadership: People who feel powerless in themselves to improve their social and personal situation can hand over that responsibility to strong leaders. Undemocratic leaders often exploit this deferral of authority from the alienated people to themselves and, ironically, turn the people's sense of powerlessness into a reality, as happened under the Third Reich.

The response to item no. 7 may be indicative of a latent sense of alienation among the vast majority of respondents. Over four-fifths of the sample (82.3%) agreed with the authoritarian view that: "*What this country needs most are a few courageous, fearless, devoted leaders in whom the people can put their faith*", while only one-in-twelve (8.8%) disagreed. A clamour for strong leadership means a definition of the citizens as principally in a passive role. A truly *adult* participating population would not seek strong leadership if they did not feel powerless to improve their situation or check its deterioration. Strong popular leaders tend to be charismatic, and there is always the danger of them resorting to demagoguery. (See Mac Gréil, 1977 pp. 116-7). Strong leadership calls for discipline and control.

Almost two-thirds of the sample agreed with the view that: "*Parents are not strict enough with their children in Ireland today*", while one-fifth of respondents disagreed. Most reasonable people would agree that discipline and self-control are essential ingredients of the socialization of the young so as to enable them to have the personal freedom to live fruitful lives. Discipline and control must be balanced by affection and space to develop creatively. The emphasis in the statement being examined here is on parents *not being strict enough* rather than not caring enough. There is a note of repression involved (not to mention scapegoating parents for the misdeeds of the young).

3.4 Anomie and Alienation Scales by Personal Variables:

The findings of Table 179 are more or less as anticipated. Variations in all personal variables for the Anomie Scale are quite similar to the pattern of the score variations of the Authoritarian Scale. The fact that the 1972-73 survey did not contain an Anomie Scale was seen at the time as an oversight. The Anomie Scale as with the Authoritarian and Alienation Scales, are both dependent and independent variables in this study.

The measures of authoritarianism, anomie and alienation in the population provide very useful information for the sociologist and for the social psychologist. They also have an anthropological significance. Where any of these factors are exceptionally high there is the likelihood of poor social integration due to mal-adaptation of economic factors or widespread social stress and personal insecurity. Measures of authoritarianism, anomie and alienation, which are measures of personal closedmindedness, of normlessness and of powerlessness respectively, are useful psycho-socio-cultural barometers. In the context of the present work they are seen as being positively correlated with social prejudice and intolerance.

TABLE No. 179
ANOMIE AND ALIENATION SCALES' P-SCORES (0-200) BY PERSONAL VARIABLES

PERSONAL VARIABLE	ANOMIE SCALE	ALIENATION SCALE
Sample Average	101.2	112.9
A. Age		
1. 35 years or less	91.7*	107.4*
2. 26 to 50 years	101.8	113.0
3. 51 to 65 years	117.0	118.7
4. 66 years plus	<u>122.7</u>	<u>119.7</u>
Range	31.0	12.3
B. Gender		
1. Females	<u>106.3</u>	N/S
2. Males	101.0*	
Range	5.3	
C. Marital Status		
1. Never Married	91.3*	108.3*
2. Married	107.4	114.2
3. Widowed	<u>117.1</u>	<u>117.9</u>
Range	25.8	9.6
D. County of Residence		
1. Dublin	95.2*	108.2*
2. Rest of Leinster	104.7	113.2
3. Munster	105.9	115.5
4. Connaught/Ulster	<u>113.1</u>	<u>115.6</u>
Range	17.9	9.6
E. Place of Rearing		
1. Large City	97.4	108.5*
2. Small City	97.2*	113.7
3. Town	97.7	113.4
4. Rural	<u>110.2</u>	<u>114.6</u>
Range	13.0	6.1
F. Education		
1. Primary Only	<u>133.3</u>	<u>126.4</u>
2. Incomplete Second	109.4	113.1
3. Complete Second	84.2	107.4
4. Third Level	64.2*	95.7*
Range	69.1	30.7

TABLE No. 179—Continued
ANOMIE AND ALIENATION SCALES' P-SCORES (0-200) BY PERSONAL VARIABLES

G. Occupational Status		
1. Professional/Executive	73.2*	104.2*
2. Inspector/Supervisor	94.1	111.6
3. Skill/Routine N-Man	116.1	120.1
4. Semi/Unskilled	128.3	114.1
Range	55.1	15.9
H. Social Class Position		
1. Class I	48.7*	85.3*
2. Class II	72.4	106.3
3. Class III	92.9	110.1
4. Class IV	111.2	118.3
5. Class V	132.4	119.4
Range	83.7	34.1
I. Political Party Preference		
1. Fianna Fáil	106.4	114.0
2. Fine Gael	103.1	111.5
3. Labour Party	106.7	111.3
4. P.Ds	81.3*	108.2 *
Range	25.4	5.8

Note: (i) Where the range is more than 5% of the average scale score of the total sample it is deemed significant.
(ii) Highest scores are underlined while lowest scores have an asterisk (*).

"Social class position", "education" and "occupational status" were the three personal variables to record the widest range of scores. "Age", "marital status", "county of residence", "place of rearing" and "political party preference" produced significant but relatively moderate ranges of variation. "Gender" recorded barely significant minimal difference in the case of social anomie and was not significant in the case of alienation. The range of variation of the Social Anomie Scale was on average two-and-a-half times that of the Alienation Scale (despite the fact that the latter's scale average was only slightly higher than that of the former, i.e., 112.9 as compared with 101.2). The lower the range of score variations, the higher the level of consensus in the population.

CHAPTER XIV

Summary and Conclusions

INTRODUCTION

In the course of the previous chapters a comprehensive range of findings was examined and analysed in an attempt to discover and explain the prejudices and related attitudes, opinions and behaviourial patterns of a representative sample of the adult (over eighteen years old) population of the Republic of Ireland. The interviews on which this work has been based were carried out during the period November 1988 until April 1989.

In addition to the presentation and analysis of the attitudes, prejudices and opinions of the national sample, a comparative study of the findings of the Dublin subsample of 1988-89 and of a Dublin sample of 1972-73 was carried out to discover the extent of change in prejudice and intergroup attitudes in the course of the intervening sixteen years. This has been a most interesting exercise in longitudinal or ongoing research into intergroup prejudices and provided the reason for the title of this book, i.e., *Prejudice In Ireland Revisited.*

In this final chapter it is proposed to summarise the main findings and interpret their meaning in the light of the application of theoretical propositions and the direction of attitudinal change in Ireland. As already indicated, the time of the national survey has been fortuitous in that it predated the collapse of the "Eastern Communist Block"; the Maastricht Treaty, the eighteen months' cease-fire (1994-96) in Northern Ireland and other internal happenings in Ireland, which may have affected Irish religious and socio-political attitudes in the short-term. The recent (1996) return to more intense hostilities inevitably leads to a hardening of attitudes more akin to those reflected in the above pages.

Just as this book analyses changes between 1972-73 and 1988-89, it is hoped that the next comprehensive survey of Irish intergroup attitudes and related issues in 2004-05 will be able to measure the changes which may have taken place because of the changing socio-cultural environment of the people due to the events referred to above. In other words, the 1988-89 survey is in itself a benchmark for further research. Hopefully, the next survey will extend the research into Northern Ireland and measure the impact of ongoing peace in a more pluralist and integrated Irish Society, that is, after the current set-back in Northern Irish affairs has been overcome.

A number of monographs on the findings of the 1988-89 survey has been already published[1] by the author and they have been incorporated into this

---

1. *The State and Status of the Irish Language*, 1990. *Educational Participation in Ireland*, 1990. *Religious Practice and Attitudes in Ireland*, 1991. *Irish Political Attitudes and Opinions*, 1992.

book. The reason for the earlier limited publication of these monographs was the desirability of informing the public of the findings closer to the time of the research. In this work it is felt that topicality is not that important and the time taken since 1992 to prepare and present the findings and analysis has been considered worthwhile because of the more longterm relevance of the analysis. Major research analysis of this nature is not conducive to instant reporting.

This book does not exhaust all the material and data of the questionnaire (see Appendix A). It is hoped that further analysis of the findings will be reported on in future articles and monographs. Constraints of space and time have inevitably resulted in a degree of selectivity of the material chosen for examination in the above chapters.

Both the conceptual and theoretical frameworks proposed in Chapter II (pages 17-54) have proven useful and satisfactory. The "momentum model of society", which facilitates the incorporation of both conflict and consent, provides a context for perpetual social change vacillating between the two extremes of anarchy and stifling conformism (see Figure No. 4, page 40). The middle-range theories of "frustration-aggression", "labelling", "the apostate complex", "anxiety", "dominant-minority postures and responses", "scapegoating", and the "functional nature of social prejudice", were reconfirmed.

"Authoritarianism", "anomie", and "alienation" as personality traits emanating from social and personal conditions have also proven very useful in explaining the differences in prejudice scores. The following paragraphs summarise the contents of each of the chapters in a systematic manner.

PART I: SUMMARY OF FINDINGS

1. APPROACH

The approach to the study of intergroup attitudes, opinions and related issues in this work has been more-or-less similar to that adopted in the analysis of the 1972-73 survey as published in *Prejudice and Tolerance in Ireland* (Mac Gréil, 1977). It was found unnecessary to repeat (in great detail) the theoretical and methodological points made in the previous publication in the introductory chapters (I and II) above.

1.1 General:

Chapter I gave the background to and outline of the present work. In so doing, the context of the findings were delineated and the reader was introduced to the overall strategy of the book which is summarised in Figure No. 33.

Figure 33: Strategic Outline of Book by Chapters

1. Background and Previous Research	
2. Theory and Method	
3. Social Distance in Ireland	
4. Ethnocentrism in Ireland	5. Racialism in Ireland
6. Religious Practice in Ireland	7. Religious Attitudes and Perceptions
8. Attitudes toward Northern Ireland and Britain	9. Irish Political Opinions and Issues
10. Sexism, Feminism and Family Life	11. Travellers and Other Social Categories
12. Underclass, Unemployment and Social Mobility	
13. General Measures of Prejudice and Tolerance	
14. Summary and Conclusions	

Chapters II and III covered more general issues while Chapters IV to XI dealt with particular areas of prejudice and social attitudes. Chapters XII to XIII returned to more general issues. Each chapter was treated as a unit in itself and as part of the overall context. This relative autonomy of each chapter enables the reader to "dip into the text" in areas of special interest without having to cover the whole text. The factual evidence (data) has been presented as close as possible to the textual commentary which enables the reader to evaluate the commentary in the light of the findings. While interpretations, arising out of the findings, are influenced by a theoretical approach, they are not intended as absolute or dogmatic. As in the case of all positivist and empirically-based commentary it is of its nature hypothetical and open to other interpretations. The reason for publishing so much detailed findings therefore, is to enable different interpretations by readers and to facilitate replication by future attitude researchers.

1.2 Conceptual and Theoretical Framework:

Chapter II gives the conceptual and theoretical frameworks and the research design of the study. The value of the *conceptual framework* is clarity of discussion and avoidance of confusion and misunderstanding by the reader. Such a framework was not presented in the 1977 publication[2] in this systematic manner and this omission may have been responsible for some controversial discussions and misinterpretations at the time. The main purpose of the conceptual framework is to enable the measurement of prejudice indicators in the responses of the sample to specially constructed questions and to make them consistent and more precise. It also provides a series of concepts which facilitates diagnosis and theoretically-based discussion.

2. The "1977 publication" refers to Mac Gréil, *Prejudice and Tolerance in Ireland.*

The advantage of the *theoretical framework* is that it provides propositions which are judged to explain variations in the levels of prejudice against a range of categories or groups. The principal macro-theories are what might be loosely called "structural" theories, i.e., functionalism and conflict theories, and the *"momentum-model theory"* (which attempts to integrate both the equilibrium and conflict theoretical approaches). The *"vacillating social situation model"* demonstrates the coexistence of both conflict and equilibrium in society and the shifts to and fro on the consensus-descensus continuum. The application of a series of social psychological middle-range theories, especially, the frustration-aggression theory, have again proven useful in the current survey. The addition of three new independent variables of theoretical significance has proven most useful both as helping the reader to understand the variations in prejudice and as findings in their own right. These three scales are *"The Anomie Scale"* (an adaptation of Srole's Anomie Scale) *"The New Alienation Scale"* (used for the first time) and *"The New Patriotic Esteem Scale"*. The absence of such independent variables for the 1977 publication was a noted deficiency.

The Research Design of the 1988-89 survey is similar to that of the 1972-73 survey. The questionnaire is printed in appendix A. The inclusion of the questions on the family and religious imagery from the *International Survey* has been a useful addition and a number of the family scales are analysed in Chapter X. The contribution the Nijmegen (Holland) questions enhanced the questionnaire, especially in the area of religious and political attitudes. The interview questionnaire has worked out very well in the field and, despite its length (averaging ninety minutes) it was favourably received by respondents who cooperated with the interviewees. There has been a minimum of missing data. The response rate at 73% (1,005 interviews) was judged quite satisfactory.

2. SOCIAL DISTANCE AND INTERGROUP DEFINITION:

In Chapter III the overall findings of question four, i.e., *social distance and rationalisation responses* in relation to fifty-nine stimulus categories, are presented. The relative level of social acceptance and rejection is recorded for each of the social categories. The standing of each category is measured by its mean social distance and by its position on the rank order of categories. The following summary table (180) gives the national ratings of the various ethnic, political, racial, religious and social categories.

It was noted in Chapter III that the stimulus categories were ranked generally to the *"principle of propinquity"* in relation to ethnic, religious, political and social categories, i.e., those closest to the respondents' ethnic, religious, racial-group, political, socio-economic, and other traits and views were most preferred and given lower social distance scores.

Intergroup definition was established by means of a Rationalisation Scale which gave the main reasons given by respondents who did not welcome members of categories into the family on the *Bogardus Social Distance Scale.* Broad categories of reasons were shown to the respondent (on a prompt card) from which he or she chose one reason or offer another not included on the precoded list. The reasons on the list included the following "religious", "racial", "cultural/ethnic/nationality", "political", "economic", "not socially acceptable" and "way of life". In some cases "way of life" was added to "cultural/ethnic/nationality". Tables 7, 8 and 9 (pp. 77 ff. above) give the findings of the Rationalisation Scale and point to the major factors which were given as reasons for excluding the various category members from kinship.

TABLE 180
SUMMARY TABLE OF SOCIAL DISTANCE BY RANK-ORDER
OF MEAN-SOCIAL-DISTANCE SCORE (1-7)

Rank Order	Category	M.S.D.	Rank Order	Category	M.S.D.
1	Roman Catholics	1.057	31	Capitalists	2.587
2	Working Class	1.210	32	Jews	2.599
3	Gardaí	1.267	33	Greeks	2.634
4	Irish Speakers	1.287	34	Socialists	2.650
5	Unemployed	1.345	35	Coloureds	2.715
6	English	1.475	36	Russians	2.882
7	White Americans	1.514	37	Africans	2.916
8	British	1.521	38	Chinese	3.009
9	Physically Handicapped	1.581	39	Blacks	3.019
10	Canadians	1.582	40	Agnostics	3.021
11	Scottish	1.592	41	Unionists	3.084
12	Church of Ireland	1.609	42	Alcoholics	3.084
13	Northern Irish	1.637	43	Indians	3.108
14	Welsh	1.641	44	Israelis	3.117
15	Protestants	1.659	45	Nigerians	3.131
16	Unmarried Mothers	1.684	46	Atheists	3.152
17	French	1.883	47	Black Americans	3.212
18	Dutch	1.946	48	Ex-Prisoners	3.316
19	Luxembourgers	1.960	49	Pakistanis	3.404
20	Germans	1.994	50	Moslems	3.420
21	Mentally Handicapped	2.010	51	Arabs	3.509
22	Trade Unionists	2.022	52	Travellers	3.681
23	Presbyterians	2.045	53	Communists	3.769
24	Danes	2.088	54	Gay People	3.793
25	Belgians	2.122	55	Sinn Féin	4.245
26	Methodists	2.128	56	Hare Krishna	4.331
27	Spaniards	2.252	57	People with Aids	4.336
28	Polish People	2.315	58	Drug Addicts	4.798
29	Italians	2.339	59	Provisional IRA	5.049
30	Portuguese	2.385			

Twenty categories were classified with *single identities*, i.e., sixteen as "ethnic" and four categories classified as "religious". Twenty-nine categories were given a *double identity*, i.e., ten were not welcomed as members of the family because of "way-of-life" and "not socially acceptable", eight because of "ethnic" and "racial" reasons, three for "ethnic" and "political" reasons and the remaining eight categories for other combinations (see Table 9, p. 77). Nine categories who elicited a *treble identity* included interesting combinations of "ethnic", "religious", "racial", "political" reasons. Finally, one category, i.e., "Communists" were excluded for four reasons, "religious", "political", "way-of-life" and "economic".

Among the notable *changes in intergroup definition*, based on the Rationalisation Scale, were the changes from *"racial"* to *"ethnic"* for the nationalities from Africa and Asia and from *"not socially acceptable"* to *"way of life"* for the relatively unpopular social categories. The shift from racial to ethnic (see Table 43, p. 153) is a clear confirmation of a reduction in racialist prejudice, i.e, prejudice based on physical appearance such as colour, lips, hair etc. over the intervening sixteen years between 1972-73 and 1988-89. It is in harmony with the shift in the United States by the Black People to see themselves as "Afro-Americans" rather than as "Negroes" or "Blacks". Such a shift in intergroup definition may not necessarily always mean a reduction in the degree of prejudice and in the discrimination arising from it. What it does mean, however, is that even in the discrimination situation the perceived difference is because of a "human trait", i.e., culture or nationality, rather than for a "non-human, non-cultural, genetically inherited" visible quality, i.e., race. It may also mean that people are becoming more politically correct, thus giving ethnic rather than racial reasons. The change from "racial" to "ethnic" rationalisation is to be welcomed.

The shift from "not socially acceptable" to "way of life" as a reason for not admitting to kinship, may indicate a drop in social snobbery as the basis of prejudice against unacceptable social minorities. This has been replaced by a widespread intolerance of groups because of their perceived life-styles or subcultural norms or values.

The special value of the findings of the Rationalisation Scale is its discovery of the dominant factor in intergroup definition which may help to explain to some extent the causes of particular prejudices. The example of social distance towards "Unionist", which is difficult to justify, is a clear case of multiple causation in the sample. Some 59.8% gave "political" reasons for not welcoming Unionists into the family while 21.2% did so for "ethnic/way of life" reasons and a further 13.6% stated it was because of "religious" reasons they would not welcome them closer (see Table 7). Awareness of this triple intergroup definition is necessary information for our understanding of the relatively negative attitudes towards "Unionists".

3. ETHNOCENTRISM IN IRELAND

Three basic measures or factors were used to examine the ethnic attitudes of the respondents, i.e., Irish nationality and ethnic self-identity, attitudes towards the Irish Language and ethnic intergroup social distance. These three factors were discussed in detail in Chapter IV.

3.1 Nationality:

Under this heading the question of Irish nationality was discussed in the context of the division of Ireland into the Republic of Ireland/Irish Free State/Twenty-six Counties and Northern Ireland/Six Counties in the early 1920s, in particular, and of the concept of "offensive" and "defensive" ethnocentrism, in general (see pages 95f.). Ireland as an ethnic entity is also a post-colonial political society and still shows some of the marks arising from that position. In relation to the division of Ireland, the vast majority could be classified as "constitutional republicans or nationalists" (see Table 94 p. 233). Irish ethnocentrism, which is measured by the social distance score towards a range of ethnic groups is largely a "defensive" ethnocentrism (see Table 28, p. 116) and a reaction to former colonisation and global media.

3.2 Ethnic Self-Identity:

The sample's ethnic self-identity has been overwhelmingly Irish, with two thirds (67.5%) seeing themselves primarily as "Irish" and a further 28.5% identifying themselves as "county/city" (20.6%) and "Southern Irish" (7.3%). Less than one percent (0.6%) identified primarily as "Northern Irish". When the above added together it is seen that 96% of the national sample saw themselves as Irish (national/provincial). This shows the homogeneity of our primary ethnic self-identity which is characteristic of an "emigrant people" (see Tables 11 and 12 pp. 97/8), i.e., a population with relatively few immigrants from other cultures.

When the ratio between "Irish" and "Internal Irish" primary ethnic self-identity scores of the 1988-89 survey are compared with those of 1972-73 (see Table 13), it is evident that a substantial change has taken place. If the hypothesis put forward and tested in *Prejudice and Tolerance in Ireland* (Mac Gréil, 1977 pp. 124 ff.) that the identification with "county or city" rather than with Ireland as a whole was more characteristic of the "working class" in contrast with the 'middle class' broader national self-identity is still true, then, the findings of the 1988-89 survey show an advance of the middle class outlook and a decline of that of the working class. "County or city" ethnic self-identity is more representative of local community identity. It is at times defined as "parochialism" or "provincialism" by "middle class" liberal critics. The decline of the community in Irish society could be associated with this change of mentality. Nevertheless, local community identity was a very strong "second" choice (see Table 13).

3.3 Patriotic Esteem:

This concept is used to depict the degree of National respect in the population. A special five-item scale has been tested. The items have been adopted from the Nijmegen questionnaire (1985). It is not easy to interpret the results in terms of their social-psychological significance. A high score could be seen, on the one hand, as evidence of self-confidence and, therefore, something very positive and not likely to be correlated with ethnocentric prejudice. On the other hand, too strong and idyllic a view could indicate either a very strong degree of nationalism or a countering of a lack of self-confidence in one's ethnic self-identity (see Rose, 1972). This could also reflect a degree of "post-colonial attitudinal schizophrenia" and ambivalence towards one's own people. Whatever the explanation, the response to the five-item scale has been most positive with a scale-score of 140 out of 200 (see Table 15 p. 102). The breakdown by personal variables followed the normal pattern but with a relatively low range of subsample variations. On analysis this scale did not show a significant correlation with "authoritarianism", which is related to prejudice.

4. ATTITUDES TOWARDS THE IRISH LANGUAGE

Table 18 (p. 107) gives the responses to a question on the restoration of the Irish Language. The findings show a positive disposition among the vast majority (94%), but the intensity of the restoration desired was mixed, mainly as a second language in a bilingual society. These attitudes had improved since the respondents were at school (Table 20). There was a significant increase in the evaluation of the Irish Language as a cultural basis of Irish unity in the longterm, since 1972-73, although it was still a minority view (see Table 22 p. 110).

Declared competence in and use of Irish were measured and the results given in Tables 23 to 27 show an increase in competence to 41% but a decrease in regular use of Irish. This lag between competence and use has a restraining effect on the survival of Irish as a widely used and accepted language. One optimistic sign may be in the positive correlations between educational and occupational status and competence in and use of the language. The importance of radio and television for the use of Irish is borne out in Table 27. In recent years the Irish speaking minority has become more vocal in Ireland and are likely to make more demands on the public authorities in the years ahead. The status of "Irish Speakers" is extremely high on the Bogardus Scale. They rank within the five "ingroups" in Table 5 (p. 65), the other four being, "Roman Catholics", "Working Class", "Gardaí" and "Unemployed".

The importance of the status of the Irish Language is very significant for the ethnic self-confidence of the Irish people. The native language of a people is their principal symbolically meaningful system and enshrines the people's nuance on reality over two-thousand-three-hundred years. As stated (pages 114f.) the attitudes are positive towards Irish and the level of competence is now sufficient for a major move forward. What is necessary is the translation of attitudes and competence into behaviourial expression in greater regular use of the language. The coming into being of the new Irish Language Television Channel may be a precipitating factor in providing a breakthrough! From the above findings it is an opportune development likely to expand the use of the latent/dormant competence in Irish within the national population.

5. ETHNIC SOCIAL DISTANCE (ETHNOCENTRISM)

Under the general heading of "ethnic social distance" it has been possible to measure Irish ethnocentrism in a very comprehensive manner. In all there were twenty-one ethnic categories including Ireland's eleven fellow members of the European Union at the time. Table 28 (p. 116) places the Ethnic categories in rank order of choice of the respondents. Categories nos. 1 to 7 could be classified as **Irish, British, (North) American**, i.e., *"English"*, *"White Americans"*, *"British"*, *"Canadians"*, *"Scottish"*, *"Northern Irish"* and *"Welsh"*. The placing of these categories in the most preferred position is a clear case of the *"principle of ethnic propinquity"*.

Categories nos. 8 to 19 are all **Continental European Nationalities** in order of preference, i.e., *"French"*, *"Dutch"*, *"Luxembourgians"*, *"Germans"*, *"Danes"*, *"Belgians"*, *"Spaniards"*, *"Poles"*, *"Italians"*, *"Portuguese"*, *"Greeks"* and *"Russians"*. With the exception of "Poles" and "Russians", the other ten categories are members of the European Union.

The third group of nationalities were categories nos. 20 and 21 and they might be classified as **Middle-Eastern Ethnic Categories**, i.e., *"Israelis"* and *"Arabs"*. The level of ethnocentric social distance towards "Israelis" and "Arabs" is quite severe with 22.6% and 26.7% respectively denying citizenship to members of these nationalities. Such a high level of hostility merits attention.

Table 31 (pp. 124/5) examines social distance mean scores by personal variables and establishes a fairly clear pattern across the twenty-one categories. "Age" is positively correlated with ethnocentrism while "education", "occupational status" and "social class position" are negatively correlated with it. In most cases the ethnic prejudice of males and females are the same. In the case of the least acceptable categories, "Italians", "Portuguese", "Russians", "Israelis" and "Arabs", males are less prejudiced than are females. Respondents from small cities were least prejudiced against ethnic groups while those from rural background were most so. In terms of "political party preferences" Fine Gael supporters were most ethnocentric while Labour Party respondents were least prejudiced.

The changes in ethnocentrism (Table 32, p. 128) since 1972-73 record a significant increase in all of the ten nationalities replicated. This is evidence of a growing *"defensive ethnocentrism"* which, while very moderate in 1988-89, could grow as has happened with the emergent revival of ethnic consciousness throughout Europe over the past twenty years.

6. RACIALISM

Racialism is examined in Chapter V by means of a special *Racialist Scale* replicated from the 1972-73 survey and a *Racialist Social Distance Scale*, measuring social distance against ten racial and ethnic-racial categories. The findings of both of these scales record a significant and substantial reduction in racialism in Ireland since 1972-73. This is confirmed in Table 33, p. 133, and Table 38, p. 144, as already mentioned above. There has been a change in the intergroup definition of ethnic-racial categories from "racial" to "ethnic" on the rationalisation scale (see Table 43, p. 153). The patterns of racialism are according to the "normal" trends given on page 122 (footnote).

The reasons for this decline in racialism in Ireland at a time of an increase in ethnocentrism have not been explicitly researched in this survey. The welcome change has probably come about due to the range of positive reference groups and role models such as the ANC, Nelson Mandela, Paul McGrath (a popular member of the Irish soccer team), Phil Lynott (see Lynott and Hayden, 1995), and other persons in the fields of music, athletics and politics. The positive influence of generations of Irish Missionaries to Africa and Asia as well as numerous volunteer aid workers must also have helped change minds. Of course, the findings of Chapter V while recording positive trends, still show an undesirable level of dormant racialism in Irish society.

7. RELIGIOUS BACKGROUND IN IRELAND

Chapters VI and VII deal with religious practice and attitudes in Ireland. The link between religious practice and social prejudice in Ireland (using the data of the 1988-89 survey) have been tested by Konig[3] and found to be neutral or positive in all cases except Anti-Semitism (see Konig 1990). The special importance of religion as a characterising factor in Irish intergroup relations has its origin in the Reformation of the 16th century and the series of dispossessions and plantations during the 17th century and the religious persecution of Roman Catholics under the infamous Penal Laws so rigorously enacted and imposed by the Irish Parliament during the late 17th and throughout most of the 18th century (see Burke, W.P., 1914). The Catholic-Protestant struggle of the 19th century was more one of social class conflict between the peasantry, who were in the main Roman Catholic, and the Landlords, who were predominantly Protestant. Also, most of the

---

3. Konig analysed the religious and prejudice scores of the 1988-89 survey and reported his findings in his master's thesis.

unskilled and semiskilled working class in the industrial conflict in Dublin in the early 20th century were predominantly Roman Catholic. Practically all of the Irish citizens who suffered during the Great Famine and those forced to emigrate were poor and dispossessed Roman Catholics. In Northern Ireland in the past Presbyterians also suffered social and economic deprivation at the hands of the Established Church, especially in the 18th century.

Later in the 19th century the religious dimension was introduced into the Home Rule equation when Randolph Churchill and others "played the Orange Card". The position of Roman Catholics in the political hierarchy was relatively speaking very low when one considers that Catholic Emancipation was not granted until 1829. By 1869 the Established Church was disestablished in Ireland and the Church of Ireland was freed from formal identity with the Colonial Government of Ireland (see Hurley, M., 1970). This enabled the development of interdenominational equality. Since the 1960s (just one hundred years after Disestablishment) an ecumenical relationship has begun to influence religious mutual attitudes. The success of this movement has been mixed and patchy to date.

The setting up of the Irish Free State and Northern Ireland in 1922 resulted in two political units in Ireland with different denominational majorities. As Tables 45 (p. 157) and 70 (p. 190) show, the Free State had a Roman Catholic majority of 92.6% to 7.0% who were Protestants and Northern Ireland had a Protestant majority of 62.2% to 33.5% Roman Catholics. This was obviously going to lead to perceived denominational dominance on both sides of the Border. By 1981 the Roman Catholic majority was to be between 93% and 95% with the Protestant minority down to from 3.5% to 4.0%. In Northern Ireland the estimated distribution of 52.7% Protestants to 38.7% Roman Catholics in 1981 had changed substantially to a ratio of 47.2% Protestants and 40.6% Roman Catholics at present (see Compton's distribution p. 190).

In Northern Ireland, despite the Disestablishment and the Ecumenical Movement, the Orange Order (a Protestant association) has continued to identify with British Rule in Ireland and the membership of the Loyalist Community continue to be predominantly Protestant (Church of Ireland and Presbyterian). Some of the more radical Protestant communities in Northern Ireland express a militant Reformationist attitude towards the Roman Catholic Church and perceive an independent integrated Ireland as a society dominated by the Roman Catholic Church. The net result of this complex interplay of religious conviction and political ideology, is the continued division of Irish society. At the time of the 1988-89 survey an intense paramilitary violent campaign had been in progress in Northern Ireland for some twenty years and was to continue for a further five years before the "cease fire" of 1994-96. The 1996 "marching season" incidents of intercommunity hostility in Northern Ireland manifest the volatile nature of the current situation despite a series of moves towards peaceful co-existence.

It is in the context of the above resume of religious-cum-political-cum-social strife that the findings of Chapters VI, VII and VIII must be evaluated. It is impossible to understand socio-politico-religious intergroup relations in Ireland without appreciating the background of the current situation.

8. RELIGIOSITY OF THE SAMPLE

8.1 Practice:

Chapter VI measures the religiosity of the people through an analysis of religious practice and the perceived importance of religion in the lives of the people. The frequency of formal religious worship has been given in detail in Tables 48 to 51 (pp. 159-162) and show a relatively high level of practice in general with evidence of a gradual decline in frequency over the previous fifteen years, where Roman Catholic weekly Mass attendance dropped from 91% to 82%, monthly Communion from 66% to 63% and monthly Confessions from 47% to 18% (over 56% of the sample went to Confessions a few times a year or more often). The latter reflected a change in norm for frequency of Confessions (see Table 55, p. 170).

When practice by personal variables is analysed in Tables 52 (p. 163), 53 (p. 165) and 54 (p. 168), it is clear that age and urbanisation are most significant variables with the younger and more urbanised practising less frequently in the case of Mass, Holy Communion and Confessions. Gender had a big influence on frequency of receiving Holy Communion and going to Confessions with females having a higher level of participation than males. There was a negative correlation between education and frequency of Confessions, i.e., those with higher education going to Confessions least frequently.

8.2 Importance of Religion:

In questions relating to the perceived *importance of religion in the lives of the respondents* there was a very positive response (see Table 56 p. 172) despite a drop in the intensity of that importance since 1972-73. A similar response was given to the question of the social advantage of one's religion and the importance of handing on one's beliefs to one's children (see Tables 57 and 58 p. 172). Very few people saw religion as an impediment to social advance which points to the absence of any significant sectarianism in the Republic.

8.3 Personal Prayer:

With regard to *prayer and closeness to God*, the findings of Table 64 (p. 181) show daily prayer at around 70% and weekly prayer at 90%. "Age" and "education" seem to be influential variables affecting prayer. Older people pray much more than younger people and those with higher education pray less than those who got less schooling. In many instances education seems to be a secularising influence in relation to religious practice. Does this mean that the religious ethos of secondary and higher schools and colleges in Ireland is diminishing in Ireland? In general, the frequency of religious practice and prayer of females is higher than that of males although the range between both subsamples is reducing. Nevertheless, the difference in the case of prayer is quite substantial. Only 1.6% said they had no belief in God.

8.4 Closeness to God:

"Felt closeness to God" was another measure of religiosity which elicited an interesting result. Some 85.7% felt close to God while only 2.9% did not feel the closeness of God at all (see Table 66, p. 184). A scale of six items replicated from the Dutch national survey (Table 67) provided interesting insights into the respondents' perception of the relationship of God to the people. The Irish sample saw God playing a greater role in the lives of the people than was the case from the Dutch respondents.

8.5 Vocations:

The attitudes towards vocations to the priesthood and religious life, i.e, towards young people dedicating their lives fully to prayer and the service of the Church, was taken as yet another indication of the degree of religiosity of the respondents. Tables 68 and 69 (pp. 186/7) give the responses to a hypothetical situation where a parent was told by a son or daughter that he or she had decided to become a priest or a nun. The response was quite positive with three quarters of the sample willing to encourage their sons or daughters to follow the religious vocation of their choice. The pattern of responses by variables was predictable in that the young, the "never married", "Dubliners", and those with "third level" education were the least supportive. At the same time the range of difference was not that substantial which meant there was a moderate high level of consensus.

9. CHRISTIAN CHURCH UNITY

Because of Ireland's unfortunate history of inter-Church conflict and misunderstanding, the progress of the ecumenical movement is of special importance. The questions addressing this issue were replicated from the Richard Rose Survey of Northern Ireland in 1968 (see Rose, 1972) and from the Dublin Survey of 1972-73 (see Mac Gréil, 1977). In response to the question on *"Christian Church Unity in principle"* there was a substantial drop

(-23%) in support for it being "desirable", despite the indications of an anticipated change in the positive direction in the 1972-73 findings. Why this decline in unqualified support for Christian Church Unity "in principle" has taken place may be due to a combination of a number of factors (see pp. 190 ff.). Another significant finding of Tables 72 and 73 is the performance of the age variable, i.e., young respondents were substantially less supportive than those of the older subsample. This does not indicate optimism for the future improvement in ecumenical outlook.

10. IMAGES OF GOD AND THE WORLD

The four continua devised by Professor Andrew Greeley to measure the people's perception of God were replicated from the International Survey. The findings were interesting in that God was seen as more a "Father" than a "Mother", more as a "Master" than a "Spouse", more as a "Friend" than a "King" and almost equally divided between a "Judge" and a "Lover". (See Table 74, p. 195).

When asked whether respondents saw the "world" and "human nature" as positive or negative, the replies were optimistic in relation to both (see Table 75, p. 197). This is an important piece of evidence which helps to balance the very negative results of the Anomie and the Alienation Scales (Table 177, p. 415 and Table 178, p. 419).

11. RELIGION IN SOCIO-POLITICAL LIFE

The attitudes and views of the sample towards the links between religion and involvement in socio-political life have been items of public discussion for many years. Opinions vary from religious/church isolationism, i.e, stick to purely spiritual and liturgical matters, to getting more involved in political and social issues and publicly campaigning for people's rights and criticising unjust systems and practices. Two of the three questions reported on Table 76 (p. 199) were replicated from the Dutch Survey. A plurality agreed with greater involvement and a majority with religious view influencing important decision. The majority disagreed with the statement that their religion had a great deal of influence on their political ideas. The pattern of responses of the Irish sample was similar to the Dutch findings.

12. SOCIAL DISTANCE OF RELIGIOUS CATEGORIES

The "principle of religious propinquity" is very evident in the rank-ordering of religious categories on Table 77 (p. 201). The main Christian denominations were most preferred in the following order: first *Roman Catholics*; second *Church of Ireland*; third *Protestants*; fourth *Presbyterians*; and fifth *Methodists*. The sixth place was given to *Jews*. The next two we general categories, i.e., seventh *Agnostics* and eighth *Atheists*. Those placed at the end of the order of preference were ninth *Moslems* and tenth *Hare Krishna*. The relative severity of prejudice (as measured by social distance) towards "Agnostics" and "Atheists" is disappointing in that most believers accept that faith is a *gift* from God. The negative attitudes towards "Moslems" and "Hare Krishna" needs serious attention also and is inconsistent with respect for religious belief in God which has been manifested in the high level of religiosity. This may in part be due to imported prejudices through the negative stereotyping on cheaper media coming into Ireland. The changes in religious social distance between 1972-73 and 1988-89 have been minimal (see Table 80, p. 205). Table 81 (p. 207) shows the difference between the National Sample and the Dublin Subsample to be significant and substantial in the percentages admitting to kinship, which means that those living outside Dublin County were more prejudiced than were Dubliners.

13. ANTI-SEMITISM

The persistence of Anti-Semitism throughout history and in all parts of the world has been one of the clearest examples of an ubiquitous social prejudice. Possible reasons are proposed for this in Chapter VII (Part IV) above (see pages 208 ff.). The overall findings of the special Anti-Semitic Scale (Table 82, p. 210) and of the Social Distance Scores (Table 86, p. 86) are compared with those of 1972-73. There was a very slight decline (-8.2 on a 1-200 anti-semitic scale score continuum) between the scale p-scores of 1988-89 and 1972-73. Table 83 (p. 211) gives a breakdown by scale item. In the case of Social Distance the position of the Jews disimproved slightly (i.e. a drop of 5% in "admission to kinship" in the case of Dubliners). The trends in "education" and "age" point to a trend towards greater tolerance (see Table 87, p. 217).

14. ATTITUDES TOWARD NORTHERN IRELAND

These attitudes have been examined in Chapter VIII under three headings, i.e., Social Distance towards Northern Irish, Special Northern Irish Scale, and views on the Northern problem. Because of the special ongoing problems of Northern Ireland it had been necessary to give special attention to the issues discussed here.

14.1 Social Distance Towards Northern Irish:

Table 88 (p. 225) shows Northern Irish as 5th in the rank order of Irish-British ethnic categories. In terms of "propinquity" one would have expected "Northern Irish" in second place after "Irish Speakers". As in 1972-73, a number of British categories are preferred to "Northern Irish". The "English", "British" and "Scottish" were ranked ahead of

"Northern Irish" and "Welsh" came after them. There was no change in the mean social distance scores against Northern Irish between 1972-73 (see Table 89, p. 226). In the Rationalisation scores (Tables 91 and 92, pp. 228 ff.) "political" and "ethnic", at 42.6% and 37.6% respectively, were the main reasons given for denying closer social distance to "Northern Irish". "Religious" reasons were given by 12.1%. This treble identity of *political-ethnic-religious* of "Northern Irish" in the mind of those prejudiced against them is central to our understanding of the degree of alienation between the minority of the sample and their Northern fellow Irish. Despite their position on the social distance scale vis-a-vis the Irish-British categories, it must be stated that there is a very high level of acceptance of Northern Irish with over 70% willing to welcome them into the family through kinship. These findings should be reassuring to the people of Northern Ireland.

14.2 Special Northern Irish Scale:

This scale was replicated from the 1972-73 survey. The findings given on Table 94 (p. 233) are worth serious study and reflection. To summarise them here would not do them justice. Three areas of significant and substantial change would be; the increase in the rejection of violence (Table 98, no. 3, p. 239), the reduction of the degree of estrangement between Dubliners and Northern Irish (Table 100, p. 242), and an increase in support for a "two-nation Ireland" (Table 96, nos. 1 and 3, p. 236).

14.3 Preferred Solutions to the Northern Problem:

Seven possible solutions to the Northern problem were suggested to the respondents and they were asked how they would see them, i.e., *"as desirable"*, *"not desirable but acceptable"* or *"as undesirable"*. The findings on Table 104 (p. 248) show very clearly that the vast majority prefer a *"Thirty-two County Republic with One Central Government"*. It was considered "desirable" by three-quarters of the sample and acceptable by a further one-eighth resulting in 88% for acceptable and desirable. Only one-in-eight saw it as unacceptable. A lesser proportion (still a majority) would accept the *"Federal Republic Solution"* and slightly more than half the sample would accept a *"Totally Independent Northern Ireland"* (22% as desirable and 33% as acceptable). The *"Power-Sharing Status Quo with Devolved Government"* option resulted in a 50/50 response. *"Northern Ireland as an Integral part of the United Kingdom"* was unacceptable to 65% while 93% rejected the pre-1922 position of reintegration of the whole island of Ireland back into the U.K. The findings show that the overall will of the National Sample is clearly nationalist and republican in aspiration but also willing to accept some form of federal solution. It is also noteworthy that when the anti-violence attitudes are taken into account, the sample are overwhelmingly what might be termed *constitutional nationalists*. The changes of attitude since 1972-73 (see Table 103, p. 246) show no change in the Republican Solution but increased in support of the Federal options.

14.4 Anglo-Irish Agreement, 1985:

The sample's reaction to the Anglo-Irish Agreement, enacted in 1985, was positive, if not enthusiastically so (see Tables 105 and 106, pp. 250, 252). The majority saw it as "providing a structure through which the Northern problem can be fairly solved". The personal variable most divided on the question was "social class position" where those with the highest status were 82% positive while those with the lowest status were least (38%) impressed (Table 106, p. 252).

15. ANTI-BRITISH ATTITUDES AND OPINIONS

Despite the fact that the *Bogardus Scale* has shown that Irish people see the British very favourably in terms of social distance, the findings of the Anti-British Scale show areas which are problematic for Irish people (Table 108, p. 259). The changes in scale scores since 1972-73 were insignificant in the overall scale score. Table 109 (p. 261) gives the variations in each item. The two new items (nos. 12 and 13) on the scale show how negative Irish people view the manner in which the British authorities have dealt with the Irish in Britain and with the Northern Ireland problem (see Table 110, p. 262).

Apart from "political party preferences", the differences between the personal variable subsamples were relatively low for scale and subscale scores. This shows a high level of consensus in Irish attitudes towards the British (as measured in the Anti-British scale) in Table 113 (p. 266). When the findings of the "hostility" and "poor esteem" subscales are examined by personal variables there is still a degree of "post-colonial attitudinal schizophrenia", although it has been significantly reduced between 1972-73 and 1988-89 (see Table 113, p. 266). This phenomenon of "post-colonial attitudinal schizophrenia" refers to an internal contradiction in the findings of the Anti-British Scale which was discovered in the 1972-73 when there was a positive correlation between "high esteem" of the British and "hostility" towards them. The interpretation of those who are hostile having a high esteem for the British is seen as indicating a low esteem of themselves and a "looking up" to the "former masters". It is not unreasonable to find this post-colonial residue of inferiority complex in Ireland. It is expected that a similar contradiction exists among recently emancipated Black people and others who have suffered the indignity of domination by colonisers or internal repression of political, racial or religious groups.

16. POLITICAL PARTY PREFERENCE

Tables 114 and 115 (pp. 269, 270) give a breakdown of *"political party preferences"* in 1988-89. The total sample's preferences are given in Table

114 (p. 269) and shows that 87% of the sample had a preference. Fianna Fáil was the choice of 52% of those expressing a preference or 45% of the total sample. Fine Gael at 29%, Labour at 8% and Progressive Democrats at 5% were the only parties to get sufficient support which was statistically significant (5% plus). The Workers Party has since split into Democratic Left and Workers' Party. The class distribution of party supporters show Fianna Fáil to be largely cross-sectional with a stronger proportion of working class and rural/town backing. Fine Gael and Progressive Democrats are under represented in blue collar, working class support when compared with Fianna Fáil and the Labour Party.

17. SOCIO-POLITICAL CATEGORIES

Table 116 (p. 272) measures the social distance towards members of five socio-political categories, i.e., "Gardaí", "Trade Unionists", "Capitalists", "Socialists" and "Communists". *Gardaí*, as already noted earlier ranked among the five most preferred out of fifty nine stimulus categories. This very high level of public respect for the *"Gardaí"* must be exceptional and reflects the positive perception of their role in Irish society. The standing of *"Trade Unionists"* is relatively good although it has declined slightly in Dublin since the time of the previous survey of 1972-73.

The social distance scores towards *Capitalists* and *Socialists* are moderately negative and quite similar. Slightly more than half of the sample would not welcome members of either category into the family through marriage. One-in-eight would deny them citizenship. When compared with the 1972-73 scores the position of Socialists disimproved somewhat, i.e., 8.1% fewer Dubliners would welcome Socialists into their family through kinship. The social distance percentages in relation to *Communists* were quite negative with only one quarter of the sample willing to welcome them into kinship while over one third (34.3%) would deny them citizenship. This relatively low score, nevertheless, has meant a substantial improvement on the 1972-73 social distance scores towards *Communists* (see Table 119, p. 278).

The position of "Trade Unionists", "Capitalists", "Socialists" and "Communists" by personal variables is given on Table 118 (p. 275). Only two of the five variables tested recorded significant differences, i.e, "county of residence" and "political party preference", in relation to Trade Unionists, with Dubliners and Labour Party supporters most favourably disposed. Males, Dubliners and members of the higher social classes were most positively disposed to "Capitalists".

All five personal variables recorded significant differences towards "Socialists" and "Communists". Younger respondents, males, those living in Dublin, Labour Party supporters and members of the upper social classes were most welcoming of members of both categories into the family through marriage. Members of the "lower class" were, surprisingly, those most hostile to both "Socialists" and "Communists", i.e., with 18.7% and 41.7% (respectively) of Class V willing to deny them citizenship.

18. NEUTRALITY AND NUCLEAR DISARMAMENT

Tables nos. 120 to 123 (pp. 280 ff.) examine Irish attitudes towards neutrality, non-alignment and opposition to nuclear weapons. The overall evidence of these four tables shows that the national sample is overwhelmingly in support of Irish neutrality and of maintaining a total ban on nuclear weapons.

18.1 Irish Neutrality:

Table 120 (p. 280) gives the overall response of the total sample to four items dealing with Irish neutrality and its involvement with the United Nations' peace-keeping role. The former was endorsed by 84% of the sample while the latter received support from 87%. These verdicts are so strong and the opposition to them so weak, 6% and 5%, respectively that there is little more an author can say. There was also a very strong expression of support for the Government actively pursuing an "*independent foreign policy*" (60% for with 11% against).

A substantial minority (31%) felt that Ireland's position as an "*independent nation*" was threatened by membership of the EEC, while a plurality of the sample (44%) disagreed. The responses to the latter issue are examined by personal variables on Table 121 (p. 281). All variables recorded significant differences between the subsamples. Fine Gael and Progressive Democrat supporters as well as those in the upper occupational status group and those with higher education were strongly in disagreement. Dubliners, males and the upper middle age respondents (51 to 65 years) had majorities in disagreement.

18.2 Nuclear Disarmament:

The strength of opposition to nuclear weapons is measured in Tables 122 and 123 (pp. 282). The opposition to nuclear weapons in the population is overwhelming, i.e., 86% in favour of banning ships and planes carrying them from passing close to Ireland and 83% holding they should never be allowed on Irish soil. There was a high degree of consensus in the personal variables in this very strong opposition (see Table 123).

19. MARITAL STATUS AND FAMILY SIZE

Chapter X deals with a number of issues related to gender and family life. Tables 124 and 125 (p. 291) give the marital status and the family size of the sample and of their family of origin. The mean family size of respondents with their youngest child over six years of age was 4.11 while the mean size of their families of origin was 5.80 which means an intergenerational drop of 1.69. The present signs of Irish fertility developments indicate a further drop of mean family size.

All respondents were asked: *"all in all, what do you think is the **ideal** number of children to have"*. The responses to this question are most revealing (see Table 126, p. 292). The sample mean family size was 3.51 children. While each personal variable recorded a significant variation the deviation from the mean was relatively small which points to an impressive level of consensus. The ideal size desired was 0.60 lower than the average size of completed families (i.e., with the youngest child over six years).

20. THE NEW FEMINIST SCALE

The findings of the *New Feminist Scale* record a very positive approach to the Feminist Movement among a large majority of the sample (see Tables 127, p. 294, and 129, pp. 300/1). Almost two-thirds (64.1%) of the sample agreed that the Feminist Movement was *"very necessary in Ireland"*, while only one-in-seven disagreed (14.6%). Other items on the scale reinforce the positive response. There may be a disagreement as to the "feminist" value of "work at home" or "excelling in the caring professions". Many who would be most positively in favour of feminism would not necessarily see women working *"better than men in the caring professions"* as negative or anti-feminist. The item failed to group with other items in the "factor analysis" (see Table 130, p. 304). For that reason it was decided to drop it from the subscales on Table 132 (p. 306).

The levels of *fundamental sexism* and *political anti-feminism* are relatively low at p-scores of 40.2 and 43.6 respectively out of a score maximum of 200. The p-score in relation to the domestic/religious factor was twice as high as the other two at 83.1 (see Table 132, p. 306). Personal variables responded in accord with the normal patterns of variation except in the case of "social class position" when those from the higher class were most negative towards items of the political feminist factor. Females were slightly more feminist than males. The greatest ranges of variation were in "education" and "age" where the direction of lower anti-feminist bias was such as to indicate further positive change in the years ahead. All in all, the results of the *New Feminist Scale* indicate a low level of anti-female sexism and the trends are in the direction of it continuing to decline in this form of prejudice in Ireland in the future.

21. FAMILY VALUES

Tables 133 to 135 (pp. 309-311) address issues of family values in relation to "working mothers" and "marriage". The scales were part of a special international study/survey carried out under the inspiration of Professor Andrew Greeley (author and sociologist, Chicago) during 1988-89. The findings of these tables proved most interesting.

21.1 Working Mothers:

The *Working Mothers Scale* is composed of ten items (Table 133, p. 309) which address a number of issues concerning working mothers and the opinions of respondents in areas of possible conflict between the demands of children and the requirements of the job. The overall result of the scale seems to give priority to the domestic obligations over the advantages of work outside the home. The majority (64.1) favoured husband/wife equality and the principle of both contributing to the household income.

Over half of the sample (52.8%) agreed that *"all in all, family life suffers when the woman has a fulltime job"* with slightly more than one third (37.0%) disagreeing. There was gender consensus in regard to the item. Almost two-thirds of the sample agreed (63.8%) that *"being a housewife is just as satisfying as working for pay"* with only one-fifth (21.0%) disagreeing. At the same time the majority agreed that "having a job" was a woman's best way of being an independent person.

Table 134 (p. 310) examines in detail the respondents' views on *when it is best for mothers to go out to work*. The following was the rank order of the most favourable time for mothers to go out to work:

	Fulltime	Part-time	Total
1st After marriage before children	74.3%	16.9%	91.2%
2nd After children are reared	63.3%	24.1%	87.4%
3th After youngest child at school	21.3%	49.5%	70.8%
4th When children are under school age	8.9%	33.4%	42.3%

These findings were as expected. They once again show the respondents' priority of the family over work while at the same time asserting the vast majority's support for a mother's right to work. This shows that the national sample is for *inclusive feminism!*

21.2 The Institution of Marriage:

Table 135, p. 311, is a ten-item scale which elicits the respondents' evaluations of marriage and examines their views on the nature and function of marriage. Only one of the ten items did not have cross gender consensus, i.e., more males (51.3%) than females (40.8%) felt that *married people were "generally happier than unmarried"* while 23.9% and 33.6% respectively disagreed with the view. The traditional values of marriage are reaffirmed in the scale while, at the same time, there is a degree of tolerance towards those in a less conventional arrangements.

22. REARING OF CHILDREN

In a short series of six statements measured on Table 136 (p. 317) five of the six items (nos. 1 to 5) are measures of importance of children *vis-a-vis*: the trouble they cause; the joy they give to parents; their burden on parents' freedom; their contribution to the completion of marriage and their financial burden. In all cases children come first with the respondents. In most instances the level of support for children is overwhelming.

The item which refers to childless marriage is also interesting in that the majority of respondents (54.4%) do not agree with the view that *"people who have never had children lead empty lives"*, with 29.4% agreeing. While a plurality (48.2%) felt that *"a marriage without children is not fully complete"*, a substantial minority (34.3%) disagreed with the view.

The basic value of children is strong in the Irish culture. To what extent this public value is getting structural support in modern society is problematic in a time when the pivotal focus has shifted from being a *domestic-centred society* to becoming a more *individualistic economy-centred society* is difficult to assess fully. In the opinion of the author, many developments are family unfriendly and, as a result, child unfriendly. Social work and professional care is an inadequate substitute for family and community support. The values expressed by the people in this survey do not seem to be receiving the appropriate support from some of the political and economic elites and media commentators in modern Ireland!

23. FAMILY STANDARD OF LIVING

A number of indicators of the material standard of living of the family in the Republic of Ireland are given in four tables in the final part of Chapter X (pages 319-322).

23.1 Household Income:

Table 137 (p. 320) gives a detailed breakdown of "take-home" (i.e., after tax), declared income for the total sample. Apart from the actual amount of money received by members of the sixteen categories, the range of income per household and per individual is given. The average individual take-home weekly income of the highest category is five times that of the lowest category's average. What is even more inequitable is the relatively low median household and individual take-home incomes. One third of the sample had take-home household incomes of less than £33 per person per week (at 1995 prices). The skewness towards lower incomes point to the relatively severe social class structure in Irish society despite protestation of social equality. In terms of income and "social class position" (see Table 155, p. 369 below) there seems to be clear evidence of an inequitable class structure in Ireland. In the opinion of the author, all relevant research points to a growing inequity between those in the bottom quartile and those in the top one. There appears to be a need for maximum and minimum levels of income to counter this inequity!

23.2 Family Accommodation:

The very high *home ownership* in Ireland is reflected in Table 138, p. 321 with *85.7%* either owning their own house (50.6%) or in the process of doing so through mortgage payment (29.0%) or buying out Local Authority houses (6.1%). Only 13.1% of the sample lived in rented accommodation. The inventory of domestic appliances given in Table 140 (p. 322) is another indicator of material standard of living of the people living in the Republic of Ireland.

24. THE TRAVELLING PEOPLE

24.1 Cultural Minority:

In Chapter XI the attitudes to Travelling People and other Social Minorities are measured and analysed. It is the contention of the author that the Travelling People are a cultural minority which have certain traits which are different from those of the Settled People. This culture is characterised by their nomadic tradition and extended family structure and community-type patterns of interaction referred to by Tonnies as *gemeinschaftlich*. It is a distinctive subculture of the broader Irish Culture. It should not be confused with the *"culture of poverty"* resulting from minority deprivation which can be removed through just and equitable treatment by the agencies of Irish Society. (See McCann, *et al*, 1994).

24.2 Government Policy and Integrated Pluralism:

Government policy to Travelling People has been largely one of "resettling" within the "Settled Community". Until recently it seems to have been more one of *assimilation* than one of *pluralism*. This does not seem to have been successful despite notable exceptions. The "Tigín" and serviced "Halting Sites" have become more accepted as transitional forms of accommodation which could lead either to genuine pluralism, on the one hand, or to full assimilation, on the other. Assimilation as an end product seems to be meeting with resistance from articulate Travellers and other committed advocates of their cause of pluralism.

24.3 Lower Caste:

The 1972-73 survey findings pointed to the status of Travellers more as a *lower social caste* in Irish society. Unfortunately, the findings of the 1988-89 have reaffirmed those of 1972-73 and require very serious attention by the Settled People to make space for this minority on the basis of pluralist equality. The treatment of the Travelling Community by some journalists, politicians and public agencies in relation to the alleged and sometimes actual involvement of a tiny minority in aggravated assault and burglary, is totally counter-productive and a gross violation of the minority rights of the members of the Travelling Community. Travellers, as a group, tend to be defined by the negative excesses of a few in some of the print media. In most just societies the Travellers could seek compensation and litigation to protect their good name. One of the best possible ways to curtail crime and deviance within the Travelling People may be to seek the cooperation of the Travelling Community itself and seek to remove the causes of any deviance.

24.4 Social Distance Towards Travellers:

Table 141 (p. 327) gives the responses of the National and Dublin Samples to Travellers on the *Bogardus Social Distance Scale*. When compared with the 1972-73 survey the social distance scores have deteriorated very substantially. Dubliners in 1972-73 were much more favourably disposed towards Travellers than they were in 1988-89. In the earlier survey 29.0% were willing to welcome Travellers into kinship and 6.6% would deny them citizenship. In 1988-89 only 16.4% would welcome Travellers into the family through marriage while 9.5% would be prepared to deny them citizenship. Those who would deny Travellers welcome in the family did so for "ethnic/way-of-life" (76.5%) and "not-socially-acceptable" (20.3%) reasons.

The social distance scale by personal variables (Table 144, Section II, p. 333) shows a high level of consensus with only four of the eight personal variables eliciting statistically significant variations. This points to the selective nature of liberalness in Irish Society today.

24.5 Anti-Traveller Scale:

The seven item *Anti-Traveller Scale* had been adapted from a previous anti-minority scale and proved most useful in measuring prejudice against members of the Travelling Community (Cronbach's Alpha = 0.80). The findings of the *Social Distance Scale* were confirmed by the findings of the *Anti-Travellers's Scale* in Tables 143 and 144 (pp. 331/3). The items which elicited most negativity were those relating to **personal contact** with Travellers which once again shows the extent of their "lower caste", if not outcaste, status in the minds of respondents. There was an extraordinary degree of consensus (Table 144) in the case of personal contact items nos. 2, 3, 5 and 7. This once again points to selective liberalness, i.e., those sub-samples which would normally express greater tolerance failed to do so. Table 147 gives a breakdown of the scale and subscale p-scores by personal variables. Young people and Dublin Residents were least prejudiced while those who were over sixty-one years old were most prejudiced. "County of residence", as in the case of social distance scores on Table 144 (Section II), had the greatest range of difference with Connaught/Ulster respondents most negative.

25. OTHER SOCIAL CATEGORIES

Social Distance toward ten special social categories were measured in the 1988-89 national survey, i.e.,

"Alcoholics"	"People with Mental Handicap"
"Drug Addicts"	"People with Physical Handicap"
"Ex-Prisoners"	"Unemployed"
"Gay People"	"Unmarried Mothers"
"People with AIDS"	"Working Class"

Table 149 (p. 343) gives the social distance scores for each social category. The range of scores covers a very wide spectrum from "Working Class" at a mean social distance of 1.210 to "Drug Addicts" at 4.798 (i.e., out of a range of one to seven from "kinship" to "debar or deport"). Six of the categories were also measured in 1972-73. Two of them experienced a slight improvement in status, "Working Class" and "Unemployed" in the intervening sixteen years. The remaining four categories, "Handicapped" (people with physical), "Unmarried Mothers", "Alcoholics" and "Drug Addicts" suffered disimprovement in their levels of social distance by mean social distance score changes of +0.192, +0.142, +0.210 and +1.020 respectively (see Table 150, p. 345).

25.1 "Working Class" and "Unemployed":

The positions of "Working Class" and "Unemployed" are so positive that they rank among Ireland's ingroups. This high ranking of "Working Class" may be in part an expression of romantic attachment to a class which only 42% of the sample identified with when asked to classify themselves according to "Class" (see Table 157, p. 372). In the case of the "Unemployed" their substantial improvement in standing may be in part due to the ubiquity of unemployment in modern Western Society (Ireland included). It is, therefore, losing its negative stigma.

The findings of the 1988-89 survey has recorded a drop of 18.6% in the proportion of the Dublin respondents whose occupations could be classified as Working Class, i.e., "skilled manual", "routine non-manual", "semiskilled" and "unskilled manual", when compared with the occupational distribution of the 1972-73 Dublin Sample. This decline of the blue-collar workers has serious consequences for the employment opportunities of tradespersons and clerical staff. The "de-manualling" of the work force in Western society leads to serious intergenerational class-culture problems.

Variations by personal variables were very modest in the few instances of statistically significant differences (see Table 151, pp. 348/49).

25.2 People Who Are Handicapped:

The position of the people who are handicapped disimproved slightly since 1972-73. They still remain a much approved category with those with physical handicap more favoured than those with mental impairment. There was practically unanimous consensus across the spectrum of personal variables. Only one variable, "county of residence", had a slight if significant variation for both categories. "Place of rearing" recorded significant differences between the subsamples in the case of "People with Physical Handicap", i.e., rural-reared being least open and those reared in small cities were most open.

The fact that each category of people with handicap (physical or mental) failed to elicit statistically significant differences in social distance scores when tested by "education", "occupational status" and "social class position", manifests the cross-class distribution of handicap and may point to this group as a socially integrating presence in society. This would be a positive interpretation of class consensus. On the negative side, however, it could be a further example of selective "liberalness" among the highly educated and those with better occupational status. See Table 151, pp. 348/9).

25.3 Attitudes towards Unmarried Mothers:

The standing of "unmarried mothers" has been moderately high at 1.684 and the rationalisation of those who would not welcome the "unmarried mother" as a member of the family has shifted from "socially unacceptable" in 1972-73 towards life-style or "way of life" in 1988-89, i.e.,

Reason	A	B	Difference
	1972-73 (Dublin)	1988-89 (national)	(B-A)
1. "Not socially acceptable"	76.2%	28.9%	-47.3%
2. "Way of Life"	8.0%	60.8%	+52.8%
3. "Religious"	5.5%	1.7%	-3.8%

The above figures show a very substantial drop in social stigma as a main reason for refusing admission to kinship and an even more substantial increase of "life style" as the principal reason.

There has been a slight drop in the percentage i.e., from 79.0% to 70.4% (-8.6%), of Dubliners welcoming "Unmarried Mothers" into the family (see Table 150, p. 345). This is in line with the overall increase in social distance towards many of the ethnic, political, religious and social categories. Six of the eight personal variables (Table 151, pp. 348/9) have recorded consensus towards "Unmarried Mothers". "County of residence" and "place of rearing" recorded a more tolerant/liberal urban attitude while in "education" the pattern of difference pointed to less tolerance among those with lower standards reached.

25.4 Alcoholics:

The level of social distance towards "Alcoholics" has disimproved significantly since 1972-73. This is seen as a counter-productive development when support for those with a compulsive addiction to alcohol is one of the requirements for successful rehabilitation. If the attitudes reported on Table 149 and on Table 151 (pp. 348/9) are reflected in social behaviour towards "Alcoholics" they may feel isolated if not ostracised. This may indeed result in even greater resort to drinking.

The level of consensus is practically universal in the social distance responses towards "Alcoholics" when measured by personal variables. Only one personal variable, i.e., "place of rearing", recorded a statistically significant variation or difference (see Table 151, pp. 348/9). The rural-reared were the most negative while those reared in "small cities" were most tolerant. Attitudes towards "Alcoholics" is a further example of the selective nature of liberalness!

25.5 Ex-Prisoners:

This category represents people who tend to be labelled negatively in society and as a result of such labelling their rehabilitation is impeded and pressure to re-commit crime increases. This in turn adds to the incidence of recidivism in the Irish prison system which was 58.4% in 1991 (see *Annual Report on Prisons and Places of Detention* 1991). The findings on Tables 149 (p. 343) and on 151 (pp. 348/9) confirm a very negative labelling of "Ex-Prisoners". The mean social distance score of 3.316 is verging on the "out-group" score of 3.500 plus.

The key personal variables of "age" and "education" report consensus which does not reflect well in Irish liberalness! Again, the variables to record the most substantial range of difference were "county of residence" and "place of rearing" where Connaught/Ulster and rural-reared respondents were the most negative subsamples.

25.6 Gay People:

The level of homophobia in the Irish population is still very high and quite disturbing. This form of prejudice seems to be cultural in origin. It may also be a reaction to a sense of insecurity in relation to the person's own sexual identity. In the stark light of what happened to homosexual males in the Nazi Concentration Camps and other ugly incidents of "gay bashing", it is disturbing to read the findings of social distance against "gay people", especially, the fact that they would be denied citizenship by quarter of the sample. This seems to be a very intolerable finding (see Table 149, p. 343).

The patterns of prejudice against "Gay People" by personal variables shows a positive trend of likely reduction in the future. "Age" seems to be a most significant variable with younger respondents more tolerant. "Education", "occupational status" and "social class position" all record positive trends towards greater tolerance. "Males" and rural-reared, residents of Connaught/Ulster all show highest prejudice scores in their respective variables. The reasons put forward by those prejudiced against "Gay People" were because of their "way of life" (75%) and their being "not socially acceptable" (20%). This would seem to indicate that recent publicity in relation to Gay life-style is not succeeding in making "Gay People" more acceptable. The association of "Gay People" with AIDS is probably another negative factor. There was a correlation of $r = 0.65$ between the social distance responses of both categories.

25.7 People with A.I.D.S.:

The attitudes of respondents towards "People with AIDS" is extremely negative at a mean-social-distance score of 4.336 which is very much an "outgroup" score. Such severity is difficult to comprehend in relation to people who are in need of community support. One third (34%) of the sample would deny citizenship to "People with AIDS". This is an attitude one would expect in the case of a political outgroup. The tragedy of the situation is that "People with AIDS" need great sympathy and understanding to help them to come to terms with their terminal illness.

This category elicited significant variations in the case of all personal variables except "marital status". All other variables differentiated according to the normal prejudice pattern. This position does show some sign of improvement by the distribution of scores between the subsamples, especially, in the case of "age" and "education".

25.8 Drug Addicts:

The social distance scores against "Drug Addicts" are even more severe than those against "People with AIDS." As in the case of "alcoholics" this negative result must militate against the rehabilitation of those who are addicted to drugs. What is probably most surprising about the findings of

Tables 149 and 151 (pp. 343 and 348/9) is the fact that "Drug Addicts" come from across the social spectrum (as is the case of "Alcoholics"). Those engaged in the rehabilitation of Drug Addicts must take the negativity of the Irish public into account when trying to cope with this problem. Many "Drug Addicts" are enticed and misled into the habit when they are young and in unreal, exotic and escapist recreational environments. The "Drug Addict" often becomes the first victim of the "Drug Pushers" who exploit the former's compulsive craving. In the attitudes of the Irish people the "Drug Addict" is treated with the negative severity one might have expected in the case of attitudes towards "Drug Pushers". This is a highly unsatisfactory and somewhat unreasonable position.

On Table 150 (p. 345) the changes of attitudes to "Drug Addicts" between 1972-73 and 1988-89 are measured. The deterioration of the situation is quite dramatic. Apart from the overal general handling of attitudes recorded in relation to other stimulus categories, there is the added association of "Drug Addicts" with "People with AIDS" (r = 0.54). Table 151 (p. 348/9) records significant differences by all personal variables except "gender" and "marital status". The variations are in line with normal prejudice trends. The variable with the widest range of difference was "social class position" with a mean social distance range of 1.70. Upper Class people are most tolerant (but, still very intolerant in real terms) at 3.55 while the "Lower Class" category were most intolerant at 5.25. While the trends are towards a reduction in the future, the current position is extremely negative and anything but conducive to the rehabilitation of the "Drug Addict" in our society!

In this context, therefore, the findings of Tables 149 and 153 are not only counter-productive in terms of rehabilitation but also, in the opinion of the author, very unjust. There has been quite a substantial increase in the mean social distance score (+1.020) in the standing of Drug Addicts among Dublin respondents between 1972-73 and 1988-89 (see Table 150, pp. 345-6). The patterns of variation in the case of the personal variables is normal and does indicate a slight trend towards greater tolerance.

26. UNDERCLASS AND UNEMPLOYMENT

Chapter XII examines the attitudes of the sample towards work, unemployment and poverty, and measures the levels of upward and downward social mobility in Ireland. In looking at the trends in inflation and unemployment in the Republic of Ireland between 1972 and 1989 it is clear from Table 152 (p. 355) that the correlation is wholly negative. In other words, as inflation decreased unemployment increased! Are the two related?

A ten-item scale was composed of specially chosen statements to measure people's views and opinions rather than their prejudices in relation to work, unemployment and poverty. Table 153 gives the results of the total sample's response to each item (see page 357).

26.1 The Earned Reputation Theory:

One of the most demoralising aspects of public opinion towards the deprived is to imply that they are responsible for their condition. Four of the eight items (nos. 1, 3, 7 and 8) set out to measure the extent of support for this theory, i.e., "unemployment is voluntary", "the poor are responsible for their poverty", "justification for State intervention to established equity", and 'the self-made man/woman psychology'. The findings show a significant minority who would seem to accept the "earned reputation theory", while the majority clearly reject it.

26.2 State Ownership and Control of Industry:

Despite the widely held identification of the Republic of Ireland as a predominantly free market, capitalist society, the findings of item no. 2 show that three-in-ten (29.3%) felt it would *"be better for the country if the State owned and controlled more businesses and companies"*, while one-in-two disagreed (53.2%). An examination of the personal variables on Table 154 (p. 358/9) clearly shows that the stronger respondents were in terms of "age", "education", "occupational status" and "social class position", the less supportive they were of State intervention, while the older, rural-reared, lower skilled, those with lower standards of education, and from the lower class (V) were strongly in favour of such initiative and support from public funds. In a sense, those who benefit most from the current system are more opposed to State intervention. This is a classical division of social opinion! Fianna Fáil supporters were those most in favour of State intervention.

Another view which indirectly refers to State ownership and control is no. 5 on the scale, i.e., *"that the private sector has failed to deliver jobs"*. The vast majority agreed (63.5%) while one-in-seven (17.1%) disagreed. The pattern of difference within the personal variables of "education", "occupational status" and "social class position" was similar to that of item no. 2 above, with the stronger subsamples more in favour of the private sector.

26.3 Trade Unions and Management:

Items nos. 4, 6, 9 and 10 on Table 153 (p. 357) address the role of Trade Unions and Management in job protection and creation. The results are mixed. A plurality of the sample (43.0%) thought Trade Unions had too much power while 36.5% disagreed. There was overwhelming support (77.1%) for the role of Unions as protectors of *"workers' welfare and rights"* while only 9.3% disagreed. The majority (52.7%) agreed that Management were more to blame than workers for "high unemployment" while slightly less than a quarter (22.4%) disagreed. Some might interpret this as scapegoating Management. The patterns in the personal variables were similar to those noted already in 24.1 above.

27 SOCIAL MOBILITY IN IRELAND

Social mobility has been measured by comparing the *social-class-position five-point scale* of respondents with that of their parents (fathers). Social class position is calculated by means of combining educational standard reached and occupational status, i.e., multiplying education by *four* and occupation by *seven* (see Figure no. 29, p. 368).

The social class distribution on Table 155 (p. 369) shows that the mean position is between Class III and Class IV, i.e., at 3.55 on a one-to-five scale. The 21.2% in the "Lower Class" (Class V) would represent approximately 800,000 people which is more or less the number of people on or below the poverty line in the State. The problem of this fifth of the population is they are likely to constitute an unorganised minority in society, that is, less likely to be a real pressure group in a situation when those above the poverty line constitutes the vast majority (78.8%) of the population. Majority democracy can militate against them in a predominantly middle-class society.

The decline of working class jobs is borne out on Table 156 (p. 370). "White collar jobs" constituted 58.8% while "working class jobs" only represented 41.3% of the occupations of the 1988-89 Dublin subsample which contrasts with the 1972-73 position when the distribution was reversed, i.e., 59% were in "working class" occupations. The overall impact of this change is likely to contribute to the "embourgeoisement" of Irish society. When asked how respondents would classify themselves, most people saw themselves as *"middle class"* (53.4%) and over two fifths (42.1%) saw themselves as *"working class"*. Very few put themselves into the *"upper class"* (0.7%) or into the *"lower class"* (3.8%). When compared with the objective classification (Table 157, p. 372) the under-rating was in the case of "upper class" (-3.1%) and "lower class" (-17.3%). Overall self-rating exaggerated slightly the social class position of the sample of +0.12 on a one-to-five class scale.

The extent of Social Mobility is given on Tables 166 and 167 (pp. 380 and 381). Some 37% experienced "upward mobility", 40% retained their father's position and 23% experienced a drop in their social class position, i.e., a net upward inter-generational mobility of 14%. When the findings of 1988-89 are compared with those of 1972-73, there was a net improvement of 2% which is not that significant. There was a significant increase in upward mobility of +7% and in downward movement of +5% while the most significant change took place in the 11% reduction in those who retained their father's status. Educational mobility has contributed much to the overall status change (see Table 163, p. 377).

Social class position by personal variables (Table 168, p. 384) is quite revealing, especially when examined by "county of residence", which confirms the internal "status drain" within Ireland. In terms of "political party preferences", the Labour Party and Fianna Fáil are more highly "Working Class" while Fine Gael and the Progressive Democrats are more "Upper and Middle Class".

28 AUTHORITARIANISM

Authoritarianism is a complex personality trait which is significantly correlated with prejudice has been examined in Chapter XIII. The scale used to measure this trait which was first devised for the 1972-73 survey (see Mac Gréil, 1977, pp. 423 ff.) was greatly influenced by the class work of Adorno, et al, *The Authoritarian Personality*, 1950. The *New Authoritarian Scale* is composed of four subscales, i.e., "religious fundamentalism", "pro-establishment conservatism", "fascist submission and aggression", and "moralism and miscellaneous authoritarianism".

28.1 Measures of Authoritarianism:

The overall findings of the scale are given on Table 170 (pp. 390/1). This table records the responses to each of the sixteen statements/items for the total sample 1988-89, the Dublin subsample 1988-89 and the Dublin sample 1972-73. The total sample's (1988-89) mean A-score is 105.1 (out of a maximum of 200). The Dublin subsample (1988-89) was significantly but not very substantially lower at 91.0. This latter score is 11.6 lower than the 1972-73 Dublin A-Score 102.6, which marks a significant but very slight decrease in authoritarianism (as measured by this scale) over the intervening sixteen years.

There is an extraordinary degree of consistency between the patterns of difference within a wide range of personal variables in the case of the sixteen individual items on Table 171 (pp. 394/5) and for the scale and subscale a-scores on Table 172 (pp. 402/3). This once again confirms the validity and reliability of the scale.

28.2 Path-Analysis:

It will be shown below that the *New Authoritarian Scale* is a valuable independent variable to explain variations in different social prejudice scales or measure, i.e., ethnocentrism, sexism, racialism, and anti-semitic scales. Regression/path-analysis[4] has clearly shown that authoritarianism is also significantly related to "anomie", "education", "age" and, to a lesser extent, "place of rearing".

4. "Path analysis is a method for presenting a causal model in which a series of independent variables is used to predict a series of dependent variables . . . A set of computation needs to be done for each step of the model but the entire model can be shown in one diagram. The dependent variable changes with each phase of the process. The actual computations involve solving several sets of simultaneous equations formed by all or some of the correlations of the independent variables with each other and the correlations of each independent variable with the dependent variable. *The results of these computations yield a numerical estimate of each independent variable on the dependent variable. The method of computation means that each estimate of direct effect, or path, is given with the effects of the other independent variables controlled"* (Spaeth and Greeley, 1970, pp. 134-5; quoted from Mac Gréil, 1977, p. 501). (Italics added.)

Figure 34: Path/Regression Analysis of Authoritarian Scale

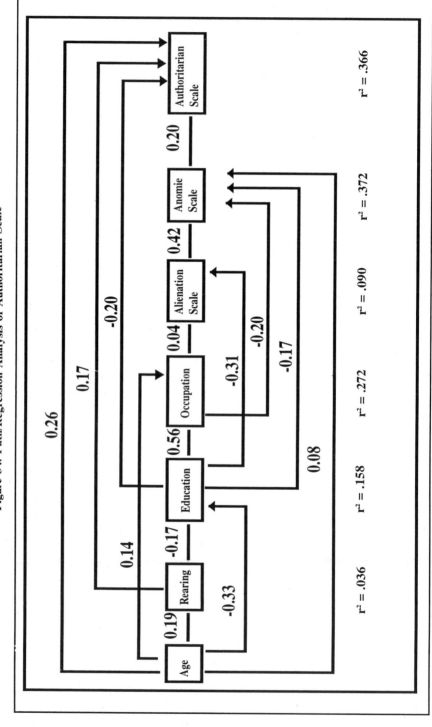

28.3 Direct and Indirect Causation:

In the above Figure no. 34* the New Authoritarian Scale is treated as a **dependent variable**. Taking 0.5 (Beta coefficient) as the minimum level of statistical significance, the direct and indirect influence of the various independent variables, i.e., "age", "rearing", "education", "occupational status", "anomie scale", "alienation scale", on the *New Authoritarian Scale* as a dependent variable leads to a coefficient of multiple correlation of r^2 = 0.366 (which means an r = 0.60). This is a relatively high level of causal explanation in social-psychological or sociological research.

The actual Beta scores between each of the independent variables are most revealing. For example, the link between "age" and "place of rearing" at 0.19 points to the fact that rural reared in the sample are older than are those reared in cities, just as the "age"/"education" relation is a negative (-.33) clearly showing that younger people are relatively more educated than are older respondents. Age/occupation scores still show that chronological seniority has the edge on education in getting to the top. It probably refers to the older educated respondents. The fact that education is negatively correlated (directly) to authoritarianism, shows the positive impact of greater participation in education on the degree of personal tolerance. The Alienation Scale was positively related to the *Anomie Scale* scores at a Beta score of .42.

In the second part of this chapter the *New Authoritarian Scale* becomes an **independent variable** as the causes of various prejudices are analysed (see Figure 7, page 142 above).

29. LIBERAL-ILLIBERAL SCALE

The original *Liberal-Illiberal Scale* was used in the 1972-73 survey and has been replicated in the 1988-89 survey. This sixteen item scale contains eight of the statements included in the *New Authoritarian Scale*. The remaining eight items are most interesting for their insight into attitudes in certain individual statements expressing "liberal" or "illiberal" views and opinions. Table 173 (pp. 406-7) is a composite table giving the responses to each of the sixteen items and the differences between the scores of Dubliners in 1988-89 and in 1972-73. These have been examined by personal variables on Table 174 (p. 409). With the exception of "gender" and "political party preference" there was significant variation in the majority of cases. Issues such as: *"Catholic priests should be free to marry"* and *"premarital sex is always wrong"* are among the eight items examined in Table 174.

Table 176 (p. 414) gives the patterns of variation of illiberalness (as measured by the *Liberal/Illiberal Scale*) which confirm the patterns of

---

*"The statistical process by which path analysis is achieved is quite complex and consists mainly of a series of partial correlations. The proportion of the variance explained is determined by the square of the coefficient of multiple correlation or r^2" (Mac Gréil, 1977, p. 502).

variation in most scales. The older respondents, the widowed, Connaught/ Ulster, rural-reared, the lesser educated, those with lower occupational status and occupying lower social class positions scored highest within the variable subsamples. Females had higher scores than had males and Fianna Fáil supporters were highest in the political party preference variable.

30. SOCIAL ANOMIE

The addition of a measure of *social anomie*, which indicates the degree of normlessness among the respondents, has been included in the 1988-89 survey primarily for the purpose of measuring its causal influence of social prejudice. The scale used to measure Social Anomie has been based on Srole's original Anomie Scale (Srole 1951) and adapted through the cooperation of the researchers of the Social Research Department of the Catholic University of Nijmegen, The Netherlands.

In terms of the overall findings of Table 177 (p. 416) it is quite clear that the level of *social anomie* in Irish society is moderately high. In instances where it has been possible to compare findings (items no. 1, 4, 5 and 6) with the Dutch National Survey (1985), the mean Irish score for the four items was 106.2 while that of the Dutch was 76.5 which is 29.7 less. These figures are out of a maximum Anomie score of 200.

The significance for Irish society of a moderately high level of *anomie* is quite serious. In his classic work on *Suicide*, Emile Durkheim, the French sociologist, discovered a link between anomie and rates of suicide in society. Among the causal factors related to anomie may be the greater degree of individualism resulting from decline of family and of community support which was more characteristic of Ireland in the past. This may well be the price of socio-economic progress in the Western liberal-capitalist free-market economy.

As already noted above, *anomie* was used in the analysis of prejudice as an independent variable with the hope of raising the level of causal explanation. *Social anomie* is both an expression of and a contributing factor to personal insecurity which, in turn, is accepted as a major cause of social prejudice.

31. ALIENATION

The findings of Tables 178 (p. 418) and 179 (pp. 422-3) are derived from a new experimental scale, *The New Alienation Scale*. The aims of this scale were to measure the extent of "alienation" (i.e., a sense of powerlessness in the sample and to explore the causal link between "alienation" and social prejudice. The findings indicate a fairly substantial degree of "alienation" in the population of the Republic of Ireland. It is particularly serious among those with lower social status and with a poor standard of formal education (see Table 179, pp. 422-3).

PART II:
PATH-ANALYSIS OF INDEPENDENT VARIABLES

As already stated (see page 455 above) the multiple-regression path-analysis discerns the nature of the influence of variations in personal variables on particular prejudice scores. Some of the influence is filtered through or by other variables in the case of each particular variable on the path while the remainder is seen to be linked directly between the variable and the prejudice in question.

In all seven independent variables have been selected to test their respective filtered and direct influence. The independent variables are:

1. Age
2. Place of Rearing   5. Alienation Score
3. Education   6. Anomie Score
4. Occupational Status   7. Authoritarian Score

'Religiosity' and 'patriotism' (as measured by the Patriotic Scale) failed to exercise significant influence on general prejudice scores. Measures of 'alienation' and of 'social anomie' are additional to those used in the earlier publication (*Prejudice and Tolerance in Ireland*, 1977) and have proven useful. Gender as a variable was excluded because of its 'nominal' nature, i.e., lacking "relationship-specification" (Mac Gréil, 1977, p. 30). Its inclusion in the 1977 publication elicited some criticism from one commentator (see Figure No. 33 on page 456).

TABLE 181: PATH-ANALYSIS SUMMARY TABLE OF BETA SCORES

Independent Variable	Ethnocentrism	Racialism	Anti-Semitism	Sexism	Anti-British	Anti-Traveller
i. Age	–	0.17	–	0.17	-0.15	0.08
2. Place of Rearing*	–	–	0.12	–	0.17	–
3. Education	-0.08	-0.08	-0.19	-0.08	–	0.08
4. Occupation	–	–	0.07	–	–	0.06
5. Alienation Scale	-0.10	0.05	0.05	0.08	0.11	0.08
6. Anomie Scale	0.09	0.15	0.15	0.07	0.08	0.07
7. Authoritarian Scale	0.34	0.26	0.29	0.32	–	0.14
R^2	0.182	0.259	0.274	0.320	0.051	0.057

Place of Rearing: 1 = Large City; 2 = Small City; 3 = Town; 4 = Rural.
Note: Beta Scores under 0.05 considered "not significant".

Table 181 summarises the direct Beta scores of each of the independent variables (listed above) on six areas of social prejudice, i.e., "ethnocentrism", "racialism", "anti-Semitism", "anti-British" and "anti-Traveller" prejudices.

An examination of the R^2 scores under each of the areas of prejudice measured gives the *extent* to which the variations in the prejudice scores is explained by the independent variables in the path analysis. Four of the six areas record a substantial R^2 score, namely, "ethnocentrism" (0.182), "racialism" (0.259), "anti-Semitism" (0.274) and "sexism" (0.320).[6] The extent of explanation derived from the seven independent variables in the case of "anti-British" scores (0.051) and of "anti-Traveller" prejudice (0.057) is barely significant, representing an R score of 0.23 and 0.24 respectively. The unique nature of "anti-British" attitudes in the Irish population has already been noted (in Chapter IV and VII above). They are completely different from the other examples of ethnocentrism and are not explained by the normal independent variables. Further research into this area of negative attitudes is called for by the failure of the standard variables to score a higher $R^2$2 score. The surviving remnant of "post-colonial attitudinal schizophrenia" may be but one element in the Irish "anti-British" attitude syndrome (see pp. 267 above). The current ambivalence towards the British role in dealing with the Northern Ireland problem also contributes to the uniqueness of Irish attitudes towards the British (see pages 257-269).

The failure of the independent variables to register higher R^2 scores or levels of explanation in the case of "anti-Traveller" attitudes may be due to two factors. In the first place there was a very high level of consensus in the level of prejudice against Travellers and this would reduce the capacity of independent variables to provide a higher level of explanation. The second reason may have something to do with the unique nature of the "anti-Traveller" bias and hostility among the Settled People in Ireland. Again, as in the case of the "Anti-British" finding, further research will be required to get at the core of this particular category of severe anti-minority hatred.

Returning to Table 181, the relative significance of direct Beta scores on the various areas of prejudice is quite impressive and, as in the case of the

6. When the R^2 is greater than 0.16 it represents an r > 0.40 and is the equivalent of stating that 16% plus of the variation has been explained by the independent variables in the 'path'. An $R^2 = 0.32$ means that 32% of the variation has been explained. These levels of explanation are significant and substantial because of the nature of the data on which they are tested in social science research. The data are mainly "ordinal data" which possess "an order of hierarchy of 'more than' and 'less than' relationship . . . (and provide) – an underlying dimension of variability along which objects are being compared" (Newcomb *et al*, 1965, p. 502). In the more precise sciences, whose subjects are not self-motivated human beings, their data are "ratio" or "interval" in nature and can produce a higher level of causal explanation. Intergroup attitudes and prejudices are not conducive to the rigorous experimental measurement one finds in other areas of the "precise sciences". Human behaviour is as prospective as it is retrospective and cannot always be explained fully in antecedent empirically measurable phenomena. For these reasons R^2 of over 0.16 are deemed satisfactory in the case of findings based on data that are, at best, "ordinal".

path-analysis of the 1972-73 data, shows the dominant position of authoritarianism in the multiple regression path (see Mac Gréil, 1977, pp. 508/9) except in the case of the "anti-British" scale. The 'alienation' and 'anomie' scales proved significant factors in the case of each of the areas of prejudice. Other variables were mixed in their levels of significance. The Patriotic Scale failed to register significant Beta scores in the multiple regression path.

Age shows a significant direct influence in the case of "racialism", "sexism", "anti-British" and "anti-Traveller" attitudes. In other words, older people are not as tolerant as younger respondents towards "Black People", "Women" and "Travellers". The opposite seems to be the case in relation to attitudes towards British, younger respondents seem to be more negative than their older contemporaries. Direct influence means that the other independent variables in the path-analysis are controlled for and the age factor is isolated. It is also noteworthy that in the cases of "ethnocentrism" and "anti-Semitism" age failed to elicit a significant direct Beta score. Its contribution to these areas of prejudice was indirectly explained by the other independent variables, i.e., education, etc. (see Figure no. 33, page 456).

The performance of **place** of rearing is interesting in its failure to show significance in four of the six areas of intolerance, i.e., "ethnocentrism", "racialism", "sexism" and "anti-Traveller" attitudes. Respondents reared in more rural or in more urban environments are neither more prejudiced or less prejudiced *because of their place of rearing* in relation to these four categories of prejudice. The two exceptions were "anti-Semitism" and "anti-British" attitudes, where the trend was in the direction of greater intolerance by the more rural the environment or place of rearing.

The performance of **education** in its direct influence of prejudice (when the other six independent variables are controlled for) is as expected except in the case of "anti-Traveller" bias, and in relation to "anti-British" attitudes. In the case of the latter it was insignificant when one would have expected it to be negative, i.e., the higher the respondents' education the weaker their negative attitudes. The finding in relation to the Anti-Traveller Scale is even more disappointing in that it indicates that education contributes to the "anti-Traveller" prejudice. In other words, the more highly educated the more negative on average were the attitudes. This is in contrast to education's performance elsewhere in relation to "ethnocentrism", "racialism", "anti-Semitism", and "sexism". In the opinion of the author this finding confirms the selective nature of liberalness.

Occupation as a personal variable has shown no direct significance in relation to "ethnocentrism", "racialism", "sexism" and "anti-British" attitudes. The two instances where significance has been recorded the results are surprising in that they indicate a positive correlation between occupational status and "anti-Semitism" and "anti-Traveller" attitudes. It is normal to expect those with strong occupational status to be more tolerant because of the security of their social positions. Do these two abnormal findings indicate that "Jews" and "Travellers" are perceived as some form of threat to the privileged positions of the stronger classes in Irish society? Could this be due to the acceptance of the Jewish-control-of-money stereotype and the Travellers-threat-to-house-values fear? Recent objections to serviced 'halting sites' for Travellers in some upper-middle class districts would seem to confirm the latter hypothesis. Whatever the explanation, its possible impact on the minorities' standing in Irish society is less than positive. Of course, the status of the "Jews" is much higher than that of the "Travellers" (see Table 5, pp. 65-7).

The **Alienation Scale** has proved a relative success in the extent of its contribution towards the explanation of prejudice directly (Table 181) and indirectly (Figure No. 32, page 456). It establishes a significant correlation between "a sense of powerlessness" (as measured by this scale, see Table 178, page 418) and prejudice. Such powerlessness is also associated with insecurity which has been long accepted as contributing to prejudice and is not synonymous with either 'Anomie' or 'Authoritarianism'. The negative Beta score (-0.10) in relation to "ethnocentrism" was not anticipated and needs further analysis and replication to establish its significance. 'Alienation' scores were positive in relation to the other areas measured in Table 181, i.e., "Racialism", "anti-Semitism", "Sexism", "anti-British" and "anti-Traveller" prejudices. Its significant direct score in relation to "anti-British" negative attitudes may once again point to the post-colonial residue of self-inferiority *vis-a-vis* our former 'masters'.

Anomie (a sense of normlessness) performed well as an independent variable in both its direct and indirect influence. It has proven to be a very useful independent variable. Table 181 shows a positive and significant direct link between 'anomie' and each of the seven areas of prejudice tested. It was noted in Chapter XIII (Part III) that there was a relatively high level of anomie in the national sample which may explain the levels of prejudice in the case of certain minorities (Beta = 0.15) in its direct link with "racialism" and "anti-Semitism".

Finally, **Authoritarianism** has very substantial direct Beta scores in the case of six of the seven areas of prejudice refuted on Table 181. The absence of a direct link with "anti-British" negative attitudes once again points to the unique nature of the Irish-British negative attitudes. These are not conducive to explanation by the normal independent variables. This repeats the performance of the variable in the case of the 1972-73 survey of prejudice (see Mac Gréil, 1977, pp. 501ff). These findings also confirm once again the theoretical propositions developed by T.W. Adorno and associates in their classic text, *The Authoritarian Personality* (1950).

PART III: CONCLUDING INTERPRETATION AND COMMENTARY

The main aim of this book has been the description, discovery and explanation of the attitudes of the people of the Republic of Ireland towards various categories (within and outside Ireland) of fellow human beings perceived to belong to different ethnic, gender, political, racial, religious, and social groupings. The major emphasis or focus in this wide range of attitudes has been on a particular type of destructive disposition known as **social prejudice** which has contributed to some of the most appalling activity of collective ostracisation, discrimination, persecution, expulsion and even extermination of various minorities in the course of human history. Unfortunately, these forms of outrageous behaviourial expression of social prejudice still continue throughout the world and are likely to do so in the foreseeable future, even in so-called 'developed societies'. Research into social prejudice, therefore, has as its therapeutic purpose and function the undermining of its grip on people through the systematic exposure of its irrational anti-social causes and inhuman effects.

It is not a pleasant task for a researcher or for an author to delve into the prejudices of his or her people and expose them for the people themselves to read and discover. Most prejudices are implicit and are not seen as prejudices by those who hold them. Just like most of our values and dispositions, prejudices are pre-reflectional. Their explicitation is a necessary stage in the process in enabling us to face up to them for what they really are, namely, a set of hate-attitudes rigidly held towards a whole range of diverse groups and categories of people. Making explicit our prejudices involves the challenging of 'dearly held myths' such as racial and gender superiority, to name but two of our cherished convictions.

In addition to the social or therapeutic aim of this book, other objectives have also been attempted. High among these has been its modest contribution to social science in providing advances in information, in methodology and in theory and explanation. The latter has been mainly in the reaffirmation of the findings of theoretical propositions long established by other authors. Also, a number of questions have been raised which need further theoretical analysis. Some new insights have emerged from the text, for example, the distinction between 'offensive' and 'defensive' ethnocentrism; the possible link between 'assimilation' or 'cultural absorption' and 'fundamentalist reaction'; and the selective nature of popular 'liberalness'.[7]

The methodology employed in this work has been an extended interview questionnaire (survey) of a randomly chosen national sample of those over eighteen years old on the electoral register of the Republic of Ireland (see Appendix A). All the norms of social survey methodology were observed. It is conceded that this method has its limitations and the findings presented

---

7. 'Liberalness' refers to 'social tolerance' as distinct from 'liberalism' which is seen as an ideology.

above inevitably share such limitations. Participant observation (as a method), for instance, may probe deeper but it too has the limitation of not being necessarily as representative of the views of the whole population as in the case of a social survey. The validity and reliability of the various scales proved satisfactory. The fact that the survey replicated the Dublin Survey of 1972-73 has added greatly to the value of the findings as measures of attitudinal change over a period of sixteen years. The overall measure of social prejudice of the 1988-89 National Survey has, in turn, provided a second bench-mark for future research. This work has also benefitted from a cross-cultural dimension, i.e., through collaboration with the Department of Sociology of the Catholic University of Nijmegen and also from the use of some questions from the (Greeley) International Survey on the family.

The profile of Irish attitudes and prejudice which has emerged from this research is quite complex and multi-faceted. In many areas the Irish as represented by the sample are a moderately tolerant people. Their high regard for the English people, for instance, is co-existing with a fairly negative opinion of the manner in which the British establishment had dealt with the 'Irish problem'. Protestant established denominations and Western European ethnic groups and nationalities are well thought of. Some disadvantaged social and domestic minorities rank among the most preferred categories, i.e., "Working Class", "Unemployed", "Unmarried Mothers" and "People with Physical Handicap". Other social minorities have a precariously low standing. Among the latter the disturbing and deteriorating position of Irish "Travelling People" merits serious attention at all levels. The position of other social categories dealt with at length in Chapter XI (Part II) manifests a relatively high level of intolerance.

Overall there has been a decrease in the level of "racialism" and a decline in "Sexism". Unfortunately there is evidence of a modest increase in Irish 'ethnocentrism' and substantial disimprovement in some areas of religious prejudice and in prejudice towards social minorities. The suggested reasons for these changes have been discussed in the course of the text. 'Authoritarianism', 'Anomie' and 'Alienation' scores are too high for complacency. Major research into these phenomena is urgently needed and the causes are probably to be found in elements of modern social structures which militate against the psychological well being of the people and lead to negative social attitudes and prejudices. It could also be hypothesised that, despite improvements in material standards of living for the majority of people, there may be lacunae in the level of 'meaning' in people's lives. There may also be a lack of support at the community and family levels.

The discovery of 'selective liberalness', especially in relation to deprived minorities who most need tolerance and support, raises serious questions for educators and community leaders, including, parents, teachers, writers, journalists, commentators, religious leaders and politicians, namely, all those agents expected to promote social tolerance. Advances in standards of education do not seem to be reflected in advances in universal tolerance.

Of course, it could be argued that the situation might have to be more extreme without such advances in public education.

In conclusion, there is sufficient evidence in this book to justify the need for the Irish people to accept and promote the model of *'integrated pluralism'* as its desired goal for the future Ireland. This model respects and promotes the authentic cultural, political and religious diversity of our people and facilitates the co-existence of the different collectivities on the basis of total equality. Where the welfare of groups is in danger there must be an effective body of **Minority Rights' Legislation** to protect the groups under threat from any form of intimidation, discrimination or harassment. 'Integrated Pluralism' is not possible without the support of such legislation. Just law, at the end of the day, is an essential condition of the possibility of achieving a tolerant society, which is the aim of this book, **Prejudice in Ireland Revisited**. A tolerant society is also promoted by opportunites of favourable contact between members of different groupings and categories. This enables the "hate-attitude" of prejudice to be replaced by the "love-attitude" of tolerance.

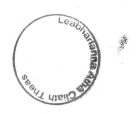

Bibliography

ADORNO, T. W., FRENKEL-BRUNSWICK, E., LEVINSON, D. J., SANFORD, R. W. (in collaboration with B. Aron, M. H. Levinson and W. Morrow), *The Authoritarian Personality*, New York, Harper, 1950.

ALEXANDER, J. E., "The New Theoretical Movement" in *Handbook of Sociology* (editor N. Smelser), 1988.

ALLPORT, GORDON W., *Personality, A Psychological Interpretation*, London, Constable, 1937 (1971).

"Prejudice: A Problem in Psychological and Social Causation", *Journal of Social Issues*, Supplement Series No. 4, 1950.

The Nature of Prejudice, Boston, Beacon Press, 1954.

Pattern and Growth in Personality, London, Holt Rinehart and Winston, 1963 (1969).

ARENSBERG, C. M. AND KIMBALL, S. T., *Culture and Community*, New York, Harcourt, Brace and World, 1965.

Family and Community in Ireland, Boston, Harvard University Press (1940) 1968.

ARON, B., see Adorno T. W. *et. al,* (1950).

ARONSON, ELLIOT, *The Social Animal*, San Francisco, Freeman, 1965.

BALLACHY, E. L., see Krech, D., *et. al.*, (1962).

BANTON, MICHAEL, *Race Relations*, New York, Basic Books, 1967.

Race and Ethnic Competition, Cambridge, University Press, 1983.

BECKLAR, see Pratkanis, *et. al.*, (1989).

BENEDICT, RUTH, "Configurations of Culture in North America" in *The American Anthropologist*, Vol. 34, pp. 1-27, 1932.

Patterns of Culture, London, Routledge and Kegan Paul (1935) 1961.

BENDIX, R. AND LIPSET, S. M. (EDITORS), *Class, Status and Power: Social Stratification in Comparative Perspective*, London, Routledge and Kegan Paul (1953) 1960.

BERKOWITZ, LEONARD, *Aggression: A Social Psychological Analysis*, New York, McGraw-Hill, 1962.

BERRY, BREWTON, *Race and Ethnic Relations*, Boston, Houghton-Milflin, 1965.

BLALOCK, H. M., *Social Statistics*, New York, McGraw-Hill, (1960), 1972.

BLEAKLEY, DAVID, *Crisis in Ireland*, London, Fabian Society (Ser. 318), 1974.

BOGARDUS, EMORY, "Measuring Social Distance", in *Journal of Applied Sociology*, No 9, 1925.

Immigration and Race Attitudes, Boston, D. C. Heath & Co., 1928.

"A Race Relations Cycle", in *American Journal of Sociology*, (Vol. 35) No. 4, January 1930.

"A Social Distance Scale", in *Sociology and Social Research*, No. 17, 1933.

"Changes in Social Distances", in *International Journal of Opinion and Attitude Research*, No. 1, 1947.

"Stereotypes Versus Sociotypes", in *Sociology and Social Research*, No. 34, 1950.

BOWMAN, JOHN, *De Valera and the Ulster Question*, Oxford University Press, 1982.

BOYD, ANDREW, *Brian Faulkner and the Crisis in Ulster*, Tralee, Anvil, 1969.

BREEN, RICHARD, HANNAN, DAMIEN, ROTTMAN, DAVID B. and WHELAN, CHRISTOPHER T., *Understanding Contemporary Ireland: State, Class and Development in the Republic of Ireland*, Dublin, Gill and MacMillan, 1990.

BRIGHAM, JOHN C., *Social Psychology*, New York, Harper Collins, 1991.

BRODY, HUGH, *Inishkillane: Change and Decline in the West of Ireland*, London, Penguin Press, 1973.

BROWN, ROBERT, *Social Psychology*, New York, Free Press, 1965.

BROWN, RUPERT, *Prejudice: Its Social Psychology*, Oxford, Blackwell, 1995.

BROWN, W. O., "Culture Contact and Race Conflict", in E. B. Reuter (editor) *Race and Culture Contacts*, New York, McGraw Hill, 1934.

BURGESS, E. W., see Park, R. E., *et. al.*, (1921) 1969.

BURKE, WILLIAM P., *Irish Priests in Penal Times*, Waterford, 1914.

CALLAN, T. and NOLAN, B., *Low Pay, Poverty and Social Security*, Dublin, ESRI Working Paper No. 36, 1992.

CHUBB, BASIL, *The Government and Politics of Ireland*, Stanford University Press, 1970.

COMPTON, PAUL, "The Demography of Religious Affiliation" in *Demographic Review: Northern Ireland (1995)*, Belfast, Northern Ireland Economic Council, 1995.

CONVERSE, P. E., see NEWCOMB, T. M., *et al.*, 1965.

COOLEY, CHARLES, H., *Social Process*, New York, Scribners, 1918.

CORCORAN, MARY, *Irish Illegals: Transients Between Two Societies*, Westport, Connecticut, Greenwood Press, 1993.

CORISH, PATRICK, *The Irish Catholic Experience*, Dublin, 1985.

COSER, LEWIS, *Continuities in the Study of Social Conflict*, New York, The Free Press, 1967.

COUNCIL FOR SOCIAL WELFARE, *The Travelling People*, Blackrock, Dublin, 1985.

CRUTCHFIELD, R. S., see Krech, D., *et. al.*, (1962).

DAVIS, E. and SINNOTT, R., *Attitudes in the Republic Relevant to the Northern Problem*, Dublin, ESRI (No. 97), 1979.

DAVIS, E., GRUBE, J.W. and MORGAN, M., *Attitudes Towards Poverty and Related Social Issues in Ireland*, Dublin, ESRI (No. 17), 1984.

DAHRENDORF, ROLF, *Class and Class Conflict in Industrial Society*, London, Routledge and Kegan Paul, 1961.

DE BLAGHD, EARNÁN, *Trasna na Bóinne*, Baile Átha Cliath, Sáirséal agus Dill, 1955.

DE PAOR, LIAM, *Divided Ulster*, London, Penguin, 1971.

D'SOUZA, DINESH, *The Earl of Racism*, New York, Free Press, 1995.

DEVLIN, PADDY, *Straight Left: An Autobiography*, Belfast, The Blackstaff Press, 1993.

DOHERTY, FRANK, *The Stalker Affair*, Cork, Mercier Press, 1986.

DOLLARD, JOHN, *Caste and Class in a Southern Town*, New York, Harper and Row, 1957.

DOLLARD, JOHN, L. W., DOOB, N.E. MILLER, O.H. MOWRER and R. R. SEARS, *Frustration and Aggression*, New Haven, Yale, 1939.

DOOB, L. W., see Dollard, J., *et. al.*, (1939).

DOUTHWAITE, RICHARD, *The Growth Illusion: How Economic Growth Enriched the Few, Impoverished the Many and Endangered the Planet*, Dublin, The Lilliput Press, 1992.

Short Circuit: Strengthening Local Economies for Security in an Unstable World, Dublin, The Lilliput Press, 1996.

DU BOIS, W. E. B., *The Negro, Black Reconstruction in America*, New York, The World, 1962.

DURKHEIM, EMILE, *On the Division of Labour*, New York, Macmillan, (1893), 1933.

The Rules of Sociological Method, New York, The Free Press (1895), 1964).

Suicide, A Study in Sociology, New York, The Free Press (1897), 1951.

EISINGA, R. N. and SCHEEPERS, P. L. N., *Ethnocentrisme in Nederland*, Nijmegen, ITS, 1989.

EVANS, E. ESTYN, *The Personality of Ireland: Habitat, Heritage and History*, London, Cambridge University Press, 1973.

EYSENCK, H. J., *The Inequality of Man*, London, Temple Smith, 1973.

FAIRCHILD, HENRY P., *Immigration*, New York, Macmillan, 1925.

FENNELL, DESMOND, *Heresy, The Battle of Ideas in Modern Ireland*, Belfast, The Blackstaff Press, 1993.

FINOT, JEAN, *Race Prejudice*, (translated by Florence Wade-Evans), London, Archibald Constable, 1906.

FITZGERALD, GARRETT, *Towards a New Ireland*, Dublin, Gill and Macmillan, 1973.

FOGARTY, PATRICIA, "Government Policy and the Travellers", Má Nuad, unpublished M.A. Thesis, 1996.

FORD, ALAN, *The Protestant Reformation in Ireland*, Frankfurt-am-Main, 1987.

FORDE, M. see Ó Nualláin, *et al*, 1992.

FOSTER, R. F., *Modern Ireland 1600-1972*, London, 1988.

FOUCAULT, MICHEL, *The Order of Things*, London, Tavidstock, 1970.

FRENKEL-BRUNSWICK, E., see Adorno, T. W., *et. al.*, (1950).

FREUD, SIGMUND, *Civilisation and Its Discontents*, London, Hogarth Press (1933), 1949.

Garda Commissioners' Reports, Dublin, Garda Headquarters, 1987, 1988, 1989, 1990.

GARFINKEL, HAROLD, *Studies in Ethnomethodology*, New Jersey, Prentice-Hall, 1967.

GIDDENS, ANTHONY, *Sociology*, London, Polity Press, 1989.

GLICK, CLARENCE E., "Social Roles and Types in Race Relations", in *Race Relations in World Perspective*, Honolulu, University of Hawaii, 1955.

GMELSH, GEORGE and GMELSH, SHARON, *The Irish Tinkers: the Urbanisation of an Itinerant People*, Illlinois, Wardland Press, 1985.

GOLDTHORPE, J. H., "Social Stratification in Industrial Society", in *Class, Status and Power* (editors Bendix and Lipset), London, Routledge and Kegan Paul, 1967.

GOFFMAN, ERVING, *Presentation of Self in Everyday Life*, New York, Doubleday Anchor, 1959.

Asylums, New York, Doubleday (1961) 1968.

GREELEY, A.M., see Spaeth *et. al.*, (1970).

GREELEY, A. M. and BAUM, G. (EDITORS), *Ethnicity*, New York, The Seabury Press, 1977.

GUILFORD, *Personality*, New York, McGraw-Hill, 1959.

HABERMAS, JUNGEN, *Theory and Practice*, Boston, Beacon Press, 1973.

HAMILTON, THOMAS, *History of Presbyterians in Ireland*, Belfast (1986), 1992.

HANNAN, DAMIEN, *Rural Exodus: A Study of Forces Influencing Large-Scale Migration of Irish Youth*, London, Geoffrey Chapman, 1970.

HANNAN, D., see Breen *et al*, 1990.

HARALAMBOS and HOLBORN, *Sociology and Perspectives*, London, Collins Educational, 1991.

HARRIS, MERVIN, *Culture, People, Nature*, New York, Harper and Row, 1988.

HARRIS, ROSEMARY, *Prejudice in Ulster*, Manchester University Press, 1972.

HAYDEN, J., see Lynott Philomena, *et. al.*, (1995).

HAYES, NICKY, *Foundations of Psychology: An Introduction*, London, Routledge, 1994.

HENRY, A. F. and SHORT, F. J., *Suicide and Homicide: Some Economic, Sociological and Psychological Aspects of Aggression*, New York, Free Press, 1954.

HITLER, ADOLF, *Mein Kampf*, London, Anchor Press, (1933), 1969.

HOLBORN see Haralambos, *et. al.*, (1991).

HOLLINGSHEAD, AUGUST DE BELMONT, *Elmstown Youth. the Impact of the Social Classes on Adolescents*, New York, Wiley, 1949.

HOLLINGSHEAD, A. B. and REDLICK, F. C., *Social Class and Mental Illness*, New York, Wiley, 1958.

HORAN, JAMES, *James Horan: Memoirs 1911-1986*, (editor M. Mac Gréil), Dingle, Brandon Books, 1992.

HURLEY, MICHAEL (EDITOR), *Irish Anglicanism 1869-1969*, Dublin, Allen Figgis, 1970.

INGLIS, TOM, *Moral Monopoloy of the Catholic Church in Modern Ireland*, Dublin, Gill and MacMillan, 1987.

I.P.A. Year Book and Diary, Dublin, I.P.A., 1992.

JOHNSON, HARRY, *Sociology, a Systematic Introduction*, London, Routledge and Kegan Paul, 1961.

JOYCE, NAN, *Traveller, An Autobiography*, Dublin, 1985.

JUNG, CARL G., *Psychological Types*, London, Routledge & Kegan Paul, 1923.

KATZ, D., "The Functional Approach to the Study of Attitudes", in *Public Opinion Quarterly*, 24, p.p. 163-204, 1960.

KEARNEY, RICHARD, (EDITOR), *Migrations: The Irish at Home and Abroad*, Dublin, Wolfhound Press, 1990.

KELLEHER, MICHAEL J., *Suicide and the Irish*, Cork, Mercier Press, 1996.

KELLY, G. A., *The Psychology of Personal Constructs*, New York, Norton, 1955.

KENNEDY, SR. STANISLAUS (EDITOR), *One Million Poor*, Dublin, Turoe Press, 1981.

KIMBALL, S. T., see Arensberg, C. M., *et. al.*, (1965 and 1968).

KLUCKHOHN, CLYDE, *Mirror for Man*, New York, McGraw-Hill, (1949), 1971.

KONIG, RUBEN, "Ethnocentrisme in Nederland en Ierland", Nijmegen, Department of Sociology, 1990.

KRECH, D., CRUTCHFIELD, R. S. and BALLACHEY, E. L., *Individual in Society*, New York, McGraw-Hill, 1962.

KROEBER, A. L., *Anthropology: Culture Patterns and Processes*, New York, Harbinger, 1948.

LECKY, W. E. H., *The History of England in the 18th Century*, London, 1890.

LEE, JOSEPH, J., *Ireland 1912-1985: Politics and Society*, Cambridge University Press, 1989.

LEICHTY, JOSEPH, *Roots of Sectarianism in Ireland*, (Pamphlet), Belfast, 1993.

LEMERT, EDWIN, M., *Social Psychology*, New York, McGraw-Hill, 1951.

LEVINSON, D. J. and M. H., see Adorno, T. W., *et. al.*, (1950).

LEWIN, KURT, *A Dynamic Theory of Personality*, New York, McGraw-Hill, 1935.

Principles of Topological Psychology, New York, McGraw-Hill, 1936.

Resolving Social Conflicts, New York, Harper and Row, 1948.

LIPSET, S. M., see Bendix R., *et. al.*, (1967).

LYNOTT, PHILOMENA and HAYDEN, J., *My Boy*, Dublin, Hot Press, 1995.

LYONS, F. S. L., *Ireland Since the Famine*, London, Weidenfeld and Nicolson, 1971.

McCANN, M., Ó SÍOCHÁIN, S., and RUANE (EDITORS), *Irish Travellers Culture and Identity*, Antrim, Prind, 1994.

McCLELLAND, D. C., *Personality*, New York, Holt, Rhinehart and Winston, 1951.

MAC GRÉIL, MICHEÁL "A Psycho-Socio-Cultural Theory of Prejudice", (unpublished M.A. Thesis) Kent State University, 1966.

"Church Attendance of Dublin Adults" in *Social Studies*, Vol. 3, No. 2, pp. 163-211, 1974A.

Educational Opportunity in Dublin, Dublin, Veritas, 1974B.

Prejudice and Tolerance in Ireland, Dublin CIR, 1977/88, New York, Praeger, 1980.

Educational Participation in Ireland (Report), Maynooth, Survey and Research Unit (Department of Social Studies), 1990.

(Editor) *Monsignor Horan: Memoirs 1911-1986*, Dingle Brandon Books, 1992.

MAIER, NORMAN R. F., *Frustration: A Study of Behaviour Without a Goal*, Ann Arbor Paperbacks (1949) 1961.

MALCOLM, X., *Autobiography of Malcolm X*, New York, Grove Press, (1964), 1966.

MALINOWSKI, BRONISLAW, *The Dynamics of Culture Change: An Enquiry Into Race Relations in Africa*, New Haven, Yale University Press, 1945.

MANDELBAUM, DAVID S., *Selected Writings of Edward Sapir in Language, Culture and Personality*, University of California Press, (1949), 1958.

MANNHEIM, KARL, *Man and Society in an Age of Reconstruction*, New York, 1942.

Freedom, Power and Democratic Planning, London, Routledge and Kegan Paul, 1951.

Ideology and Utopia, London, Routledge and Kegan Paul, (1929) 1960.

MARDEN, CHARLES F. AND MEYER, GLADYS, *Minorities in American Society*, New York, American Book Company, 1962.

MANSERGH, MARTIN, "The Background to the Peace Process", *Irish Studies in International Affairs*, Dublin, R.I.A., Vol. 6, 1995 (pp. 145-158).

MARX, KARL, *German Ideology*, London, (1845-46), 1938.

Karl Marx: Selected Writings in Sociology and Social Psychology (edited: T. B. Bottomore and M. Rubel), London, 1956.

Karl Marx: Early Writings (edited: T. B. Bottomore) London, 1963.

MASLOW, AMBROSE H., *Motivation and Personality*, New York, Harper, 1954.

MEAD, GEORGE H., *Mind, Self and Society: From the Standpoint of a Social Behaviorist*, (ed. C. W. Morris), University of Chicago Press, 1934.

MERTON, ROBERT K., "Discrimination and the American Creed" in *Discrimination and National Welfare* (editor: R. M. McIver), New York, Harper Brothers, 1949.

 Social Theory and Social Structure, New York, Collier Macmillan, 1957.

MILES, ROBERT, *Racism After Race Relations*, London, Routledge, 1993.

MULLER, N. E., see Dollard J., *et. al.*, (1939).

 "Minor Studies in Aggression: The Influence of Frustrations Imposed by the Ingroup on Attitudes Towards Outgroups" in *Journal of Psychology* 25, pp. 437-442, 1948.

MISCHEL, WALTER, *Introduction to Personality*, New York, C.B.S. College Publishing, 1981.

MONTAGUE, ASHLEY, *Man's Most Dangerous Myth: The Fallacy of Race*, Cleveland, The World Publishing Company, 1964.

MORROW, W., see Adorno, T.W., *et. al.*, (1950).

MOWRER, O.H., see Dollard, J. *et. al.*, (1939).

MYNDAL, GUNNAR, *An American Dilemma: The Negro Problem and Modern Democracy*, New York, Harper and Row (1944) 1962.

NEWCOMB, T. M., TURNER, R. H., and CONVERSE, P. E., *Social Psychology: A Study of Human Interaction*, London, Routledge and Kegan Paul, (Tavistock), 1965.

NEWMAN, WILLIAM, M., *American Pluralism: A Study of Minority Groups and Social Theory*, New York, Harper and Row, 1973.

NOLAN, see Callan, *et. al.*, (1992).

NUNNALLY, J. C., *Psychometric Theory*, New York, McGraw-Hill, 1967.

O'MAHONY, PAUL, *Crime and Punishment in Ireland*, Dublin, The Round Hall Press, 1993.

Ó NUALLÁIN, S., and FORDE, M., *Changing Needs of Irish Travellers*, Galway, Woodlands Centre, 1992.

Ó SÍOCHÁIN, SÉAMUS, see McCann *et al*, 1994.

PARK, ROBERT E., "Our Racial Frontier on the Pacific", in *Survey Graphic*, Vol. 9, 1926.

 Race and Culture, New York, McGraw-Hill, 1950.

PARK, ROBERT E. and BURGESS, E. W., *Introduction to the Science of Sociology*, University of Chicago Press, (1921), 1969.

PARSONS, TALCOTT, *The Structure of Social Action*, New York, McGraw-Hill, 1937; Free Press, 1949.

 The Social System, Glencoe, Illinois, Free Press, 1951.

PEILLON, MICHEL, *Contemporary Irish Society: An Introduction*, Dublin, Gill and MacMillan, 1982.

PRATKANIS, BECKLER and GREENWALD, (EDITORS), *Attitude, Structure and Function*.

RADCLIFFE-BROWN, A. R., *Structure and Function in Primitive Society*, 1952.

RAJECKI, D. W., *Attitudes*, Sunderland, Massachusetts, Sinauer Associates, Inc., Publishers (2nd Edition), 1990.

REDDING, SAUNDERS, "Ends and Means in the Struggle for Equality", in *Prejudice U.S.A.* (editors Glock and Sligelman), New York, Praeger, 1969.

REDLICK, F. C., see Hollingshead, A. B., *et. al.*, (1958).

Report of the Steering Committee on the Future Development of Higher Education, Dublin, H.E.A., 1995.

REX, JOHN, *Race Relations in Sociological Theory*, London, Weidenfeld and Nicolson, 1970.

Race, Colonialism and the City, London, Routledge and Kegan Paul, 1973.

ROGERS, CARL, *Counselling and Psychotherapy*, Boston, Houghton-Milflin, 1942.

ROLTER, J. B., "Generalised Expectations for Internal Versus External Control of Reinforcements", in *Psychological Monographs 80* (No. 609), 1966.

ROSE, ARNOLD and CAROLINE, *America Divided*, New York, Knopf, 1953.

ROSE, RICHARD, *Governing Without Consent*, London, Faber, 1971.

ROTTMAN, D. B., see Breen *et al*, 1990.

RUANE , see McCann *et al*, 1994.

RYAN, LIAM, "Irish Emigration to Britain Since World War II" in *Migrations: The Irish at Home and Abroad* (Ed. R. Kearney), Dublin, Wolfhound Press, 1990.

SANDFORD, R.N., see Adorno, T. W., *et. al.*, (1950).

SANTA CRUZ, HERMAN, *Racial Discrimination*, New York, United Nations, 1971.

SAPIR, EDWARD, see Mandelbaum, David (1949), 1958.

SCHEFF, THOMAS, *Being Mentally Ill*, London, Weidenfeld and Nicholson, 1966.

SCHEEPERS, P. L. H., see Eisinga *et al*, 1989.

SCHERMERHORN, R. A., *Comparative Ethnic Relations*, New York, Random House, 1970.

SEARS, R. R., see Dollard, John, *et. al.*, (1939).

SHELDON, W. H., *Varieties in Delinquent Youth: An Introduction to Constitutional Psychiatry*, New York, Harper, 1949.

SIMMEL, GEORG, *Conflict and the Web of Conflict Affiliations*, (translated and edited by Wolff and Bendix) New York, Free Press, (1908), 1953.

SIMPSON, G. E. and YINGER, J. M., *Racial and Cultural Minorities: An Analysis of Prejudice and Discrimination*, New York, Harper and Roe, 1965.

SKINNER, B. F., *Science and Human Behaviour*, New York, MacMillan, 1953.

About Behaviourism, New York, Knopf, 1974.

SMELSER, NEIL J., *Theory of Collective Behaviour*, New York, Free Press, 1962.

The Sociology of Economic Life, New Jersey, Prentice-Hall, 1976.

(Editor) *Handbook of Sociology*, London, Sage, 1988.

SPAETH, J. L. and GREELEY, A. M., *Recent Alumni and Higher Education: A Study of College Graduates*, New York, McGraw-Hill, 1970.

SROLE, L., "Social Dysfunction, Personality and Social Distance Attitudes" paper read before the *American Sociological Society*, 1951.

STEWART, A. T. Q., *The Narrow Ground: the Roots of Conflict in Ulster*, London (1977), 1989.

SUMMER, W. GRAHAM, *Folkways: A Study of the Sociological Importance of Usages, Manners, Customs and Morals*, New York, Ginn 1906.

THOMAS, W. I., *The Unadjusted Girl*, Little, Brown, 1923.

THOMAS, W. I. and ZWANIECKI, *The Polish Peasant in Europe and in America*, (5 vols.), Boston, Badger, (1918-1920), Knopf 1927.

TONNIES, FERDINAND, *Community and Association*, (English translation), London, Routledge and Kegan Paul, 1955.

TURNER, R. H., see NEWCOMB, T. M., *et al.*, 1965.

TYLOR, EDWARD BURNETT, *Primitive Culture*, London, Murray, 1871.

VANDER ZANDEN, JAMES W., *American Minority Relations*, New York, Ronald Press, 1972.

VEBLEN, THORSTEIN, *The Theory of the Leisure Class*, New York, Vanguard Press, 1928.

WALDRON, JARLATH, *Maamtrasna Murders*, Dublin, Burke, 1992.

WARNER, W. L. and SROLE, L., *The Social System of American Ethnic Groups*, New Haven, Yale University Press, 1945.

WEBER, ANN, *Social Psychology*, New York, Harper Perennial, 1992.

WEBER, MAX, *Essays in Sociology* (edited by Gerth and Mills), London, Routledge and Kegan Paul, (1948), 1970.

WHELAN, C. T., see Breen *et al*, 1990.

WHITE, LESLIE, *The Science of Culture: A Study of Man and Civilization*, Toronto, Doubleday (1949), 1969.

The Evolution of Culture: The Development of Civilization until the Fall of Rome, New York, McGraw-Hill, 1959.

WHYTE, JOHN, *Church and State in Modern Ireland 1923-1970*, Dublin, Gill and MacMillan, 1971.

WILLIAMS, ROBIN, *America, A Sociological Interpretation*, New York, Knopf (1951), 1958.

Strangers Next Door: Ethnic Relations in American Communities, New Jersey, Prentice-Hall, 1964.

WISTRICH, ROBERT S., *Anti-Semitism: The Longest Hatred*, New York, Schockin Books, 1994.

YABLOWSKI, LEWIS, *The Violent Gang*, London (Pelican A802), Penguin, 1962.

YINGER, J. MILTON, *The Scientific Study of Religion*, New York, Macmillan, 1970.

see Simpson, G.E. *et. al.*, (1965).

ZANGWILL, ISRAEL, *The Melting Pot: Drama in Four Acts*, New York, Macmillan, 1921.

ZWANIECKI, F., see Thomas W. I., *et. al.*, (1918).

Appendix A:

Questionnaire

SURVEY OF ATTITUDES IN IRELAND

Area Code: _____ Respondent Code: _____ Interviewer No: _____

Introduction: Hello, my name is _____. I am a member of a research team from The Economic and Social Research Institute. We have been commissioned by the Research Unit at Maynooth University to carry out a social survey of a representative sample of adults in the Republic.

The main purpose of the survey is to find out people's opinions, attitudes and values, so that we can get a better understanding of how people see the problems and challenges facing Irish society.

Your name has been chosen as part of a random sample from the Electors' Register. It is very important for us that you co-operate so that our sample will be completely representative. I can assure you that strict confidentiality and anonymity will be maintained with regard to all of your answers. I would be most thankful if you could spare me about an hour of your time to answer a questionnaire.

1.   Respondent's sex: Male 1   Female 2

2.   (a)   Could you tell me where you were born? (Complete line a. below). If you are married, where was your spouse born? (Complete line b. below). And where were your parents born? (Complete lines c. and d.)

	Place	Category*	County or Country
a. Self	_____	1 2 3 4	_____
b. Spouse	_____	1 2 3 4	_____
c. Father	_____	1 2 3 4	_____
d. Mother	_____	1 2 3 4	_____

*1 = City of 100,000 plus;   2 = Large Town of 10,000 to 99,999
3 = Town of 1,500 - 9,999;   4 = Rural or town of under 1,499

(b)   Where were you reared (i.e., principal town and county of residence up to 16 years)?

_____

(c)   [If respondent not born in this area.] How many years have you been living here? _____ No. of years.

3.   (a)   Which of these terms best describes the way you usually think of yourself? (Show Card A and Circle one number in first column below).

(b)   Of the remaining categories, which would be closest to the way you see yourself? (Circle in second column below).

	First Choice	Second Choice
Anglo-Irish	1	1
British	2	2
County/City of Rearing	3	3
European	4	4
Irish	5	5
Northern Irish	6	6
Southern Irish (Republic of Ireland)	7	7
Other (specify)	8	8

(c)   Would you say you are a strong or average   _____ ?

        Strong 1   Average 2   I don't know 3

(d)   Of which country are you a citizen?   _____ country.

(a)   People have different views about certain groups in society. I am going to read ou
a list of groups and I would like you to tell me how close you would be willing t
allow members of each group. The main idea here is to get your first reaction
therefore, it would be better if we went through the list fairly quickly. (Show Car
B and explain it).

Stages of Social Distance

1.   "Would marry or welcome as members of my family".
2.   "Would have as close friends".
3.   "Would have as next-door neighbour".
4.   "Would work in the same work-place".
5.   "Would welcome as Irish Citizens".
6.   "Would have as visitors only".
7.   "Would debar or deport from Ireland".

gory	Kinship	Friendship	Neighbour	Co-Worker	Citizen	Visitor Only	Debar or Deport	Reason See Q.4 (b)
Africans	1	2	3	4	5	6	7	A B C D E F G H
Agnostics	1	2	3	4	5	6	7	A B C D E F G H
Alcoholics	1	2	3	4	5	6	7	A B C D E F G H
American Negroes	1	2	3	4	5	6	7	A B C D E F G H
Atheists	1	2	3	4	5	6	7	A B C D E F G H
Arabs	1	2	3	4	5	6	7	A B C D E F G H
Belgians	1	2	3	4	5	6	7	A B C D E F G H
Blacks	1	2	3	4	5	6	7	A B C D E F G H
British	1	2	3	4	5	6	7	A B C D E F G H
Canadians	1	2	3	4	5	6	7	A B C D E F G H
Capitalists	1	2	3	4	5	6	7	A B C D E F G H
Chinese	1	2	3	4	5	6	7	A B C D E F G H
Church of Ireland	1	2	3	4	5	6	7	A B C D E F G H
Coloureds	1	2	3	4	5	6	7	A B C D E F G H
Communists	1	2	3	4	5	6	7	A B C D E F G H
Danes	1	2	3	4	5	6	7	A B C D E F G H
Drug Addicts	1	2	3	4	5	6	7	A B C D E F G H
Dutch	1	2	3	4	5	6	7	A B C D E F G H
English	1	2	3	4	5	6	7	A B C D E F G H
Ex-Prisoners	1	2	3	4	5	6	7	A B C D E F G H
French	1	2	3	4	5	6	7	A B C D E F G H
Gardai	1	2	3	4	5	6	7	A B C D E F G H
Gay People	1	2	3	4	5	6	7	A B C D E F G H
Germans	1	2	3	4	5	6	7	A B C D E F G H
Handicapped (physically)	1	2	3	4	5	6	7	A B C D E F G H
Greeks	1	2	3	4	5	6	7	A B C D E F G H
Hare Krishna	1	2	3	4	5	6	7	A B C D E F G H
Indians (Non-Am.)	1	2	3	4	5	6	7	A B C D E F G H
Israelis	1	2	3	4	5	6	7	A B C D E F G H
Italians	1	2	3	4	5	5	7	A B C D E F G H
Itinerants/ Travellers	1	2	3	4	5	6	7	A B C D E F G H
Irish Speakers	1	2	3	4	5	6	7	A B C D E F G H
People of Lux.	1	2	3	4	5	6	7	A B C D E F G H
Jews	1	2	3	4	5	6.	7	A B C D E F G H
Methodists	1	2	3	4	5	6	7	A B C D E F G H
Mentally h/capped	1	2	3	4	5	6	7	A B C D E F G H
Moslems	1	2	3	4	5	6	7	A B C D E F G H
Nigerians	1	2	3	4	5	6	7	A B C D E F G H
Northern Irish	1	2	3	4	5	6	7	A B C D E F G H
Pakistanis	1	2	3	4	5	6	7	A B C D E F G H
People with Aids	1	2	3	4	5	6	7	A B C D E F G H
Polish people	1	2	3	4	5	6	7	A B C D E F G H
Presbyterians	1	2	3	4	5	6	7	A B C D E F G H
Portuguese	1	2	3	4	5	6	7	A B C D E F G H
Protestants	1	2	3	4	5	6	7	A B C D E F G H
Provisional IRA	1	2	3	4	5	6	7	A B C D E F G H
Roman Catholics	1	2	3	4	5	6	7	A B C D E F G H
Russians	1	2	3	4	5	6	7	A B C D E F G H
Scottish	1	2	3	4	5	6		A B C D E F G H
Socialists	1	2	3	4	5	6	7	A B C D E F G H
Spaniards	1	2	3	4	5	6	7	A B C D E F G H
Members of Sinn Féin	1	2	3	4	5	6	7	A B C D E F G H
Trade Unionists	1	2	3	4	5	6	7	A B C D E F G H
Unemployed	1	2	3	4	5	6	7	A B C D E F G H
Unionists	1	2	3	4	5	6	7	A B C D E F G H
Unmarried Mothers	1	2	3	4	5	6	7	A B C D E F G H
Welsh	1	2	3	4	5	6	7	A B C D E F G H
Working Class	1	2	3	4	5	6	7	A B C D E F G H
White Americans	1	2	3	4	5	6	7	A B C D E F G H

(b)   Looking over your answers to this question, there are a number of categories which you would not welcome into kinship. Which of the following would you say was your main reason for placing them at the distance indicated? (Show Card C and explain it). Then circle <u>one letter</u> under Reason for each group <u>not</u> circled 1.)

A.	Religious Beliefs and/or Practices	E.	Economic danger to us
B.	Racial - colour of skin, etc.	F.	Not socially acceptable
C.	Political views and/or methods	G.	Way of life
D.	Nationality and culture	H.	Other (specify ____)

5.   (a)   Let's go back and talk about yourself again. What is your date of birth?

Month _____   Year _____

(b)   Could you tell me if you are?

Married.................	1
Widowed.................	2
Divorced................	3
Separated...............	4
Never married........	5

(c)   How many children do you have, if any _____

(d)   And how old is the eldest? _____ And the youngest? _____

(e)   How many children were there in your family of origin? (count in yourself and all your brothers and sisters (incl. any adopted) _____

6.   Thinking now of the household in which you live, could you tell me the ages and sex of all the members and their relationship to the Head of the Household?

Member (give initials)	Age	Sex		Relationship to Head of Household					
		M	F	Self	Spouse	Son/ Daughter	Father/ Mother	Other Relative	Not Relative
Respondent	___	1	2	1	2	3	4	5	6
_____	___	1	2	1	2	3	4	5	6
_____	___	1	2	1	2	3	4	5	6
_____	___	1	2	1	2	3	4	5	6
_____	___	1	2	1	2	3	4	5	6
_____	___	1	2	1	2	3	4	5	6
_____	___	1	2	1	2	3	4	5	6
_____	___	1	2	1	2	3	4	5	6
_____	___	1	2	1	2	3	4	5	6
_____	___	1	2	1	2	3	4	5	6

7.   <u>Family Life Today:</u> I would now like to ask you a number of questions about your views or opinions about family life today. *This is part of an international study and the questions are being answered in nine different countries,* so they might not fit every country perfectly, but I would be grateful if you would answer them as completely as you can.

Do you agree or disagree with each of the following statements

Statement		Strongly Agree	Agree	Neither Agree Nor Disagree	Disagree	Strongly Disagree	Can't Choose
A.	A working mother can establish just as warm and secure a relationship with her children as a mother who does not work.	1	2	3	4	5	8
B.	A pre-school child is likely to suffer if his or her mother works.	1	2	3	4	5	8
C.	All in all, family life suffers when the woman has a full-time job.	1	2	3	4	5	8
D.	A woman and her family will all be happier if she goes out to work.	1	2	3	4	5	8
E.	A job is alright, but what most women really want is a home and children.	1	2	3	4	5	8
F.	Being a housewife is just as fulfilling as working for pay.	1	2	3	4	5	8
G.	Having a job is the best way for a woman to be an independent person.	1	2	3	4	5	8
H.	Both the husband and wife should contribute to household income.	1	2	3	4	5	8
I.	A husband's job is to earn money: a wife's job is to look after the home and family.	1	2	3	4	5	8
J.	I would enjoy having a job even if I didn't need the money.	1	2	3	4	5	8

8. Do you think that women should work outside the home full-time, part-time or not at all under these circumstances:

Circumstances		Work full-time	Work part-time	Stay at home	Can't choose
A.	After marrying and before there are children.	1	2	3	8
B.	When there is a child under school age.	1	2	3	8
C.	After the youngest child starts school.	1	2	3	8
D.	After the children leave home.	1	2	3	8

9. Think of a child under 3 years old whose parents both have full-time jobs. How suitable do you think each of these childcare arrangements would be for the child?

Child Care Arrangement		Very Suitable	Somewhat Suitable	Not very Suitable	Not at all Suitable	Can't Choose
A.	A public, state or local authority nursery.	1	2	3	4	8
B.	A private creche or nursery.	1	2	3	4	8
C.	A childminder or babysitter.	1	2	3	4	8
D.	A neighbour or friend.	1	2	3	4	8
E.	A relative.	1	2	3	4	8

10. (Not included in survey of intergroup attitudes).

11. Do you agree or disagree with each of the following statements?

Statement		Strongly Agree	Agree	Neither Agree nor Disagree	Disagree	Strongly Disagree	Can't Choose
A.	Married people are generally happier than unmarried people.	1	2	3	4	5	8
B.	Personal freedom is more important than the companionship of marriage.	1	2	3	4	5	8
C.	The main advantage of marriage is that it gives financial security.	1	2	3	4	5	8
D.	The main purpose of marriage these days is to have children.	1	2	3	4	5	8
E.	It is better to have a bad marriage than no marriage at all.	1	2	3	4	5	8
F.	People who want children ought to get married.	1	2	3	4	5	8
G.	A single mother can bring up her child as well as a married couple	1	2	3	4	5	8
H.	A single father can bring up his child as well as a married couple.	1	2	3	4	5	8
I.	Couples don't take marriage seriously enough when divorce is easily available.	1	2	3	4	5	8
J.	Homosexual couples should have the right to marry one another.	1	2	3	4	5	8

12. (a) All in all, what do you think is the <u>ideal</u> number of children for a family to have? Ideal number of children _____

    (b) In general, what do you feel about each of these family sizes? (Show Card D) It is........

Family Size	Very Desirable	Desirable	Neither Desirable Nor Undesirable	Undesirable	Very Undesirable	Can't Choose
A Family with:						
A. No children	1	2	3	4	5	8
B. One child	1	2	3	4	5	8
C. Two children	1	2	3	4	5	8
D. Three children	1	2	3	4	5	8
E. Four children or more.	1	2	3	4	5	8

13. Do you agree or disagree with each of the following statements?
     (Show Card E and circle <u>one</u> number on each line).

Statement		Strongly Agree	Agree	Neither Agree nor Disagree	Disagree	Strongly Disagree	Can't Choose
A.	Children are more trouble than they are worth.	1	2	3	4	5	8
B.	Watching children grow up is life's greatest joy.	1	2	3	4	5	8
C.	Having children interferes too much with the freedom of parents.	1	2	3	4	5	8
D.	A marriage without children is not fully complete.	1	2	3	4	5	8
E.	It is better <u>not</u> to have children because they are such a heavy financial burden.	1	2	3	4	5	8
F.	People who have never had children lead empty lives.	1	2	3	4	5	8

14./17. (Not included in survey of intergroup attitudes).

18. [If respondent is a married woman who had children]
     Did you work outside the home full-time, part-time or not at all........

Circumstances		Worked Full-time	Worked Part-time	Stayed home	Does not Apply
A.	After marrying and before you had children	1	2	3	8
B.	And what about when a child was under school age	1	2	3	8
C.	After the youngest child started school	1	2	3	8
D.	And how about after the children left home	1	2	3	8

19. (Not included in survey of intergroup attitudes).

20. With regard to the role of men and women in society, I would be interested to know if you
     would agree or disagree with each of the following statements.

	Statement	Agree	Neither A nor D	Disagree
1.	A woman's proper place is in the home	1	2	3
2.	It is bad that there are so few women in Government in this country	1	2	3
3.	Generally speaking, women think less clearly then men	1	2	3
4.	Women work better than men in the caring profession	1	2	3

	Statement	Agree	Neither A nor D	Disagree
5.	People should be employed and promoted strictly on the basis of ability, regardless of sex or gender	1	2	3
6.	The Feminist movement is very necessary in Ireland	1	2	3
7.	Some equality in marriage is a good thing, but by and large the husband ought to have the main say in family matters	1	2	3
8.	Education and vocational training is less important for girls than boys	1	2	3
9.	A woman should be as free as a man to propose marriage	1	2	3
10.	Husbands and wives should have an equal say in how to spend the family money, irrespective of who earns it	1	2	3
11.	Women should be allowed to become priests in the Roman Catholic Church	1	2	3
12.	The emigration of young women from Ireland is less serious for the country than the emigration of young men	1	2	3

21.   Now, I would like to ask you a number of questions in relation to religion.

Could you tell me the religion or denomination to which yourself, your spouse and your parents belong?

     (a)   Self   _____

     (b)   Spouse   _____

     (c)   Father   _____

     (d)   Mother   _____

22.   (i)   Is this the religion in which you (and your spouse) were brought up?

     (a)   Self   Yes 1   No 2

     (b)   Spouse   Yes 1   No 2

If YES for both, go to Q. 23.

    (ii)   If NO please give religion of rearing

     (a)   Self   _____

     (b)   Spouse   _____

    (iii)   What was the main reason for change?

     (a)   Self   _____

     (b)   Spouse   _____

23.   Now, could we go on to talk about other religions? With regard to the Jews, would you agree or disagree?

	Statement	Agree	Neither A nor D	Disagree
1.	That it would be good for the country to have many Jews in positions of responsibility in business	1	2	3
2.	That Jews are a bad influence on Christian culture and civilisation	1	2	3
3.	That Jews may have moral standards when dealing with each other, but with Christians they are ruthless and unscrupulous	1	2	3

	Statement	Agree	Neither A nor D	Disagree
4.	That it is wrong for Jews and Christians to intermarry	1	2	3
5.	That golf clubs or similar organisations are justified in denying membership to a person because he or she is a Jew	1	2	3
6.	That the Jews as a people are to be blamed for the crucifixion of Christ	1	2	3
7.	That Jews do not take a proper interest in community problems and government	1	2	3
8.	That Jewish power and control in money matters is far out of proportion to the number of Jews	1	2	3
9.	That Jews are behind the money-lending rackets	1	2	3
10.	That we should encourage Irish Jews just as much as anybody else to take up positions of importance in Irish society	1	2	3

4. Would you say that the religious beliefs in which you were brought up influenced your growth or development as a person?

An essential help to me	1
Important but not essential	2
Helped me somewhat	3
Neither a help nor a hindrance	4
Hindered me somewhat	5
A serious hindrance	6
A grave hindrance	7

5. Would you say being a _____ (Respondent's Religion) is an advantage or disadvantage to you in getting on?

A great advantage	1
A slight advantage	2
Neither an advantage nor disadvantage	3
A slight disadvantage	4
A great disadvantage	5

6. (a) How often do you attend Church or place of Worship? (USE CATEGORIES AS PROBES IF NECESSARY)

Daily	1
Several times a week	2
At least once a week	3
Once to three times a month	4
Several times a year	5
Less frequently	6
Never	7
No answer	9
Not applicable	0

(b) [If codes 4 to 6 at (a)] Is there any particular reason why you don't go more often?

Ill	1
Working	2
Just don't bother	3
Other reason (specify)	4

27. <u>For Roman Catholics Only</u>: Could you say how often you go to Mass, to Holy Communion and to Confession? (Circle <u>one</u> number in each column - USE CATEGORIES AS PROBES AS NECESSARY)

	Mass	Holy Communion	Confession
Daily	1	1	1
Several times a week	2	2	2
At least once a week	3	3	3
Once to three times a month	4	4	4
Several times a year	5	5	5
Less frequently	6	6	6
Never	7	7	7
No answer	8	8	8

28. There are many different ways of picturing God. We'd like to know the kinds of images you are most likely to associate with God.

Here is a card with sets of contrasting images. On a scale of 1-7, where would you place your image of God between the two contrasting images?
(HAND CARD. F)

The first set of contrasting images shows Mother at 1 on the scale and Father at 7. If you imagine God as a Mother, you would place yourself at 1. If you imagine God as a Father, you would place yourself at 7. If you imagine God as somewhere between Mother and Father, you would place yourself 2, 3, 4, 5 or 6. (REPEAT EXAMPLE AS NECESSARY FOR EACH ITEM A-D, SUBSTITUTING IMAGES B-D FOR "MOTHER" AND "FATHER").

Where would you place your image of God on the scale for .... (READ EACH SET OF IMAGES AND CIRCLE ONE CODE FOR EACH).

a. Mother _____ Father
1   2   3   4   5   6   7

b. Master _____ Spouse
1   2   3   4   5   6   7

c. Judge _____ Lover
1   2   3   4   5   6   7

d. Friend _____ King
1   2   3   4   5   6   7

29. People have different images of the world and human nature. We'd like to know the kinds of images you have.

Here is a card with sets of contrasting images. On a scale of 1-7, where would you place your image of the world and human nature between the two contrasting images? (HAND CARD G)

Look at the first set of contrasting images. If you think that "The world is basically filled with evil and sin", you would place yourself at 1. If you think "There is much goodness in the world which hints at God's goodness" you would place yourself at 7. If you think things are somewhere in between these two, you would place yourself at 2, 3, 4, 5 or 6 (REPEAT FOR B).

Where would you place your image of the world on the scale for .... ?
(READ EACH SET OF IMAGES AND CIRCLE ONE CODE FOR EACH).

a.
The world is basically filled with evil and sin		There is much goodness in the world which hints at God's goodness.				
1	2	3	4	5	6	7

b.
Human nature is basically good			Human nature is fundamentally perverse and corrupt			
1	2	3	4	5	6	7

9. About how often do you pray? (USE CATEGORIES AS PROBES IF NECESSARY.)

Several times a day..	1
Once a day...	2
Several times a week..	3
Once a week..	4
Less than once a week...	5

1. How close do you feel to God most of the time? Would you say extremely close, somewhat close, not very close, or not close at all?

Extremely close..	1
Somewhat close..	2
Not very close..	3
Not close at all..	4
Does not believe in God...	5
Don't know..	8

2. Now I would like to read you a few statements about beliefs that some people hold. After I read each statement could you tell me whether you agree or disagree?

	Statement	Agree	Neither A nor D	Disagree
1.	Everything that happens must be accepted as God's will	1	2	3
2.	The more active you are in politics, the harder it is to be a good Christian	1	2	3
3.	The miracles in the Bible happened as they are described there	1	2	3
4.	People whose doctrines are false should not be allowed to preach in this country	1	2	3
5.	My (Christian) religion has a great deal of influence on my political ideas	1	2	3
6.	If I have to make an important decision my (Christian) religion would play an important part in it	1	2	3

33. How important would you say it is for children (USE CATEGORIES AS PROBES IN EACH CASE)

		Very Important	Fairly Important	Not very Important	Let them make up their own minds	Don't know
A.	To be brought up with the same religious views as their parents?	1	2	3	4	8

		Very Important	Fairly Important	Not very Important	Let them make up their own minds	Don't know
B.	To be brought up with the same views as parents on the Border question?	1	2	3	4	8
C.	To be brought up to vote for the same party as their parents do?	1	2	3	4	8

34. (a) Imagine, if you had a son and he came to you and told you that he had decided to become a priest, how do you think you would respond? (Circle one number on first line below).

    (b) And if you had a daughter and she came to you and said she had decided to become a nun, how do you think you would respond? (Circle one number on second line below).

	Greatly Welcome	Welcome with reservations	Neither welcome nor discourage	Would discc
Son's decision to become a priest	4	3	2	1
Daughter's decision to become a nun	4	3	2	1

35. (a) There's a lot of talk these days about uniting the Protestant Church and the Roman Catholic Church into one. What do you think of this idea? (Let me make sure I have this clear).

    Do you think that in principle uniting the Protestant and Catholic Church is:

    Desirable.. 4
    Depends.. 3
    Don't know, no opinion............................. 2
    Undesirable... 1

    (b) Do you think that in practice uniting the Churches is:

    Possible... 4
    Depends.. 3
    Don't know, no opinion............................. 2
    Impossible.. 1

36. That's very interesting. Before going on to the next subject, I would like to get your opinions on a number of general views held by some people. Would you agree or disagree or have no opinion about each of the following statements?

	Statement	Agree	Neither A nor D	Disag
1.	With everything so uncertain in these days, it seems as though anything could happen	1	2	3
2.	These days a person doesn't really know whom he/she can count on	1	2	3
3.	Most people can still be depended on to come through in a pinch	1	2	3
4.	Everything changes so quickly that I often have trouble deciding what are the right rules to follow	1	2	3
5.	Everywhere in the world Irish people are loved	1	2	3

6.	If you try hard enough, you can usually get what you want	1	2	3
7.	In striving for international co-operation we have to take care that no typically Irish customs get lost	1	2	3
8.	People were better off in the old days when everyone knew just how (s)he was expected to act	1	2	3
9.	We, the Irish people, are always willing to put our shoulder to the wheel	1	2	3.
10.	There is little use writing to public officials for anything	1	2	3
11.	The lot of the average person is getting worse not better in Ireland today	1	2	3
12.	It's hardly fair to bring children into the world with the way things look for the future	1	2	3
13.	Generally speaking, Ireland is a better country than most other countries	1	2	3
14.	Most people don't care what happens to the next fellow	1	2	3
15.	You sometimes can't help wondering whether any effort is worthwhile	1	2	3
16.	We, the Irish people, have reason to be proud of our history	1	2	3
17.	Parents are not strict enough with their children in Ireland today	1	2	3
18.	Other countries can learn a lot of good things from our country	1	2	3
19.	Nowadays, more and more people are prying into matters that should remain personal and private	1	2	3
20.	What this country needs most, more than laws and political programmes, are a few courageous, fearless, devoted leaders in whom the people can put their faith	1	2	3

(a)   Thank you. I wonder if we could now talk about how you got on in school/college? What age were you when you left school/college (for the first time)?

Age _____ Years

(b)   Did you return to school/college later?   Yes 1   No 2

(c)   Total number of years spend in full-time education   _____

(a)   What type of second-level school did you attend (for the last two years of your time in second-level education)?

Secondary Free... 1
Secondary Fee Paying...................................... 2
Vocational.. 3
Comprehensive.. 4
Community... 5

(b)   Name of Second Level School   _____

(a)   [Did you go on any further?] So what level did you reach? How was it in the case of your wife/husband? Could you tell me about your parents? (Circle one number in each column below).

	Self	Spouse	Father	Mother
None	1	1	1	1
Incomplete Primary	2	2	2	2
Complete Primary	3	3	3	3
1-2 Secondary School	4	4	4	4
3-4 Secondary School	5	5	5	5
Finished Secondary School	6	6	6	6
Some Vocational Education	7	7	7	7
Completed Vocational Education	8	8	8	8
Some University/Third Level	9	9	9	9
Completed University/Third Level	10	10	10	10
Post Graduate (M.A., Ph.D. etc.)	11	11	11	11

(b)   Please list the educational (i.e., certificates, diplomas, degrees, etc.) and professional qualifications you received.

1.   Degree _____

2.   Diplomas   _____

3.   Certificates   _____

4.   Professional Qualifications   _____

(c)   Have you attended adult education courses since finishing your formal education

Yes 1   No 2

(d)   Most important course in adult education you completed

_____

_____

40.   So much for education. Now, I would like to get your views in relation to Black people
Could I ask you a number of questions.

	Statement	Agree	Neither A nor D	Di
1.	If you had a boarding house would you refuse digs (accommodation) to Black people?	1	2	
2.	Do you think that because of their basic make-up Black people could never become as good Irish people as others?	1	2	
3.	Do you believe there should be a stricter control on Black people who enter this country than on Whites?	1	2	
4.	Do you believe that the Black person is basically or inherently inferior to the White person?	1	2	
5.	Would you stay in a hotel or guest house that had Black guests also?	1	2	
6.	Do you believe that the Black person deserves exactly the same social privileges as the White person?	1	2	
7.	Do you hold that by nature the Black and White person are equal?	1	2	
8.	Do you believe that Black people are naturally more highly sexed than White people?	1	2	
9.	Would you hold that Black people should be sent back to Africa and Asia where they belong and kept there?	1	2	
10.	Do you agree that it is a good thing for Whites and Blacks to get married where there are no cultural or religious barriers?	1	2	

41.   (a)   That's fine. The next thing I'd like to talk about is community involvement. A
you a member of any voluntary organisation/association/society?

Yes 1   No 2

(b)   If yes, are you a member of any of the following types of voluntary organisation
(Circle all those that apply).

1. Tenants/residents Assoc.	6. Trade Union	11. Sports Club/Association
2. Golf Club	7. I.C.A.	12. Snooker/Darts Club
3. Political Party/Movement	8. Music/Drama Soc.	13. Irish Language Assoc.
4. Peace Movement	9. Prayer Group	14. Social Club
5. Pro Environment Society	10. Social Action Group	15. Other _____

42.   Thank you. Now, let us go on to discuss your views and opinions on issues relating to defence and peace. Do you agree or disagree with the following statements?

	Statement	Agree	Neither A nor D	Disagree
1.	The Irish Defence Forces should continue their peacekeeping work with the United Nations	1	2	3
2.	Irish Governments should be more actively pursuing an independent foreign policy	1	2	3
3.	Every Irish person ought to pay honour to our national symbols like the national flag and the national anthem	1	2	3
4.	The presence of nuclear weapons is more a threat to peace in Europe than its guarantee	1	2	3
5.	Ireland should continue to maintain its neutral stance in wars between other countries	1	2	3
6.	I am proud to be Irish	1	2	3
7.	Ships and planes carrying nuclear weapons should be banned from visiting or passing close to Ireland	1	2	3
8.	Ireland's position as a distinct and independent nation is threatened by our membership of the EEC	1	2	3
9.	Nuclear weapons are necessary for our protection	1	2	3
10.	A nuclear war is likely in my lifetime	1	2	3
11.	Ireland should never allow nuclear weapons on its soil	1	2	3

43.   (a)   Thank you. Now I would like to ask you a few questions about the Irish language. With regard to the future of Irish which of the following would you like to see happen? (Show Card H and circle only <u>one</u> of the following).

The Irish language should be discarded and forgotten	1
It should be preserved for its cultural value as in music and art	2
Spoken Irish should be preserved only in the Gaeltacht	3
Ireland should be bilingual, with English as the principal language	4
Ireland should be bilingual, with Irish as the principal language	5
Irish should be the principal language of use (like English is now)	6
Other	7

(b)   Which of the following best describe the way you felt about Irish while in school? And the way you feel now? (USE CATEGORIES AS PROBES)

	When in School	Now
Strongly in favour	1	1
Somewhat in favour	2	2
No particular feelings	3	3
Somewhat opposed	4	4
Strongly opposed	5	5

(c)   [IF CHANGE RECORDED] What brought about this change?

_____

_____

(d)   (i)   Have you studied any other languages besides Irish and English?

Yes 1   No 2

(ii)   If yes: Which ones?   _____

(e)   What would you say your standard is in these languages? (USE CATEGORIES AS PROBES)

Language	Very Fluent	Fluent	Middling	Not So Fluent	Only a Little	None
Irish	6	5	4	3	2	1
French	6	5	4	3	2	1
German	6	5	4	3	2	1
Other (Specify)	6	5	4	3	2	1

44.   (a)   How frequently would you say you use Irish? (i.e. read, listen to or speak)

Daily....1   Weekly....2   Occasionally....3   Rarely....4   Never....5

(b)   [If codes 1-4 circled at (a)] When would you normally use Irish?

		Yes	No
1.	When meeting Irish-speaking friends	1	2
2.	At work	1	2
3.	All possible opportunities	1	2
4.	At home	1	2
5.	Listening to programmes TV/Radio	1	2
6.	Reading (specify)	1	2
7.	Communicating with officials	1	2
8.	Other (specify)	1	2

45.   (a)   Northern Ireland is a topic of interest and concern for many people. I would like to get your views on some aspects relating to the Northern problem. Would you agree or disagree with each of the following statements.

	Statement	Agree	Neither A nor D	Disagree
1.	Catholics in Northern Ireland have more in common with Northern Protestants than they have with Catholics in the Republic	1	2	3
2.	Northern Irish Protestants have more in common with the rest of the Irish people than they have with the British	1	2	3
3.	Northern Ireland and the Irish Republic are two separate nations	1	2	3
4.	Having separate Catholic and Protestant schools (Primary and Secondary Schools) has been a major cause of division in the Northern Irish community	1	2	3
5.	The use of violence, while regrettable, has been necessary	1	2	3
6.	A return to the Irish language and culture could provide a good basis for Irish unity in the long term (even though it might present difficulties in the short term)	1	2	3
7.	The position and influence of the Catholic Church in the Republic is a real obstacle to Irish unity	1	2	3
8.	National unity is an essential condition for the just solution of the present Northern problem	1	2	3
9.	Protestants in the Republic have more in common with Catholics here than they have with Protestants in Northern Ireland	1	2	3
10.	There should be increased co-operation across the Border with the people in Northern Ireland	1	2	3
11.	Northerners on all sides tend to be extreme and unreasonable	1	2	3

6. To continue with Northern Ireland, I would like you to tell me what you think of the following possible solutions to the present problem. Would you consider each of them to be desirable, not desirable but acceptable, don't know, unacceptable?

		Desirable	Not Desirable but acceptable	Don't Know	Unacceptable
1.	N. Ireland an integral part of the united Kingdom	4	3	2	1
2.	Totally independent Northern Ireland	4	3	2	1
3.	Federal Republic of Northern and Southern Ireland	4	3	2	1
4.	A thirty-two county Republic with one central government	4	3	2	1
5.	A thirty-two county Republic with provincial and central government.	4	3	2	1
6.	The status quo with a devolved power-sharing northern administration.	4	3	2	1
7.	The whole island of Ireland to become part of the United Kingdom again	4	3	2	1
8.	Other (specify) _____	4	3	2	1

7. How would you rate the ANGLO-IRISH AGREEMENT as providing a structure through which the Northern problem can be fairly solved? Please indicate your opinion on the following seven point scale (Show Card I)

Prevents progress   Promotes progress
towards a solution   towards a solution

Negative   -3   -2   -1   0   +1   +2   +3   Positive

8. (a) If there were a General Election today and you were voting, which party would you be inclined to vote for (first preference)?

_____

(b) Have you voted for this party in the past?

Regularly............ 1

Occasionally........... 2

Never............... 3

9. (a) Are you involved in politics at all (apart from voting)?

Yes 1   No 2

(b) If yes, could you please say in what way? (Circle all that apply)

1. Have contested National Elections 1
2. Have contested Local Elections 2
3. Member of Cumann/Branch Officer 3
4. Canvass and help on election campaign 4
5. Contribute money to party/organisation 5

50.   Did you vote in the:

Occasion	Did Vote	Did not Vote	What was the main reason you did not vote?
1.	Referendum on the Single European Act in 1987	1	2	_____
2.	General Election in 1987	1	2	_____
3.	Referendum on Divorce in 1986	1	2	_____

51.   Can you remember which party you voted for in the last General Election in February 1987 (first preference)?

1.	Fianna Fáil	1	6.	Sinn Féin	6
2.	Fine Gael..............	2	7.	Independent...........	7
3.	Labour Party..........	3	8.	Other (specify) ____	
4.	Progressive Democrats......	4		_____	8
5.	Workers' Party...........	5			

52.   Now, I'd like to read you a few things that people sometimes say in favour of our system of government. After each statement can you tell me whether you agree, disagree or have no opinion?

		Agree	No Opinion	Disagree
1.	Our system of government is good because it is traditional	1	2	3
2.	It keeps things peaceful here	1	2	3
3.	Its goals are usually good ones	1	2	3
4.	It is in the hands of people who are good leaders	1	2	3

53.   Now I would like to read you a number of statements about the opinions that some people hold. After I have read each statement could you tell me whether you agree or disagree or have no opinion?

	Statement	Agree	Neither A nor D	Disag
1.	If Ireland did not have its own team in the Olympic games or international sports, I would cheer for the British	1	2	3
2.	The British are pretty decent people	1	2	3
3.	Some British qualities are admirable but on the whole I don't like them (the British)	1	2	3
4.	I'd rather live in Britain than any other place abroad	1	2	3
5.	The British are inferior in every way	1	2	3
6.	British people are slow and unimaginative	1	2	3
7.	I don't object to the British people but I don't like the British government.	1	2	3
8.	The world owes a lot to Britain	1	2	3
9.	I am happy to see British people get on in Ireland	1	2	3
10.	I would never marry a British person	1	2	3
11.	I would be happy if Britain were brought to its knees	1	2	3
12.	The British Government has been evenhanded when dealing with Northern Ireland since 1969	1	2	3
13.	The British have little respect for the Irish	1	2	3

54. In recent years the problem of the Travellers or Itinerants has been discussed widely in Ireland. I would be very thankful if you would let me know if you agree or disagree in relation to each of the following statements referring to an average member of the Travelling People. (USE CATEGORIES AS PROBES)

		Agree			Disagree		
		Strongly	Moderately	Slightly	Slightly	Moderately	Strongly
1.	I would respect this person	6	5	4	3	2	1
2.	I would be reluctant to buy a house next door to this person	6	5	4	3	2	1
3.	I would be hesitant to seek out this person's company	6	5	4	3	2	1
4.	I would be willing to employ this person	6	5	4	3	2	1
5.	I would exclude this person from my close set of friends	6	5	4	3	2	1
6.	I would consider this person competent to serve on a jury	6	5	4	3	2	1
7.	I would avoid this person in social situations	6	5	4	3	2	1

55. Thank you. Again, I would like to read you various statements about people's attitudes and opinions on a wide range of issues. After I have read each statement could you tell me whether you agree or disagree.

	Statement	Agree	Neither A nor D	Disagree
1.	There should be a very strict control of RTÉ	1	2	3
2.	Communism should be outlawed in Ireland	1	2	3
3.	There is a God who occupies himself with every human being personally	1	2	3
4.	An applicant's religion should be considered when considering him or her for a responsible public position	1	2	3
5.	A person with bad manners, habits and breeding can hardly be expected to get on with decent people	1	2	3
6.	God takes care that good will finally overcome evil	1	2	3
7.	Only if you believe in God, death has a meaning	1	2	3
8.	Catholic priests should be free to marry	1	2	3
9.	Homosexual behaviour between consenting adults should not be a crime	1	2	3
10.	Obedience to the directives of the clergy should be the hallmark of the true Catholic	1	2	3
11.	Gardaí should be armed always	1	2	3
12.	Itinerants/Travellers should be facilitated to live their own way of life decently	1	2	3
13.	The dole should be abolished	1	2	3
14.	Punks and skinheads should be locked up	1	2	3
15.	In my opinion, sorrow and suffering only have meaning if you believe in God	1	2	3
16.	To me, life is meaningful only because God exists	1	2	3
17.	A thing is either right or wrong and none of this ambiguous woolly thinking	1	2	3
18.	There is a God who wants to be our God	1	2	3
19.	Women should get equal pay for equal work	1	2	3
20.	The unmarried mother is more to blame than the unmarried father	1	2	3
21.	Premarital sex is always wrong	1	2	3
22.	Prostitution should remain a prosecutable offence	1	2	3
23.	Student protests should be outlawed	1	2	3

56.   (a)   That is very interesting. Now could you tell me something about your occupation
              and employment. Which of the following would best describe your present
              situation?

              Permanent, full-time employee..   1
              Temporary, full-time employee...   2
              Part-time employee...   3
              Self-employed on your own..   4
              Self-employed with paid employees...   5
              Self-employed with others in a co-op or partnership...............   6
              Self-employed working for somebody else on a contract or
              fee-paid basis...   7
              Permanently ill/disabled...   8
              Retired..   9
              Student (full-time)..   10
              Home (domestic) duties...   11
              Unemployed (seeking work)...   12

       (b)   How long have you been in this situation?

                                  _____   Years/months

       (c)   Could you describe exactly what your occupation is? (If farmer, state acreage and
              farm type. If manager/supervisor state number supervised).

              _____

              _____

       (d)   Where do you work?   _____

       (e)   What job or occupation would you be most suitably qualified for? (Describe
              exactly)

              _____

              _____

       (f)   Which sector of the economy do you work in?

              Agriculture/Forestry/Fisheries....   1   Industry............   4

              Mining/Turf etc.   2   Distribution
                                                             (shop, pub etc.)   5

              Building and Construction........   3   Other services........   6

       (g)   Do you work in: Public Sector? 1   Private Sector? 2

       (h)   Are you a member of a Trade Union?   Yes 1   No 2

       (i)   About how many hours per week do you work on average? _____ hrs

       (j)   Do you supervise others at work?   Yes 1   No 2

(k)   How old were you when you got your first full-time job?
        (exclude vacation employment while a student)   _____ yrs

.   Could you tell me about the occupations of your spouse and your parents? (Describe <u>fully</u> -
    If farmer state acreage and type of farm)

1.   Husband   _____

        _____

2.   Wife (after marriage)   _____

        _____

3.   Wife (before marriage)   _____

        _____

4.   Own Father   _____
        (after you left school)

        _____

.   Thanks for all that information. I would now like to get your reactions to a number of
    views relating to unemployment, personal income, standard of living etc. Do you agree or
    disagree with each of the following statements?

	Statement	Agree	Neither A nor D	Disagree
1.	There are plenty of jobs in this country for those prepared to work	1	2	3
2.	Emigration is a disastrous drain of the country's best talents and brains	1	2	3
3.	Trade Unions are essential for the protection of worker's welfare and rights	1	2	3
4.	The difference between social classes ought to be less than they are at present	1	2	3
5.	It would be better for the country if the State owned and controlled more businesses and companies	1	2	3
6.	Young people should get out of this country whenever they can get more highly paid jobs abroad	1	2	3
7.	The differences between high and low incomes in this country should be greatly reduced	1	2	3
8.	Trade Unions have too much power in Ireland	1	2	3
9.	The private sector of Irish industry has failed to deliver on jobs	1	2	3
10.	If we want to create real jobs we must attract the multinational companies to this country	1	2	3
11.	Management is more to blame than workers for high unemployment	1	2	3
12.	The poor person is generally responsible for her/his state of poverty	1	2	3
13.	Only the tough and resolute get on in this country	1	2	3
14.	The government should see to it that differences between higher and lower incomes are greatly reduced	1	2	3
15.	Priests, brothers and nuns should become more directly involved politically in fighting for social justice in Ireland	1	2	3
16.	Trade Unions should advise their members on how they should vote in General Elections in the light of workers' interests	1	2	3

59.   (a)   How about your material standard of living? Would you say that your (family's) income at present is:

Very satisfactory......................... 5
Fairly satisfactory....................... 4
Not very satisfactory.................. 3
Poor.. 2
Very poor.................................... 1

(b)   With regard to the years ahead, do you expect the standard of living of the average person in this country to improve or disimprove over the next five years?

Improve greatly.......................... 5
Improve somewhat..................... 4
Neither improve nor disimprove.. 3
Disimprove somewhat................ 2
Disimprove greatly..................... 1

(c)   How would you rate yourself on the following social class scale?

Lower class................................. 1
Working class............................. 2
Middle class............................... 3
Upper middle class.................... 4
Upper class................................ 5
No answer................................... 6

Thanks very much for your views. I would now like to ask you a few questions about your income.

60.   (a)   Could you tell me what your <u>personal income</u> has been over the past three months, i.e., your average weekly or monthly income? (Show Card J and get income for <u>both</u> before and after tax).

Income Code _____ (Before tax)   Income Code _____ (After tax)

(b)   Could you tell me what was the average weekly/monthly <u>income of your household</u> over the past three months?

Income Code _____ (Before tax)   Income Code _____ (After tax)

(c)   Number of persons in your household with an income?   _____ (No.)

61.   (a)   With regard to your accommodation, would you tell me if it is:

Owner occupied (fully paid for)................................... 1
Being bought out (by mortgage)................................. 2
Tenant Purchase Scheme (from Local Authority)....... 3
Privately rented... 4
Local Authority Rented... 5

(b)   Is it?   Detached.............. 1   Other flat........................ 5
              Semi-Detached........ 2   Caravan.......................... 6
              Terraced................. 3   Other.............................. 7
              High-rise flat........... 4

52. With regard to domestic amenities, do you have (Circle all mentioned)?

Indoor flush toilet.............	1	Washing Machine..........	6
Bath or Shower................	2	Spin Dryer......................	7
Central Heating................	3	Video.............................	8
Telephone.........................	4	Micro-Wave Oven.........	9
Colour T.V.	5	Hi-Fi Stereo...................	10

GO RAIBH MAITH AGAT   THANK YOU

63. (a) Where interview took place:

Living room......................	1	Kitchen...........................	3
Hallway.............................	2	Doorstep.........................	4
Other place (specify)..........	5		

(b) Reception:

Excellent...........................	1	Fair, improving later.......	5
Very good.........................	2	Cool...............................	6
Good.................................	3	Hostile............................	7
Fair....................................	4		

(c) Amount of explanation needed:

General introduction...	1
General introduction and further explanation at beginning.....	2
General introduction and further explanation at.....................	3

(d) Acquaintance with survey:

Had heard of survey from person previously interviewed......	1
Had heard of survey from other sources (specify) _____	2
Had not heard of survey...	3

(e) Call on which Interview as Obtained (Circle No.)

     1   2   3   4   5   6   7   8   9   10   11   12   13   Over 13

(g) Duration of Interview: When begun   _____
     (24 hour clock)
                         When ended   _____

(h) Date of Interview: Day _____   Month _____

Int. Rate   _____   Coder _____

Appendix B:

Correlation Matrix of Social Distance Responses

TABLE 182: PEARSON PRODUCT-MOMENT CORR

STIMULUS CATEGORY	1	2	3	4	5	6	7	8	9	10	11	12	13	14	15	16	17	18	19	20	21	22	23	2
1 Africans	1.00	.59	32	.77	.53	.64	.49	.73	.30	.39	.34	.63	.36	.70	.51	.46	.32	.45	.29	.46	.44	.19	.40	.4
2 Agnostics		1.00	.30	.64	.81	.61	.52	.64	.31	.39	.51	.60	.47	.62	.66	.51	.34	.49	.31	.50	.47	.19	.50	.4
3 Alcoholics			1.00	.35	.31	.31	.22	.28	.16	.21	.24	.30	.22	.27	.27	.24	.47	.20	.12	.39	.21	.13	.28	.3
4 Amer. Negroes				1.00	.65	.71	.54	.84	.32	.42	.45	.71	.42	.78	.61	.55	.36	.51	.31	.51	.52	.21	.50	.5
5 Atheists					1.00	.65	.54	.63	.33	.42	.53	.60	.47	.59	.68	.54	.36	.51	.22	.52	.49	.18	.53	.4
6 Arabs						1.00	.52	.71	.30	.39	.46	.70	.41	.67	.64	.49	.41	.47	.27	.52	.47	.18	.49	.4
7 Belgians							1.00	.57	.44	.60	.55	.56	.49	.55	.46	.74	.28	.74	.40	.42	.71	.31	.41	.6
8 Blacks								1.00	.34	.44	.47	.76	.43	.82	.61	.55	.35	.54	.32	.52	.54	.19	.52	.5
9 British									1.00	.62	.40	.36	.48	.32	.26	.43	.19	.44	.80	.25	.43	.42	.26	.4
10 Canadians										1.00	.49	.49	.49	.40	.36	.61	.22	.61	.54	.32	.65	.35	.31	.6
11 Capitalists											1.00	.52	.46	.46	.56	.54	.27	.51	.39	.41	.49	.30	.37	.5
12 Chinese												1.00	.49	.74	.62	.60	.38	.58	.35	.52	.57	.23	.51	.5
13 Church of Ireland													1.00	.46	.41	.54	.26	.53	.50	.40	.52	.33	.35	.5
14 Coloureds														1.00	.59	.58	.36	.57	.33	.50	.54	.21	.50	.5
15 Communists															1.00	.49	.41	.46	.25	.53	.45	.15	.52	.4
16 Dames																1.00	.28	.85	.48	.42	.77	.32	.42	.7
17 Drug Addicts																	1.00	.27	.15	.48	.25	.08	.47	.2
18 Dutch																		1.00	.49	.41	.80	.29	.41	.7
19 English																			1.00	.25	.44	.47	.25	.4
20 Ex-Prisoners																				1.00	.38	.15	.49	.3
21 French																					1.00	.35	.38	.8
22 Gardai																						1.00	.11	.2
23 Gay People																							1.00	.2
24 Germans																								1.
25 Handicapped (Phy.)																								
26 Greeks																								
27 Hare Krishna																								
28 Indians (Nth. Amer.)																								
29 Israelis																								
30 Italians																								
31 Itinerants/Travellers																								
32 Irish Speakers																								
33 Luxembourgians																								
34 Jews																								
35 Methodists																								
36 Mentally H/capped																								
37 Moslems																								
38 Nigerians																								
39 Nth. Irish																								
40 Pakistani																								
41 People with AIDS																								
42 Polish People																								
43 Presbyterians																								
44 Portugese																								
45 Protestants																								
46 Provisional IRA																								
47 Roman Catholics																								
48 Russians																								
49 Scottish																								
50 Socialists																								
51 Spaniards																								
52 Sinn Fein																								
53 Trade Unionists																								
54 *Unemployed																								
55 Unionists																								
56 Unmarried Mothers																								
57 Welsh																								
58 Working Class																								
59 White Americans																								

Note: Correlations 0.50 plus are in bold print.

CIENT BETWEEN ALL STIMULUS CATEGORY RESPONSES

31	32	33	34	35	36	37	38	39	40	41	42	43	44	45	46	47	48	49	50	51	52	53	54	55	56	57	58	59
.39	.19	.44	.50	.43	.34	.57	.68	.34	.63	.40	.47	.39	.52	.34	.23	.12	.54	.35	.44	.49	.29	.37	.28	.38	.37	.35	.24	.33
.36	.20	.47	.57	.57	.30	.60	.62	.36	.59	.39	.54	.51	.58	.46	.26	.13	.59	.38	.50	.52	.34	.39	.28	.43	.43	.37	.22	.34
.31	.14	.22	.29	.26	.30	.28	.30	.22	.28	.39	.26	.25	.25	.22	.22	.10	.22	.18	.19	.22	.24	.18	.20	.23	.28	.22	.18	.21
.44	.23	.51	.59	.52	.35	.65	.78	.38	.70	.48	.56	.47	.58	.38	.25	.12	.61	.39	.52	.56	.30	.37	.28	.42	.44	.41	.26	.39
.34	.23	.47	.57	.58	.32	.59	.61	.38	.60	.43	.56	.52	.59	.47	.28	.14	.61	.36	.54	.53	.34	.40	.29	.45	.44	.38	.25	.37
.44	.25	.47	.56	.50	.36	.66	.71	.36	.73	.48	.54	.48	.56	.41	.30	.12	.62	.36	.53	.51	.37	.42	.28	.48	.40	.39	.23	.34
.25	.34	.71	.59	.52	.28	.50	.53	.42	.49	.34	.68	.51	.66	.47	.20	.19	.58	.54	.52	.67	.24	.43	.36	.39	.44	.58	.34	.50
.46	.23	.53	.58	.49	.35	.63	.77	.35	.72	.47	.57	.48	.61	.39	.27	.13	.62	.40	.53	.58	.32	.39	.31	.42	.45	.44	.27	.40
.19	.34	.42	.34	.41	.25	.29	.34	.42	.32	.19	.42	.42	.41	.44	.06	.19	.35	.49	.35	.42	.14	.40	.34	.34	.41	.49	.33	.43
.20	.37	.60	.45	.47	.25	.40	.45	.46	.42	.24	.56	.48	.57	.50	.17	.27	.46	.57	.48	.57	.20	.43	.39	.33	.41	.61	.41	.55
.21	.31	.52	.53	.51	.22	.50	.47	.38	.48	.28	.53	.49	.56	.43	.24	.18	.53	.44	.57	.52	.31	.42	.33	.44	.39	.46	.30	.39
.41	.28	.58	.61	.54	.37	.65	.73	.41	.71	.49	.62	.53	.65	.49	.28	.15	.67	.44	.56	.62	.33	.44	.34	.45	.46	.49	.29	.44
.23	.34	.47	.54	.62	.30	.43	.45	.46	.42	.28	.53	.62	.53	.72	.20	.21	.48	.48	.45	.51	.27	.39	.39	.39	.43	.50	.39	.41
.41	.22	.55	.60	.50	.35	.65	.77	.35	.68	.47	.59	.46	.64	.41	.22	.14	.62	.42	.49	.58	.29	.34	.26	.40	.44	.45	.25	.38
.37	.23	.44	.57	.52	.33	.66	.63	.36	.64	.47	.51	.48	.53	.41	.37	.10	.65	.35	.62	.49	.43	.42	.27	.48	.43	.35	.22	.32
.30	.34	.80	.59	.55	.32	.53	.60	.50	.55	.35	.75	.55	.73	.52	.22	.22	.63	.60	.58	.75	.26	.47	.38	.41	.46	.63	.36	.57
.39	.12	.27	.34	.28	.22	.39	.36	.23	.38	.54	.30	.28	.32	.26	.26	.06	.34	.20	.32	.30	.28	.21	.20	.31	.28	.21	.16	.19
.27	.36	.78	.57	.53	.29	.48	.55	.46	.49	.32	.73	.52	.71	.51	.19	.18	.58	.61	.54	.75	.25	.48	.37	.38	.44	.64	.37	.55
.16	.41	.45	.36	.42	.23	.29	.36	.47	.35	.19	.44	.44	.42	.45	.07	.23	.36	.55	.38	.45	.15	.39	.37	.34	.35	.50	.34	.47
.46	.23	.38	.49	.48	.31	.48	.52	.38	.52	.49	.47	.44	.49	.42	.37	.11	.46	.33	.47	.44	.44	.35	.32	.38	.42	.37	.25	.29
.28	.37	.80	.55	.51	.30	.49	.54	.45	.50	.30	.70	.51	.69	.50	.20	.19	.57	.63	.52	.73	.23	.46	.38	.39	.44	.66	.39	.57
.13	.41	.34	.25	.26	.18	.19	.23	.32	.22	.09	.33	.29	.29	.32	.05	.24	.26	.37	.26	.34	.13	.36	.36	.23	.28	.34	.35	.34
.35	.17	.42	.52	.45	.33	.48	.49	.33	.48	.62	.44	.43	.45	.38	.25	.10	.49	.28	.44	.44	.32	.30	.20	.35	.37	.31	.19	.28
.27	.36	.77	.56	.53	.29	.51	.56	.48	.53	.30	.70	.53	.69	.51	.17	.21	.59	.59	.55	.71	.23	.44	.34	.42	.42	.63	.41	.56
.26	.36	.36	.39	.43	.57	.36	.39	.36	.34	.25	.43	.43	.41	.41	.20	.16	.34	.34	.38	.37	.24	.33	.37	.30	.43	.38	.32	.32
.34	.31	.66	.63	.53	.34	.64	.72	.46	.69	.38	.68	.55	.75	.47	.23	.15	.70	.49	.61	.71	.30	.45	.32	.51	.44	.52	.30	.45
.40	.20	.43	.53	.47	.32	.62	.60	.34	.63	.46	.47	.44	.51	.37	.36	.10	.58	.34	.55	.47	.40	.38	.25	.44	.38	.33	.20	.29
.43	.27	.56	.63	.54	.38	.68	.77	.39	.77	.45	.62	.53	.67	.44	.29	.16	.66	.45	.56	.63	.33	.44	.31	.49	.43	.47	.27	.41
.44	.25	.59	.68	.56	.35	.69	.75	.38	.75	.45	.66	.54	.68	.45	.27	.15	.72	.43	.61	.65	.35	.48	.34	.48	.44	.46	.27	.41
.36	.34	.73	.62	.54	.31	.57	.65	.46	.63	.37	.73	.55	.74	.49	.21	.18	.66	.56	.58	.77	.29	.52	.36	.46	.43	.60	.33	.50
1.00	.15	.27	.33	.29	.29	.40	.43	.26	.45	.40	.30	.26	.30	.26	.31	.08	.34	.22	.34	.31	.36	.26	.22	.30	.28	.22	.18	.23
	1.00	.41	.29	.37	.24	.21	.25	.41	.25	.12	.36	.36	.35	.37	.14	.26	.26	.44	.32	.35	.20	.40	.50	.28	.36	.44	.43	.40
		1.00	.53	.52	.32	.52	.56	.47	.53	.33	.72	.53	.73	.50	.18	.25	.59	.62	.56	.75	.23	.41	.32	.41	.50	.62	.38	.53
			1.00	.70	.33	.65	.66	.45	.61	.43	.66	.62	.67	.55	.25	.18	.69	.45	.59	.64	.36	.45	.32	.44	.48	.61	.38	.52
				1.00	.37	.60	.60	.51	.53	.36	.61	.78	.63	.68	.22	.20	.60	.50	.56	.64	.36	.46	.34	.49	.46	.48	.35	.44
					1.00	.40	.39	.29	.36	.32	.34	.35	.35	.35	.21	.11	.33	.24	.28	.32	.27	.26	.30	.24	.36	.27	.29	.29
						1.00	.77	.37	.76	.46	.57	.54	.63	.43	.31	.13	.70	.39	.61	.56	.38	.39	.26	.51	.46	.39	.24	.35
							1.00	.41	.82	.49	.66	.55	.70	.44	.27	.16	.71	.43	.60	.64	.36	.45	.32	.49	.44	.46	.28	.40
								1.00	.41	.24	.42	.52	.50	.52	.18	.13	.70	.42	.60	.59	.39	.44	.31	.43	.42	.44	.24	.44
									1.00	.48	.61	.52	.64	.42	.31	.13	.70	.42	.60	.59	.39	.44	.31	.51	.41	.41	.25	.37
										1.00	.38	.32	.38	.30	.25	.06	.41	.22	.38	.37	.30	.24	.20	.29	.35	.25	.16	.21
											1.00	.63	.79	.53	.23	.20	.70	.60	.62	.75	.31	.54	.43	.44	.50	.62	.38	.53
												1.00	.68	.74	.19	.21	.59	.53	.56	.58	.29	.48	.40	.48	.48	.61	.38	.52
													1.00	.58	.22	.19	.71	.57	.63	.81	.33	.52	.44	.44	.45	.54	.41	.44
														1.00	.19	.26	.50	.52	.49	.52	.27	.40	.41	.44	.45	.54	.41	.44
															1.00	.04	.26	.15	.31	.21	.73	.24	.16	.27	.23	.17	.17	.18
																1.00	.12	.25	.18	.20	.10	.15	.23	.11	.15	.26	.29	.27
																	1.00	.44	.67	.34	.48	.33	.52	.46	.46	.26	.41	
																		1.00	.50	.60	.21	.48	.46	.38	.44	.74	.45	.56
																			1.00	.62	.39	.56	.39	.56	.44	.56	.33	.50
																				1.00	.28	.54	.42	.45	.45	.62	.38	.55
																					1.00	.33	.22	.34	.31	.24	.22	.23
																						1.00	.45	.44	.42	.51	.42	.46
																							1.00	.30	.43	.47	.57	.42
																								1.00	.37	.38	.26	.34
																									1.00	.46	.43	.44
																										1.00	.48	.63
																											1.00	.54
																												1.00

List of Tables

504

List of Figures

Index